FIRST CLASS
COMRADES

FIRST CLASS COMRADES

THE STASI IN THE COLD WAR, 1945-1961

J. BOULTER

Oldcastle Books

First published in 2025
by Oldcastle Books Ltd,
Harpenden, UK

oldcastlebooks.co.uk
@OldcastleBooks

A CIP catalogue record for this book is available from the British Library.

ISBN
978-0-85730-520-6 (Hardcover)
978-0-85730-609-8 (Trade Paperback)
978-0-85730-521-3 (Ebook)

2 4 6 8 10 9 7 5 3 1

Typeset in 11 on 13.7pt Garamond MT Pro
by Avocet Typeset, Bideford, Devon, EX39 2BP
Printed and bound in Great Britain by
TJ International, Padstow, Cornwall

The manufacturer's authorised representative
in the EU for product safety is
Easy Access System Europe, Mustamäe tee 50, 10621 Tallinn, Estonia
gpsr.requests@easproject.com

Contents

Abbreviations

ACC Allied Control Council

ADN East German news agency (Allgemeiner Deutscher Nachrichtendienst)

APN Early name for East German foreign intelligence (Aussenpolitischer Nachrichtendienst)

BDJ Nationalist youth organisation in West Germany (Bund Deutscher Jugend)

BfV Federal security service (Bundesamt für Verfassungsschutz)

BND Federal foreign intelligence service (Bundesnachrichtendienst)

BOB Berlin Operations Base – US intelligence office

BV Stasi regional office (Bezirksverwaltung)

CDU Christian Democratic Union (Christlich-Demokratische Union)

Cheka The first Soviet secret police – term remained in use thereafter

CIA Central Intelligence Agency

CIC Counter Intelligence Corps of the US army

Comintern Moscow-led confederation of national communist parties (Communist International)

DBD Democratic Farmers' Party of Germany (Demokratische Bauernpartei Deutschlands)

DDR German abbreviation for East Germany (Deutsche Demokratische Republik)

DGB Federal trade union federation (Deutscher Gewerkschaftsbund)

DP West German nationalist party (Deutsche Partei)

DST French domestic security service (Direction de la surveillance du territoire)

DVdI German Administration of the Interior (Deutsche Verwaltung des Innern)

FDGB East German trade union federation (Freier Deutscher Gewerkschaftsbund)

FDJ East German youth organisation (Freie Deutsche Jugend)

FDP Free Democratic Party (Freie Demokratische Partei)

GDR German Democratic Republic – East Germany

GI Stasi secret informer (Geheimer Informator)

GM Stasi secret co-worker (Geheimer Mitarbeiter)

GPU Soviet state security service 1922-23 – term remained in international use thereafter

GRU Soviet military intelligence service

GST Society for Sport and Technology (Gesellschaft für Sport und Technik)

Gulag Directorate of Soviet penal labour camps

HA Prefix for a Main Department of the Stasi (Hauptabteilung)

HUMINT Human intelligence

HVA Stasi foreign intelligence service (Hauptverwaltung A)

IRD Information Research Department

IWF Cover name for GDR foreign intelligence (Institut für wirtschaftswissenschaftliche Forschung)

K5 Secret police in Soviet Occupation Zone of Germany

KD Stasi district office (Kreisdienststelle)

KGB Committee of State Security – Soviet intelligence and security service

KgF League of Struggle Against Fascism (Kampfgemeinschaft gegen den Faschismus)

KgU Combat Group Against Inhumanity (Kampfgruppe gegen Unmenschlichkeit)

KI Soviet foreign intelligence service 1947-1951

KJVD Youth wing of the KPD 1920s-30s (Kommunistische Jugendverband Deutschlands)

KPD German Communist Party (Kommunistische Partei Deutschlands)

Kripo Slang term for German police criminal investigation department (Kriminalpolizei)

KVP East German paramilitary police (Kasernierte Volkspolizei)

LDPD Liberal Democratic Party of Germany (Liberal-demokratische Partei Deutschlands)

MfS East German Ministry for State Security; the Stasi (Ministerium für Staatssicherheit)

MGB Soviet state security service 1946-1953

MI5 British state security service

MI6 British foreign intelligence service

MID Military Intelligence Department of US army

MVD Soviet interior ministry (from 1946)

NATO North Atlantic Treaty Organization

NDPD National Democratic Party of Germany (National-Demokratische Partei Deutschlands)

NKGB Soviet state security service 1943-1946

NKVD Soviet interior ministry ('people's commissariat') and term for state security from 1934-1943

NSA National Security Agency; US SIGINT organisation

NSDAP Nazi party (Nationalsozialistische Deutsche Arbeiterpartei)

NTS Anti-communist Russian émigré organisation

NVA East German army (Nationale Volksarmee)

NWDR Nordwestdeutscher Rundfunk – radio station based in Hamburg

OG West German foreign intelligence service (Organisation Gehlen)

OGPU Soviet state security service 1923-1934 – term remained in international use thereafter

OMGUS US Office of Military Government

OMS Secret service of the Comintern

OPC Office of Policy Coordination – branch of CIA

Ostbüro The 'eastern office' of a West German political party, focused on work in the GDR

PET Danish intelligence and security service (Politiets Efterretningstjeneste)

PiD Political deviance (Politisch-ideologische Diversion)

POZW Cooperation between the Stasi and other agencies (politisch-operatives Zusammenwirken)

Profintern Interwar communist trade union organisation

RFB Interwar German communist paramilitary organisation (Rotfrontkämpferbund)

RGO Communist trade union organisation (Revolutionäre Gewerkschafts-Opposition)

RIAS Radio in the American Sector

RU Interwar Soviet military intelligence service

SA Nazi paramilitary organisation – the Brownshirts (Sturmabteilung)

SBONR Anti-communist Russian émigré organisation

SBZ Soviet Occupation Zone of Germany (Sowjetische Besatzungszone)

SD Intelligence and security service of the Nazi party (Sicherheitsdienst)

SDECE French intelligence service (Service de documentation extérieure et de contre-espionnage)

SED East German communist party (Sozialistische Einheitspartei Deutschlands)

SfS Name for the Stasi from 1953-55 (Staatssekretariat für Staatssicherheit)

SIGINT Signals intelligence

SIS Secret Intelligence Service, aka MI6

SMAD Soviet Military Administration (Sowjetische Militäradministration in Deutschland)

SMERSH Soviet military counter-intelligence service 1943-1946

SPD Social Democratic Party (Sozialdemokratische Partei Deutschlands)

SSD German term for the Stasi – State Security Service (Staatssicherheitsdienst)

TBK Stasi term for a dead letter box (tote Briefkasten)

UfJ Investigative Committee of Free Jurists (Untersuchungsausschuss Freiheitlicher Juristen)

VEB State-owned company in the GDR (Volkseigener Betrieb)

VEG State-owned agricultural concern in the GDR (Volkseigene Güter)

VOS Association for the Victims of Stalinism (Vereinigung der Opfer des Stalinismus)

VPO Association of Political Refugees from the East (Vereinigung Politischer Ostflüchtlinge)

WU Western Union – postwar west European military alliance

Note on the text

Selected German and Russian terms, such as *Grossaktionen* ('big operations') and *razvedka* ('reconnaissance'), are in italic font for the sake of emphasis. For the sake of less cluttered pages, most text in German and other languages is in ordinary font. The term 'spy' usually refers to a gatherer of information, the term 'agent' to a person performing other intelligence tasks, such as a courier or observer. 'Agents' is used as the umbrella term. Terms such as 'social democrats' are not usually capitalised because, in the context of this book, such people were not necessarily members of a Social Democratic Party. The term 'eastern Germany' refers to the territory of the GDR before 1949, when the GDR was founded; after that date, it is East Germany. Wherever they are known, translators of text have been credited in the notes. Other translations are the responsibility of the author.

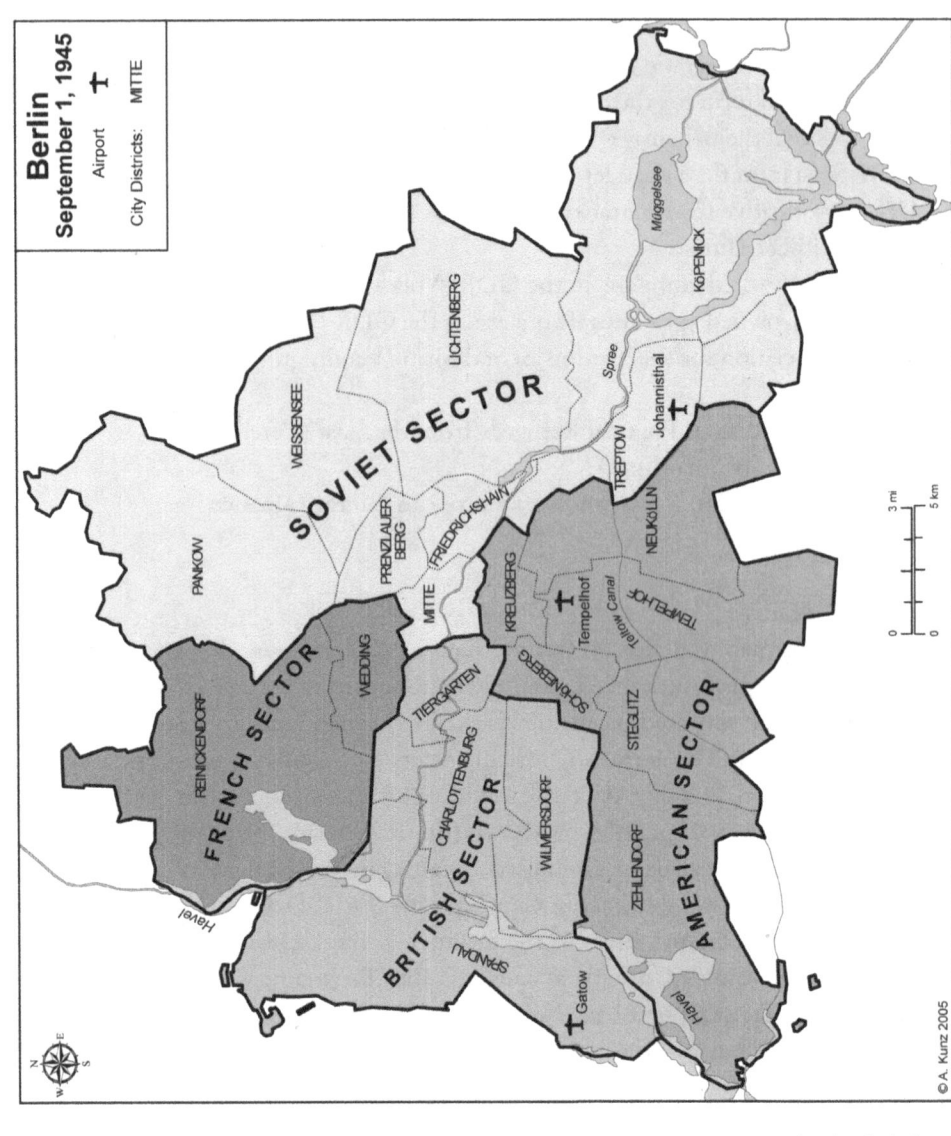

Berlin, 1 September 1945
Source: Original cartography
by IEG-MAPS, Institut für Europäische Geschichte, Mainz,
A. Kunz, 2004. Revised cartography (WCAG-compliant) by
Gabriel Moss, 2021.

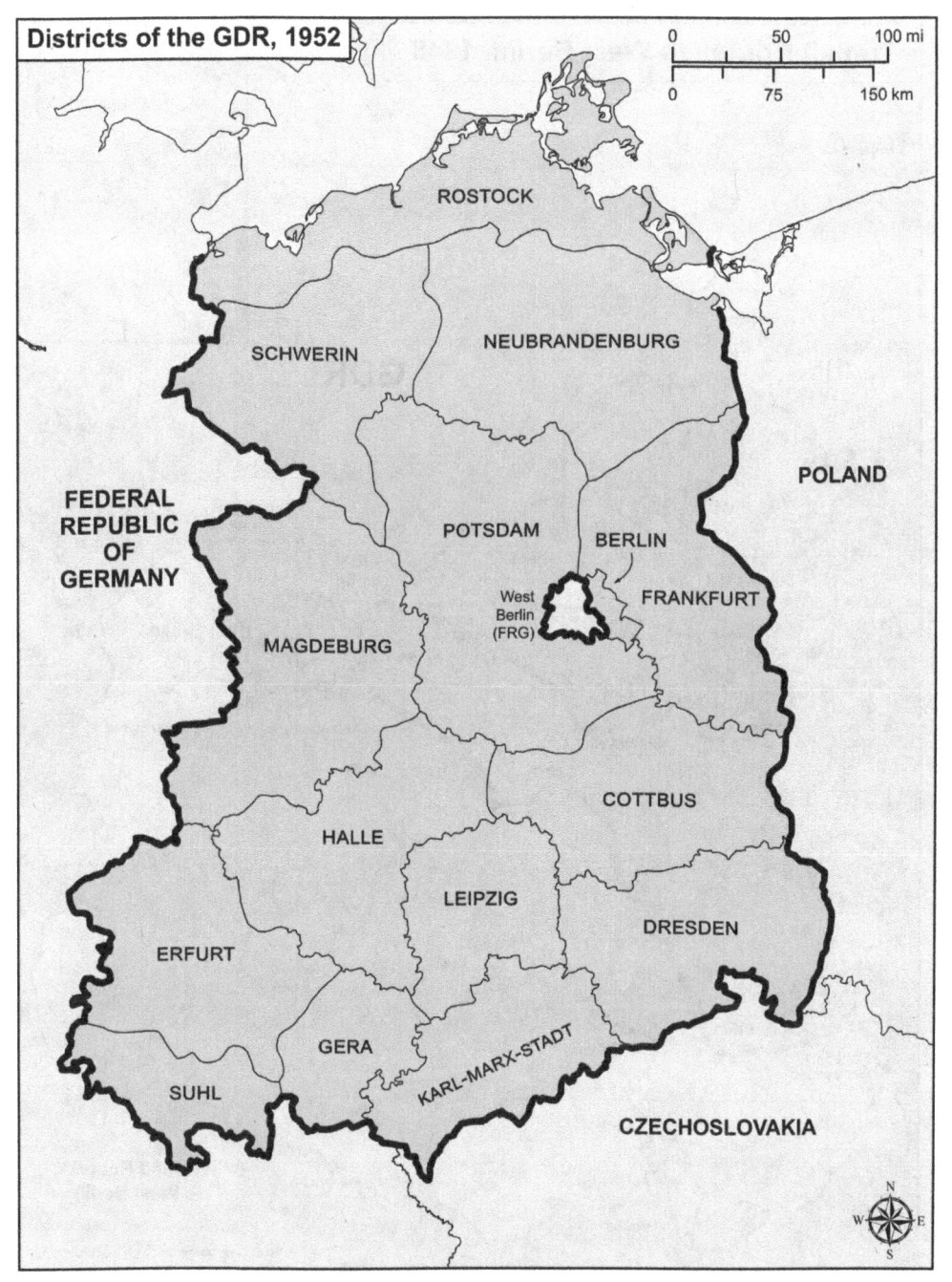

Districts of the GDR, 1952

Source: Original cartography by IEG-MAPS, Institut für Europäische Geschichte, Mainz, A. Kunz, 2005. Revised cartography (WCAG-compliant) by Gabriel Moss, 2021.

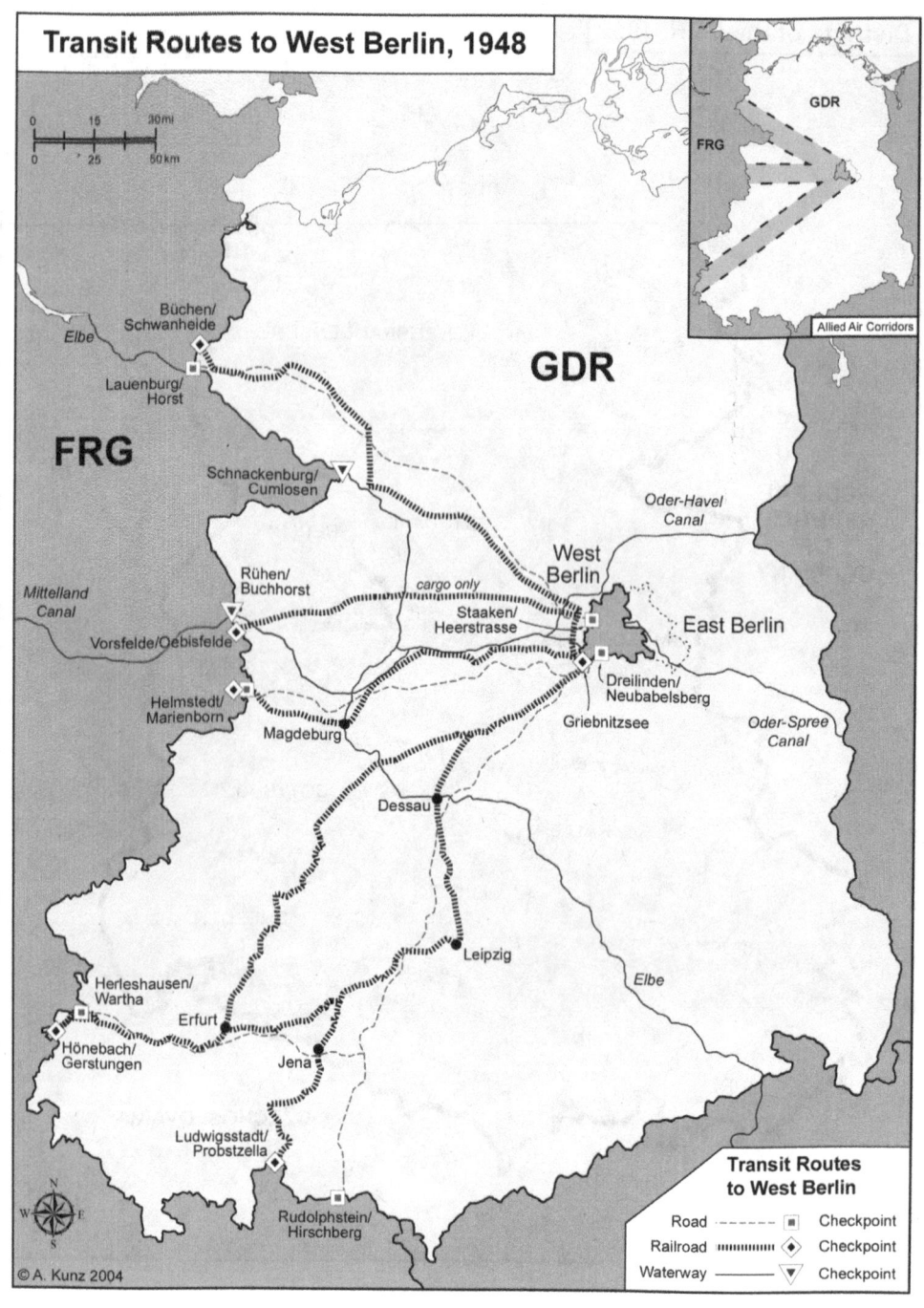

Transit routes to West Berlin, 1948

Source: Original cartography by IEG-MAPS, Institut für Europäische Geschichte, Mainz, A. Kunz, 2005. Revised cartography (WCAG-compliant) by Gabriel Moss, 2021.

Prologue

In the sunny garden of a medieval chapel, now a private home on the edge of an East Anglian village, a group of academics, soberly dressed and mostly grey-haired, stand in small knots or sit on deck chairs. They talk, debate, reminisce, smoke. The air is filled with the sounds of multilingual chat and clinking cutlery.

At intervals the academics stop to listen to a lecture. When each lecture finishes they heap praise upon one Joseph Stalin. They praise Stalin's wisdom regarding ethnicity and autonomous peoples. They laud his 1939 pact with Adolf Hitler, as it prevented bloodshed between 'Russian brother-worker and German brother-worker'. Several times Stalin is referred to as 'Uncle Joe'.

This isn't the 1950s. It is 1982 or thereabouts, and two young children – my sister and I – are trying to amuse ourselves in a corner of the garden, chucking balls and sniffing flowers; anything to temper the grown-up talk we don't understand.

This scene was a gathering of communist academics. My family, neither communist nor academic, had received a friendly invite. The host, resident of the chapel, was an elderly English historian who had joined the Communist Party of Great Britain in the early 1920s, and whom my parents had befriended. Every Saturday morning he would come to our house for coffee and push a copy of *Marxism Today* on my father, who was less than convinced.

On the way home from that garden party I asked my mum who Uncle Joe was. She seemed embarrassed – keen to imprint the message that Uncle Joe, long since dead, was a monster who brought suffering and death to innocent people.

Still – if I had understood the lectures correctly – this Stalin had built a number of countries, including one called East Germany. My mum said he ruled ruthlessly; that East Germany was a frightening place whose citizens were trapped inside it: they couldn't leave. She said the East German people at the garden party were different. They had been given special permission to travel, but they would have to go back. They, too, couldn't leave.

I was gripped. So began a lifelong interest in communism and its opponents, in Stalin and the societies he made. Their ideology and leaders, their abuses and excuses, their armies and, above all, their spies; some of whom were at that garden party, among the funny old academics given leave to travel abroad. Who were these people? And what had brought them to the Suffolk-Essex border?

Introduction

This is a book about spies and secret police agents.

Spies, thousands of them, who stole military secrets and priceless technologies, who interfered with the running of political parties, who spent decades reporting on their friends, or who married unsuspecting spouses just to gain information.

Secret police agents who shadowed suspects and made threats and gathered dirt, who infiltrated underground groups and burgled and kidnapped, who spread false rumours and killed.

This all happened in living memory and in the very heart of Europe. For this book concerns the spies and agents who worked for and against the Stasi, the intelligence and security service of communist East Germany.

East Germany – formally the Deutsche Demokratische Republik (DDR) or German Democratic Republic (GDR) – existed from 1949 to 1990. Before that the country had been the Soviet Occupation Zone of Germany, the territory won by the Red Army in 1945. With the collapse of Soviet communism in Europe, the GDR reunited with West Germany – the Federal Republic – to form today's Federal Republic of Germany.

The Stasi had a slightly shorter lifespan than its host country – 1950 to 1989. For most of that time it was a government ministry, the Ministry for State Security or Ministerium für Staatssicherheit (MfS); the slang term Stasi derives from 'staatssicherheit'. In Germany it was commonly referred to as the Staatssicherheitsdienst or SSD, meaning State Security Service. Some people, including its employees, knew it as Die Firma: The Firm.

The Stasi was a leading security service of the Soviet Bloc, the group of countries in central and eastern Europe that were occupied by the Soviet Union after the Second World War and which remained, to varying extents, obedient to Moscow. During the late 1940s the world became divided in a conflict of systems, capitalist 'West' versus communist 'East'. However spurious these geographical labels, the conflict itself was real enough: bad-tempered, dangerous, sometimes deadly.

The Stasi's main purpose, in the early Cold War and beyond, was to defend and strengthen the rule of the East German communist party, the Socialist Unity Party (Sozialistische Einheitspartei Deutschlands, SED). The Stasi was kept busy tackling real and perceived opponents of the SED, for the party's rule was resented by much, though not all, of the East and West German populations. In time the Stasi evolved into its mature role as a mass surveillance agency. This role, heavily reliant on informers, is captured in the well-known film *The Lives of Others*. It depicts the Stasi invigilating a nightmare land where husbands snitch on wives, neighbour denounces neighbour, and workmate reports on workmate. Thus the Stasi's name evokes Big Brother, the surveillance state, a malign authority constantly watching citizens and bullying them in covert ways.

Certainly the Stasi had an unpleasant habit of putting the evil eye on ordinary working Germans. Its victims, often religious or political dissidents, could find themselves hounded in all sorts of ways: sacked from a job without explanation, or forever at the bottom of lists for housing or healthcare. There was a Kafkaesque spookiness to some Stasi methods.

In 1977, for example, the East German actor and singer Manfred Krug applied for an exit visa to resettle in West Germany. Krug had fallen foul of the SED after signing a petition against the deportation of a fellow dissident. In his application he described how his career and sense of well-being had taken a sudden, eerie nosedive. Without explanation, he had been excluded from East German television productions. A music album, ready for release, was shelved. His most recent film wasn't entered into a major film festival, as had been promised. A previously agreed tour of West Germany was cancelled. Representatives of the Ministry of Culture, probably working for the Stasi, had spread false rumours that Krug had forced other people to sign the petition. Mysterious officials had made enquiries in Krug's neighbourhood about 'whom I visit, when and how often'; and a man from Erfurt, 'known to be employed by State Security', had circulated a story that Krug scorned socialism and had a dollar account in Switzerland.

Even worse was the foul play around Krug's concerts. 'Although all my jazz concerts have been sold out in recent years,' he wrote, 'there have been no new offers. Of 15 promised concerts this year, 9 have been cancelled without explanation and not rescheduled.' During a recent concert tour, Krug had been 'openly observed by detectives', his onstage patter 'demonstratively written down'. Friends had 'complained that no open ticket sales took place', and photographers had been ejected from every venue. Krug described the attendees:

> a carefully selected audience, primarily in the front rows, who all had dark looks
> on their faces and demonstratively did not applaud during the programme; there
> was arranged hostility from the audience, which makes it impossible for a stage

artist to work, which breaks him. I know now what a huge number of possibilities there are to discourage and depress people.[1]

Krug's story epitomises the sinister reach and 'demoralisation' tactics of the Stasi in the 1970s and 1980s. But all this was to come. This book tells the story, for the first time in English, of the Stasi's earlier, 'Stalinist' years, when for various reasons its behaviour, while no better, was somewhat different. It shines new light on a little-known period that began with the Allied victory over Nazi Germany and ended in 1961 with the construction of the Berlin Wall.

The story is told chronologically, with a few diversions along the way. First, the Stasi's predecessors – especially a secret political police outfit known as K5 – helped to establish the authority of the Soviet Union and SED in eastern Germany. They played a vigorous role in the 'denazification' of German society carried out by the victorious Allies. Once created, the Stasi tackled political resisters and Western agents, and helped to enforce the SED's radical policies. At the same time, East Germany created its first, tentative foreign intelligence service. The Stasi had to react to a rebellion in 1953 – the first revolt against communist rule to occur in the Soviet Bloc. In the mid-1950s it tried to rid the country of enemy spies by carrying out massive counter-espionage operations, known as the *Grossaktionen* ('big operations'). It also developed its foreign intelligence service, now led by the renowned spymaster Markus Wolf. Towards the end of the decade the Stasi focused increasingly on ideological dissidence, and on the immense problem of East Germany's porous borders, especially in the divided city of Berlin; for unsealed borders made it virtually impossible for the SED to govern as it wished.

During these years the Stasi wasn't ubiquitous; it was far from being an all-seeing eye. Instead it performed 'classic' espionage and secret police functions. It spied on enemy countries, caught real enemy spies, and tackled real armed opponents of the East German government (as well as total innocents). It was founded and led by devout German communists who had somehow survived the violence and misery of the preceding years, and who now craved the chance to create their own Marxist-Leninist state. Contrary to Western accusations, the Stasi rarely employed former Gestapo or SS personnel; Western intelligence services hired a far greater number of Nazis. The Stasi wanted its officers to be so-called 'first class comrades' – the best the communist movement had to offer.

No country in history has been more deeply penetrated by spies than divided Germany after the Second World War. The intelligence historian Paul Maddrell writes that 'it is hard to think of a state which has suffered an espionage and subversion crisis as grave as that which crippled the GDR in the years up to 1961.'[2] The Berlin Wall was a way of ending this crisis.

Throughout the 1950s, Western countries, above all Britain, France, the United States and West Germany, deployed thousands of spies in the GDR. Western intelligence services co-opted opponents of communism living in West Berlin or the Federal Republic, grooming them as saboteurs and subversives. There were semi-constant fears that the division of Germany would ignite a new land war in Europe, with both sides wary of attack by the other. This period of almost mass-scale spying came to an end with the building of the Berlin Wall.

After the Wall went up, it was much harder to infiltrate East Berlin and East Germany; and, by extension, the Soviet Bloc, for Berlin was rivalled only by Vienna as a gateway to the wider Soviet world. The Wall is thought of as a means of keeping East Germany's citizens locked inside their unwanted republic. It was, but it was also a means – and a successful one – of keeping out foreign spies and agents.

Not that the Stasi deserves a reputation as a noble spy-catching service. Throughout its history it 'acted beyond the rule of law and in flagrant disregard of human dignity and civil rights'.[3] The Stasi answered to two authorities. The first was the Soviet Union and its security service, the KGB. Secondly, and most significantly, it served the SED. The Stasi was known as the 'Shield and Sword of the Party', and it copied the shield and sword imagery of the Soviet secret police: 'the shield to defend the revolution, the sword to smite its foes.'[4]

On paper East Germany was not a one-party state; parties other than the SED were allowed to exist. But it was a party dictatorship. With the consent and direction of Moscow, the SED ran East Germany. Its members held every important position and made every meaningful decision. The party's leaders were greatly influenced by the personality and policies of Soviet dictator Joseph Stalin, and the SED often acted with a similar cruelty and ruthlessness towards opponents and dissidents.

This cruelty and ruthlessness was reflected in the Stasi. It is said that the spirit of Stalin survived in the Stasi 'like nowhere else in the GDR'.[5] At its height there were five Stasi employees for every 1,000 East Germans, dwarfing the ratio for the security services of the Soviet Union or Czechoslovakia. When East Germany collapsed, besides its employees the Stasi had on its books at least 170,000 informers and helpers – its notorious Unofficial Co-workers or IM (Inoffiziellen Mitarbeitern).[6] Other statistics are equally sobering. Over the course of East Germany's history, it is estimated that some 250,000 people were imprisoned for political offences – 'state crimes', as the Stasi knew them – and that 25,000 died in jail.[7] More than 75,000 were imprisoned for trying to flee the GDR or helping others to do so.[8] In the immediate postwar years, more than 60,000 internees died in Soviet-run camps in eastern Germany, and 20,000 Germans died in the USSR's Gulag camps.[9] Many of these people had been identified or arrested by the Stasi's precursor organisations. At its very worst, the Stasi killed people or stole their children, consigning them to state orphanages. Meanwhile, the Stasi's foreign intelligence service became one of the most invasive and problematic in the world. In the 1990s more than 3,000 legal proceedings were initiated against people accused of spying for the Stasi in West Germany,[10] although relatively few were convicted.

More than any other European country, Germany was deeply troubled and badly scarred by the Cold War. The conflict played out with a vengeance in Germany; in comparison, a place like Britain was relatively unaffected by it. For years Germany was hit by a blizzard of clandestine activity – an almost ludicrous amount of espionage, counter-espionage and geopolitical intrigue. Many Germans, then as now, were uninterested in such things and resented their country being used as an arena for secret warfare. Yet throughout the 1950s, the Stasi didn't need to look far to find those it considered its enemies – the 'terrorists' of the capitalist West, plotting the downfall of East Berlin and Moscow. The East German authorities inherited the Soviet mentality which had, since the days of Lenin, been:

> shaped by greatly exaggerated beliefs in an unrelenting conspiracy by Western governments and their intelligence agencies… The Soviet propensity to conspiracy theory derived both from the nature of the one-party state and from its Marxist-Leninist ideology. All authoritarian regimes, since they regard opposition as fundamentally illegitimate, tend to see their opponents as engaged in subversive conspiracy. Bolshevik ideology further dictated that capitalist regimes could not fail to be plotting the overthrow of the world's first and only worker-peasant state. If they were not visibly preparing an armed invasion, then their intelligence agencies must necessarily be secretly conspiring to subvert Soviet Russia from within.[11]

Such convictions came naturally to East Germany's rulers. Even so, when playing the 'paranoia' card against authoritarian states which rely on strong security services, it should be borne in mind that, largely due to their own untenable forms of governance, the existential threats faced by such states can be real enough. Thus 'vulnerable' is perhaps a more accurate word than 'paranoid'. In the case of East Germany, fears of plots and overthrow were not necessarily delusional.

The Cold War is commonly seen as a straight fight between a heroic West and the evil empire of communism. Yet when it came to spying and subversion, both sides in the conflict tended to do, and to accuse each other of doing, much the same things. They invaded each other with prying eyes and covert interference. While the West's incursions into East Germany don't provide an excuse for what the Stasi did, they did provide a reason for it. Like other ruling communist parties, the SED was acutely aware of its limited popularity and the frailty of its position. So when the Western powers inveigled ordinary Germans into spying on or subverting the East German state, the SED took it seriously and had an answer in the form of the Stasi, one of the pillars of the party's rule.

The moral tightrope walked by the competing Cold War powers brings up the tricky issue of comparison: the temptation to compare the Stasi's actions in the Cold War with those of, say, Britain's MI6 or America's CIA. Most books on the Stasi, in German and English, tend to present the Stasi's foul deeds with no context from the wider world of intelligence and security. This book aims to give the political and intelligence contexts in which the Stasi's actions occurred. This means showing, at least to an extent, what the Stasi's adversaries were doing to incur its wrath.

Comparisons are problematic, and arguably are outside the scope of a subject history. Undoubtedly there were fundamental differences between the Stasi and the intelligence and security services of properly democratic countries: differences in powers, remit, and constitutional standing, in internal culture and the behaviour of individual staff members. There were differences even in a technical, potentially unpolitical field such as counter-espionage. The Stasi was often responsible for the entire life-cycle of a counter-espionage case, from arrest to detention to trial to incarceration. The size and pervasiveness of the mature Stasi also differentiated it sharply from Western counterparts. Nevertheless, some comparisons between the various intelligence services are unavoidable, and a few are essential. Comparisons help to provide a fuller picture of the Cold War, the nature of authoritarian regimes, and the activities of both Western and Soviet Bloc intelligence services – activities that can look very similar on paper, even if the causes they served were different.

Of course, some intelligence and security services, including the Stasi in its earlier years, indulge in outright criminal violence. Others do not. Perhaps, though, the starkest difference between intelligence services lies in their taskers more than their tasks. The novelist Alan Judd, who worked for Britain's Foreign Office, has made this point: 'If intelligence is controlled by [an authoritarian] government [the results] won't be very nice. But if it is under proper democratic control, generally it aims to be better. It's a reflection of the political culture that it serves.'[12]

Much of the research in this book is based on documents provided to the author from the Stasi files, which are maintained by Germany's national archive, the Bundesarchiv. When East Germany collapsed, the Stasi's paper records – some 111 kilometres of them, if laid end-to-end – were preserved mostly by members of the public, who seized them from Stasi offices, determined to secure evidence of its abuses. In the 1990s, under new laws and the direction of a new government body, the files were made available for study – including by German citizens who were monitored by the Stasi or otherwise impacted by it, although that use of the files has now been curtailed.

Although the Stasi is the only intelligence and security service in the world to have its history laid bare in this way, there is an element of myth around the openness of its archive. If granted access, researchers give archivists a list of the names and topics in which they are interested. The archivists then do their best to meet the requests. Some of the documents they provide are apt and some are not. Some persons and topics are definitely off-limits; there's no point asking for them, because you won't get them. Moreover, all Stasi files must be assessed with due scepticism, although this isn't as tricky as it sounds. It is fairly easy to spot the biases and made-up nonsense contained, for example, in the files on arrested Western agents – like classifying arrestees as dangerous state enemies merely because they happened to have West German relatives. Equally discernible is the Stasi's general insistence on accuracy and the citing of credible evidence in its investigations.[13]

The archive's relative accessibility has obscured an important fact about the Stasi: the fact that in its lifetime, and especially in its early years, the Stasi was an utter mystery. Until quite recently, almost everything written about in this book was a secret. Today we can piece together the Stasi story with great accuracy. Its operations and intimate details, including the names of its staff members, are knowable. When the Stasi existed, however, these operations, details and staff members were unknown and undiscoverable. This should be kept in mind when reading.

There were some surprising things about the Stasi's 'public' face in East Germany, like its regular appearances in the press, or the fact that citizens could drop into their local Stasi office to discuss or report something. The majority chose not to. Often the Stasi would come to them anyway, like when its officers paid visits to factories to hector the workers about the threat from Western spies. But the Stasi's intelligence-gathering and other operations were carried out in great secrecy – 'conspiratorially', as the Stasi put it. Therefore, what it actually did, on a day-to-day basis, was to most people opaque, and not to be enquired into.

East Germany, too, is a character in this book, and it was a bizarre and baffling place. To understand the double-think and double-talk of the Stasi, one must understand the double-think and double-talk of the GDR. It was a deceitful state from its name onwards: the German Democratic Republic was, in fact, partly Russian and wholly undemocratic. It had a thoroughly martial atmosphere, yet official texts constantly employed the word 'peace'; the GDR sold itself, including *to* itself, as Europe's leading country of peace. In the later Cold War it became a hub of European anti-nuclear protest, yet it was the first territory outside the USSR to host Soviet nuclear missiles. The SED regime's constant repetition of such phrases as 'our peaceful democracy' or 'our peaceful, democratic economy' comes across like neuro-linguistic programming, as if repeating these falsehoods enough times would somehow make them true.

In some ways, then, East Germany was a psychologically disorientating dreamland. This was a state where people sent to prison for political crimes were never to be called political prisoners; where Article 10 of the 1949 constitution gave everyone the right to emigrate, but an average of seven people per day were imprisoned for trying to do so.[14] And so on. When reading about it, one has to accustom oneself to a society where nothing is at it seems.

Neither historians nor former residents can agree on whether East Germany was an example of totalitarianism. Many say it was not. Some don't even concede that it was authoritarian. 'The SED state' is a useful descriptor for the GDR. This term, favoured in Germany, conveys the supremacy of the party throughout East German life. Ultimately the party decided and guided most practical, cultural and intellectual matters in the life of every East German citizen. If the citizen resisted, the party had recourse to a firm-handed police force and an especially vigorous state security service to sort out the problem.

There are those who continue to argue that the Stasi wasn't so bad. Some retired personnel still claim that, far from being a force of oppression, the Stasi was honourable and necessary. After all, nearly every society has a secret intelligence service and makes use of covert policing, especially for crimes that are connected with politics or national security, even if they aren't political crimes in the East German sense. Other commentators – including some who stand by the Marxist intentions of the GDR, and admire what they see as its socialist achievements – claim that the Stasi was neither evil nor good, but innocuous. They insist that it did not impact ordinary people's lives to anything like the extent that has since been alleged. If a person was a decent citizen, the story goes, the Stasi wasn't interested; it left the innocent alone, having bigger fish to fry. This explains why the Stasi kept a file on around six million East Germans but not on the remaining nine million.

If there is any truth in this claim, it applies especially to the period covered by this book, when the Stasi had to deal with an infestation of real Western spies.

In the words of one historian, the 'East German authorities wanted their country to be perceived as a *German* state founded on *German* traditions – and supporting the idea of German unity.'[15] It is often overlooked that Germany, for all its urbanity, is a strongly religious and agricultural land. Thus life in East Germany was more parochial and traditional than might be imagined. While the vast majority of Stasi officers were male, women are largely missing from the Stasi story because they have been overlooked, and not because they were not there. It is true that most women employed by the Stasi held a secretarial or medical job. But where are the recollections of these women, their experiences, the insights they gained into notorious people and historical events? This store of knowledge appears to be untapped.

While it was never intended for this book to fill that gap, certain points have become clear in writing it. The Stasi's famous 'Romeo' spies – men sent into West Germany to seduce women with access to classified information – had their female equivalents, and the latter became active before the Romeos did. Some women were not expected to seduce anyone, and instead were well-trained in spycraft before being sent abroad. Just one example is Rosalie Kunze, agent 'Ingrid', who obtained military information for Stasi foreign intelligence. Women took an active part in the Stasi's security and counter-espionage operations. In so doing, they deceived and infiltrated and tricked and plotted, like any other secret police agent. And the 'conspicuously high proportion' of woman secretaries who spied for the Stasi in West Germany is explained partly by the fact that they did a good job. From 1949 to 1987, fifty-eight secretaries were identified by West German security services as Stasi spies – the mere tip of the iceberg.[16]

The gap that *is* filled by this book, at least in English, is for a comprehensive account of the Stasi's formative years: its birth and growth. An abundance of books, films and articles cover the Stasi of the 1970s and 1980s, but it is quite difficult to find substantive material on what the Stasi did in the 1950s. There wasn't a book in English devoted to the subject, so I wrote one. I wanted to collate all that is known about it. The events of the period are, among other things, a lesson in how to create and maintain a political and economic system that is unwanted by at least half of a population. One gets to see the Stasi's key role in fashioning a new state – a role that, again, differentiates the Stasi from its Western counterparts. The closer one looks at the Stasi's first years, the more one understands the particular conditions of the early Cold War, and how these conditions affected not just the global powers but the ordinary Europeans – especially Germans – who were caught up in them.

Furthermore, there is a need for more books that explain *how* the Stasi did what it did, books that include its operational details. German histories tend to focus on two things: the Stasi's bureaucratic evolution and its abuses of the law, the latter based on voluminous court records. This book tries to cover the operational detail – the tradecraft, if you like – that is largely missing elsewhere. As well as its intrinsic fascination, operational detail puts the sinister nature of the Stasi in its proper place. Another aim of the book is to position the Stasi, as it should be, within the continuum of communist espionage and security activity which predated the creation of East Germany by decades; and within the continuum of national security practices, with which most of us still live today.

First Class Comrades was commissioned originally as a 'true crime' book with a focus on espionage. Its true crime origins no doubt show through in some ways. It is a specialist study but not an academic book; it isn't intended to fulfil academic criteria. There were no research grants, no lengthy periods of uninterrupted study. As well as the Stasi archives, primary sources include the files of Britain's security service, MI5, held at the UK National Archives; publicly released CIA documents; and documents made available by the Wilson Center and Germany's Bundesarchiv. The latter has released hundreds of publications in which original Stasi and SED documents are reproduced, thus becoming a proxy primary source.

Information from the available literature in English and German, including recent German academia, has been gathered and reinterpreted in *First Class Comrades*. The book is indebted to such German authors as Susanne Muhle, Hanna Labrenz-Weiss, Helmut Müller-Enbergs, and many more; and, in English, to Paul Maddrell, Gary Bruce and others. To quote the historian Blair Worden, 'though it draws pervasively on the work of others, I hope that it brings some fresh findings and perspectives'.[17]

Arguably there are some issues with the historiography of the Stasi. Much of the fine detail on what the Stasi really was, and what it really did, has been obscured by a justifiable anger in the German histories and by a degree of Reaganite sensationalism in some of the English ones. In a British television documentary of 2023, the politician Ben Wallace opined that when the Berlin Wall fell, the people of eastern Germany were released from 'the most brutal torture known to humanity'.[18] The SED regime is interesting precisely because it was *not* the most brutal torture known to humanity. That is what makes it instructive and worth studying. Being clear about the nuances of the Stasi's actions – say, the ways in which it tried to earn support from among the general public – makes the Stasi more comprehensible, not less reprehensible.

On a similar note, it should be remembered that the SED regime was not detested by everyone who lived in the GDR. By the 1980s, one fifth of East German adults had joined the party.[19] According to Jens Gieseke, a leading historian of the Stasi, as much as fifty percent of the population either tolerated or in some way appreciated the East German system. It was opposed, to varying degrees, by the other fifty percent. The regime faced armed resistance organised by diehard anti-communists, but much of the political opposition tackled by the Stasi came from people who wanted to improve East German socialism, not overthrow it; hence the phrase 'resisters and reformers' used in this book.

Some potentially unwelcome subjects are covered in the following pages, like the question of whether the Stasi faced armed opposition organised by unrepentant Nazis. But in all that follows, every reader should keep in mind a simple fact. The Stasi was never a legitimate intelligence and security service, because it served an artificial state, a government that was never freely and fairly elected, and a political system that was too unfair, too harsh, and too flawed to be sustained.

Part I

Death to Spies:
The Descent of Eastern Germany

'Everyone imposes his own system as far as his army can reach.'

Joseph Stalin[1]

'It's got to look democratic, but we must have everything in our control.'

Walter Ulbricht, German Communist Party[2]

1

Stunde null

East Germany was created from the wreckage of a broken world. Defeat in the Second World War left the Thousand Year Reich in a state of ruin, deprivation, lawlessness and social brutality; a direct result of unleashing one of history's most popular destructive ideologies. In Germany this moment in history is known as *Stunde null*, 'zero hour': the end of twelve years of Nazi belligerence and its consequent total war, and the beginnings of a cowed, horizonless future.

The unreal and hellish conditions of *Stunde null* are captured in a 1948 novel by Hans Fallada, *Der Alpdruck*.[1] With the war over – at least on paper – the protagonist, Doll, navigates a blasted landscape populated by suspicious and traumatised citizens, all searching desperately for food, housing and medical treatment. There is little, if any, to be found. Returning to Berlin, Doll finds his apartment occupied by menacing squatters who ridicule the idea of his ownership and refuse to leave. The city itself is transfigured, now a place where 'Doll, who knew Berlin like the back of his hand, actually had no idea where he was.' Even so, the city's rubble and fear are considered preferable to life in the countryside. At a housing office, a pompous clerk dismisses the paperless Doll with an angry rebuke: 'You just want to worm your way into Berlin, that's all!'

As Doll surveys the global devastation wrought by National Socialism, he reflects that the word 'German' has 'become a term of abuse throughout the world'. It is 'a fatuous hope' to try to prove there are 'still some decent Germans'; and if he were to drop dead, 'not a heart in the world would grow heavier on his account'. Suicide is everywhere. At one point Doll talks with a doctor who mentions, 'out of the blue: "My wife killed herself out on the highway, by the way."' From another doctor Doll prises the best methods for killing oneself, learning of 'cyanide, morphine, scopolamine, about dosages that were guaranteed to be fatal... about insulin, which enabled someone to commit suicide in a way that was virtually undetectable later'.

The governmental authority of this nightmare landscape is the Red Army. Abjectly, Doll accepts their presence: 'The world, and his fellow countrymen in particular, were not yet ready for a life without constant supervision, without the threat of force… his dear fellow countrymen would doubtless smash each other's heads in if they were left unsupervised.'

The black market, however, is the real ruler of people's lives. It doesn't offer luxury; this is an economy where cigarettes are traded for drinking water. Everyone is torturously hungry. Doll's former home in the country is looted: 'They had not left him a single sock or shoe, not a shirt or a suit.' This brings home 'how feral and depraved this country had become: people felt they had a perfect right to plunder and steal, since the war had robbed them of so much'. With no functioning police service or judiciary to intercede, 'Who was going to stop them helping themselves?' And so people with nothing steal from those with almost nothing; 'Germans against Germans, every man for himself, and every woman, too, keeping up the fight against the whole world and everyone else.'

The police force – such as it is – is flooded with denouncements. An embittered Doll considers ratting on an acquaintance for her Nazism, remembering her pleasure when Hitler famously swerved assassination in 1944: 'Do you think I've forgotten how you rejoiced over the divine deliverance of your beloved Führer after the 20th of July?' Aside from food, medicine is the most coveted commodity, rare as hen's teeth and chokingly expensive. Treatments for venereal disease are disastrously absent, for this is a place of indiscriminate sexual violence inflicted by the victors. There are signs outside every communal toilet: 'Not to be used by gon. or syph.!'

And yet, despite or because of it all, the flame of Nazism flickers on. Doll 'often had the feeling that deprivation and hardship were simply turning them into better Nazis than they were before… To all of them, including many who had not been Nazis before, the years of the Hitler tyranny suddenly seemed like some sort of golden age'. For Doll, this nostalgia, and the surviving faith in Nazism, are the most shocking aspects of this land of shocks, but they do not inspire anyone to action. Dejection and apathy are total, for this is a 'world in ruins, which will take everyone's determination, everyone's hands, to rebuild. But instead [the people] are lying on their backs… They have nothing now, and they are nothing now'.

Der Alpdruck was based closely on Fallada's experience. In an example of the abrupt turnarounds of circumstance so common in continental Europe at the time, Fallada had been released from a Nazi psychiatric prison in late 1944 only for conquering Soviet troops to appoint him mayor of the small town of Feldberg. The dazed and drug-addicted author was in no condition to perform this task, which consisted of adjudicating pointlessly on the distribution of non-existent resources. The townspeople, frightened and angry, lobbied him with unmeetable needs. Those with Nazi pasts – and there were many – did their best to deny them or explain them away. As *Der Alpdruck* records, a familiar mantra arose. 'There were only ever three National Socialists in the world; Hitler, Göring and Goebbels.'

Fallada's appointment as mayor was based partly on the premise that, having been incarcerated during the Third Reich, he must have been a political enemy of the regime. He was no admirer of it, but the reality is messier. Although he was later celebrated as a humanist 'people's writer', Fallada, like many others, had tried to keep life simple by burying his feelings and coming to an uneasy accommodation with Nazism. He had been locked up not for political resistance but because of his poor mental health, his criminal record, and an inebriated attempt to shoot his wife.

Der Alpdruck provides important clues for the history of the Stasi. The novel captures the conditions and motive forces that underlay the creation of the German Democratic Republic and its state security service. It is all discernible here: the ruin and hardship, the need to rebuild and to heal; the bartering among the victors; the social and political suspicion, accusation, about-turning; the blurred line between Allied reparation and revenge; a desperate, difficult desire to put things right; the craving for a new meaning to life; violence and its numbing effects; the harsh watchful eye of Soviet Russia; and the feelings of war guilt, vying with an awesomely inappropriate war pride.

There are telling omissions from Fallada's novel, however. One is the destruction of European Jewry, which is mentioned only briefly, in passing. Another is the powerful presence and importance of Soviet security services. In 1945 there were three such services at work in Germany: the NKVD, the NKGB, and SMERSH, the latter acronym formed from the Russian for 'death to spies'.* As well as their security functions – some of which were also performed by Soviet diplomats and communist party officials – these agencies were responsible for governance and administration. They impacted the daily lives of working Germans, often deciding their physical fate. So before the GDR even existed, those who were to become East Germans lived in a militarised, 'securitised' territory. It was a place of stiff rules, severe authority, harsh punishments, and arbitrary power in the hands of security forces. This, then, was the material from which a new state was formed: East Germany, strange and blighted, where the Second World War didn't end until 1990.

*

---

* SMERSH, a contraction of the phrase Smiert' Shpionam, was the Soviet military counter-intelligence service. The NKVD was the Soviet interior ministry (Naródnyy komissariát vnútrennikh del' or People's Commissariat for Internal Affairs); the NKGB was the state security ministry (Naródnyy komissariát gosudarstvennoy bezopasnosti or People's Commissariat for State Security). The NKVD and NKGB were forerunners of the KGB.

To understand the 'securitisation' of eastern Germany, we should consider the bleak and distressing state of Europe after the war. Arguably, we continue to pay too little attention to the history of the postwar years. While the historiography of the Second World War keeps growing, our knowledge of the war's after-effects remains inadequate. A simplistic idea has prevailed that humanity was saved, and 'evil' defeated, in May 1945; that the celebratory scenes of VE and VJ Day were universal and lasting, marking the endpoint of struggle and the start of joyous rejuvenation. On the contrary, many societies faced some of the most traumatic moments in their history after the war against the Axis had been won. For most Europeans, the late 1940s and early 1950s were a time of problems and hardships, not the least of which was hunger.

Keith Lowe's book *Savage Continent* is a valuable account of this postwar grimness. Lowe details how Europe 'remained economically, politically and morally unstable' well into the 1950s. Rupture and disorder ruled the day. Much of the continent saw the collapse of its food supply, transport systems, medical services, and state structures. Even as people struggled to overcome individual and collective trauma, political extremism continued to flourish. The 'civilised world' grappled with its dawning knowledge of the Holocaust, scrambling to put in place international rules and organisations to prevent anything similar happening again. The continent's population shifted and diffused on a pre-viously unimaginable scale, for this was Europe's time of the camps. Prisoners of war, displaced persons, forced labourers awaiting repatriation, former Nazis and war criminals: all spent years in massed captivity, especially 'Jews and Poles, [who] would languish in camps of Nissen huts well into the 1950s.'[2]

Jews continued to be vilified and attacked. The historian Lawrence Rees has detailed the stories of Slovakian Jews who, having barely survived concentration camps, were beaten and driven away when they tried to re-occupy their former homes.[3] Dutch Jews returned to Amsterdam to find the locals had looted their houses and didn't want them back. While some spectators wrung their hands over the destruction of European Jewry, others lamented its curtailment. The psychiatrist R.D. Laing recalled a Glaswegian neighbour saying that 'the only trouble with the war ending when it did was that [Hitler] "didn't have a chance to finish the job".'[4] This breathtaking hatred, expressed with full knowledge of the death camps, was not so rare.

Lowe describes how the black market pullulated, as 'all semblance of law and order vanished'. Europe experienced a crime wave that 'dwarfed that which had occurred during the war, and has never been equalled since'. The 'massive movements of refugees provided an excellent cover for those seeking revenge (just as it provided cover for escaping war criminals), and the lack of any form of law and order meant that murders went unreported, uninvestigated and often unnoticed.' These were circumstances in which 'far from being shocking, acts of extreme violence became quite unremarkable across much of the continent.'

Women suffered grievously. The mass sexual violence inflicted by the Red Army upon German and Austrian women – which mirrored the violence inflicted by Axis soldiers on women in Ukraine, Belorussia, Poland, Russia and elsewhere – is still topical and still discussed. Yet sexual violence increased everywhere, including in the United Kingdom and the country that came out of the war in by far the strongest position, the United States. Lowe records that in Britain and Northern Ireland, 'sexual crimes, including rape, increased by almost 50 percent... a fact which caused huge concern at the time'. In June 1948 *The Times* covered the continuing rise in sexual violence in an article called 'A Problem Picture'. In America, the 'picture' was never to be the same again.

Despite the United States' continued economic success, American society was infused with a certain morbidity, caused partly by the presence of nuclear weapons. Popular films of the period, especially in the film noir genre, are dominated by new themes, many inspired by the return home of military personnel: the rise in alcoholism, the surge in crime and violence, the pervasiveness of psychosis and mental distress. In Britain the amount of juvenile delinquency – especially the crime of burglary – rose by almost forty percent.[5] The war did have some silver linings. One example is the focus on medical care and hygiene that, together with the creation of the wildly popular National Health Service, made public health in Britain better and fairer than it had ever been. Nevertheless, there was a widespread awareness that society was more dangerous than it had been in the 1930s.

Gradually the people of Europe tried to work out political answers to this mess. One result was the popularity of communism, Nazism's apparent antithesis. Lowe notes that 'the single most important task of every European government in the aftermath of the war was to keep the economy afloat... The Communists therefore gained a stranglehold on industry and transport by infiltrating trade unions and workers' committees in factories.' Membership of communist parties boomed. In 1944 the Romanian Communist Party had eighty members in Bucharest and fewer than 1,000 nationally; by 1948 there were more than one million. Within a year the party membership in Hungary rose from around 3,000 to half a million. The most dramatic increase was in Czechoslovakia: 50,000 members in May 1945, one and a half million by 1948.[6]

In part these increases were due to Soviet occupation, and working people's attempts to indemnify themselves, but they were prompted by idealism too. At this grim time, the more naïve communists believed that they could bring an end to war and even militarism. As in earlier decades, communists thought they could fashion a new type of human who would be organised in a new and faultless way. Crucially – especially for Germany – communists believed that it was only they who could offer redemption.

The parlous state of Europe in the 1940s and 1950s brings to mind Aleksandr Solzhenitsyn's pithy comment on the need to avoid war in the first place: 'Any idiot can bomb a train, but just try sorting out the mess!' It takes one generation to start a war; it can take several generations to overcome the damage, as eastern Germans were about to discover.

2

Circles of Hell: Postwar Germany

It is difficult to associate contemporary Germany with spying and harsh political policing, never mind chaos and collapse, for the country has come to stand for the opposite of those things – for openness, justice, efficiency and prosperity. Germany is Europe's flagship democracy. As well as its war guilt, and the desire to forget its trauma, it is probably Germany's success as a nation and a society that results in the relative lack of attention given to its dire postwar circumstances.

Yet this is starting to change. In 2019 a book by Harald Jähner called *Wolfzeit*, an account of Germany's postwar rebirth, became a bestseller in the country. There was an appetite among Germans to understand how their country had dealt, or not dealt, with its immediate past, and then risen from the ashes. Today, some Germans can be cynical on the matter, believing that their country flourished mostly because it allowed the big businesses of the Nazi era – the likes of BMW, Messerschmitt, Siemens – to flourish.[1]

Either way, Germany's roaring success began with austere military occupation. At the Yalta conference of February 1945 the Allies decided on a four-power occupation of the country after their coming victory. On 5 June 1945, in the Berlin suburb of Karlshorst – soon to be notorious as the headquarters of the Soviet occupation – the victors signed the 'Declaration in Consideration of the Defeat of Germany'. In the absence of any tenable German government, the governments of the United States, the Soviet Union, Britain and France were now the governing authorities of Germany, with each administering its own zone. Berlin, where the Soviets had been the sole Allied authority since storming the city in May, lay inside the Soviet zone and was to be administered by a Kommandatura of the four Allies. Issues concerning the whole of Germany were to be addressed by the four powers in the Allied Control Council, a body constituted on 30 July at Schöneberg in the American sector of Berlin.

The confusion and tensions set to arise from this arrangement – not to mention the long-term rupture of an entire country – might have been predicted. In 1961 the writer of an official British government publication passed the following verdict on the division of Germany:

> The provisions for the exercise of supreme authority in Germany as a whole – that it should be exercised on instructions from three, later four, governments, by three, later four Commanders-in-Chief whose decisions in the Control Council were required to be unanimous – would have been difficult enough to work if the governments concerned had enjoyed a common approach to their task, confidence in each others' intentions and a determination to succeed. When these were found to be lacking the provisions agreed upon immediately became unworkable. For anyone who did not wish them to bear fruit they could hardly have been better designed.[2]

Moreover, conditions on the ground were desperate. From the start the Allied armed forces struggled to carry out the unfamiliar duties of governance and policing. Ordinary soldiers and their commanders were now obliged, as Keith Lowe puts it, 'to act as a police force in a continent that had descended into chaos and lawlessness, and where weapons of all kinds were freely available'. During the war it had been anticipated that much of Germany's administration and infrastructure would survive. Instead they had been obliterated, compelling an unexpected degree of Allied involvement in salvaging and running the country. Military governments had to restore electricity, gas, water and coal supplies, to provide food and healthcare, to rehouse displaced persons, to clear roads and railway lines, and to recruit civic mayors and makeshift police forces. It was impossible to perform these tasks adequately. Everything had crumbled in Zusammenbruchsgesellschaft – the collapse of society.

Hunger was a killer. In all four occupation zones, most people had to survive on far less than 2,000 calories of food per day. Adding to the five million internal refugees in Germany were almost eight million forced labourers awaiting repatriation. Hailing from every corner of Europe, these former slaves were brutalised, hungry, and angry. A British military observer in Schwerin, a regional capital in north-east Germany, noted displaced persons 'roaming around in their thousands, murdering, raping, looting – in short, away from the main streets, law did not exist'.[3] The violence was exacerbated by the Soviet habit – not entirely dissimilar to that of the Western Allies – of allowing 'liberated' forced labourers a brief period of carte blanche in which to avenge themselves on the surrounding German population. These free-for-alls ended with the mass internment of labourers that soon followed, an internment in which some experienced worse conditions than they had during their enslavement.

Damage to roads and railways was so extensive that for years travelling anywhere in eastern Germany remained a slow, stressful ordeal. Attempts to repair railway tracks were scuppered when the Red Army pulled up big sections of the line to take to the USSR, an early example of the plundering Soviet approach to reparations which was to cause much economic grief. On receiving reports from Germany, Guy Liddell, deputy chief of MI5, Britain's security service, wrote that:

> Russian behaviour is to say the least peculiar. The whole of their zone is being stripped of machinery. The impression is that they intend to create a belt of Germany which will be devoid of any war potential. This in addition to Poland will act as a protective barrier between Russia and the Germans. The policy is being carried out in the most ruthless manner.[4]

Neither was the countryside spared. According to one rural mayor:

> Bringing in the harvest and threshing the grain gave us great difficulties, as most of the machines had been confiscated and most of the horses had been driven away... the Red Army took without payment and without receipt [from] 72 communities [a total of] 1,767 cattle, 896 pigs, 4,106 sheep, 32 calves, 2,221 chickens, 100,997 eggs, 282 geese and 142,200 kilograms of grain.[5]

Such confiscations of produce were supervised by the newly recruited local police forces – a foretaste of the Soviet-driven, German-against-German actions that would follow.

Another item on the police agenda was overseeing compulsory testing for sexually transmitted disease. The same mayor recorded that an 'examination of all inhabitants between 15 and 45 years of age for venereal disease has been ordered and will be carried out with the help of police control points'.[6] Even so, Keith Lowe writes that venereal disease was 'generally incurable, since the price of a single injection of antibiotics in Germany in August 1945 was two pounds of real coffee' – one of Europe's scarcest commodities. This situation had almost unthinkable effects on the millions of German women who had been raped. It took years for the threat of Red Army violence to recede. Women living near Soviet barracks had reason to be fearful until at least 1948.

Germany was now a country of women and girls, old men and boys. The Foreign Office registered more than 300,000 orphans in the British zone of north-western Germany; across the whole country there were probably two million.[7] In June 1945 a *Newsweek* article described 'groups of "child gangsters" [in] the Soviet zone mugging and sometimes killing people for food and money'.[8] Many German prisoners of war didn't return home for several years. Some of those held in the Soviet Bloc were not to see Germany until the mid-1950s, if at all, for the mortality rate among German soldiers captured in the east of Europe was ninety times higher than in the west.[9] Thus in the new Germany, a land without fathers, there was great potential for older German communists – those released from Nazi prisons and camps, for example – to perform an authoritative and avuncular role.

Even the reassurance of Marxism-Leninism couldn't help Berlin, however, which became Europe's most crime-infested city. By early 1946 there was a daily average of 240 robberies.[10] At first there was little the German police could do. The Allies had decreed they should be armed only with truncheons, and they faced dozens of criminal gangs, and mobs of displaced persons, who were armed to the teeth. Some crimes were spectacular, like the hold-up of a train at Anhalt station by 100 armed fugitives.[11] This gutsy, touchy, unorthodox city had always boasted a lively criminal underworld. In time, Berlin's gangsters, grifters, thugs and smugglers would prove to be trusty recruits for carrying out the dirty work of the Stasi and other intelligence services.

As noted, at the end of the war many Germans – probably a majority – were still not opposed to the Nazism that had brought them to this hellish state. Surveys conducted by an American agency in 1947 found that 'more than half of Germans considered National Socialism a fine idea poorly implemented'.[12] Thus the ruthless persecution of political dissent by the Soviet authorities, covered in the next chapter and beyond, had a rational basis of sorts. Moreover, it wasn't just the Soviets who governed firmly, for it was generally agreed, including among some Germans, that a degree of suffering was in order, as punishment for what Europe and the world had just endured. In all four occupation zones, military courts were given recourse to the death penalty for Germans guilty of such offences as the unauthorised possession of weapons or assaulting a member of the Allied forces.

Yet the overall impression of eastern Germany in 1945 is of a territory where brutality was simply placed under new management. The symbols on the flags changed; and the residents were plunged, without any meaningful consultation, straight into another authoritarian and belligerent regime.

3

SMERSH

In the aftermath of the war, life in eastern Germany was profoundly affected by the presence of SMERSH. When the Stasi was founded, its officers were expected to revere and emulate the work of SMERSH; 'Death to Spies', as Russian speakers knew it. Some of those Stasi officers had even served SMERSH as auxiliary personnel. Furthermore, SMERSH made a wider mark on the mentality and expectations of the people who were to become East Germans.

SMERSH was the counter-intelligence service of the Soviet armed forces. It had a short life: created in 1943, dissolved in 1946. Its original purpose was to catch German spies and root out traitors in the Red Army. As the Soviet military behemoth crashed westwards, SMERSH was tasked with vetting Soviet prisoners of war and forced labourers before they were repatriated. Like so many security services of authoritarian states, SMERSH then pushed at the boundaries of its remit, expanding almost organically. By the time the Red Army had overrun Ukraine, Belorussia and Poland, SMERSH had assumed the task of removing from society almost anyone whose face didn't fit.

In the James Bond novels, Ian Fleming used the name SMERSH as the assassination department of the KGB. This helped to confuse Western understanding of the organisation. Much of its work was bureaucratic. It played a role in the denazification of German society and at the Nuremberg trials in 1946. Moreover, the impact of SMERSH on eastern Germany, and on the Stasi story, has gone largely unremarked. This is partly because SMERSH was often misidentified by its victims. Its personnel wore the uniform of the military formation in which they served, and so were visually indistinguishable from other Soviet soldiers, sailors and aircrew. Many of those who fell into its hands believed their cases were being handled by the better-known NKVD. The confusion is understandable, for scores of experienced NKVD officers had been transferred into SMERSH when it was founded, and they transferred back to the state security service after its disbandment. This included the SMERSH chief, Viktor Abakumov.

In the twenty-first century, Abakumov has been exalted in hagiographical Russian television documentaries and dramas. He is held up as an example of a noble security official, foiling the plots of despicable fascists, as if his role in the war made him somehow cleaner than the known rapists, drunkards and hoarders of pornography who had previously led the Soviet counter-espionage effort.* This upright reputation is undeserved. Early in his career Abakumov was demoted for forcing female informers into sex and making false denouncements. He thus found himself, aptly, working as a Gulag guard.[1] But his comfort with violence helped him climb back up the ladder, as did his greatest qualification – the fact he was an ethnic Russian. If an organisation's values are spread downwards by its executives, there was little hope for SMERSH. Or for eastern Germany, given that Abakumov was to be a master of the region's fate for a lengthy period; as head of SMERSH in 1945-6, and as head of Soviet state security – known at this stage as the MGB – from 1946 to 1951.

The brutality of SMERSH was one aspect of the purportedly righteous violence of the Soviet assault on Germany. The Red Army's advance was described by one Soviet officer as a 'gory, drunken wave of debauchery' that 'rose high and swept over the dam of official orders'.[2] Although rape and other crimes potentially were punishable by death, Soviet troops understood that they were unlikely to face any penalty for committing them. The peoples of the Soviet Union, including ethnic Russians, had suffered on an unimaginable scale. It was time for the Germans and their Axis partners – especially Hungarians and Romanians – to pay the price.

To this end, political officers held 'revenge meetings' in Red Army units, where soldiers would describe what the Germans had done to their families and villages, and pledge to even the score once on German soil. The desire for revenge was whipped up in propaganda campaigns that included the exhortations of celebrated Soviet writers. Hundreds of thousands of Red Army troops were familiar with such works as Konstantin Simonov's poem 'Kill Him!' ('If your brother kills a German/He's a soldier, you are not... So kill at least one of them/And as soon as you can'), and Ilya Ehrenburg's famous article 'Kill The Germans' ('If you kill one German, kill another – there is nothing more amusing').

Large Red Army formations were augmented with commissions tasked with confiscating German property and valuables. Stalin's government was intent on seizing German assets, both as compensation and to boost Soviet industry and technology. While some items ended up in official hands, others

---

*   This refers to Lavrenti Beria, Nikolai Yezhov and Genrikh Yagoda.

were claimed by the rank-and-file. This could make an unreal spectacle of advancing Soviet columns: trucks loaded with paintings, carpets and grandfather clocks; soldiers with top hats and musical instruments, their arms ringed with wristwatches.

The underlying point is that the Red Army advance, and the early days of Soviet occupation, created an outlandish situation. Those responsible for ferocious vengeance against the German population were also responsible for governance and rebuilding civil society. The Red Army officer who might steal your furniture and assault your relatives was the person you went to with suggestions and complaints. And so, from the start, the social and political atmosphere of eastern Germany pulsed with this peculiar tension.

Of course, there were problems with corruption and violent incidents in all the occupation zones, and SMERSH did carry out some real counter-intelligence work against real Nazis, especially during the war. Vadim Birstein, the author of a major study of the organisation, writes that 'at the beginning of 1945, the activity of groups of German terrorists in the rear of advancing Soviet troops intensified.'[3] Joint operational groups were formed, consisting of SMERSH, NKGB and NKVD personnel, the latter usually security troops. Viktor Abakumov reported to Lavrenti Beria that these groups:

> were told to find and immediately arrest spies, saboteurs, and terrorists of the intelligence organs of the enemy; members of the bandit-insurgent groups; members of fascist and other organizations; leaders and operational staff of the police, and other suspicious individuals; and also to confiscate depots of weapons, radio transmitters, and technical equipment left by the enemy for [sabotage] work.[4]

By the autumn of 1945, nine camps had been opened in Germany for those apprehended by the operational groups. Three were former concentration camps: Buchenwald, Sachsenhausen and Jamlitz.

The Soviets began to prosecute war crimes with more alacrity than the Western Allies. This was partly because the Soviet theatre of war provided the opportunity to do so. Birstein quotes a section called 'Statement on Atrocities' in the Moscow Declaration, signed in November 1943 by Stalin, Franklin Roosevelt and Winston Churchill. It sanctioned the removal of suspected war criminals from Germany to the USSR and elsewhere:

> Those German officers and men and members of the Nazi party who have been responsible for or have taken a consenting part in [the] atrocities, massacres and executions will be sent back to the countries in which their abominable deeds

were done in order that they may be judged and punished according to the laws of these liberated countries and of free governments which will be elected therein.[5]

It was the job of SMERSH personnel to identify such culprits, prepare indictments, and provide evidence at their trials. They set to work quickly, for in December 1943 the Soviets held the first ever trial of German officers for war crimes, after SMERSH had indicted four men taken prisoner at Stalingrad the previous January. At this trial, in the testimony of SS-Obersturmbannführer Georg Heinisch, the first public evidence of mass killing with gas at the Auschwitz concentration camp emerged, although this revelation went unreported by all of the foreign correspondents who attended.[6]

On 9 June 1945, Order Number 1 established eastern Germany's new government: the Soviet Military Administration in Germany or SMAD.* Based at Karlshorst, SMAD was responsible for the administration, economy, infrastructure and justice system of the Soviet occupation zone, which was known in German as the SBZ (Sowjetische Besatzungszone). The first head of SMAD was Marshal Georgy Zhukov, hero of Stalingrad and commander of the Soviet forces in Germany – although, since 1939, the NKVD and then SMERSH had collected compromising materials on Zhukov, of whom Stalin was wary. Another Soviet official who was to play a big role in Germany's future was Ivan Serov, who was appointed 'NKVD Plenipotentiary in Charge of Combating Spies, Saboteurs, and Other Enemies on German Territory'. This position gave Serov the right to arrest anyone and to create prisons and camps, but it also made him responsible for local civil administrations. Jealous of Serov's power, Viktor Abakumov insisted on founding a SMERSH department under SMAD, with operational groups in every region and city.

The occupying powers were in a position to augment German laws with their own. One of the laws that applied in the SBZ – the infamous Article 58 of the Soviet Russian penal code – had already been in use in the USSR for almost two decades in cases of 'counter-revolutionary activity'. Designed to incriminate political 'enemies of the people' – spies, saboteurs and 'wreckers' of socialist industry – in the late 1930s Article 58 had given Stalin a spurious legal basis for the mass persecution of his own people. Now it was to cut a legalistic swathe through the population of eastern Germany.

Birstein notes that 'local citizens arrested by SMERSH were charged, mostly as spies [under] Article 58-6'. Cases could be dealt with locally, but SMERSH

---

* SMAD for Sowjetische Militäradministration in Deutschland; in Russian, SVAG, for Sovyetskaya Voyennaya Administratsiya v Germanii.

'sent many of those suspected of espionage to Moscow'.[7] Some of those arrested were, if not actual spies, at least active Nazis. Others were neither, as subsequent chapters will indicate, but it was the extra-curricular activities of SMERSH personnel that caused the most grief.

In June 1945 an official policy was introduced to regulate the acquisition of German goods by Red Army personnel. It set out a (rather un-communist) hierarchy for the items obtained. Private soldiers 'were permitted to take whatever they could carry in their arms, officers could utilize a bicycle or motorcycle, and generals could use a car to transport whatever they wanted'.[8] Abakumov, usually loath to criticise his own workforce, was compelled to order SMERSH personnel to be more scrupulous in recording their personal possessions.

Even Marshal Zhukov and the hard-nosed Ivan Serov grew uneasy about the abuse of the German population. In June and September 1945, Zhukov issued orders to tackle the problem. The first order stated that, 'Local authorities, peasant communities, and individuals continue to complain about numerous acts of violence, rape, and robbery… Women do not mow hay or work in the fields, for fear of being raped or robbed.'[9] According to the September order, 'Marauding, hooliganism, and violence against the German population have not stopped; on the contrary, crimes committed by servicemen have increased. This behaviour [must] stop immediately at all costs.'[10] Stalin's response was to reprimand Zhukov and make him withdraw the September order.

Ivan Serov resented having to clean up the messes made by SMERSH. In 1946 he complained to Stalin about two incidents from the previous year. One was a botched kidnapping of some women from the British occupation zone. The intended victims, who were probably Soviet labourers due for repatriation, gave their abductors the slip and then pointed the finger at SMERSH operatives. The second incident occurred when a Soviet military tribunal had pronounced death sentences on some residents of the city of Halle. One night the prisoners were escorted into the fields outside of town to be shot by SMERSH officers. Not unusually, the executioners were staggering drunk. In burying the corpses, they left two hands and a head sticking out of the ground. These were spotted the following morning by locals passing by on a nearby road. The locals dug up the corpses, found bullet holes in the heads, gathered witnesses, and went to the police.[11]

Serov's reaction to this and other complaints involving SMERSH was to organise a series of show trials against the German complainants. The trials, which took place towards the end of 1946, were held throughout the Soviet zone. Sentences were publicised in the local press. For the accused, the most likely outcome was incarceration in a camp for arrested Nazis. This invidious method paid off. Birstein notes that 'after this, Germans were afraid to report the atrocities.'[12] Thus, several years before the Stasi existed, one of its major fields of activity had emerged: the harsh and corrupt justice system of eastern Germany, and citizens' doomed attempts to challenge it.

For their part, Soviet military and security personnel were accustomed to arbitrary and violent political repression. They had grown up with it. Some relished the task put before them in Europe, like the SMERSH and MGB officer Colonel Georgy Yevdomimenko, who wrote: 'For some people, perhaps, the war was over, but for us... the real war, to bring about the final destruction of the capitalist world, was only just beginning.'[13]

4

Anti-fascist Unity: The New Politics

At the end of April 1945, the Red Army soldiers fighting their way towards the heart of Berlin were joined by a team of foreigners armed mostly with loudhailers, registration forms and stocks of leaflets. In the first week of May, two similar teams joined the Soviet troops in the eastern German states of Mecklenburg and Saxony. These teams were made up of communists: around thirty hand-picked German communists, most of whom had spent the war in exile in the Soviet Union. They and the remnants of their German Communist Party, the KPD (Kommunistische Partei Deutschlands), had managed to survive one of the most turbulent and bloody eras experienced by any political movement. Now they were to go to work, and help to build the country of their dreams.

These teams were known as initiative groups (initiativgruppen). Some of the members were Wehrmacht prisoners of war who had undergone political re-education in Soviet captivity. For some time, the exiled KPD leadership in Moscow had been debating Germany's postwar future. One result was a large scheme of political re-education, implemented across the USSR's prisoner of war camps with the aim of 'denazifying' the inmates.

The main task of the initiative groups was to support the Soviet authorities and help them to communicate with a frightened and suspicious public. They were also to help create new civil institutions – including, crucially, police forces – and to join the hunt for important Nazis and war criminals. Another task was to identify anti-Nazi Germans who might prove useful to the Soviet administration.

The groups were led by fifty-one-year-old Walter Ulbricht, head of the group for Berlin-Brandenburg. Ulbricht was second only to Wilhelm Pieck in the KPD hierarchy. Pieck, twenty years his senior, remained in Moscow for a little longer. It was Ulbricht, a moaning Stalinist whose eyes never quite managed to meet anyone else's, who was destined to spend the next two decades as the most powerful German in East Germany.

Some of the other group members had a notable future in store. Twenty-four-year-old Wolfgang Leonhard, the youngest, was destined to flee eastern

Germany a few years later. He went on to write one of the key eyewitness accounts of twentieth century communism, published in English as *Child of the Revolution*. Later, as a Yale professor, Leonhard was able to provide the Western democracies with much-needed information on the mysteries of the Soviet Bloc. Then there was Gustav Sobottka, a miners' agitator who had run to Moscow in 1935; he led the initiative group for Mecklenburg. By the end of the war Sobottka had seen two of his sons die at the hands of Europe's extremist regimes, one in Moscow's Butyrka prison, the other at the Nazis' Fuhlsbüttel concentration camp. Sobottka himself only survived exile in the USSR by the skin of his teeth, his prestige boosted when the Nazis sentenced him to death in absentia. After working at an East German government ministry he was to die, reputedly of grief, the day after learning of Stalin's death in 1953.

Anton Ackermann, leader of the group for Saxony, was another highly experienced KPD functionary. A decade later, as East Germany's deputy foreign minister, he would fall victim to the factional infighting typical of a communist party; fired from his job, his name ruined, he was then – almost as suddenly – forgiven and rehabilitated in a classic Bolshevik about-turn. Rudolf Herrnstadt was to lose his job in the same purge, despite his legendary career as a spy for Moscow during the 1930s. Fred Oelssner, a prominent figure in the early days of the GDR, would also be a purge victim. Another seasoned Soviet spy, Kurt Fischer, who was in Ackermann's group, would reach the heights of East German police chief, only to die at a Stasi health spa in 1950.

Some group members were to experience smoother lives. Artur Hofmann would spend nearly twenty years as a Stasi colonel. Hermann Matern was to play a key role in the East German leadership. Karl Maron would be serving as interior minister when the Berlin Wall was built. Otto Winzer was to spend much of the 1960s and 1970s as foreign minister; and by the 1980s his fellow diplomat, Peter Florin, would be serving as East Germany's permanent representative to the United Nations.

Wolfgang Leonhard claimed that it took the initiative groups just two weeks to ensure communist control of eastern Germany.[1] This was an exaggeration, but it does suggest how avidly the communists sought power. They were equipped with a KPD manual, 'Guidelines for the work of anti-fascists in areas occupied by the Red Army', which set out the rules for new anti-Nazi newspapers; for the closing of schools and the discarding of their textbooks, to be replaced by newly written books propounded by newly trained teachers; for the formation of committees and personnel departments, led by returning exiles, to purge institutions of active Nazis. At this early stage, local citizens were to be reassured that mere membership of the Nazi party wouldn't necessarily result in punishment; it was acknowledged that some had joined the party for reasons of safety and conformity.

To create a framework for their own dominance, the Soviet authorities and their German helpers used at least two Stalinist methods. Both were honed during the Soviets' earlier involvement in the Spanish Civil War; and both were designed to give communists the real power in what looked like a coalition of several political parties.

The first was to appoint communists not to the top political positions but rather to deputy positions, especially as provincial interior ministers and police chiefs. The post-holders thus had control over such areas as security, press censorship, job appointments and identity papers. This tactic enabled communists to enact their programme without appearing to be overly dominant. The second method was Stalin's 'National Front' strategy. This meant creating a coalition or block of political parties that could be dominated by communists, by various means and with varying degrees of subtlety. This strategy was applied in the countries that came to make up the Soviet Bloc.

There is still debate about when Stalin began to plan for a Soviet empire in Europe – a plan based on the assumption that Hitler would lose the war, and one that called for expansion in order to protect Stalin himself, his territory, and his ideology.[2] But the formation in 1943 of the National Committee for Free Germany, a future-focused resistance organisation with its headquarters in Moscow, is a strong indicator that Stalin's secret plans for the continent were already being hatched. The committee was a manifestation of the emerging National Front strategy.

Stalin wanted the new governments of central and eastern Europe to be friendly to the Soviet Union, and biddable, but he didn't intend to impose the Soviet system on Germany. Such a move was considered unrealistic, and likely to antagonise the Western Allies and the German population unnecessarily; perhaps even to render the German people ungovernable. Conscious of the need to soothe the fears of the bourgeoisie, at one point Stalin told German communists, 'You should advance towards socialism not by taking a straight road but move in zigzags.'[3] Initially, then, Germany was to be rendered compliant, but not a replica of Soviet Russia.

In fact, all the Allied leaders, including Stalin, had rather vague ideas about what to do there. Stalin's policies are difficult to trace, partly because he adopted his masterly habit of remaining aloof from the matter while his subordinates ran around like headless chickens, all trying to implement conflicting approaches. But it is safe to say that stealth and opportunism ruled the day, for Stalin's main concerns, it seems, were practical rather than ideological: first, to secure massive reparations, on an ongoing basis, from Germany; and second, to prevent the creation of an eastwards-facing military alliance in western Europe – in short, to prevent the emergence of a West Germany.

This is where the National Committee for Free Germany came in. On paper, the committee was intended to usher in a future German democracy. It was dedicated to the notion of a united Germany, and its membership supposedly was pan-political. Branches were set up anywhere in the world where there were exiled anti-Nazi Germans, and most members of the initiative groups had been involved with the committee while living in the Soviet Union. Given their subsequent careers in East German politics, however, it is fair to see the National Committee as a Stalinist ruse – a way of creating a pro-Soviet government-in-waiting, but one which gained the acceptance of the Western Allies, at least while the war was still being fought.

On 10 June 1945 – the day after Order Number 1 had created SMAD – Stalin's ideas for a new order in eastern Germany began to take shape. Marshal Zhukov issued Order Number 2, which permitted the founding of an 'anti-fascist block' of political parties and trade unions. Members of the National Committee were expected to take leading roles in the block, which was formally constituted in July as the United Front of Anti-fascist Democratic Parties; the Antifa Block for short. Later the Antifa Block was to evolve into the National Front, a sham coalition that dominated electoral politics in East Germany for the duration of its history. Initially the block had four parties, all founded or refounded over the summer of 1945.

The most influential and best-supported parties in eastern Germany were the KPD and the Social Democratic Party, the SPD. The Nazi defeat led to a surge in Marxist confidence; by the end of August the KPD had 150,000 members, the SPD 375,000.[4] The Christian Democratic Union (CDU), which grew from the remnants of the pre-war Centre Party, also had large support. Somewhat smaller, though constitutionally significant, was the Liberal Democratic Party of Germany (LDPD), which adopted the left-liberal position of a Weimar-era predecessor.* The CDU and LDPD were slated to be the Antifa Block's non-Marxist participants. According to the Soviets, these four were the acceptable parties in what they were already calling 'the democratic zone', a new kind of territory where parties representing fascism, nationalism, and bourgeois conservativism would never be welcome.

On 11 June 1945 the KPD issued a proclamation that hinted at the realities and deceits which were to follow. 'We are of the opinion that it would be wrong

---

* SPD: Sozialdemokratische Partei Deutschlands. CDU: Christlich-Demokratische Union Deutschlands. LDPD: Liberal-Demokratische Partei Deutschlands.

to force the Soviet system on Germany,' read the preamble, 'as the present conditions of development in Germany are not suitable for it.' As noted, such caution was shared by many Soviet and German communists, who had no desire to make enemies among the population or the Western Allies. The KPD's ten-point programme called for the restoration of 'democratic rights' and an end to racial discrimination. It stressed the party's willingness to join with others in a united front, which ultimately would result in a blissful 'anti-fascist, parliamentary, democratic republic'. The declaration said nothing about freedom of speech or religion, however. Nor did it give details about the party's proposed remoulding of the judicial system 'according to the people's new democratic way of life'. It was equally vague about the party's plans to redistribute land, which apparently was to be confiscated from landowners without compensation.[5]

When it came to denazification, the KPD showed its teeth. There was to be a 'complete liquidation of the remains of the Hitler regime and the Hitler party', the 'complete cleansing of all public offices of active Nazis', the 'expropriation of the entire property of Nazi bigwigs and war criminals', and the 'liquidation of large estates'. For many eastern Germans these were welcome aims. They tallied with the goals set out at the Potsdam conference that summer, which manifested in the International Military Tribunal set up for the Nuremberg trials.[6]

The other Antifa Block parties soon issued their own proclamations. The SPD stated its willingness to work with communists, blaming Hitler's success partly on the divisiveness of the political left, but its proclamation put more emphasis on democracy. While it pledged commitment to a socialist economy – more than the KPD did, at this point – it rejected the notion of class struggle or the imposition of the Soviet system. The CDU gave its theoretical blessing to some state-owned industry and to the redistribution of land, partly to accommodate the millions of Germans being expelled from Czechoslovakia and Poland. More boldly, it demanded that the Soviet occupiers release prisoners, restore access to bank accounts, return stolen livestock, and meet the population's fuel and food needs. Unlike the Marxist parties, the CDU also insisted on having an independent judicial system. It stressed that the rule of law and 'legal security' (Rechtssicherheit) – an important concept for Germans to this day – must be scrupulously observed. Similarly, the LDPD called for a spotless and independent judicial system 'to safeguard justice'. At a meeting in July 1945 a liberal official declared that Rechtssicherheit was 'not merely a legal issue, but rather a requirement of life in a modern parliamentary democracy'.[7] The LDPD also recognised the right to private property; it was cautious on the topics of redistributing land and nationalising industry.[8]

Despite the divergences within the Antifa Block, the Soviets were quick to use this oddly-shaped alliance for propaganda. Press and radio boasted that the Soviet zone was the first in which anti-fascist Germans could resume some form of political expression. In reality, this didn't amount to much more than being corralled into joining one party or another. And, predictably, there were great internal tensions and contradictions in this 'democratic' fellowship; although, to be clear, the communists were not using the word 'democratic' in the Western sense – in Soviet use, it implied 'not fascist'. Still, in promoting the block concept, and spraying around the word 'democracy', the communists were, of course, initiating a vast deception. In the years to come, those who happened to oppose the one party selected by Moscow to govern eastern Germany, the SED, were routinely accused of being 'anti-democratic'.

Meanwhile, the chaotic and inefficient structures of the Soviet zone were put in place. During May 1945, seventy German communist exiles and 300 former prisoners of war had been brought to eastern Germany to head local administrations, though, of course, they were subordinate to Soviet military commandants.[9] The US army vacated eastern areas such as Thuringia to make way for the Red Army, but not before removing human and material assets of all kinds; in a similar vein, the British 'evacuated' tremendous stocks of sugar from Magdeburg. As further compensation for their loss of territory, the Western Allies then occupied parts of Berlin, creating the city's eccentric layout, with the British, American and French sectors effectively islands in a Soviet sea.

It was soon established, albeit rather loosely, that Allied personnel were entitled to travel between Berlin and western Germany using the main Helmstedt-Berlin highway, or by train on the railway line adjacent to it. Three more roads, and alternative rail routes, were available to other travellers. There was extensive access via canal and river systems; in due course almost 4,000 barges were licensed to carry goods between the zones and, later, between the two German republics. And in the years before the Wall was built, the three Berlin air corridors came to be used by Pan-Am, British European Airways and Air France, as well as military aircraft.

The Soviet sector of Berlin was by far the largest, partly in recompense for the Red Army's losses. Significantly for the Stasi story, Soviet Berlin encompassed Lichtenberg, a traditionally left-wing district where communists of the 1920s had gathered in the beer halls to plot revolutionary violence. The Stasi would make its headquarters there. Another left-wing area, Wedding – 'Red Wedding' to the pre-war working class – fell in the French sector. It was the birthplace of a certain Erich Mielke. In time, British personnel would warm to their sector, which encompassed the nightclubs of Charlottenburg – 'Grotty Charlotty' to British soldiers – as well as 'Dickie Heinrich's little cabin' on the Kurfürstendamm, where one could 'get a smashing goulash [at] four or five in the morning after a heavy night out'. One British intelligence officer recalled that 'newcomers [to the city] were usually initiated at the Golden Hufeisen where they were never quite the same after discovering that their gorgeous dancing partners were actually transvestites.'[10] In 1945, however, there were no hints of such abandon. Adding to the sense of desolation and isolation, the western sectors of Berlin were bounded by Soviet, and later East German, territory. In the south-western suburbs these borders ran across a lake system, which was to see much illicit activity in the years to come.

On 9 July, SMAD Order Number 5 divided the Soviet zone into five traditional provincial states known as Länder, each with its own president, vice presidents, and administration.* The KPD did not push for its members to be appointed president of any Land, for ceding the presidency to social democrats and liberals gave the appearance of democracy and broad representation. Instead, communists were appointed as vice presidents, the position that came with control of each state's interior ministry and police service. Soon after the founding of the Länder administrations, a number of central administrations were created in Berlin. But they were not empowered; at first they just advised SMAD in such matters as the railway system, supplies, and the postal service.[11]

In all four occupation zones, land reform was one of the first major shake-ups of Germany's society and economy. The need to house and feed a homeless population pushed it to the top of the agenda. In the Soviet zone, ostensibly land was to be appropriated from war criminals and members of Nazi organisations such as the SS, and redistributed in five-hectare plots. In preliminary discussions, Christian democrats and liberals insisted that landowners with a non-Nazi past be compensated if their land were taken. The co-chair of the LDPD, Andreas Hermes, tried to publish an article in the zone's Soviet-run newspaper, *Tägliche Rundschau*, to air his concerns about the potential lack of compensation. He also warned that class warfare in one part of Germany might jeopardise the reunification of the country. Hermes had already raised Soviet hackles by petitioning SMAD, as early as July 1945, to release all arrested persons, restore access to bank accounts, and 'satisfy the fuel requirements of the German population and German industry'. Clearly, Hermes didn't get it:

---

* The five Länder were Mecklenburg, with its seat of government in the city of Schwerin; Brandenburg (Potsdam); Thuringia (Weimar); Saxony (Dresden); and Saxony-Anhalt (Halle). Formally the latter was a Provinz, not a Land.

in the eyes of SMAD officials, Germany was guilty of trying to destroy Russia, and even-handedness wasn't called for. When the Soviet authorities refused to publish his article, Hermes – in an early sign of the brewing systemic conflict – published it in the American-licenced *Allgemeine Zeitung.*

For the Marxists, land reform was a vengeful as well as a practical step, and one of many in the coming socialising of the economy. As one communist official put it, 'it is imperative to fill the higher and middle level posts in the economy with our people in order to create a new order in the means of production.'[12] When it came, the KPD-driven land reform was insatiable. Although the party scrupulously avoided any talk of 'class warfare', social background tended to be the deciding factor in who lost land and who did not. According to a CDU statement, social criteria saw 'thousands of completely untainted families, themselves fierce opponents of the Nazi system and recognised victims of fascism... expelled from their homes and unjustly ordered out of their towns'. Unlawful actions saw people 'not only robbed of their land, but of all their personal belongings'.[13]

In November 1945 the CDU lodged a formal protest on the matter. By this time the Soviets had started to subvert the CDU by inserting articles praising the land reform, published initially in the communist press, into the CDU's main newspaper without attribution. Low-level coercion of members of the non-Marxist parties had also begun. Soviet officials urged CDU activists to challenge the party's leadership. At least one CDU group was granted a newspaper licence as a reward for endorsing the landgrabs.[14] When these tactics failed to unseat the party's leaders, the Soviets sent out a loud and clear message by simply removing them from their posts.[15]

5

The Police Reborn

For the Soviet authorities, the police force of eastern Germany ultimately was to be a communist police force. However, it was not to *look* like a communist police force, especially in its early days. It was to appear democratic and pluralistic. The tricky job of arranging this was dumped on the German communists who were chosen to fashion the new police. Arguably, they didn't manage to fool anyone.

At the time, there was a genuine and widespread desire to create a fairer, proletarian, anti-fascist police service. This was true among social democrats as much as communists. During 1945, SPD members were still at liberty to play a leading role in the new police organisations. As well as anti-Nazis returning from exile, and those released from prisons and camps, there were up to 18,000 candidates for police work among the prisoners of war who had been re-educated by KPD instructors.[*] Adding to this number were those who had been lectured by German communists at 'field schools' during the final days of the Soviet advance.[1] However, senior positions in the police were to be filled by proven anti-Nazi resisters: 'the only people who had the moral authority to take charge'.[2]

In the months after the Nazi defeat, many administrative tasks in eastern Germany, including rebuilding the police, were carried out by means of the venerable 'anti-fascist committee'. Throughout the zone these committees sprang up to purge and restructure every locality, site, and activity: offices, apartment buildings, schools, police stations. This was another echo of the Spanish Civil War, where committees of leftists and democrats had purged every conceivable institution in the wake of the Nationalist coup. In eastern Germany, the committees contained anti-Nazis of various stripes, although the 'Red Kapos' of Buchenwald and Sachsenhausen – communist trusties liberated

---

[*] The KPD ran an extensive programme in Soviet POW camps. During the war, some 2,000 retrained Wehrmacht officers who had renounced Nazism were assigned to frontline Soviet forces, often partisan units. Prisoners who were especially promising and trustworthy could find themselves being trained in intelligence tradecraft at the KPD's 'Institut 100', or in propaganda broadcasting at 'Institut 205' – both under the watchful eyes of Soviet security personnel.

from the camps – tended to take prominent positions.[3] So too did communists released from prisons who, together with camp inmates and others who had suffered under the Nazis, now made up the Association of Victims of the Nazi Regime,* an organisation that would come to play an important role in East German civic life.

Another priority for the anti-fascist committees was to set up new residents' registration offices (Einwohnermeldeämter). The practice of registering one's home address with the local authorities, including the police, was traditional in Germany and many other European countries. Now it was to provide the Soviet occupiers with vital information on who was who and who was where.

None of this reorganising was easy. The newly appointed anti-fascist administrators 'had to deal first with a bureaucracy inherited from the hated Nazi regime and then with the lack of trained personnel once the old guard had been removed'.[4] Often there were great tensions between the anti-fascist committees and local people, many of whom were scornful of returning left-wing exiles.[5] A considerable number of Germans were uninterested in shedding their National Socialism. Visceral hatred of Russians, stoked by years of racist propaganda, was probably even more indelible. Thus, anger towards the Red Army's perceived sidekicks took a range of forms, from mockery in fast-spreading jokes to physical violence. Moreover, the committees were shot by both sides; they were disliked by Walter Ulbricht and other KPD high-ups, who were wary of their independence and revolutionary naiveté.

In fact, efforts by the KPD, and above all Ulbricht, saw the committees steadily shut down in favour of Soviet-appointed administrations answerable to a local Soviet commandant, of whom there were some 500 at first. As in the other occupation zones, for Germans it was an offence, triable in a military court, to fail to support these newly appointed administrations. And week by week, month by month, KPD members got the positions that really counted at police departments.

Special efforts were made in Berlin. The city's first postwar mayor was the politically colourless Arthur Werner, but the Soviet commandant, Nikolai Berzarin, appointed two communists to the more hands-on roles beneath Werner. Karl Maron, who had joined the KPD in 1926, was made deputy mayor, and so responsible for the city's internal affairs. Paul Markgraf, a Wehrmacht officer who had undergone political re-education in Soviet captivity, was appointed Berlin police chief.[6] His staff included Hans Fruck, later to be a Stasi general, and Erich Mielke, who would lead the Stasi to its bitter end; Mielke was commissioner for police affairs. The secretary of the Berlin police union,

---

* Vereinigung der Verfolgten des Naziregimes (VVN).

Walter Mickin, was another veteran communist who had spent ten years in Nazi prisons. Richard Staimer, soon to marry the daughter of KPD leader Wilhelm Pieck, headed the police in the Prenzlauer Berg district; later he would lead East Germany's paramilitary police. Richard Grosskopf, freed from twelve years of Nazi imprisonment, headed the police department for identity papers; a few years later he would help to build the Stasi's foreign intelligence service. Alfred Schönherr was released from Waldheim prison to lead Berlin's detective police, the Kriminalpolizei or Kripo; he was to become an SED invigilator within the Stasi.

Reports found their way to MI5 concerning the appointment to an important police role of Hans Kahle, a German revolutionary communist with whom Britain's security service was already well acquainted. The Metropolitan Police Special Branch told MI5 of 'information received' – probably from German communists still living in London – that Kahle:

> the military expert of the German Communist Party, and a former G.P.U. [Soviet security] agent in Spain during the Civil War, has now been appointed Police-President of the German Province of Mecklenburg, in the Russian occupied zone.
>
> Kahle is said to have been directly responsible for the murder of a number of non-Communists fighting with the Republican Forces in the International Brigade in Spain.[7]

An officer noted a 'most significant' point about this development in Kahle's MI5 file: that 'here was a communist returning to Germany who had spent the whole war in the West but who was at once given a big police appointment by the Russians.'[8]

It should be remembered that all of these police appointees answered to the Soviet military administration. These were not Germans whom the Soviets trusted – the Soviets didn't trust any German – but they were considered the least likely to cause trouble. Soviet officials arbitrated on all appointments and made every important decision. The police, formally subordinate to local army commanders, existed to assist the Soviet military, on demand; and they had to get the approval of the Soviet military for anything else they might want to do.

Nevertheless, from their sectors of Berlin and the west of Germany, the Western Allies watched the steady appointment of communists to run the Soviet zone's police. This creeping development meant something. It was intriguing, disconcerting. Something was coming.

*

From the summer of 1945 onwards, the new police force in the Soviet zone had two priorities. One was to tackle the raging black market and the outbreak of smuggling between the occupation zones. The other was to help the Soviet security forces to order the population. In particular, this meant enforcing confiscations of property, and arresting Nazis and war criminals.

The new police were not proficient. The fight against crime was hopeless. Experienced officers had been arrested by SMERSH or the NKGB, helped by the members of anti-fascist committees. Despite the high ideals set by the Soviets and German left-wingers, many local police stations employed drifters and thugs. The desperate need to tackle crime and disorder led to an unfussy recruitment drive which netted former Wehrmacht soldiers and Nazis,[9] even members of the SS and old Brownshirts from the SA. Communist police officers complained about the hiring of 'older comrades whose mental abilities were not sufficient to master service in the police'.[10] Other recruits joined up, in the words of one historian, 'neither out of political conviction nor out of some altruistic desire to serve the public but primarily in order to gain food (ration cards), clothing (uniforms, boots) and shelter (police barracks) during a time of terrible shortages'.[11]

These benefits weren't always on offer. The Allies had agreed that the German police should not be armed; in many cases, neither were they clothed, fed or housed. Uniforms were in short supply and many officers were identifiable only by an armband, their sole defence against the gun-toting criminals terrorising the land. Not until January 1946 did the fight against criminals get a bit fairer, when the Allied Control Council lifted the ban on carrying firearms. Police officers faced great danger when trying to arrest the many Red Army soldiers who were looting and assaulting the locals. The few who were arrested successfully were handed over to Soviet commanders whose only action, usually, was to dismiss the case.[12]

Being under Soviet military leadership didn't rule out police corruption; far from it. There were cases of extortion, theft, the settling of personal scores, and ill-discipline – including a tendency for police officers to simply drift away from guard duty whenever it suited them.[13] Women recruits were underused, although those who weren't palmed off with directing traffic were allowed to take part in campaigns to combat prostitution and venereal disease.

All four occupying powers struggled to achieve competent policing. At Wildflecken in the American zone, for example, the police force serving a large displaced persons' camp had to be sacked and replaced five times in eighteen months due to corruption.[14] But such was the organisational nadir that was postwar Germany. Rather than trying to implement effective consensual policing, the police in the Soviet zone probably found it more straightforward to act as translators and muscle for Soviet arrest operations, which was one of their major duties.

These operations were led by SMERSH or NKGB counter-intelligence officers, with the NKVD responsible for guarding and transporting prisoners. From April 1945 onwards, the initiative groups had trained German communists in the techniques of house searches and making arrests. One of the first big arrest campaigns took place after SMAD issued its Order Number 42 in late August. It stipulated that all Wehrmacht officers, Nazi party members, Gestapo employees, and members of the SS and SA were to report to the local Red Army command. Having identified themselves, around 150,000 were arrested.[15]

In every locality the SMAD security forces drew up lists of persons of interest. As well as their own intelligence they collected information from concentration camp survivors, freed prisoners and forced labourers, and denunciations from the public. The German police officers who assisted SMAD in political operations were something of a clandestine elite within their own stations. They worked with Soviet liaison officers and carried Soviet identity cards. These small teams acquired the name of S Departments (Abteilungen S), with S standing for special or security tasks (Sonderaufgaben, Sicherheitsaufgaben). In Saxony-Anhalt they were named Police Political Departments (Polizei Politische Abteilungen), making their role even more explicit. It is surprising, at this point, to find such obvious reference to the notion of a German political police. The idea was completely taboo, and ran counter to everything the Allies had agreed about defeated Germany. Although the Allies intended to encourage Germans to gradually adopt independent political activity, as well as freedom of speech and thought, the occupation zones were not supposed to be politicised, and were certainly not supposed to host German security agencies.

At the end of October 1945, two more SMAD orders led to new waves of arrests. Order Number 124 announced the takeover of all assets possessed by the former government, the Wehrmacht, and militant Nazis. Order Number 126 mandated the same thing for the Nazi party and its affiliated organisations, such as the Hitler Youth and the League of German Girls. These orders clarified the legal basis for the seizure and redistribution of land, which was already underway. On 3 December, Order Number 160 criminalised 'encroachments against economic measures' by any German corporate body, and established stiff prison sentences for offenders.[16] This gave some legal weight to the summary takeover of industrial and commercial concerns, including stripping them for removal to the Soviet Union.

Although equivalent measures were taking place in the western occupation zones, they were being carried out in a markedly different spirit – one of sober recompense rather than vengeful oppression. But then, the theory and practice of policing changed in every place where the Soviets ended up with the biggest say. Just one example is Finland, where by December 1945 communists made up almost sixty percent of the police force.[17] The British, Americans and French started to redress the balance in Germany; for example, communists were removed from all twelve chief inspector posts in the western sectors of Berlin. But even as these officers lost their jobs, the communist takeover of the police in the state of Saxony was at its most decisive and prophetic.

The early communist police force in Saxony became a model for East German law enforcement. In later years, Stasi case studies and police lectures would celebrate its heroic figures and deeds. Moreover, the Stasi's origins can be traced in the personalities and bureaucracy of Saxony's police departments.

It is understandable that Saxony witnessed this special effort. It is a German heartland, a traditional principality, its cities proud and distinctive: Leipzig, the largest, with a centuries-old reputation of friendliness and culture and music; Chemnitz, soon to be renamed Karl-Marx-Stadt; and Dresden, city of poetry, painting and moonlit spires, a seat of Romantic beauty and wisdom.

The place was still burning when the Red Army and KPD arrived. Veteran communists were given the key administrative posts. Kurt Fischer, who had spent much of the 1930s spying for Soviet military intelligence throughout Europe and Asia, was appointed mayor of Dresden and then Saxony's interior minister. Hermann Matern led the city's office for 'instruction and coordination', from which he re-established the KPD and built up the police;[18] every district KPD cell was ordered to provide three members for police service. Artur Hofmann was chief of police; he would take over from Fischer as Saxony's interior minister before entering the Stasi. And they all worked with Max Opitz, who advised SMAD on personnel policy and the prosecution of political crimes. Opitz would spend much of the following decade as head of East Germany's presidential chancellery.

Another future Stasi officer, Erich Glaser, opened an office on Bautzner Strasse to coordinate the activities of the city's anti-fascist committees. These committees did their best to help the survivors of Dresden's firestorms, organising street cleaning, rehousing, health and social care, the distribution of ration cards, and the registering of businesses and trades. Any foodstuffs found in Nazi party premises were given to the needy, especially the hordes of homeless, while milk for infants was procured from the surrounding areas.[19]

Other measures were ideological. The Antifa Block parties were established in factories and workplaces, and new workers' councils were set up, regardless of the views of business owners. Whenever the anti-fascist committees faced resistance, such as a refusal to hand over requisitioned supplies, they would threaten the non-compliant with 'severe penalties'. One former committee member admitted that these penalties 'were actually a bluff because as an Antifa committee we didn't have the slightest right to impose prison sentences or carry out [any punishments]'.

The mass registration of former Nazi party members was begun by small security teams within the anti-fascist committees. Questionnaires were given to every household, requiring everyone above the age of fifteen to state their affiliation with any Nazi organisation. Only by completing this checkable survey could a person get a resident's registration form which, in turn, was necessary for claiming a ration card. The information from these questionnaires was used to create an index of the population. The historian Thomas Widera notes that this system blended pragmatism with 'the intention to collect information that would be useful later', although it wasn't unique to the Soviet zone; for understandable reasons, similar measures were enacted throughout occupied Germany.

In July 1945 the Soviets ordered the creation of a new department in Dresden's Kriminalpolizei to deal with 'fascist, militarist and reactionary criminals'. A month later this 'special unit' (Sonderstelle) was involved in at least one operation that left a paper trail. A campaign of arrests, based on lists drawn up by the Soviet authorities, took place over two days in August. These arrests set a pattern which was to be repeated throughout eastern Germany in the following years. Twenty-five suspects were apprehended. Twenty-three were former members of the Nazi party, SS, or SA; two were not. The arrestees were interned, but their families and associates weren't informed of their whereabouts, in some cases for several years. This was to become one of the biggest complaints about the justice system in eastern Germany: the withholding of information about arrested persons.

By October 1945 the special unit had been replicated throughout Saxony's Kriminalpolizei. Its officers supported the Soviet authorities in investigations of 'fascist and reactionary organisations', 'economic sabotage', and crimes against humanity. At the same time, Artur Hofmann founded a department at Dresden police headquarters for 'close cooperation with police stations in all political matters' and 'the monitoring of all organisations and parties and their assemblies'. Explicit political policing had come to eastern Germany – and very quickly. By the end of the year, Saxony's special units had been consolidated into so-called 'K5' detachments, thus establishing one of the direct forerunners of the Stasi.

Denazification in Saxony set a template. It was a way to eliminate not just Nazis but other potential opponents of communist authority. Thomas Widera notes that 'numerous police actions in 1945 were directed against criminalised representatives of other political programmes'. Although the Soviet authorities were in charge, 'without the purposeful energy of German communists [these actions] would not have been so dynamic'. Communist officials' disregard of civil rights 'corresponded to their revolutionary self-image'. For Widera, the behaviour of Saxony's 'political police demonstrated the KPD leadership's deep distrust of the German population and their own doubts about the persuasiveness of their future utopia... they especially feared the democratic parties and dissenting opinions among communists or social democrats'. The result was that 'a free decision about the re-creation of society was ruled out'. Such was the ethos of Saxony's communist police officers: we are, they told themselves, an extraordinary vanguard entitled to use extraordinary means.

Communist domination of the police shows up in the numbers. In November 1945 Dresden's civil police service – the beat coppers – comprised 587 communists, 182 social democrats, and 337 'independent' officers. Within a month, Marxist representation had increased to 756 KPD and 288 SPD members. The number of independents shrank quickly, and there was only one CDU and one LDPD member in the entire force. KPD officials then embarked on a successful policy of shuffling social democrats from the police into the fire brigade.

Again, the reality of policing didn't live up to the idealism. Reckless hiring led to all sorts of undesirables joining up, from common criminals to rabid Nazis, many of whom then had to be removed in tricky purges. In the unarmed days, the job was unacceptably dangerous; far too many officers were killed on raids. But the crucial work got done. At a police conference in November, Max Opitz proclaimed that every resident of Dresden had now been registered. His speech isolated and threatened the unregistered: 'If you don't have a resident's registration certificate,' said Opitz, 'you have not registered for malicious reasons.' By the end of December, 45,000 members of the Nazi party had declared themselves. Another 40,000 people had 'politically undesirable' behaviour recorded against them, usually some kind of Nazi association.

By the end of 1945, then, the Soviet and German communists who wished to dominate central Europe had achieved much in eastern Germany. They had a democratic-looking selection of political parties that could be steered by communists. They had police forces led by communists, indexes of the population, and camps starting to fill with former Nazis and other potential opponents. This was the framework for the Soviet occupation zone. Now secret political policing could begin in earnest.

6

Ordering the Occupation Zone

About eighteen million people lived in the Soviet zone, a number that dropped steeply over time. Although East Germany conjures up images of cheap, ugly architecture and sulphurous industry, the zone's 108,000 square kilometres, while in a ruinous state, encompassed some of central Europe's prettiest, most culturally significant, and most productive places. As well as the important port and university town of Rostock, the Baltic coast in the north-east had sandy resorts and idyllic holidaymakers' islands like Rügen, the vertiginous grandeur of its chalk cliffs once immortalised in a Romantic masterpiece by Caspar David Friedrich. Heading south one threaded through the lakes and forests of Mecklenburg, thinly populated and atmospheric, sprinkled with old Hanseatic settlements like Greifswald. The zone had Dessau, where the Bauhaus design school had made its civilised stand against rising Nazism, and the site of a world-leading Junkers aircraft factory; and Weimar, where Goethe had conjured up *Faust* and encouraged a young Mendelssohn to compose. Jena boasted one of Germany's flagship manufacturers, the Carl Zeiss optics firm. There was plenty of agricultural land – traditionally, grain and potatoes from eastern Germany had fed the miners of the Ruhr – but the zone's south-eastern border with Czechoslovakia was mountainous. Here, in the Erzgebirge, there was uranium ore, and the region's mines were soon to see feverish espionage and counter-espionage activity. The zone's other eastern border was with Poland, and after the war it was the scene of bad-tempered exchanges of land and population; Germany's loss of Pomerania and Silesia to Poland was to remain an inflammatory issue for years to come. Across the western border was the British zone of Germany, to the south-west the American. Elsewhere in the zone, mining was focused on the region's peculiar brown coal. When burned it gave off a weird acrid smell that many came to associate with East German towns and cities.

Nearly forty percent of the Soviet zone's residents had lost all their possessions in the war.[1] Much of the frightened populace rushed westwards. It is estimated that by mid-1946 more than one and a half million people

had run to western Germany.[2] In response, the Soviets made a few efforts
to calm the nerves of eastern Germans. For a while, token goodwill was
shown towards diverse cultural and ideological interests. The churches were
allowed to exist. Soviet-run media emphasised Germany's cultural heritage
of philosophers and composers; the Goethe museum in Weimar was rebuilt,
and a Bach museum was opened, based around a collection of eighteenth
century instruments that had survived the war in a cellar. Soviet officers
with degrees in German literature publicly praised the strength of eastern
Germany's literary scene. German communists took up the call, with Anton
Ackermann pledging that artistic freedom would be respected in the zone.
Yet all of this hid a creeping Stalinism that, by 1948, had seen socialist realism
come to dominate the arts. By that point, 'American cultural barbarism' –
which meant the art and culture of Western countries, basically – was being
thoroughly denigrated. And it was with their security agencies that the Soviets
really made their presence felt.

Moscow established an intelligence and security foothold in eastern Germany
that was to remain for forty-six years. The former St Antonius hospital at
Karlshorst, where SMAD was based, came to house the biggest and most
important KGB outpost in the world. Karlshorst was a large site, patrolled by
sentries and dogs, surrounded by high walls crested with barbed wire. Behind
the walls were administrative and medical buildings, garages and sports
facilities, not to mention the spacious villas where KGB officers would make
their homes, living more comfortably than almost anyone else in the region.
In time, the KGB contingent at Karlshorst would number 1,500 people.[3]
Meanwhile the headquarters of the Soviet occupation army and the military
intelligence service – the latter with some 250 officers – were established
in the towns of Wünsdorf and Zossen, to the south. The KGB's immediate
forerunners, the MGB and MVD, also had offices in every Land and district
(Kreis) of eastern Germany.

The Soviet embassy on Unter den Linden in Berlin came to host another
large contingent of intelligence and security officers. Yet more worked from
the Soviet trade delegation and, later, at the Soviet consulate in West Berlin and
the offices of Aeroflot in the city. Furthermore, the Soviets benefited from the
use of safe houses, vehicles and communications facilities throughout eastern
Germany. Its importance as a strategic territory is clear.

The Soviet security forces had a broad and challenging remit after the war.
They were to carry out denazification, oversee political parties, trade unions and
civil organisations, cement Soviet ownership of the zone, and get intelligence

on the Western Allies, especially on the dreaded prospect of another European war. It was equally important to supervise the creation of a strong, ruling pro-Soviet party, ensure its primacy and, in time, augment it with a powerful right hand: a German security service.

In January 1946 there were some 2,200 NKVD and 400 NKGB personnel in the zone, as well as nine regiments of NKVD security troops comprising 15,000 soldiers.[4] At Karlshorst the first NKGB 'resident' – the Soviet term for the head of an espionage station – was Aleksandr Korotkov. A highly experienced and decorated intelligence officer, during the war Korotkov had masterminded 'radio games' in which captured Axis agents had been made to transmit false reports back to their German handlers, in which they implied that large Wehrmacht forces, still loyal and still fighting, were trapped behind Red Army lines. The Germans would then waste time, troops and supplies trying to sustain or rescue these non-existent forces.

The appointment of the feted Korotkov set a vigorous tone for the work of Soviet security in Germany. An equally appropriate tone was set by Korotkov's reported involvement in political assassinations in Paris in the late 1930s. The recollections of one former NKVD executive put Korotkov at the scene of the killing of Soviet defector Georgi Agabekov, who was knifed to death by Korotkov's fellow NKVD employee, 'a former officer of the Turkish army'. According to this account, Agabekov's corpse was then 'stuffed into a suitcase, thrown into the sea, and never found'. The same pair are said to have killed the leading Trotskyist Rudolf Klement, who was lured to an apartment on the Left Bank, supposedly for dinner, only to find Korotkov and 'The Turk' lurking inside: 'The Turk stabbed Klement to death, cut off his head, and put his body into a suitcase and threw it into the Seine.' By the time the French police had found and identified Klement's decapitated corpse, his killers reportedly had made a smooth return to Moscow.[5] Korotkov, suitably inured to such violence, was to exercise considerable influence in postwar Germany.

In spring 1946 the People's Commissariats of the Soviet Union adopted the more familiar name of ministries, a move which transformed the NKVD into MVD and the NKGB into MGB.* Their division of labour remained. The MGB was responsible for secret policing and some foreign espionage, while the MVD mostly provided security foot soldiers, as well as running camps and prisons. SMERSH was absorbed into the MGB as its Third Main Directorate, for military counter-intelligence. Unsurprisingly, its personnel continued to be especially active in places that had been vacated by the US and British armies. Cementing these changes, Viktor Abakumov was appointed chief of state security.

---

* Ministerstvo vnutrennikh del and Ministerstvo gosudarstvennoy bezopasnosti.

Abakumov's power had now reached its zenith, as stressed by Vadim Birstein: 'For the next five years, Abakumov was in control of the life of almost every Soviet citizen and his MGB could arrest any citizen it chose to – without waiting for an order from Stalin. Through the MGB branches in occupied countries, Abakumov also controlled half of Europe.'[6] Crucially for eastern Germany, in November 1946 Abakumov created an in-house, quasi-legal Special Board* in the MGB, with the power to sentence the ministry's own prisoners. This meant 'the MGB became a closed institution: it arrested people on political charges, investigated cases, tried the arrestees, and put the most important convicts into its own special prisons.'[7] This set-up was to greatly influence the Stasi. It affronted many Germans and Western observers.

Some Germans signed up, though. The Red Army and security forces quickly recruited Germans as undercover informers. In early 1946 more than 2,000 Germans were registered as Soviet agents; by 1949 the number was 3,000.[8] So began a phenomenon that didn't end until the collapse of East Germany itself; eastern Germans working directly for Moscow, and having little or nothing to do with the Stasi or any other East German authority. The Soviets never let go of these private assets, who tended to be used for the secret work that Moscow considered most critical.

By March 1946 the Social Democratic Party had nearly 700,000 members in the Soviet zone. Communism was suddenly popular too – the KPD's membership in the zone was now 600,000.[9] The fear that the KPD might be dwarfed by the SPD was a major motivation for merging the two parties.

Debates about the potential merger had begun to rage the previous year. Many communists still hated the 'social fascists' of the SPD. Social democrats wanted neither Stalin nor Soviet-style communism. The elections held in Austria in November 1945 had a decisive effect on events. Social democrats won seventy-six of the 165 seats in Austria's national assembly. Communists won four.[10] It was clear the KPD would need a big injection of social democracy to achieve any kind of mandate for rule.

At a December 1945 meeting attended by thirty executives from each party, known thereafter as the 60er Konferenz, the social democrat leader Otto Grotewohl had explained why merger was unacceptable. His main complaint was that it should not occur solely in the Soviet zone; if it was going to happen, it should be an all-German development. He also disagreed intensely with the communist plan to present a so-called 'unity list' at elections. Under this

---

*   The MGB 'Osoboe Soveshchanie' or OSO.

system, the electorate would not vote for an individual party or candidate but only 'for' or 'against' the pre-selected delegates of the entire Antifa Block.

SMAD sprang into action to steer things the communist way. Local officials put pressure on social democrats, banning the meetings of SPD groups that opposed the merger and rewarding groups that favoured it. Opponents of the merger were slurred as fascists and saboteurs; some of the more vocal dissenters were arrested.[11] These subtle and not-so-subtle tactics paid off. Support for the merger appeared to spread upwards from the SPD's grassroots, forcing the hand of opponents such as Grotewohl. Reputedly he claimed to have agreed to the merger only because he was being 'tickled by Russian bayonets'.[12] In the western zones of Berlin and throughout western Germany, the SPD – still intact in its pure form – braced itself for the inevitable. On 21 April 1946, at the Admiralspalast theatre in Berlin, Otto Grotewohl and Wilhelm Pieck shook hands on the foundation of a new party for the Soviet zone: the Socialist Unity Party of Germany or SED.

Support for the merger was patchy and varied from place to place. Vociferous objections could prove fatal. A month after the merger, five rebellious SPD officials were detained by Soviet security officers in Rostock. In unclear circumstances Erich Krüger was summarily shot, while three others subsequently received twenty-five-year prison sentences; one managed to flee westwards to tell the tale.[13] Inspired by this and other incidents of repression, Kurt Schumacher, leader of the western SPD, angrily condemned the merger. He spoke out against what he already recognised as the deceit and hypocrisy of the SED, stating that, 'One cannot declare the principles of democracy, of socialism, of freedom, of the right to self-determination, and then adopt policies which are the opposite.'[14] Wisely, Schumacher took to being escorted by British guards whenever he travelled to Berlin. He soon became a glaring public enemy to the SED, which watched aghast as Schumacher presided over the creation of the SPD's Eastern Office (Ostbüro).

Headquartered in Hanover in the British zone, with much of its logistics organised in Berlin, the SPD Ostbüro was given a set of demanding tasks. It was to be a contact point for social democrat resisters in eastern Germany; to gather information on developments in the Soviet zone, and use it for propaganda; to identify and thwart communist subversion among social democrats in western Germany; and to help re-home social democrat refugees.[15] Sir William Strang, Britain's top political adviser in Germany, expressed his approval of the Ostbüro.[16] And from the start its leaders, especially Siegmund 'Siggi' Neumann and the pseudonymous Stephan Thomas, who was born into a working-class Berlin family called Grzeskowiak, proved themselves to be doughty, highly motivated activists. The communist authorities of eastern Germany feared and detested the SPD Ostbüro, and battle was joined.

Merging the left-wing parties of satellite countries was a favourite Stalinist trick. The socialist parties of Romania, Hungary, Czechoslovakia, Bulgaria and Poland all disappeared into new communist-run concoctions. As Keith Lowe notes, 'Despite such deft manoeuvres, none of the Communist parties of Europe ever managed to attain enough popularity to win absolute power at the ballot box.'[17] Always a conduit for Soviet influence, to an extent the SED was the KPD by another name. At first its social democratic members were able to question hardline policies, or put forward more liberal arguments, which certainly would not have happened in the original KPD. Nevertheless, former KPD members were expected to dominate. Like so much in East Germany, the SED was something of a reality-warping lie – just a way for communists to launder their communism, although those on the party's far left were disappointed by its apparent caution and lack of revolutionary intent. Its artificiality meant the SED was always dependent on the coercive threat of a strong security service, whether Soviet or German.

Some of the party's early initiatives were popular. A referendum instigated by SMAD and the SED resulted in the sequestering of more factories owned by former Nazis and war criminals. This move met with much public enthusiasm, despite being a German rubber-stamp for the Soviet reparations that were already gutting the zone's industry and infrastructure. The initiative's popularity had waned by the autumn of 1946, thanks to the unlawful and arbitrary way it was implemented. Helped by the police, the authorities seized property from people who were neither Nazis nor criminals. Again the CDU and LDPD made official complaints, to no avail. And when innocent property owners who disputed the sequestration were thrown into camps, or simply disappeared after being sentenced by a Soviet military tribunal, opposition to the Soviets and SED began to intensify.

7

Denazification

An official history of the British military government in Germany sums up the denazification tasks which faced the occupying powers:

> First, to destroy the Nazi Party and its numerous subsidiary organizations, second, to eliminate objectionable Nazi laws and Courts from the legal system of Germany, and, third, to ensure that no Nazis of any importance and no member of the German General Staff should be retained, in, or appointed to any position of authority.[1]

The Western powers failed miserably on all counts. In the French zone, denazification never really got going. The British and Americans gave up when they realised the complexity and unpopularity of the scheme, which threatened western Germany's absorption into the democratic order, especially as a military partner. As a result, Wehrmacht generals and former Nazis would become rich and powerful figures in West German politics and business, thriving in the judiciary, armed forces, and intelligence services. This was a Cold War propaganda gift to the Soviet Bloc. Although Western propaganda tried to argue the contrary, it was only in the Soviet zone and East Germany that denazification was pursued relentlessly, and ruthlessly.

However, all four powers exempted German scientists from denazification, especially those who could make rockets. Western claims that the Stasi employed many former Nazis, and was thus a 'Red Gestapo', are dealt with later – they are wrong. Moreover, America's use of former Nazis in an intelligence capacity is occasionally shocking. Klaus Barbie, the Butcher of Lyon, was utilised; so too was Josef Mengele, one of history's most revolting criminal sadists.[2] The intelligence gained was surely not worth this moral abjection. But then the American intelligence services were in their infancy, and perhaps believed they had to play dirtier than was necessary.

Britain, too, felt compelled to 'deal with some pretty unattractive former (and not so former) Nazis,' to quote Keith Jeffery in his history of MI6. One of them, Sturmbannführer Horst Kopkow, was deemed so valuable a source of information on communists – despite being implicated in the extrajudicial killings of captured Allied servicemen – that MI6 faked his death in order to continue the intelligence relationship unhindered. Jeffery writes that 'a cover story was invented that he had died while interned in the United Kingdom, a death certificate was issued to that effect and a false identity was created for him as "Peter Cordes". He lived under this name for a while, but later appended his real name to the alias and settled openly in West Germany.'[3]

The employment of former Nazis by intelligence services wasn't altogether sinister. Originally they were co-opted not for their anti-communism but, as a historian of the French secret services puts it, 'to guard against the revival of Nazi networks in the West, and to track down collaborators. These activities, common to Soviet and Western agencies, spawned lingering accusations [in France] that notorious collaborators had found asylum under the protective umbrella of the secret services'.[4] In a similar vein, before its dissolution Britain's Special Operations Executive took to infiltrating German recruits known as 'Bonzos' into POW camps, 'to identify unregenerate Nazis who might be planning to form a resistance movement'. MI6 then took over this activity.[5] Allied security operations such as Nursery and Selection Board, which targeted underground Nazi groups, were based on information gained from cooperative war criminals.[6]

As for the destruction of the Nazi party, it began similarly everywhere.[7] Offices, records and party property were seized, and senior officials arrested – if they were found. The Western Allies' Central Registry of War Criminals and Security Suspects contained the names of more than 30,000 wanted persons. This giant index, carried by intelligence and security officers in the field, was recalled as being 'pretty much like a telephone directory'.[8] But confusion soon arose about what to do with those arrested and interned. If they were suspected war criminals they should be put on trial; if they were not, what then? In the British zone there were more than 68,000 internees by the end of 1946; only 2,100 were 'individual security suspects'.

In the Soviet zone, the KPD tried to resolve this dilemma by drafting definitions of 'active' and 'nominal' Nazis. The former were Nazi militants, to be pursued and prosecuted. The latter were passive party members who were entitled to start a new life under Soviet occupation, provided they had the right attitude. Law Number 10 of the Allied Control Council – 'Punishment of Persons Guilty of War Crimes, Crimes Against Peace and Against Humanity' – was an attempt to shed further light on the matter. Persons accused of 'Crimes against Peace' or 'Crimes against Humanity' were to be tried by a national (e.g., British) court or military government court; or by a German court or tribunal, depending on the offence. Evidence was expected to come from the victims of Nazism, the records of the former Reich Ministry of Justice, and the records of the infamous People's Courts created by Adolf Hitler. The law divided the accused into such categories as prison employees, 'proven helpers' [of Nazism], witnesses, informers, participants in court proceedings, lawyers, judges, and public prosecutors.[9] Those facing lesser charges were to go before review boards and German-led panels, with a range of lesser punishments at hand: up to ten years in prison, confiscation of property, loss of civic rights, 'exclusion from employment above that of ordinary labourer', residence restrictions, or compulsory reporting to the police.

This all sounded good, but implementing it proved a knotty and thankless slog. Even so, sincere efforts were made. The Nuremberg tribunal ruled that mere membership of certain Nazi organisations amounted to a war crime. By the end of 1946, one and a half million persons had been evaluated in each of the British and American zones, mostly in the context of job applications. The Americans had passed their Law for Liberation from National Socialism and Militarism, which decreed that everyone over the age of eighteen must fill in a questionnaire (Fragebogen) detailing their past. This went beyond the measures encouraged at Potsdam, and was similar to the approach taken by the communist police of Dresden.

Nevertheless, for the Western Allies it proved too difficult to interpret and judge people's personal histories. The purge was unrealistic. Nazis who had worked in electricity plants, for example, were needed to supply electricity. In many workplaces and professional fields, such as the civil service, membership of the Nazi party had been a condition of employment; it wasn't necessarily enthusiastic. And the increasing number of German-led tribunals tended to be more lenient than those of the Allies, leading to uneven and incoherent judgements.

By late 1947 denazification was being described in Britain's House of Lords as 'a horrid tiresome business'.[10] By that time, most rank-and-file Nazis held in the British zone had been released to get on with their lives. Five hundred or so had been declared dangerous, but their cases were under review, and 'considerable numbers' were then set free. All four occupying powers had wanted to prevent a Nazi insurgency in Germany, for no one had known how long it might take for Nazism to die. But apart from a few isolated incidents, the feared uprising didn't materialise. There were a few tense moments still to come. One was the British army's arrest in 1953 of a far-right group around the former Nazi functionary Werner Naumann, an action prompted partly by fears that German neo-Nazis might enter a marriage of convenience with the Soviets in order to expel the Western powers from Germany. But in general, the Western Allies put denazification early to bed.

This didn't happen in the Soviet zone. It wasn't just the scale and duration of Soviet denazification that was different. For example, the conditions in prisons and camps run by the Western Allies were not necessarily bad, and those that were bad were unlikely to be intentionally cruel or vengeful. This cannot be said of the Soviet camps, which were steeped in death.

Soviet internment camps were not places to intern people. They were places to punish and kill. This was a moral and political mistake, though perhaps an understandable one, for the Nazis had tried to wipe the Slavic peoples off the world map.

From 1945 to 1950 the Soviet authorities interned 154,000 Germans and 35,000 foreigners in ten special camps – 189,000 people. One third of them – 63,000 – died there.[11] Hunger and disease were the biggest killers, followed by maltreatment. Over the harsh winter of 1946-7, rations in the camps were reduced to the level of the Soviet Gulag. Some internees were Nazis, but others were prisoners of war who had been released by the Western Allies, or opponents of the KPD-SPD merger, or critics of the falseness of Stalin's block politics. Homeless or rowdy youths were interned on the mistaken suspicion that they were 'Werewolves' – Nazi 'stay-behind' saboteurs. The NKVD was even known to arrest people on the street to make up the numbers in columns of prisoners.[12]

The Soviets could claim some legitimacy for the camps as defence against Nazi insurgency. But, for historian Jens Gieseke, internment in the Soviet zone was 'in effect unlimited punishment without trial'.[13] Moreover, internees tended to just disappear from society, without notice or explanation. And so rumours began to spread of the 'Schweigelager' – the 'silent camps'. The main Soviet interrogation prison at Hohenschönhausen in Berlin also acquired a deeply sinister aura.

Within a year, Soviet military tribunals had passed more than 17,000 sentences. By 1955, when such tribunals finally stopped operating in East Germany, the number was 40,000. Nearly 2,000 death sentences were pronounced, of which 1,201 were carried out: 1,140 men and sixty-one women. Gieseke argues that some of those executed were convicted of trumped-up crimes against the Soviet authorities, and were completely innocent of the Nazi war crimes of which they were accused.

Many of these sentences were underpinned by Article 58 of Soviet Russia's criminal code, which detailed fourteen 'counter-revolutionary' offences punishable by law. Counter-revolutionary activity included 'propaganda or agitation which incites the overthrow, undermining or weakening of Soviet political authority... as well as the spreading, production or storing of materials with similar contents'.[14] According to Gieseke, 'A great many Social Democrats as well as Liberal and Christian Democrats were convicted for "counter-revolution" because they resisted being co-opted by the SED and tried to engage in independent politics.' Soviet security agencies 'increasingly targeted the representatives of other political currents and social forces [including] bourgeois politicians who refused to be co-opted into a bloc [and] entrepreneurs and tradespeople who disagreed with nationalisation'.[15]

Directive 38 of the Allied Control Council – titled 'The arrest and punishment of war criminals, Nazis and militarists, and the internment, control and surveillance of potentially dangerous Germans' – proved to be another useful catch-all instrument for SMAD. One of its articles established that individuals could be punished if they 'endangered the peace of the German people or of the world [by] spreading National Socialist or militaristic propaganda, or by inventing and spreading tendentious rumours'.[16] The Soviets, with their long experience, were able to fit this definition to all kinds of misdemeanours and behaviours.

MGB arrest figures from the first half of December 1946 indicate the scale of punitive actions against liberal and left-wing undesirables. Of the 432 Germans arrested, thirty-seven were said to be spies and 191 former members of Nazi organisations. No reason was given for the arrest of the 204 others.[17] By the start of the 1950s, when the campaign against unyielding social democrats ended, more than 5,000 had been sent to prisons and camps. At least 400 were executed or died of maltreatment.[18] Moreover, from 1948 to 1950 there were 597 documented arrests of Christian democrats. Many of these unfortunates were sent to Gulag camps in the Soviet Union, a potentially deadly punishment.[19] Yet throughout East Germany's history, the plight of Germans who had been held in Soviet camps remained a sternly taboo subject.[20]

8

The German Administration
of the Interior

Summer 1946 saw a big step taken towards the creation of the Stasi, with the founding of the German Administration of the Interior (Deutsche Verwaltung des Innern, DVdI).

A prototype interior ministry for eastern Germany, the DVdI was responsible mostly for policing. The Soviet authorities wanted to create an efficient, centralised, politically reliable police force. They had form for doing so, for this desire was the same as that of the OGPU in Russia in 1930, or the Spanish Republican government in 1936. And Soviet dissatisfaction with the weak, chaotic and corrupt Länder police forces had reached a critical point. The crime rate remained astronomical. Only forty percent of crimes were solved. This malaise led to the creation of the DVdI.

It was founded in great secrecy, for Allied Control Council regulations forbade the existence of 'all German police agencies and bureaus which have as their purpose the supervision or control of the political activities of persons within Germany'.[1] Flouting this rule with cold-blooded calculation, the Soviets appointed four diehards of German-Soviet communism to run the DVdI. Its president was Erich Reschke, who had been thrown into Buchenwald before the war and remained there for its duration. He was promoted to the DVdI from his position as Thuringia's police chief. Reschke couldn't then have foreseen the hard times in store for him; a few years later he would plummet from grace, first sentenced to the Gulag and then forced to eke out a living as a boilermaker, though at least he lived.

Kurt Wagner, latterly Saxony's interior minister, was a DVdI vice president responsible for certain branches of the police, including the Kripo (the detective department), the water police, and the fire brigade police. The railway and traffic police also fell under the DVdI, and it was to acquire responsibility for the border police. The latter force was established in December 1946 on SMAD orders; each Land formed a Grenzpolizei department to patrol the border areas previously guarded by Soviet troops. The personnel were poorly clothed, housed and equipped, and in 1947 the DVdI took over the service, with orders to strengthen it.

Another DVdI vice president, Willi Seifert, had been in Buchenwald with Reschke. Seifert was responsible mainly for administration, a role he was to continue as East Germany's deputy police chief and then deputy interior minister; he occupied the latter position into the 1980s. The third vice president was Erich Mielke.

Mielke's main job at the DVdI was to increase the political awareness and loyalty of police officers. He warmed to the task, declaring that the police were 'the sharpest military-political fighting weapon of the working class'.[2] Just as the spirit of land reform was distinctive in the Soviet zone, so too was the class consciousness imbued in police recruits. Mielke illustrated this in a speech with a hypothetical story of two drivers pulled over for a motoring offence: 'In one case we are dealing with an honoured worker or workers' functionary and the other person is known to us as an arch reactionary... It is clear that we take care of the case of the worker through a few friendly words, and we jack up the fine as high as possible for the enemy of democratic development.'[3]

From a Soviet perspective, the DVdI was quite successful in centralising the zone's disparate police forces and ensuring they were dominated by communists. By the end of 1946 it had seventy employees,[4] and had been granted 'supreme authority' for every provincial department that dealt with 'internal police administration, public order [and] security'.[5] Walter Ulbricht and the SED had been pushing for tighter control of Länder interior ministries, and the DVdI was a useful way to align their work. The process was overseen by the SED's head of police affairs, Robert Bialek, who a decade later would pay the ultimate price for his disillusionment with East German policing.

The DVdI also took on some specialist roles, such as monitoring and censoring the media. For the first time since the war, German police officers were empowered to tackle some of the zone's afflictions: the flight of the population, Western infiltration across the borders, the black market, the vulnerability of industrial sites. The first school to train new police officers opened in Saxony in March 1946. Before long the school had a political department, staffed by stalwart SED members, to teach recruits the fundamentals of Marxism; an initiative based explicitly on Soviet practice. Indeed, almost all of the police school's property, vehicles and weapons were provided by the Soviets, as was much of the police budget.[6]

Behind closed doors the DVdI was sold to everyone concerned as being a 'German' agency. This was important internal propaganda, but misleading. It was tightly controlled by the Soviets. Erich Reschke reported directly to the internal affairs department of SMAD. Erich Mielke, as the Soviets' most loyal asset at the DVdI, had a direct telephone connection with Karlshorst – although one assumes it was not connected to Kremlevka, the closed telephone system for Soviet government officials.[7]

While the DVdI set about centralising the police force, the justice system was being remodelled to meet communist requirements. Legal practitioners in the Soviet zone tended to be 'rechtsbewusst' – respectful of the law – which was a problem for the Soviets and the SED.[8] When the Central Administration for Justice was formed, the KPD, and subsequently the SED, insisted that their members should head the personnel department and the department of criminal law. Again, this infiltration tactic meant that members of other parties would be visible as the top post-holders, while communists would control the things which, to them, really mattered: judicial appointments, the debates around new laws, decisions on what constituted a crime. Hilde Benjamin was appointed head of personnel; as 'Red Hilde' she was to become one of East Germany's most resented authority figures. Courses were set up to train new 'people's judges' and 'people's public prosecutors'.[9] By 1947 almost eighty percent of the pupils on these courses were SED members.[10]

None of this boosted the communists' public popularity, however. The first elections in postwar Germany, for the membership of local councils, took place in September 1946. In the Soviet zone the SED did quite well, with fifty-seven percent of the vote; it won more than five million votes overall, with the LDPD and CDU winning three and a half million. Nevertheless, there were worrying signs for the SED. One was the widespread spoiling of ballots in places where the preferred CDU candidates had been disallowed by the Soviet authorities.[11]

The following month, the SED failed to win an absolute majority in elections to the Länder and district assemblies, taking forty-seven percent of the vote. Between the two elections, the party lost 430,000 votes and the LDPD and CDU gained 750,000. Even more ominous were the results in Berlin, where the SPD still existed thanks to an American-sanctioned referendum that saw an overwhelming rejection of its merger with the KPD. The SPD won forty-eight percent of the vote, the CDU twenty-two percent, and the SED nineteen percent.[12] Berliners had made their feelings clear. The Soviets and SED were shaken. Never again were elections in eastern Germany to be so free.

9

New Cloaks and Daggers

In spring 1946 the US army's Counter Intelligence Corps – at that time America's main espionage and counter-espionage agency – launched Operation Bingo. This was the first mass campaign to thwart communist spies in the west of Germany. Almost 400 infiltrators were identified.[1] Many were Soviet citizens biding their time in camps for displaced persons. Some were trained Red Army intelligence officers who had allowed themselves to be captured by the Wehrmacht in order to penetrate German society in the long term.

This came as a shock. These were the earliest days of the Cold War – it was in March 1946 that Winston Churchill gave the famous speech in which he coined the term 'the Iron Curtain'. In some settings, such as the UN Security Council and the Berlin Kommandatura, the four victorious powers were still making a token effort to get along. The large haul of hostile agents in Operation Bingo was one motivation for the Western Allies to employ the controversial Reinhard Gehlen as a spy chief, capable of counteracting communist penetrations. Gehlen's expertise and detailed archive, acquired as head of Wehrmacht intelligence on the so-called Eastern Front, overrode any squeamishness about making use of him.

Incursions in the east by Western intelligence services began more modestly. In summer 1945, three officers of the OSS German Mission* went through the Red Army lines and made their way to Berlin. They were seeking potential agents among the managers of a factory which one of them had owned before the war.[2] The American intelligence agencies working from the Berlin Operations Base (BOB) evolved steadily; from OSS to SSU to CIG to CIA, the latter founded in mid-1947.† But it took time for BOB to develop a long-term strategic mission. It wasn't assigned a Russian speaker until two years after the war.[3] Initially BOB carried out background checks on Germans and monitored

---

* The Office of Strategic Services was America's wartime espionage and sabotage agency, and a forerunner of the CIA. Allen Dulles established its German Mission at Biebrich, near Wiesbaden.
† SSU: Strategic Services Unit. CIG: Central Intelligence Group.

the activities of local officials. Some rare bursts of excitement were provided by 'occasional acts of violence by diehard Nazis', as well as its officers' greedy involvement in the black market.[4] But it then dawned on the US authorities – as it did on the British and French – that they knew very little about the political and economic changes taking place in the Soviet zone, and lacked details of the Soviets' military strength there.

So began the interrogation of refugees – which was to continue for four and a half decades – and the acquisition or placing of spies in eastern Germany. A secret report from January 1947 lists some of the objectives of America's spies:

> Clandestine coverage of three major political parties [SED, CDU, LDPD] and trade unions in Soviet Zone of Germany, including secret directives, connections with Russian, British, and other governments, financial aid, aims and their general place in the long-range political plans of the Soviet Union...
>
> Coverage of land administrations in the Russian Zone of Germany...
>
> Dismantling of factories in the Russian Zone of Germany...
>
> Nuclear physics, coverage of raw material needed for research and production, as well as installations, laboratories, personnel, etc., participating in research or contemplated production in the Russian Controlled Economy.
>
> Research on supersonic devices, rockets, jet propulsion, and other special devices or weapons...
>
> Information on research on biological warfare...[5]

Quickly BOB built up good coverage of eastern Germany's railway system. As well as being susceptible to material rewards, many railway employees no doubt resented the Soviet takeover of the railways. It was also important for BOB to find agents at Karlshorst, not just among officials but among the local maintenance staff – cleaners, caretakers, decorators, grocers – many of whom were more than ready to be paid for information or stolen paperwork. As early as September 1945 BOB was able to acquire the minutes of a meeting between Soviet executives and the German staff of the Central Administration for Industry. Presumably the dismantling of industrial equipment and its removal to the USSR were high on the agenda.[6] One US source at Karlshorst, a Soviet official codenamed 'Buick', used his mistress as a courier to take SMAD documents to the western sectors of Berlin. His activity ceased in 1948, when he was resettled in the American zone.[7]

It was probably 'Buick' who in September 1947 provided BOB with an insider report of a meeting of the SMAD executive council. This report is noteworthy because it gives an account of Soviet officials discussing sabotage by German workers at industrial sites. Although several workers at an Audi plant had been arrested on suspicion of sabotage, the officials admitted that the plant's production problems didn't result from politically motivated sabotage, and instead were caused by 'a shortage of raw materials' and other, apolitical factors.

Industrial sabotage was a festering obsession of the Stasi in its early days; indeed, it was one of the main reasons the Stasi was created. The SED's first Two Year Plan for economic recovery, launched in 1948, appeared to be met with an increase in sabotage and even shootings of party activists. That year the police recorded fifty-one explosions and 300 suspicious-looking incidents in workplaces.[8] Smaller but still worrying numbers were recorded throughout the 1950s. But it is difficult to find corroborating evidence of real, politically motivated sabotage in eastern Germany, whether organised by unrepentant Nazis, repressed social democrats, or Western secret services. Doubtless many alleged cases were as innocuous as the one discussed by SMAD in 1947.

The Soviets were quick to seize upon the unique potential for intelligence and security operations in divided Germany, with its porous borders, interconnected populations, and temptingly close Western administrations. Counter-espionage agencies like the CIC had a difficult task; in June 1947 the US authorities in Frankfurt reported the arrest of 516 Soviet Bloc agents, most of them German. But typically, one of Moscow's first concerns was to devise a scheme to expose and entrap disloyal Soviet officials posted to Germany: an elaborate sting of its own people. It worked like this: Soviet officials would have the carrot of defection to the West dangled in front of them by a recent German acquaintance, a person who appeared to have entered their life by chance. Those who expressed an interest would be introduced to further contacts – Germans who seemed to hail from the western sectors of Berlin – who would then organise their defection. On the fateful day, having got into a car in the Soviet sector, accompanied by their new German friends, the defectors were driven to a sumptuously decorated villa. There, plied with food and drink, and relaxing on a velvet sofa, they were debriefed by American soldiers. Some way into this debriefing the disguises would be dropped: these were MGB officers in American uniforms; the villa was in the Soviet zone, at Mühlenbeck; and the defector had been exposed as a runaway and a traitor.

In the following decades, this scheme of stage-managed defection was used throughout the Soviet Bloc to identify the users and organisers of escape routes. In postwar Berlin, the trick had a counter-intelligence function. The MGB's goal was to smoke out Soviet citizens who had, or wanted to have, contact with Western intelligence services. According to one KGB veteran, among some thirty-five cases of duped defectors, only one was found to be in contact with

American intelligence. By 1949 the expensive and fiddly scheme had been put on ice.[9]

Immediately after the war, General Lucius Clay, the top American official in Berlin, demanded restraint in intelligence operations. He was wary of harming relations with the Soviets, and he made an agreement with Zhukov's deputy, Marshal Vasily Sokolovsky, to return wanted persons to the Soviet zone.[10] But from autumn 1945 onwards, BOB developed a few double agent cases, usually by turning refugees who had been sent by the Soviets to spy on the western sectors.

BOB's main goal was to understand the Soviet security services and, ideally, to recruit their personnel. This proved difficult. BOB officers discovered that their Soviet counterparts knew 'all the tricks of agent handling: neutral meeting points, aliases, red herrings, keeping the agent in blinders so far as concerns the location of headquarters and identity of other agents or staff personnel'.[11] The British gained rather more information by debriefing wartime forced labourers who had been recruited by SMAD as translators before running westwards.[12] But Britain's MI6, too, was forced to adopt a somewhat hit-and-hope approach. One of its operations, 'Tamarisk', involved raking through the dustbins outside Soviet offices at night.[13]

BOB pursued its double agent cases as best it could. The plans for one operation, named with brutal honesty 'Sitting Duck', envisaged using a German woman called Hildegard Beetz to fool Soviet security:

As an aid to current and prospective double agent operations against Soviet Intelligence Stations lying outside Berlin it is proposed to place Frau Beetz in OMGUS [Office of Military Government, United States] as a secretary in the near future. As is now well known, one of the principal targets of the Soviet Intelligence System is the penetration of important American offices at OMGUS. In the process of doubling back Soviet agents dispatched on such a mission, it almost inevitably becomes necessary to use a cutout, someone actually employed inside the Soviet target-office, in order to give the Soviet controlling officers the illusion that their agent has in fact contacted a well-placed source of information. Such a decoy or 'sitting duck' placed inside the Soviet target would be subject to our complete control and, by giving the Soviets increasing confidence in the success of their operation, enable our penetration of their service to achieve greater results.

In the past friendly and secure American officers have sometimes cooperated with us as 'sitting ducks,' but the Soviets do not, for understandable reasons, appear to trust such a contact of their agent as much as a well-placed German secretary. It is therefore deemed imperative to have at least one, but preferably two or three, German decoys inside the target. Newly discovered Soviet agents can then be directed – probably unconsciously – to the decoy for neutralization, and doubled agents already under our control can use the sitting duck as camouflaging support for their delicate double role.[14]

Within five months the project had been declared a failure, although Beetz became well-liked at OMGUS; she later won awards for her journalism.

The central figure of another case, Hans Kemritz, codenamed 'Savoy', was a Berlin lawyer and former Abwehr officer who had been threatened with arrest by the Soviets and pressed into their service, only to be similarly threatened by BOB and doubled against his NKGB handlers. In a city that would soon experience a seedy free-for-all of intelligence black-marketeering, Kemritz was the archetype for all Berlin's intelligence-pedlars: individuals with a shady past, present and future, prone to blackmail, playing all sides for money or favours or their own furtive survival. This was a milieu in which, in the words of a senior MI5 officer, it was 'possible to buy up almost anybody with a packet of cigarettes or a hunk of bread'.[15]

Kemritz gathered information for the Soviets, but they also used him to lure former Abwehr colleagues from the western sectors of Berlin to the Soviet zone – colleagues that, strictly speaking, should have been returned to Soviet jurisdiction anyway, under the Clay-Sokolovsky agreement. Meanwhile, the Americans used Kemritz in repeated attempts to bring his Soviet case officer to the western sectors. Every attempt failed, though narrowly. Eventually it became clear that Kemritz's Soviet handlers had realised his duplicity, and he was resettled in the American zone for his own safety. It didn't prove very safe. In November 1950 Kemritz was arrested by the local authorities for his role in luring fellow Germans into Soviet captivity. His case was taken over by an American district court, however, and was resolved by the application of what became known as 'Kemritz law': a German could not be prosecuted for obeying an instruction from an occupying power, if it resulted in the capture of wanted war criminals.[16]

As always with espionage, there was tragi-comedy too. BOB began to get information on Soviet policy from a Major General Leonid Malinin, without ever realising he was the regional chief of Moscow's new foreign intelligence service, the Committee of Information (KI).* Malinin shone at clubby dinner

---

* Komitet Informatsii. The KI combined the intelligence directorates of the MGB and GRU, and fell under the Soviet Council of Ministers and, later, the Foreign Ministry. It existed from 1947 to 1951, creating overlap and rivalry with the MGB and MVD.

parties hosted by US ambassador Robert Murphy, but he tried to play things too cleverly; under an alias, he was simultaneously trying to influence German politicians in the Soviet zone, pushing his own points of view and disregarding Moscow's instructions. He paid the price for his presumptuousness and inexperience. When Stalin heard of the naïve diplomatic games he was playing, Malinin went before an officers' court and was demoted. After summer 1948 he was never seen in Berlin again.[17]

BOB developed good sources to cover uranium mining in eastern Germany, vital for understanding the Soviet nuclear programme. It also played a key role in an intelligence-collection campaign called Grail, which the US hoped would fill its blank pages on the Soviet order of battle. This was the espionage of the ancient world: where is the enemy, how many are they, and how are they armed? The work required 'tough, unsentimental' German head agents, many of them veterans of the war with the Soviets, who in turn could recruit networks of friends in eastern Germany as intelligence-gatherers; friends they were prepared to sacrifice. A BOB report of the period suggests that the main motivations for Grail spies were money and revenge on the Red Army.[18] Around 250 were involved, the majority living close to Soviet barracks, airfields or military transport routes. Arrest rates were high, but replacements seemed to be plentiful enough.

This was fortunate, because security among the Grail spies was minimal and tradecraft virtually non-existent. Up to twenty-five agents at a time would get together at morale-boosting parties held in safe houses in the American sector of Berlin, all raising jaunty toasts for the camera. Head agents and sub-agents from throughout the Soviet zone got to know and like one another. This proved unhelpful when in autumn 1946 the MGB – assisted by the emerging communist police force, and surely lashing back at the West for Operation Bingo – began to roll up the Grail networks.

A later head of BOB admitted ruefully that 'the old Vetting Desk of X-2 [the counter-espionage section of the OSS] had broken down under the load of new recruitments.' This meant the 'bill for overexpansion was presented at the end of 1946 and we have been paying it in instalments ever since'. He reported:

> Generally a single weak link was detected by Russian counter-intelligence: sometimes by chance, perhaps as the result of a routine pick up for black market or other charges, and sometimes through an agent gone sour and bought over. Only rarely if ever does the initial break seem to have come from a deliberate penetration.

Either way, these arrest operations displayed that cornerstone quality of counter-espionage, patience:

Usually the Russians avoided direct action until they had learned almost all the details of [each spy] chain's makeup. Sometimes we were even able to follow their progress through attempts at kidnapping, luring agents into the Russian Sector or Zone, and arrests which were followed by attempts to double the agents and their subsequent release to work against us... once the Russians had a sizeable group of men within their grasp they were usually able to make effective concerted swoops.[19]

Most of the Grail arrestees ended up in the Gulag. The survivors were not to see Germany again until the mid-1950s.

By late 1947, Ernest Bevin, Britain's foreign secretary, had seen enough Soviet truculence to believe 'that there was no longer cause for optimism that friendly relations could be maintained in the face of their anti-Western and expansionist campaigns'.[20] In at least one Cold War activity, however – covert propaganda – Britain itself led the rest of the West. Its Information Research Department (IRD), the creation of which was signed off by the British Cabinet in January 1948, slightly predated similar American endeavours in 'psychological warfare', although it came to work closely with the US State Department. (The Soviets were ahead of the game, though; in 1947 Vyacheslav Molotov, the minister for foreign affairs, had stipulated that the KI should have a disinformation unit to 'influence the public opinion of other countries, and compromise anti-Soviet officials and public figures of foreign governments.')[21]

The founding of the IRD was driven by Christopher Mayhew, an anti-communist MP in Britain's Labour government. This is unsurprising, for moderate socialists, tired of the corruption of their creed, had long been fierce opponents of Moscow. The IRD's purpose was to gather confidential information about communism and use it to produce fact-based but unattributable 'publicity'. This was to be disseminated – knowingly or otherwise – by 'politicians, trade unionists, journalists and intellectuals.'[22] Among other goals, its propaganda aimed to foster nationalism in Soviet Bloc countries, in accordance with Britain's policy of the 'containment' of Soviet power. The IRD had close ties with MI6, which was perhaps unfortunate in its earlier years, for the British traitors Kim Philby and Guy Burgess were both in a position to feed information about it to Moscow.

In the late 1940s MI6 operated in Germany in the guise of 'No. 1 Planning and Evaluation Unit'. The service also ran the Technical Section of Intelligence Division, the latter a part of the Control Commission for Germany (British Element). Thus MI6 officers worked under both military and Control Commission cover, mostly from their headquarters at Bad Salzuflen or from innocently-named offices at Hamburg (purportedly covering 'regional rehabilitation') and Düsseldorf (the 'Rhineland Statistical Recording Unit').[23] At the same time, an analytical hub, the Joint Intelligence Committee (Germany), was assigned to collate and interpret material from 'the four zones of Germany and all countries bordering, plus the Soviet Union'.[24]

Both MI6 and Intelligence Division sought information on scientific and technical developments in Soviet Russia's weaponry. Such information did not necessarily come from spies; much of it came from debriefing the panic-stricken German scientists who herded into the British zone when the Soviets carried out a mass deportation of scientific workers to the USSR in October 1946. Shortly afterwards the British authorities launched an operation called Matchbox to entice yet more scientific and arms-production specialists to head westwards. They were offered jobs 'either by coded letter or by telegram or, most commonly, by an agent who did not know for which country he was working'.[25] Prisoners of war returning to western Germany were another important source of information, especially on the Soviet Union's 'topography, industry, military installations and growing military-industrial complex'.[26] Furthermore, spies were run in eastern Germany by all of Britain's intelligence players: MI6, Intelligence Division, Naval Intelligence, Air Force Intelligence, and the British component of FIAT – the 'Field Information Agency, Technical', collector of scientific intelligence for the Allied military. By January 1947 the British section of FIAT in Berlin claimed to have a spy inside 'most of the more important factories engaged in warlike production' in the Soviet zone.[27]

British intelligence professionals were inclined to see the emerging Cold War in slightly less apocalyptic terms than some of their American counterparts. While acknowledging a brooding clash of civilisations, Guy Liddell, deputy director of MI5 and a good barometer for the British intelligence community, made an assessment that:

> Stalin is determined that Soviet Russia should be strong enough to prevail in the decisive struggle which [he believes] should result from the next and inevitable crisis of monopoly capitalism... This clash is not, however, necessarily imminent and in the meantime the Soviet Union is prepared to rub along with the rest of the world, provided of course that this entails no weakening of her position in the ultimate struggle...
>
> The most that we can hope for is that the passage of time without a collision will of itself induce greater elasticity in the Soviet mind and consequent recognition of the mutual advantages that lie in the conception of one world as opposed to two... although Soviet policy is conceived as strategically defensive, its execution involves the same military preparations, the same striving after self sufficiency, the same propaganda campaigns and the same tactics of stalling intervention

and attempts at disruption as would a policy planned for aggression. It therefore carries with it the same dangers and forces upon us preparedness and vigilance.[28]

Liddell thought it regrettable that certain British hawks, for example in the Air Ministry, were:

> too much inclined to think in terms of a direct act of aggression. Things are much more likely to happen by subversive means when it will be made to appear that Russian domination of any particular country has been brought about through the will of the people. The issue will be clouded and the machinery of the United Nations Organisation will be brought into action. There will be long discussion and any action will be vetoed. It is only when this has happened three or four times that the limit will be reached and the Russian bluff will be called. The danger is that the Russians will miscalculate on the extent to which they are going to be allowed to get away with it.[29]

Some of Liddell's words were borne out by events; others were not.

Whatever the far horizons, British intelligence officers, like their US counterparts, had to tread carefully when it came to the aching sensitivities of early Cold War diplomacy. This was a real bind, especially because 'intelligence-gathering from human sources assumed disproportionate importance in the early years of the Cold War because of the difficulty of penetrating the Soviet Union by other means'.[30] When questioned by Foreign Office officials about the extent to which MI6 agents were operating in the Soviet Bloc – their concern was the possible diplomatic repercussions if such agents were discovered – Stewart Menzies, chief of MI6, replied that he would be failing in his duty if he 'did not encourage the rapid building up of organisations within the satellite countries [to] obtain information from within Russia'.[31] Somewhat outside the scope of this reply was the activity of the MI6 agent 'Merrick', who had been parachuted into Hamburg in 1944 only to disappear when the war ended. Having remade contact, he pulled off such coups as carrying a Soviet 85mm shell and a helicopter propeller across the border into the British sector of Berlin. MI6 also debriefed a major military defector to Britain, Lieutenant Colonel Grigori Tokaev, an accomplished aero engineer, before using him to try to lure other Soviet officers to the West. For this work, a new post was established at Bad Salzuflen 'to co-ordinate policy and the efforts of outstations to provoke defectors'.[32]

Some youthful residents of the occupation zones were arrested as 'spies' and 'terrorists' when they were little more than unfortunate delinquents. Originally, the Edelweiss Pirates movement was a subversive anti-Nazi creed that had given teenagers a chance to kick back at the thick-headed orthodoxies of the Hitler Youth. But in the postwar climate, the rowdiness of the Pirates, and their independence of mind, were beyond the pale. While some groups undoubtedly drifted into common crime, more for the sake of survival than ideology, it is unlikely they were guilty as charged; in one MGB document the Pirates were accused of 'organising terrorist acts' and 'training armed groups to fight the Soviet army'. In the American zone, Pirates were 'reported to be harassing German girls dating American soldiers, beating up Polish Displaced Persons, and engaging in extensive black market activities'. It was also noted that they 'spouted Nazi rhetoric'.[33]

Over the winter of 1946-7, the MGB arrested sixty youths belonging to fourteen groups of Pirates.[34] For the Soviets, these arrestees undoubtedly were the agents of German fascism, or Western countries, or both. Hundreds more Pirates were arrested in the American zone by the CIC, which launched Operation Valentine to 'infiltrate and incapacitate' the groups. In subsequent interrogations it became clear to CIC officers that the Pirates were not 'an all-powerful, well-organized Nazi subversive movement', but rather a bunch of marginalised orphans who had fashioned 'a primitive nationalistic creed to create a sort of *ersatz* community'.[35] The situation was complicated, however, by the loyalty to Adolf Hitler shown by many young Germans. An adolescence spent in the Hitler Youth left its mark. Sometimes gangs of youths in the Soviet zone would beat up lone soldiers or SED activists, daub swastikas on Antifa Block buildings, or vandalise Red Army war graves. To the MGB this made every German youth fair game for internment as a fascist and, in due course, thousands were arrested for 'relatively minor infractions'.[36]

Politically motivated kidnapping was another grubby manifestation of the emerging secret war. In 1946, 3,439 people disappeared from the streets of Berlin; in 1947 the number was 2,586.[37] This implies that the Soviets were busily snatching persons of interest – war criminals, Soviet expatriates, dissidents, and useful professionals. Western agencies knew it was happening and understood the implications. The intelligence historian Thomas Boghardt writes that in autumn 1947, 'the 970th CIC detachment in Berlin reported that Soviet intelligence had abducted six German employees of the Civil Administration Branch of the Office of Military Government for Berlin Sector... "It is therefore reasonable to conclude," the CIC noted, "that an almost complete penetration of subject office has been successfully effected by Soviet Intelligence."'[38]

Western services seized persons of interest too, especially valuable scientists. For example, William Blume, an important designer of U-boats during the war and latterly employed at a research facility in the Harz mountains, was arrested when visiting family in the British sector of Berlin, interrogated, and then prevented from returning to the Soviet zone.[39] French secret agents 'snatched the engineer Ferdinand Porsche on German territory'; he was subsequently put to work for Renault. A French military intelligence officer recalled of this period that it 'was a real race to capture "brains", people who would help us to make the atomic bomb. We succeeded in bringing back two or three scientists whom we had snatched from the Russians'.[40] Berlin was to remain a kidnapping hotspot, and the Stasi would come to specialise in it.

This was the dirtier end of postwar intelligence operations, and it set a tone. Yet much of the intelligence activity of the early Cold War was conducted by educated professionals at a high, strategic level. This, after all, is where you really want your spies: in the room at government meetings, inside intelligence services, international organisations, manufacturers of weapons; or working discretely at laboratories, military installations, political parties. By 1948 the Soviets 'had infiltrated the major West German political parties and had penetrated Allied military administrations... the quantity of agents [then] rose significantly to include government officials, financiers, politicians, and important journalists'.[41] As they grew more aware of Soviet atomic research, America and Britain focused their espionage on bomb-making materials and activities: uranium mining, the distillation of calcium, the production of wire mesh, ore concentration facilities. The Soviets had to buy much of the equipment they needed, such as vacuum pumps, from western Germany.[42] Because such items were subject to export controls, the Western powers were able to stop the shipments – leading, no doubt, to a busy clandestine effort to get hold of them.

When it came to gathering high-level intelligence, there was a big imbalance in the Soviets' favour. They had spies in places of which the West could only dream. The KI obviously had good coverage of French politics. Its sources included a French diplomat in Germany who reported his information to the KI residency in Paris; among other things, he gave notice of early attempts to draft a new constitution for Germany.[43] And from the end of the war until the 1980s the Soviets enjoyed the services of a cipher clerk at the Quai d'Orsay, codenamed 'Zhur', who provided Moscow with copies of communications between Paris and French embassies worldwide.[44] The KGB recorded that 'Zhur' used a 'special container' to transport these copies – this implies the use of microfilm messages concealed in a hollowed-out item such as a clothes brush or a coin, but there are other possibilities.

Meanwhile, from his desk at MI6, Kim Philby was happily smashing to pieces the British and American attempts to insert guerrillas into Soviet-dominated countries, condemning to death dozens, perhaps hundreds, of Western agents as he did so. Thanks to his role for the Foreign Office in America, Philby's fellow traitor Donald Maclean had freer access to the Atomic Energy Commission building in Washington than did FBI boss J. Edgar Hoover. Maclean was able to give the Soviets reams of 'information about American atomic energy projects, the British atomic energy programme, and the political differences arising between the two countries out of atomic energy matters'.[45] Just as significant was Maclean's knowledge of uranium ore supplies and the West's pre-emptive purchasing of uranium from the Belgian Congo. Presumably this intelligence led to even greater exploitation of the Wismut mines – and their bedraggled workforce – in the south-east of the Soviet zone. In 1948 Maclean told his Soviet handlers 'exactly how much uranium Britain and America thought they would need during the next four years'. This made it possible for the Soviets to estimate 'with reasonable accuracy how many bombs the West planned to make'.[46]

Guy Burgess, at this point an *éminence grise* at the Foreign Office, was every bit as valuable a spy for Stalin. Burgess received copies of 'almost all papers that came to the Foreign Office ministers, including the minutes of meetings of the Cabinet [and] Defence Committee'.[47] His in-tray contained 'cables from embassies and foreign governments' revealing 'the positions of Western countries on the post-war settlement in Europe'.[48] All of this was shared with Moscow. Furthermore, Burgess attended the Council of Foreign Ministers conference in London in late 1947, and accompanied the British delegations to important meetings in Paris and Brussels. In each case he gave advanced warning to the Soviets on the British bargaining positions. He took minutes at the talks that led to the creation of the Brussels Treaty Organisation, and 'passed across information about [the] founding meetings of the United Nations, NATO and OECD'.[49]

For the Soviet Union, the telegrams, papers, minutes and gossip retailed by Guy Burgess were vital for negotiating Europe's future. Espionage is sometimes criticised for being inconsequential, as if it affects nothing and might as well be dispensed with. But the information provided by Burgess and Maclean didn't just make a difference to the geopolitical wrangling over Europe. It directly affected the lives of ordinary Germans, especially Berliners, helping to decide the everyday reality of their divided home.

10

Germany's New Political Police: K5

The first major forerunner of the Stasi was a secret political police force known as K5. Fittingly, its origins were rather obscure. By autumn 1946 the new police service for eastern Germany, which came to be known as the Volkspolizei or People's Police, was starting to take shape under the direction of the DVdI. Its detective branch, the Kripo, was organised into 'K' departments – K1 for capital crimes, K3 for economic crimes, and so on.[1] The K5 designation was open-ended. In some provincial forces it was the department responsible for juvenile delinquency; in others, for house searches. Basically, 'work area number five' of the Kripo was a miscellany, a dump for 'any other business'. To an outsider the classification meant nothing: the perfect cover for a secret police.

The first K5 unit with a political role was set up in Dresden during 1945. Other cities and regions followed, and from autumn 1946 there were bureaucratic moves, propelled by Erich Mielke, to centralise and expand K5.[*] For most of its life it had a strength of around 1,000 officers. Top positions were the preserve of former KPD members, proven anti-Nazi resisters, and wartime partisans with the Red Army. Its task, broken down into a brusque ten-point programme,[2] was to assist MGB-MVD operational groups in the investigation of:

- Political assassination
- Acts of sabotage, including against 'reconstruction efforts'
- Surviving Nazi organisations
- Deceit or misinforming by former members of the Nazi party
- Crimes against humanity
- Weapons and explosives violations
- 'Removal and besmirching of democratic propaganda'
- Spreading rumours or slogans

---

* In cities, towns and districts, the agency's units were known as K5 commissariats (Kommissariate K5). At provincial and headquarters level they were known as K5 departments (Dezernate K5). This naming has led to a mistaken idea that the formal title of the agency was Kommissariat 5: it was not.

- Disobeying orders of the Soviet Military Administration
- 'Other violations against the establishment of the new order'

While the MGB was busy recruiting moles inside the CDU and other block parties, K5 concentrated on monitoring police officials and the SED, whose members had been subject to stringent background checks ever since the party was founded. One K5 veteran noted that if the party leadership lacked compromising evidence against a political undesirable, K5 officers might be told to 'construct a case'.[3] A sharp lookout was kept for unenthusiastic social democrats and unorthodox Marxists. Saxony's K5 officers set another precedent by carrying out surveillance of judicial officials, providing the MGB and MVD with a dossier on every provincial judge and prosecutor.[4]

Here a key point arises about communist security services. For all their hostility towards enemy countries, one of their biggest concerns – sometimes to the exclusion of all else – was to watch and harass their own side. Communist authorities didn't just distrust their subordinate populations – they distrusted themselves. The successive counter-intelligence departments of the NKGB, MGB and eventually KGB were forever watching the staff of SMAD, or Soviet foreign intelligence, or the so-called 'Soviet colony' of several thousand professionals working in Germany. For their part, East German security agencies learned quickly that they were expected to devote much time and energy to invigilating East German communists. The personnel of K5 were guided in this task by the Soviet advisers placed at every level of the organisation.

The first head of K5 was Ernst Lange, a communist activist since the age of eighteen. By the time he was thirty, Lange had endured incarceration in some of the Third Reich's most sinister locations; the Plötzensee and Spandau prisons, Gestapo headquarters on Berlin's Prinz-Albrecht-Strasse. During the war he had been pressed into service in the Todt Organisation, the Nazi construction agency, working in France while doing his best to carry out communist agitation. But Lange wasn't trusted by the Soviets or by the Moscow-based German exiles, who were suspicious of anyone who had spent time in western Europe, and in 1948 he was replaced as K5 chief by Erich Jamin.

Jamin's war experience had been even more traumatic. An inmate of concentration camps and prisons since 1933, he had then been corralled into the infamous Dirlewanger SS penal brigade; it is possible his capture by the Red Army in 1944 brought him some respite. Despite his lengthy track record of communist devotion and persecution by the Nazis, Jamin wasn't released from Soviet captivity until 1947. When he returned to Germany he was appointed straight to the DVdI, which needed tough, not to say brutalised, people.

The leaders of K5 in Saxony, Thuringia and Mecklenburg – Rolf Markert, Jean-Baptist Feilen and Rudolf Wunderlich – were all survivors of Buchenwald and Sachsenhausen. Another K5 executive, Martin Weikert, was a Sudeten German who had received clandestine training in Moscow during the 1930s and served as a radio operator for Slovakian partisans during the war. These men knew heroism and courage, but they had also experienced the very worst in violence, callousness, deprivation, and political intrigue. Within a few years, Jamin would be leading the Stasi department responsible for monitoring social democrats, Markert would be head of the Stasi in Dresden, and Weikert a deputy minister of security.

Although it worked under strict Soviet supervision, K5 had special powers to deal with political criminals and opponents. The historian Norman Naimark has called the agency 'a specialized MGB task force among the German population'.[5] K5 acted above the law and sometimes outside the control of the SED.[6] Its files were housed separately from those of other police departments, which were forbidden to enquire into its work, and it had sweeping powers to arrest suspects, seize their property and bring charges,[7] especially when enforcing SMAD directives or Law No. 10 of the Allied Control Council.

The term 'political police' was forbidden, and the existence of K5 was a tightly guarded secret – one kept not only from the Western powers. Markus Wolf, the Stasi's legendary spymaster, recalled that when he was working as a young party official in eastern Germany:

> the West Berlin Social Democratic paper, *Telegraf*, published a story that in the cellar of the residential house where I lived people were being interrogated and tortured by a police section known as K5. I publicly denied this completely and accused the paper of inventing not only torture but the very existence of a section K5. Only later, when I was appointed to the Ministry for State Security, did I discover that K5 did indeed exist and it had been torturing suspects in that very basement.[8]

Usually K5 investigated and detained suspects identified by the MGB. It would then hand over suspects' cases to the Soviet authorities, to conclude as they saw fit. Sometimes Soviet personnel would arrest suspects investigated by K5, partly to limit the public's perception of German-on-German policing. To obscure the fate of arrestees, K5 officers had to sign forms given them by the MVD, confirming that a particular individual had fled to western Germany; the real fate of the person was unknown to them.[9] Some of these individuals died and some were thrown into camps. Others became Soviet agents.

In due course K5 began to monitor Länder assemblies and ministries, city and district councils, and mayoral offices. A range of entities and activities fell under its scrutiny: 'the judiciary, railways, postal services, health care [providers], credit institutions'. K5 headquarters at the DVdI housed files on 'state-owned, sequestered and private companies, trade and commercial [concerns], parties, organisations, associations and clubs, the press, radio, theatres, cinemas, the hotel industry, churches and certain groups of people [such as] re-settlers and returnees'.[10] Detailed files were kept on employees of the Länder interior ministries, including police officers. The Soviets, of course, were privy to all of this information and could use it to recruit, purge or punish anyone they chose, including those who merely made negative remarks about SMAD or the SED.[11]

There were several different types of K5 report: they were divided into such areas as activity reports, arrests for the German authorities, arrests for the occupation authorities, confiscations and seizures, and searches.[12] Two further types of K5 report were portentous – political situation reports and informer reports, both of which would come to be the bread and butter of the mature Stasi.

Vetting by K5 unearthed plenty of undesirable personal backgrounds, and led to numerous expulsions from the Volkspolizei, the SED, and judicial positions. But it was as an auxiliary force for MGB operations, ostensibly as part of denazification, that K5 really earned its spurs – kicking down doors, punching faces, and slinging class enemies into the dark interiors of vehicles and cells.

From 1946 to 1948, underground resistance by social democrats was one of the biggest concerns for the security authorities of the Soviet zone. SPD members who had spurned the merger with the communists were branded 'Schumacherites', after the leader of the western SPD, Kurt Schumacher. For years they were demonised in the screaming denouncements of SED-run media; Erich Mielke, in particular, would spray around the term in a state of near apoplexy. Mielke stressed that Schumacherites had infested political parties and mass organisations, determined to undermine 'the economic rebuilding of the SBZ'. The job of K5, he said, was to defend 'democratic institutions' against such 'enemies'.[13]

In Berlin the SPD continued to thrive thanks to the city's four-power status. Party headquarters at Zietenstrasse, in the American sector, became a meeting point for disgruntled social democrats. Among other things, they could pick up leaflets and newspapers to distribute in the Soviet zone, although this was a risky activity. The fate of an underground SPD group based in Halle is typical. The group agitated against the SED using materials picked up from Zietenstrasse by one of its members, Hans Behle; because of the war-ravaged transport routes, the journey would take him several days. In late 1946 Behle was contacted by an SPD Ostbüro courier from Hanover. The courier was not who he seemed. The end result, on 9 April 1947, was Behle's arrest by Soviet personnel. He was taken to the cellars of a notorious prison in Halle, the Red Ox (Rote Ochse), which played a big part in repression after the war. (Having been run by the NKVD-MVD and hosted Soviet military tribunals, the Red Ox was to become a women's prison run by the Stasi. Five protesters were shot dead while trying to storm it during the June 1953 uprising.)

To make him reveal his accomplices, Karl Behle was beaten up almost every day for five months. After being detained at Sachsenhausen for a while, he was sentenced to ten years' hard labour. Behle's recollections of Sachsenhausen are interesting; he complained about the lack of food but was impressed by the Soviet practice of granting prisoners three newspapers a day, and the opportunity to watch films in the 'non-political' wing of the prison.[14]

Like many other stories of repressed SPD members, Behle's experiences only came to light in the 1950s, when the lucky ones were released from prisons and camps and were able to emigrate. In the late 1940s, the disappearance of social democrats was a mysterious and unnerving phenomenon. Their fate was unknown. It was difficult for everyone, including the Western powers, to see what was going on. One indicator, however, was the continuing capture or treachery of Ostbüro personnel. Over Easter 1947, presumably as part of the same operation that netted Behle, the Soviets arrested 130 social democrats in Halle, Gera, Leipzig and Dresden.[15] On 8 April the main Ostbüro courier, Waldemar Kasparek, was arrested. He revealed the names of SPD resisters throughout the Soviet zone. There were some surprises. The director of government publications in Halle turned out to be an Ostbüro activist. So did an SED city councillor in Magdeburg.[16]

Clearly there were problems with Ostbüro security. There were incidents of childlike guilelessness. Even the inexperienced Ostbüro staff expressed unease when an SPD activist from a small town near Dresden posted to Hanover a list of the members of his resistance group.[17] In its favour, the Ostbüro was one of the only sources of information on K5, which it noted was responsible for the 'constant surveillance' of 'all the leading personages in public life' – another hint of the Stasi's later ubiquity, though an exaggeration of K5's capabilities.[18] In due course the Ostbüro was boosted by the craft and professionalism of the likes of Günther Weber, a former Präsident of the Leipzig police who fled from the Soviet zone.[19]

There is no doubt that some SPD members were organising significant underground political resistance to communism in postwar Germany. This is apparent in the arrests made later by the Stasi, which were not random arrests of everyday social democrats; they were targeted. Sometimes SED officials would take part in K5's interrogations of suspects, for they wanted to understand the political thinking of those ranged against them.[20] And political opposition arose in diverse places. The chair of the LDPD in the Mecklenburg assembly, Dr Scheffler, a devotee of culture and the arts, refused a bribe of extra rations to stop criticising the confiscation of privately owned theatres. He was arrested and tried as a Nazi.[21] The CDU youth organisation Junge Union attracted lasting SED hatred. During June 1947 a CDU pamphlet was distributed at dozens of meetings by the Junge Union leader in Thuringia, Wolfgang Seibert. Part of it read, 'We did not fight against terror in order to watch new despotism emerge.'[22] Early the following year the Junge Union was banned, but underground groups sprang up. Some collaborated with social democrat resisters, but Soviet and K5 arrest operations broke up much of this activity.[23]

A CDU student group led by Georg Wrazidlo at the University of Berlin inflamed the Soviets when it pushed through a resolution against decorating the campus with communist imagery. Wrazidlo and twenty others were arrested, and he was sentenced to nine years in prison for 'conducting underground fascist activity' and possessing weapons. The first charge, and probably the second, was trumped up, for Wrazidlo was no fascist; he had been persecuted for his anti-Nazi resistance during the war. More recently he had, however, published a student journal in which he criticised communism. Christian democrats in the Berlin senate were so disturbed by these arrests, and the unlikeliness of the crimes, that they demanded the Allied Kommandatura investigate them.[24] If an attempt was made to do so, it didn't get anywhere.

Yet in some respects things weren't going so well for the Soviet and German communists. Although Stalin tried to win approval by abolishing the death penalty in 1947, this led to a sharp increase in Gulag sentences of twenty-five years, a punishment that wasn't necessarily preferable. The experiment didn't last anyway, and the death penalty was reinstated three years later. Furthermore, the geopolitical situation was worsening. At their 1947 summit in Moscow, the Allied foreign ministers failed to agree on a plan to run Germany as a whole. A meeting held in Munich in May 1947, which convened the heads of every German provincial state, was similarly fractious. The representatives from the Soviet zone left after a few hours when there was no agreement on the agenda.[25]

Meanwhile K5 was going through its first re-organisation. Political offences were on the rise, and there was deemed to be an 'increasing severity of crime' of all types. The Volkspolizei was proving unreliable and unpopular. Because police units were placed in factories to keep order and prevent stealing, or to confiscate stashes of surplus food or privately traded supplies, huge resentment built up towards them.[26] The police lacked experience too: a DVdI report from June 1947 found that of the roughly 39,000 Volkspolizisten, only some 2,000 – six percent – had worked in the police before 1945.[27] In another report, SED officials commented on the lamentable state of the force: '[The police] deal with not only criminal and traffic matters, but rather I see one of their most important tasks as constantly protecting [against] attacks on our young democratic state. The imperative precondition for this is the absolute political reliability of all of those in the service of the police.' There were disturbing signs that this reliability was lacking. The report continued, with some foresight, that 'there is a great danger that if a sudden political situation occurred, we [the SED] would not have enough control of the police [to] use them as a protective instrument.'[28]

The communists pushed on regardless with their programme. In June 1947 SMAD ordered the creation of the German Economic Commission (Deutsche Wirtschaftskommission, DWK) as 'the first central administrative organ' in the Soviet zone. This proto-government was a big step towards German governance of eastern Germany. And the SED announced at its second party congress that it was to become a 'Party of a New Type' – a 'vanguard of the working class', like the Soviet communist party, rather than the 'people's party' it had previously claimed to be.[29] Among other things, this meant that distinctions between its communist and social democratic members would no longer be observed. Subsequently it was established that all party business was to be based on Lenin's autocratic principle of 'democratic centralism' – the rank-and-file may get to debate an issue, but only the top leaders get to decide it.

For the SED, the tricky thing was that many eastern Germans didn't want any part of this. Something had to be done.

11

Order No. 201

In August 1947 a notice was pasted onto every suitable wall that remained standing in the cities, towns and villages of the Soviet zone. It read:

Proclamation
Order No. 201 of the Supreme Head of the Soviet Military Administration and Commander-in-Chief of Soviet occupation troops in Germany

The population is called upon to submit all available documents that lead to the identification of all:

Nazi activists
Nazi leaders
Nazi criminals
War criminals
Reactionaries
Militarists
War profiteers

The sessions of the De-Nazification Commission are public; the population is requested to take part in the meetings.

At the same time, K5 was mandated to pursue its own investigations. No longer was it to serve merely as an SED vetting service, or to provide the muscle on operations led by the MGB and MVD. Now, the German personnel of K5 were encouraged to go after any suspect they wanted to; that is, to pursue other Germans of their own choosing.

Order 201 signified both the climax and the long drawn-out end of denazification. All Nazi militants, big and small, were to be swept from the political, economic and civil administrations of eastern Germany. After being assessed, so-called 'nominal' Nazis were to be offered the chance of rehabilitation. But as well as subjugating real Nazis – who, it seems, were still at large in considerable numbers – the order was to be a smokescreen for the removal of dissenting or merely unenthusiastic people from responsible positions in society.

This morally doubled-edged campaign brings up difficult, probably unanswerable questions. How many committed Nazis remained in eastern Germany in 1947? In what ways were they defying the new authorities? We know that some 5,000 former members of the SPD were incarcerated in this period, and an estimated 100,000 fled the Soviet zone, but what was the position, and the conduct, of the 595,000 former SPD members who were not incarcerated and who remained in the zone? How many citizens were genuinely supportive of the new authorities, or such measures as Order 201? After all, left-wing Germans – numerous since the nineteenth century – had waited a long time to see their form of politics implemented in their own country. Furthermore, many people agreed that a measure of retribution should be inflicted on Nazis. Thus to some, Order 201 might have appeared progressive and just – provided one didn't look too hard behind the scenes.

In addition to extending its political tasks and regional presence, Order 201 gave K5 a range of judicial functions. In the instructions that accompanied the order, K5 officers were granted the right to issue their own arrest warrants. They could conduct legal investigations and prepare indictments without the involvement of a prosecutor, who need only be brought in at a late stage to rubber-stamp their work. And K5 had considerable influence over the punishments of convicted Nazis. New denazification commissions were formed,* with seats reserved for delegates from the local Kriminalpolizei. These, of course, were K5 officers, meaning that the police both arrested and judged suspects. This was precisely the type of situation that was being avoided in the British zone, for example, where the intention was to steer Germans away from totalitarian practices and instead attract them to 'the British way of life', with its checks and balances, and its separation of powers.[1]

The powers now enjoyed by K5 led to protests from 'bourgeois' and even SED lawyers. Some challenged the practice of making prisoners perform 'hard and heavy' forced labour while awaiting trial, a measure advocated strongly by Erich Mielke. To legitimise it, SMAD issued the instruction 'Transfer of investigation procedures for crimes against Control Council Law No. 10 to the investigative bodies of the criminal police'. Much of the activity around Order 201 was underpinned by such Allied Control Council instruments, especially Law No. 10 and Directive 38, which were applied indiscriminately, and arbitrarily. According to the Soviet and SED interpretation of Directive

---

*   Entnazifizierungskommissionen or EK.

38, it criminalised those who 'somehow express a positive attitude to the Nazi state' or 'somehow oppose the pronouncement of a new democratic state or try to undermine its authority'. This effectively meant carte blanche to arrest a person who, although never a Nazi, was not wild about Soviet communism or the SED.

The Länder interior ministries were made to answer a lengthy questionnaire about the progress of denazification under Order 201. Offices for housing and sequestered assets had to disclose their compliance with the order; failure to do so was deemed sabotage and invited the criminal prosecution of Länder officials. This approach suggests that the Soviets and SED were aware that their commands were not being obeyed. In a speech Erich Mielke hammered home the importance of the current measures: 'The course of denazification until now shows that we as German bodies have not worked properly so far. The empty words will now finally be put to an end. Order 201 concerns the issue of the struggle for power. Order 201 concerns the question of national independence and the unity of Germany.'[2]

Within a year of Order 201 being issued, the number of suspects tried as a Nazi or war criminal rose from 873 to more than 4,500.[3] The SED supplied most of the judges, lawyers and lay judges (representatives of the public) for these proceedings. All were given classes in how to 'see things from the Party's viewpoint'.[4] At the same time, the incarceration of thousands of social democrats in Soviet camps and prisons occurred largely under Order 201.

There are various pieces of evidence for this wayward use of the order. A section of K5 was given the job of tackling 'Schumacher supporters and Trotskyists',[5] as well as churches, suspect members of Antifa Block parties, and the members of 'sects' (which usually meant Jehovah's Witnesses). K5 in Saxony reported that the number of incidents of subversive leafletting had risen from 160 in 1946 to more than 500 the following year;[6] but the same report claimed that Order 201 was helping to quell this 'SPD resistance'. Clearly the order was being applied to social democrats and not Nazis. Moreover, Saxony's K5 department opened 23,017 cases in 1947, of which 5,760 fell under Order 201. In 1948 it opened 51,236 cases of which 12,674 concerned Order 201.[7] These figures indicate that many other political 'criminals' and opponents of the SED were being dealt with in cases that weren't classified under Order 201.

Some operations under the order targeted underground SPD groups explicitly, for it was possible to accuse such groups of harbouring unrepentant Nazis who were cloaking themselves as social democrats. It is extremely difficult to test the truth of such allegations. Either way, a wave of arrests in May 1948, of democrats with connections to the SPD Ostbüro, and an even bigger wave in the autumn, which rounded up democrats in Magdeburg, Halle, Frankfurt an der Oder and Dresden, both took place under Order 201.[8]

The order also led to developments within K5. Its ranks were boosted with hundreds of Volkspolizei officers from around the Länder.[9] A new recruitment drive sought to enlist working-class personnel, and special schools were set up to teach officers how to enforce Order 201. In one of the first examples of security agents going undercover to monitor the political system of eastern Germany, handpicked specialists were chosen for the clandestine 'penetration and investigation' (Durchdringung und Durcharbeitung) of central and Länder administrations.[10] Growing concerns about Western espionage saw K5 ordered to monitor the manufacturers and repairers of radios and writing equipment.[11] And all forms of policing took a step forward when in August 1947 a telex system for the whole zone came into operation.[12] Before this, the Soviets had been reluctant to give telephone lines to the police and other agencies, making communication difficult and – in the case of the police – disastrously slow. Now, better communications began to strengthen the fight against political troublemakers.

Even as Order 201 targeted serious political offenders, milder forms of political dissent were punished harshly. During summer 1947 leaflets appeared in Saxony campaigning against 'Ivan the Terrible', and a police station had anti-communist slogans daubed on its outer walls. An underground SPD group was found responsible; its members were arrested and received sentences of ten to twenty-five years' hard labour.[13] SED members also had to be on their toes. That November, following a hopeful rumour that the SPD might be relicensed in the Soviet zone, an SED member from Cottbus visited the SPD office on Berlin's Zietenstrasse for instructions. He was told to gather and prepare associates in the Soviet zone who might be interested in re-founding the party. In May 1948 he and the four friends who had joined him were arrested, presumably after months of observation.[14]

In terms of security, the SPD Ostbüro was not covering itself in glory. In January 1948 an Ostbüro courier called Richard Lehners fluffed the name he gave to Soviet personnel during an identity check. The Soviets played dumb and let him go, in order to observe his movements and contacts. Having kept his blunder to himself, Lehners returned to the Soviet zone two months later and stayed in the homes of some SPD resisters, at least two of whom were then arrested.[15]

Another Ostbüro courier, Ernst Knippel, was smuggling leaflets and secret reports with the use of a forged ID, which allowed him to travel between Hanover and the Soviet zone. One day in February 1948 he aroused suspicion at the zonal border and was arrested by Soviet personnel. Under interrogation he revealed the names of the resisters he was servicing around the town of Gardelegen in Saxony-Anhalt. The MVD blocked off the roads around Gardelegen and rounded up the group; several were imprisoned in the cellars of the Red Ox.[16]

A month after this, MVD plainclothes officers arrested Arthur Liebknecht, who had been distributing Ostbüro leaflets. Liebknecht's capture resulted from his renewed acquaintance with one Arthur Reich, an old friend who managed to convince Liebknecht that he had joined the Ostbüro. Liebknecht duly shared some of his pamphlets with Reich. An MVD raid soon followed; leaflets, false IDs, maps, and records of clandestine meetings were found on Liebknecht's desk. After receiving severe beatings while in detention, Liebknecht was sentenced to twenty-five years' hard labour.[17] The same sentence was handed to the members of an underground SPD group in Thuringia, who had been making use of a contact in the Soviet zone's economic bureaucracy because of his access to telephones. The group's leader told his captors that he had chosen to resist the Soviet authorities because of unfair trials and the denial of freedom of expression.[18]

The arrest of Ostbüro activists impacted on two of the organisation's sponsors, the CIC and CIA. For example, two CIC agents recommended by the Ostbüro, Alfred Lippschütz of the Volkspolizei and Walter Willfahrt of the DVdI communications department, were both arrested and given lengthy Gulag sentences. In its postmortem the CIC bemoaned the 'severe indiscretion and total lack of security consciousness on the part of Willfahrt and Lippschütz'. Also culpable was the 'very sloppy handling' and 'complex tangle of sub-sources' of Region VIII – the CIC's Berlin branch – and in particular its agent O-35-VIII. The latter was Willy Brandt, future mayor of Berlin and West German chancellor.[19]

Given the creepy disappearance of many of their comrades, SPD resisters showed considerable courage in persisting at this time. At one Leipzig trade fair – an event that was soon to be a showcase for East Germany, and something of a spies' annual general meeting – a social democrat activist slipped leaflets into copies of the programme, and covered telephone kiosks and Leipzig's main train station with anti-communist stickers; among the leaflets were copies of Kurt Schumacher's speeches. The culprit was an SED member, and he had recently asked the party to do something about the harsh conditions at the Soviet-owned Wismut uranium mines, where more than 100,000 conscripted and forced labourers had been put to work. The SED had told him to drop the matter, inciting him to resistance; he was identified, arrested, and sentenced to eight years in prison.[20] In general, social democrat detainees were treated harshly and unfairly. One SPD activist later complained that he had signed the Soviet interrogation protocol placed before him because he had been interrogated at night, kept awake all day, and given a Russian text to sign without any idea of what it said.[21]

Some social democrat resisters and reformers held high office in the SED. Max Fank, a party functionary in Stralsund, was arrested in March 1949 and sentenced to twenty-five years' hard labour for promoting the cause of social democracy.[22] Two SED executives in Saxony, the former SPD members Fritz Drescher and Arno Wend, had both been notable anti-Nazi resisters. Wend was arrested in July 1948 and sentenced to twenty-five years' hard labour. He was to spend seven years in the barbarous Gulag camp at Vorkuta. Meanwhile, Drescher and fourteen members of his covert social democrat group were accused not only of spreading anti-Soviet propaganda but, portentously, of espionage. They may or may not have been genuine spies; certainly, political resisters were being used in increasing numbers by Western intelligence services. Every member of Drescher's group was sentenced to twenty-five years' hard labour. Like so many others, their ordeals only came to light in the mid-1950s when, lucky to survive, they were released from the camps in post-Stalin amnesties, and managed to escape the Soviet Bloc.[23]

Principled members of the CDU were also refusing to buckle under. Angered by all the repression, in mid-1948 the eastern CDU temporarily refused to participate in the Antifa Block. Over the previous year, arrests of its members had gone up by forty percent.[24] The Soviets had already removed one party leader, Andreas Hermes, from his job. In December 1947 they removed his replacements. One of them, Jakob Kaiser, was to become an influential figure in West Berlin, where he orchestrated vociferous Christian democrat opposition to developments in eastern Germany.

As part of the Soviet drive for 'remaining bourgeois politicians' to be 'liquidated from leading positions',[25] the CDU vice-chairs elected in Saxony and Mecklenburg were forbidden to take office.[26] The entire CDU executive in the district of Niederbarnim was arrested.[27] In an incident that might repay further investigation, Dr Wilhelm Wolf, a critic of the Soviet authorities, died in a car accident in Berlin five days after being elected CDU chairman in Brandenburg.[28] Other leading CDU officials, such as Dr Rudolf Paul of the party's disobedient Thuringia branch, were smuggled out of eastern Germany, together with their documents, by the CIC.[29]

In October 1948 SMAD forced the resignation of Arthur Lieutenant, leader of the liberal democratic LDPD. He was replaced by Karl Hamann, who would himself feel the force of communist disapproval a few years later. But Hamann lived; others died. The CDU mayor of Falkensee, Hermann Neumann, died in prison soon after his arrest;[30] and in spring 1948 a CDU district chairman, Hans Georg Löser, was shot dead in his apartment by the Soviet personnel who had gone there to detain him.[31]

The arrest campaigns under Order 201 were only supposed to run for three months. Extended in November 1947, they ran for much longer. Their collected data were evaluated well into the following decade, especially by the Stasi, which continued to base its operations on the information.[32] At certain points Order 201 was refocused. In his annual report for 1947, the chief of police in Saxony urged his K5 officers to concentrate less on workers, minor entrepreneurs and former mid-level Nazis, and instead to target the Nazi high-ups who 'because of their economic position [had] supported fascism materially, gave financial assistance and received personal benefits'.[33]

Yet according to historian Monika Tantzscher, an expert on the political policing of the time, 'The work of K5 was made more difficult by the lack of help from the population in implementing Order 201.' The authorities noted that throughout the campaign there was a 'strong, steady increase in cases of sabotage and the spreading of fascist and anti-democratic propaganda, as well as agent activity'.[34] While this might be put down to public disgust at the iniquitous actions of SMAD and the SED, it again raises one of the big questions about the period: how much latent, organised Nazism was there? Denazification was deeply unpopular in the western occupation zones too, where it was seen to target 'token' party members who were not convinced Nazis, penalising the small fry while the high-level culprits went unpunished. Still, surviving Nazi faith is a possible explanation for the public's resentment.

Order 201 was the making of K5, however. By 1949 it had 1,500 personnel and a headquarters staff of around fifty. In operations connected with the order, some 7,000 private companies had been expropriated, of which almost 5,000 were now state-owned and 2,000 converted into various forms of cooperative. K5 in Thuringia had confiscated assets worth more than sixty-four million marks, K5 in Saxony more than thirty million, all of it now publicly owned.[35] And K5 had attracted renown. The West Berlin radio station RIAS (Radio in the American Sector) started to broadcast warnings about individual K5 officers who were known to have a close relationship with 'NKVD' personnel and to hand over arrested Germans to the Soviet authorities.[36] And in his Whitsunday sermon of 1949, Bishop Otto Dibelius of West Berlin denounced K5 by name. The only thing K5 officers could do in response was dash off a livid internal memo.[37]

12

Developments in the Zone

SMAD disbanded the Soviet zone's denazification commissions in February 1948. One month was put aside to assess appeals. By this point around half a million people had been removed from their jobs, especially in civil administrations, although the need for qualified staff meant that many nominal Nazis stayed in work. Despite the disbandment of the commissions, though, the arrests and confiscations continued, with K5 reporting that at least twenty-eight underground Nazi groups were still active.[1]

The complement of Antifa Block parties increased that spring, with the founding of the National Democratic Party of Germany (NDPD) to represent the middle classes and former right-wingers, and the Democratic Farmers' Party of Germany (DBD).* One idea behind the DBD was to cater for the formerly landless citizens who had been given five-hectare plots in the land reforms. Soviet fears over the growing popularity of the CDU and LDPD provided an equally strong motive for founding the new parties, which fragmented some of the opposition to the SED.

It is rare for an authoritarian regime to be purely oppressive. Unending oppression makes a regime's life more difficult and its overthrow more likely. Instead, authoritarian rulers have to strike a balance. If struck successfully, they are much harder to remove. Thus, ruling an authoritarian society involves a constant segue between carrot and stick. The rulers have to know when to hit, and when to reward, the population. During the 1930s, Stalin learned that the margins are fine. Just a bit too much oppression, for just a bit too long, might create enough public resentment to inspire more active and widespread opposition than existed in the first place. Just a bit too much reward, and the people start asking for too many things that can't be delivered – thus exposing the inadequacy of the dictator's rule, and perhaps triggering more opposition.

SMAD was walking this line in the Soviet zone of Germany. Some SMAD executives pleaded with Moscow to try a more lenient approach. The head of SMAD in Thuringia, Ivan Kolesnichenko, although no liberal, wrote that

---

* National-Demokratische Partei Deutschlands and Demokratische Bauernpartei Deutschlands.

'the "disappearance" of people because of the activities of our [MGB-MVD] Operational Sectors is still arousing major discontent among the German population and providing every hostile element with ammunition for anti-Soviet propaganda'.[2] In his appeals it is apparent that Kolesnichenko, who had probably never left the Soviet Union until his posting to Germany, was making a clumsy but sincere effort to understand concepts that were thoroughly alien to him – compassion, the presence of civil society organisations, jurisprudence and, above all, the rights of the individual, for which he used the term 'freedom of personality':

> In Germany it has long been the rule, incidentally even under fascism, that when a citizen was arrested because of a criminal or political offence, family members and organizations that take an interest in the fate of this arrested person were informed. Family members were allowed to visit the arrested person, members of the clergy were allowed to visit them in order to pray and hear their confessions... the Germans have got so used to this order of things that they associate it with the idea of 'freedom of personality'. They see this 'freedom of personality' in the fact that an arrest can only take place if a judge who has evidence of the arrested person's guilt [issues] an arrest warrant, and that the arrested person always has the right to legal counsel.[3]

The MVD's special internment camps were also attracting troublesome attention. In the words of Jens Gieseke, 'this impenetrable complex inadvertently evoked associations with the recently defunct Nazi regime'.[4] This put the SED, defender of Soviet policy, in an uncomfortable position. The Soviets responded with a spasm of clemency. In summer 1948, 28,000 prisoners were released from the camps: those serving less than one year for Nazi crimes, and those awaiting sentence for minor crimes.[5] Eight of the camps were then closed, and two years later the whole camp system was dissolved. The remaining inmates were disposed of in abrupt fashion, however, some to the Gulag and others to the contentious Waldheim trials.

As part of managing their image, the Soviets began increasingly to hide behind the indigenous authority, the SED. This was another favoured tactic in the countries dominated by Moscow. In the gradual course of being granted powers, by the end of 1948 the SED controlled the Administration for Justice. This was partly because SMAD had removed at least nine of its leading officials. Every visible opponent of the SED's hold on the judiciary had now been ousted.[6] The SED had also created its own Soviet-style Politbüro and a Party Control Commission, the latter a salivating internal watchdog with departments at all levels. Within two years it purged some 200,000 party members.[7]

Steadily the SED was claiming the right to direct the economy, regardless of the views of the other Antifa Block parties.[8] As well as devising the Two Year Plan, the party's members saturated the zone's proto-government body, the German Economic Commission, although they managed to stage a puppet show of democratic discussions. At cagey and indecisive conferences of the Allied foreign ministers held during 1947, it had probably dawned on SMAD and the SED that their vision of a united but demilitarised Germany, in which pro-Moscow Marxists would play a leading role, was a fantasy. So to further secure their hold on eastern Germany, they took the step of initiating a proto-parliamentary forum to be hosted in the Soviet sector of Berlin, known as the Volkskongress. It was planned to convene the congress occasionally, with delegates from the block parties and civil organisations in attendance. Representatives of western German parties would also be invited, though few had the stomach to attend when their chance came. Many members of the non-Marxist block parties were against the Volkskongress; their biggest complaint was that it didn't represent the entire country. At this point it was impossible for most Germans to foresee, never mind to accept, that their country was to remain divided for decades.

The Volkskongress laid some foundations for the German Democratic Republic. To ensure its domination by SMAD and the SED, the Volkskongress of 1948 was attended not by elected candidates but by delegates appointed by the leaders of the block parties. At the congress these delegates duly elected a Volksrat or People's Council, which began to draft a new German constitution. For the third Volkskongress, the zone's authorities trialled a version of the electoral system that would later be used to steer the outcome of every East German election. Anyone of age was entitled to vote, with the exception of the 'mentally ill', those convicted of crimes under Order 201 or Allied Directive 38, and those 'sentenced for "sabotaging" the new anti-fascist democratic order, or for adopting a "confrontational attitude" towards the occupying power'. Voters were given a pre-selected list of candidates from the block parties and were posed a quasi-patriotic statement with which to agree or disagree: 'I support the unity of Germany and a just peace treaty. I therefore vote for the following list of candidates for the Third German Volkskongress.'[9]

In a contested result, which saw the CDU, in particular, accuse the SED of tampering with the results – which it did, especially by counting spoiled ballots as 'agree' votes – sixty-six percent of voters answered 'agree'. It was a majority, but nothing like the majority that SMAD and the SED had hoped for. Predictably, they grew fearful about the dissenting thirty-four percent living in the Soviet zone.[10] Elections for local councils were postponed until late in 1949 (and subsequently postponed again), a decision that proved fiercely unpopular.

Georg Dertinger, who had replaced the bravely anti-Soviet Jakob Kaiser as CDU chair, explained that it was lack of 'legal security' that had led to the lukewarm election result, and was the biggest complaint of the zone's residents, who could see all too clearly that law and legal proceedings were not being respected.[11] Grotewohl and Pieck of the SED took a different view. They lashed out publicly at the 'enemies' responsible for the lacklustre vote – reactionaries in the CDU and LDPD and, above all, the SPD Ostbüro.[12]

There were continuing problems with the police. In summer 1948, having doubled the strength of the force in one year,[13] the SED decided it had to subordinate it to the party more explicitly. Senior officers now had to swear an oath of loyalty to the SED and its policies.[14] The name Volkspolizei was now widely used, and became official in 1949. It was accurate; almost ninety percent of police recruits in the Soviet zone were manual workers or farmers.[15] But the Volkspolizei was far from being the sharp, shining weapon of working-class justice it was intended to be. As late as October 1948 the force in Saxony-Anhalt was complaining about its lack of bicycles and bike tyres; officers were in no position to protect farmers' fields from thieves who, thanks to having bicycles, were 'far better equipped'.[16]

Erich Reschke was replaced as head of the DVdI by Kurt Fischer, supposedly because of questions about Reschke's conduct as a wartime inmate of Sachsenhausen. Moscow-trained and a veteran of the Spanish Civil War, Fischer had already shown his proficiency in centralising the police system in Saxony. The SED inserted Fischer in his new role without consulting the other block parties. This prompted complaints from the CDU that the police should be under 'parliamentary control' rather than that of one party.[17] But the deed was done, and Fischer was able to enact the policies required of him.

By this point, the secretly founded DVdI was sufficiently well known to be described in a Western newspaper as 'one of the most important prerequisites for the absolute rule of the SED'; part of 'an apparatus that will ensure the absolute primacy of the SED, even if Soviet troops withdraw from the eastern zone'.[18] Apparent proof came with Fischer's Command No. 2 of 14 January 1949, which triggered the biggest purge yet seen in the police force. One in ten police officers in Berlin lost their job, one in five in the Länder.[19] The purge rumbled on for several years, extending to any 'undesirable officer'. Mostly this meant former members of the Nazi party, but it also meant those who had served in the Wehrmacht, or been a POW in an Allied country other than the USSR, or who had come to the Soviet zone as a refugee from territory once held by the Germans, or who had relatives in western Germany.

For practical reasons, former members of the Hitler Youth were exempted from the purge. So were especially useful Nazis. Their continuing employment was justified when Erich Mielke prohibited the purging of officers 'who have demonstrated their anti-fascism by putting their lives on the line'. Non-Marxists and former social democrats were vulnerable to the purge if they maintained 'ties to the enemies of the democratic order'.[20] In the draft of one guideline, Mielke wrote that every police officer must be 'a conscious hater of international imperialism and reaction'.[21] (Later he replaced the word 'hater' with 'enemy', and deleted the word 'international'.) Mielke stressed that it was time for the police to perform the political duty of tackling secret agents, saboteurs and Schumacherites, given that – according to him – the fight against ordinary crime was being won.[22]

In autumn 1948 the DVdI created its Main Department for Political Culture (Politkultur). Based on equivalent organs in the Soviet police and armed forces, its purpose was to improve the political knowledge and reliability of police officers. The first Politkultur chief was the veteran communist Erich Wichert, a crony of Mielke's who, with unbeatable irony, had been sentenced to fifteen years in prison in 1933 as an accessory to the murder of two policemen. In due course there was one Politkultur officer for every 100 police officers. They held training and morale-boosting sessions, and made sure that appointments and promotions were in line with SED interests. Mielke insisted that Politkultur officers be 'the best and most reliable sons of the working class'.[23] Having written some hack journalism before the war, he now appointed himself executive editor of the staff magazine *Die Volkspolizei* – a publication no one would have foreseen running for four decades.

The police leadership started to hammer the point that the Volkspolizei was to be explicitly political. The force's unpredictable workers' councils were shut down. Instead, officers were herded into the Soviet zone's trade union federation, the FDGB,* a solidly SED creation. Crime and its prevention, as well as the behaviour of individual police officers, were now to be assessed against political criteria and from a 'class standpoint'. New recruits had to swear an oath of allegiance recognising that 'the Volkspolizei was created in order to protect the interests of the working people from all fascist, reactionary and other elements'.[24] A special school to train Politkultur officers was set up under the watchful eyes of Soviet instructors. In a training manual, officers were told to inculcate 'pitiless opposition to the forces of reaction'.[25] They also learned Russian history and the essentials of Marxism-Leninism-Stalinism.

None of this boosted the popularity of the authorities. Every stern or sneaky move by SMAD or the SED, every campaign to imbue citizens with an iron

---

* Freier Deutscher Gewerkschaftsbund.

class-consciousness, seemed to prompt more dissatisfaction. There were already widespread complaints from much of the population about what were seen as the SED's 'Might over Right' methods.* According to the SPD Ostbüro, the biggest public complaints in eastern Germany at this moment concerned the 'terror methods' of the Soviets and SED, and – never to be underestimated – the lack of food.[26]

In the face of these developments, how did the Antifa Block survive? For a start, many of those arrested by the Soviets and their German helpers really were former Nazis. Other arrestees, for reasons of political resistance, had begun to work illicitly for Western secret services, as charged. The zone's more conformist residents were able to distance themselves from such arrestees, and instead to hope that the Antifa Block would succeed, in the interests of rebuilding eastern Germany. There was also a desire among centrist politicians to work constructively with the occupation authorities, and try to preserve an element of liberalism in the coalition. And it is likely that war guilt, fatigue and apathy made many people disinclined to push their political demands too hard; in the end, they just did what SMAD told them to.

It is also likely that many members of the block's non-Marxist parties couldn't quite see the bad times coming their way. A one-party dictatorship in eastern Germany seemed so stunningly inappropriate that there was a tendency to believe it couldn't happen.[27] Moreover, certain Soviet political initiatives continued to be welcomed. Provided they really were owned by proven Nazi criminals, the confiscation of factories still enjoyed some popular support. And for all their unlawfulness and targeting of innocent smallholders, the expropriations of land resulted in 14,000 landowners in the Soviet zone losing their property. In contrast, some 560,000 landless farmers, refugees and labourers each received their five hectares,[28] for which many were grateful. In the process they became a heralded new social group, the 'new farmers' or Neubauern, who were to be almost deified in the GDR – although their good standing with the authorities didn't prevent them from suffering terrible hardships in the years ahead.

It wasn't just new structures of society and governance that were being put in place. Communist security was being strengthened by the creation of paramilitary police forces that eventually would evolve into the East German army. Similar developments were taking place in the West. Problems with elections, food supply, property ownership and the justice system were one thing, but the worst-case scenario was war.

---

* 'Gewalt geht vor Recht'.

13

The Cold War Hits New Depths

1949 was a bad year for humanity and planet earth. The founding of communist China caused global tensions to rigidify. Major wars were brewing in east Asia. The North Atlantic Treaty drew battle lines for the nuclear age. The division of Europe into capitalist West and communist East was symbolised by three events – the ongoing blockade of Berlin by the Soviet Union, the founding of West Germany in May, and the founding of East Germany in October. It was six years before either state achieved sovereignty; West Germany remained subject to the interests of Washington, London, Paris and Brussels, East Germany to those of Moscow. Communist fortunes appeared to dip when the insurrection in Greece ended in failure. But on 29 August, Soviet Russia exploded its first atomic bomb. The speed of its development, assisted by a foreign legion of scientific spies, shattered Western estimations. At the same time, military intelligence suggested that Soviet long-range bomber aircraft were now capable of reaching the US and dropping nuclear loads onto American cities.[1] Perhaps they wouldn't need to, for advances in biological and chemical weapons presaged a comparable devastation. This was Cold War, but everywhere one looked it threatened to turn hot. The world braced itself. The threat hung especially heavily over the American military and intelligence establishments; and over Germans, a majority of whom believed in 1949 that another war was imminent.[2]

The escalation of the Cold War, and the worsening of the Berlin crisis, unfolded inexorably, almost in spite of the humans affected by them. The causes were many: Stalin's expansionism, irreconcilable national interests, unshakeable faith in incompatible political and economic systems, the unstoppable generation of new military technologies; not to mention bloody-mindedness and big doses of anger and fear. Every move made by one of the occupying powers in Germany seemed to result in a rival power throwing a spanner into the works.

This intractability had become obvious in the preceding years. The US and British administrations had merged their zones in the Economic Council of

'Bizonia', an entity which furthered the regeneration of western Germany and served as a tentative prototype for a West German government. In March 1947 the US administration had adopted the Truman Doctrine, vowing to contain any further Soviet expansion. The immensity of the Soviet army presence in Europe, facing the West's more modest land forces, wasn't lost on the countries of the Western Union, which had begun to discuss the formation of a West German government at their meetings.[*] The US had started to pump economic aid into Europe with its Marshall Plan, which came with the caveat that communists be ousted from the governments of France and Italy. Communists around the continent were told to resist; French and Italian dockers refused to unload Marshall-laden ships. And in a knee-jerk reaction, the Sovietisation of eastern Europe accelerated. As the former NKVD officer Pavel Sudoplatov noted in his memoirs, 'Six months after the Marshall Plan was rejected by the Soviet Union, multiparty rule in Eastern Europe came to an end'.[3] Initiatives such as Marshall's angered and scared the Soviets, whose representative on the Allied Control Council, Vasily Sokolovsky, stormed out of its final four-power meeting in March 1948. Shortly before this, 400 MGB troops had been dispatched to Prague in plain clothes to invigilate the communist takeover of the Czech government.[4] Everywhere one looked there were agendas and bellicose confrontations.

In June 1948, with hyperinflation and the black market still running out of control, the Western powers had replaced the Reichsmark with the deutschmark. The Soviets duly introduced a new mark for their zone and, to stop the Western currency coming into Berlin, finally made the move that had suggested itself for the past three years: they closed off the roads, railways and waterways into Berlin. The Western Allies responded by supplying the city's western sectors by air, an effort which at its height saw an aircraft landing at the Tempelhof and Gatow airfields every thirty seconds.[5]

The Berlin blockade and airlift were to become symbols of broken international relations and a responding heroic altruism. Today it is easy to lose sight of the very great, and very real, fear of war that lurked behind it all, although there were divergent opinions in the West about the likelihood of war, and the conclusion drawn by US and British intelligence services was that Stalin would not go to war over the blockade itself. Nevertheless, the creeping, almost helpless sense of escalation was heightened when new paramilitary police forces – embryonic armies – were created in Germany's occupation zones.

Summer 1948 saw the founding of the 'standby police' (Bereitschaftspolizei)

---

* The Western Union, a response to the threat posed by the Soviet Union or a potentially rearmed Germany, was a military alliance of the UK, France, The Netherlands, Belgium and Luxembourg, established in September 1948 to implement the Treaty of Brussels signed earlier that year.

in the Soviet zone, a force that was soon subordinated to the stalwart communists of the DVdI. The Bereitschaftspolizei were given military training and housed in barracks, while leading officers were sent to study at Soviet army academies. They were envisaged as German auxiliaries for the Soviet armed forces; at this point, the need to use them to suppress internal rebellion was less obvious. To imbue the force with a suitably martial communist ethic, Wilhelm Zaisser was appointed as chief. He was a veteran of communist insurrections on three continents, as well as the Spanish Civil War, and more will be seen of him.

Zaisser built up the standby police under his euphemistic 'Administration for Training' at the DVdI. Soon some 10,000 armed police were under his command, divided into units of 250 and equipped with trucks, armoured personnel carriers, artillery pieces and even a few tanks. Recruits took an oath to fight alongside the troops of the 'People's Democracies' to repel the attacks of 'the reaction'. Meanwhile, further recruitment was boosted by sharp practices. It was said that 1,000 German prisoners working in the mines at Stalino in the USSR were pressed into service.[6] Wehrmacht prisoners of war returning to Germany were offered a stark choice when they reached Frankfurt an der Oder railway station – work in the mines of the Erzgebirge or join the Bereitschaftspolizei. Some of these recruits had been senior officers. The head of the DVdI's Department of Border and Standby Police, Polizei-General Hermann Rentzsch, had served on the Stalingrad front. A former Luftwaffe general was in charge of supply, while a former Wehrmacht colonel was a top adviser.

As with so many of the zone's new institutions, SMAD and the SED were instantly dissatisfied with both the proficiency and the political reliability of the standby police. Although former Wehrmacht personnel were needed to make the force effective, they were inherently unreliable. The SED chose effectiveness over reliability. When Walter Mickin, who had helped to build a distinctly communist police force in the Soviet sector of Berlin, queried the decision to appoint former Wehrmacht officers to key positions, he was removed from his post in the personnel department of the DVdI and sent on a six-month course at an SED school. At the same time, Robert Bialek was removed from his position as the party's functionary for police affairs – a decision that would have dramatic repercussions some years later.

In addresses to their officers, Berlin's police chiefs thundered that 'pacifist ideas within the Volkspolizei cannot be tolerated... The uproar about supposed 'Militarism' from among imperialists and warmongers inside and outside [the Soviet zone] means we are doing things right'.[7] Pompous ceremonies were held, with much flag waving and podium gesticulating, where weapons were presented to the paramilitaries by representatives from factories and the SED.

Hectoring speeches damned Western aggression and heaped effusive praise on the Soviet authorities for their trust and support of the new German democratic order.[8] The admiration wasn't reciprocal, however. One Soviet official wrote to another, 'We cannot allow the kind of situation like the one used by the Teutons against the Romans, when they stabbed them in the back... We have to keep our eyes wide open. We give weapons to the police, and [we] must deal with them strictly and watch [them] carefully.'[9]

It wasn't easy for the Western powers to get accurate information on these developments. For the Americans especially, peering into the Soviet zone and trying to make sense of it all, this was a disconcerting time. Reports confirmed that the Bereitschaftspolizei were holding field exercises and learning to use mortars and anti-tank guns. Soviet officers and even heavy tanks were said to be involved.[10] During the Berlin blockade the strength of the border police rose from 7,000 to 10,000; armed with Soviet weapons, they helped to encircle the city. On the other hand, the Americans' Berlin Operations Base (BOB) had a source at Dresden, a Soviet major, who insisted that the standby police were not preparing for war.[11] Still, the Western powers were catching glimpses of an apparent rearmament in the Soviet zone, at precisely the same time as Berlin was being sealed off. This was unsettling.

There was a silver lining for the West: the fact that the standby police had an obvious problem with low morale and desertion. These desertions led to security leakages that took time and painstaking effort to repair. They also slowed the process of recruitment, which had to be ever more rigorous. Nevertheless, big numbers were being achieved. By September 1948 almost 81,000 Germans were serving in the security apparatus of the Soviet zone.* During the great manufactured pageantry of May Day 1949, an attempt was made to paper over any cracks; the ranks of police marched and sang heartily, as ordered.

Changes to policing were also occurring in the western sectors. The Soviets had left the Berlin Kommandatura in summer 1948, but all sides were supposed to continue respecting the quadripartite agreements already in place. However, when Berlin police chief Paul Markgraf broke one such agreement by dismissing three senior police officials on Soviet orders and without consultation, it led directly to the founding of a West Berlin police force with its own chief.

As the Berlin blockade dragged on through spring 1949, BOB had at least two useful sources inside the SED who reported on the party's schemes to thwart

---

* This figure includes the various branches of the Volkspolizei (administrative, criminal, civil, railway and standby police), the border police, K5, the DVdI department for protecting sensitive sites, and several new intelligence departments. The latter are discussed below.

the airlift and win the stand-off. BOB learned of a plan for communist militants from factories to stage demonstrations and stir up riots against the Western powers, to make it look like the ordinary Berliner didn't want them in the city. The riots never occurred, however, and deep down the SED was sufficiently pessimistic to prepare for being banned in the western sectors, where it planted stay-behind activists and set up covert communications routes.

The closing of access to Berlin proved indecisive. One thorny issue was highlighted by a US-supported strike of Berlin railway workers, who were demanding payment in the new deutschmarks rather than eastern marks. The Soviets reasoned that because they owned the land that the railways ran across in West Berlin, they should control the policing of railways throughout the whole city. The point was not conceded, and the debate carried on causing problems for years.[12] Faced with the unsatisfactory border closures, Paul Markgraf convened meetings at which communist police officials pondered new ways to seal off the sector boundaries or, failing that, to be a nuisance to the Western powers and public. A complete sealing of the borders looked unlikely; when reporting on one such meeting, a CIA source commented that 'police officials are sure that it is impossible to hermetically seal the sectoral boundaries'. Being a nuisance, on the other hand, was pretty easy. Plans were made to close more streets to the western sectors with wooden barriers. Foot patrols were instructed to stop more vehicles on the main thoroughfares, and to seize those driven by anyone who didn't have a correct police permit. Volkspolizei officers began to confiscate any luggage larger than a briefcase from passengers on the U-Bahn and S-Bahn urban railways. This caused some angry confrontations – there was no legal basis for the East Berlin police to seize such belongings – and railway personnel began to warn travellers of the new rules and to hide their baggage for them.[13]

This wasn't the only popular resistance to the blockade. Soviet belligerence proved a useful recruitment tool for the CIA and others, as public resentment saw an increasing number of Germans volunteer their services to Western intelligence agencies.[14] Their willingness endured beyond the end of the blockade in May 1949.

14

Clean and Dirty Spying

In one of its intelligence digests, the CIA had laid it on the line: 'the possibility must be recognized that the USSR may resort to direct military action in 1948.' Another of its predictions was that 'the Soviet zone must be placed under the permanent control of a well organized German group, loyal to the USSR, and supported by police state measures.' These estimates, distributed in April of 1948, capture the mentality of the moment. Given 'the disposition and combat readiness of its forces', Soviet military expansion into western Europe was considered inevitable. Even if the Soviets didn't attack, the CIA believed that war might easily be touched off by 'miscalculations', such as the West wrongly interpreting a Soviet move as a conscious step towards conflict.[1]

These were hard-won divinations for, even at this early stage, the perennial disparity in Cold War intelligence-gathering had already kicked in. It was relatively easy for the Soviets to acquire agents in the West by inserting them in refugee flows, or planting plausible defectors, or by recruiting from among Western anti-capitalists and anti-imperialists of various stripes; the West was open, democratic and self-critical. In contrast, it was difficult for the Western powers to acquire agents inside the governments, armed forces and sensitive industries of the Soviet Bloc, and especially in Russia itself, which was closed, authoritarian and 'securitised'. The biggest chink in this armour, however, was Berlin. Here, both sides enjoyed illicit access to one another's territory.

When the CIA was founded in 1947, it is said that US secretary of state George Marshall declared, 'I don't care what the CIA does. All I want from them is twenty-four hours' notice of a Soviet attack.'[2] Similarly, at a 'heated session' at the Pentagon a US army colonel reportedly demanded 'an agent with a radio on every airfield between Berlin and the Urals'.[3] The CIA, of course, could meet neither of these demands. Despite a belief within the US military that it 'wasn't a matter of whether the Soviets would attack or not, but of when', clearly the young CIA faced a struggle to enlarge on 'the very little information that the US possessed on Soviet capabilities and intentions'.[4]

So began 'the largest expansion of CIA covert action and capabilities in the agency's history', wherein 'the main challenge was to penetrate the Iron Curtain'. The chief purpose of this 'vast covert effort', which was at its height from 1948 to 1953, was to spot early warning signs of a Soviet attack on western Europe.[5] In terms of human intelligence (HUMINT), the chief method was the mass recruitment of low-level German informants who happened to live near military sites in the Soviet zone, and who could make emergency contact with the West if they saw any signs of mobilisation. Next came the use of defectors, refugees, and political opponents of communism as amateur – or, at best, semi-professional – spies.

American espionage went hand-in-hand with other covert operations designed to either contain or 'roll back' Soviet expansion; there were advocates of both policies in the US, although containment eventually won the day. Efforts were made to discredit communism and Soviet authority, to urge the population to come westwards, to poach educated professionals – especially scientists – and to prepare for guerrilla actions behind the Iron Curtain if war should come.

From 1947 onwards there was an official means for observing military capability in Germany, in the form of the Military Liaison Missions (MLMs) agreed between the four occupying powers. These missions, which had the right to inspect certain military sites and were staffed by some sixty officers at a time, were based at West Berlin and Potsdam for the Western powers and Frankfurt am Main and Bünde for the Soviets. In time, the MLMs became a form of semi-legitimised spying, although on occasions the Stasi was to interfere in the West's use of them. But the MLMs were never likely to provide the kind of apocalyptic intelligence that the US and USSR were seeking.

Undeclared services had more chance of getting at the enemy's secrets. One of them, Britain's MI6, based its head station for Germany at Bad Salzuflen, with Simon Gallienne in charge. By November 1947 he was leading a staff of thirty-eight officers and fifty-three administrators. In the words of MI6 chief Stewart Menzies, Gallienne was focused on gathering intelligence on 'the Russians' and 'international communist parties and the degree of Russian influence over them'.

To this end, the KPD in western Germany was heavily infiltrated. A woman agent codenamed 'Cook', who had served in Britain's Special Operations Executive during the war, penetrated left-wing circles in Hamburg, although she died before fulfilling her great promise as a spy.[6] Markus Wolf recounted other British successes. When Wolf was appointed head of the GDR's foreign intelligence service in the early 1950s, he assessed the suitability of an agent he calls 'Merkur' – real name Hans Joachim Schlomm – for further employment as a spy in West Germany. Since 1948 'Merkur' had been employed by the intelligence service of the western KPD, on whose orders he penetrated the far-right Socialist Reich Party, gaining a position in Bonn as secretary to its chairman. Under intense questioning by Wolf, 'Merkur' admitted he had been infiltrated into the KPD by the British, that he was still working with them, and that he had been reporting British disinformation to both the KPD and SED.[7]

Lothar Weirauch was another example. After the war, during which he had served as an official in Nazi-occupied Poland, the KPD had ordered him to join a western liberal party, the Free Democrats (FDP).* During this penetration he was run by some highly experienced communist handlers – Walter Vesper, who had served as an undercover agent for the Republican security service during the Spanish Civil War, and Bruno Haid, a leader of the SED's intelligence work in western Germany and head of counter-espionage for the KPD. After some examination, Weirauch, like 'Merkur', was deemed to have been working for British intelligence all along.[8] These incidents saw West Germany's communist party ruled off-limits as a source of recruits for Markus Wolf's intelligence service.

The authorised history of MI6 notes that its further interests, 'mostly common to all SIS stations', included:

> "the scientific development by any country of new weapons or methods of war" and "the intention and capability of any foreign country to wage war, together with its economic potential and relations with the economies of other countries". As for special operations, Gallienne was instructed to plan for action to be taken in the event of a Soviet invasion of the West, probably including scorched-earth policies, sabotage and stay-behind organisations.[9]

Western intelligence services made themselves useful during the Berlin blockade. BOB was able to provide reassurance that the Soviets weren't prepared to use force to resolve the crisis. MI6, under its operation Easy Exercise, had set up eight covert transit routes to the city for the use of high-grade agents. Several of these routes were used successfully and repeatedly.[10] But the West couldn't hope to match the Soviet Union's ongoing, high-level strategic spying. In September 1948, probably courtesy of Guy Burgess or their agent in the French government telegraphy department, or both, the Soviets had read telegrams sent by British foreign secretary Ernest Bevin, in which he discussed meetings of the Western foreign ministers held in Paris. Moscow also received reports on the deliberations of the UN Security Council over the

---

* Freie Demokratische Partei.

Berlin problem. These materials gave important negotiating power to Soviet foreign minister Vyacheslav Molotov and his deputy Andrei Vyshinsky when attending the UN General Assembly.[11] At around the same time, a Soviet mole inside the Western Union reported on a meeting of European defence ministers held at Melle in Lower Saxony where – at least according to the mole – it was agreed to create military forces for western Germany. Already the Soviets knew all about Britain's spending on research into military technology, thanks to the Cambridge spy John Cairncross, whose main job at the Treasury in London was to sign off on the research budgets (before sharing them with Moscow).

Throughout this period, the views of French political adviser François Seydoux were always known to the KI residency in Paris. Among other things, Moscow learned that Seydoux had crowed over the elections held in West Berlin in December 1948, in which the staunchly anti-Soviet SPD had trounced all-comers.[12] KI had coverage of the meetings and opinions of the French High Commissioner for Germany, André François-Poncet, and the French commandant of Berlin, General Jean Ganeval. The secretary of one Colonel Black, deputy head of the French signals intelligence facility at Mont-Valérian, was a Soviet asset.[13] More KI sources reported from inside French diplomatic offices in Berlin and Bonn.[14]

These were all examples of espionage conducted among executives and governmental bodies. Yet the period also witnessed an explosion of quick and dirty spying – a low-level scramble for basic military information. This activity was to draw in, and spit out, many ordinary Germans.

In mid-1948 the head of the MGB in Germany, Nikolai Kovalchuk, reported to his boss Viktor Abakumov that 549 people had been arrested for espionage in the first half of the year. Of these, 391 were recorded as spying for America, 121 for Britain, thirty-one for France, and six for 'other services'. Whether they really were spies for these countries, or were just accused of being such, is impossible to confirm. Given that information on the Soviet order of battle was to remain the Western powers' top priority for some time, it is likely that most of the genuine spies were gathering intelligence on Soviet garrisons and other military sites.[15]

In June that year, Kovalchuk's MGB had launched an arrest campaign targeting an underground organisation called Immer Bereit Sein (Always Ready), headquartered apparently in Thuringia. Having identified two agents of Immer Bereit Sein when they botched an attempted recruitment, the MGB watched as the network's members steadily gathered military information. It then stepped in and made eighty-eight arrests. Under interrogation the arrestees said that Immer Bereit Sein was funded and directed from Frankfurt am Main by the US intelligence services. When BOB found out about the arrests, an officer reported rather dolefully that the Berlin branch of the CIA 'could not provide the backup these operations apparently required'. This was an admission that once such agents were even under the threat of arrest, they were finished – there was simply no way of supporting them. In fact, Immer Bereit Sein was one of the earliest networks established by the Organisation Gehlen, of which more will be seen.[16] The networks' liquidation, therefore, was symbolic. War had now been declared between General Reinhard Gehlen and the secret services of the Soviet Bloc, a war that would blaze on for decades.

In this period, most of the clandestine activity undertaken by eastern Germany's communists was focused on fostering the communist movement in the western zones of Germany. One means of doing so was a secret section of the SED known as the Transport Department. It was run by a long-time, hardcore communist operator who had adopted the name Richard Stahlmann. More will be seen of Stahlmann, who would end his days as a veritable legend of the Stasi.

When it came to arranging communist affairs in the western zones, normal means of communication, such as the postal and telephone system, were insecure. Thus the formal, but secret, task of Stahlmann's outfit was 'to ensure connection with the [KPD] executive committee [in Frankfurt am Main] under all circumstances, and above all to ensure that leading party officials, couriers and materials of a wide variety of kinds could be brought illegally across the border'.[17] With his secret headquarters at 1 Lothringer Strasse in Berlin, disguised as the anodyne 'Interzonal Bureau', Stahlmann was joined by the likes of photographer Walter Tygör, who twenty years previously had been a passport forger for the KPD. Tygör now did a roaring trade in fake interzonal passes. Also useful was a communist of Italian descent called Camillo Scariot who, having been persecuted by the Nazis during the war, had landed a job with the police in Essen, in the British zone. Scariot was able to secure a big supply of 'deregistration' forms – certificates which suggested that an individual had been given permission to relocate from one part of Germany to another. Lieutenant Colonel Vladimir Mulin, head of radio propaganda at SMAD and an old friend of Richard Stahlmann, oversaw the whole operation for the Soviets.

At a time when petrol was scarce, Stahlmann's fleet of six cars and several trucks, stashed at the SED motor pool on Alte Jakobstrasse,[18] enjoyed a guaranteed supply. Stahlmann established clandestine crossing points along the zonal borders, especially in Saxony-Anhalt and Thuringia; one example was the Ellrich railway tunnel in the southern Harz mountains. Some of

Stahlmann's crossings were still in use by the Stasi forty years later. Stahlmann also exploited a system of care homes which had been established after the war. These were places where mentally and physically damaged victims of the Nazis could recuperate. Stahlmann used those located in border areas as safe houses for clandestine people and goods.

A British military intelligence report from 1949 suggests good knowledge of Stahlmann and the Transport Department. It was noted that 'shortly after the currency reform, considerable quantities of cigarettes were smuggled to the KPD in place of funds'; and that 'Stahlmann himself bought western deutschmarks on the Berlin black market in order to provide the KPD with financial support.' Stahlmann was known to appear in western Germany in 'a dark coloured Mercedes limousine, 2 Liter model', while one of his aides, Hans Rosenberg, used 'an old type Horch, a big conspicuous sedan with a roll-back fabric top'.[19] A report written for MI5 described Stahlmann's system for micro-photographing and transporting secret text:

> By this method not less than 80 closely written foolscap sheets could be reproduced on each plate size 9 x 12 cm! When the intended material had been photographed, the thin layer of film on the photographic glass plate was separated from it. By this method an extremely thin negative was obtained, which most closely resembled a charred piece of thin paper. This negative was later hidden in books which were to be given to certain recipients.[20]

These, then, were the low-level beginnings of what amounted to a foreign intelligence service for eastern Germany. The SED was to maintain its secret Transport Department until the 1970s.

One dirty operation of this period highlights the confusion that was to prevail in so many cases of inter-German spying. It concerns Heinz Kühne, a functionary of the SPD Ostbüro. Kühne's story has similarities with the more famous case of Otto John, which occurred some years later and has baffled intelligence enthusiasts for decades. Information on Kühne's case is even harder to confirm. The matter seems to have been somewhat obliterated, rather than clarified, by the existence of the internet.

Well into the 1950s, Western publications were reporting that Heinz Kühne had been kidnapped in Berlin in 1948 by communist agents – probably from the MGB and K5 – and that during his kidnapping he had been subdued with an injection of morphine. A *Reader's Digest* article from 1957 asserts that 'Kühne's kidnapping was capped by a 25-year, living-death sentence to Siberia.'[21] Yet during 1949, Kühne played a part in a considerable propaganda campaign to discredit the Western powers. He conducted this campaign in articles and open letters to newspapers. He even published a shamefaced autobiography in which he admitted spying against the Soviets and 'democratic Germany'.[22]

Much of this was repeated in the Otto John case of 1954, when John, head of the nascent West German security service, disappeared from West Berlin only to resurface in the east as a supposed admirer of Moscow. In both cases, it was unclear if the apparent defection was voluntary or a kidnapping; and if Kühne and John had then been threatened or coerced into delivering anti-Western propaganda.

John, who survived the ordeal, always insisted he had been kidnapped and coerced. As for Kühne, little doubt remains that he was kidnapped and tortured, and that his fulsome admissions of spying for the West were dictated to him by the Soviet authorities. One result was an 'open letter to the Social Democratic Party', published on 9 April 1949 and aimed at West German social democrats. Kühne claimed that after spending some time as a courier between the British zone and repressed social democrats in eastern Germany, he had been horrified to realise that he had been 'turned into an espionage agent for the Western Powers':

Under the pseudonym of Heinz Mueck, I went for the first time into the Soviet Zone in the beginning of March, 1948... This round trip made it clear to me that leading members of the [SPD] Eastern Bureau were in regular contact with the English and Americans. Apart from the fact that we had false identity documents that the British helped us obtain, we were also provided from the same source with food, cigarettes and ready money. We travelled in an English military train which could pass the frontier without any control... After this first trip I made fifteen more. I travelled to Mecklenburg and Saxony, to Thuringia and Saxony-Anhalt, visited the agents in each of the Lands and in Berlin. [Ostbüro couriers] constantly used forged papers that we received through an English agent, to legalise our presence in the Soviet Zone... The travel documents for the interzonal and military trains were provided by the deputy leader of the Eastern Bureau [who] maintained constant contact [with] the British occupation authorities. The representative of these authorities at the Eastern Bureau [sometimes] provided the couriers with forged passports of officials of the Swiss Red Cross. I myself once had one of these, issued in the name of Lieutenant Jean Andre...[23]

Kühne's letter went on to describe his affront at the thought of being a spy rather than an honourable political activist, although he seems to have done a thorough job:

I was repeatedly given the task on my trips of collecting military information that would be useful to the English and Americans. Thus for [the British] I had to check about warships at Rostock harbour and at Warnemünde, about their types and armament, about the type of coastal fortifications, the loading capacity of the harbours and the cranes, as well as the type of radar antennae used on any Soviet warships.

Kühne followed up his letter with more revelations in the main SED newspaper, *Neues Deutschland*, explaining that the 'refugee welfare office' on Kuno-Fischer-Strasse in Berlin's Charlottenburg district was the SPD Ostbüro's main centre for recruiting secret agents.[24]

The case of Heinz Kühne raised issues that were to remain pertinent for decades. At what point did political resistance to the east's repressive politics become espionage and criminal subversion? Did the protagonists know and understand that they were spies? Was it morally correct to subvert and spy upon the communists? Or was it naïve and unhelpful? Was it appropriate for the Western intelligence services to recruit such large numbers of ordinary working Germans? Was it appropriate for Germans to give information about other Germans to those Western intelligence services? Or was it treacherous?

For good measure, Kühne's admissions were republished in such Moscow-sponsored productions as a book by Wilfred Burchett, an Australian journalist then famous for his reporting on the bombing of Hiroshima. Published in 1950, *Cold War in Germany* – which is pretty crude propaganda, replete with sycophantic references to Stalin – contains a litany of Soviet complaints against the West. These complaints are interesting, for they provide insight into the geopolitical beliefs of the early Cold War.

Burchett wrote that Western countries were run by militarists and warmongers. He insisted the West wanted to rearm Germany and then attack the Soviet Union; that the West wanted to reinstall the Nazis; that the West wanted Germany to remain divided and was making it impossible to pursue Soviet proposals for unification; that the West had reneged on the Potsdam agreements; that the West had thrown away the opportunity to create benign social democracy in Germany; that the British and Americans were using the uncooperative French to thwart every Soviet suggestion for Germany's future; and so on.

Although Burchett used Heinz Kühne's admissions to support these arguments, Kühne himself would not have chosen to endorse them. Soviet torture was effective; detainees might be made to stand in filthy water up to their necks for days on end, or to sit in it without changing position, risking death from exposure or illness. It is unsurprising that Kühne signed off on all the anti-Western propaganda. And his case wasn't the only example of the dirty war unfolding in divided Germany.

15

The Murder That Wasn't

One evening in early May 1949, in the basement of a house in Lehnitz, just north of Berlin, Oberkommissar Siegfried Krause of the Volkspolizei stood looking at a selection of tools.[1] By his side stood Erich Jamin, chief of K5. The basement belonged to Jamin's house, where Krause was staying. The pair considered the implements laid out before them; perhaps a mallet, a wrench, hammers. Jamin prompted Krause – choose one. The best one for smashing a man's skull. Krause chose a blacksmith's hammer.

Siegfried Krause was part of the young generation of Volkspolizei officers who epitomised the aims and ideals of the service. At twenty-five, he was already a chief inspector. He worked diligently in an 'operative group' of the Dresden police, charged with investigating economic crimes. The Soviets obviously had noticed his potential for, in late April, Krause had been summoned to the MGB office on Dresden's Bautzner Strasse. There he had found himself before one Major Bayabeyev, who instructed him to report immediately to Erich Jamin in Berlin, and not to breathe a word to anyone.

Jamin had wasted no time in explaining Krause's task. He was to go to West Berlin and find a man called Gerhard Schütt, a disabled bookseller and the leader of an anti-communist group. He was to lure Schütt to a quiet spot and beat him to death. Then he was to take Schütt's wallet, so the killing looked like a violent robbery, and dump his body in the Teltow canal.

Gerhard Schütt lived at 104 Kommandantenstrasse, in the American sector. He sold his books from a stall which he would trundle through the local streets, despite the inconvenience of his crude wooden leg. Following Jamin's instructions, Krause met with two plainclothes K5 officers with whom he was already familiar, Pauke and Wisotzki. Together they reconnoitred Schütt's neighbourhood and assessed the best places along the Teltow canal for committing a murder and disposing of a corpse. Krause was given a map showing the locations of American and West Berlin police stations, so he could avoid them when making his escape back to East Berlin. The murder plan was taking shape.

Erich Jamin came up with the specific approach. Krause was to befriend Schütt by selling him some books, thus lowering his defences for a subsequent meeting. Krause was sent to a second-hand bookshop near Friedrichstrasse station to pick up some books reserved under Jamin's name – a Karl May adventure story and two historical novels. He then made his way to Steglitz, not far from Schütt's home, and met Pauke and Wisotzki in a pub garden. This time they were joined by twenty-year-old Ursula Hahn, an Oberwachmeister – roughly, a senior sergeant of police – who usually worked as a stenographer at K5 headquarters. In the early afternoon, when Schütt emerged from his home and set up his stall, Krause and Hahn were the pleasant young couple who approached him to sell some books. They all got along fine.

The next day Krause and a driver made their way back to Steglitz in a small delivery van. Erich Jamin had told them to look out for a third man who would help Krause with the job – a 'good SED comrade' identifiable by his great height and bulk. They spotted the man on Schloss Strasse. He got into the van, introduced himself as Müller. He asked how they were going to kill Schütt. With a hammer, Krause told him. Müller didn't like it. 'Wouldn't it be better to shoot him?', he protested.

Ensconced in the back of the van, Krause and Müller settled down to watch Schütt's home. The mood was bad, nervy. After just half an hour Krause made up his mind to send away Müller, telling him he was unneeded. Müller didn't argue – he was delighted. Then Krause sent away the driver and van, too. He spent the next six hours wandering the streets of Berlin. That night, when he reported to Jamin, he said that he hadn't seen Schütt all day. Jamin was unfazed – the Soviets had extended the deadline for the operation. He told Krause that he could kill Schütt any time in the coming days.

Two days later Krause was driven back to Kommandantenstrasse. This time he was accompanied by another K5 officer, Erwin Ulrich. Krause's assistants were growing in seniority – Ulrich held the rank of Polizeirat, equivalent to a captain. The pair were told to confer discreetly with another man who was likely to emerge from Schütt's home. After two hours or so, he did – a smooth-faced young man with a trim moustache and deep-set, burning eyes. They followed him to Friedrichstrasse station. Ulrich went to speak with him. It transpired that the young man, whom Ulrich referred to only as 'He', was demanding to talk to 'Martin'. This was one of Erich Jamin's codenames.

So Krause telephoned Jamin. Jamin told Krause to bring 'He' to Potsdamer Platz. When they got there, Jamin arrived in his chauffeur-driven car. He told the pair to get in, sent his chauffeur for a walk. Krause listened as 'He' explained to Jamin that he had earned Gerhard Schütt's complete trust. Schütt believed 'He' to be the organiser of an 'anti-Bolshevik' organisation. Jamin told 'He' to go away and write a report. Then Jamin took Krause back to his home in Lehnitz, where Krause was still spending his nights.

The next day Krause snuck away and called on Gerhard Schütt. He told him about the murder plot and showed him the hammer. Schütt was greatly alarmed. The pair talked for a couple of hours. Krause was able to enlighten Schütt about the false role played by 'He' – who, it turned out, Schütt knew as 'Hecht'. Krause assured Schütt that he had no intention of killing him. On the contrary, he would do his best to warn Schütt of any coming attempt on his life.

At this point, however, the plan changed. Krause was ordered to a secret meeting in Jamin's office at K5 headquarters, in the DVdI building in Berlin's northeastern suburb of Wilhelmsruh. Present were the K5 employees with whom Krause was already acquainted – Pauke, Wisotzki, Hahn and Ulrich – and five others: two women and three men. Jamin explained that Schütt was now to be taken alive. He was more valuable that way. With Siegfried Krause as leader, the assembled K5 employees were to deploy around the area of Schütt's home – on the street, at railway stations and tram stops – and ensure that Schütt made his way into the Soviet sector. Measures were being taken to confirm Schütt's likely movements over the coming days. Ideally, the K5 employees should manoeuvre Schütt towards Rummelsburg station, where Jamin himself would be waiting to make the arrest.

Jamin had prepared detailed maps of where each individual or pair should station themselves in Schütt's neighbourhood. He then opened a safe, took out Walther PP handguns and ammunition, and gave them to four of the K5 officers. A couple of them – Polizeioberrat (major) Robert Hahnheiser and Polizeimeister (detective constable) Richard Kluckert – queried this. They were not authorised to operate in the American sector, never mind carry firearms there. Jamin dismissed their qualms. He also made it clear that the operation was being carried out at the behest of 'the friends' – the Soviet secret services.

The first attempt, on 10 May, failed. Siegfried Krause was now collaborating with Schütt, who knew very well that his fellow anti-communist 'Hecht' was really an agent provocateur. When 'Hecht' invited Schütt to accompany him on a visit to a mutual friend being treated in the Charité hospital, hoping thus to deliver Schütt into the arms of the waiting K5 officers, Schütt was forewarned by Krause. He managed to find something else to do that day.

A week later the K5 team tried again. This time Schütt was even better prepared. Some time earlier, he had made an arrangement to travel to the town of Erkner with 'Hecht'. When 'Hecht' arrived at Schütt's home to pick him up, he was confronted by Schütt and four others, who pushed pistol muzzles into his chest and took him prisoner. Out on the streets, detective Leske and his team from the West Berlin police arrested the entire complement of seven K5 employees, as well as Siegfried Krause. Leske said later that Robert Hahnheiser of K5 was easy to identify – a Walther pistol could be seen bulging in his breast pocket.

Over July and August 1949, a trial of 'Hecht' and the seven K5 employees was held at the American military court in Lichterfelde West. All but forgotten today, the trial was an early Cold War sensation in Berlin. The defendants were charged with conspiracy and attempted kidnapping. 'Hecht' turned out to be twenty-six-year-old Wilke Henke, a senior official of the CDU in Brandenburg. Press and public made much of the fact that three of the accused were women – Polizeirätin (captain) Frieda Schlegel, Polizeikommissarin (inspector) Helene Taube, and Ursula Hahn. Gerhard Schütt, the intended victim, and Siegfried Krause, his would-be killer, were the main prosecution witnesses. Krause had been placed under American protection ever since his arrest.

The trial was full of fascination; the emerging Cold War in miniature. Although the K5 employees had been returned to the Soviet sector after their arrest, unusually the Soviet authorities had decided to allow their extradition back to the American sector to stand trial. Possibly this was because K5 was soon to be wound down and was thus, in a way, expendable; also, perhaps, because a lesson had been learned, and serving police officers were never again to carry out such kidnapping operations. The Soviet authorities appealed for the trial to be held behind closed doors, so as not to embarrass 'more than one occupying power'. This was refused, as no doubt they had wished. For both sides intended to use the trial to shame the other. Both sides largely failed.

Krause's tale of the hammer was ridiculed in the Soviet zone's press. After an initial flurry of headlines – 'Ordered to murder', 'Hammer and sickle', 'K5 ordered me to kill' – the Western press went curiously quiet on the matter of the hammer. Given that much of the West Berlin newspaper coverage was American-sponsored, it is possible that instructions went out to editors to drop the hammer angle; it wasn't working. Meanwhile, the accused K5 employees conducted themselves with the unfussed cynicism that would become a hallmark of Moscow's secret agents when caught red-handed. When first asked to explain their presence around Schütt's home, one of the K5 officers, mocking West Berlin's boasts of material plenty, replied with 'we were just there to see all the oranges'.

The cross-examination of 'Hecht' – Wilke Henke – proved more compelling. A former Hitler Youth, Wehrmacht officer and Nazi party member, he had joined the CDU after the war and quickly risen in its ranks. The MGB recruited him as an informer in 1947, probably by applying pressure over his political past. He hadn't wanted to work for the Soviets, he explained. In fact, he had wanted to leave eastern Germany, but he had had to obey orders – a line of argument that stirred up much talk about Nuremberg, where 'obeying orders' had been deemed no defence. Henke was then incriminated by his wife, who was appearing ostensibly in his defence. A Russian interpreter often came to their house, she said. She had known her husband worked for the 'NKVD', and that 'his assignment was to monitor an organisation that was working in the eastern zone against the occupying power'.[2]

Things looked bad for the CDU's rising star, but gradually Henke began to turn the tables. Far from being an innocent, he explained, Gerhard Schütt was the ringleader of a violent political group. At meetings Henke had heard the group's members discussing how best to assassinate political figures in the Soviet zone. He had already thwarted one of their terrorist plans by deliberately bungling the acquisition of some ammunition on their behalf. Finally, following Soviet instructions, he had sold the group the idea of bombing the railway facilities at Erkner. Schütt had been enthusiastic about this act of sabotage, and had tasked Henke with procuring the explosives. To satisfy Schütt's demand, the Soviets had given Henke a substance that could pass as nitrotoluene, but was rendered harmless with an infusion of soap powder. Henke claimed that it hadn't been at all necessary to coerce Schütt into visiting Erkner; Schütt had been eager to go, to scope out the railway depots and finalise the bombing plan. Furthermore, on the day of the attempted kidnapping, Schütt and his friends had effectively kidnapped Henke, holding him at gunpoint for hours. During that time they had forced Henke to write a list of some thirty anti-communist activists he had denounced to the MGB (or 'NKVD', the commonly used term of the time).

Even *Der Tag*, a Western newspaper despised in the Soviet zone, sympathised with Henke's allegations:

> The "Schütt case" is just an eruption of the huge volcano on which Berlin diligently and peacefully tries to earn its hard living… a *faux pas* of the so-called Cold War, where the NKVD and K5 clash with one of the emerging anti-Soviet groups or with the CIC, whenever it sheds its diplomatic reserve… The book dealer Gerhard Schütt has long been suspected of being the head of such an organisation. After [an earlier] major operation in Charlottenburg, in which no fewer than 17 NKVD agents were involved, and in which a defected Turkish-Russian NKVD driver was abducted, never to be seen again, the name Schütt appeared in the interrogation files, so there is much uncertainty about him…[3]

The prosecution pointed out that Schütt was not on trial. What mattered was the guilt or innocence of those accused of conspiring to kidnap him. Henke said he knew nothing of K5's intentions and manoeuvres, which was probably true. Throughout the trial, the principle of compartmentalisation was seen to pay off; none of the accused had known the bigger picture of what they, as individuals, were doing. Faced with this, the prosecution tried to twist the word 'conspiracy' into meaning behaviour 'not directly connected' with other people, carried out with no knowledge of 'any co-conspirators'. This nonsense was treated with the contempt it deserved by judge John A. Sabo: if Henke had not conspired then he was not a conspirator. It began to look as though the American authorities had simply chosen the wrong charges. The K5 personnel were likely guilty of two things that could be proven: illegal possession of firearms and carrying out a police operation in the US sector, where they had no authority. If they had planned to arrest Schütt within the Soviet sector, that, in itself, wasn't necessarily a kidnapping.

In all of this, both sides had their own agendas. The Americans wanted to do something about the wave of Soviet kidnappings. The Soviets wanted to show they had been carrying out a necessary police operation to prevent a terrorist attack by political extremists. When they came, the verdicts were a let-down – an archetypal Cold War lose-lose. Wilke Henke was sentenced to two years in prison, with a further year on probation, for violating public order and the interests of the American military government. The K5 employees received sentences of between six months and one year for violating public order and illegal possession of weapons. The sentences were probationary, so six of the seven were released immediately. The Soviet zone's media clamoured for action against Schütt for his planned sabotage attacks, but he and his friends subsequently received only short probationary sentences, for unauthorised possession of the guns with which they had threatened Wilke Henke.

For a trial that had caused uproar, conducted in a tense atmosphere, with a heavy police presence around the court building and American soldiers searching every attendee, this was all rather flat. The trial had been timed to help push through new legislation in the West Berlin senate, as described in *Die Welt* as the court proceedings were taking place:

> The new bill on the abduction of people from the western sectors of Berlin, which will be submitted to the senate for approval on Thursday, provides for prison sentences for anyone who uses deceit, threats or violence to take control of a person in order to take them to an area outside the western sectors of Berlin against their will, or who provides assistance in such an operation. If the death of a person occurs as a result of the attempted or implemented kidnapping, the perpetrator should be punished with life in prison.[4]

The legislation was passed, but didn't prevent the kidnapping pandemic that blighted Berlin in the following years. The trial's biggest losers were probably the West Berlin public, left with a feeling of vulnerability due to the failure of the American authorities to secure conspiracy and kidnapping verdicts. Not that this mattered to at least one American-sponsored paper, the *Telegraf*, which announced the verdicts under the headline 'Three years in prison for kidnapper Henke', when he had just been found not guilty of precisely that crime. The *Sozialdemokrat*, West Berlin's most popular political newspaper, articulated the mood in an article called 'K5 in the dock':

> 'Berliners will not be able to understand this verdict even if they approach the matter dispassionately. Mildness should be exercised where appropriate. Justice should prevail instead of terror. But! Human abduction, in the form in which it is used as a political tool by the communists, is a crime that is in no way lesser than murder... In the case of the verdict for Henke, the punishment is too minor in relation to the crime...[5]

The article insisted that the agencies responsible for giving the orders should be on trial, not random individuals: 'The case of the defendants should have been separate from an accusation against the commissioning organisations, and a verdict passed against the latter that was just as clear as the Nuremberg verdict. This was the expectation of the Berliners and others tormented by the NKVD and K5.'

The trial raised plenty of other issues. K5 was exposed. Erich Jamin, personally, was badly exposed. A letter from a former acquaintance published in the *Hamburger Echo* criticised Jamin's behaviour as a KPD operative in the Nazi period: 'Even back then – in 1936 – there was an opinion in the circles of illegals that Jamin handed over to the Gestapo people whose political views were inconvenient to the [KPD] "apparatus".' The letter-writer went on to blame Jamin for the arrest of one Gustav Ulfert, whom Jamin had 'counted as part of the opposition within the communist party... For this reason, Jamin revealed his knowledge of Ulfert's activities to the Gestapo... It seems to me that these methods also exemplify the Jamin of today'.[6]

To Berliners, the involvement of senior police officers in the Schütt case was deeply shocking. In court, the K5 employees defended themselves tersely, revealing what they thought of their work. 'My task,' said Erwin Ulrich, 'is based on the laws and directives of the Control Council.' He described his main job at K5 as checking 'leading personalities' to ascertain if they had 'disqualified themselves because of their political past'. Robert Hahnheiser said his job concerned 'the general fight against crime, in particular the prosecution of crimes against humanity in accordance with Directive 38'. Richard Kluckert opined that the 'dangerous criminal Schütt naturally falls under the provisions of Control Council Directives 24 and 38, and Law No. 10'. When the prosecutor said he had proof that K5 was controlled by the 'Russian' authorities, Ulrich gave the rehearsed and untruthful reply that he was 'an employee of a German authority, and have never been aware that I was working for an occupying power'.

The women officers came across as fierce and flippant. Frieda Schlegel, a devoted communist who served in the SED committee at the DVdI and in the Democratic Women's League, said that she and the other female officers had only been in West Berlin 'to brighten up the streets'. Helene Taube kept it simple, saying only that 'Schütt is a fascist'. A comment by young Ursula Hahn – 'We're all quite proud to be in the Volkspolizei, you know' – caused approving chuckles from the communists in attendance.

One striking feature of the trial was the difference in press coverage between Western and Soviet zone newspapers. Articles in the Western press tended to stick to the subject at hand: the trial, the charges, the testimonies. The Soviet-sponsored press flew into a wild spree of obfuscation. The specifics of the case were swept aside by counter-accusations and political rants. The Reichstag Fire trial of the early 1930s was invoked at length; capitalism, imperialism and fascism were decried as the true evils; the allegations were said to be part of the West's 'barrage of hate and lies'; Siegfried Krause, it was claimed, had done a deal with the *Telegraf* while under US protection; Jakob Kaiser of the CDU must be behind all this, somewhere, and was no better than Joseph Goebbels; Carl-Hubert Schwennicke of the Free Democratic Party was a former Gestapo agent; the Americans were just trying to raise support for 'the Atlantic Pact' in their House of Representatives; and so on. All these charges, and more, were thrown at readers. There was little or no mention of an attempted murder or kidnapping.

16

The Final Steps Towards the Stasi

K5 wasn't the only German-staffed security body operating in the Soviet zone. In August 1947 an agency called the Offices for the Protection of National Property had been formed under the German Economic Commission. Significantly, Erich Mielke, vice president of the DVdI, was appointed its chief. Its main task was to investigate apparent cases of sabotage and 'wrecking' at industrial sites. In practice, Mielke's 'Offices' were a second, parallel security service that augmented the work of K5. Their similarity to K5 may have been the result of organisational un-coordination, but the separateness might also have given the Offices more autonomy and secrecy than was afforded the police.

The work of the Offices was overseen by the Committee for the Protection of Public Property,* a body formed to oversee the numerous state-owned companies being created through expropriations. More than 200 large industrial companies had also been given a new form, becoming Soviet stock companies.† These entities were entirely Soviet-owned and were run from Moscow, opaquely, by the Chief Directorate of Soviet Property Abroad.‡ The Wismut AG mining concern was a flagship example. But conditions were tense at the stock companies. Although their German workers sometimes received above-average pay and provisions, the heavy-handedness of Soviet directors, and the silencing and occasional arrest of German union representatives, went down very badly.

There were grievous problems with resuscitating the zone's economy. It was largely agricultural, with just a few centres of heavy industry. Most of the decent plant was uprooted and taken to the USSR as war reparation. Factories and farms were left with ancient and faulty equipment, making workplaces dangerous and productivity an unattainable fantasy; but the logic of Stalinism meant that economic and supply failings had to be blamed on malicious sabotage, instigated by foreign enemies.

---

* Ausschuß zum Schutz des Volkseigentums.
† Sowjetische Aktiengesellschaften, SAG.
‡ GUSIMZ, for Glavnoe upravlenie sovetskogo imushchestva zagranitsei.

Erich Mielke was especially vociferous on this issue. In internal communications, he insisted that it wasn't just factory fires or damaged stock that required investigation by secret police; it was 'lazy work habits' and 'undisciplined attitudes' among workers.[1] For Mielke, the prevailing go-slow mentality was organised from top to bottom by a minority of counter-revolutionaries. Although small, his Offices were a potential solution to the problem. This is a feature of communist and authoritarian states: security police being sent in to deal with socio-economic problems which, in properly democratic countries, are addressed openly by government and civil agencies.

As well as the fight against industrial 'wrecking', the period witnessed other security activities that would come to be absorbed by the Stasi. One was the gathering of intelligence on the popular mood. Another was countering Western propaganda. Activity in both areas began promptly in the Soviet zone. In 1945 the Soviets created Information Offices (Ämter für Information), staffed mostly by KPD members, which disseminated positive news about the occupation. In Saxony and Saxony-Anhalt these offices also collected information on the political atmosphere and reported it to the Länder interior ministries. Sometimes they tipped off the police about residents who were known to consume 'reactionary' media, such as the Berlin newspapers *Tagesspiegel* and *Telegraf*; the police would then visit and warn the transgressors.[2] Thus, one agency gathered political intelligence while the resulting actions were executed by the police; an example of separate functions that were soon to be united in the Stasi.

During 1947, when the British and Americans began to broadcast radio propaganda in earnest, the Soviets responded by setting up another agency under the DVdI, the Intelligence and Information Department (Abteilung für Nachrichten und Information). Yet again, Erich Mielke was appointed as chief. He saw the new department's task as fighting back against the 'enemies' who were using media, rumours, and illegal propaganda to slander the Soviets and SED. He wanted the department to take hold of the zone's press and sponsor the writing of positive articles, with its personnel entering 'the closest personal dealings with reporters and editors'.[3] Mielke also saw the value of spreading disinformation and 'black' propaganda about the Western powers.

Besides the typically pugnacious tasks conceived by Mielke, the Soviet authorities also needed, in the words of a DVdI report, 'to be constantly informed about the positive as well as the negative occurrences in the country, in order to be able to undertake [the] necessary adjustments and measures'.[4] Therefore, Mielke's new department was also tasked with collecting information on political opponents and developments. To do this, it was mandated to create a 'network of confidants and informers' who could report anti-Soviet and anti-

SED statements and activities, especially if they were coordinated by groups based in western Germany.[5] Existing intelligence sections of the DVdI, such as N-2 (political information) and N-2b (observation of underground movements), were thus incorporated in the new department.

By this point there was a glut of intelligence-gathering agencies operating in the Soviet zone, including secret departments of the SED and the other block parties. Because the remit of Mielke's Intelligence and Information Department – to collect information 'on any intentional or unintentional activities designed to damage the SED' – included coverage of western Germany, it was, in effect, another early foreign intelligence service. It also anticipated the Stasi by making use of informers 'in all branches of the economy, society, mass organisations, and political parties'.[6]

It was around this time that Erich Mielke drafted the phrase used by Norman Naimark as the title for a pioneering research paper: Mielke wrote that his Intelligence and Information Department was 'to know everything and to report everything worth knowing'.[7] Despite the small size and unrealistic workload of the agencies under his command, Mielke was already picturing an omniscient organisation. And he was already dissimulating about it. In one speech he reassured listeners that 'a huge police and spy apparatus' was not being built up in eastern Germany, as this would remind people of the bad times under Hitler. Instead he called for 'anti-fascist vigilance', suggesting that it was an honourable public duty, and in no way distasteful, to report any 'anti-democratic' activity by one's fellow citizens.[8] This reasoning anticipated the claims made later by the Stasi that it performed a noble role, essential for the public good.

By late 1948, then, Erich Mielke was responsible for every security function that the Soviets considered vital. He oversaw the selection of police personnel and their indoctrination in Marxism-Leninism, directed much of the work of the secret political police, dealt with alleged sabotage in industry, organised responses to the West's ideological propaganda, and gathered information on the public mood. Mielke also had a say in the personnel policies of the German Economic Commission, central administrations, and provincial authorities.

At the end of 1948, four of the SED's top executives – Otto Grotewohl, Wilhelm Pieck, Walter Ulbricht and Fred Oelssner – visited Moscow for a series of audiences with Stalin. They reported on the successes of the Volkspolizei and of the three, parallel German intelligence services – K5, the Offices for the Protection of National Property, and the Department for Intelligence and Information. They also posed a question to Stalin: 'How can we consolidate our state security?'[9] Notably, it was these German Marxists who sought to create a consolidated security service to protect their own Marxist territory; it was not a development imposed on them by Moscow.

As a result, it was decided to combine all the overlapping functions in one agency. The description of its mandate was similar to that of K5 two years previously. Its tasks would include 'defence against sabotage (arson, destruction of factories and other acts of sabotage against people's property), assassination attempts and other crimes, violations regarding explosives and weapons, combatting illegal organisations, as well as the fight against anti-democratic activities'. It was to operate 'independently, under the direct management of the Soviet occupation organs as well as the President of the DVdI'. As well as a headquarters it was to have corresponding offices in the Länder, each to include a 'Representative for Defence against Sabotage' to cover industrial sites.

Between this proposal and its realisation, one thing changed. Originally it was planned to place the new agency within the police bureaucracy. In the end this didn't happen. The change of plan might have been due to the escalation of the Cold War, and the fact that any pretence about forming a German-staffed security agency could now be abandoned. It might have been to enhance the new agency's security, or to simplify its command structure, making it directly responsible to its chief and the Soviets.

Either way, this final step towards the creation of the Stasi occurred in May 1949, when K5 was detached from the Kriminalpolizei to become 'an independent organ'. After intense scrutiny of its personnel, it emerged five months later – with the founding of the GDR – as the Directorate for the Protection of the National Economy.* Led by Erich Mielke, the Directorate was placed under the interior ministry (Ministerium des Innern), which had been formed from the nucleus of the DVdI; East Germany's first interior minister was a former social democrat, Karl Steinhoff. After just a few months, the Directorate was elevated to the level of a government ministry, becoming the Ministerium für Staatssicherheit or Stasi.

From the start, the Stasi took exceptional care over who it employed. Rigorous vetting was carried out at each stage of the evolution from K5 to Directorate to Stasi, with more than 100 Soviet security officers brought to Germany to assist in the vetting process. Only ten percent of K5 personnel made it into the Stasi.[10] The remainder were transferred to other branches of the police or discharged altogether. After all, K5 had continued to include former Wehrmacht officers, or those with contacts in Western countries, or youths of doubtful allegiance; even the occasional SS member, either undiscovered or for some reason tolerated. In the new ministry, these losses were replaced with

---

* Verwaltung zum Schutz der Volkswirtschaft. The organisation's name changed during its short life. In its earliest days it was referred to as the Main Department for the Protection of the National Economy and the Democratic Order (Hauptabteilung zum Schutz der Wirtschaft und der demokratischen Ordnung).

trusted SED functionaries brought in from around the Volkspolizei and other administrations.

At first, not every intelligence and security activity was absorbed by the Stasi. Exceptions included the SED's secret departments for communications and for gathering information in western Germany. The Offices for the Protection of National Property continued to exist as a standalone agency, albeit a very small one. Confusingly, the designation K5 also survived, as a police department for any matter involving the top SED leadership. But most of East Germany's existing security tasks were taken over by the new ministry. Political crime, economic crime, industrial sabotage, the countering of seditious propaganda, checking the population's mood; the Stasi took on all of these jobs, and it was to take on much, much more.

Part II

United at Birth: The GDR and the Stasi

'We East German Socialists tried to create a new kind of society that would never repeat the German crimes of the past. Most of all, we were determined that war should never again originate on German soil.'

Markus Wolf, head of Stasi foreign intelligence

17

The Firm

The German Democratic Republic was founded on 7 October 1949. Four months later, on 8 February 1950, its security ministry – the Stasi – was established.

In the preceding weeks, East Germans had been alerted to the dangerous security situation. Alarming articles about spies and saboteurs had appeared in the press. On 26 January the government published a resolution on the matter in *Neues Deutschland*. It stated that 'the cases of sabotage have been prepared for by increased propaganda, the rabble-rousing of RIAS and the other enemy radio stations, by the distribution of illegal leaflets, and by the overt and secret enemies of our democratic order, who live within our republic and who are partly even active in state positions.'

The threat was to be met with greater public and institutional vigilance, starting with the police:

> Through constant instruction and schooling for all Volkspolizisten, the latter must become the first admonishers about vigilance. No measure of the enemy, no propaganda measure must go unobserved. [Police and security leaders must] organise the system for reporting cases of sabotage, espionage, etc., in such a way that [for both] enemy propaganda from abroad and the activities of agents inside the country, a general overview is constantly gained.

To beguile the working classes, the main victims of sabotage, especially fires, were said to be the Neubauern, the low-income farmers whose lot had been improved by land reform. Wealthy peasants were blamed for these incidents – that is, farmers whose circumstances were probably reduced by the reforms. (In an echo of the USSR, allegedly 'rich' farmers were among the most vilified class enemies in East Germany and every other communist country.)

Two days after this, *Neues Deutschland* published an article by Erich Mielke, reiterating the message. Mielke thundered that the 'gangsters and murderers' of terror and espionage groups, directed by the British and American intelligence services and staffed by unrepentant Nazis, were causing explosions in factories, inciting war in their leaflets, subverting East Germany's youth, and planning to kill government figures. He pointed out that 'the Constitution of the German Democratic Republic says in Article 6: "Incitement to the boycotting of democratic institutions and organisations, incitement to the murder of democratic politicians, the propagation of religious, racial, and national hatred, military propaganda and the incitement to war [are all] offences under the Criminal Code."'[1] Given that most of Germany and the world did not recognise the GDR's right to exist, and might have passed comment on the matter, Mielke's pronouncement criminalised a considerable number of people. In the years to come, the sweeping offences of Article 6 would underpin many prosecutions of real and imagined political opponents.

Mielke's claims contained useful grains of truth, but he didn't give any evidence for them. In some cases, there wasn't any. There were no known attempts to assassinate leaders of the East German government, and one historian has described the genuine incidences of Western sabotage as 'little more than nuisance actions',[2] although at least one anti-communist organisation, the Combat Group Against Inhumanity, certainly did some damage; this is covered in subsequent chapters. Above all, Mielke's pronouncements employed Stalinist thinking as well as Stalinist language. Ominously, he concluded that to 'preserve the full effectiveness of our Constitution it is necessary to put [Article 6] into practice through the creation of suitable organs for waging a battle against agents, saboteurs, and diversionists, as well as through relevant criminal laws which give the judiciary the possibility to justly punish the perpetrators apprehended and found guilty by these organs'.[3]

The next day, two pieces in *Neues Deutschland* drove the point home. The lead article asserted that most of the sabotage, subversion and spying was sponsored by the United States; that 'American imperialism' was 'the chief enemy of our republic and our people'.[4] The second article, titled 'Danger, Agents!' ('Achtung, Agenten!'), announced that the government had decided to establish a state security ministry to deal with the problem.

On the evening of Wednesday 8 February, interior minister Karl Steinhoff took the floor in East Germany's provisional parliament, the Volkskammer, and announced that the Directorate for the Protection of the National Economy was to be transformed into a new ministry – the Ministerium für Staatssicherheit. His speech cited the alleged arson attacks and bombings taking place at state farms and industrial sites, and on the transport system. In tone-perfect Stalinist language, Steinhoff – the former social democrat – blamed 'criminal elements in the employ and under the direct guidance of the Anglo-American imperialists and their henchmen'.[5]

Steinhoff explained that the new ministry was to 'protect national enterprises and factories, transport and national property from attacks by criminal elements... to combat activities of enemy agencies, subversives, saboteurs and spies, to wage energetic battle against bandits, to protect our democratic development and to safeguard our democratic, peaceful economy and the undisturbed fulfilment of our economic plans'.[6] No one knows exactly why the East German security service was created as a standalone government ministry rather than being an agency under the interior ministry, as in the other Soviet Bloc countries, but eastern Germany's strategic importance is one likely motive.

Underlying the creation of the Stasi was the combination of factors that underlay the creation of its host country, the GDR: a mixture of chance, thwarted aims, administrative confusion, ideological dogma, hunger for power, foreign interference, and irreconcilable interests among the world powers – interests that were national, political, economic, military, and geo-strategic. The law creating the Stasi was passed quickly and stirred little protest, although a few politicians from the block parties left East Germany in disgust. The speaker of the provisional Volkskammer, Johannes Dieckmann of the LDPD, briefly questioned the bill's validity on a technicality; it didn't name the new ministry's leaders, as required, for they would automatically join the government cabinet, the Council of Ministers (Ministerrat).[7] Reflecting its envisaged role as an auxiliary of the Soviet security service, there was no detailed legal basis for the Stasi's activities. It wasn't until late 1953 that a general definition of its competences was drafted.[8] However, this vagueness, and lack of statutory footing, is common to intelligence and security services the world over – a point that German historians have tended to ignore.

The first the public heard of the Stasi was on 18 February, when announcements were made by East German president Wilhelm Pieck. The Stasi was sold to the populace as a necessary defensive measure, as the new state faced mortal threats from Western aggression and subversion. Pieck swore in the two men chosen to lead the new ministry – Wilhelm Zaisser, the security minister, and his deputy Erich Mielke, state secretary. Zaisser thus became a member of the SED Politbüro, the party's highest governing body, demonstrating East Germany's close alignment with the Soviet political system.

To pursue its 'founding cause and main purpose', once described as 'detecting and fighting any kind of resistance or rebellion against the SED regime',[9] the Stasi began life with around 1,100 employees, some 600 of them officers.[10] Its headquarters occupied a former tax office at 22 Normannenstrasse in Lichtenberg, a working class and historically left-wing district of eastern Berlin.

On Prenzlauer Allee there was a separate office, the Administration for Greater Berlin, with responsibility for the Berlin area. Regional headquarters were set up in the five Länder, and smaller offices in 100 districts. A special department called Verwaltung Wismut was established to protect the uranium mines of the Erzgebirge. (The Stasi was to continue this practice of establishing a fixed presence at a so-called Objekt – an industrial or sensitive site with special security needs.) The Normannenstrasse headquarters expanded over time, as an increasing number of rectilinear office blocks and even streets – Helmutstrasse, Müllerstrasse – were consumed by the Stasi's swelling departments. Centred on three streets – Normannenstrasse, Ruschestrasse and Magdalenenstrasse – the complex grew into a semi-sealed citadel, encircled by the low-rise suburbs.

Originally there were sixteen Stasi departments (Abteilungen). Their designations and roles changed regularly, and in some cases quickly, starting in 1951. At first its key branches included Department II ('intelligence operations in West Germany'), tasked with gathering information on political opponents in West Berlin and the Federal Republic; Department IV (counter-espionage); Department V, responsible for tackling underground political movements; and Department VI ('state apparatus'), responsible for the security of East German ministries and state bodies, as well as the churches and judiciary. Although the latter had a sub-department, VIa, which was supposed to monitor the broader population, it was 'very small' at first; this function wasn't developed until some years later. The departments for cadres and training, which were soon united in a so-called Main Department (Hauptabteilung), were of obvious importance, for they selected and trained the Stasi's employees. And although the Stasi's department for propaganda ('agitation') wasn't founded until the mid-1950s, from the start its more experienced propagandists tried to support the efforts of the SED Central Committee to demonise foreign opponents using disinformation and influence campaigns.

Franz Gold, a Sudeten German, was to lead the Stasi's VIP protection branch – known as Main Department PS for 'Personenschutz' – from its foundation until his retirement in 1974. Gold had been captured by the Red Army and politically re-educated during the war; after it he had worked for an organisation established by the Soviets at Weissensee, the Institute for Social and Economic Problems, which was a front for espionage.[11] Gold's subordinates guarded SED and other officials, secured sites and travel routes, and inspected premises, vehicles and shipments. They were also assigned to some twenty-five holiday destinations used by party functionaries.[12]

Also important was Department III, responsible for securing the economy. It had four sections: planning and finance, industry, light industry and trade, and agriculture. Its work was determined by SED policies and the government's

Soviet-style economic plans. In East Germany, companies and industrial activity were organised into a system of nationalised entities called 'publicly-owned enterprises' or VEB.* The agricultural version, VEG,† mirrored the system of Kolkhoz and larger Sovkhoz in the Soviet Union.

When the Stasi was founded, VEB accounted for more ·than half of the country's 'total social product' – the proportion in industry was seventy-six percent and that in the transport sector eighty-two percent. Agriculture lagged behind, with only ten percent of farming organised into VEG – a deficit that was soon to be addressed in abrupt collectivisation campaigns. The Stasi was given the task of 'protecting state-owned companies and worksites, [and] state-owned goods from attacks by criminal elements'.[13]

Department III was helped in this task by other departments whose remits sometimes touched on matters of supply and state property, such as Department XIII, responsible for securing the transport system.[14] In most of its activities the Stasi worked high, aiming to tackle security threats at managerial and executive level, and so focusing its efforts inside the ministries and agencies that ran things. At this point it spent little time grubbing around among the general population looking for miscreants; the miscreants it was seeking were in the GDR's administrative and economic hierarchies. As well as their potential treachery or political opposition, senior officials were watched for signs of an 'immoral' lifestyle, alcoholism, corruption, or incompetence. Usually, information would be collected over a lengthy period of time, and deployed only when an official was to be sacked, reprimanded or recruited as a Stasi asset.

Department VII monitored the interior ministry and police. While it concentrated chiefly on the Volkspolizei, it had specially focused sub-departments. VIIa under former K5 executive Rolf Markert invigilated the paramilitary police; VIIb, the maritime police headquarters (Hauptverwaltung Seepolizei), which in effect was the camouflaged beginnings of the East German navy; and VIIc, the earliest units of what would become the air force.‡ The leader of Department VII from July 1950 was Wilhelm Enke, another former inmate of Nazi prisons and camps, and an unwilling wartime conscript to the Dirlewanger SS brigade. Enke had deserted and presented himself to the Red Army. After the war he had helped to run K5 in Thuringia, where he had specialised in tracking down and prosecuting former Nazis.[15]

---

* Volkseigener Betrieb.
† Volkseigene Güter, 'publicly-owned goods'.
‡ Known as the Referat zur besonderen Verwendung der Hauptverwaltung Ausbildung, or 'Special-Purpose Department of the Main Administration of Training'.

Department VIII (observations) contained the Stasi's foot soldiers – the personnel who watched suspects, carried out searches and arrests, and sometimes took part in kidnappings and other dirty operations. Led by Hans Morgenthal, the department was divided into three sections for observation, detection, and arrests and searches. Like so much of the Stasi, its beginnings were limited and surprisingly tiny. Just twenty-nine staff members worked from headquarters: twelve observers, four investigators, six arrest and search operatives, an administrator, a mechanic, and two drivers.[16] Although every Stasi department was subject to Soviet direction, the MGB's experience of selecting squads of tough operators for clandestine actions meant that it was closely involved in building Department VIII. The department was staffed exclusively by proven anti-Nazi resistance fighters, police officers hired after 1945, and the sons of trusted party members.[17]

Department IX (investigations) questioned arrestees and prepared cases for trial. Its main goal was to secure convictions. The department was to become notorious, largely because it employed the Stasi's prison interrogators, who would earn the disgust of the many dissidents and innocents they mistreated. Most of the department's early personnel came from the Kripo and K5. According to recollections and German-language histories, one of the department's most detested activities – although it is a practise used throughout the world, underpinning many criminal convictions in the United States to this day – was the use of so-called 'room agents' (Kammeragenten), later renamed for what they really were: cell informers (Zelleninformatoren). The practice was introduced to Department IX by the Soviets, who for decades had been planting sympathetic-looking cellmates to elicit information and confessions from prisoners.[18]

Although drunken ill-discipline behind the scenes was probably more common than the leadership liked to think, the Stasi's overriding atmosphere was hard, military, and driven. Personnel had the principle of unconditional obedience (unbedingte Gehorsamkeit) drummed into them.[19] The Stasi was organised on the 'line' principle, whereby each department, such as counter-espionage, extended out in a line from its headquarters staff through its regional staffs to its smallest staffs in the districts. If officers believed an order to be wrong, in theory they had the right to say so, but they had to carry it out anyway. No Stasi employee was allowed to shift 'responsibility upwards or downwards'.[20] Stasi officers had police ranks – after a couple of years these were changed to military ranks – and took an oath at the start of their service. It concluded: 'If I ever break this, my solemn oath, I may be punished severely under the laws of the Republic and by the contempt of the working people.'

East German organisations, like those in the Soviet Union and other communist countries, were great coiners of jargon. The Stasi had its own lexicon from the start. One of its favourite in-house phrases was 'Wer ist wer?' or 'Who is who?'. It captured the idea that the SED and Stasi needed to know about every person's qualities and reliability. The phrase also related to the chaos of postwar Germany, and the fact that so many people's personal histories and past movements had been rendered obscure or unknowable. 'Who is who?' was used repeatedly as a kind of operational mantra for the duration of Stasi history. Another favourite phrase was 'all-round battle against the enemy' ('allseitige Feindbekämpfung'), to which the Stasi was dedicated.[21] Influenced by the insecurity of the SED, throughout its history the Stasi stuck rigidly to a 'friend-enemy' image of the world which miscast independent thinkers, political agnostics, harmless foreigners, dissatisfied workers, and even peace and environmental campaigners as dangerous state enemies who had to be taken down in aggressive, prophylactic security operations.

Although the Stasi was later to develop an entire dictionary of terms for its part-time collaborators, initially two terms dominated. These were 'secret informer' (Geheimer Informator, GI), which denoted a spy or provider of information, and 'secret co-worker' (Geheimer Mitarbeiter, GM), which applied to other Stasi hirelings such as couriers and getaway drivers.

The term 'political-operative' (politisch-operativ) also crops up incessantly in Stasi communications: 'political-operative measures', 'political-operative requirements', and so on. Most agencies would just use the term 'operational'. The Stasi's term was a way of reminding personnel they were serving in a 'fighting organ of the proletariat'; everything they did was political, designed to protect the workers' and peasants' state from class enemies. In the words of one historian, 'East Germany's motto as the "workers' and peasants' state" captured the essence of the Stasi, a secret police of and for the working class, one that looked on previous intellectual achievements with disdain.'[22]

The Stasi exercised a strict 'need to know' policy. Most employees had only a sketchy idea, and knew no details, of the activities conducted elsewhere in the organisation. Of course, this disciplined secrecy is common to all intelligence and security services and is a key part of any successes they enjoy. Information gathered by the Stasi was provided above all to the general secretary of the SED – Walter Ulbricht – and to senior officials in the Politbüro and, at a stretch, the Central Committee. Only in later years did the Stasi properly develop its units for analysis and interpretation. In the earlier period, raw data was given to members of the party leadership because – according to Leninist principles – they were deemed the wisest judges of it. When Erich Mielke became chief in the late 1950s, it was he who presented the Stasi's findings to their end users. This was a disadvantage. Mielke wasn't stupid, but neither was he thoughtful or sceptical. An organisation is only as strong as its weakest link; and who knows what nuances of Stasi analysis were lost, or corrupted, in Mielke's deliveries to the party leadership? But much of the Stasi's information stayed in-house anyway – it was a major consumer of its own intelligence.

As well as being resolutely working class, the Stasi's world was overwhelmingly male. In the years covered by this book, the proportion of women on its staff decreased. In 1954 a quarter of the personnel were women, working mostly in medical services and administration. Occasionally women performed party work or analytical roles, but they were rarely employed in operational or regional departments. Very few women ran informers, for example, and no woman ever led a Main Department in the mature Stasi.[23]

Contrary to the Western propaganda that labelled the Stasi a 'Red Gestapo', teeming with former SS people, only the occasional former Nazi served in it. The 'Red Gestapo' propaganda was propelled by a book of that title by Bernard Sagolla, published in 1952 by Hansa Druck of West Berlin. This effort, which cast the Stasi as a Nazi old boys' club and was probably US-sponsored, was wide of the mark. If no specific crime were recorded against them, former Gestapo employees were sometimes recruited as informers; after all, they were more likely to associate with far-right opponents of the SED regime. Despite the fact that every security service wants to acquire trustworthy contacts inside the enemy camp, German historians tend to single out the Stasi as especially dishonourable and hypocritical in this respect, as if the security service of an 'anti-fascist state' should never have countenanced dealing with former fascists.

It is a naïve criticism. For a start, around one and a half million residents of the GDR had been members of the Nazi party. This was an obvious source of potential trouble. The advantages of gaining information from former Gestapo employees are apparent in a Stasi assessment of one Franz Bienert, aka GI 'Schmidt'. Bienert, who had reached the rank of SS-Obersturmführer, had been arrested by the Soviet authorities after the war. Not untypically he had agreed to work for them, tracing former Gestapo colleagues. Later he was passed on to the Stasi. Department V reported that Bienert had been 'checked by other GI and his honesty was established'. He fulfilled his assignments 'well and conscientiously', providing 'information about his work with the Gestapo' and naming old cohorts. This was security work as it should be – has to be – performed. Partially rehabilitated, Bienert even appeared as a key witness at a trial in West Germany, where he helped to convict Gestapo war criminals.[24]

Louis Hagemeister, formerly an SS-Hauptsturmführer, is a rare example of a full-time Stasi officer with a Nazi past. He headed the Stasi's interrogation department for the Schwerin area.[25] More typical is Albert Schuster, who had joined the Nazi party in 1933 yet was hired by the fledgling Stasi as a low-level informer at the Wismut mining complex. Although he had been censured by a denazification commission, there was no evidence that Schuster had been a 'criminal' Nazi. However, in 1969 firm information came to light about Schuster's role in atrocities committed in Poland. The Stasi sacked him, and he was executed in 1973.[26]

It will take further scrutiny of Moscow's archives to understand why a few former SS officers such as Hagemeister managed to thrive in the Stasi. After all, former Wehrmacht officers mostly were rejected for employment, and many former SS officers were incarcerated or executed during denazification. The reasons for hiring a few of them might range from the personal – say, candidates being let off the hook by friends in the authorities – to the conspiratorial. It is quite possible that some had been communist infiltrators in the Nazi movement.

The issue raises a key point about totalitarian and authoritarian regimes; they are inconsistent. They never implement their socio-political programmes thoroughly; they always let some things slide, or leave at liberty some of their rigorously defined enemies. For example, most aristocrats in the Soviet Union were purged from society, but a few ended up serving in the NKVD. In the 1960s and 1970s, the Stasi made increasing use of former Auschwitz guards who were blackmailed into becoming informers. Just one example is Josef Settnik, an SS volunteer who worked at the camp from 1942 onwards. He was pressured by the Stasi into reporting on his Catholic church community.[27] If the East German authorities had followed their own rhetoric, Settnik would have been in prison, or dead. Perhaps the explanation for these authoritarian blind spots is mere incompetence. Perhaps they simply exploit whoever is useful to them. Still, the inconsistent behaviour of extremist regimes begs for more analysis.

From the start, human intelligence (HUMINT) – the use of spies, moles, informers – was the Stasi's bread and butter. This never really changed, even with the growth of electronic eavesdropping and other advances in technology. One former Stasi officer described running informers as 'the Alpha and Omega of operational work'.[28] But the Stasi learned quickly that the practice doesn't necessarily generate information worth having. It was always easier to recruit informers who were pro-regime enthusiasts, and they were unlikely to know the details of subversive plots. Moreover, the SED regime, while contentious, engendered a certain amount of popular loyalty. It was not uncommon for smaller, district Stasi offices to find themselves hunting in vain for active political opponents.[29]

Despite its reliance on spies and informers in the field, Stasi jobs could be rather desk-bound. Like all workplaces prone to sloppiness, it was heavily bureaucratic. Stasi leaders, especially Mielke, constantly disseminated advice and best practice in guidelines (Richtlinien). Details or changes in method were explained in implementation guides (Durchführungsbestimmungen) and service guides (Dienstanweisungen). Instructions were given in official orders (Befehle) and directives (Direktiven). For security reasons, copying machines were rare or non-existent in Stasi offices. This resulted in the practice, well remembered among former personnel, of exhaustively retyping or hand-copying immense piles of paperwork.

One of the Stasi's first internal communications clarified the rules for its Registration and Statistics department, which was to hold all the files about suspects and operations. (Within a couple of years, employees had been provided with an almost maniacal level of detail on the construction and annotation of files.) Another early communication was the 'Provisional business and office regulations of the Ministry for State Security', issued on 18 April 1950.[30]

This regulation captures the Stasi's nature as a top heavy, sternly hierarchical organisation, with its number two, state secretary Erich Mielke, in the role of disciplinarian: 'the Secretary of State has the delegated right to exercise disciplinary powers'. The Stasi's working hours, 'set uniformly by the Ministry', were Monday to Friday from 8.30 a.m. to 5.30 p.m., and Saturdays from 8.30 a.m. to 2.30 p.m., with a half hour break each day; a forty-eight-hour week. Sunday work would be performed as needed, while 'the working hours for personnel in telephone, security and driving duties [are organised] according to special regulations'. All these rules were set in stone: 'Any violation of the working time regulations will [result in] disciplinary punishment.' This contrasts sharply with the likes of MI6, which until at least the 1980s was doing much of its business over five-hour lunches.

Stasi personnel were paid above the East German average, and enjoyed a system of 'finely tiered access' to scarcer goods. Still, they tended to see the pressures of their job, with its frequent unpaid overtime and need for twenty-four-hour readiness, as rendering their salaries fairly average.[31] Nevertheless, the regulation made it clear that they were not to grab any respite by slinking away on work-related travel:

> A special authorisation order is required for each work-related journey, which must be completed and presented to the head of main department or his deputy before the start of travel. The order must contain the name [and] rank of the traveller [and the] purpose and destination of the trip. Arrival and return must be certified by the offices visited.

The regulation also covered one of the strangest features of the Stasi – the fact that it was open to visitors: 'Visiting days at the Ministry are the Tuesdays and

Fridays of each week, from 8:30 a.m. to 5:00 p.m.' Anyone feeling brave enough to enter a Stasi office was 'not allowed to remain unattended... Documents or files may not be inspected without special permission [which] can be granted by the head of each main department. The provision of documents, files or parts of files [to] visitors is strictly prohibited'. This suggests there had already been some sloppiness and violations of security.

The same document contains page after page of regulations around the writing, copying, marking, and signing of postal correspondence. Again, administrative chaos must have reigned in the Stasi's early months. Some of the disorder was to be resolved with the use of coloured pencils: 'The State Secretary and heads of department [mark their approval] with coloured pencil... the Secretary of State, black... the main department manager, green. All other employees are forbidden to use coloured pencils for the purpose of signing.'

18

Party, Partners, and the Law

The SED was represented at every level of every East German ministry; indeed, any workplace with more than three employees had to have a delegated party representative to encourage productivity and promote SED policies. Thus the party maintained a discrete administration, led initially by Sachsenhausen survivor Otto Walter, which ran from top to bottom of the Stasi. But it should be remembered that the Stasi was the party's 'shield and sword', and the two had a special relationship.

As well as party membership being almost universal in the Stasi, party loyalty was exceptionally strong, especially in later years. For a short period the SED ran the 'Felix Dzerzhinsky' school to educate Stasi personnel; after its closure, political education became more general and hands-on. The SED's role within the Stasi was further defined in a Politbüro directive of 1954. The party organisation was to educate employees 'in patriotism as well as in love for and devotion to the GDR and its government, to the SED, to the conscientious fulfilment of duties and to the uncompromising fight against agents, spies, saboteurs and all enemies of workers' and peasants' power'.

In a copy of Soviet practice, in all East German institutions a party official was usually in the room whenever important decisions were taken. The SED representatives in the mature Stasi's Central Party Organisation, who numbered 150 or so, enjoyed high rank. Their presence was augmented, especially at lower levels, by a larger number of 'honorary' party representatives; again, a Soviet practice. Their job was to 'ensure that the MfS faithfully, enthusiastically and creatively implemented the policies of the SED'. As well as monitoring discipline and adherence to the party line, they maintained political morale by 'clarifying ideological matters, helping in the selection of the best cadre for promotion and dealing with the problems of SED members within the MfS'.[1] If an employee had to be disciplined – the most common transgressions being drunkenness, extramarital affairs and embezzlement – this was done by the Stasi's Party Control Commission, which could impose punishments in collaboration with the Main Department for Cadres and Training. And there was reciprocity in the Stasi-SED relationship. Although formally the Stasi wasn't allowed to 'spy' on SED officials, there were plenty of Stasi informers within party organisations.

Mostly these informers were looking for the same things as their counterparts in the Soviet Union, for there was a set list of communist transgressions. 'Diversion', which often referred to foreign-sponsored subversion, could also mean deliberate attempts to pollute party bodies with criticism and doubts. 'Faction-forming' was a serious offence; coined by Lenin and prohibited by party statutes, it meant forming a group in opposition to the party executive, thus upsetting the processes of democratic centralism. 'Counter-revolution' could encompass any preference for the deposed exploiting classes. 'Revisionism' was the liberal tendency to revise Marxism-Leninism in the interests of the intelligentsia and bourgeoisie. 'Opportunism' was just as bad; this meant a lack of principles, an empty and cynical careerism.[2]

For a year or so, starting in autumn 1952, a high-ranking woman sat at the top of the Stasi party organisation for Greater Berlin: Polizei-Oberrat Isolde Sobeck, who with the change to military ranks became an Oberstleutnant, or lieutenant colonel. Although nearly lost to history, Sobeck occupied the highest position held by a woman in the Stasi's first decade. Born in Altenburg to working-class parents in 1922, before the war she went to clerical school. After it she joined the KPD, segued into the SED, and was appointed head of the police affairs department at Altenburg town council. She enjoyed a spotless political ascent: assistant to the SED chairman for Thuringia, Werner Eggerath; party secretary for women's affairs in Suhl; teacher at a party school, and student at the main SED school; then the Stasi, joining its party organisation in 1951.

Sobeck aimed to steer party work in the Stasi by writing such tracts as 'The lessons of the XIX Party Congress of the Communist Party of the Soviet Union for the construction of socialism in the GDR, and the conclusions for the work of the party organisation in the MfS'.[3] She also tried to adjudicate on the tricky issue of whether party workers should be given details of investigations and operations,[4] although the matter was never resolved satisfactorily and remained a fudge until the Stasi's final days. Sobeck resigned from the Stasi in 1954, probably to have children, which the party wanted from women more than anything else. However, she continued to perform gritty work for the SED, serving on its Control Commission for the city of Gera.

The Stasi's party organisation was one of several bodies that, in theory, maintained a form of oversight on its activities. Founded in 1954 (with seven members), the fourteen-member Kollegium of the Stasi, which included Markus Wolf and other service heads, was supposed to advise the security minister on policy. In reality, by the time Erich Mielke was security minister, Kollegium meetings seem to have consisted of fourteen subdued executives listening to him pontificate, and then clapping whatever he had said. Two party bodies, the Politbüro's Security Commission and the Security Secretariat of the SED Central Committee, also had a kind of strategic seniority over the Stasi. But from 1956 to 1971 the prime mover at these bodies was Erich Honecker, with whom Erich Mielke was politically chummy, and they tended never to meddle in any operational matter. There was a Control Department at the Stasi, which carried out spot checks of its personnel and operations, but this was with a view to refining techniques, not curbing powers. Finally, from 1961 there was the National Defence Council of the GDR, tasked with guiding East Germany's defence in the event of crisis or war. However, the Stasi chief was a leading member, and the other members of this body were unlikely ever to contradict him.

Therefore, the oversight of all these bodies was nominal. While they had some formal authority to invigilate the Stasi, they exercised it rarely, if ever. There is consensus among historians that throughout East Germany's history, the party and government averted their eyes and let the Stasi get on with doing whatever the SED Politbüro had tasked it with. The Stasi had freedom of action; the only firm brakes on it were the Politbüro and the security minister himself, although the Soviets also exercised a certain power of veto.

Throughout its history the Stasi had a network of MGB, and then KGB, liaison officers. In its earlier years the MGB 'held the reins' of the Stasi.[5] Instructors and role models from the Soviet secret services were peppered throughout its offices. The heads of operational departments were supervised by a Soviet chief instructor, and numerous Soviet representatives observed, guided and sanctioned operations right down to the district level. The Soviets were well-known for spying on their 'friends' and 'brother organs', as they called the Soviet Bloc's intelligence services, and the KGB laced the Stasi with 'informal sources' who kept Karlshorst and Moscow informed of everything of note.[6]

The Soviets also tended to take over the Stasi's most important security cases, and to run the most significant foreign spies. It became common practice for the Stasi, as the junior partner, to take a fall for the KGB whenever the latter's operations were busted. If caught in the West, spies and agents of the KGB would claim to be working for East Germany, which would then admit its guilt.[7] This was a thin pretence, however, and one which was unlikely to fool Western security services for long.

The Stasi could also rely on 'political-operative collaboration' (politisch-operatives Zusammenwirken, POZW) with partner agencies. Its main partner was the Volkspolizei, regarded by the SED as another vital organ of state security.[8] Like the Stasi, the police had the aura and trappings of a military service. While its lower levels had traditional police ranks such as Wachtmeister, in time its officers came to have military ranks – Leutnant, Major, and so on. Other partners included provincial government ministries, state employees, and workplace managers, any of whom might be co-opted by the Stasi to help with its operations or investigations. The Stasi had clout. It could get information and help, and when necessary hide behind, state agencies like the Workers' and Peasants' Inspectorate, judicial bodies, prosecutors' offices, mass organisations, local councils, banks and insurance offices, educational establishments, utilities providers, hospitals, and libraries.

East Germany's judicial system comprised the Ministry of Justice, the Department of State Prosecutors, and a range of military, lay, regional and district courts, with the Supreme Court, the highest organ of justice, at its head. In theory 'an elaborate corpus' of civil, family, labour and criminal law, as well as the constitution, 'provided the legal and regulatory framework'.[9] In reality, these instruments tended to be trumped by political factors imposed by the SED, as part of defending and extending its rule. The SED Central Committee, which was founded in summer 1950 on the model of the Soviet communist party, controlled all judicial appointments with its Department for Organs of State and Legal Questions.

Klaus Marxen, a professor of criminal law at Berlin's Humboldt University, has argued that the SED treated 'law as an instrument of politics'.[10] By the late 1970s, Erich Mielke was making this explicit in conference speeches; that in order to fulfil the 'historical mission of the working class' – the establishment of communist society – 'Socialist law is an important instrument of exercising, enhancing and consolidating power.'[11] The German ideal of the Rechtsstaat – a state based on a transparent and honourable legal system – was scorned as 'bourgeois' by the SED. The party considered the separation of state powers to be a sham, serving only to strengthen the rule of the hated exploiting classes. This approach was to be replaced by 'socialist legality', once described by the SED as 'an expression of the will of the working class and its Marxist-Leninist party'. It has been noted that the 'ideologically driven idea of a unitary will of the whole society also functioned as a cloak for obscuring arbitrary practices'.[12]

Nevertheless, 'socialist legality' was heralded as a superior and robust form of justice. As the Cold War dragged on, and the Soviet Bloc tried to improve its image, the demonstrable practice of 'socialist legality' became ever more important. When Western journalists were admitted to trials in East

Germany, rehearsed members of the jury would ask staged questions as to whether certain procedures were being followed correctly or not. Everyone present would then be reassured that every procedure was being followed scrupulously.[13]

Despite the pressures placed on the Stasi to observe 'socialist legality', ultimately both the SED and the Stasi manipulated the legal system and judiciary for their own ends. Powers were concentrated and human rights ignored. Whatever the SED claimed in public, several key principles were simply dispensed with: equality before the law, the subordination of the administration to the law, trials conducted with demonstrable integrity, and the independence of the judiciary. Any person accused of a crime in East Germany could rely on none of the above. Police detectives were often Stasi collaborators or subordinates. Judges, prosecutors and tribunals were groomed by the Stasi;[14] prisons and detention centres were run by it. Hearsay was admissible as evidence, meaning that convictions could be secured by third-party gossip. Interpretations of 'attempting' or 'preparing' a crime were very broad. This made it easy to accuse suspects of political conspiracy, even when their behaviours were apolitical and humdrum; phoning a relative, stopping to chat with someone in the street.

The GDR criminal code, which evolved over time, was uncompromising when it came to alleged spies, saboteurs and political subversives. Eventually, the maximum possible sentence for the crimes of treason, passing secret information, recruitment to a spy ring and sabotage was death. Passing non-secret information could mean twelve years' imprisonment; taking part in an illegal demonstration, eight years; and unauthorised contact with Western journalists or political groups, five years.[15] However, as time passed it became less common for suspects to face the more severe accusations of espionage or sabotage. They were unnecessary. It was much simpler to get undesirables off the streets by convicting them of public order offences, or of attempting to flee East Germany.[16]

19

A New European Country

The constitutions of the GDR, especially the 1968 revamp, illuminate the country's official political system. They also highlight the disparity between East Germany's political ideals and the realities of living there.[1]

In Article 1, the GDR was defined as 'a socialist state of the German nation': a fudge. Its system was described as 'the political organisation of the working people in town and country, who together under the leadership of their Marxist-Leninist party, are realising Socialism'. By not naming the SED as the Marxist-Leninist party, the authorities left open the possibility of renaming the party, or of reforming it if deviationists ever happened to ruin the original. Furthermore, in the commentary that accompanied the constitution, the party was named. Thus Article 1, in effect, established the 'legal' pre-eminence of the SED in all areas of society.

Article 2, however, stated that 'all political power is exercised by the working people'. This point was clarified in Article 48; the people exercised their power through the Volkskammer, 'the highest organ of state of the German Democratic Republic. It decides in its plenary sessions the basic questions of state policy'. Article 47, meanwhile, stipulated that 'the Sovereignty of the working people realised on the basis of Democratic Centralism is the governing principle of the structure of the state'.

Taken together, these articles meant that while, in theory, voters and lower bodies elected the memberships of every higher body, the higher bodies dictated policy downwards to the voters and lower bodies. As the SED itself was subject to democratic centralism, these articles also meant that the ultimate decision-making power lay firmly in the hands of the party's Politbüro. (For many, the Leninist concept of democratic centralism was never anything other than a fig leaf to conceal the reality of top-down government by a tiny minority.)

Article 3 united all parties and 'mass organisations' in a coalition, the National Front, which was to decide on candidates for the Volkskammer. No other candidates were permitted. As well as the five parties of the National Front – the SED, CDU, LDPD, DBD and NDPD – the Front's mass organisations also had seats in the Volkskammer. These were the Free German Trade Union Federation, the Free German Youth, the Democratic Women's League of Germany, the Cultural Association of the GDR, and the Peasants' Mutual Aid Association.* These SED-dominated organisations were critical, because it was their votes that gave the SED its *de facto* majority in the Volkskammer for the entire history of the GDR.

Standard constitutional fare – the freedoms of speech, assembly, and association – were enshrined in Articles 27, 28 and 29. Article 20 established freedom of conscience and belief, and Article 39 religious freedom. The privacy of postal and telephone communications was guaranteed in Article 31. This was all eyewash; not one of these rights was respected in East Germany. And in some ways, the 1968 constitution was even harsher than that of 1949; by that time, for example, freedom of movement had been restricted to travel inside the GDR.[2]

As well as the Volkskammer or parliament – which was replicated at regional levels as a 'council' – the government of the GDR had a Council of Ministers (Ministerrat) and, later, a State Council (Staatsrat). Ostensibly the latter was a collective head of state, while the former was the government cabinet, which 'led, coordinated and checked the activities of the ministries, other state organs and district councils'. But the Council of Ministers certainly didn't lead, coordinate or check the activities of the Stasi – ever – and the real government was the SED Politbüro under the party's general secretary (a position renamed first secretary in 1953).

To work around the fact that the constitution guaranteed free elections, the SED and the Soviet Control Commission, which replaced SMAD when East Germany was founded, ensured that 'unity lists' became the basis of elections. Under this system the electorate did not vote for an individual party or candidate. Instead, voters supported or rejected the appointment of an entire list of pre-selected candidates, representing every National Front party and organisation.

In March 1950, after months of opposition, the non-Marxist parties finally accepted the use of unity lists. It was announced that this system would be used for all elections.[3] Before every election the Volkskammer would pass an election act, stating in advance the number of seats allocated to each party. For the 1950 election, the allocations were set at fifteen percent each for the CDU and LDPD, seven and a half percent each for the NDPD and DBD, and twenty-five percent for the SED. Given that the NDPD and DBD were little more than SED front parties, this made forty percent of seats subordinate to

---

* In German, the FDGB or Freier Deutscher Gewerkschaftsbund; the FDJ or Freie Deutsche Jugend; the DFD or Demokratischer Frauenbund Deutschlands; the KB or Kulturbund der DDR; and the VdgB or Vereinigung der gegenseitigen Bauernhilfe.

the SED. The remainder of seats – thirty percent – were given to the mass organisations. These were also run or dominated by the SED, thus making seventy percent of seats subordinate to the party. And that was how the SED ruled East Germany.

From the start, the ambition of the SED and Soviets was for ninety-nine percent of the population to vote in agreement with the unity lists. Candidates for the lists were assessed by panels made up mostly of members of the SED, the trade union federation and the Free German Youth (FDJ). Candidates who didn't conform to SED requirements were rejected. On election days, voters were given a ballot paper upon arriving at the polling station. If they agreed with the unity list, they simply put the paper unmarked and unfolded into the ballot box, and went on their way. Only those who did not agree with the list went into a booth to mark their vote.

However, FDJ members would supervise entry to the booths, taking voters' names and sometimes asking them to fold their ballot paper, to ensure it was counted as a 'disagree' vote.[4] All of this was done in an atmosphere of intimidation and suggested reprisal. Moreover, those 'disagree' voters who forgot, or were not told, to fold their ballot paper ran the risk of having it counted as an 'agree' vote; this was a widespread practice.[5]

In theory, there were other ways for East German citizens to express a view. From 1949, according to GDR law, the republic adopted the use of Eingaben, a form of written or oral petition with which citizens could address their frustrations to party and government leaders or to institutions. They were widely used; statistically, every household in the GDR submitted an Eingabe at some point in the republic's history. In the earlier years, the most frequent recipients of Eingaben were president Wilhelm Pieck, prime minister Otto Grotewohl, and SED general secretary Walter Ulbricht who, in effect, was the country's ruler. Other frequent recipients included the state security chief, Wilhelm Zaisser, although few people addressed him by name; media outlets, especially the *Neues Deutschland* newspaper; and the Council of Ministers. Over time, the most common complaints were the lack of decent housing, the restrictions on travel and emigration, and the scarcity of consumer goods.[6] Although the use of Eingaben offered citizens a chance to air their views and lobby for improvements, it was rare for top executives to respond to them. Moreover, the Stasi had a nasty habit of twisting information from the Eingaben for security purposes, or launching investigations into the senders.

In some ways, the SED tried to introduce a little colour into East German life, and whip up some public enthusiasm. Markus Wolf recalled that the new state was founded with 'torchlight processions, mass marches and patriotic songs'.[7] A Free German Youth rally held in May 1950 in the Soviet sector of

Berlin attracted hundreds of thousands of attendees.[8] Art, music and literature were encouraged to flourish, albeit under SED scrutiny. Newspapers and journals were founded, and East German graphic design, in particular, attained a world-class beauty and skill. To some, the early 1950s might have looked like the dawn of a vibrant cultural renewal. Mass organisations encouraged citizens into sport and games, leisure activities, and numerous forms of education; and East Germany's boy scouts and girl guides, the blue-scarfed Thälmann Pioneers, named after the pre-war leader of the KPD, were founded in 1948 as a subdivision of the Free German Youth.

On 7 October, 'the birthday of the Republic', the SED sometimes tried to curry favour by granting amnesties to the political prisoners who, officially, were said not to exist. This happened in 1951, 1956 and 1960, and continued into the 1970s and beyond. As well as demonstrating the compassion and progressiveness of the party and its penal system, released prisoners added to the labour pool in times of need.[9] And May Day, like the state's birthday, was always celebrated noisily. For much of its party paraphernalia, the SED eschewed the use of the colour red, with its pre-war communist associations; the national colour of East German communism was a bracing royal blue.

From the start, the notion of international peace was fetishised in the GDR. While this was partly a lame self-justification for the state's right to exist – and reflected Soviet fears of Western attack – many East German citizens were deeply committed to peace, and motivated by it. Even so, the promotion of peace was riddled with mixed messages. West German rearmament was criticised but matched, step for step; thumping military music was played throughout the Soviet-backed World Youth Festival, supposedly a paean to peace, held in Berlin in 1951.

Foreigners were never liked or trusted by the SED regime. The Second World War was followed by a period in which the 'contrast between foreign evil and homegrown nobility was hugely important in the rebuilding of national identities... and one of the principal ways in which Europe's battered nations chose to lick their wounds'.[10] Thus the war encouraged, rather than deprecated, nationalistic thinking. East Germany had its own important version of patriotism. By celebrating what it saw as its highly moral political philosophy, and criticising the imperialist instincts of other nationalities, including western Germans, the GDR was able to demonise foreigners and champion its own national correctness. Although it sat uneasily with Marxism, this was a feature of the entire Soviet Bloc; the growth of a kind of 'socialist patriotism' that cast foreigners as 'fascists' or bourgeois counter-revolutionaries, alien and dangerous.

Thus in-house Stasi manuals told employees they must be 'imbued with love for our homeland, with love for our people... You must be real, true patriots

[and] never allow comrades to sway from our patriotic duty'.[11] This echoed the way in which Stalin had mobilised his population to defend the USSR, and his regime, against the invading Axis; by appealing to people's Russianness and love of homeland, rather than their devotion to Marxism-Leninism.

Another major rhetorical claim in the GDR was the idea that German reunification was the strongest desire and foremost aim of the SED and the Soviet Union. The SED framed its role in divided Germany in almost regretful terms, as if to say, 'We're having to do this, but we'd rather not – we actually want the superpowers to leave and to be part of a united, but unarmed, Germany.'

As for East Germany's reputation as the quintessential land of Big Brother, security vetting was indeed ubiquitous and intensive. From the GDR's earliest days, checks were carried out on those applying to join the SED, enter a university, or start an apprenticeship; to those wanting to travel abroad, be promoted at work, receive foreign visitors, or live near a border.[12] Purges were a regular and obviously Stalinist feature of life. The East German vilification of 'fascists, imperialists, Schumacherites and Titoist agents' – the latter being alleged supporters of Yugoslavia's Marshal Tito and his breakaway version of communism – was similar to the demonisation of Trotskyists in Stalin's Soviet Union.

Another distinctly Soviet element of East Germany's makeup was 'cadre policy', a cornerstone of Leninism imported from Moscow. Appointing a cadre, or small elite, to operate every lever of power meant that a minimal personnel could run everything. For Leninists this was 'a proven method for accelerating social transformation from a minority position using forcibly seized powers of the state'.[13] While public opinion towards the regime might have ranged from uncritical support to outright opposition – taking in doubt, scepticism and uninterest along the way – with 'cadre policy' in place it didn't really matter. If a small number of people can use the reins of power to make the voicing of dissent inadvisable, then dissenting voices will stay silent.

The feelings and opinions of GDR citizens, and the ways in which they related to the SED regime, are huge areas of study and argument. Dissatisfaction with the regime, or aspects of it, has been divided by academics into a range of terms: opposition, resistance, dissidence, 'immunity'. For Jens Gieseke, the spectrum of opinions among citizens consisted of 'an aversive half, from militant system hostility to disgruntled loyalty, and a sympathetic half, from partially well-meaning acceptance to "150 percent participation" in the exercise of [SED] power'. Gieseke points out that the extremes of this spectrum have been well studied, but the less distinct 'centre' positions had many nuances and permeations in terms of citizens' feelings.[14] One of the most patient opponents of the GDR was West Germany, which never properly recognised its eastern neighbour and, given that they were fellow Germans, extended the same rights to East German citizens as it did to its own. In theory, any East German was welcome to make a new life in the Federal Republic.

Active and organised resistance (Widerstand), aimed at overthrowing SED rule and dissolving the GDR, was especially strong in the 1950s. Most participants wanted to bring back free market economics, a 'bourgeois' social order, and a more representative government, as well as a reunited Germany without Russians in it. Some wanted a kinder and fairer form of socialism; others wanted the return of National Socialism, at least as an influence. (In West Germany, this nostalgia for Nazism was reflected in such organisations as the League of German Youth, which was initially sponsored by the American authorities.)

Once the Berlin Wall was built, and the GDR looked set to last a while, a sense of resignation overcame East German society. For a few years, and to an extent, people and leadership tried to get along. The first West German ambassador to the GDR, Günter Gaus, said that East Germany became a country of 'niches', although 'boltholes' might have been more apt. Many people turned inward – to the extent that the SED allowed them to – and concentrated their lives on family, hobbies, church, sport, the occasional holiday. When they weren't required to pay lip service to the superiority of socialism, the greatness of the SED, the magnanimity of Moscow or the evil of the West, they didn't bother. They were people, and they just lived.

In a properly democratic country, intelligence and security services occupy a peripheral position in the structure of the state. They are necessary but mostly reactive; they respond to threats that come and go; and they are not expected to play a leading role in the life of the country.

In a Soviet Bloc domain such as the GDR, the security service was an intrinsic part of the state, one of the necessary pillars upon which the republic was built. Without a KGB there was no Soviet Union; without a Stasi there was no East Germany.

To this day, some people – especially some of its former citizens, interestingly – consider East Germany to have been an honourable attempt to create a well-run Marxist country in postwar Europe. In an interview with the BBC, the former footballer Uwe Rösler, who played for East Germany, described himself as 'fortunate' to have grown up in a different political system where money and materialism were not the most important things in life.[15]

Throughout the twentieth century there were those who misjudged the Soviet version of socialism – who were swayed by its purported idealism and anti-fascism, and were prepared to excuse at least some of its failings. This still happens. In her book on the communist atomic spy Klaus Fuchs – a proud resident of East Germany once he was released from a British prison – Nancy Greenspan writes that Fuchs 'was consistent and constant to his unwavering set of ideals. He sought the betterment of mankind that transcended national boundaries. His goal was to balance world power and prevent nuclear blackmail. As he saw it science was his weapon in a war to protect humanity'. Greenspan suggests that Fuch's espionage 'might have kept the United States from dropping an atomic bomb on North Korea. If so, was that a bad outcome? Was the person who made that happen evil or good, guilty or innocent, traitor or hero?'[16]

It is true that the international communist movement was populated by many sincere believers. Although there was plenty of evidence that Stalin's communism was oppressive, violent and hypocritical, postwar communists continued to be motivated by anti-fascism and a keen sense of working people's exploitation and colonial peoples' subjugation. Many of those who worked for communist intelligence services were recruited to work 'for the international workers' movement' and, like Fuchs, saw themselves as serving the cause of world peace, or national liberation from colonialism, or the final end of fascism.

To our twenty-first century ears much of this sounds good, but it was all specious, for there was little that was pacifistic, and nothing that was humanist, about Soviet communism. It was never intended to be a humanist creed. Under its aegis, millions of working people continued to be exploited (and, for that matter, brutalised), and ultimately Moscow was itself the centre of a vast – and vastly inefficient – empire, despised by many of its subjects.

Behind all the talk of peace and 'transcending national boundaries', true communists believed, above all, in class warfare and a planned, centralised economy. To understand the Stasi and the party that tasked it, we must understand that *work* and *workers* were the most important things in life.

The founding of the GDR, a state in which work and workers were to be preeminent, was opposed by some members of the non-Marxist parties. For example, the provincial assembly of Saxony, steered by its CDU members, refused to issue a resolution supporting East Germany's foundation. In response, members of the SED and FDGB began to pay home visits to the dissenters, the majority of whom then changed their minds.[17]

Questions were also raised about the Waldheim trials. In September 1949, in an attempt to boost the party's popularity, the SED had asked Stalin to order the closure of the three remaining special internment camps in eastern

Germany. The MVD released around 5,000 prisoners, and 10,000 more were transferred to the jurisdiction of the GDR's interior ministry. Some 3,400 were then put on trial at the Chemnitz Provincial Court in Waldheim, Saxony, before handpicked SED judges and prosecutors.

The defendants were alleged to be dangerous and unrepentant Nazi war criminals, but it was hard to say. The trials were held behind closed doors, with a few minutes devoted to each case. No new evidence was provided, and sentences were passed on the basis of old Soviet interrogation protocols. The trials attracted so much criticism, including internationally, that the SED tried to prove its judicial propriety by staging a few show trials of selected convicts. SED-vetted crowds were bussed in to Waldheim town hall to witness these retrials, with the whole charade aiming to prove that the original sentences had been correct. It was not an auspicious start for the young GDR's legal system. Also ominous was the membership of a special panel convened to review the cases of other former internees – Erich Mielke, the future interior minister Karl Maron, and 'Red Hilde' Benjamin.

For some, opposition to the new state proved fatal. Arno Esch was a youthful leading light of the liberal democrats, and a campaigner for all-German elections, individual freedom, and the deprecation of nationalism. He had refused to take part in the Volkskongress and he walked out of the session at which the LDPD accepted the founding of East Germany. On the night of 19 October 1949, Soviet security officers arrested Esch as he left a party meeting. With capital punishment reinstated, a Soviet military tribunal sentenced Esch and six others to death for 'preparing an armed revolt' under Article 58 of the Russian criminal code. Seven of his associates were sentenced to twenty-five years' hard labour. Esch was shot in the USSR on 24 July 1951.[18]

Interlude

The DNA of the Stasi

'What is conspiracy? It is self-defence from our enemy. We are an army against the bourgeoisie so we must keep secrets the same as an army. The enemy is everywhere.'

Unnamed Comintern official, 1933[1]

20

Conspiracy

Every Stasi office was decorated with a portrait of Felix Dzerzhinsky, the first chief of the Soviet secret police. The Stasi drew inspiration from Dzerzhinsky's outfit – the Cheka – and from the subsequent Soviet intelligence and security services of the interwar years: the OGPU/NKVD, the RU, and the secret service of the Communist International, the OMS. As well as the direct influence of these agencies, the Stasi inherited many features and habits of the interwar communist movement. Above all, this meant the use of 'conspiratorial methods', known as *konspiratsia* from the Russian. Communists' lives were full of secrecy and intrigue. Many rank-and-file communists were exposed to the harsh discipline and repressive measures that would later be inflicted on the East German public. And specific creation myths fed into the Stasi – especially stories of the suffering and resistance of German communists during the Nazi era. Furthermore, the Stasi was heavily influenced by German experiences of the Spanish Civil War.

In the first part of Victor Serge's novel *Unforgiving Years*, set in the late 1930s, a Soviet spy called D flees from Paris to escape the clutches of his bosses in Moscow.[1] Serge knew his subject well. An anarchist-communist revolutionary who had converted ultimately to Trotskyism, he wrote *Unforgiving Years* in Mexico during the Second World War, in exile and in fear of his life. After performing secret work for the communist movement in Weimar Germany, Serge had fallen foul of the Stalinist authorities, for in the late 1920s Stalin had begun to persecute real and perceived supporters of Leon Trotsky, his political nemesis. As a result, Serge, like many others, had gone from being a trusted secret operative to a prime target for assassination. After his fortuitous release from a spell of forced labour in the USSR, he had run for his life.

The account of D's defection reveals many examples of *konspiratsia,* the security practices to be used by communist spies and underground revolutionaries. The rules of *konspiratsia* included the use of dead letter drops, where secret materials could be stashed by one person and picked up by another; of safe houses, and codes and ciphers; of intermediaries ('cut-outs') to relay money and messages. Also important was the strict compartmentalisation of underground networks and their participants, so that the arrest of one member, with limited knowledge, might cause only minor damage. This rigorous system was designed to thwart hostile surveillance and investigation. From the late nineteenth century onwards, any breach of these conspiratorial rules by a revolutionary communist was seen as tantamount to treachery, and could prove fatal for transgressors.

In Serge's novel, D takes three taxis to make a short journey, to avoid being shadowed. He deposits suitcases at a hotel under one name and rents a new apartment under another. We learn that a female cut-out attends meetings on D's behalf with an attaché at the Soviet embassy. She also meets with D's sub-agents, who include an antique dealer, a painter, and a scholarly member of the Philatelist Society. We're told that D sometimes hires a private detective to tail the cut-out, to check her trustworthiness and her observance of *konspiratsia*. The woman has a fiancé; on D's instructions, the detective has unearthed every humdrum detail of the fiancé's life.

Steadily we learn more. D's spy network uses city names as ciphers: 'I'm in Strasbourg' means 'unforeseen complications'; 'I'm in Mulhouse' – a phrase 'known only to five people' – means 'Danger!'. D discourages his circle from writing down anything. He urges his sub-agents to 'watch out for anyone taking photos'; to make themselves harder to recognise during a mission by wearing unfamiliar clothing; to turn off the lights before looking from any window at night. In public they pass signals to one another by blinking, or lighting a cigarette in a particular way. No one uses their real name, ever; everyone has two, three, four aliases.

D is wary of surveillance when walking down the street. He suspects all passers-by; a young cyclist 'with a small yellow parcel dangling from the handlebars – maybe a signal'; a woman who slows down and fumbles in her handbag – 'a good way to survey the street in a pocket mirror'. We also learn that D worked previously in the 'postal interception department of the Secret Service'; that he has bribed 'savvy intermediaries' at big newspapers to carry stories; and that he doesn't trust his youngest sub-agent, whom he employs only for minor tasks such as meeting the communist militants 'embedded in arsenals and shipyards'.

This catalogue of clandestineness tells us much about the life of communist spies and militants before the Second World War. For the rules of *konspiratsia* were not restricted to Soviet secret agents. Instructions from Moscow ensured they were observed by many rank-and-file communists all over the world. Later, they would be learned by Stasi recruits.

*

Like any belief system, the interwar communist movement had its legends and a pantheon of revered figures. In Germany, the legends included the story of the Spartacist uprising of 1919 that gave birth to the German Communist Party, the KPD. The KPD's heroes included such founder members as Rosa Luxemburg and Karl Liebknecht. Communists had their own terminology and familiar institutions, which were replicated all over the world. Communist parties made use of fixed structures, based largely on their parent party in Soviet Russia. Many features of the interwar communist movement carried over into the Cold War era; and it is important to understand this communist universe, because it was inhabited by the people who created and led the Stasi.

The highest decision-making bodies in a communist party were its central committee, composed of dozens or hundreds of favoured party leaders, and – higher still – its political bureau or politburo. In communist states these bodies trumped the authority of the government and ministries. While there might be a nominal head of state, such as a president, the *de facto* national leader was the general secretary of the party. Stalin, for example, ran the USSR from his position as general secretary of the communist party.

The politburo, an 'inner cabinet' of the most senior communists, was in most respects the highest authority in the land. Lenin's first politburo after the Russian Revolution consisted of just ten members. The primacy of a politburo was one aspect of the Leninist principle of democratic centralism; a decision can be debated but, once approved at the highest level, must be obeyed unquestioningly by party, state, and people.

Most communist parties had a Central Control Commission, an internal watchdog that monitored the ideological correctness of members. In the Soviet Union, investigations by the Control Commission were the usual means by which purges of unwanted party members were carried out. Furthermore, communist parties, and the movement in general, were obsessed by the concept of 'cadre' – a hardcore of especially reliable, well-trained party activists who might be given any tough task, and could be relied upon to complete it to the letter. Like the party's control commission, its cadre department assessed the loyalty of members and the distribution of jobs. Before their appointments to lead the Stasi, Wilhelm Zaisser and Erich Mielke had played important roles in the cadre work of the DVdI.

The communist universe was home to a range of organisations beyond the party. Some assisted the party overtly. Others pretended to be apolitical or non-partisan; these were the 'front organisations' so beloved of communist (and Western) intelligence services. Many of the Stasi's early leaders cut their teeth in these organisations between the wars. Overtly communist bodies included the Profintern, which supervised communist activities in the worldwide trade union movement.* There was also the Young Communist International or KIM.† Among the most important and active was Red Aid – in German, Rote Hilfe – and its international version, known as MOPR.‡ Supported by socialists and leftist free-thinkers as well as communists, Red Aid raised money and gave legal help to the many communists who fell foul of the authorities in their home countries. It also provided for their families.

Interwar front organisations included the League Against Imperialism, the Friends of the Soviet Union, and the League for Peace and Democracy. A postwar example was the original World Peace Council. These groups posed as pan-political and, of course, many of their supporters believed passionately in their aims. The problem, however, was not necessarily what they said, but who they really were. Such organisations surreptitiously pushed communist party agendas, recruited members, and – above all – acted as an undeclared arm of Moscow's foreign policy. If anything, they proliferated in the later Cold War. One study notes that in the early 1980s, fifty-three KGB front organisations were run from the Soviet embassy in New Delhi alone. They included friendship societies, youth and student organisations, workers' and farmers' associations; and between them, they were responsible for publishing more than forty newspapers and periodicals.[2]

Media organisations were a favourite front. The bias of an interwar service such as the Moscow Round World News Agency was obvious, but the British authorities initially were shocked to discover that Moscow funded the likes of the Federated Press of America, with its offices in London and Paris.[3] The German communist Willi Münzenberg, a former KPD member of the Reichstag, became an acknowledged master of attractive-looking Soviet propaganda. He oversaw an empire of newspapers, illustrated magazines and publishing houses, and later went into film production. The skill, imagination and striking aesthetics of Münzenberg's products helped to attract what Christopher Andrew has called 'a galaxy of "uncommitted" writers, academics and scientists' to the communist cause.[4] These sympathisers, naïve but useful, were dubbed 'innocents' by Münzenberg, who targeted their support relentlessly.

Throughout their histories, all communist parties used such subterfuge. It might be argued that communists, like any revolutionaries, were forced into using sharp methods because they were persecuted by bourgeois capitalist governments. This self-pitying argument is naïve and, at most, half true. Communists sought to topple those governments, and it would be odd for

---

*   Derived from Krasnyi internatsional profsoyuzov or Red International of Labour Unions.
†   Abbreviated from Kommunisticheskiy Internatsional molodozhi.
‡   Abbreviated from Mezhdunaródnaya organizátsiya pómoshchi bortsám revolyútsii or International Organisation for Helping Revolutionary Fighters.

any elected authority to ignore those who use illegal means to bring about its destruction.

Furthermore, even when pro-Moscow communism enjoyed mass support in a European country – such as in France and Italy after the war, or the highpoint of Czechoslovakia in 1946, when the party won thirty-eight percent of the vote in a fair election – communists always knew and admitted that they would have to rely on coercion or force to achieve their ultimate political aims. This was not because of unjust persecution, but because of the extremity of their programme and the wariness it engendered.

Pro-Moscow communism, then, always had a dual nature; an overt side and a – perhaps larger – covert side. Its clandestine devotees spied on the military secrets of their host countries, or tried to disrupt the armed forces, or hampered the output at industrial sites, or cached arms for use in a potential uprising – one in which all communists were expected to fight and to kill. To be a communist between the wars was to be a member of an elite revolutionary vanguard that would save and transform humanity. In practice, it also meant being a self-declared fighter, living a variety of lies, and being suspicious of every human being who happened to cross one's path.

Put simply, by the time the Stasi was created, communists had been sneaking around the planet for more than half a century. *Konspiratsia* was in the blood. Furthermore, the Stasi was influenced by specific models and creation myths.

21

Chekists: The OGPU and NKVD

Before the 1917 Bolshevik Revolution, Lenin declared that a police force was unnecessary in a communist state, for the workers would maintain their own form of class justice.[1] Six weeks after the revolution Lenin founded the Cheka, one of the most notorious secret police forces in history.[*]

The Soviet state security service and its personnel – the 'Chekists' – were the most important models for the remit, structure and personnel of the Stasi. From the Cheka's earliest days, a fearsome cult grew up around its first leader, Felix Dzerzhinsky, who exemplified the ruthlessness and prim socialist morality expected of every Chekist. This burning-eyed revolutionary, dutiful and ascetic as a Christian saint, was said to forego sleep, and any form of aimless entertainment, in favour of rooting out the enemies of the revolution; and all this on a penal diet of tea, black bread and cheap tobacco. Dzerzhinsky was well aware of his own reputation and power, once boasting to his sister that 'for many people there is nothing so frightening as my name.'[2]

Another phrase attributed to Dzerzhinsky was displayed on the walls of many Stasi offices: that the true Chekist should have 'a burning heart, a cool head, and clean hands'. To this day the hero-myth of the Chekist pervades the Russian intelligence community, as it did the Stasi and other Soviet Bloc intelligence services. More than a spy or secret police officer, a Chekist was a revolutionary fighter. Chekist values were duty, vigilance, toughness, effort, iron discipline. 'Chekist methods' – a widely used phrase in the Soviet era – were the means by which secret police officers and other communist functionaries were expected to carry out their work; means that were conspiratorial, arbitrary, extra-legal, and violent when necessary.

Of course, any newly established revolutionary authority must defend itself, but it is significant that, from the start, the Cheka alarmed many communists, never mind their opponents. In February 1918 it was granted, albeit temporarily, the formal right to shoot suspects without charge, trial, or the sanction of any

---

[*] Cheka is a Russian contraction of the words 'extraordinary committee'; the agency's formal name was Extraordinary Committee for Combating Counter-revolution and Sabotage.

other authority. As time passed the Cheka began to persecute those left-wing revolutionaries who were not Bolsheviks – anarchists, Social Revolutionaries, Mensheviks. This cannibalism caused the penny to drop among many who initially had approved of the Cheka. As early as 1918, one pro-Bolshevik lawyer complained to a colleague of Lenin: 'I strongly believe that the activities of the Cheka will inevitably be the strongest element discrediting Soviet power.'[3] Seventy years later, some East German communists would express identical opinions about the Stasi.

The Cheka grew into the security service of the Soviet Union, which over the twentieth century was known successively as the OGPU, NKVD, NKGB, MGB and finally KGB. By the 1920s, Soviet state security had acquired a broad remit – just as the Stasi did, decades later. The OGPU was responsible for foreign espionage and domestic counter-espionage; the security of the railway system and armed forces; postal interception; the protection of officials and industrial sites; the political loyalty of the press and public; the militarised border guard service and the prison camp system. As a ministry – or 'people's commissariat', to use the Soviet term – the NKVD was even more sprawling. The OGPU evolved into just one of its departments, the Main Directorate for State Security or GUGB.* Also controlled by the NKVD were the civil police force, the penal system, the fire brigade, orphanages, the building of infrastructure, and numerous industrial concerns. When criticising the laxness of the NKVD under Genrikh Yagoda, Lavrenti Beria insulted it as 'a company for producing worsted wool'.[4]

The tone of the organisation was set by the Cheka's first mass operation. From 1918 to 1922, Cheka officers – many of them untrained and unvetted, or newly released from prisons – enforced Bolshevik rule throughout Soviet Russia and beyond. They did so by carrying out acts of barbaric violence in the name of revolutionary law; what Donald Rayfield has called 'an explosion of criminal sadism'.[5]

This was the Red Terror. It was aimed mostly at class enemies and the Whites, the latter being those Russians or imperial subjects who were opposed to Bolshevism. Among the Whites were many Tsarist officers and right-wing nationalists. Less politically coherent was the Cheka's violent subjugation of dissenting national and ethnic groups who wanted neither communism nor rule by Russians.

The Red Terror also saw the first implications of the communist mania for dividing the population into official categories. Farmers who owned property or employed labourers were 'kulaks'. Aristocrats and minor Tsarist officials

---

* Glavnoe upravlenie gosudarstvennoy bezopasnosti.

– civil servants, accountants, lawyers – were 'former people'.* Other, vaguer classifications were to follow, including 'socially distant' and 'socially harmful' people. These terms were applied to recidivist criminals, the unemployed, prostitutes, the families of political opponents, and unreliable national minorities. By contrast, Russian manual workers were classified as 'socially close' – that is, sympathetic to the Bolshevik regime, and trusted by it.

The Red Terror saw many Russian subjects flee across Europe, Asia and the Americas. In the early 1920s, an estimated 400,000 Russians lived in the city of Berlin alone.[6] Some of them formed White paramilitary organisations, dedicated to the overthrow of the communist regime from afar. For years, the OGPU and NKVD foreign intelligence effort was directed mainly at these émigré groups. The Soviet secret police were similarly preoccupied with scouring Europe for Soviet defectors and opponents to assassinate. The deaths of Ignace Reiss, Georgi Agabekov, Rudolf Klement, Dimitri Navashin, Yevhen Konovalets, Yevgeni Miller, Georg Semmelmann and Alexander Kutepov – all of which occurred from 1930 to 1938 – are unfortunate examples.

To understand the Stasi, it's also useful to consider Stalin's Great Purge of 1936 to 1939. Carried out mostly by the NKVD, it was the apotheosis of Soviet terror by category and quota.

The purge began with a campaign to remove alleged political deviationists from the Soviet communist party, the Red Army, and state institutions. The NKVD's infamous Operational Order No. 00447, which accelerated the purge, added more social groups to be repressed: former kulaks, recidivist criminals, members of 'anti-Soviet parties', former Whites, repatriated émigrés, religious believers, 'speculators', and former officials of the tsarist government.

Order No. 00447 stemmed from a plan devised by the NKVD in early 1937 – a plan designed to remove politically undesirable people from Soviet society 'once and for all time'. After approval by Stalin, the plan was handed to the authorities of sixty-five Soviet regions. It stipulated that the victims were to be arrested in mass round-ups. Their cases were to be dealt with administratively, in huge batches, by specially appointed tribunals. There would be no personal hearings.

Furthermore, the arrestees were to be split into two categories. Category I suspects were to be shot. Category II suspects were to be sent to labour camps. Before a single arrest had taken place, every region received set quotas for these categories. Initially the quotas totalled 249,250 individuals, of whom 72,950 were to be shot.[7] By 1938, these figures had been grossly exceeded.

---

* 'Byvshie liudi'.

The Great Purge is sometimes described as an inexplicable, chaotic event; something illogical that spun out of control. Why would a dictator attack his own people in peacetime, including many of his own loyal supporters? Millions of people were arrested or saw their lives ruined. It is possible that more than one million were shot.[8]

In the past, the destructiveness of the purge was put down to its being a demented personal campaign; a result of Stalin's sadism and paranoia, and one that mostly affected leading communists, army officers, industrial bosses and intellectuals. Certainly, the purge was the act of a cruel and violent dictator, and it ripped through the upper echelons of Soviet society. But thanks to more recent scholarship, we now know that it was not so random or uncontrolled. On the contrary, it was bureaucratic, methodical and – in Stalin's eyes – logical. We know that it victimised many working people, and that it was part of a cycle of repressive state campaigns dating back to the 1920s.* We also know that much of the brutality was aimed at national and ethnic minorities.[9]

The purge had several triggers. By the mid-1930s, Stalin's USSR was malfunctioning. Soviet society was deprived, inefficient, hungry, and violent. This was largely the result of Stalin's policies. Earlier campaigns to collectivise agriculture, and to remove the kulaks as an entire class from the countryside, had caused grievous upheaval. They had entailed the forcible deportation of millions of people, the execution of tens of thousands. They had also led to the famine of 1932 and 1933 that particularly afflicted Ukraine and southern Russia. At least six million people starved to death, possibly ten million. Millions more were displaced by this violent economic and social engineering. Soviet cities and the railway system were flooded with hungry peasants, itinerants, and criminals. They were joined by big gangs of orphaned children and youths.

For Stalin and his entourage, the most convenient response was to blame this nightmare scenario on other people. By this time, real Trotskyist opposition to Stalin within the USSR had been obliterated. Undeterred, Stalin alleged a vast conspiracy among dissident communists, supported by fascist foreign powers – 'the Trotskyite-Zinovievite Centre'. Huge numbers of loyal Soviet citizens were persecuted in the name of this conspiracy, which existed only in the minds of Stalin and his cowed servants. Their persecution was enabled partly by sweeping definitions of political crimes, which saw the victims accused of sabotage, 'wrecking' or 'anti-Soviet activity'. Most of these alleged political criminals were not criminals at all. As in East Germany decades later,

---

* For example, from 1932 to 1935 hundreds of thousands of people were swept up in mass arrest operations that targeted 'socially marginal' groups of people – common criminals, orphans, the unemployed, the homeless.

euphemistic political crimes were a convenient way to eliminate free-thinkers and nonconformists as well as potential political opponents.

At the time, Stalin was increasingly fearful that his rule was under threat. In 1936 he had tried to win favour, at home and abroad, by issuing a new constitution that re-enfranchised many formerly persecuted people. This move coincided with mass releases from penal institutions. Those released began to seek work, housing, and the few remaining civic services that the country had to offer, putting an unbearable strain on infrastructure. Meanwhile, elections for a new governing body, the Supreme Soviet, were scheduled to take place in late 1937. Given that these elections were set to include many people who had been re-enfranchised or released from prisons – resentful victims of dekulakisation and other mass operations – it seemed to Stalin that it was best to silence them before they could make their feelings known, by voting or any other means.

Simultaneously, and with world war looming, Stalin had learned of the fascist spy and sabotage networks operating behind Republican lines during the Spanish Civil War – the so-called 'fifth column'. The existence of the fifth column convinced him that he should strike at potentially 'hostile' categories of people before the expected world war began. Partly as a result, national and ethnic minorities in the USSR became prime targets for persecution.

The ferocity of the purge, and the choice of victims, are explained by this combination of factors. For Stalin, a bureaucratic cull of the population seemed the best idea. At local NKVD departments, the selection and number of victims were influenced by other factors – personal animosities, officers' ambitions, the need to fulfil the quotas. Yet for Stalin the purge was a roaring success. By 1939, every class of person he suspected of being likely to oppose him had been decimated, guilty or otherwise.

Some aspects of the purge were echoed in East Germany. For a start, the SED had a similar tendency to purge its out-of-favour officials, and to blame its failures on internal 'enemies' and their foreign sponsors. The Stasi inherited the belief that when carrying out political and social cleansing, it was 'better to do too much than not enough'. NKVD boss Nikolai Yezhov used this phrase during the purge when it became clear that his execution quotas were being exceeded. It captured a principle: that an excessive amount of persecution was acceptable, provided that among the masses of innocent victims there was a smattering of genuine political enemies.

Among the victims of the purge were many loyal KPD members who had sought safety in the Soviet Union. Between 1936 and 1938, around seventy percent of the exiled party membership was arrested.[10] Most of the German communists who survived the purge were enthusiastic participants in it. This included Erich Mielke, who briefly recounted the period in an autobiographical statement he wrote many years later for the Soviet authorities.

Surrounded by blood, terror, and the arbitrary killing of illustrious party comrades, Mielke described his role in the slaughter thus: 'During my stay in the Soviet Union I participated in all Party discussions of the KPD and also in the problems concerning the establishment of socialism.'

22

RU

Before the Second World War, the Soviet military intelligence service was known as the Fourth Department or, more formally, the RU. Its name derives from *razvedka*, a Russian term that translates roughly as 'scouting' and encompasses espionage, military reconnaissance, and information-gathering. Today, known as the GRU, the agency is notorious for its operations against expatriate opponents of the Kremlin.*

The RU was not created to carry out political killings, however. Founded soon after the Bolsheviks seized power, it was tasked with collecting military, political and economic information in foreign countries. Traditionally, its employees were considered more sophisticated and erudite than those of its 'neighbours', the OGPU and NKVD, although their work and personnel overlapped. Some of the most celebrated spies in Soviet history worked for the RU, including the Second World War heroes Leopold Trepper and Richard Sorge.

Trepper was a leader of the large Soviet spy network in western Europe that the Nazis dubbed the Red Orchestra. Many of its members were later commemorated on East German postage stamps and other such items. Trepper was a remarkable survivor who endured spells of incarceration by the British authorities in Palestine, the Gestapo, and the NKVD; surprisingly, he lived to publish an entertaining autobiography in the 1970s.

Richard Sorge, the first spy in history to be featured on a postage stamp,[1] has been the subject of a seemingly endless string of biographies for almost eighty years. He too was honoured in the GDR; an award for Stasi officers was named after him. Most famously, Sorge operated in Japan, where he posed as a Nazi journalist and churned out highly regarded articles on Asian politics and economics. Some of his espionage coups are said to have changed the course of the Second World War.[2]

---

* RU for razvedyvatel'noye upravleniye or intelligence directorate, usually shortened to razvedupr; officially, the IV Directorate of the General Staff of the Red Army. GRU stands for Main Intelligence Directorate. The agency's name changed several times over the years.

According to one historian of the RU, it was:

> an uncharacteristically cosmopolitan organization, with members from almost every ethnic background. Many of them were highly educated, and from middle- or upper-class families. This was especially notable when compared to the frequently humble origins of the Chekists... This enhanced its ability to successfully operate on a global scale. The relative sophistication of the RU's officers and agents also gave them access to the aristocratic circles of western Europe in a way that was impossible for the Cheka.[3]

After the collapse of East Germany, the Stasi's Markus Wolf would make a similar distinction when praising and exonerating his own foreign intelligence service. In his interviews and writings, Wolf implied that his intelligence officers were equivalent to the RU personnel of the interwar years; that they had inherited the RU tradition of cleverness and worldliness, altogether superior to the Stasi's domestic security officers. As a corollary of this, Wolf insisted that his outfit was not involved in oppressing the East German public. This argument is given short shrift by Jens Gieseke, who asserts that Wolf's foreign intelligence service 'was involved in persecuting East German citizens to the extent that it was able'.[4]

The leaderships of the RU and the Soviet security service were closely connected, sometimes interchangeable. Just as Chekists were placed within military units to ensure loyalty and catch spies and traitors, OGPU-NKVD oversight of the RU was 'achieved by the practice of appointing senior members of the security organ to the directorship of the [RU]'. According to one defector, the Soviet communist party 'hoped that this arrangement would keep the Cheka, Red Army and RU at odds with one another and thus ensure the primacy of the Party'.[5] The SED was to adopt similar tactics of divide and rule. Furthermore, the practice of 'watching the watchers' – placing secret external observers within security agencies and other organisations – was rife throughout the interwar communist movement, and was to become a deeply engrained habit of the SED.

The notable interwar Soviet defector Walter Krivitsky spent most of his career in the RU. In 1940 he was debriefed by Jane Sissmore, the first female officer in Britain's security service, MI5. Like many defectors Krivitsky invented things, but he also provided or clarified some of MI5's fundamental information about Soviet espionage. This included, for example, the Soviets' simultaneous use of legal and illegal *rezidents*, or spy-runners, in foreign countries. A 'legal' resident operated from a legitimate position in the host country, such as a diplomatic post. 'Illegals' operated under false identities and pretences.

Certainly, the Stasi learned from the patience of the RU when it came to placing long-term sleeper agents in foreign countries. Krivitsky explained how the RU liked 'to grow up agents from the inside'. While it took years to get results, the RU 'was prepared in some instances to wait for ten or fifteen years for results and in some cases paid the expenses of a university education for promising [recruits] in the hope that they might eventually obtain diplomatic posts or other key positions in the service of the country of which they were nationals'.[6]

Most tellingly, Krivitsky described the RU's use of 'demoralisation'. Such operations are known in German as Zersetzung. In MI5's report the Russian term is translated as 'decomposition', which tallies with the German and is surprisingly accurate given MI5's linguistic shortcomings of the time.

Krivitsky described RU decomposition work as 'the creation of situations [in] foreign countries to provide favourable military factors for the Soviet Union in case of need'.[7] This meant sowing disinformation and fear in target countries, harming their public and political morale, weakening their institutions by stoking personal rivalries or provoking alarming incidents. Yet here there was a crucial difference between the RU and the Stasi. The RU carried out decomposition operations against hostile countries. Stasi officers were to apply them to their own compatriots.

23

The Comintern and the OMS

Archives in Moscow show that in 1942 the leader of the British communist party, Harry Pollitt, was in direct contact with Pavel Fitin, chief of NKVD foreign intelligence.[1]

The Pollitt-Fitin connection was evidence for something that Western intelligence services had been trying to understand and prove for years – that national communist parties were directed by Soviet intelligence officers as well as by the Bolshevik leadership in Moscow. The Soviet Union's domination of foreign communist parties is important not only for understanding the Stasi, but the whole of twentieth century geopolitics.

Based in Moscow, the Comintern was the organisation that co-ordinated the work of communist parties outside the Soviet Union. In the years before its dissolution in 1943, it was a prime means for Stalin to control the global communist movement. Formally called the Third Communist International, the Comintern was created in 1919 to foment worldwide revolution based on the Russian example.* At first it had a small and varied membership. There were socialist parties, radical workers' groups, trade unions. Many of these organisations were soon consolidated into new national communist parties. As its membership of orthodox communist parties increased, the Comintern underwent a steady process of 'Bolshevisation', followed inevitably by Stalinisation during the 1930s.

The Comintern's staff was fluid. Communist parties would send batches of representatives for spells of duty with the Comintern's fixed employees in Moscow; the Comintern would dispatch trusted emissaries in the other direction, to supervise national parties on the spot. Like a communist party, the Comintern had a cadre department, training schools, and a tough Control Commission to ensure its members toed the line. It also had an autocratic Executive Committee, the ECCI. By the mid-1930s one of its leading figures was Wilhelm Pieck, future president of East Germany.

---

* The First Communist International was born and died in the nineteenth century; the Second was dismissed by the Bolsheviks as overly social democratic.

On one level, it is quite possible to write a history of the Comintern without once mentioning spying or sabotage. Historians of the labour movement have tended to do so. But choosing to focus solely on its overt activity is to practice self-deceit. Despite the diversity of its initial revolutionary membership, from the start the Comintern 'was closely tied to Soviet foreign policy'.[2] Communist parties were illegal in various countries at various times; partly as a result, the Comintern was steeped in *konspiratsia*. It conducted an exponential amount of spying on behalf of Stalin and the Soviet secret services, and was a major sponsor of criminal activity all over the world.[3]

The Comintern's principal clandestine body was its International Liaison Department, the OMS.* Its ostensible purpose was to enable 'confidential contact' between Moscow and foreign communist parties.[4] Mostly it did so via covert radio transmissions or with secret couriers who transported party funds, equipment, and propaganda. OMS agents performed a variety of other roles. They assisted fugitive revolutionaries by supplying false papers and running international escape lines; disseminated Moscow's policy decisions and assessed the loyalty of local party members; collected the information gathered by communist spies; and helped to prepare national parties for paramilitary operations in the event of crisis or war. These watchers could themselves expect to be watched; according to Walter Krivitsky, 'like every other body in Soviet Russia' the OMS was 'honeycombed with OGPU agents'.[5]

Moscow mandated foreign communist parties to have a military section – an 'M-Department' or, in Germany, 'M-Apparat'. These units were expected to be ready to carry out armed uprisings or acts of sabotage, or to confront political opponents in open civil warfare. Members of the M-Department were trained in battle tactics and the use of firearms and explosives. Many were former First World War soldiers and sailors. Although mainland Britain was less troubled by political violence than continental Europe, even the interwar Communist Party of Great Britain had a secret paramilitary outfit, the Workers' Defence Corps. Investigations by MI5 revealed its links with Soviet espionage inside the United Kingdom and with Irish Republican Army gunrunners, highlighting the collaboration between insurrectionary organisations.[6]

By 1930 the M-Apparat was frequently referred to as the 'military-political' apparatus; 'military-political' being a widely used term in Soviet and German communism. The concept was important. Many communists underwent 'military-political' training in Russia, which meant taking courses in military skills – weapons, explosives, reconnaissance, range-finding, communications equipment – and, concurrently, on ideology, studying Marxist-Leninist

---

*   Otdel mezhdunarodnoi svyazi.

literature and the history of Russian Bolshevism. Communist activists were expected to know how to fight, but also to understand and remain loyal to the ideology they were fighting for. Years later, in a direct copy of such Soviet institutions as the Red Army, the Stasi would help to run political departments within the Volkspolizei and, later, in the East German army and border troops.

Towards the end of the 1920s, when Moscow decreed that the German Communist Party should adopt a more defensive approach, its military department generated the 'anti-military' department (Anti-militarischer or AM-Apparat). Its small cells agitated within the Weimar-era police and armed forces, aiming to sap the morale of 'imperialist' troops and to instigate strikes and desertions. They were also responsible for warning communists who faced arrest, for arranging emigration routes, and for the security of their local party, above all by identifying and neutralising police spies. The rise of Nazism saw AM operatives doing their best to root out infiltrators within local KPD branches, and propagandising among Nazi groups and the police. This was dangerous work. AM-Apparat agents who managed to survive the Third Reich were considered trustworthy recruits for the Stasi and other East German institutions.

All such covert functions in communist parties were overseen by the Comintern-OMS, just as the parties' overt activities were. Furthermore, the Comintern sponsored insurrection wherever it could; China in the late 1920s, Brazil in 1935, India continually. The future Stasi chief Wilhelm Zaisser spent three years as a Comintern agent in Manchuria. This period of revolutionary war in China, and the travails of its communist participants, is the setting for *Man's Estate* by André Malraux, considered a masterpiece of twentieth century literature.

With the communist party banned in British India, the Comintern wooed Indian communists in Europe, enticing some to Moscow. The Comintern's attempts to disrupt British rule followed Soviet foreign policy, which decreed that Britain was an arch enemy, its empire an Achilles heel. As well as Britons and Indians, German communists were favoured for despatching to India as underground organisers.[7] There they disseminated agitational propaganda or agitprop – a Bolshevik term that entered the left-wing lexicon. This was not the last time that German communists would be sent to developing countries to support uprisings and mess with Western interests. From the 1960s onwards, the Stasi specialised in doing so.

Perhaps the Comintern's most significant clandestine activity was talent-spotting or nurturing spies. Numerous RU officers – including Trepper, Sorge and Krivitsky – began their careers in the Comintern. Once noticed, promising agents were not necessarily recruited in the name of the Soviet Union.

Recruitments were often mysterious and insinuating. Communist sympathisers who might not be amenable to working for Moscow were asked to do 'secret work' for the Comintern, 'the party', or even 'the workers' movement'; they weren't always aware that the USSR was their ultimate employer.

Nevertheless, avowed communists proved to be reliable recruits for the Soviet Union for the remainder of the twentieth century. Their political affiliations made things tricky, however. Soviet intelligence services knew that communists were under suspicion in their home countries. Both the RU and OGPU ruled that no one with known communist associations was to be recruited. In practice this rule proved impossible to follow. After all, thanks to foreign communists the Soviet ability to spy on Western military technology, for example, was exponentially greater than the ability of the Western powers to spy inside the Soviet Union.

Decades later, the Stasi foreign intelligence service was highly prized by the KGB partly because, unlike other Soviet Bloc agencies, it could sidestep this problem. For several reasons, the Stasi was better able to recruit spies – especially in West Germany – who had no connection whatsoever with communism.

Many foreign communists recruited for covert activity were trained in the Soviet Union at schools either run by the Comintern or connected with it. The most renowned was the International Lenin School (ILS). Others were the OMS institution known as the Wilson School, the Communist University for National Minorities of the West, the Communist University for the Toilers of the East, and the Sun Yat-sen University of the Toilers of China. Between them these schools educated future national leaders of China, Vietnam, Kenya, Azerbaijan and Greece, as well as Markus Wolf and other Stasi and SED notables.

Regardless of its earlier, more idealistic aims, by the late 1930s the Lenin School had become a production line for 'assault troopers of Stalinism'.[8] The school was clandestine – all students used pseudonyms and, according to one study, 'the code of *konspiratsia* bound all involved to treat the school as a secret organization.' Furthermore, 'as Stalinism tightened its grip, an ILS Cadre Department reported to the Comintern Cadre Department which reported to the NKVD.'[9] Today the school is best remembered as the place where interwar communists learned spycraft and skills in guerrilla warfare; an academy for spies and saboteurs.

After several months of political education, the less promising ILS students were placed in factories to gain experience of Soviet industry. More promising pupils were selected for military training. This meant living 'like soldiers', being 'drilled, taught to shoot, [and learning] street fighting'. Following this, 'a limited number of the ablest students' were chosen for the all-important intelligence courses. Among other skills, such as using codes and ciphers, they were 'taught radio work, the use of secret inks and the technique of obtaining false passports'. They 'acquired a knowledge of chemicals and explosives, how to cut water supplies, wreck machinery and disconnect telephone wires'.[10]

The KPD sent more pupils to Moscow than any other party.[11] The biographies of the Stasi's early leaders often refer to military training at the Lenin School. There are frequent references to taking a 'short course' or a 'long course' in the USSR. Usually, the former signifies a 'conventional' political education. A 'long course' meant that a student had gone through every component of the Lenin School curriculum, emerging as a fully-fledged communist secret agent.

The 'disciplined orthodoxy' of Stalinism was at its steeliest in the trinity of Soviet secret agencies described in the preceding pages. Whether or not communists liked or admitted it, these clandestine services, with their subterfuge and violence, were a fixed part of the international communist movement. In the three decades before the Stasi was created, many of its founding executives served the OGPU or NKVD, the RU, and the OMS. By the time they became Stasi officers, they had tales to tell and advice to give. Two creation myths in particular were fostered within the Stasi by these Old Comrades.

24

Stasi Creation Myths

A Stasi creation myth (1): Communist resistance in the Third Reich
When Adolf Hitler acquired full power in Germany in March 1933, KPD members were under instructions from Moscow to resist openly. This meant printing and handing out anti-Nazi leaflets, shouting down Nazi speakers in public places, removing and detaining important Nazis in the factories. The KPD leadership called for mass petitioning, mass deputations to the Justice Department, mass strikes and sit-downs. For the KPD was not under orders merely to resist; it was under orders to seize power.

Communist calls for open resistance and 'mass action' were leftovers from the turmoil of the first months of 1933. Once Hitler was made chancellor in January, the Nazis embarked on a campaign of violence to kill, detain or deter KPD members and voters, and to wipe out the labour movement and left-wing organisations in general. It worked. They were helped by Moscow insisting to the KPD that this was a good moment for a communist insurrection. Party leader Ernst Thälmann, a working-class Stalinist from the Hamburg shipyards, gave rousing speeches in which he insisted that the new regime was unstable, that the economy would continue to falter, leaving the Nazis vulnerable to overthrow. But the KPD, badly advised by Moscow, was making a terrible mistake. By taking to the streets, agitating in the factories, and even using constitutional means such as petitions, the party was almost obliterated. As well as conveniently identifying its members to the waiting hordes of stormtroopers and Nazi-inclined police officers, the KPD's open insurrection gave Hitler a pretext to destroy the party, by official and unofficial means.

The idea that the KPD could have formed the German government at this moment was preposterous. The party was popular; it had 360,000 members at the start of 1933, and had achieved a high of nearly six million votes in the election of the previous November. It enjoyed strong traditional support in Berlin, the Ruhr basin and Lower Rhine area, and in certain other cities: Leipzig, Stuttgart, Hamburg. By the March 1933 election, however, which the Nazis won with their coalition partners, the situation had changed completely.

Once in power, Hitler issued a string of decrees that allowed him to dismantle the KPD and other parties. Emboldened by their election victory and growing popularity with the public and police, the Nazis set about persecuting communists with sickening relish. Unsurprisingly, many communists recanted and swapped sides. Others fled Germany. The remainder suffered grievously. Entire working-class suburbs were sealed off by the SS, the Brownshirts and the police; their populations were attacked, intimidated, and subjected to violent searches. Communists were tortured in ways that paralyse the mind. They were beaten, stabbed, shot to death; they were thrown from the highest windows of police stations, beheaded in the cellars. A particularly distressing assault occurred in the Berlin suburb of Köpenick in June 1933, where 'a week-long orgy of bestial atrocities left seventy dead, most though not all of them communists'.[1]

Those who remained alive were thrown into Germany's first concentration camps, including Oranienburg and Dachau. The Nazi camp system was created chiefly for members of the KPD. By the end of 1933, as many as 100,000 party members had been interned. Communists and socialists were locked up ostensibly for their own safety, initially under the rubric of 'protective custody' – a trusty concept for any government that wants to remove an entire constituency from the streets.

After a year or so of open bloodletting, the penny dropped in Moscow that the policy of seizing power from the Nazis wasn't altogether satisfactory. By 1935 Moscow's policy had shifted to urging underground resistance. Again, this reveals characteristics of the Bolsheviks and, later, of the SED in East Germany: about-turns in policy; autocratic policies that end in disaster; attempts to mitigate the disaster with more reversals of policy; and all of it dumping a ton of intractable problems on the heads of rank-and-file communists.

However, once they were no longer obliged to hurl themselves publicly at millions of Nazis, German communists did a fair job of regrouping and functioning. Living and resisting covertly, they were able to use every trick of the *konspiratsia* that was their inheritance.

When it came to rucking with the Nazis, the KPD was proud of its belligerent traditions. Weimar Germany was scarred by political street violence. On the communist side, the Red Front Fighters League (Roter Frontkämpferbund, RFB) was formed in 1924, in the wake of a failed communist coup the previous year. The RFB had two aims: to protect KPD members against assault, and to prepare for the guerrilla warfare the party considered inevitable. Many RFB members had fought in the First World War, hence the reference to 'front fighters' – veterans. As one of the KPD's 'mass organisations', it played an important role in the life of the party. When it was banned in 1929 – chiefly due to its bloody confrontations with socialists rather than Nazis – the RFB mutated into the League of Struggle against Fascism or KgF. Though illegal, the KgF continued the work of the RFB, specialising in caching weapons for use in future conflicts.*

The RFB wasn't the only party organisation to fight physically for communism. KPD meetings were protected by the Party Self-Defence organisation (Parteiselbstschutz). The ranks of these armed bouncers included the likes of Erich Mielke, a man who could start a fight in an empty room. A combative culture infused the party's main youth organisation, the KJVD, and its main organisation for agitating within trade unions, the RGO.† Throughout the 1920s, there was a big increase in the number of workers' sports and hiking clubs, mostly under the umbrella of the communist-run Combat Group for Red Unity in Sport, known as the KG.‡ As well as satisfying a vogueish demand for workers' health and fitness, these clubs were a good way to give surreptitious combat training. They anticipated the mass organisations of East Germany, especially the Association for Sport and Technology or GST.§

The use of paramilitary groups was common to all pugnacious ideologies of the period. In early 1930s Britain, for example, the proto-fascist New Party was accompanied on the campaign trail by a protective mob called the Biff Boys. Yet for the KPD, the situation was especially loaded. Faced with vitriolic opposition from conservatives and socialists, and psychopathic hatred from fascists and nationalists, the RFB and other communist groups found themselves having to punch, kick, stab and cosh their way through the 1920s.

The use of force by communists had at least one unwanted side effect: it enabled the supremely violent Nazis to claim they were the victims of violence. The author Rebecca West commented on this phenomenon in the British context:

> The proper course for those who were anti-Fascist was to abstain from all action on the day of [a fascist] meeting, to stay in their houses and ignore it; but the idea of violence would enter them also, and they would feel under a compulsion to attend the meetings and interrupt and provoke the stewards to throw them out... if the Communists had ignored the Fascist meetings and refrained from interrupting them, the Fascists would have been checkmated, since they would

---

*   KgF for Kampfgemeinschaft gegen den Faschismus.
†   KJVD for Kommunistischer Jugendverband Deutschlands or Young Communist League of Germany; RGO for Revolutionäre Gewerkschaftsopposition or Revolutionary Trade Union Opposition.
‡   Kampfgemeinschaft für Rote Sporteinheit, commonly called Rotsport.
§   Gesellschaft für Sport und Technik.

not then have been able to exercise violence and plead that they were defending the right of free speech.[2]

Of course, West's view didn't account for the particular conditions of Germany, where it was difficult, perhaps impossible, for anti-fascists to see how best to challenge the rise of Nazism. Arguably, communist violence was not as strategically disastrous as the bitter feud between communists and socialists, which prevented any meaningful coalition of left-wing forces.[3] But it did mean that many floating voters came to associate the Nazis with the promise of civil order, and an end to political bloodshed.

By 1935 the KPD had re-established itself with a new 'conspiratorial' structure. Most of its members, and all of its leaders, lived in exile. Its secretariat was in Paris. 'Sector headquarters', each corresponding to an area of Germany, were set up in five European cities – Amsterdam, Brussels, Copenhagen, Prague and Zurich. As well as trying to direct the dispirited bands of communists who remained in Germany, the sectors printed and distributed propaganda, organised anti-Nazi activities around Europe, and smuggled people – fugitives out of Germany, undercover activists in.

Ironically, given what happened later in East Germany, the Prague sector was celebrated for its clandestine border-crossing activities. Eleven frontier posts were set up adjacent to Silesia, Saxony and Thuringia. In mountainous spots, large groups were able to meet under the guise of being trekkers or mountaineers. From 1933 to 1936, a stretch of the Czech frontier saw more than 1,000 crossings without loss. One devout communist, a former school cleaner called Minna Fritsch, was said to have made more than forty clandestine journeys into Germany.[4]

Communists who remained in Germany lived miserable and perilous lives. By the mid-1930s, some had been freed from prisons and camps. But their release was followed inevitably by Gestapo monitoring, often by re-arrest. Mostly they were unable to revive the pre-1933 networks that had reported from within companies and factories. Before the Nazi victory, several thousand 'worker correspondents' – known by the Russian term Rabcors, or the German term Betriebs-Berichterstatter or BB – had provided the communist press with details about the conditions at factories, and gathered useful technical information for Soviet industry. Later, the Stasi was able to resurrect the practice of mass covert reporting from within workplaces.

Brave and hardy communists formed small cells in which to continue their anti-Nazi propaganda – now usually conducted by word-of-mouth – and to organise subtle forms of resistance and non-compliance. Cells were restricted to three or five members. The latter, known as fünfergruppen or 'groups of five', became the stuff of KPD legend. Only one member had contact outside the group, making any breakthrough by the police easier to seal off. A form of rendezvous called a treff also became renowned – an apparently random meeting between two underground party members in a street or square, from which one could follow another to a park or café. The Stasi continued to use the term until the end of the 1980s.

Most communists were well-versed in the *konspiratsia* that could aid survival under the Nazis. They understood how to circumvent bans, thwart interrogators, avoid self-incrimination, and use aliases and false papers. By now, their typewriters and printing presses were hidden from prying eyes. Yet these heightened security measures were only partially successful. Although Gestapo informers – the notorious vertrauensmänner or V-Men – were not numerous within the underground KPD, they were well placed. For one historian, 'most of the mass arrests and trials by which the Gestapo broke up successive clandestine Communist Party organisations were probably the work of a few such individuals in each area.'[5]

The daring efforts of the fünfergruppen were proclaimed in the world's press, with some articles even claiming they were close to destroying the Nazi regime from within. But today the fünfergruppen are disparaged by historians, some of whom insist they were a pure invention. However, their myth 'proved very attractive not only to German communists, but to many other Germans distressed at the absence of any armed resistance to Hitler before the end of 1944... surely a singular achievement of the KGB and Stasi who assiduously spread the story of the fünfergruppen'.[6]

The torturous experiences of KPD members in the 1930s make it even more remarkable that resistance groups continued into the Second World War. Most were composed of party members who had been incarcerated in the early 1930s and somehow lived to tell the tale. Many of these groups were honoured in East Germany, as were the information-gathering networks around Harro Schulze-Boysen, a lieutenant who worked at the Ministry of Aviation, and Arvid Harnack, an official in the Ministry of Economics. The efforts of exiled party leaders in the USSR were also celebrated. Markus Wolf and other Stasi high-ups served with Soviet partisan units, while Walter Ulbricht and his associates were at Stalingrad, yelling defeatist propaganda at the German lines through loudhailers.

Yet there was another side to the stories of some KPD members who lived through these years, a side that the SED regime did not memorialise. As noted, many terrified communists dropped their political activities or joined the Nazis. Furthermore, communists in concentration camps, in the words of historian Allan Merson, 'achieved by co-operation some degree of control of their environment'. Given that 'the SS could not run the camps in the long run without some degree of collaboration on the part of the prisoners', those 'who took office under the SS had to walk a moral and political tightrope'.[7] Usually these communists became hut leaders (Kapos) or camp seniors (Lagerälteste), or procured jobs in useful places such as sick bays and kitchens. When it worked, collaboration with the camp authorities meant that communists might receive treatment which, however rough, was preferable to that meted out to other inmates. In fact, the 'moral tightrope' may have amounted to the largescale denunciation of those fellow inmates who were not communists.

Another problem with the SED's memory of anti-fascist resistance was its suppression of the role played by German Jews. The Nazis' cornerstone claim that Bolshevism was 'Jewish' was always nonsense; a research paper published by the German Resistance Memorial Center has shown that 'most of the Jewish Communists, Socialists and Social Democrats who joined the illegal resistance [were], at least initially, on the margins of the Jewish community.' Even so, it is now established 'that the proportion of Jews active in the whole range of illegal groupings [after] the Nazi seizure of power was very considerable indeed, and [that] certainly more Jews than non-Jews quickly decided to resist actively'.

As the paper's author notes, in East Germany 'any special emphasis on the Jewish contribution to the resistance would not have conformed to the Communist party line.'[8] Similarly, after the war Stalin did not encourage publicity about the extermination or resistance of Soviet Jews, preferring to commemorate the suffering of Russians or 'the Soviet people'. What mattered to the SED regime – a lot – was the KPD's resistance to Nazism. Communist resisters were sanctified. To this day, to be remembered in Germany as an 'anti-fascist resistance fighter' (antifaschistischer Widerstandskämpfer) can be a powerful compliment. KPD resisters were commemorated on East German stamps, or with portraits and monuments, or in the names of streets, schools, clubs and awards. To new generations of GDR youth, they were presented as unimpeachable idols.

Stasi officers, too, were inspired by the KPD's anti-fascist heritage. Their mentality is captured in the reminiscences of deputy security minister Rudi Mittig. Recalling his induction into the Stasi in 1952, Mittig described the almost mystical gravitas of communists who had fought against Hitler:

> The question was, to whom do I subordinate myself? My superiors at that time, it is important for me to emphasise, [were] without exception anti-fascist resistance fighters who had taken part in the Spanish war of liberation, in the fight of the Red Army against fascism, people who had been in concentration camps… I gave

them my complete trust. In those days there was a definite difference between a GDR staff officer and a fascist… Yes, I had great respect for them. They had, unlike me, proved themselves during the time of fascism.[9]

The KPD's anti-fascist history lent some moral weight, however specious, to the pronouncements of the East German authorities. Whenever the Stasi or SED condemned an adversary – individual, organisational, national – as 'fascist', for some East Germans the word carried real force and evoked real horror. The word 'fascist' was not a petulant, empty insult. Anyone or anything 'fascist' was steeped in the blood of their national heroes.

A Stasi creation myth (2): The Spanish Civil War

Five thousand German volunteers fought for the Republic in the Spanish Civil War. Some were social democrats and libertarians. The majority were communists.

Most foreign volunteers served in the International Brigades. Organised by the Comintern from a clandestine office in Paris, the brigades are still a treasured memory for left-wingers the world over. While it is important not to demean those left-wing and social democratic volunteers who fought and died in Spain in the name of anti-fascism and democracy, there was a disturbing underside to communists' involvement in the war. This was thanks largely to Joseph Stalin.

At the very least, many communists joined the International Brigades under false pretences. They were not fighting for the liberty of the Spanish people but for something else. One veteran of the Lincoln Brigade, composed of American volunteers, commented wryly, 'Yes, we went to Spain to fight fascism, but democracy was not our aim.'[10] Instead, communists fought for the Comintern's goal of imposing a 'new type' of republic in the country. If successful, this would give Stalin his first satellite state in the west of Europe.

By dressing up this goal as a fight for peace and democracy, Stalin greatly enhanced his international reputation. As the war raged, the Great Purge was underway in the USSR. Yet partly thanks to his Spanish endeavours, Stalin was considered the main bulwark against Hitler and fascism. Most Western newspapers were reluctant to publish criticism of him. His lunatic accusations against the Red Army leaders he executed in 1937 may have disenchanted some communists and socialists, but they were reported without comment in much of the world's press.

The influence of Stalinism in the Spanish Republic led to the system of strict political indoctrination which gained a chokehold on the International

Brigades. Much of this was overseen by the Comintern's main invigilator, the French communist André Marty, who by his own count sentenced to death some 500 brigade volunteers during the conflict. While transgressors were often charged with cowardice, desertion or ill-discipline, in some cases political dissent or independence were probably closer to the mark. Marty's bloodlust is noted in Ernest Hemingway's great novel of the war, *For Whom The Bell Tolls*, in which a character opines that Marty has 'a mania for shooting people' and 'kills more than the bubonic plague'.

This ferocious political control could be passed off as legitimate in wartime. Less excusable was Stalin's covert campaign to assassinate left-wing opponents. With factional violence erupting among left-wing Spanish Republicans, Stalin and his security commissar Nikolai Yezhov spotted an opportunity to get rid of some perceived enemies in the international socialist movement. The chaotic civil war conditions were perfect for justifying or covering up the killings. While the Spanish communist party conducted its own campaign of political murder, a contingent of NKVD officers liquidated at least twenty of Stalin's critics.[11]

German communists played a leading role in these activities. The tough reputation of KPD members meant that a dozen or so German communists served as personal bodyguards to senior NKVD officers. Others worked their way into influential positions in Republican security and counter-espionage agencies, or carried out conspiratorial tasks as rank-and-file brigade soldiers. Wilhelm Zaisser and Erich Mielke are said to have served in the Servicio de Investigación Militar or SIM, a fearsome counter-espionage agency that hunted Francoist spies and saboteurs. When it comes to the DNA of the Stasi, it is striking how many leaders of the East German security and interior ministries were veterans of Spain.

What methods did German communists learn or refine in Spain? What behaviours did they acquire, or come to rationalise? Arguably, all those they later used to subjugate the people of East Germany. They learned to root out enemies without compunction, to combat individualism and enforce a party line. They learned to litter organisations with informers, to cover criminal or immoral acts with a veneer of legality, and to infiltrate rival or non-partisan organisations in order to take control of them.

The creation of the Spanish Republic's wartime police force, the Cuerpo de Seguridad, is significant. Once the war was underway, the Republican government wanted to create a new, centralised, anti-fascist police force. It had to be trusted by the entire range of Republicans while effectively fighting crime as well as the Nationalist enemy. Above all, it had to be seen as a police force *of the people*. This task was more-or-less identical to that faced by the East

German leadership at the end of the 1940s. It partly explains why so many German volunteers were involved in creating and running the Volkspolizei.

Once the Stasi was formed, its leaders spread their knowledge and experiences from the Spanish Civil War downwards, through the lower ranks of the service. They told stories and made myths. They developed strategy and practices from the lessons of this brutal political conflict. Veterans of Spain were national heroes in the GDR, and German experiences of the Spanish war fed into the lifeblood of the Stasi.

25

First Class Comrades:
The Stasi's Early Leaders

The phrase 'first class comrades' was used by Stasi chief Wilhelm Zaisser at an SED congress in 1953. He was talking about the stringent vetting applied to all Stasi officers before they were accepted into the service. Zaisser said: 'We have been specially checked. We are especially good comrades. We are, so to speak, first class comrades.'

Zaisser believed that he and his colleagues were the cream of the SED – the toughest, most experienced, most reliable communists – and first among equals in the party. What, for Zaisser, made for a first class comrade?

Based on an awareness of interwar communism, and the lives lived by its adherents, it could be said that a first class comrade was someone who:

- was working class
- was a Stalinist and loyal to the Soviet Union
- had some knowledge of Marxism–Leninism
- was prepared to carry out covert, illegal or paramilitary operations
- had fought in wars, or been in prison or concentration camps, for their political beliefs
- preferably had a background in security, intelligence or disciplinary work
- was prepared to remove, or conspire against, unwanted party colleagues
- understood that SED policies would not be adopted gladly, and must be imposed; at least some of the population would need to be coerced or forced into accepting these policies
- understood the need for subterfuge in electoral politics and civil life; for example, elections could be held but SED candidates must win them
- was dedicated to the remoulding or – preferably – the eradication of 'enemy' classes of people
- was *vigilant* – intent on unearthing and fighting attempts to undermine the SED.

The Stasi was created and led by individuals who met these criteria; individuals who came from the communist universe of *konspiratsia*, secret agencies, and struggle. What were their life stories? How did the turbulence and tragedies of interwar communism shape their experiences?

Some idea can be gained from the following biographies of notables from the Stasi and East German interior ministry.[1] These biographies are not intended as a reference, which might otherwise be placed at the start or end of a book. They are part of this book's narrative; an introduction to those who built the Stasi. Most of them served in Spain. While the details of their service there can be obscure, it is likely the majority served in security and counter-intelligence roles behind the lines, and not as frontline soldiers.

THE LEADERS OF THE STASI

Wilhelm Zaisser: first chief of the Stasi, 1950-1953

Wilhelm Zaisser (1893-1958) was born in Germany's industrial heartland, the Ruhr. His father served in the local gendarmerie. Unusually for someone of his class, Zaisser was able to attend university, and by the time the First World War began he was working as a schoolteacher.

Zaisser served in the German army throughout the war, reaching the rank of lieutenant. While serving on the Russian front he witnessed what he saw as the positive effects of the revolution. In 1919 he returned to Essen and joined the KPD.

Zaisser served as an officer in the paramilitary Red Ruhr Army which fought against nationalists during the Kapp Putsch of 1920. The following year he was arrested for this activity and spent four months in prison; upon release he was barred from the teaching profession.

Zaisser then eked out a living as a journalist and KPD propagandist, editing the *Ruhr Echo* and another paper. At the same time, he was a leader of the local party's military department (M-Apparat), in which role he agitated against the French forces then occupying the Ruhr. He travelled to Moscow twice, attending the second congress of the Profintern in 1922 and receiving military-political training at a Comintern school in 1924.

Thus qualified, the RU sent Zaisser to Syria as an adviser to the Druse tribes fighting against French colonial troops. He performed the same advisory role for Abd el-Krim, leader of the Rif tribes in Morocco, who was battling French and Spanish forces. Once back in Berlin he became one of the KPD's leading intelligence officials, overseeing the party's military-political training throughout Germany.

In July 1927 Zaisser returned to the Soviet Union and became a full-time agent of the Comintern. This role trumped and ended his direct employment by the KPD. He was sent by the RU to China, which was then undergoing revolutionary upheavals. For three years, posing as a conservative arms dealer, he spied at the court of the puppet leader of Japanese Manchuria. Zaisser was a successful deceiver; he founded a Shanghai branch of the right-wing military association, the Stahlhelm, and he and his wife entertained diplomats, army officers and visiting dignitaries. His cover was blown in 1930, however, and he was forced to return to Moscow.

Zaisser then spent nearly two years as a Comintern instructor in Prague. In 1932 he was back in Russia, where he acquired Soviet citizenship and joined the Soviet communist party. Using the alias Werner Reissner, he ran a Comintern military-political school at Babovka outside Moscow for several years. Erich Mielke was one of his pupils.

In summer 1936 Zaisser travelled to Spain in the guise of 'General Gómez', a military adviser to the Republican forces. Initially he commanded the XIII International Brigade, composed mostly of Slavic and French-speaking volunteers. When the brigade was battered in the Brunete campaign of summer 1937, Zaisser was moved to a more significant – and largely punitive – role: commandant of the International Brigade base at Albacete. In other words, Zaisser was a senior military security officer.

Zaisser thus began to impose the harsh political discipline for which the International Brigades became notorious. He was joined in this work by other important German communists – Erich Mielke, Anton Ackermann, Franz Dahlem, Karl Gaile and, reportedly, Walter Ulbricht. Zaisser's authoritarianism went hand-in-hand with his striking appearance. An acquaintance from Spain wrote that 'the general is a gigantic man. His eyes lie deep in his massive face... [whoever] has seen the hard, strained eyes of General Gómez, and his hard, scar-cut face, feels that [his] pleasantness is only put-on and the brutality is genuine.'[2]

Under the auspices of the War Commissariat – the Republican body responsible for the army's political loyalty – Zaisser's headquarters staff had carte blanche to imprison and execute brigade soldiers without referral to any other authority. The close relationship between the work of the War Commissariat and the military counter-intelligence service, latterly the Servicio de Investigación Militar, meant that some veterans recalled Zaisser and Erich Mielke as SIM operatives. Whether or not this was true, Zaisser certainly answered to the NKVD contingent in Spain. Any brigade member accused of Trotskyism, or any other strain of non-Stalinist socialism, was in mortal danger.

At the end of the war Zaisser returned to Moscow to continue working for the Comintern. He briefly suffered in Stalin's purges; having been thrown into prison, he was released on the orders of Lavrenti Beria, the new NKVD chief. Zaisser resumed work as a writer and editor, and eventually helped to develop the political re-education programme that was applied on a mass scale to German prisoners of war.

Zaisser returned to Germany and joined the SED in 1947. Within a year he was chief of police in Saxony-Anhalt; subsequently he was appointed interior minister for Saxony. In 1949 he became head of training and cadres at the German Administration of the Interior (DVdI). This role included overseeing the paramilitaries of the new 'standby police' (Bereitschaftspolizei), an early precursor to the East German army.

In February 1950 Zaisser was appointed – reputedly against his wishes – as GDR security minister: the first chief of the Stasi. While Erich Mielke may have been the more logical choice for the job, Mielke wasn't altogether trusted by the Soviets. Zaisser was. This didn't prevent him falling from grace and being replaced in 1953.

Ernst Wollweber: second chief of the Stasi, 1953-1957
Ernst Wollweber (1898-1967) was the son of an alcoholic miner from Silesia. He escaped his unhappy family life by becoming a sailor on Germany's inland waterways. He was then called up by the navy, and served in the submarine fleet from 1916 to 1918. In November that year, by now serving as a stoker on a light cruiser, he took part in the fabled communist mutiny at Kiel. He joined the KPD the following year.

Wollweber rose quickly in the party, becoming a Central Committee member and a regional leader of the M-Apparat. Walter Ulbricht, then party secretary for Thuringia, recommended Wollweber for military-political training in Moscow. Upon returning to Germany, Wollweber was slated to lead paramilitary forces in the KPD uprising of 1923, but was arrested and detained before he could go into action.

From this point onwards Wollweber, like Zaisser, was a Soviet asset under the direct orders of the RU. In 1924 he was denounced by a police spy in the KPD, and after more than a year in custody awaiting trial he was sentenced to three years in prison. However, his sentence was cut short when the impropriety of the state prosecutor came to light, enabling Wollweber's release for wrongful conviction.

Wollweber then became a KPD parliamentary candidate, partly for tactical reasons; election to office guaranteed immunity from arrest. He was elected to the Prussian Diet in 1928 and the Reichstag in 1932. When Hitler seized power, Wollweber was one of very few KPD leaders to remain in Germany organising resistance, a fact which earned him great respect in later years. However, the futility of the task soon dawned on the KPD and Comintern, and Wollweber was relocated to Copenhagen.

The Danish capital now became a major centre of KPD and Soviet activity. Previously based in Berlin, the Comintern's Western European Bureau reopened there under the guise of an engineering firm – it was housed in a prestigious office building, the Vesterpoort. Copenhagen had many advantages. It lay on a rail and sea route from Moscow to western Europe that took just forty-eight hours and ran through fairly 'safe' territories – as far as the Comintern was concerned – such as Finland. Furthermore, communists were a strong presence among Scandinavian sailors, which enabled smuggling and illicit communications.

Wollweber was already leader of an important Comintern front organisation, a trade union called the Seamen's and Dockers' International, usually known by its German initials ISH.* Founded in 1930, the ISH was funded by Moscow – although its rank-and-file members did not necessarily know it – and had 16,000 German members; there were branches in more than twenty countries. Its activists smuggled people, propaganda and weapons, carried out maritime espionage, and fomented industrial action. In 1935 the Soviet leadership decided to make the ISH the starting point for a new maritime sabotage agency under Wollweber's command.

The 'Wollweber League' – referred to in Moscow as Organisation 'Bernhard' – became a major clandestine agency, operating well into the Second World War. Its several hundred members resigned from their national communist parties and severed all links with the workers' movement. Wollweber created units in the Baltic States, Scandinavia, the Netherlands, Belgium, France, Germany and China. His sabotage operations targeted the ships of the Anti-Comintern Pact countries – Nazi Germany, fascist Italy and Japan. During the Spanish Civil War the organisation sank around 250,000 tons of shipping, hampering the transport of arms to the Nationalist insurgents. One spectacular bombing occurred at Frederikshavn in Denmark in 1938, when several vessels destined to supply General Franco were sunk.

Following the Axis invasion of the Soviet Union in 1941, Wollweber's saboteurs turned their attentions to the rail network in Scandinavia, blowing up several troop trains destined for Russia. A prominent Norwegian saboteur, Asbjørn Sunde, kept the network alive in his 'Osvald Group', with small cells in Oslo, Narvik, Bergen and other ports. It claimed responsibility for 200 sabotage attacks during the German occupation, more than any other Norwegian resistance organisation. At least two Dutch members of Wollweber's

---

* Internationale der Seeleute und Hafenarbeiter.

network, Jan Cornelis van Schaik and Theodorus Fleeré, who had operated in Rotterdam in the 1930s, were killed by the Nazis in 1943; van Schaik was beheaded in Plötzensee jail and Fleeré died from medical experiments with TB at Sachsenhausen concentration camp.[3]

Wollweber, too, did not remain at large. He was arrested in Sweden and sentenced to three years in prison for his bomb-making activities. His release was secured by the Soviet Union, from where Wollweber returned to Germany in March 1946.

Wollweber soon joined the SED, and spent several years attempting to rebuild the shipping industry for eastern Germany. This was good cover for reviving his maritime sabotage network, which was said to be active during the Korean War. In summer 1953 he was appointed chief of the Stasi, which had been demoted from its status as a ministry and was now an agency under the Ministry of the Interior. As chief, Wollweber concentrated on counter-espionage operations against Western intelligence services, including West Germany's Organisation Gehlen and its successor, the Bundesnachrichtendienst (BND).

Erich Mielke: third chief of the Stasi, 1957-1989

Erich Mielke (1907-2000) formally became leader of the Stasi at the end of 1957, after Ernst Wollweber's resignation. He had already been substituting for Wollweber for some time. Once appointed chief, Mielke had fulfilled his life ambition; as he saw it, he was finally occupying his rightful place in the East German hierarchy. For the next three decades, he presided over an exponential growth in the Stasi's size and power.

Erich Mielke had impeccable credentials. He was redoubtably working class, came from a family that boasted several KPD members, and was renowned as a communist street fighter. He was born in the Wedding district of Berlin, the son of a cartwright and a seamstress. His mother died when Mielke was two; at the age of fifteen he saw his father, a party member, imprisoned for eighteen months for political street fighting. Mielke was bright enough to earn a scholarship to a good school, but had to abandon his studies due to his family's poverty. He found a job as a despatch clerk, and embarked on his career as a hard-bitten party militant.

First, Mielke joined the communist youth and trade union organisations, the KJVD and RGO. Upon joining the KPD in 1925 he became the leader of a street cell. He was rescued from unemployment by a spell as a reporter for the party daily paper, *Red Flag*. He also joined the Party Self Defence organisation (Parteiselbstschutz), a bunch of armed bouncers who protected KPD meetings.

Mielke's main claim to fame as a communist militant was his involvement in the murder of two police officers. In August 1931, two KPD members of the Reichstag, Heinz Neumann and Hans Kippenberger, decided to target Captain Paul Anlauf, a widower with three daughters, who was known by Berlin communists as 'Pig Face'. The KPD headquarters was in Anlauf's district, and he often led the police charges that would break up communist demonstrations. Mielke and a fellow youthful KPD member, Erich Ziemer, volunteered as assassins.

On a Sunday evening in August 1931, Anlauf was lured to Bülowplatz by a violent KPD rally. Spotting Anlauf and two other officers in front of the Babylon Cinema, Mielke and Ziemer approached and opened fire at point blank range. Anlauf and Captain Franz Lenck fell dead in front of the cinema entrance; a Sergeant Willig, though badly wounded, managed to return fire at the assailants. Mielke and Ziemer swiftly fled Europe. Helped by Comintern agents, the pair boarded a merchant ship at Antwerp and sailed for Leningrad.

Back in Berlin, a small group of communists was arrested and convicted for the murders; one died in prison and another was executed. Safely in Russia, Mielke – using the alias 'Paul Bach' – attended Wilhelm Zaisser's military-political school at Babovka, and then the Lenin School.

Mielke went to Spain in 1936. Joining the International Brigades under the alias 'Fritz Leissner', he worked at Albacete for the War Commissariat, possibly the SIM, and very likely the NKVD. Undoubtedly his main role was to silence non-Stalinists. It is notable that Mielke requested the transfer of Erich Ziemer, his accomplice in the police murders, to the Albacete base where he worked. Within two months of arriving Ziemer was dead, reportedly killed in action.

After the defeat of the Republic Mielke was ordered to Belgium, where under the alias 'Gaston' he edited a propaganda newspaper and serviced the underground KPD apparatus. He then went to France where, using yet another alias – this time 'Richard Heller' – he built up an underground communist cell in Toulouse. During the Second World War, his work as a woodchopper saw him co-opted as a labourer for the Todt Organisation, which carried out construction work throughout Nazi-occupied Europe. When the organisation's labourers retreated with the Wehrmacht into Germany during 1944, it is likely that Mielke was among them. Yet these years of Mielke's life were always shrouded in mystery. As Stasi chief, he stuck to the story that he had been in the Soviet Union throughout this period. Yet he was almost certainly in the American occupation zone of Germany in spring 1945; a fact that Mielke tried to conceal in the early 1950s by having other 'western emigrants' arrested as Anglo-American or 'Zionist' spies. Occasionally, doubts were raised about his suspected collaboration in wartime France. The Soviet authorities were never quite able to trust him; they distrusted anyone who had spent time in western Europe.

Either way, during 1945 the Soviets brought Mielke to eastern Germany as a leader of Berlin's nascent police administration. It helped that he was renowned for his obsequiousness to superiors, and skilled at reading the bureaucratic infighting intrinsic to Soviet communism. Mielke's connections were impressive; Walter Ulbricht sponsored him, and he was reputedly a protégé of Ivan Serov, NKVD plenipotentiary in the Soviet zone.

Among other benefits, his connections helped Mielke to swerve an early attempt to bring him to justice for the 1931 police murders. In January 1947, two Weimar-era police officers recognised Mielke at an official function. Informing the head of the Kriminalpolizei in the western sectors of Berlin, the officers demanded that Mielke be arrested and prosecuted. Wilhelm Kühnast, chief prosecutor in the west of the city, was brought in. Having ordered a search of the archives, he was astonished to find that the files of the murders had survived the wartime destruction of Germany.

Finding ample evidence of Mielke's involvement, Kühnast ordered his arrest, but a Soviet representative on the Allied Control Council alerted the MGB. This led to protests by Marshal Vasily Sokolovsky, then commander-in-chief of the Soviet occupation troops. Meanwhile, Soviet representatives at the Control Council launched a virulent campaign to discredit Kühnast. It worked – Kühnast was suspended from his position and placed under house arrest at his home in the Soviet sector. Although Kühnast managed to extricate himself from this predicament, foiling an attempt to forcibly detain him, the Soviet authorities successfully shut down further investigations.

From July 1946 to October 1949 Mielke served as a vice president of the German Administration of the Interior, a top position in security and policing. From October 1949 to February 1950 he headed the Directorate for the Protection of the National Economy, the direct forerunner of the Stasi. From 1950 to 1957 he was permanent secretary in the Stasi; by the end of 1957, he was minister for state security.

By the time he was ruler of the Stasi, Erich Mielke had demonstrated all the attributes that would keep him in the job until the late 1980s. He was intelligent but not an intellectual; a good organiser but an arbitrary one; ruthless and devious, but unswervingly obedient to the people who mattered. He adored Joseph Stalin, and for the rest of his life did not waver from devout Stalinism. Mielke also exemplified the (somewhat superficial) cleanliness and healthiness of the ideal Chekist. A lifelong fitness fanatic, he was a long-term executive of the German Gymnastics and Sports Association,[*] swam every day before work, and neither drank nor smoked. His main recreation was deerstalking. As

---

[*]   Deutsche Turn- und Sportbund or DTSB.

Stasi boss he was able to indulge this passion at a private country estate, often hosting Soviet Bloc dignitaries there. Mielke's biggest sporting love, though, was the Dynamo Berlin football club, of which he was vice-chairman for twenty years.

THE STASI'S FIRST REGIONAL CHIEFS: THE HEADS OF THE LÄNDER ADMINISTRATIONS IN APRIL 1950

Hermann Gartmann

Hermann Gartmann (1906-1972) was a farm labourer and builder who became a deputy minister of security and a deputy interior minister in East Germany. In 1950, with the police rank of Chefinspekteur – equivalent to a major general of the army – he led the Stasi in Brandenburg.

Gartmann joined the KJVD as a nineteen-year-old and the KPD two years later. From 1928 to 1931 he was an agent of the AM-Apparat, the KPD's counter-intelligence and 'demoralisation' service, for Berlin and Brandenburg. Sentenced to two years in prison for agitating in the police force, he spent his term at Strehlitz fortress.

After release Gartmann found a job in a steel factory. In 1937 he left for Czechoslovakia and then Spain, where he joined the International Brigades. Given his later career, it is likely he served under Wilhelm Zaisser and Erich Mielke in a counter-intelligence role. He was then interned in France until 1941, at which point he was handed over to the Nazis and sent to the Dachau concentration camp, where he managed to survive until liberation in 1945.

After the war Gartmann returned to Brandenburg, working initially for the KPD and then the SED. In 1948 he became deputy chief of the political department at the Brandenburg Volkspolizei. He then led the Brandenburg administration of the short-lived Directorate for the Protection of the National Economy before entering the Stasi, in the same role, in 1950.

Gartmann was a deputy minister of security for several years. He was appointed chief of the border police in 1952 when the Stasi assumed responsibility for that service. The following year he became a deputy minister of the interior and, from 1955, built up the Interior Security Headquarters (HVIS),[*] a composite head office for the border, transport and standby police.

In 1957 Gartmann moved to the National People's Army (NVA) as a major general, before spending two years as military attaché in Moscow. Later he was commander of an NVA officers' school at Frankenberg and the 'Rosa

---

[*]   Hauptverwaltung Innere Sicherheit.

Luxemburg' school for border troops at Plauen. After retiring in 1964 he served as secretary of a political aid organisation for Spain, which was still enduring the Franco dictatorship.

Otto Last

Otto Last (1906-1990) was a wheelwright who became a deputy minister of security in East Germany. In 1950, with the rank of Chefinspekteur, he led the Stasi in Mecklenburg.

A worker's son from the island of Rügen, Last learned the trades of wheelwright and coachbuilding, which he practised for a while as a migrant in Brazil. Returning to Germany at the end of the 1920s, he joined the KPD, for which he carried out propaganda work.

When the Nazis seized power Last continued his activities in the communist underground, but he was arrested by the Gestapo in 1935 and sentenced to three years in prison. Having served his sentence at Gollnow, he spent time in Sachsenhausen and other concentration camps. Released in spring 1939, he worked as a furniture maker in Stettin, but was then drafted into the Wehrmacht's 999th Light Afrika Division, a penal formation, and deployed to Greece. Last's life may have been saved by contracting malaria, for he spent the last two years of the war in hospital.

After serving as a KPD and then SED district secretary, Last became a member of the Mecklenburg assembly in autumn 1946, concurrently attending an SED school. In July 1949 he was appointed head of the Directorate for the Protection of the National Economy in Mecklenburg. Last is a good example of a trusted party official brought into the Stasi at its inception in preference to former K5 officers.

In 1951 Last became a deputy minister of security in Berlin. At different points he was responsible for the Stasi's Main Departments III (securing the economy) and XIII (transport), as well as its file registry and the transport police. He fell from grace in 1957, mostly for his association with the out-of-favour party functionary Gerhart Ziller. He was transferred to lead the Stasi's office at the Wismut mining operation, then further demoted to colonel and assigned to the Schwarze Pumpe industrial concern as an undercover Officer on Special Assignment. He retired in 1966.

Rudolf Menzel

Rudolf Menzel (1910-1974) was a pre-war office clerk who became a deputy minister of security, deputy interior minister, and deputy defence minister in East Germany. In 1950, with the rank of Chefinspekteur, he led the Stasi in Thuringia.

The son of a Dresden factory worker, Menzel joined the KPD in 1928. Two years later he became a political leader of the KJVD, which had been banned. Menzel was arrested and detained when the Nazis seized power. Released at the end of 1933, he emigrated for Czechoslovakia before moving on to the Soviet Union, where he attended the Lenin School.

Menzel was in Spain from 1937 to 1939, serving mostly in the Thälmann Battalion and XI International Brigade. He worked in the brigades' cadre department and for the War Commissariat, probably under Erich Mielke, where he would have been responsible for the political loyalty of brigade soldiers and the removal of undesirables. After the Nationalist victory Menzel fled to Belgium, was then interned in France, and finally was extradited to Germany. After a period at Buchenwald concentration camp, in 1942 Menzel was sentenced to two and a half years' imprisonment for treason, which he spent at Waldheim prison. He was then returned to Buchenwald, where he was active in the camp's communist resistance organisation.

After the war Menzel worked briefly for the Thuringian office of economics, but was then assigned to the Volkspolizei. By 1948 he was deputy chief of police for Thuringia. In late 1949 he joined the Directorate for the Protection of the National Economy, before entering the Stasi as its chief for Thuringia.

Rated as 'too soft' by his superiors, Menzel completed a correspondence course at the SED's 'Karl Marx' party school from 1951 to 1954. In 1953, having been appointed a deputy minister of security, like Hermann Gartmann he transferred from the Stasi to the Ministry of the Interior. As a deputy interior minister he helped to build up the infrastructure of the Kasernierte Volkspolizei (KVP). In 1956 he was appointed deputy minister of defence, in which role he helped to develop the National People's Army (NVA), but he was removed in 1959 due to 'lack of professional qualifications'. After studying at the NVA's military academy in Dresden, Menzel spent two years as director of the Strausberg military library. He then spent six years as military attaché at the East German embassy in Moscow, before retiring with the rank of lieutenant general.

Martin Weikert

Martin Weikert (1914-1997) was a former commercial apprentice who became a deputy minister of security in East Germany. In 1950, with the rank of Chefinspekteur, he led the Stasi in Saxony-Anhalt.

Born in Bohemia to a shoemaker and a weaver, Martin Weikert attended a business training college before becoming a senior functionary of the youth wing of the Czech communist party. When the Nazis seized power he carried out illegal cross-border work between Czechoslovakia and Germany, then went to Moscow to study at the Lenin School. He joined the Czech army in 1936, but remained a clandestine communist agitator. In 1939 Weikert emigrated for the Soviet Union, where he worked as a locksmith. After attending a guerrilla warfare school in Ufa, he was deployed to a partisan formation of the Red Army's 4th Ukrainian Front (army group), serving under Rudolf Slánský in 1944-45.

Having worked in the resettlement of refugees after the war, Weikert joined the SED and became head of police affairs in the Land government of Saxony-Anhalt. In 1947 he was appointed chief of K5 in Saxony-Anhalt; the following year he began attending the Higher Police School in Berlin. After leading the Directorate for the Protection of the National Economy in Saxony-Anhalt in 1949, Weikert entered the Stasi in the same role.

Transferring to Berlin in 1952, Weikert was made a deputy minister for security with formal responsibility for various departments, a position he occupied until 1957. (From 1953-55, with the change in the Stasi's status, he was a deputy state secretary.) In 1956 he became head of the Stasi administration for Greater Berlin; he then transferred to lead the Stasi office in Erfurt, a position he held for twenty-five years. The recipient of numerous awards from the East German and Czech governments, Weikert ceased working for the Stasi in 1982.

Joseph Gutsche

Joseph Gutsche (1895-1964) was a bookbinder who became a leading Stasi officer. In 1950, with the rank of Chefinspekteur, he led the Stasi in Saxony.

The son of a worker, Gutsche's bookbinding apprenticeship was cut short by the First World War. He joined the German army in 1915. Having been captured by the Russian army, Gutsche escaped and made his way to Rostov-on-Don. He then became a very early member of the Red Army, in which he fought against counter-revolutionaries; he also joined the Bolshevik party.

After returning to Germany Gutsche took part in two notable armed uprisings, in Berlin and Hamburg. He received military-political training in Moscow in the mid-1920s, but once back in Germany was imprisoned for three years for his political activities. After release he went back to the Soviet Union and was given the (high) rank of Regimental Commissar in the Red Army; he then spent a decade carrying out special tasks (Sonderaufgaben) in China and other countries, probably for the RU.

As a highly experienced guerrilla fighter and intelligence specialist, in 1942 Gutsche and his son Rudolf joined a Soviet partisan unit operating behind German lines in Ukraine. In this role Gutsche saw in his fiftieth birthday. Father and son then took leading positions in Saxony's postwar security police, Joseph as president of the Kripo in Dresden, Rudolf as head of K5 in Leipzig.

Both entered the Directorate for the Protection of the National Economy in 1949, and the Stasi upon its foundation a few months later.

Gutsche, who was said to speak Russian better than German, was something of a Stasi legend. As well as serving as Stasi chief for Saxony, Gutsche's other roles included leading the Stasi in Dresden, running one of the Stasi's principal special tasks units, heading the internal information department, and finally running its control inspectorate, in which role he spot-checked Stasi operations and personnel. He retired in 1957.

Karl Kleinjung

Karl Kleinjung (1912-2003) was a hairdresser who became chief of the Stasi's military counter-intelligence department. In 1950, with the rank of Chefinspekteur, he led the Stasi's Greater Berlin office.

Kleinjung joined the KJVD in 1929, following his hairdressing apprenticeship. The next year he joined the KPD and the Rotfrontkämpferbund. In 1933 he was involved in the murder of an SA Brownshirt during a street fight, and fled to the Netherlands. He helped to organise an illicit KJVD congress in Holland, for which he and Albert Hössler were arrested; Kleinjung was interned in Fort Honswijk and later deported to Belgium. (Hössler was killed in the Second World War after being parachuted into Germany as a Soviet agent.)

While serving in the International Brigades in Spain, Kleinjung reportedly served as personal bodyguard to Naum Eitingon, a senior NKVD officer stationed in Barcelona. Towards the end of the conflict Kleinjung took up a counter-intelligence role, which presumably involved repressing – and perhaps executing – political deviationists. After the war he made it to the Soviet Union and for a time worked in a car factory at Gorky. When the Axis invaded he was trained in codes, ciphers and radio operations, and from 1943 to 1945 he served with Belorussian partisans and was involved in NKVD special operations. According to one account he took part in the assassination of Wilhelm Kube, a top Nazi official.

Kleinjung then received further political education in Moscow before returning to Germany in 1946 and joining the SED. He became district police chief for Nordhausen and then chief of the border police at Mühlhausen. In 1947 he was appointed deputy head of the Volkspolizei in Thuringia and then Volkspolizei chief in Mecklenburg. At the end of the decade he was back in Russia, taking a course for Volkspolizei officers at the Military Academy in Saratov.

In 1950 Kleinjung joined the Stasi as its chief for Greater Berlin. He then led the office at the Wismut mining concern. By 1955 he was head of Main Department I, responsible for military counter-intelligence. He held this post until his retirement in 1981. Kleinjung's later career was overshadowed by his involvement in attempted and actual killings. He helped devise a plan to assassinate Rudi Thurow, a deserter from the border troops. Reputedly at least three attempts were made to kill Thurow in West Berlin, although the plan was ultimately abandoned. In 1976 Kleinjung drafted an internal instruction called 'Plan of action to prevent further border provocations'. This document appeared to prompt the killing of Michael Gartenschläger, who was shot dead by Stasi special forces in a border area as he tried to dismantle weapons systems as a protest.

Kleinjung's connection with Gartenschläger's death saw him charged with manslaughter in the 1990s, but after many interruptions the case against him was dropped in 2002 due to his ill health. He died the following year.

MORE FIRST CLASS COMRADES

Bruno Beater

Bruno Beater (1914-1982) was a carpenter and delivery driver who became a deputy minister of security in East Germany.

The son of a worker, Beater trained as a carpenter and drove a bread delivery van, but also experienced spells of unemployment. He joined the KJVD and RGO in 1928. He did some military service in the emerging Wehrmacht during the 1930s, and by 1939 had properly joined the force.

Beater's Wehrmacht service is highly unusual among Stasi executives. He reached the senior NCO rank of Oberfeldwebel and won an Iron Cross. One possible explanation of this anomaly is that Beater was reporting to communist secret agencies the whole time; certainly in his later Stasi career he was welcomed in Moscow. In 1944, having defected to the Red Army, he was quickly admitted into the National Committee for Free Germany, which he served as a political re-educator in POW camps.

After the war Beater was given a series of police jobs: chief of the Kriminalpolizei in Hennigsdorf, chief of police in Schönwalde and then, until 1949, chief of the Kripo in Nauen. He then entered the Directorate for the Protection of the National Economy. He joined the Stasi upon its foundation, working first under Karl Kleinjung in its administration for Greater Berlin, where he headed Department V, responsible for tackling political opposition. He led Main Department V for the entire Stasi from 1953 to 1955, and was then appointed a deputy security minister, with various responsibilities. He performed this role until 1974, when he retired, although he continued to work informally for the Stasi until his death.

Gustav Borrmann

Gustav Borrmann (1895-1975) was a stonemason who became the first head of general administration at the Stasi, and its first head of propaganda.

Born into a working-class family in Halle, Borrmann joined the Socialist Working Youth, the youth wing of the Independent Social Democratic Party, in 1911. He was drafted when the First World War began and fought until 1918. While in the army Borrmann joined the Spartacus League and, in 1919, was among the founders of the KPD in Saxony-Anhalt. In 1921 he was sentenced to eighteen months in Coswig prison for fighting during the Kapp Putsch.

From 1923 onwards Borrmann was an energetic figure in the KPD. As a district party secretary, he agitated against the occupying forces in the Ruhr and was managing director of the local KPD publishing service. He then became head of distribution for the Neues Deutschland publishing house and an important party newspaper, the *Arbeiter Illustrierte Zeitung*. He was also a regional chairman of the Rotfrontkämpferbund and its successor organisation, the KgF, from 1924 to 1933.

Borrmann was arrested in March 1933 and held in concentration camps for a year. After his release he worked for the illegal KPD. In 1935 he emigrated for Czechoslovakia, before moving on to Moscow. From this point until the end of the Second World War he worked variously as a stonemason, a proofreader of German publications, and an organiser of the German communist exiles living in Kazakhstan. Although accounts differ, it is possible he served in the International Brigades around 1937-38.

In 1946 Borrmann returned to Germany, joined the SED, and became deputy chief of the Volkspolizei in Saxony-Anhalt. In 1950 he entered the Stasi as head of its general administration department. He was promoted to colonel and in 1954 became leader of the new Agitation Department, responsible for propaganda. He retired in 1958 and died in 1975. Like those of other Stasi and SED notables, Borrmann's ashes were interred in the Memorial of the Socialists at the Friedrichsfelde cemetery in Berlin. In 1951 the East German authorities rededicated this cemetery, which was built in the nineteenth century, installing a large stone monument with the inscription 'The dead exhort us'.

Friedrich Dickel

Friedrich Dickel (1913-1993) was a metal worker who became East German interior minister.

The son of a bricklayer, Dickel was active in the KJVD from 1928. He joined the KPD in 1931 and the KgF, successor to the Rotfrontkämpferbund, in 1932; he also worked for Red Aid.

When the Nazis came to power Dickel continued to perform undercover work for the KPD and was arrested twice. After a three-month prison term in 1935 he emigrated for France and then the Netherlands, where for a year he was a communist activist. In 1936 he went to Spain and became a company commander in the Thälmann Battalion. He then attended an RU guerrilla training school at Benimàmet near Valencia. Withdrawn from Spain, Dickel carried out covert missions for the RU in Finland, China and Japan, where he was arrested in 1943 and incarcerated. In May 1946 he made it back to Moscow, and from there to Berlin.

Dickel joined the SED and held a senior position in the Leipzig Volkspolizei until 1949. After studying at the police officers' school at Kochstedt he became a leader of the Department of Political Culture at the interior ministry. In 1952 he was promoted to the rank of major general, and for four years headed the political administration of the Kasernierte Volkspolizei.

When the NVA was created, Dickel became deputy defence minister and head of the army's political administration. At the end of the 1950s he was posted to the General Staff Academy in Moscow, where he took a diploma in military science. He was then made permanent representative to the staff of the Soviet armed forces in Germany.

Dickel was one of the SED executives to oversee the construction of the Berlin Wall. Once it was built he reached the highpoint of his career, serving as East German interior minister from 1963 until 1989. By 1984 he had attained the GDR's highest military rank, army general. He was also a member of the SED Central Committee and a deputy of the Volkskammer for more than twenty years.

Heinrich Fomferra

Heinrich Fomferra (1895-1979) was a miner and factory worker who became head of the minister's secretariat at Stasi headquarters. A leading instructor of sabotage and guerrilla warfare, for much of his life Fomferra was a trusted subordinate of Wilhelm Zaisser.

Fomferra was born in Essen in the Ruhr, and followed in his father's footsteps as a miner; he also worked as a labourer in a brick factory. He joined the Social Democratic Party in 1912 and fought as a conscript in the First World War from 1915 to 1918. Dissatisfied with the SPD, Fomferra joined the more radical Independent Social Democratic Party in 1919. The following year he fought in the Red Ruhr Army during the Kapp Putsch. He also joined the KAPD or Communist Workers' Party of Germany, an independent communist party that advocated workers' councils and syndicalism.

Fomferra was given an eighteen-month prison sentence for raiding the cash office of a tram depot to get funds for the KAPD. Once released he worked as a builder in Essen and a carpenter in Jena. Returning to the Ruhr, he left the KAPD and joined the KPD, leading a local paramilitary group, the Proletarian Hundred, until its dissolution by the authorities in October 1923. A few months later he was imprisoned again; sixteen months in Bielefeld jail for possession of weapons and explosives.

Just as Fomferra's first incarceration had led to his joining the KPD, his second led to another hardening of his communist faith. After release he worked as a builder, roadmender and printer, became a leader of the Rotfrontkämpferbund in Essen, and subsequently a KPD functionary for the Ruhr region.

In 1930, using the alias Karl Schwarzmann, Fomferra received military-political training at a Comintern school in Moscow, probably the Lenin School. After graduating he became an agent of the KPD's AM-Apparat for the Ruhr, and organised a reporting cell at the Krupp works in Essen. In 1932 he returned to Russia, where he spent three years giving explosives and weapons training under Wilhelm Zaisser at the Comintern school in Babovka. He also worked as a secret courier for the OMS.

Fomferra went to Spain when the civil war broke out, serving as a captain and battery commander in the XIV International Brigade. Then, posing as an Austrian called Hans Laber, he became an instructor at the RU guerrilla training school at Benimàmet. The school had a dual purpose: to train partisans for frontline operations, and to gather a reserve of saboteurs and radio specialists for use by the Soviet Union outside Spain. Every senior instructor at the school was German. Richard Stahlmann led one section, and Friedrich Dickel was among Fomferra's top pupils.

By now Fomferra was an especially trusted Soviet asset. Ordered back to Moscow in May 1937, he undertook radio technology training with the RU. In 1938 he was sent to work as an illegal radio operator in Germany and then Belgium. After another spell of RU training in Moscow, he carried out secret missions to Paris, Brussels and Switzerland during 1939. Undoubtedly these concerned the establishing of radio networks for the Red Orchestra, the well-known Second World War spy ring.

In November 1939 Fomferra was sent to Hungary to set up an RU sabotage network in the armaments industry. The following year he was ordered to Slovakia, where he helped to form 'sleeper' guerrilla units and prepare them for use in the forthcoming war. By this time the Nazi authorities knew of Fomferra's importance, but not his whereabouts. In 1940 his name appeared on the SS blacklist of nearly 3,000 people to be arrested after a German occupation of Britain.

In February 1942 Fomferra was arrested by the Gestapo in Bratislava and sentenced to twelve years' imprisonment. Under torture he revealed much information about his clandestine work and colleagues. This understandable indiscretion was later used against him in the political infighting of East Germany. He was freed from prison by Slovak partisans in 1944 and took part in the Slovak National Uprising, serving as political commissar of a partisan unit and then briefly in the interior ministry of the new provisional government.

Fomferra returned to eastern Germany in 1945 and began working for the forestry administration in Brandenburg. In 1946 he was employed in the German Administration of the Interior (DVdI). By 1947 he was a senior police official in K5, in which role he sharply criticised the practice of hiring former Nazis and Wehrmacht personnel for administrative positions in the Soviet zone. He subsequently led the Department of Political Culture at the DVdI and, in 1949, was in the small minority of K5 personnel selected to serve in the Directorate for the Protection of the National Economy.

In 1950 Fomferra was appointed head of statistics for the newly founded Stasi. The following year he became head of the secretariat of minister Wilhelm Zaisser, continuing decades of the pair's relationship as boss and deputy. Fomferra was made chairman of the SED's internal watchdog, the Control Commission, within the Stasi. Yet because of his proximity to Zaisser, when the latter was disgraced Fomferra had to resign.

However, Fomferra remained trusted by the East German authorities. He was retained by the Ministry of the Interior and entered the border police as a lieutenant colonel, also leading the Control Commission for his unit at Pätz. In 1957 the Ministry of National Defence appointed Fomferra deputy chief of Gustav Röbelen's Dienststelle R, which trained guerrilla fighters for acts of sabotage in West Germany in the event of war. Röbelen's outfit of around sixty personnel ignored officialdom and became something of a law unto itself. Partly as a result, it was investigated by the Stasi and reorganised under the misleading name of the Administration for Patriotic Education. Röbelen and Fomferra were retired from active service.

In retirement Fomferra was made a full colonel of the National People's Army, lived mostly in Berlin, and received two high awards for his role in the liberation of Slovakia. His ashes were interred in the Memorial of the Socialists at the Friedrichsfelde cemetery.

Hans Fruck

Hans Fruck (1911-1990) was a lathe operator who spent more than two decades as deputy chief of Stasi foreign intelligence.

Born into a working-class Berlin family, Fruck joined the Socialist Working

Youth in 1925. Like many of those whose biographies appear here, he dropped his socialism in favour of communism, joining the KJVD in 1927 and the KPD in 1929. From 1930 to 1933 Fruck worked as a clerk and sub-editor for the RGO. When the Nazis seized power he participated in the underground resistance, working illegally for a Berlin metalworkers' union, the RGO, and the Federation of German-Jewish Youth.

Fruck then went into exile, and served in the International Brigades from 1936 to 1938. After the Spanish war he returned to Germany, where he found work as a carter, locksmith and machinist. During the Second World War, together with his wife Carmen, Fruck joined the renowned resistance group led by Herbert Baum, and organised a cell at the Raboma factory in Berlin. He was arrested in 1943, convicted of high treason, and sentenced to five years' imprisonment. He managed to survive his term at Brandenburg-Görden prison, although his mother-in-law was murdered in the Plötzensee jail.

In 1945 Fruck was appointed chief of a Berlin police station. The following year he joined the SED and was given responsibility for locating and chasing wanted persons for the Berlin Kriminalpolizei. He was deputy chief of the Berlin Kripo from 1948 to 1950.

Fruck joined the Stasi upon its founding, working first in its Greater Berlin administration under Karl Kleinjung. In 1952 he replaced Kleinjung as chief and was promoted to colonel; the following year he was made a major general. Fruck then moved to the foreign intelligence service, and from 1956 was a deputy chief of its mature version, the HVA. After serving under Markus Wolf for more than twenty years, he retired in 1977.

Erich Jamin

Erich Jamin (1907-1976) was a baker and builder who became chief of K5 and head of the Stasi's department for invigilating the East German police and interior ministry.

The son of a locksmith, Jamin performed the above jobs as well as enduring lengthy periods of unemployment. He joined the KPD in 1929. In 1933 he was arrested and sent to the Brandenburg (Havel) concentration camp. Although he emerged and survived for a year or so, he was rearrested and spent six years in Brandenburg prison, then two years in Sachsenhausen.

In 1944 Jamin was conscripted into the Dirlewanger SS penal brigade, but was captured by the Red Army and incarcerated. Having returned to Germany in 1947, he was appointed chief of K5, thus becoming a senior secret police officer. He entered the Directorate for the Protection of the National Economy in 1949 and the Stasi upon its founding, working for Departments VI ('state apparatus') and V (political opposition). For some years he led the section of

Department V that dealt with social democrats. In 1959 he became chief of Main Department VII, which secured the police and interior ministry. He performed this role until his retirement in 1965.

Karl Maron

Karl Maron (1903-1975) was a machinist who became East German interior minister.

A keen wrestler in the workers' sport movement, Maron joined the KPD in 1926, becoming leader of a party cell at the Siemens works in Berlin. In 1931 he took on a senior role in the Rotsport organisation. When the Nazis seized power Maron spent a year as an underground party activist; he then emigrated for Copenhagen, where he became an editor at the press service of Red Sport International, a Comintern organisation. In 1935 Maron relocated to Moscow and represented Red Sport International on the Executive Committee of the Comintern, the ECCI. He then worked in the ECCI press and information department. In the Second World War, he was a war reporter and an editor at *Freies Deutschland*, the newspaper of the National Committee for Free Germany.

Maron returned to Germany in 1945 with Walter Ulbricht's initiative group. He became a senior SED councillor for Berlin and also worked as an editor at *Neues Deutschland* for a year or so. In 1950 he was appointed chief of the Volkspolizei, and from 1955 to 1963 was East German interior minister. He resigned the post due to ill health – Friedrich Dickel replaced him – but continued as a member of the Volkskammer until 1967. He also led the SED Central Committee's public opinion research department. Maron's ashes were interred in the Memorial of the Socialists at the Friedrichsfelde cemetery.

Gustav Röbelen

Gustav Röbelen (1905-1967) was a clerk who eventually led the East German programme to train guerrillas and saboteurs for use in West Germany.

An ironmonger's son, Röbelen was born in Bregenz in western Austria. In 1929 he joined the KPD in Bremen and became leader of a party cell. He also worked for the RGO and Red Aid, and was a member of the KgF, the successor organisation to the Rotfrontkämpferbund.

After the Nazi seizure of power, Röbelen was arrested and charged with assault and explosives violations. He fled to Belgium, where he carried out clandestine cross-border work for the KPD. He was arrested again in 1934, but managed to escape and went on to lead a group of German emigrants in Ghent.

Röbelen went to Spain in 1936 and received training as a guerrilla and saboteur. In February 1937 he took command of a special partisan armoured group. He joined the Spanish communist party, and subsequently carried out a number of covert missions around Europe for the NKVD. In 1939 he made it to the Soviet Union, where he worked as a locksmith and briefly attended a Comintern school. When the Axis invaded he was mobilised as an NKVD officer; his expertise in explosives and sabotage meant he probably entered the NKVD's foreign brigade for special operations, the OMSBON. From late 1941 to 1943 he performed clandestine work in Iran. He then served briefly as a political re-educator in POW camps before taking part in NKVD partisan operations in Belorussia and Lithuania.

Röbelen returned to Germany in 1946. Initially he worked in a commission for sequestration and confiscation, in which role he helped the Soviet authorities to punish and dispossess war criminals. In 1948 he was made deputy chief of the German Economic Commission, the DWK, and the following year became a security representative in the SED Central Committee. It was in this party position – and eventually holding the rank of major general – that Röbelen played a key role in building up the Stasi, Volkspolizei, Kasernierte Volkspolizei and National People's Army. He was considered a close ally of Walter Ulbricht, serving as secretary to Ulbricht's Politbüro Security Commission.

Röbelen was then given command of his own agency, the Dienststelle R, responsible for planning guerrilla warfare and sabotage in the Federal Republic. When this unit was reorganised, he was transferred to run the training programme of the Ministry of Transport. He retired in 1964. His ashes were interred in the Memorial of the Socialists at the Friedrichsfelde cemetery in Berlin.

Richard Stahlmann

Richard Stahlmann (1891-1974) was a carpenter who became an early leader of Stasi foreign intelligence.

Stahlmann – an alias that honoured Stalin – was born Artur Illner in Königsberg. Following military service and British captivity during the First World War, he joined the KPD in 1919. He rose quickly in the party's military department, and in 1923 joined the KPD Military Council as a specialist in weapons smuggling.

The following year Stahlmann emigrated for the Soviet Union, where he was granted Soviet citizenship and joined the Bolshevik party. He underwent further military-political training and for several years was employed as an agent of the Comintern and RU. Under the cover of a member of Soviet trade delegations, Stahlmann carried out missions in France, the Netherlands and Czechoslovakia; his task was to create communist cells within those countries' armed forces. In 1927 the RU sent him to China, where he was to support the communist insurrection in Canton and agitate among Kuomintang (Chinese nationalist) soldiers. This episode resulted in messy failure, but Stahlmann managed to escape and return to Moscow, accompanied by some Chinese delegates to the Comintern.

Stahlmann attended the Lenin School in the early 1930s, and became a secretary to Comintern leader Georgi Dimitrov, in which role he specialised in propaganda aimed at the Balkans. In 1933 Dimitrov and Stahlmann were arrested by the Gestapo after the Reichstag Fire incident. Reputedly, Stahlmann toughed out his subsequent interrogation with great verve, contributing to his legend; a later MI6 report described him as 'a man of daring and brutality'.[4] During the Spanish Civil War, in which he was known as Richard the Partisan, Stahlmann served as a sabotage instructor and commanded the '1er Batallón Motorizado de Guerilleros'. This unit of around eighty brigade soldiers, mostly Scandinavians, waged partisan warfare behind Nationalist lines. Some of its members later joined Ernst Wollweber's maritime sabotage network.

During the Second World War, Stahlmann tried to organise communist resistance inside Germany from a base in Sweden. He was said to have escaped to Moscow on the day he was due to be arrested by the Swedish police. After the war he performed intelligence tasks for the SED, building up its secret Transport Department to smuggle funds and propaganda to the KPD in western Germany. In this capacity Stahlmann helped to organise the 1950 abduction of Kurt Müller, deputy leader of the western KPD, who then spent five years as a prisoner of the Soviet Union.

In 1952 Stahlmann briefly succeeded Anton Ackermann as head of the GDR's first foreign intelligence service. From 1956 until his retirement in 1960, Stahlmann served as a deputy chief of foreign intelligence, now known as the HVA, under Markus Wolf. After his death in 1974, his ashes were interred in the Memorial of the Socialists at the Friedrichsfelde cemetery. In 1986, the Stasi published a hagiography called *The life of a professional revolutionary – the memories of Richard Stahlmann*.

Gustav Szinda

Gustav Szinda (1897-1988) was a machine fitter who became the first head of counter-espionage in the East German foreign intelligence service.

A carpenter's son, Szinda served as a frontline infantryman in the First World War, and in 1920 fought in the Red Ruhr Army against the insurgent nationalists. He joined the KPD and the Rotfrontkämpferbund in 1924. After the Nazi seizure of power Szinda carried out underground party work for almost two years.

In 1935 Szinda emigrated for Amsterdam. Already known as a streetfighter, he became an operative of the KPD's intelligence service. He served in Spain from 1936 to 1938; he was briefly chief of staff and then commander of the Thälmann Battalion. In 1937 he took a leading role in counter-intelligence for the International Brigades, a job that fell under unofficial NKVD direction and meant working closely with Wilhelm Zaisser, Erich Mielke, and top KPD officials. Emphasising the importance of his position, Szinda became a member of the Central Committee of the Spanish communist party.

With the defeat of the Republic Szinda emigrated for Moscow, where he worked for the Comintern. His reputation as a tough interrogator and investigator saw him tasked with vetting the émigré German communists in the Soviet Union. He was said to be suspicious and scathing about many of his party comrades.

In 1943 Szinda was assigned to a partisan unit in Ukraine. After a few months he was parachuted into the Berlin area as an RU agent, but was unable to establish his contacts as planned. He was picked up by the advancing Red Army in spring 1945, and briefly imprisoned by the NKVD. He was then released to work at 'Antifascist School No. 12', where he politically re-educated Wehrmacht prisoners.

Upon returning to Germany in January 1946, Szinda was appointed to the police presidium in Berlin. He then served as the Volkspolizei's head of personnel for Mecklenburg. He became a member of the SED Central Committee, leading its Department for Security Questions from 1949 to 1951. He was then appointed as the first head of counter-espionage for the East German foreign intelligence service, a role he performed for two years. From 1954 to 1958 he headed the Stasi's Department VII, responsible for security in the Volkspolizei and interior ministry. Succeeded in that role by Erich Jamin, Szinda then became chief of the Stasi in Neubrandenburg, where he stayed until his retirement in 1965. His ashes were interred in the Memorial of the Socialists at the Friedrichsfelde cemetery.

Otto Walter

Otto Walter (1902-1983) was a carpenter who became a deputy minister of security in East Germany.

A carpenter's son, Walter took up his father's trade in Upper Silesia. In 1920 he joined the KJVD and KPD, subsequently performing a series of district leadership roles for both organisations. When the Nazis seized power Walter tried to continue underground work, but was arrested in December 1933. Thereafter he was incarcerated, serving three years in prison and then being transferred to Sachsenhausen, where he spent the remainder of the Nazi era.

After liberation from the camp, Walter became a leading KPD and then SED functionary in Saxony-Anhalt. Like Otto Last, he was a favoured party member brought into the Directorate for the Protection of the National Economy when it was founded in 1949. Walter then spent three years as head of the SED administration within the Stasi. In 1953 he was promoted to deputy minister of security, with responsibility for various functions, and later became a member of the Stasi Kollegium. Walter left the Stasi in 1964, reportedly due to differences with Erich Mielke.

Part III

Stalinism in Action

'[It is said] that we have hired comrades who can't write. It seems to me that what is important is that this comrade, who perhaps can't write, knows how to win and what to do to destroy enemies. Let's see how many can write splendidly and how wonderfully they can blather on, and then let's check to see how many enemies they've destroyed... [if a comrade] can't even sign his own name, that's not important. If he knows who the enemy is, he's on the right path.'

Erich Mielke to a meeting of SED activists in the Stasi[1]

26

Rostock, 1950

A photograph exists of the personnel at the Stasi's Rostock office in 1950. They are enjoying what looks like a celebratory meal; fourteen men and twelve women, some of the men in uniform and others in plainclothes, some standing and others seated at long tables covered with plates, ashtrays, vases of flowers and bottles of beer. On the wall behind the group hangs a large hand-painted banner, framed by the GDR and Soviet flags and topped with a medallion with the Stasi's shield and sword emblem just visible upon it. To one side of the banner hangs a portrait of Stalin. On the other side hangs a portrait whose subject has been inked out, probably in the years after the photo was taken; a common sight in communist photographic portraiture, where it was often necessary to doctor images showing heroes who had since fallen from grace. The banner proclaims: 'State security is the highest duty, so relentlessly fight all spies, agents and saboteurs, for the peace, freedom and unity of Germany'.

Some of these Stasi officers are grinning, perhaps drunkenly; their eyes are shining and their arms are draped around colleagues. Others look solemn and uneasy and avoid looking directly at the camera. There are, no doubt, Soviet liaison officers among the group; perhaps they are the older men dressed in dour civvies. A row of younger men, standing at the back, probably comprises personnel from Departments VIII and IX – the Stasi's foot soldiers, responsible for watching suspects, making arrests and interrogating prisoners. At least two of them appear to have a broken nose. The women are probably secretaries, nurses and wives – the Stasi in Rostock had no female officers at this time – and they are dressed in as much finery as they can muster in postwar Germany: dresses with frills, pearl necklaces. One holds hands, surreptitiously, with an older man. Another tries to lean out of the photo frame, reluctant to be included.

This unintentionally eerie image, taken possibly on May Day or on the first birthday of the GDR, is made eerier with the knowledge that, two years later, the head of the Stasi in Rostock – who could be the central figure in this group – was dismissed for his excessive use of torture.[1] The image depicts the Stasi in the first months of its existence. It is under close Soviet direction. It is establishing its role and tasks. Most of its personnel are young working-class men who previously were working as manual labourers, or have just left school with few qualifications. Most have no experience of secret police work, and are undoubtedly going through a baptism of fire. At this point in its history, the Stasi kills if it has to.

The early 1950s were bloody years of Stalinism in action.[2] The Stasi set about silencing real and perceived enemies of Moscow and the SED with apparent relish. Its leaders were poachers-turned-gamekeepers, a situation that tends to arise after a revolution or civil war. The criminals become the lawmakers; the hunted, the hunters. Stasi operations were yet to acquire the creepy subtlety for which they are renowned. Instead, violence, blackmail, humiliation and sleep deprivation were applied routinely to suspects and prisoners, whose relatives usually were not told of their arrest or whereabouts.[3] According to Jens Gieseke, 'The main methods of the State Security Service during this phase consisted of arbitrary arrests and extorting confessions using unceasing nightly interrogations and other torture methods.'[4]

The experiences of a worker from Erfurt, arrested by the Stasi for alleged sabotage in the workplace, are characteristic. Forced into signing a confession, he recalled that 'I was beaten during my questioning' by two Stasi employees 'with their hands and with a hose with a [metal] spiral inside it. For this reason and because they didn't believe me I said yes to everything.'[5] Another arrestee, who was to face an accusation of spying, recounted the moment of his arrest, with 'a blanket over my head, a very severe reception'. He was bundled into the back of a van; after a drive, he was dragged from the van to a cellar. His cell had no windows, just an air vent high on one wall. There was a plank bed and a bucket. He was then kept in solitary confinement for one and a half years, and tortured by being locked for lengthy periods inside a cell of only one square metre. He recalled German jailers taking part in this torture, but his interrogations were conducted by Soviet personnel; from February 1950 until October 1951, there were only three occasions when he met a German interrogator.[6]

Anyone accused of spying for the Western 'fascists' and 'imperialists' could expect similar treatment. Increasingly, opponents of the SED were getting involved in this perilous activity. Unlike in Ukraine, Poland and the Baltic states, there were no sustained armed attacks on communist authority in East Germany.[7] Most resistance groups were unarmed, but many had contact with, or could find themselves being coordinated by, Western parties and organisations that were considered arch enemies of the East German state. Above all, these were the Ostbüros (Eastern Offices) of the SPD and the western CDU, which had followed the SPD's example in creating an Ostbüro; and two anti-communist organisations operating from West Berlin, the Combat Group Against Inhumanity (KgU) and the Investigative Committee of Free Jurists (UfJ).*

Of course, the Soviet security forces and the Stasi also persecuted individuals and unorganised resisters. The members of Leipzig's so-called 'Belter Group' – which wasn't truly a group – were discovered quite by chance, when in October 1950 two students were taken into police custody for failing to carry identity papers. Discovered in the pocket of one of them, Herbert Belter, was a letter in which a friend opined how much pleasanter it was to live in western Germany. The discovery led to a Stasi investigation which found that some of Belter's friends were in possession of anti-SED and anti-Soviet leaflets. A Soviet military tribunal sentenced eight of them to twenty-five years' hard labour and Belter to death. He was shot in Moscow, although his fate was only clarified in the 1990s.[8]

The Stasi was greatly influenced by the MGB's fast and loose manipulations of the law. For the first couple of years of its existence, Stasi investigators 'worked practically in a legal vacuum'.[9] In theory, the Reich code of criminal procedure still applied in the GDR. But the legal grounds for many cases continued to be SMAD Order 201, Allied Control Council Directive 38, and – especially when it came to defining crimes and their punishment – Article 58 of the Soviet Russian penal code. Even when the Stasi was formally subjected to the supervision of public prosecutors' offices, which occurred when a new code of criminal procedure was enacted in 1952, this 'changed little in the practices of MfS investigators'.[10]

Article 6 of the East German constitution was to be another indomitable instrument in the hands of the Stasi, prosecutors, and judges. The article didn't contain concrete definitions of offences or a framework for punishments. But it did criminalise 'incitement to the boycotting of democratic institutions and organisations, incitement to murder democratic politicians, expressions of religious, racial, or national hatred, [and] military propaganda and warmongering'.[11] As such, the article enabled the authorities to prosecute 'espionage', 'sabotage', 'diversion' and 'terror' as anti-state crimes (Staatsverbrechen), mostly by employing 'incitement to the boycotting of democratic institutions' and 'warmongering' as, technically, the offence in question. Offenders were subject to open-ended sentences that included the death penalty.[12]

In March 1951, ominously, the Soviet authorities handed over Hohenschönhausen prison in Berlin to the Stasi. For the next decade East Germany's

---

* KgU: Kampfgruppe gegen Unmenschlichkeit. UfJ: Untersuchungsausschuss Freiheitlicher Juristen.

most important political prisoners were kept in its basement wing, known as the 'U-boat' for its wetness, darkness, and metallic austerity. Prisoners held elsewhere in Hohenschönhausen suffered from too much light. Cells were lit day and night by 'incandescent' bulbs over their doors, causing inmates to lose all track of time.[13]

27

Cleansing the SED

In time-honoured communist fashion, among the first to suffer the wrath of the SED were its own members. In August 1950 the Central Committee ordered a clean-up of the party's ranks. The purge was directed chiefly at 'western émigrés' – those KPD members who had spent the war years exiled in countries other than the Soviet Union. Former SPD members and prisoners of war held by the Western Allies were also targeted. They were all considered tainted with the deviant ideas of bourgeois societies.

The SED's most influential leaders, Walter Ulbricht and Wilhelm Pieck, were determined to create an ideologically pure party, a 'monolithic, hierarchical body' that could dominate 'an increasingly centralised economy and administration'.[1] In their eyes it was vital to crack down on members who expressed forms of ideological difference, or even personal independence. At least, this was one motivation for the purge. Another was anti-Semitism. Taking a lead from Stalin's postwar disparagement of Soviet Jews, including the preposterous 'Doctors' Plot' in which the MGB slandered the Jewish doctors working at the Kremlin, the SED, helped by the Stasi, purged a conspicuous number of Jewish SED members.

The pretext for much of this persecution was the Rajk and Slánský show trials held in Hungary and Czechoslovakia, and the related investigations into Noel Field. Field was an American aid worker who had been acquainted with intelligence officers from several combatant countries during the war, and had been lured into detention behind the Iron Curtain in 1949. Many of those affected by the Field affair were Jewish, and some were accused of being run by Field as agents of US intelligence. One notable victim of the trials was the interwar communist propaganda expert Otto Katz, who was executed after the Slánský debacle.

In East Germany, friendship or association with SED executive Paul Merker proved especially dangerous; he was arrested in another wave of anti-Semitic operations towards the end of 1952. Also arrested was Bruno Goldhammer, deputy head of the government press office, who was sentenced to death by a Soviet military tribunal, although his sentence was then commuted to twenty-five years' hard labour. Merker, a western émigré, was something of an independent soul, with a long history of disciplinary problems behind him; in the early 1930s he had been expelled from the KPD secretariat.[2] Now he was accused of Zionism, among other offences. Trotskyism and Titoism were also common allegations of the period; the MGB claimed it had evidence that Noel Field was helping Marshal Tito to undermine the Soviet Bloc.

Starting in 1950, SED members began to be expelled from the party only to be arrested several months after their expulsion. At least four of the SED functionaries arrested that year lost their lives. Lex Ende of the *Neues Deutschland* newspaper died of heart failure at a smelting works in Saxony after being sent there as a labourer on probation. A colleague on the paper, Rudolf Feistmann, whose journalism had taken him on trips to London and Prague, was adjudged to have committed suicide after being investigated. So too was Paul Bertz, a party official and pre-war member of the Reichstag who died in custody in Chemnitz. The most well-known case is that of Willi Kreikemeyer, the disgraced president of East Germany's railway system, Deutsche Reichsbahn.

In 1957, after spending years claiming variously that Kreikemeyer was still alive and awaiting trial, or had been executed by the KGB in Moscow, the Stasi finally came out with a semi-official version of his death. It was said to have occurred in custody in August 1950. While in detention Kreikemeyer apparently had asked for some confiscated handkerchiefs to be returned to him; he had knotted three of them together and hanged himself in his cell. His widow Marthe had spent years writing to the SED Central Committee to enquire about her husband's fate. Her letters were ignored, mostly on the advice of Walter Ulbricht, who told colleagues it was unwise to respond to queries from a 'foreigner' – Marthe had never given up her French passport, and had returned to France after her husband's disappearance.

The story is darkened further by the presence of Erich Mielke. During the war he had worked as a conscripted labourer for the Todt Organisation in France. Some of the western émigrés had also been there, and later had given unfavourable reports about Mielke's conduct. It was said that during his interrogation Kreikemeyer had claimed that one 'Leissner' – an alias used by Mielke before the war – had acted as an agent of US intelligence in France, and had received money for this work from Noel Field. So it is thought that Mielke may have used the party purges of the early 1950s to silence the western émigrés, some of whom were unwanted witnesses to his wartime behaviour; hence Kreikemeyer's mysterious death in a Stasi cell.

In some respects, it doesn't look good for Mielke. On at least two occasions in the 1950s he wrote letters to Walter Ulbricht in which he lied about Kreikemeyer's fate, claiming that Kreikemeyer had been transferred to Moscow. However, it is possible that Kreikemeyer was not murdered and indeed killed himself – he was known to be deeply depressed by his fall from grace and expulsion from the SED.

The purges saw the Stasi flaunt legal norms with abandon, as shown in the case of Helmut Brandt. A CDU executive and state secretary in the Ministry of Justice, Brandt was arrested in September 1950 after criticising the Waldheim trials. He was held in the basement of Hohenschönhausen for almost two years before the Stasi obtained an arrest warrant, which it did on 6 August 1952.[3] (A torrid decade followed for Brandt, in which he was routinely abused in prison, released and then rearrested; eventually, in 1964, he became one of the first political prisoners in the GDR to be bought out of jail by the West German government.) Some SED officials were caught in covert contact with Western organisations, like the mayor of Rathenow, Paul Szillat, who carried out unofficial duties for the western SPD. In 1951 he was sentenced on charges of espionage and 'social democracy', although it is unclear how the latter charge was made to stick as a crime.[4]

It wasn't just party officials in East Germany who were purged. The repression extended to the communist party in West Germany, still known as the KPD and, for those in Moscow and East Berlin, worryingly independent. In March 1950 Kurt Müller, deputy chair of the KPD and member of a provincial assembly, was lured into East Germany to attend a meeting with Walter Ulbricht. He found himself accused of Trotskyism, 'brutally' interrogated by Stasi officers – among them Erich Mielke – and thrown into Hohenschönhausen, where he spent the best part of three years in solitary confinement. This was followed by three years in the Gulag, until he benefited from the amnesties granted after Stalin's death and was released. On returning to West Germany he joined the SPD, his communist days over.

Adding to the intrigue around Müller's case was the fact that one of his accusers, Max Reimann, a representative of the western KPD in East Germany, may have denounced Müller in an attempt to secure lenience for his son Josef, a Volkspolizei officer who had defected to the British sector of Berlin in 1949, only to disappear in mysterious circumstances. Josef was thought to have been kidnapped and brought back to East Berlin. If Max Reimann's aim was to save Josef, he failed; it is said that the latter was held for three years in Stasi prisons before being sentenced to fifteen years in the Gulag.[5]

Leo Bauer was another communist with close links to West Germany to suffer in the purges. After the war Bauer spent much time in the western zones, and liaised with the KPD once the SED had been formed, although at the time of his arrest and that of his wife, Margarete, he was living and working in East Germany as editor-in-chief of the Deutschlandsender radio station.

Bauer later alleged that he had been beaten during interrogations – including personally by Erich Mielke – and deprived of sleep for days on end. It isn't difficult to see why Bauer might have aggravated Mielke. He was a western émigré with some knowledge of Noel Field, although Bauer had compounded his problems by unwisely criticising Walter Ulbricht. Accused of being an 'imperialist agent', and suffering physical abuse, Bauer signed a confession that he later retracted as 'entirely exaggerated or fabricated'. A Soviet military tribunal sentenced him to death for counter-revolutionary activities under Russia's Article 58.[6] This was commuted to a Gulag sentence, and Bauer was pardoned in 1955; upon returning to West Germany he too joined the SPD, which was fast becoming a refuge for Marxists who had learned hard lessons about Soviet communism.

Bauer's wife Margarete, typically for the time, was arrested without a warrant and held in a pretrial detention centre for more than a year and a half. During this time she was not interrogated and had no contact with the outside world. This changed in March 1952, when she was taken to the offices of the Stasi administration for Greater Berlin on Prenzlauer Allee and 'thoroughly interrogated'. Although there was no evidence that Margarete had committed any act besides marrying Leo, she was to spend another year and a half in prison.[7]

The chair of the Hamburg KPD, Willi Prinz, and Kurt Müller's successor as deputy chair of the KPD, Fritz Sperling, were also invited to East Berlin for inscrutable reasons and arrested there. Sperling was apprehended at a party clinic where he was receiving medical treatment offered by the SED. Prinz's arrest was less subtle; after getting into a car to be taken to an SED meeting, he was driven straight to prison. Both later alleged torture by the Stasi and MVD.

Prinz faced the standard accusations wheeled out for a communist purge. He had not followed the party line correctly; he had been too lenient towards ideological transgressors; etc. Sperling was accused as part of the Noel Field conspiracy, and vividly described his torture; beaten with fists and steel objects, kicked in the shins, his hair pulled out, his glasses smashed and their platinum frames stolen. Knowing that he had had two heart attacks, one MVD interrogator slapped him repeatedly on the chest.[8] After several years Prinz and Sperling were freed from prison, but neither recovered well. Prinz headed back to West Germany to a subdued life as a manual worker. Sperling died of a heart attack two years after his release.

28

Neutering the National Front

Even as the Soviets and SED were cracking down on unorthodox Marxists, they continued to face opposition from the members of East Germany's non-Marxist parties, and increasingly from the wider population. The Stasi, their guided weapon, was now targeted at CDU and LDPD members in order to silence the dissent.

In August 1950 Günter Stempel, general secretary of the LDPD, was arrested by the Stasi after protesting the use of unity lists in elections. A Soviet tribunal sentenced him to twenty-five years' hard labour, some of which he served at the Vorkuta camp.[1] Stempel survived this ordeal to be amnestied in the mid-1950s. Others were less fortunate. Frank Schleusener, the CDU mayor of Brandenburg, arrested in March 1950, didn't live long enough to face trial. Although the Stasi claimed Schleusener committed suicide in his cell in Potsdam, it is firmly believed he died under torture.[2] In a similar incident Ludwig Baues, CDU city councillor in Cottbus, died in custody shortly after his arrest.[3] The CDU was seen as especially troublesome in Brandenburg, where Stasi chief Wilhelm Zaisser singled out the party for punitive actions. Thus the mayor of Potsdam, Erwin Köhler, and his wife Charlotte, were arrested at the same time as Schleusener. Having confessed to spying and disseminating 'anti-Soviet propaganda', almost certainly under torture, the pair were sentenced to death by the same Soviet tribunal that convicted Stempel. It is possible the Köhlers were accused of espionage because they had been sharing information with the western CDU, an activity that probably hadn't struck them as treacherous. They were shot in Moscow in April 1951.[4] It took almost a decade for their four children to discover anything concrete about their fate.

The unnerving disappearances of National Front politicians, and the harshness of Soviet and SED justice, began to make their mark. During the elections of October 1950, so many SED posters were torn down or defaced that special detachments of the Volkspolizei were formed to guard them; nearly 2,000 incidents of graffiti or damage were reported.[5] The dissatisfaction didn't show in the election results, however, which to the untrained eye looked like an SED triumph. It helped that the party had run a weird pre-election campaign in which a vote for the unity lists was called 'a vote for peace'. Though specious, this concept had perhaps resonated with some of the public, who were greeted at polling stations by imploring groups of flower-bearing Young Pioneers. Ninety-eight percent of the electorate voted, supposedly returning 99.72 percent approval for the unity lists. The pre-allocation of seats in the Volkskammer meant the SED gained 100 seats, the CDU and LDPD sixty each, and the NDPD and DBD forty each. Of the 'mass organisations' in the National Front, with their numerous overt and covert SED members, the trade union federation, the FDGB, was granted forty seats; the Kulturbund and Free German Youth twenty each; the Democratic Women's League and Association of Victims of the Nazi Regime fifteen each; and the Peasants' Mutual Aid Association and Committee of Antifascist Resistance Fighters five each.[6]

This apparent public endorsement of the unity lists was deceptive. SED activists and Stasi collaborators swayed the election results. One method was to deny voters the use of private booths, for a public vote tended to be a fearful and conformist one. The Stasi's Department VI had been tasked, secretly but officially, with vetting the candidates on the unity lists, overseeing the printing of ballot forms, and checking the members of the SED-dominated electoral committees which prepared local constituencies and returned results. Counting was organised in such a way that, right down to the smallest districts, the only two people who knew the final truth of the voting were the local Stasi chief and a returning officer from the Ministry of the Interior.[7] And before a vote had even been cast, the Stasi was putting the frighteners on known troublemakers – pastors, mayors, former landowners. Otto Last, Stasi chief in Mecklenburg, reported to Berlin that 'all people who have shown any negative tendencies and have influence among the population have been warned by us and held responsible for the good conduct of the election.'[8]

After the election the Stasi carried out a big information-gathering effort, unusual for its time, on how the whole event had been managed. Senior officers around the country assessed the performance of the functionaries who had organised the voting. This was a chance to criticise and gather dirt on any official who had been unenthusiastic or disobeyed the instructions of the interior ministry. It was also the start of the long-term practice of keeping a secret record of abstainers. More than anything, the inquiry revealed the utter chaos reigning throughout the young republic.

Numerous undesirables, among them 'Schumacherites' and former Nazis, had made it onto unity lists and election committees. Numerous officials had ignored, or been ignorant of, the people-pleasing measures brought in before the election, such as price cuts, tax breaks and wage increases for state employees. Numerous National Front officials had been assaulted by angry constituents. Many of the National Front speakers sent to pre-election meetings had had no understanding of the GDR government or the election itself. There were many cases of speakers not turning up. The same was true of constituents: at a pre-election rally held in the Neptun shipworks at Rostock, thirty employees from its 6,000-strong workforce made the effort to attend. There was open dissent too. In Mecklenburg, for example, the Stasi and police arrested 361 people for election-related offences; 130 of them were Jehovah's Witnesses who made a protest of abstaining.[9] Viewed like this, the election result was a miracle. Certainly it baffled some of the high-ups at the Stasi and SED.

In fact, there was so much popular discontent around the election, and such a surge of opposition from former social democrats and West German political parties, that the Volkspolizei had launched three operations – codenamed 'Gustav', 'Heinrich' and 'Fritz' – to stop a glut of subversive publications entering East Germany. Those caught distributing such material faced the charge of 'smearing democratic institutions'. The police knew that some of it was coming in by train from the western sectors of Berlin, and that this traffic was organised by activists living in, among other places, Halle, Weimar and Leipzig. During the operations, undercover police officers travelled on trains to these cities while others patrolled their station platforms and waiting rooms. All were looking for suspect travellers or luggage. Huge amounts of leaflets and Western newspapers were seized, and at least one CDU courier was arrested while attempting to meet a contact.[10]

This kind of police activity only exacerbated dislike of the Volkspolizei. Almost certainly it aroused more dissidence than it quelled. The hatred erupted in the town of Saalfeld in August 1951, when a small protest against the arrest of some drunk and disorderly workers from the nearby mines escalated. Armed with picks and axes, townspeople and workers from the Wismut mining complex stormed the police station, where they threatened officers, demanded the release of all prisoners, and insisted that two particularly obnoxious officers be turned over to the mob. Despite reinforcements arriving from the surrounding areas, and the appearance of 2,000 SED activists with instructions to placate the crowd, the disturbances continued into the following day. The mob's fury now centred on the town's court prison; the historian Gary Bruce has noted that popular anger at this point focused on the police and judiciary, given that the Stasi was in its infancy and somewhat obscure. The seriousness of the disturbances, and their incendiary potential, led to the deployment to Saalfeld of almost 800 Volkspolizei officers from Erfurt and Gera, including paramilitaries.[11]

The SED struggled to understand the nature and extent of public opposition. General surveillance of the population was still at a low level. It wasn't until 1952 that the Politbüro set up a department for evaluating the climate of East German society, known as the Leading Organs of the Party and Mass Organisations or LOPM.* Reporting on the mood inside workplaces, organisations and state institutions, the LOPM became one of the most important departments of the SED's Central Committee. It encouraged the deployment of 'brigades' of party activists to trouble spots, to urge greater productivity or impose consensus on the local population – a practice copied directly from the Soviet Union.

Compared to invigilating the public, the task of removing problematic National Front officials from office was perhaps more straightforward. The Stasi engaged in targeted political spying, prompted by Erich Mielke's November 1951 order to its Brandenburg office, to collect information and photographs of the leading provincial members of the non-Marxist parties, the Free German Youth, and the Peasants' Mutual Aid Association. Of the 78,000 people tried during 1950 for political offences – 'state crimes' – many were independent or critical members of National Front parties and organisations.[12] CDU archives record the arrest of more than 400 party members that year, although this figure is almost certainly too low.[13] Pressure from the Soviets and SED saw communist-friendly candidates rise to the top of CDU bodies. The Stasi reported approvingly on those who were 'advancing the progressive line' and helping to 'exclude reactionary forces from the party'.[14] And the more compliant CDU administrations did the SED's job by silencing their own dissenters. For example, when Peter Bloch, member of a provincial assembly, complained of injustice and despotism at a meeting of his CDU group, he was removed from his position and expelled from the party.[15]

This, in its way, is another demonstration of the confusion that reigned in the early days of East Germany. Vocally opposing the Soviet Union or SED wasn't necessarily seen as a good or constructive approach. Some non-Marxists thought that a measure of acquiescence might strengthen their position. Yet slowly and surely, the entities of the National Front became accessories of SED rule. Their more querulous members found themselves arrested, demoted or sacked, or decided to vote with their feet and leave the GDR. From 1950 to 1952, the CDU and LDPD lost at least 70,000 members.[16] Characteristically, Erich Mielke insisted that fleeing CDU members had left behind 'subversive bases' in East Germany. He called for Stasi informers to penetrate CDU bodies and to investigate the former associates of refugees.[17]

---

* Leitende Organe der Parteien und Massenorganisationen.

The growing conformity of those who remained in East Germany can be seen in the CDU's adoption of its 'Christian realism' programme, which made its support for the SED more explicit. By the time of its sixth congress in September 1952, the party officially was recognising the leading role of the SED in all areas of government and society.[18] The SED believed that most of the leading Christian democrats had been brought into line; they were now 'gleichgeschaltet' – 'synchronised'.

However, even as the CDU was affirming the primacy of the SED, the latter was being instructed by the Soviets to carry out another round of arrests and show trials. In December 1952 a court in Erfurt handed prison sentences of between eight and fifteen years to seven Christian democrats accused of maintaining contact with the CDU in West Germany.[19] The Stasi carried out searches of CDU offices, including its headquarters, and sensationally arrested Georg Dertinger, East German foreign minister and a co-founder of the eastern CDU, for allegedly conspiring with the Federal Republic to absorb the GDR. He and five co-defendants were each sentenced to fifteen years in prison.[20]

Dertinger had indeed been striving for a united Germany. After all, that was the policy of the GDR government, albeit with unrealistic conditions attached. The same charge couldn't really be levelled at Dertinger's family; nevertheless, his wife and a fifteen-year-old son were also arrested, his daughter placed in a children's home, and his youngest son put up for adoption. Dertinger didn't benefit from the post-Stalin amnesties of the mid-1950s, and spent almost ten years in a notorious prison at Bautzen. There were two prisons in the town; one, slightly older, was known as the 'Yellow Misery' for the colour of its bricks. Bautzen II was a special Stasi prison for serious political offenders. Dertinger was held at Bautzen II. Only in 1964 was he pardoned.

The public response to a major show trial held in spring 1950 shows the extent to which the populace was already weary of political coercion, even at this early stage of the GDR's history. Among the defendants were the CDU minister for work and social policy in Saxony-Anhalt, Leo Herwegen, and the SED official and former social democrat Dr Willi Brundert. They were accused of economic sabotage and, at this time of collectivisation and the nationalising of industry, their trial was used as a warning to dissenters. Held at the largest theatre in Dessau, it was accompanied by a vigorous propaganda campaign. Every day 1,400 SED activists were bussed to the venue, and proceedings were broadcast simultaneously on the radio. The defendants' opposition to the SED's economic measures was said to have been organised by West German and American 'imperialists', determined to restore capitalism to eastern Germany. Yet when the people of Dessau were exhorted to head to the city's main square to hear the pronouncement of fifteen-year prison sentences, only 300 showed up.[21]

By the autumn of 1950, the residents of East Germany were already complaining of a 'complete overdose of political events'.[22] Their heads were spinning with posters, meetings, trials and directives; as one historian puts it, instead of letting 'the people under their control rebuild their lives in peace, East German Communists (supported by the Soviet occupiers) imposed a regime of continual mobilisation and upheaval'.[23] Already there were at least three discernible forms of public discontent. First there was disgruntlement over 'too much politics', at the way ideology was interfering with everyday life and pleasures (such as being able to travel freely). Then there was disgruntlement over the poor living conditions and material scarcity. Finally, among the politically engaged there was disgruntlement over specific aspects of SED rule. Whenever these three strands coalesced, the SED regime tended to experience its most challenging insurrectionary moments.

People's major political complaints of the early 1950s included the abolition of the SPD, the imprisonment of democrats and members of other National Front bodies, the apparent rearmament that was taking place (especially when armed conflict with West Germany was one of the biggest fears of the moment), the lack of 'legal security' and widespread abuse of the law, the heavy-handed media censorship, and the absence of free elections in which parties could compete with one another. No less galling was the rarity of meat and dairy products, the shockingly poor conditions of housing, the high prices and paucity of goods in state-run shops, and – never to be underestimated – the overbearing presence of Russians.

East Germany, Europe's new flagship of consensual socialism, was beginning to attract international opprobrium. In 1951, Nobel Laureate Thomas Mann sent a 228-page letter to Walter Ulbricht criticising the Waldheim trials and comparing them to the conduct of Hitler's People's Courts.[24] Anger and deprivation led to an increase in clandestine opposition groups inside the GDR. By the end of 1950, Christian democrat resisters and reformers had gathered themselves into an abundance of networks: the Jakob-Kaiser-Gruppe, Arbeitsgemeinschaft Alte Union, Christlich-Demokratischer Kampfbund in Mitteldeutschland, Deutsche Freiheitsliga, Deutsche Widerstandsbewegung gegen den Kommunismus.[25]

These groups, which often worked with the anti-communist organisations springing up in West Berlin and the Federal Republic, distributed leaflets, listened to Western radio broadcasts, defaced SED posters and graffitied government buildings. Crucially, however, some of their members were also prepared to radio secret reports to the Western powers about conditions in East

Germany, or to give political and economic information to such agencies as the CDU Ostbüro, which had joined the SPD Ostbüro as a major hub of organised opposition to the SED.

It was in these activities that political opposition dovetailed with crimes against the state, at least as far as the SED and Stasi defined them. Some CDU activists reported the number of Soviet tanks or fighter aircraft at bases, the frequency of landings at airfields, the layout of Soviet and East German barracks. Much of this activity was part of the US programme of gathering military intelligence. It was a pervasive and fairly successful effort, but one with heavy losses among its amateur spies, and not just because of inexperience and cavalier attitudes to security. Most Germans had not adjusted to the idea of a divided country, and many did not see the GDR as a legitimate state; thus from their perspective, how could they possibly be considered guilty of 'anti-state' crimes? Motivated as they were by Christian, social, or liberal democratic beliefs, and inspired by hopes of peace and German unification, many political resisters and reformers did not see or understand that they were spies.

The CDU had created its Ostbüro to support the party's breakaway faction led by Jakob Kaiser in West Berlin, which offered a home for those Christian democrats who could no longer stomach the East German version of their party. Like its SPD precursor, one major role of the CDU Ostbüro was to vet the Christian democrats who were fleeing East Germany. Suspicions of them were at fever pitch, and were justified. The Ostbüro's leader, Werner Jöhren, was soon the object of malign attention from the Stasi, which for years plotted endless permutations of his downfall.

In late 1950 Erich Mielke issued a two-part guideline to the Stasi's provincial chiefs.[26] Followers of Jakob Kaiser were to be targeted specifically. Shortly beforehand, Kaiser had been placed in charge of the Bonn government's Ministry for All-German Affairs. According to Mielke, in this capacity Kaiser had met with 'representatives of the Anglo-American secret service' with whom he had developed 'criminal schemes' to 'sabotage the 5-year plan' in the GDR. For the Stasi, this was a counter-espionage matter; and so Christian democrat campaigners were to be tackled by its Department IV.

'Kaiser is no longer obscure,' Mielke wrote bitchily. 'He has managed over the past few years to steer a number of leading reactionary CDU officials to the West, who in turn have left behind their bases in the GDR.' His guideline continued:

In order to put a stop to this criminal activity, the following must be reported by 25 December 1950:
1) All CDU officials who have fled to the West in recent years are to be recorded in a list, specifying where they were employed and where they lived and what

their profession was. What function did they exercise within the CDU and for how long? When and why did they flee? Where are they now and where are they employed now? Are their family members also in the West or are they still living in the GDR?

2) For each individual who has fled, it is to be determined with which people he had private, business or political connections before he fled, and with whom he still maintains connections today.

Once these connections have been established, secret co-workers are to be deployed in order to determine with their help what influence these refugees still have on certain circles within the GDR today, and who is working for them.

Mielke was quick to praise the achievements of the SED, and suggested they were causing unease in Western countries:

The successes achieved thanks to the activist movement... the early fulfilment of the two-year plan, and the associated improvement in the material situation of the population of the GDR, are the best proof that the slogan of the SED ['To better one's life under one's own power'] was correct and the time of success has begun. Even the Anglo-American's attempts to disrupt it with their West German lackeys could do nothing to change that. The American imperialists see, however, that the greater the successes in building up a peaceful economy in the GDR, the greater their difficulties in exploiting the West German population for their war aims, and that finally the GDR's successes will be reflected in other Western countries, states under American influence, against the ruling class there and especially against the war plans of American imperialism. Recognising this, the Anglo-Americans are now trying with all the means at their disposal to hinder the peaceful reconstruction in the GDR.

Mielke's instruction reveals that political opposition groups, which the Stasi considered 'espionage centres' run by America and Britain, were springing up faster than the Stasi could cope with them. It also betrays his lack of confidence in the spy-hunters of Department IV. Their work was not yet thorough or systematic. Neither were they keeping the Stasi leadership in Berlin sufficiently informed:

In each new case where concrete findings on espionage are made, a report is to be made [to Berlin HQ] according to the following scheme:

1. When and how did the incident arise (incl. secret co-workers, anonymous notifications, statements)?

2. Which people appear in the case (name, possibly alias, personal details and personal description)?

3. What is known about the connection of the above persons or groups with the enemy espionage service?
4. What specific espionage activity did the individuals engage in:
   a) Industrial espionage (production capacity, workforce, branch of industry, etc.)?
   b) Military espionage (such as airfields, troop movements, armaments, Volkspolizei units, etc.)?
5. Which people have been arrested so far, and which people are under surveillance?
6. When interrogating the previously detained persons, the following points must be observed and excerpts from the interrogation submitted here:
   a) By whom was this person recruited?
   b) When and where were they recruited?
   c) What is the name of the apparatus for which they are working?
   d) Who works for this apparatus, who are the leading persons (name, address, etc.)?
   e) With which persons of the apparatus in question was the person in direct contact?
   f) What did the people look like (personal description), if not known by name?
   g) Which departments of the opposing espionage services or meeting places were created in West Berlin, West Germany or even in the GDR?
   h) Precise information about all locations (street, house number, telephone number, etc.)
   i) Which motor vehicles of the apparatus are known (description with number)?

Department IV personnel were to report the number of secret collaborators being used on each case, explain their instructions, and state where they had been deployed: 'West Berlin, West Germany, [GDR] administrations, etc.' Regular supplementary reports were to be submitted. 'Only if all MfS offices work on this basis,' concluded Mielke, 'is it possible to gain an intimate insight into the enemy's apparatus, as well as an overview of the working methods and tactics used by him, and their goals.'

The results of this counter-espionage approach, no doubt insisted upon by the Soviet authorities, were assessed in an MGB report. Based on the interrogation of prisoners and, possibly, reporting by Stasi agents, the report concluded that the CDU Ostbüro had formed a covert party executive in Thuringia that was trying to attract dissident members. As a result of this intelligence, forty Ostbüro activists, including teachers, mayors, town councillors and civil servants, had been arrested for 'espionage-diversionist' activities.[27]

These resisters sound peaceable, but some resistance groups really were armed and dangerous. One notable case was the 'Michael Group', which consisted of former Wehrmacht personnel who were now members of the CDU and LDPD. When the group's weapons cache in the foothills of the Harz was unearthed, it was found to include grenades, a machine gun, two artillery pieces, and 300 light firearms. Some of these veterans doubtless were motivated by hatred of Russians, or by latent Nazism, or both; the Michael Group, in fact, was the type of outfit that lent weight to the SED's claims that fascists were trying to destroy the GDR. Whatever their motivations, the group was liquidated when two of its members, Engelbert Lohse and Rudi Fuhrmann, were arrested in December 1950 after making a trip to Berlin; shortly afterwards, more than fifty group members were rounded up. It is possible they were exposed by Fuhrmann, who was said to have been released rather quickly. Their fate is unknown, which indicates that they were sent to the Gulag.[28]

Like all vigilant communist authorities, the SED always kept a close eye on the young. Loyal youths needed to be nurtured and promoted; the disloyal needed to be hit hard. In 1951 the party made its first reforms to the university system to encourage working-class students and technical subjects. Six universities and fifteen technical colleges already existed, and twenty-five more were founded. Covering such subjects as medicine and electrical engineering, they were intended to help fill the skills gaps in the GDR. There were several new institutes for physical education too, created in the hope that East Germany's young would attain the corporeal robustness of the communist ideal.

The results looked good on paper. By the end of the decade the number of students in East Germany had risen from the 28,000 of 1951 to 100,000. By 1953 more than half of students were the offspring of manual workers – in 1945 the figure had been nineteen percent.[29] But try as it might, the SED could never quite silence the political dissent emanating from classrooms, or educate enough people to make up for the loss of the professionals who were fleeing westwards.

East Germany hosted the third World Youth Festival in 1951 – the previous editions had been staged in Prague and Budapest – and, as well as serving as a showcase for the GDR and the superiority of socialism, the event gave the Stasi one of its first tastes of a mass operation. The festival, with its motto of 'Peace and Friendship against Nuclear Weapons', was well supplied with delegates from around the Soviet Bloc and east Asia, but many youths and youth leaders from left-wing organisations in West Germany were prohibited from attending. An ambitious plan was hatched to smuggle groups of delegates across the borders. At the same time, it was considered vital to prevent any

Western organisation from disrupting the event with what the Stasi called 'Wühl- und Zersetzungsarbeit' – 'digging and decomposition work', where digging means undermining.

This was Aktion Morgenröte: Operation Red Dawn. Watchers from the Stasi's surveillance branch, Department VIII, joined an operational task force composed of Free German Youth activists and units of the Volkspolizei and Kripo. A measure of paranoia is discernible in the operational plan; for instance, to prevent attacks on SED officials, the Stasi headquarters in the Länder were instructed to reinforce 'guards and the checking of passes in the buildings of ministries, administrations and [state-owned] companies'. The Stasi was also to use secret informers (Geheime Informatoren or GI) to discover any 'preparations or measures' being planned by student and youth groups, for the authorities were determined that the festival should present the world with a slick ideological unity.

Another task was to arrest unwelcome attendees and seize the opportunity to recruit others. After crossing the demarcation line between West and East Germany in rural corners of Mecklenburg, Saxony-Anhalt and Thuringia, West German delegates were to be brought to assembly points where they would be registered and checked against lists drawn up in advance by the Kripo. They would then be accompanied on to Berlin. Meanwhile, undercover Stasi officers at the assembly points were to record the number of infiltrators arrested, and the number of secret collaborators recruited from among the socialist youth of West Germany. To the authorities' delight, the festival ran smoothly. Erich Mielke took personal pride in the Stasi's performance in Operation Red Dawn, afterwards praising Department VIII for its 'successful fight against the enemy'.[30]

Students and youngsters accused of political crimes in the GDR got short shrift. One night in October 1950, in the town of Olbernhau in Saxony, an eighteen-year-old student called Hermann Flade set out to distribute leaflets he had written himself, criticising the Volkspolizei and the GDR's rigged electoral system. He was caught in the act by a police patrol and drew his pocketknife; in the ensuing scuffle a police officer was lightly wounded. Flade managed to get away, but he was identified and arrested two days later.

For weeks Herman Flade was interrogated by the Stasi in preparation for his show trial. (In such a situation, the Stasi would always seek to link a suspect with conspiracies organised by Western powers, and look for chances to brand the accused as fascistic or militaristic.) In most European societies of the early 1950s, any youth who pulled a knife on a police officer could expect rough treatment at the hands of the police. But Flade was sentenced to death for 'incitement to the boycotting of democratic institutions' and attempted murder. The publicity around his show trial misfired, however, sparking protests in the GDR, and even bigger protests in West Germany, over the severity of his sentence. It was commuted to fifteen years in prison, of which Flade served nine.[31]

One of the major iniquities of Soviet and SED rule was becoming more apparent all the time: the exaggeration of crimes and sentences, and the fact that people who were not involved in serious political activity were said to be state enemies and dangerous criminals despite the relative mildness of their acts. The severity of the authorities' legal interpretations and punishments, and the terrible distrust of the population revealed by them, must have taken many East Germans by surprise.

One day in May 1953 a medical student at the University of Greifswald called Horst Erdmann scattered leaflets around the town calling for free elections. The next morning he was awoken by five men with drawn pistols pounding at his door. He was shown an ID; it was the Stasi. At the local headquarters he was stripped naked and then held overnight in a cell. The next day he was put into a 'Green Minna' van, with small compartments for five prisoners, disguised as a bread van. After several hours' drive he was shoved into another Stasi cell, windowless and filthy.

Erdmann endured weeks of sleep-deprived interrogation, followed by weeks of total isolation, with food slipped into his cell by unseen guards. The interrogations then resumed, more violently; and after being kicked repeatedly in the kidneys, and threatened with the arrest of his mother, Erdmann signed a confession. He was tried before a judge and two lay attendees – a female social worker and a stonemason – under the ageing Directive 38 of the Allied Control Council. Convicted of 'Sabotage and spreading fascist propaganda that endangers the peace', he was sentenced to eleven years' hard labour. In a way, Erdmann was lucky. His trial judge was Götz Berger, who the previous year had handed out thirty-two death sentences for political crimes.[32]

Erdmann had made the mistake of asking publicly for a democratic change. Like so much dissidence of the period, his actions were rather innocuous and undirected. At the same time, organisations had become active outside the GDR – especially in West Berlin and West Germany – with the stated aim of challenging Soviet communism and disrupting SED rule. Many of them were collaborating with Western intelligence services. These organisations earned the implacable hatred of East German communists in general, and of the Stasi in particular; and it was with these organisations that the Stasi entered some of its bitterest conflicts.

29

Enemies

During 1950 a number of West German campaign groups and intelligence agencies were classified by the Stasi as major enemies. Notable among them were the Ostbüros of the SPD, the CDU, and a West German liberal party, the Free Democrats (FDP), whose Ostbüro worked closely and covertly with members of East Germany's liberal party, the LDPD. Perhaps the most detested enemies were two anti-communist political organisations, the Combat Group Against Inhumanity (KgU) and the Investigative Committee of Free Jurists (UfJ).

Not that the Stasi forgot its erstwhile fascist opponents. By all appearances, latent Nazism was continuing to make its presence felt in the GDR. In guidelines issued in September 1950, which called once again for the largescale registration of former Nazis, the Stasi listed the state's enemies: terrorists, saboteurs, participants in 'illegal Schumacher work', Trotskyists, former members of illegal fascist organisations, former members of the Gestapo, SD and Abwehr, leading administrators of Nazi camps and prisons, former members of the SS and SA, leading functionaries of the Nazi party and government, members of religious sects, and – just to be on the safe side – 'other people'.[1] Former Nazis and agents of Western intelligence services were given top priority for arrest. In practice the two tended to be conflated, although being an 'Agent of the USA' was deemed a 'more important' crime than being a former Gestapo officer.[2]

Furthermore, the guidelines stated that the 'enemy bases' (Feindzentrale) being built up in West Berlin and the Federal Republic were home to a range of worrying new organisations intent on challenging SED rule. They included the League of German Youth (BDJ), the Association of Political Refugees from the East (VPO), the Association for the Victims of Stalinism (VOS, believed to have been founded by British intelligence officers), and the Federal trade union organisation, the DGB.* Even foreign companies whose assets had been appropriated in East Germany were considered nests of clandestine opposition. Furthermore, the Stasi was expected to help the MGB and MVD in their fight

---

* BDJ: Bund Deutscher Jugend; VPO: Vereinigung Politischer Ostflüchtlinge; VOS: Vereinigung der Opfer des Stalinismus; DGB: Deutscher Gewerkschaftsbund.

against anti-communist Russian émigré organisations, especially the National Labour Alliance of Russian Solidarists (NTS), the Union of the Struggle for the Liberation of the Peoples of Russia (SBONR), and the Central Association of Post-War Emigrants (ZOPE).

As time passed, it became more common to blame any questioning or dissenting views held by East German citizens on the conspiratorial work of these organisations. Some of them ran on American money and CIA advice, a result of the US policy of 'liberating captive peoples'. All available forces were mobilised to denounce the lack of democracy in the Soviet Bloc, destabilise the ruling communist parties, and help restrict the USSR's regional power.[3] The Stasi, with its Stalinist mindset, was convinced that these organisations, and the East Germans who engaged with them, were inextricably bound together under the leadership of Washington.

Some of the connections pictured by the Stasi were correct. When it came to information-gathering, for example, there were close links between the UfJ and the FDP Ostbüro. Other Stasi perceptions were wrong, like its belief that the Association for the Victims of Stalinism carried out sabotage attacks in East Germany.[4] Bitter hatred, Stalinist language, and sweeping judgements of the enemy are obvious in a Stasi directive of 1952, in which the military veterans' societies of West Berlin, the Soldatenbünde, are castigated as 'a run-off trough for every sort of failed life: down-at-heel officers and NCOs, former Gestapo and Abwehr officers, their female so-called "assistants", Red Cross nurses and homosexuals, as well as criminals and delinquent orphans'.[5]

In this period, the Stasi's Department IX – responsible for interrogations, collecting evidence and preparing cases for trial – divided suspects into three categories: those accused of either espionage, underground activity, or 'various crimes'.* Spies were classified as working either for America, 'England', France or West Germany. Activists of the UfJ, KgU or the Ostbüros might also be considered spies, but tended to be classified as 'agents' conducting underground activity. 'Various crimes' applied when a transgressor had no apparent connection with a Western organisation. Usually this meant that a person had been accused of 'anti-democratic agitation' for criticising the SED, or of 'sabotage' for some perceived failing in the workplace.[6]

The Stasi even had ethno-national enemies. The Sorbs, a Slavic people traditionally inhabiting Saxony and Brandenburg, were considered 'Titoists'. Erich Mielke wrote that 'the areas inhabited by Sorbs' needed special attention, and a new section of Department V was set up to monitor them. It was led initially by Oskar Worrack, the Stasi's only speaker of Lower Sorbian.[7]

---

*   Spionage, Untergrundtätigkeit und diversen Straftaten.

*

Some of the East Germans who had contact with Western organisations saw their actions as neither political resistance nor secret service. One example is the regional judges and court employees who felt they had a professional duty to interact with the UfJ.[8] Many East Germans made contact with such organisations merely to seek information. Others were contracted to make emergency contact with a Western agency if they ever happened to see a sudden build-up of Soviet armed forces; they didn't report information regularly and probably believed that, far from being spies, they were helping fellow Germans to avoid a disastrous surprise war.

On the other hand, there were activists of Western organisations who were conscious spies and saboteurs. In the name of political resistance, they were prepared to report regularly on military sites or to lay explosives on railway lines. Many members of the League of German Youth (BDJ), for example, understood they were taking part in a form of guerrilla warfare in the name of far-right, nationalist politics. Conceived by such CIA officers as Henry Sutton, but founded officially by the German, Paul Lüth, a rabid anti-socialist, the BDJ was intended as a West German rival to the Free German Youth. Despite its disguise as a kind of posh hiking club, the BDJ's older members were gathered into a potential stay-behind partisan formation to be activated if the Soviets invaded western Europe.[9] Klaus Barbie helped to recruit this cadre, most of whom had served enthusiastically in the Wehrmacht or Waffen-SS.[10]

The BDJ's 'Technical Service' oversaw its most ominous activities, for which it rented a remote villa, the Wagner-Haus, in the wooded hills of Hesse. Sterling Garwood, liaison for the CIA, adopted the guise of a painter and moved into the place with his family. The guerrilla trainees were then brought in by bus, masked as holidaying employees of Johann Saxer GmbH, a CIA front company.[11]

These activities aroused seething fury in the Stasi. Its consequent penetration of the BDJ is obvious in its Directive 7/51, which indicates the presence of informers in the West Berlin branches.[12] The BDJ's East German collaborators began to be arrested. In an operational case called Zentrale Kurier, at least twenty members of the 'Gräf underground group', created 'on the orders of the BDJ or UfJ', were arrested for 'spying for America'.[13] In a draft government statement, an SED official explained that:

in June 1951, on the instructions of the American secret service and the fascist organisation BDJ, a criminal group made up of former fascist officers under the direction of [an arrested agent] was formed in the territory of the GDR. At secret meetings [in] West Berlin as well as in the headquarters of the fascist organisation [BDJ] in Frankfurt/Main, which were attended by a liaison officer from the American secret service, concrete measures were determined for the immediate preparation of war. In addition to fulfilling their espionage mission, the fascist group was supposed to set up a well-functioning courier network, reconnoitre entire sections of the border areas, and prepare border crossings for people and the transporting of illegal arms.

The [head agent] was also given the task, together with his group, of setting up assembly points that would serve as a starting point for armed raids on the GDR when an invasion was triggered.

All members of this fascist organisation were arrested.[14]

The BDJ's paramilitary endeavours came undone in September 1952 when Hans Otto, chief of staff of the Technical Service and a former SS-Hauptsturmführer, admitted its illicit activities to the Frankfurt police. He revealed the whereabouts of weapons caches and the extent of American funding, reported variously as 50,000 deutschmarks or dollars per month. Worse still were the blacklists drawn up by Otto, containing the names of West Germans who were to be silenced in the event of war with the communists. Ironically – stupidly – most were high-ranking SPD members, who would hardly have abetted an invasion by the SED. The following year, mercifully, the BDJ was banned. Even so, four of its arrested leaders were promptly released from custody. Further investigations into its activities were quashed by both Konrad Adenauer, the West German chancellor, and the US authorities.[15]

A similarly sanguine approach was taken by the NTS, an anti-communist Russian émigré organisation that had championed Hitler's rise to power in the 1930s. In the postwar years, with MI6 and the CIA jointly handling its funding, one of the organisation's activities was running a group of agents in Berlin who had contact with Soviet officials and soldiers based in East Germany. The CIA's Berlin Operations Base (BOB) benefited greatly from these Soviet assets; on one occasion, BOB acquired from them a telephone directory stolen from one of its key targets, the Administration for Soviet Property in Germany. The CIA co-opted the NTS for various tasks, like encouraging defections by distributing leaflets that described easy ways to cross into West Berlin. However, MI6 pulled out of its involvement with the NTS, leaving it to the Americans. The CIA was under no illusions about the organisation. As early as April 1948 an Agency report had concluded:

These groups [of émigrés] are highly unstable and undependable, split by personal rivalries and ideological differences, and primarily concerned with developing a secure position for themselves in the Western world...

They have been completely unable to provide intelligence of real value since they are rarely able to tap useful sources of information within the USSR, and generally concentrate on producing highly biased propaganda materials in place of objective intelligence.[16]

It is significant that the CIA continued to fund and employ such a group as the NTS in the face of its own misgivings. Predictably, the Agency struggled to comprehend or control the fanaticism of some of the émigrés. In time, NTS activists proved rash and extremely vulnerable to capture and turning by the Soviets; the organisation, in fact, was riddled with communist spies.

The CIA similarly was burned by its sponsorship of another anti-communist Russian group, SBONR. This was largely because one of the group's key players, who ended up working for the CIA in Berlin for the best part of a decade, was a Soviet mole. Born in the Bryansk region of Russia, during the war Aleksandr 'Sasha' Kopatzky had served in Soviet military intelligence until his capture by the Germans. Subsequently he had fought against the Red Army in Andrei Vlasov's collaborationist Russian Army of Liberation. Although the Americans briefly interned Kopatzky at Dachau after the war, like other Soviet soldiers who had fought alongside the Germans he was hired by the fledgling Organisation Gehlen. Presumably the OG was reassured, not to say delighted, by Kopatzky's next move – marrying the daughter of a former SS officer who herself had been imprisoned for her activities as a Hitler Youth.

By 1949, however, Kopatzky had made contact with his former comrades and begun working for Soviet intelligence. Karlshorst and Moscow profited from his infiltration of SBONR, but better was to come; he was signed up as a 'principal agent' by the CIA under the alias 'Franz Koischwitz'. Principal agents were German go-betweens who hired and ran networks of Berliners and East Germans on the Agency's behalf. This was a necessary risk, as CIA officers tended to struggle either with the German language or the Berlin accent. Kopatzky specialised in recruiting East German women who were prepared to have relationships with Soviet men in order to instigate their defection. Such defectors would then be processed at the Americans' Defector Reception Center near Frankfurt am Main.

Kopatzky soon began to betray. One night in November 1951 he went on a drinking spree with a fellow principal agent, got him blind drunk, manoeuvred him into East Berlin, and gave him to the MGB. In time, Kopatzky revealed to the Soviets the identities of more than 100 American intelligence officers and agents, many of whom were then arrested or turned. He also took part in a staged defection, in which the Soviet agent 'Viktor' was smuggled westwards and planted at the Voice of America radio station.

In 1954 the CIA changed Kopatzky's name to 'Igor Orlov', to help him abrogate a drunk-driving conviction. He spent a short period in Washington, but soon returned to take part in CIA operations in Germany and Austria. Only in 1960 did the CIA begin to suspect him. He was brought to the US, where he could do less damage, but despite years of investigation by the FBI it proved impossible to charge him with an offence.[17]

The likes of the NTS and SBONR proved risky as intelligence-gatherers, partly because of their preference for action over spying. But the most active spies and saboteurs operating in East Germany were probably those of the Combat Group Against Inhumanity: the KgU.

The Combat Group Against Inhumanity was founded by Rainer Hildebrandt, who liked to tell tales of his anti-Nazi resistance. During the war he had served as a Wehrmacht interpreter for a while, but he was arrested by the Gestapo – perhaps due to the discovery of some Jewish heritage – and, apparently, imprisoned without charge. He was then put to work as a guard in a POW camp in Poland where, it was said, he maintained connections with some of the military resisters who tried to kill Hitler in 1944.

After the war Hildebrandt lived in West Berlin and published books about the anti-Nazi resistance. He became increasingly concerned about developments in the Soviet zone, and during summer 1948 began to urge Radio in the American Sector (RIAS) to broadcast appeals to eastern Germans either to leave the zone or fight for change. He also started to document the repression by interviewing socialists, liberals and Christian democrats who had been released from Soviet camps.

SMAD remonstrated with the Americans about Hildebrandt's activities, but to no avail. In October 1948 he helped to convene a rally at West Berlin's Titania Palast cinema with representatives from the Free University, the SPD, and the CDU's youth wing, Junge Union. Under the slogan 'Inaction is Murder' ('Nichtstun ist Mord'), the assembly heard how the 6,400 inmates of Sachsenhausen, some of whom were innocent of any charge of Nazism or war crimes, were dying at the rate of sixty to eighty per day, mostly of malnutrition and tuberculosis.

The following year, the Western Allies signed off on the creation of the KgU. In its founding proclamation of 25 April 1949, the organisation urged eastern Germans not to vote in the upcoming elections to East Berlin's Volkskongress, as this meant voting for a 'system of inhumanity'.[18] Hildebrandt set out the KgU's two main goals: freeing all those unjustly imprisoned in the Soviet zone – soon to become the GDR – and documenting the crimes against humanity taking place there.[19]

Within a few months the KgU had received 12,000 missing persons enquiries and had been notified of the circumstances of 8,500 arrests in the Soviet zone. It soon had eighty employees, including its deputy chief Ernst Tillich, a social democrat and Christian who had spent much of the war in Nazi prisons and camps. Reportedly, Rainer Hildebrandt at first rejected offers of American money to finance his organisation. But as the KgU formed more underground groups in East Germany, which set about reporting on arrests and distributing anti-communist propaganda, he accepted funding from the US army's Counter Intelligence Corps (CIC).

Young adults in eastern Germany rushed to the KgU flame, availing themselves of its help and literature. In a characteristic case, one bunch of youths in Schwerin had started a protest group of their own accord. They liked to gather in front of the main train station, then set off hundreds of fireworks which showered their fellow citizens with homemade leaflets criticising the Soviets and SED. Then the group discovered the KgU, which began to provide a better class of leaflet.

This leafletting campaign was one of the first cases ever to be investigated by the Stasi officers of Schwerin. Oppositional flyers were showing up everywhere, but they couldn't find the culprits. Until a slip-up; during a leafletting action, a member of the group let a passport photograph of his girlfriend fall from his pocket. It was recovered, and quickly he was identified. The Stasi arrested him and searched his parents' home. They found 15,000 leaflets provided by the KgU and SPD Ostbüro.

The Stasi then arrested another fourteen young adults. Among them was twenty-year-old Erika Bludschun, who was unfortunate; she had once stood guard on a night-time leafletting action, but had declined to do so a second time 'out of fear'. She had, however, typed up more leaflets for the group's supply. When Bludschun heard that her friends were being arrested, she asked her brother to bury her typewriter in the family's garden, but this attempt at concealment failed. She and her boyfriend, Hans-Jürgen Jennerjahn, were taken by Stasi personnel to the offices of the Soviet administration on Demmlerplatz. After intensive questioning, with not a German in sight, they and their friends went before a Soviet military tribunal. They were sentenced to twenty-five years' corrective labour – the Gulag. Jennerjahn went to the camp at Vorkuta, Erika Bludschun to a factory in Siberia. Two years later her father was still writing to the authorities for information on her whereabouts; he sent some letters to prime minister Otto Grotewohl, who ignored them. Although Bludschun and Jennerjahn were released early in a mid-1950s amnesty, they never really recovered from this trauma, despite resettling in West Germany.[20]

There are similarities in the case of a resistance group known as 'Antikominform' in the town of Altenburg in Thuringia. The group grew up around a couple of social democrat schoolteachers and their pupils, some of whom had fathers who had been arrested as active Nazis by the Soviets; at least one had died in internment. Having made their own leaflets for a while, the group likewise discovered the KgU and took part in its 'F' campaign, painting the letter F for Freedom on public buildings and noticeboards. Some of the group's handier members then built their own radio transmitter, intending to disturb the official broadcasts on Stalin's birthday.

The arrests began in March 1950. After he had been spied upon and denounced by colleagues, one of the teachers, Wolfgang Ostermann, was lured to a non-existent work meeting in Weimar. There he was detained by a fellow teacher and a Stasi employee disguised as an official from the Ministry of Education. This was followed by the arrest of more than two dozen youths and townspeople from Altenburg. At least one arrestee had nothing to do with the group; she had somehow picked up one of its leaflets and accidentally left it inside a returned library book. Some group members, no doubt hoping to avoid further punishment, were released after being recruited as informers. Three of the leaders, including Ostermann, were sentenced to death by a Soviet military tribunal and shot in Moscow. In a further measure designed to bring the local National Front parties to heel, the chairpersons of the CDU and LDPD in Altenburg were replaced.[21]

This, then, was how the Stasi and Soviet authorities dealt with perceived KgU supporters. Meanwhile, the KgU's deputy chief Ernst Tillich was urging the organisation to become more radical. He succeeded. Spurning their initial actions, such as throwing stink bombs into SED offices or burning Soviet banners, its underground groups began to prepare for paramilitary sabotage. The Stasi in Thuringia reported the arrest of some KgU activists in possession of acid 'disguised as state-made schnapps', intended to 'render the ball bearings of valuable machines unusable'.[22] In Leipzig, ampules of phosphoric acid were used to set fire to state-run shops.[23] (The devices were planted at a time when the shops were busy with customers; this, then, was indeed an act of 'terrorism', the word used so frequently by the East German authorities.) A KgU agent called Albrecht Gessler was adjudged to have twice planted explosive devices on the Halle-Magdeburg railway line, one of which was detonated by a passenger train. Walter Gennrich, leader of a KgU cell, was sentenced to fifteen years in prison for commissioning sabotage schemes: he had planned to blow up a turbine at the Agfa film works in Wolfen and set fire to the coal heaps at a nitrogen plant.[24] And the KgU engaged in some fiery propaganda. In the course of 1950, it collaborated with Western radio stations to name 20,000 suspected Stasi spies.[25] This, of course, was an exaggerated figure; one wonders about those accused in error.

The newborn Stasi reacted to all this by creating an anti-KgU task force under Otto Knye of Department V. Knye had served in the Wehrmacht throughout the war, and was only returned to Germany from Soviet captivity in 1949, having undergone extensive re-education. His unit set about arresting KgU sympathisers and infiltrating the organisation by turning captured activists. Those who went to trial usually were convicted, like Bludschun and Jennerjahn, of 'anti-Soviet' offences under Russia's Article 58.

Before long Rainer Hildebrandt ceded leadership of the KgU to Ernst Tillich. Hildebrandt later claimed he had been troubled by the growing violence and intrigue. Already there had been several failed attempts to kidnap him from West Berlin, for he had a reward of 15,000 marks on his head. As early as July 1949, four men in possession of a Mauser pistol had been arrested when their car was seen circling Hildebrandt's residence; they were Germans from the Soviet sector, and each was given a two-year sentence for attempted kidnapping. On at least three more occasions Otto Knye's unit was ordered to kidnap Hildebrandt but, reputedly, a CIC spy within the Stasi's planning group was able to sound the alarm.

Responsibility for funding the KgU soon passed from the CIC to the CIA. Although unsure about the organisation's discipline, and never in direct control of its activities, the Agency valued having, in the words of a CIA participant, 'a flexible instrument for conducting a full range of covert operations against the East German regime'. One US-sponsored activity that especially riled the SED was the KgU's fabrication of East German documents and publications, including a postage stamp depicting Walter Ulbricht with a noose around his neck, which saw circulation.[26] In its operation Osterhase (Easter Bunny), the KgU sent 150,000 forged letters to state-owned shops in East Germany with instructions to slash prices, causing a run on goods that shook the supply chain.[27] On another occasion the KgU forged faultless release papers for an activist incarcerated in the GDR. The attempt failed only because the papers were sent to the wrong prison.[28]

Operating under his CIA alias of 'Charles E. Newham', Ernst Tillich soothed American consciences, and stoked righteous American anger, by constantly comparing the SED regime to that of the Nazis. He told Joseph McCarthy's House Committee on Un-American Activities that 'Communism in Germany is nothing more than a continuation of Nazism.' He pointed out that East

German youth organisations drilled their members in the 'goose-step, the jack-booted leitmotif of Nazi conquest'. Tillich was a major source for the West's fallacious claims that the Stasi comprised former Nazis. This was ironic, and hypocritical. One important founder member of the KgU was Heinrich von zur Mühlen, a Nazi 'ethnicity expert' who had served in the elite Brandenburg Division during the war. Another executive, Leo Wolfgang Miller, had served in the SS security service, the Sicherheitsdienst. The KgU campaigned hard in West Germany for the amnesty of certain imprisoned Nazis, and former Waffen-SS and Wehrmacht personnel could often be found in the KgU groups which planned the most serious armed actions.[29]

Also problematic, given Tillich's righteous posture, was the KgU's information-gathering on left-wingers living in West Germany. This activity encompassed not just KPD members but those of the Independent Social Democratic Party as well as Jewish Auschwitz survivors and foreign nationals. Sometimes intelligence on these individuals was shared with the West German security service, the BfV, and other Federal agencies. As always with the Cold War, the political morality of these activities was complicated. For instance, there were examples of East German refugees who, having been debriefed by KgU members, were refused entry to West Germany and sent back to the GDR, at the behest of the CIA. Yet this, in the end, was the KgU fulfilling its assigned task – spotting potential communist agents before they could embed themselves in the West.[30] And the organisation had some clear successes; it was indicated in a CIA report that the KgU had persuaded at least two Stasi officers to defect.[31] However, such achievements didn't prevent Ernst Tillich being expelled from the SPD, which wanted less and less to do with him.

Questionable judgements by the KgU were just one problem affecting the West German refugee system. An SPD report noted that some refugees 'had to stop at no fewer than 68 locations, including 22 offices of Western secret services'.[32] In February 1952, interviews by KgU members, who initially had been delegated by the Americans to vet refugees at an office on Kaiserdamm in West Berlin, were made a formal part of the Federal admission process. A KgU unit was set up at the Marienfelde reception camp, where members of the SPD, CDU and UfJ were similarly employed. KgU expertise was valued for assessing defectors from the Volkspolizei and the GDR's emerging armed forces. When Stern magazine accused the KgU of effectively carrying out mass-scale espionage with such refugee interviews, the KgU issued a statement denying any interest in military information. This was a standard rebuttal and untrue; the KgU collected great sprawling mounds of military information.[33]

There was much diversity among the KgU's East German collaborators, though they tended to be young. October 1951 saw a well-remembered trial at which eighteen people from the Saxon town of Werdau – teachers, teenaged students and their parents – were sentenced to a combined total of 124 years' hard labour for offences supposedly inspired by the KgU. The students had made leaflets protesting the death penalty and East Germany's rigged elections; the teachers and parents were guilty of not stopping them.[34]

In contrast to such mild resistance, some of the KgU networks proliferating in the GDR continued to damage industrial machinery, bring down power lines, and destroy communist monuments. Reportedly, the CIA considered the KgU to have caused millions of dollars-worth of damage.[35] And the organisation was capable of unnerving the communist leadership. When four masked KgU activists carried out an attack on a workers' holiday home in Liebenberg in February 1951, the incident fuelled SED claims that Western organisations were trying to kill East German officials. Apparently the assailants had known that GDR interior minister Karl Steinhoff was visiting the home. They cut the electricity and telephone lines leading to the premises, fired leaflet-spreading rockets into its courtyard, and – according to the KgU's own report – threw twenty 'bombs' in through the windows, although it isn't recorded whether these were of the stink or explosive variety. The perpetrators were executed after going before a Soviet military tribunal.[36] This was the period of the 'Walter Affair', named after the codename of a captured KgU activist, in which Soviet security forces rounded up more than 200 KgU supporters in East Germany.

In April 1952 Wilhelm Zaisser reiterated that fighting the KgU was one of the Stasi's 'most important tasks'. His Order Number 60/52 – perhaps the first Stasi order to be issued independently of Soviet instructors – urged a concerted effort. It stressed the need for Department V to be supplied with timely information from informers run by other Stasi departments. All cases 'in which connections to the KgU have been determined' had to be reported to the Lichtenberg headquarters within three weeks, 'with a description of their current status and the measures taken'.[37]

Just as Zaisser's order went out, the MGB showed the Stasi how it was done by kidnapping the secretary of a KgU official, acquiring the official's briefcase, and using the consequent haul of information to arrest more than sixty of the KgU's 'active diversionary agents' in East Germany.[38] In May and August two important show trials of KgU defendants were staged at the Supreme Court. Presiding over them was 'Red Hilde' – Hilde Benjamin, soon to be minister of justice. The first trial saw the Supreme Court impose its inaugural death sentence, on KgU activist Johann Burianek. Intent on demolishing a bridge, he had smuggled a suitcase full of explosives into East Berlin.[39] A key defendant in the second trial was Wolfgang Kaiser, victim of one of the Stasi's more bizarre kidnappings.

At about 3 a.m. on 8 May 1952, Wolfgang Kaiser and his friend Wolfgang Baumbach had presented themselves, staggering drunk, at a Volkspolizei station in East Berlin. Kaiser was in possession of a pistol, a cosh, and a cigarette soaked with knockout anaesthetic. Baumbach had a pistol too. Kaiser told the astonished police officers that he wanted to work for the Stasi, like his friend Baumbach did. He said that Baumbach had relayed to him an offer of employment from the Stasi. They were both arrested.

This odd scene was the culmination of a Stasi operation to entrap Kaiser, who was an illicit chemist for the KgU. The substances Kaiser concocted in his homemade laboratory in West Berlin could be used to poison water systems or make explosives, but they also went into less sinister products; stink bombs, or the fuses for leaflet-dropping devices in the balloons which the KgU kept launching over the German borders.

To get Kaiser, the Stasi used a number of secret informers (GI) and secret co-workers (GM), in what would become its textbook fashion. One GM, Gustav Buciek, was a KgU courier whom the Stasi had recruited with blackmail, threatening him with knowledge of his criminal past. Another GM, Herr Gläser, owned the pharmacy where Kaiser bought the substances he needed for his work; potassium chlorate, ammonium nitrate. Buciek and Gläser were two regular sources of information on Kaiser's activities. A third was Kaiser's old friend, the East Berlin resident and Stasi GM Wolfgang Baumbach.

Kaiser and Baumbach liked to drink. Kaiser used their inebriated friendship to prise money and free booze from Baumbach. Baumbach used it to buy information on the KgU from Kaiser, although the Stasi at first did not realise this was how Baumbach was acquiring his intelligence. Baumbach also exhorted Kaiser to work directly for the Stasi. Two occurrences prompted the Stasi to wrap up the case. First, Gläser reported the fact that Kaiser knew Baumbach worked for the Stasi. Second, Kaiser told Baumbach that he was due to help out in a big KgU leafletting campaign planned for May Day. Baumbach was told to get Kaiser into East Berlin, fast. He did so by persuading Kaiser to come and talk to his friends the Stasi about becoming a mole inside the KgU. Although his drunkenness makes it difficult to judge, Kaiser's probable intention was to become a double agent, working illicitly for the KgU within the Stasi set-up.

Kaiser was tried with several other captured KgU activists. He was said to have been supplying them personally with secret inks, poisons and incendiary devices, although in reality they were all strangers to each other. The prosecution also claimed that a small amount of cantharidin, a neurotoxin possessed by Kaiser, could in theory poison 25,000 people. For the gravity of this and other charges Kaiser was sentenced to death, reputedly on the insistence of the Soviet authorities. He was guillotined at an execution site in Dresden.

During these years, many ordinary Germans would learn the hard way that the East-West intelligence war was hazardous. Making bombs for a US-funded sabotage outfit, or playing around with a pretended recruitment by the Stasi, wasn't a game – this was dangerous stuff. Some, like Kaiser, went about things in a spirit of drunken bravado. Others, like Rainer Hildebrandt's nineteen-year-old housemaid Helga Ramm, probably had no idea of the risks they were running. On occasion Hildebrandt would ask Ramm to deliver letters to American military personnel. One such delivery involved a brief trip through East Berlin, where Ramm was arrested, allegedly tortured, and ultimately sentenced to twenty-five years' hard labour.[40]

The CIA department responsible for supervising the KgU, in a project it codenamed DTLINEN, was the semi-independent Office of Policy Coordination. The OPC had a range of tasks: creating media disinformation campaigns and anti-communist front organisations, supporting subversive groups, harming the Soviet Bloc's economy, and founding underground paramilitary units. It was obvious from the number of arrests made in East Germany that Otto Knye's Stasi unit had thoroughly penetrated the KgU and was aware of these CIA plans. According to the files for Aktion Karo, an anti-KgU operation launched by deputy security minister Mielke, the Stasi knew the locations of alarm switches in the KgU headquarters, and the names of the chemicals stored in its laboratory fridges. Nevertheless, Ernst Tillich and Henry Hecksher, 'executive officer' of the Berlin OPC (and remembered as 'a nut' by some of his colleagues),[41] persisted in sending KgU activists into East Germany on clandestine missions. The beheading of two of their agents was no disincentive.

Meanwhile, Rainer Hildebrandt had been forced out of the KgU, and even out of West Berlin altogether. This was due to CIA doubts about his claimed past. According to one CIA officer, Hildebrandt's 'world-wide advertised activities as a resistance fighter and concentration camp victim were a complete myth'. When the Agency confronted Hildebrandt with its suspicions, it was noted that he 'did not refute a single accusation'.[42] Of a sudden, he was persona non grata.

However untruthful he may have been, Hildebrandt surely had never expected his organisation to get so blood-soaked. Over time, more than 1,000 KgU-linked suspects were arrested by communist security services. Five were executed by the East German state. The Soviets put at least 500 before military tribunals, of whom at least 121 were shot.[43] Of the 927 Germans who were executed or died in Moscow from 1950 to 1953, associates of the KgU were the biggest single group. The severity of their deeds varied wildly. KgU supporters who had plausible connections with Western intelligence services tended to receive the harshest punishments. One KgU activist had bragged, perhaps falsely, about killing two Soviet soldiers. Another, a Jewish student called Fritz Flatow, who had been persecuted by the Nazis, had tried to cultivate an MGB interpreter as a spy. The former paratrooper Alfred Weigel had possessed an incendiary device with which he had intended to destroy a high-voltage pylon. But some of those executed were guilty of no more than distributing leaflets. In such cases it was wartime background, such as voluntary service in the Waffen-SS, which really counted against them.[44]

Eventually the heavy losses sustained by the KgU at the hands of the Stasi proved to be a major cause of the organisation's downfall, but there were fierce battles to come before the end.

The other major political group to be engaged in combat by the Stasi was the Investigative Committee of Free Jurists (UfJ).

In the years after the Second World War, a lawyer called Horst Erdmann ran a small practice in Belzig, south-west of Berlin.* The town also happened to accommodate a big contingent of MGB personnel. In 1945 the local authorities had vetted Erdmann who, like thousands of others in this time of refugees, drifters and returning prisoners of war, was paperless. Erdmann explained his background. Born in Lübeck, and a law graduate, he had lost his job as a courtroom assistant during the Third Reich because of his Jewish heritage. Later, an anti-Hitler remark had seen him sent to a concentration camp in Silesia, from which he was liberated by the Red Army.

For several years Erdmann had a close-up view of Soviet occupation and the rise of the SED. He was appalled, and he had an idea. If a group of like-minded lawyers could get together in the western sectors of Berlin – still accessible from Belzig – they could start to record cases of legal malpractice by the Soviet authorities, and give advice to the beleaguered residents of the Soviet zone. They might even be able to take action against those German prosecutors and judges – usually SED members – who were helping the Soviets to do their dirty work. And so, in 1949, Erdmann took his idea to the American sector of Berlin.

Before long he had secured CIC funding for a new organisation – the Investigative Committee of Free Jurists. Using the cover name Theo Friedenau, Erdmann published articles in West Berlin papers and distributed leaflets in eastern Germany, exhorting citizens to tell the UfJ about unlawful arrests and prosecutions. Based initially in a two-room apartment on Troppauer Strasse, and with a staff of two, the UfJ grew quickly to become a significant presence

---

* A different Horst Erdmann to the one mentioned previously.

in the fight against communism. Its campaigning attracted widespread support and admiration. It also attracted the CIA, which took over its funding. The previously mentioned Henry Hecksher, who used the aliases 'Mr Henry' and 'Vane', would hand over the Agency's cash personally to Erdmann, in an arrangement that the latter kept secret from even his closest UfJ colleagues.[45] The CIA disguised its payments behind a front organisation, the Society for a United Germany, purportedly run by a German-American family of brewers in Wisconsin.[46]

CIA cash, and affiliation with western Germany's Institute for All-German Affairs – later to be a Federal ministry – allowed the UfJ to upgrade its premises to a plush villa on Limastrasse. With eighty permanent staff members at its height, it had sections covering criminal law, civil law, tax and labour law, refugee issues, and youth affairs. In terms of activity, the CIA got its money's worth. Throughout the 1950s, thousands of East Germans flooded to the UfJ to report abuses of the law and seek advice. As well as reinforcing the organisation's ironic claim to being 'the largest law firm in the GDR', this enthusiastic take-up turned the UfJ into a notable press agency for Western media. In 1953 and 1954, for example, more than 1,500 news articles and radio reports were generated by its work.

At the same time, the UfJ built up a network of more than 10,000 informants inside East Germany.[47] They supplied not only evidence of legal malpractice but information on the GDR's economy, infrastructure, and political hierarchy.[48] A former employee, while denying that UfJ activists gathered military intelligence, remembered collecting data on election fraud, the illegal seizure of private assets, forced collectivisation, the suppression of dissenting workers, and criminal convictions for 'boycott' agitation, *Republikflucht* (the SED's term for fleeing East Germany), and other spurious GDR-only crimes.[49] UfJ information went into a register of tens of thousands of East German state functionaries, who would otherwise have been unknown in the West. The UfJ was also asked to screen refugees arriving in West Berlin, reflecting justified fears about infiltrators planted by the communist secret services. In 1955 the UfJ carried out nearly 9,000 vetting procedures.[50]

Some of the organisation's activities inflicted real damage on the GDR, and on some of the less scrupulous West German merchants who did business with it. An MGB report from 1952 described how the UfJ had been able:

> through its agents in GDR enterprises, to expose more than four hundred transactions between GDR offices and West German firms that violated the American ban on trade. This resulted in the detention of about eight hundred traders involved in these deals and the interruption of receipt by GDR industry

of goods and raw materials from West Germany in the amount of eight hundred million marks.[51]

Perhaps the UfJ's most striking activity was sending threatening 'indictments' to East German legal professionals who were known to abuse the law. The tone was set with the first of these missives. It was sent in November 1949 by Erdmann, alias Friedenau, to Bernhard Bechler, the former interior minister of Brandenburg. Drafted and printed like an official prosecutor's indictment, it charged Bechler on counts of kidnapping, crimes against humanity, falsified paperwork, deprivation of liberty, embezzlement, bribery, and election fraud.

More of these postal warnings soon followed – they were sent to the East German finance minister, the attorney general, the Volkskammer president and, of course, to security minister Wilhelm Zaisser. The UfJ used *konspiratsia* to deliver these items, which were sent in unmarked envelopes and signed by bogus authors. Its couriers, some of them students earning pocket money, would enter the Soviet sector of Berlin on the S- or U-Bahn and use postboxes there, avoiding the scrutiny given to mail posted in West Berlin. One historian of the Stasi has reproduced a typical message sent to a lawyer suspected of human rights abuses: 'Someday you will be held to account not because you are a communist but because you are committing wrongful acts. It is up to you to decide whether or not you want to carry this guilt on your shoulders.'[52]

These postal threats had a dual purpose: to warn human rights abusers they would be held to account whenever possible, and to dissuade them from continuing to abet Soviet and SED injustice. They were an emphatic success. Reputedly, it wasn't uncommon for recipients to travel to West Berlin to explain themselves to the UfJ, hoping to forestall any future consequences.

Unsurprisingly, such a successful and popular anti-communist agency was soon in the frontline of the spy wars. Starting in summer 1952, *Neues Deutschland* embarked on a vigorous counter-propaganda campaign, accusing the UfJ of espionage and sabotage, and of using bribery and threats to recruit 'criminal' agents in East Germany. Horst Erdmann denied repeatedly that his organisation received CIA funding, or that it engaged in intelligence-gathering – both lies.

In fact, the CIA was getting more than just information and propaganda from the deal. Under CIA projects called TPEMBER and CADROIT, the UfJ was sponsored to publicly expose injustices. Sometimes it carried out such covert actions as an attempt to thwart the prosecution of a lawyer imprisoned in Gera. It also secured the release of a few prisoners. The Stasi, unnerved that legal professionals could be swayed by the UfJ, arrested the likes of Götz Schlicht, a senior judge in Potsdam, for interacting with the organisation.[53]

In 1952 the CIA added another component to its sponsorship, known as project CADROWN – a plan to create a paramilitary UfJ underground in East Germany, which would organise escape lines and other resistance activities in the event of war.[54] Unfortunately for both CIA and UfJ, most of these cells were rolled-up in a string of security operations carried out by the MGB.[55] UfJ supporters in East Germany, many of them completely unsuited to handling a weapon, were easy meat for Soviet security personnel. By 1955 the CADROWN project had been scrapped.

Even the UfJ's gentler activities could be deeply problematic for the SED regime. Simply by studying the Western press, the Stasi learned of the UfJ's efforts during 'Green Week', a regular agricultural fair held in West Berlin. To mark the event the UfJ published an 'inflammatory' newsletter, *Der Bauernbrief*, and hosted an advice centre at the Haus Tannen hotel on Karolingerplatz. Visiting East German farmers received counsel on such matters as 'securing assets in the event of escape from the Soviet occupation zone', what to do if they couldn't meet a production quota, how to get compensation for losses incurred due to East Germany's dilapidated infrastructure, and 'how to behave in the event of political and judicial coercive measures'.[56]

Steered by MGB hands, the Stasi reacted viciously to the Free Jurists. One action, on 8 July 1952, proved to be one of the most notorious inter-German kidnappings of the Cold War. Early that morning, Walter Linse, head of the UfJ's economics section, left his home on Gerichtstrasse in the American sector of Berlin and headed down the street. Within a few seconds he was asked for a light, then grabbed and punched by two men, who bundled him into a nearby taxi with its engine running. Some passers-by shouted and screamed. A Volkswagen van tried to block the taxi's escape. Two pistol shots were fired from the fleeing vehicle. The struggling Linse made his legs stiff so that the taxi door couldn't be closed on him; he was shot in one leg and fainted. Any chance of pursuit ended when tyre-bursting tetrahedron spikes were thrown from the taxi's windows as it sped away.

This was Operation Lehmann. It had been devised by Otto Knye and Bruno Beater in response to an order from Wilhelm Zaisser to apprehend Linse; Zaisser, in turn, was acting on orders from the head of the MGB apparat at Karlshorst, Mikhail Kaverznev. The kidnappers, and several lookouts who helped them, were petty criminals hired by the Stasi. These hired thugs delivered Linse into the Stasi's custody at Hohenschönhausen prison.

The US High Commissioner for Germany protested Linse's disappearance to the head of the Soviet authorities, at this point the war hero General Vasily Chuikov. Chuikov claimed to have no idea what had happened. Linse's wife wrote to East German prime minister Otto Grotewohl, who ignored her. For the first time, West Berlin began to protect itself against East; barriers were erected on the western side of the Schwelmer Strasse border crossing, where the kidnappers had escaped into East Berlin. The placing of these barriers was featured in a newsreel, which commented that West Berlin now had to defend itself against kidnappers like 'a patch of peaceful countryside against poaching wolves'.[57]

At Hohenschönhausen, Linse shared a cell with stool pigeons and hidden microphones. By December 1952 he had undergone more than thirty gruelling interrogation sessions. The following year he was handed over to Soviet Military Tribunal No. 402. In the course of his trial, Linse named more than thirty UfJ collaborators living in East Germany, and admitted that he had gathered economic intelligence on his visits there.[58] It was alleged that when he was abducted he was carrying a report on GDR trade and industry which was intended for a US intelligence service.[59]

The MGB and Stasi moved quickly against Linse's associates in East Germany, arresting twenty-seven in an initial round-up. This led to the discovery of more names, and by the end of the year a total of eighty-four Free Jurist 'agents' had been apprehended. Some turned out to be professionals 'employed in responsible positions in the state apparatus of the GDR'. Soon after Linse's abduction his secretary, Ruth Schramm, had disappeared from West Berlin. Almost certainly an MGB agent, Schramm then turned up as a prosecution witness when seven Free Jurists were tried before 'Red Hilde' Benjamin at the GDR Supreme Court. Two were given life sentences and the remainder lengthy prison terms. Following this trial, an approving MGB report noted the Stasi's plan to penetrate the UfJ with new moles, who were to be sent into West Germany in the guise of refugees.[60]

Walter Linse had been targeted both by chance and design. West Berlin was due to host a congress of international lawyers in summer 1952, at which the UfJ was to play a leading role. The MGB staff at Karlshorst planned various measures to disrupt the event, one of which was a scheme to kidnap the UfJ founder Horst Erdmann. But Erdmann had taken an unexpected trip to Sweden before he could be seized; thus the kidnap plan had shifted to Linse, who had aroused Soviet displeasure with his work on such touchy subjects as the expropriation of property without compensation, and the shocking plight of workers at the Wismut uranium mines.[61]

There was outrage at Linse's brazen kidnapping. Willy Brandt, a member of the Bundestag and future chancellor, declared in a speech that 'kidnapping is the worst violation of human rights, kidnapping [is] at least attempted murder. Organisations that kidnap people are criminal institutions.'[62] For decades, Linse remained just one of the disappeared. Although the Red Cross acquired some information in the early 1960s, the details of his fate weren't clarified until 1996. Convicted of 'espionage', 'anti-Soviet propaganda' and 'formation of an anti-Soviet organisation',[63] Walter Linse was shot in Moscow on 15 December 1953.

During his interrogation, Linse had talked about the plans to set up a secret network of paramilitaries in East Germany under the CIA project CADROWN. It transpired that the head agent of these groups was a retired Kriegsmarine officer who had connections with the Organisation Gehlen, West Germany's nascent foreign intelligence service. Thus when some of the UfJ 'guerrillas' were arrested in 1953, the MGB and Stasi were able to claim a conspiratorial link between the CIA, West German intelligence, and the UfJ. Furthermore, their arrest was too easy. In theory, the groups were organised into unconnected three-person cells. In reality, almost all the participants were known to each other, and the groups were liquidated after the arrest of just one member.[64] The collapse of these networks forced the CIA to devote heavy resources to what has been called 'a cauldron of security investigations'.[65]

30

Re-ordering the Stasi

There is no doubt that in its first years the Stasi, with its under-educated workforce and reliance on Soviet advisers, got off to a chaotic, even unruly start. This is illustrated by the glut of internal guidelines about paperwork, legal requirements, and arrest procedures that were issued from 1950 to 1952. These documents betray an urgent need to regularise the behaviour of Stasi personnel.

Too many loose cannons were serving in the Volkspolizei as well. In a speech to the Rostock police in August 1950, Walter Ulbricht, while cannily implying that German reunification was just around the corner, urged police officers to clean up their act, to look less thuggish in the eyes of the public. Undoubtedly his comments applied equally to the Stasi:

> To win over patriotic [i.e., anti-Western] forces in West Germany, the question of how things look in the German Democratic Republic is of the utmost importance. Is it orderly and democratic? Are democratic laws upheld? Our recommendations for unity will have greater resonance if things look orderly, than if the population talks [about] conflicts with the police, etc. This means that each police officer must be aware of the heavy responsibility he has with regard to upholding democratic laws, and the importance this has for peace, the unity of Germany, and the preparation for all-German democratic elections.[1]

Here, Ulbricht was hinting at the East German version of nationalism: socialism equals patriotism, and opposition to socialism is unpatriotic. Given that the SED had set out to defend itself with tough extra-legal security forces, his speech was also an example of an old communist habit: blaming the population and subordinates for the failings of the leaderships' untenable policies. State employees throughout the Soviet Bloc were to become wearily familiar with this cycle. First, subordinates were given a command; then they were given a contradictory command that made the first command unfulfillable; finally, everything that had gone wrong was blamed on the fact that subordinates hadn't fulfilled the two commands.

A slew of instructions issued in September 1950, in which the hand of deputy security minister Erich Mielke is more discernible than that of minister Zaisser, established some of the Stasi's fundamental, long-term practices.* They also mark the historical beginnings of the Stasi's immense registry of suspects and investigations.

These documents established that an investigation of a lone person was to be known as an individual process (Einzelvorgäng), while the investigation of a circle of people would be a group process (Gruppenvorgäng). Before being opened, every process needed the sign-off of a top Stasi leader; the security minister or a provincial minister.[2] For the purposes of 'maintaining conspiracy' and 'ease of use in correspondence', every process was to be given a cover name – formally, these were 'designations' (Bezeichnungen).

Investigations could only be based upon 'verified documents', 'reports from secret co-workers and informers', and 'investigative, denunciatory and other official material suggestive of hostile activity'. If the investigation of an individual revealed suspect contact with others, the individual process was to become a group process. The files on all investigations were to be stored in metal safes as 'secret classified information' (GVS).† If a suspect died or there was insufficient evidence of 'underground activity', senior officers could end an investigation. And, above all, everything was to be recorded by the Registration and Statistics department, which had at least one staff member at every Stasi office.

It is clear from these documents that there was a lack of uniformity and conscientiousness among Stasi personnel when making arrests, detaining suspects, and ticking legal boxes. They are also notable for giving instructions on how to do the paperwork of secret policing, not how to do the work itself. The nitty-gritty of the work was being learned in the field, off the record and by word of mouth, from Soviet personnel. At this stage, no doubt due to concerns about the perceived illegalities of the East German state – not to mention the obvious administrative chaos – it was office procedures that the Stasi wanted to drum into its employees' heads; especially, how to manage the paper trail around arrests and detentions.

The September 1950 guidelines paid lip service to legality and due process. An order to arrest a suspect had to be approved by the security minister or state secretary (Zaisser or Mielke), a provincial minister or deputy minister, or a head of department. A judge or public prosecutor was to be informed of the arrest

---

* These included 'Order No. 1/50 on the Creation of a Registration and Statistics Department and the enactment of its guidelines'; 'Guidelines on the registration of persons who carry out hostile activity and are identified by the organs of the Ministry for State Security of the GDR'; 'Guidelines for registering persons arrested by the organs of the Ministry for State Security of the GDR'.

† Geheime Verschlusssache.

in advance. One guideline mentions, almost as an afterthought: 'According to the applicable code of criminal procedure, it is necessary to contact the public prosecutor or judge to obtain an arrest warrant for the criminal.'

Having obtained an arrest order (Haftbefehl) and an arrest warrant (Haftbeschluss), Stasi personnel were to hand over arrestees to detention centres with an admission order. Operational units at every Stasi office were obliged to notify the Registration and Statistics department within twenty-four hours of any arrest they made. An index card for the arrested person would then be completed, in triplicate. Before freeing anyone, it was necessary to obtain a release order (Entlassungsbefehl). And the security minister or deputy minister had to approve the sharing of any paperwork about an arrest, a stipulation which suggests that legal professionals were causing trouble by demanding information the Stasi didn't want them to have.

In practice, these procedures tended to go out the window. Stasi arrest teams continued to apply Order 201 from years earlier, which allowed them to issue their own warrants. The Stasi was stocked with a hotchpotch of old arrest warrants, some of which only required the signature of a Stasi officer. It was noted frequently by arrestees that the space on a warrant for a public prosecutor's signature was blank.[3]

These guidelines show the Stasi trying to cover itself, and they indicate the lack of experience and education of its personnel. They also reveal that there was a concerted effort at this time to use legal means to thwart Stasi investigations, to intercede in its operations. Some of this effort was encouraged or conducted by the likes of the UfJ and KgU. But who knows what lay behind the activities of every legal practitioner within East Germany who tried to hamper the Stasi's work? The example of West Germany would indicate that a fair proportion of legal professionals had been committed Nazis in the recent past.

Lawyers and members of the public challenged Stasi practices, or what they knew of them, in various ways. As previously mentioned, a major complaint was that no information was given to the families of arrestees, who had a right to this information under Article 136 of the East German constitution. In an attempt to put the issue to bed, in May 1951 the Supreme Public Prosecutor's Office announced that neither the constitution nor the Reich criminal code applied in this matter, as arrest procedures were subject to the old military instruments – SMAD Order 201 and Control Council Directive 38. An even older law, Control Council Order No. 2 of January 1946, applied in cases of illegal possession of firearms.

Thus the arrest squads of the Stasi's Department VIII continued to issue their own warrants, the investigators of Department IX to write their own indictments. In November 1951 Wilhelm Zaisser ordered that arrests could only be made 'if all the available material on the person to be arrested has been thoroughly checked and the conditions for an arrest have been met'. He wasn't bothered about the suspects; he was bothered that enemies were slipping through the Stasi's fingers because of inadequate paperwork, and vowed to 'hold accountable the person responsible for every unfounded arrest that results in the arrested person being released'.[4]

Guidelines and orders issued in spring 1952 reflect the need to improve the Stasi's conspiratorial practices while at least pretending to follow the criminal code; a tricky balancing act. In March, instructions were issued about the materials given to prosecutors and courts.[5] Stasi offices were being careless, which was not in Stasi interests:

> It has repeatedly occurred that departments of the Ministry for State Security, when handing over completed investigation processes to the responsible courts, submitted documents from which the working methods, the order of business and contexts of the ministry's work are discernible. To preserve conspiracy in the working methods of the Ministry for State Security, such [negligence] must be put to an end... processes submitted to the public prosecutor's office and the courts must contain [only] the following documents in the following order: table of contents, summary document, arrest and detention warrants, records of personal and property searches.

Interrogation protocols (transcripts) were to be 'written cleanly', with no strikethroughs or underlining; and only the first page of any anti-SED hate mail ('Hetzschriften') was to be photographed and shared – not the entire letter. In general, Stasi offices were to stop giving the game away:

> All those documents that provide insight into the working methods of the Ministry for State Security [and] which could jeopardise operational measures are not allowed to be included in the court file. This [includes] information breaking down the work of the Ministry for State Security, such as names of employees and secret co-workers or informers, methods of working with them, and indications of the structure of the ministry...

Reports by collaborators and cell informers, observation reports, search logs, operational plans, 'documents on planned or initiated operational measures against persons who are still at liberty', Stasi internal correspondence: all of this was to stay 'in the reference file of the employee who conducts the investigation'. If necessary it could be summarised, for it was 'categorically forbidden for the supervising public prosecutor to get into this reference file'.

These instructions were followed two months later by Order No. 74/52 on investigation procedures.[6] It insisted that Stasi employees demonstrate their respect for the law. The GDR constitution and codes of criminal procedure were to be 'strictly observed'. 'Democratic legality' was an obligation when conducting investigations – especially for 'employees charged with conducting investigations into criminal cases [and] the management of prisons' – and any deadlines set by judicial bodies were 'absolutely to be observed'.

These communications show the unwinnable position in which the SED's 'shield and sword' found itself. On the one hand the Stasi was to reinforce opacity, secrecy and its arbitrary freedom of action; on the other, it was subject to judicial oversight and under pressure to show its correctness. It still had more basic problems, too: an accompanying instruction pointed out that 'appropriate rooms' for interviewing suspects must be made available to judges, and that the 'aim must be to obtain [an] arrest warrant before arrest'.[7] Crucially though, the Stasi had power of veto over the prosecutors who were to be appointed, supposedly, by the attorney general: 'The names of public prosecutors appointed for individual administrations and districts are to be announced to those administrations by the Ministry for State Security.'

Stasi instructions reflect the turmoil and contradictions of the young GDR, the unreasonable expectations of the Soviet authorities, and the impossible aims of the SED. Put simply, the state they were trying to create didn't fit together. It couldn't be explained properly. It didn't convince. One reason was that nothing could be seen to be what it really was; everything had to pretend to be something else. Meanwhile, the Stasi increasingly was being identified and held responsible for the obvious lack of 'legal security'. This made the authorities more cautious; but only until their blood began to boil over the 'bourgeois tendencies' still prevalent in corners of the judicial system, which were preventing a complete subjugation of the law to the needs of the SED.

Contradiction followed contradiction. The Soviet Control Commission did not trust East German judges and prosecutors to deal firmly with political resistance; this was one reason why the most important political cases were handled by Soviet military tribunals until the mid-1950s. But in the autumn of 1951, the Soviet authorities – perhaps blaming the SED and Stasi for things that were their own fault – expressed concern that arbitrary repression was damaging East Germany's image, at home and in the West.[8] A Soviet Control Commission memo spoke of 'shortcomings and mistakes' in law enforcement, which were causing 'a certain dissatisfaction among the population' and being 'exploited by the domestic and foreign reaction'. The commission called for 'an end to arbitrary arrests, notification of the relatives of detainees, and public prosecutor oversight of criminal investigations and pretrial detention'. Yet these were the very public prosecutors who simultaneously were being castigated in SED reports for their 'objectivism' and reactionary views.

At the end of 1951 a resolution issued by the SED Politbüro reiterated that judges and prosecutors had 'weaknesses in the ideological field', were 'reluctant to impose even minimum fixed sentences', were 'not resilient and alert enough to Western tendencies', and held 'the mistaken opinion [that] the judge and prosecutors have to be neutral'. Their 'lack of class and party affiliation' meant they were 'not in a position to view every judgement as a political decision'. It was these criticisms that prompted the legislative changes of 1952, and led to the wave of guidelines that crashed through the Stasi, both of which attempted 'to integrate the criminal investigative activities of the State Security Service into the judicial system of the GDR'.

As well as introducing new training programmes to eliminate 'bourgeois legalism' in the judiciary, the Politbüro placed 'the judiciary on a completely new normative basis [with] a new code of criminal procedure, a new penal code, a law on the organisation of courts and a law on prosecutors'. The attorney general now had formal 'supervision of all criminal investigations and all prisons and pretrial detention centres, including those of the MfS'. Ultimately, these changes had two results: they made the judiciary more partisan and the Stasi more legalistic, in its paperwork if not its conduct.

The first recorded attempt to address the Stasi's use of torture dates from October 1952. Wilhelm Zaisser announced to all Stasi offices the dismissal of Eduard Switalla, chief of the Stasi in Rostock. Switalla had 'grossly violated democratic legality' and was 'guilty of "abuses" during interrogations'. The same period saw the first internal prosecutions of officers for extorting confessions and causing bodily harm to pretrial detainees.[9] Switalla and his fellow offenders were probably made an example of for being too obvious and cocky. There is no doubt that torture continued to occur. To an extent the Stasi's reputation, like that of its mentors in the Soviet Union, was saved by the tendency of victims to think that Stasi abusers were rogues, their behaviour unseen by superiors; 'the tough people who do not rule for long', as one suspect called them during interrogation.[10] And meanwhile, Erich Mielke had won an argument against the rule that Stasi arrestees had to be dealt with by the nearest district court. He got his way; the Stasi gained the right to choose which district court it worked with. This meant it could pick sympathetic judges and prosecutors for every case, and make it less likely that defendants' complaints would be listened to. Mielke failed in his campaign to extend the forty-eight-hour detention limit for arrestees who hadn't been charged, but this scarcely mattered. It was a rule the Stasi hardly ever followed anyway.[11]

Historians of the Stasi have argued that 'the acceptance of Soviet uncompromisingness and harshness in political criminal justice' was 'the fundamental prerequisite for [the Soviets granting] greater judicial independence in the GDR'.[12] But even as it struggled to strike the right balance between covert harshness and overt faultlessness, the Stasi's evolution from a tool of Soviet security to something stronger, and more independent, is illustrated in its first in-house instructions for one of its treasured specialisms: the running of informers.

The Stasi issued its first secret manuals on how to run informers in 1950 and 1952.[13] Over this period the number of informers shot up. According to the guidelines, which were signed by Erich Mielke, 'The main goal [of informers] is always to penetrate the centres of the enemy or the groups set up by him, in order to determine enemy plans early, make enemy activity impossible, and expose agents.' 'Enemy centres' meant the headquarters of West German parties and anti-communist groups, and the bases of Western intelligence services – all of whom were conniving together, as far as the Stasi was concerned.

The 1950 guidelines were issued just seven months after the Stasi was founded. Instigated by the MGB to foster the Stasi's 'creative initiative', they were drafted with the help of Soviet officers and used simple examples and case studies to make their points. They gave instructions on how to screen, recruit, and run informers, who at this time were split into the two main categories of secret co-worker (known as GM) and secret informer (GI); terms that came directly from the Soviet secret police term 'sekretnye sotrudniki' or 'seksot'.[14] It would be many years before these designations were replaced by the more famous, or infamous, IM (Inoffizieller Mitarbeiter or unofficial co-worker).

According to the guidelines, a GM was someone who carried out a range of tasks for the Stasi but was neither a full-time employee nor a straightforward source of information. GM were expected to have access to individuals or groups who were known or suspected of hostility towards East Germany. In practice, this meant recruiting people who were well-placed to take part in communist skulduggery, including the petty criminals hired for dirty jobs. Many GM were located in West Berlin and western Germany, where they were expected to observe or interfere with 'enemy centres', and to carry out supporting roles in operations against suspects and 'enemy factions'.[15]

A GI was someone who could give the Stasi information, especially in the course of everyday life. Many GI were the likes of waiters, teachers, hoteliers, or business travellers. As time passed, GI became more important to the Stasi and took on more of its work, reporting on the mood within workplaces and institutions, identifying political wrongdoers, and gathering information on suspects under investigation. When the term was changed in the late 1960s, the GI became IM; East Germany's ill-famed snitches, grassing on their colleagues, neighbours or family members. The early guidelines also set out the role of 'persons who maintain conspiratorial apartments' or KW.* This practice, which was developed and renamed over time, meant letting the Stasi use your property, contact address or belongings in the course of its work.

This last role is something of a forgotten corner of espionage, one that remains as vital today as it was for the Stasi in 1950. Intelligence services need the use of safe premises, messengers, and innocent-looking vehicles. They also need assets inside innocuous bureaucracies. In the mid-1950s, for example, the KGB planned to recruit more than 100 'documentation agents' around the world. This meant the employees of local councils, or registrars of births, deaths and marriages, whose only job for the KGB would be to provide paperwork as bogus evidence of spies' 'legends' (false identities).[16] Subsequently the KGB made great use of a clerk in the vehicle registration department of the Greater London Council.

The guidelines emphasised that, ideally, more than one informer should be recruited in any opposition group, and that these informers should be unknown to one another, enabling comparisons of their information. This is standard for any security service. However, right from the start it was difficult for the Stasi to acquire informers in the places that really mattered. Most people willing to supply information were supporters of the SED regime and uninvolved in any opposition. Compared to recruiting new informers, it was easier, and more common, to 'turn' arrestees and use them as information sources, despite the complexity and hazards of doing so.

It was especially difficult to entice professionals and highly educated people into becoming informers. In advice tailored for recruiting informers inside the UfJ, the 1952 guideline stated:

> The search for suitable persons to work against the so-called 'Free Jurists', for example, must be conducted among the group of persons from which the [UfJ] itself selects its agents. Of the criminals from the so-called Investigative Committee of Free Jurists convicted in the last trials,
>
> 32 percent were in ministries and the state apparatus
>
> 31 percent were engineers and designers in state-owned enterprises
>
> 10 percent were department heads in state-owned enterprises
>
> 10 percent were self-employed craftsmen and businessmen
>
> 17 percent were jurists, lawyers, and legal consultants.[17]

---

* 'Personen die konspirative Wohnungen unterhalten'.

In a similar vein, because the Stasi perceived the KgU to be a neo-fascist organisation, it was to be penetrated by the recruitment of former Nazis and Wehrmacht officers.[18] To expedite recruitment, the guidelines stated that a formal declaration of engagement as an informer – which most were expected to sign – could be waived, if doing so created a better bond between informer and handler. Informers within the churches and religious circles tended to make use of this caveat, partly in the hope of not leaving a paper trail on their activity.[19] The guidelines also reminded handlers to create a relaxed atmosphere by providing cigarettes and snacks at meetings. Still, many recruitments weren't so sensitive; throughout the 1950s blackmail was a common and accepted way for the Stasi to force cooperation.

On the first page of the 1952 guidelines, political opponents were described as 'reserve troops of the Anglo-American secret services'. Other suspect social groups, on whom information was desperately needed, were said to be former Hitler Youth leaders and SS officers, former Wehrmacht soldiers, 'morally depraved' youths, engineers, technicians, and managers in state enterprises: all difficult environments from which to recruit admirers of the SED. For the remainder of the decade and beyond, and despite the fact that recruiting SED members as informers was frowned upon except in special cases, Stasi officers protested: we have to recruit SED members as informers because we are unable to recruit anyone else.[20]

Even so, the Stasi had great freedom of action to stage events or co-opt citizens. To fool the fellow members of an opposition group, for example, informers would be pulled in for rough interrogation. To obscure the fact there was a traitor in the ranks, the Stasi would subtly spread knowledge about investigations or coming arrests among a number of group members, making it difficult to tell that a particular member was interacting with the Stasi. If needed, it would protect informers by simply planting evidence on the person, or in the home, of those it wanted to arrest, although it was far more interested in convicting people perceived as genuine opponents than in framing the innocent. And all the time, box-ticking bureaucracy was never far away. Every informer had to be recorded in the central Department of Registration and Statistics on a 10cm by 15cm card, giving first and last name, place and date of birth, address, class, occupation, nationality, political affiliation, date of recruitment, the name of the Stasi recruiter, and codename. Signed statements of cooperation would then be attached to the card.

The historian Gary Bruce has detailed several informer recruitments in the early days of the Stasi. In December 1949 – before the Stasi's founding and the use of the term GI – the communist Karl Ehmann was identified as a potential 'V-Mann' by a district office of the Directorate for the Protection of the National

Economy. (It isn't surprising the Stasi soon came up with its own designations for such collaborators, given the term V-Mann was strongly associated with the Gestapo.) Under the Nazis, Ehmann had done time in three prisons for his communist beliefs. He had a job in a sensitive place – the tractor depot on a collective farm, where sabotage might occur or dissatisfaction surface. The Stasi adopted the procedure it was to follow for the next forty years: officers discreetly approached local party officials for their view of the candidate, of course without telling those officials that a recruitment was in the offing. These enquiries always covered the individual's personality, relationships and conduct, their class background and financial situation, and any vices such as drinking; information the Stasi routinely wanted to possess, about anyone.

A local SED member vouched for Ehmann. Like most recruited informers, he was made to hand-write and sign a declaration of commitment to the Stasi. It was these declarations, lodged in Stasi files, which caused such havoc in the 1990s, when former Stasi collaborators were being unmasked. As the Stasi knew at the time, it was hard to deny or walk away from one's cooperation when a written statement of commitment was on record. Ehmann's commitment from 1950 sets a familiar template:

> I declare myself prepared to fulfil to the best of my knowledge and conscience the duties given to me by representatives of the Ministry for State Security as, being an [SED] member, I recognise the political necessity of this work. Since I recognise this importance, I also feel duty-bound not to mention this matter to anyone, not even to family members. If I do not abide by this, I am aware that I can be brought to justice.[21]

Having chosen the cover name 'Vogel' (Bird), Ehmann went on to a lacklustre career as an informer. He was sacked from the tractor depot for using its official stationery to acquire lightbulbs for his flat. Tellingly, the Stasi retained his services despite him leaving this useful position. His subsequent jobs at a rayon factory and a community college turned up little of interest, however, and the Stasi dropped contact a few years later, concluding that Ehmann 'lacked a view'.[22]

A recruitment of 1953 also shows the Stasi focusing on a sensitive site. The SED and Stasi had got wind of political 'grumbling' at a river port in the small town of Wittenberge. A colleague of the complainers, Kurt Wollschläger, was targeted for recruitment. After secretly gathering opinions on Wollschläger, including from a party official at the port and his landlady, the Stasi planned to make its pitch at the local council's housing office. Wollschläger would be enticed to enter a conversation with an undercover Stasi employee about the paucity of housing in West Germany. If he spoke positively about the situation in the GDR, his interlocutor would reveal his Stasi connections and try to recruit him as an informer.

This plan changed when Wollschläger left his job at the port and found work at a school. Again, the Stasi remained interested in him, despite the fact that he no longer worked at a significant place; even in 1953, the seeds were being sown for an all-round observation of society. Instead of being lured into a conversation about housing, one day at the school Wollschläger was drawn into a chat with a visiting official about the Western corruption of East German youth. When he expressed vaguely sympathetic views, the official revealed himself as a Stasi officer. At first Wollschläger wasn't keen on informing, but he was flattered into agreement; he liked it when he was told that the Stasi recruited 'only the best'.[23]

In the early guidelines, officers were urged to make the moment of recruitment 'a work of art'.[24] Everything had to be right; the chosen approach, the setting, the cover story and, if necessary, the means of diffusing or escaping the situation. Recruiters had to be able to read the subtle responses of the candidate. If a candidate declined, recruiters might change tack and bring up something threatening about a past misdemeanour, such as membership of a Nazi organisation.

Bruce recounts the tale of a Stasi officer tasked with recruiting a land-owning farmer as a source. First the officer chose his approach; he would pose as an agricultural official at the local council, and invite the candidate to the council offices to discuss his work. The conversation would start with the importance of large-scale farmers, who produced most of the food that was feeding the workers. The official would then mention that it was necessary to combat sabotage on farms. He would claim that enemies of socialism were introducing diseases to livestock, or milking cows so roughly that they stopped producing milk. If this failed to get a positive response, the recruiter would change tack and point out that the candidate's wife was known to possess leaflets issued by an anti-communist group in West Berlin; she would be charged if the farmer didn't cooperate. The pitch was successful.[25] In later years, it became more common for citizens to refuse to inform. In the early 1950s, with the Soviets still holding military tribunals, most were too scared to say no.[26]

The early guidelines didn't mention contact persons (Kontaktpersonen, KP), a vague category of Stasi helper. A KP was not formally registered as an informer, but might provide occasional information and assistance. Later guidelines referred to them as 'trustworthy citizens' who could be 'approached to fulfil specific tasks'. Often they were people in an official capacity who might help the Stasi with the likes of vetting, especially schoolteachers and workplace managers. Another example – which shows the pull the Stasi had, in all walks of life – was a funeral director who complied with the Stasi's request to prevent mourners from getting too close to the body of a loved one in an open coffin, so they wouldn't see the injuries he had sustained in Stasi detention. In the same incident, the backgrounds of the hearse drivers and gravediggers were thoroughly investigated by Stasi collaborators.[27]

The Stasi was to become famous for listening to private phone calls and reading private letters. The origins of this core activity were typically modest, and illustrate how the Stasi managed to transform itself over time.[28]

In 1950 the Stasi's Department VI, responsible for the security of state institutions, had a small sub-department, VIa, whose head and his deputy worked at the Normannenstrasse headquarters. Other employees of Department VIa worked undercover at postal sorting offices in Berlin, in what were secretly called 'Collection centres for anti-democratic correspondence' or AFaS.*

The thirty-odd personnel of the AFaS had two tasks. 'Anti-democratic writings' criticising the SED, East Germany, or the Soviet Union, and known as 'hate material' ('Hetzmaterial'), were to be removed from the postal system, undelivered. Secondly, citizen's private correspondence was to inform regular reports on the mood at workplaces and governing bodies.

The regular postal workers at each depot would be given quotas of mail – say, 1,000 letters posted to students at Humboldt University – which they would turn over to the Department VIa employees. They were not given a reason for doing so. Each Department VIa employee was expected to scrutinise 500 letters per day. The first such Stasi outpost was at the Nordbahnhof post office, and was referred to as Objekt A or ANTON. Another was created at Ostbahnhof – this was Objekt C or CAESAR. Both operated almost to the end of the GDR, as did a third on Gotlindestrasse (BERTA), which provided coverage of the telegraph traffic in the Greater Berlin area.

Similar interception procedures were set up on a smaller scale by provincial Stasi offices, where personnel of Department VIa would compile their mood reports (Stimmungsberichte) to be forwarded on to Berlin headquarters. In a glimpse of the Stasi's long-term ambitions, these reports were intended, in the Stasi's words, to 'give a perfect picture at all times of the mood of the population from various social classes on individual political and economic issues'. As for the letters and parcels withdrawn from circulation, there was no slick system for transporting or storing them – individual officers of Department VIa had

---

* Auffangstellen für antidemokratischen Schriftverkehr.

to lug them around and stash them, taking personal responsibility for their safety.

A Stasi instruction of May 1951 reveals the targets of postal interception at the Stasi's Länder administrations. In Brandenburg, the post of 1,000 workers from each of two industrial sites, Hüttenkombinates Ost and the Brandenburg steel works, was to be intercepted, as well as that of 1,000 farmers, including some of the supposedly loyal Neubauern. The targets for Mecklenburg were 1,000 workers from the Rostock shipyards, and 500 students and fifty lecturers at Rostock University; in Saxony-Anhalt, 1,000 workers in both the chemical and heavy engineering industries, 1,000 farmers, and 800 students and 100 lecturers at Halle's Martin Luther University; in Saxony, 1,000 workers from the Riesa steelworks, some commercial and tradespeople, and 800 students and 100 lecturers at the University of Leipzig; and in Thuringia, 1,000 workers from both the Unterwellenborn steelworks and Carl Zeiss in Jena, some tradespeople, and 800 students and 100 professors at the University of Jena.[29]

Correspondence involving the Stasi's sworn enemies soon became the top priority – the Ostbüros, UfJ, KgU and League of German Youth – as well as that of the Jehovah's Witnesses, of which more below. Letters and parcels sent by these organisations were easy to spot. Thanks to the naiveté of their senders in West Berlin and the Federal Republic, they always had the same weight, sizes, ink, fonts and franking. (For the remainder of the 1950s, the thoughtless use of the postal system meant that trained spies of Western intelligence services, including the Organisation Gehlen, continued to be caught due to the obviousness of the letter-senders.)

At the start of 1952 Department VIa became Department M. This remained the designation of the Stasi's postal interception branch until the demise of East Germany; in its mature phase it functioned covertly as the mysterious Unit 12 (Stelle 12) within the structure of Deutsche Post. And another development proved helpful. In the summer of 1952, the Länder – the five provincial states of the GDR – were dissolved and reorganised into new regions and districts. The main reason for the change was to create a progressive new structure for a progressive new state, but it also enabled closer control of the postal system, a welcome side effect.

31

Ulbricht's Acceleration of Socialism

In summer 1952 Walter Ulbricht, from his position as general secretary of the SED, began to push through an extreme ideological programme to transform East Germany's society and economy – a process known in his words as 'the building of socialism' and 'an intensification of the class struggle'. Earlier that year he had shared details of the country's new Five Year Plan. Announcing it in a mass-produced pamphlet,[1] Ulbricht had generously let his readers know that this 'is no ordinary reading material, no brochure like many others that one leafs through and sets aside. It contains your fate'. He had pledged the end of rationing within one year and, by 1955, 'more meat, sugar, milk, etc., per capita than we had in 1936', promises that proved hollow. Ulbricht had followed this up by announcing the building of socialism (Aufbau des Sozialismus, or Aufbau for short) at the SED's second party congress. One of its cornerstones was a more radical collectivisation of agriculture. One of its results was a busier Stasi.

Moscow was horrified. With the Korean War raging and nuclear weapons proliferating, the defensive Soviet foreign policy of the moment was to present the GDR in a fairly moderate light, as a place the West could talk to and do business with. Yet here was Ulbricht pushing forward with hardcore socialism, alienating Western countries and stirring up more resentment, and potentially revolt, among the population. But Walter Ulbricht had been waiting for a lifetime for the chance to implement Marxism-Leninism-Stalinism in his own country. Now he could.

The Aufbau saw private businesses and the middle classes, especially shopkeepers and manufacturers, hit by punitive legislation, high taxes, and the denial of credit. The self-employed were excluded from health and social care. Half of all businesses with fewer than fifty workers had already ceased to exist in their original form; now the remainder were to be brought to heel.[2] Those who refused to comply with the centralising of the economy were liable to have land or property confiscated, or be denied access to subsidies, benefits or education.[3]

On a more sinister level, charges of sabotage or hoarding saw recalcitrant farmers and entrepreneurs put through harsh interrogations and local show trials, often resulting in prison sentences. Stasi arrests increased – 1,500 were made from August to December 1952. Despite the Stasi's behind-the-scenes attempts to foster probity, many arrestees were subjected to harsh physical treatment, sleep deprivation and other forms of torture.[4] Therefore, in the minds of the East German public, the acceleration of socialism was seen to go hand-in-hand with an acceleration in aggressive, arbitrary policing – just as it had in the Soviet Union when Stalin had enacted similarly harsh campaigns.

Not every opponent of the Aufbau was blameless. Collectivisation was met with violence. Some of the hated directors of state farms were murdered in East Germany, like they were in Bulgaria.[5] Privately owned farms, still in a large majority, were encouraged to 'voluntarily' form 'agricultural production co-operatives' or LPGs, with collective ownership.* The LPGs aroused such bitter opposition that by January 1953 more than 1,200 trials had been conducted against farmers,[6] and the programme was temporarily shelved, eventually taking a decade to complete.

Given the way that socialist societies everywhere have tended to initiate it, often at terrific human cost, it is safe to say that collectivised agriculture, badly and rashly implemented, is one of socialism's fatal addictions. In East Germany it led to shortages as well as social disruption. The first half of 1953 was marked by the virtual disappearance of meat, butter, fruit and vegetables.[7] At least, this was true for the person in the street; for according to a CIA report of the time,[8] the GDR's State Planning Commission prioritised the distribution of home-produced and imported foodstuffs as:

a. Red Army in the Soviet zone
b. State Reserve
c. Export and Reparations
d. Privileged circles (party and government functionaries, working intelligentsia)
e. General population

The same report noted that private businesses were at the bottom of the list for wholesale supplies. Meanwhile, urban workers were hit with extreme production quotas and the clumsy nationalisation of industry which, among other things, saw a severe drop in health and safety standards. Many people were killed in avoidable accidents. The production of consumer goods was deprioritised to rock bottom, and everyday items for an acceptable quality of life became ever scarcer. Heavy industry and the expansion of paramilitary forces were the new

---

*   LPG: Landwirtschaftlichen Produktionsgenossenschaften.

priorities; but so were social initiatives such as the public promotion of working-class people and culture, an accompanying public denigration of the middle class, and a drive to maintain at boiling point the hatred of Western-sponsored 'fascism'.

Ulbricht and his Politbüro colleagues knew they were ushering in a hard, unpopular era. Part of Ulbricht's resolution on the Aufbau read, 'The party and each individual member of it must exercise great revolutionary attentiveness and conduct a decisive battle against tendencies of forgiveness towards enemies of the party and the people.'[9] To pay for the acceleration of socialism, stiff cuts were made in social funding. Two million people – those considered socially suspect by the SED – had their ration books withdrawn; a good example of communism in practice, wherein a desperate economic measure is conflated with the exercising of class hatred. There were many corollaries to Ulbricht's central policy. Ideological pressure on the churches increased, and the SED aimed to make Marxism-Leninism the basis of all higher education.[10] Predictably this inspired new resistance among hitherto inactive students, such as a notable CDU group at the University of Leipzig, thus generating new enemies for the attention of the Stasi.

Perhaps the most hated measure of the Aufbau was the Law on the Protection of National Property, which came into force on 2 October 1952. Its first paragraph proclaimed that 'theft, embezzlement or any other removal of state property or collective property, or of property belonging to social organisations, will be punished with one to five years imprisonment'.[11] In practice, the law criminalised anyone who tried to beg, borrow, deal or steal food, or innocuous items for daily use, as well as anyone who was accused of slacking at work.

Within five months more than 10,000 East Germans had been proceeded against under this law. Absurdly harsh prison sentences were handed down. Just one example is the woman sentenced to six (rather than five) years for selling eggs on the streets of West Berlin. Another is the workers at a Schwerin cigarette factory sentenced to three years for smoking during a break.[12] From July 1952 to May 1953 the country's prison population increased from 30,000 held in 150 prisons to more than 60,000 held in 200 prisons.[13] All of this upheaval stirred up virulent popular resentment.

At Christmas 1952 large bonuses were awarded to some of the factory bosses who had met SED quotas. This led to strikes by workers in Berlin, Cottbus and notably Magdeburg, where 2,000 walked out of the Karl-Liebknecht-Werk.[14] Three brigades of SED agitators were sent to quell the disturbance, but in the following months the complaints and unrest rumbled on. Economic grievances were mixing potently with political demands, especially for free elections, for the workers understood that free elections were likely to remove the SED from power.

By February 1953 the party was sufficiently fearful of popular anger to make new efforts to protect its leadership. According to a resolution, 'Uninterrupted day and night protection is to be guaranteed to all members of the Politbüro [by having] escorts from the Ministry for State Security.'[15] In all districts, party secretaries were authorised to carry arms. And, echoing the social cleansing that took place in the USSR in the 1930s, known or suspected 'undesirables' were rounded up and kicked out of the Pankow district of Berlin, where many of the SED's top officials lived.[16]

Ulbricht's Aufbau had numerous repercussions on the Stasi and East Germany. As mentioned, the territory itself was rearranged, for the SED wanted its citizens to see the GDR as a fresh start, and to wean them off parochialism. To inculcate a sense of novelty, the five Länder were replaced by fifteen regional administrations (Bezirke) subdivided into more than 200 districts (Kreise). The population was thus grouped into new, strangely-named locations. From this point onwards, the historical Länder of Mecklenburg, Brandenburg, Saxony, Thuringia and Saxony-Anhalt were rarely mentioned in official texts, although they made a brief reappearance in a set of 1960s postage stamps celebrating their traditional costumes.

An equally big jolt to the population was the creation in May 1952 of a five-kilometre-wide prohibited zone (Sperrzone) along the length of the inter-German border. At a meeting at the Kremlin the previous month, and in the wake of his failed attempts to lure the Western powers with a plan for German reunification that favoured Soviet interests, Stalin had told Ulbricht, Pieck and Grotewohl that the 'line of demarcation between West and East Germany must be seen... not as a simple border but a dangerous one'.[17] Planned by the Stasi and executed by the Volkspolizei, Operation Vermin (Aktion Ungeziefer) saw the unfurling of 1,000 kilometres of barbed wire through town and country.

In his order initiating the operation, Wilhelm Zaisser blamed the Western powers for introducing 'a strict border and customs service along the demarcation line', by which they had 'set themselves apart' and 'deepened the division of Germany'. Up to this point, travellers between the different zones of Germany had needed an interzonal pass, valid for thirty days. In the wake of Aktion Ungeziefer, this system was replaced in East Germany by the use of exit permits, for which anyone wishing to leave the GDR had to apply. For Zaisser, the new measures were aimed more at Western intelligence services than East Germans. He wrote that the 'lack of adequate protection' was 'being exploited by the Western powers to smuggle ever greater numbers of spies, diversionists [and] terrorists' who, 'after carrying out their criminal tasks', could 'return unhindered across the demarcation line to West Germany'. The new border zone, complete with its fortified 500-metre wide 'protective strip' leading up to the demarcation line, and a ten-metre wide 'control strip' on the borderline itself, was intended to render impossible 'the penetration of enemy agents into the territory of the German Democratic Republic'.[18]

Aktion Ungeziefer saw at least 10,000 people evicted from their homes in the border areas.[19] Before the operation the Volkspolizei checked all residents, fast-tracking political undesirables for resettlement: former Nazis, families with contacts in West Germany, common criminals, and farmers resisting collectivisation ('reactionary peasants'). Rumours spread that these were deportations to Poland and Siberia, and when the police and trucks arrived there was some violent disorder, egged on by the likes of RIAS. In many areas, church bells pealed to warn adjacent villages. In Thuringia, nearly 2,000 people escaped eviction by running into West Germany. In the Sonneberg district, seven cases of suicide were reported, including of a family of four. The mood quietened when re-settlers learned of the 500 marks compensation coming their way, and when resettled persons were brought back to the border areas to show that 'they were well accommodated and already inducted in new jobs'.[20]

In most places the Sperrzone made it more difficult and dangerous to cross the borders. There were, however, patchy spots, and the sector crossings of Berlin's streets, alleys, waterways and bomb-blasted voids remained as porous as ever. But the psychological sense of separation was heightened. In both republics the slang phrase 'drüben', meaning 'over there', grew up in reference to the other. Given that the 'Berlin corridor' was now the only place for refugees to abandon East Germany with relative ease, many did just that; over winter 1952-53, more than 130,000 crossed into West Berlin.[21]

The SED and Stasi discussed further measures to stop this exodus. A CIA source in the East German government reported new instructions from the Politbüro to newspaper editors, who were now to refer to refugees as 'fugitives'. Another instruction demanded that 'particular emphasis [must] be placed on the danger facing young male refugees that upon their arrival in the West they may be shanghaied by the French Foreign Legion', a claim that might have had some truth in it. And, at least according to the CIA source, the same directive declared that no one should mention the internment of returnees to the GDR:

> ...the fact that every such person returning to East Germany is immediately arrested and confined for a period varying from two weeks to three months must be kept quiet. This imprisonment is considered to be for "re-educational

purposes", while allowing sufficient time for an investigation of the person's activities during his [sic] stay in the West. In case of acquittal, the confinement is to be regarded as a police punishment for failure to register the change of address with the local police.[22]

Other Stasi-related developments illustrate the severe climate of the Aufbau period. For a while, telephone connections between East and West Berlin were severed, with the Stasi monitoring the disconnection. By August 1952 the border and transport police had been subordinated to the Stasi, although their boss, deputy security minister Hermann Gartmann, allowed them some operational autonomy. Furthermore, the tightening of the borders went hand-in-hand with a growing militarisation. After the April meeting between Stalin and the SED top brass, the government of the GDR – blaming similar moves in West Germany – announced the build-up of 'national armed forces'.

The first manifestation of this was an enlargement and empowerment of the paramilitary police, now renamed the Garrisoned People's Police or KVP (Kasernierte Volkspolizei). This was a prototype army, ready to receive the armaments that were supposed to start tumbling from East Germany's clanging production lines. The Stasi, too, had armed soldiers on strength; guard units garrisoned in the Adlershof area of Berlin and at provincial administrations, tasked with protecting government buildings. By late 1952 the Stasi's Berlin Guards Regiment, later renowned as the Felix Dzerzhinsky Guards, comprised 154 officers, 537 NCOs, and 2,329 troops. But the same old problems with morale and desertion continued. Or rather, they worsened, for the new deprivations and pressures created by Ulbricht's policies saw an increase in desertions from the paramilitary police, from 600 in 1950 to nearly 1,200 two years later.[23]

Despite the dwindling number of National Front politicians and party members who were able to overcome their fear of reprisals, a few voiced opposition to the rearming of East Germany. One district CDU office gave four reasons why its members were against the creation of a 'Volksarmee': it would increase the risk of civil war, entail ongoing domination by Russia, have harmful impacts on the economy, and – with beautiful simplicity – was unnecessary.[24] But the SED, like so many authoritarian rulers, was prepared to sacrifice a great deal for the sake of numerically strong armed forces and a well-resourced security service.

Thus the Stasi strengthened and grew through the Aufbau. Because of the enlargement of its Administration for Greater Berlin, and the subdivision of the GDR's new regions into 211 districts, the number of Stasi offices had to be more than doubled. The new local offices were known as 'district service units': Kreisdienststellen (KD). Within a couple of years, enlarged offices had been set up in some of the regional capitals – Leipzig, Karl-Marx-Stadt, Dresden, Halle, Magdeburg, Rostock. The number of full-time Stasi personnel duly increased from 4,500 at the end of 1951 to almost 9,000 a year later;[25] within a few more months it hit 10,000.[26]

Although in theory the district offices followed the line principle, whereby every department at Stasi headquarters was replicated throughout the lower-level sites, in practice they tended to bundle activities and personnel rather than follow the lines. Typically a KD would assign personnel to what were seen as the four most important functions performed at the Berlin headquarters: analysis, counter-espionage, political opposition, and the economy.[27]

The average KD had a staff of fifteen, plus a chief and a deputy ('operational') chief, although some of the larger and more important districts had more than forty employees. Support staff included drivers, secretaries, radio operators, medics, and building guards. The inhabitants of smaller districts tended to know that someone was a full-time Stasi employee but not, of course, who was an informer.[28] The Stasi's premises were identifiable, thanks to their external Ministerium für Staatssicherheit plaques and small advertisements for opening hours. But the details of the work done inside these buildings remained obscure – the subject of hints, intimidating whispers, and fleeting facial expressions.

The steep rise in the number of Stasi employees resulted from a big influx of young working-class men, most with only elemental education, poached from around the SED, the Free German Youth and the Volkspolizei. Almost overnight these young adults became the large majority of Stasi employees: brawny, grateful, and with unsullied minds, for most had 'no personal experience of the Communist labour movement before 1945'.[29] In internal reports the Stasi classified its staff as being ninety-two percent working class, ninety-two percent SED members, and fifty percent under thirty years' old.[30]

It was reckoned that youths from underprivileged families would be able to carry out arrests and interrogations with the required force. There was a good chance they would buy into the Stasi's 'friend-enemy' ethos; its Stalinist worldview of deadly foes requiring merciless liquidation. However, two problems arose rather quickly. First, many of the new recruits were not sufficiently educated to write the transcript of an interrogation.[31] Secondly, there was a very high turnover, due especially to rapid dismissals for ill-discipline.

Several initiatives aimed to correct these faults. During 1951, on the site of the former Prussian Police Officers' School at Potsdam-Eiche, the Stasi founded its own educational establishment, the MfS School (Schule des MfS). As well as offering the obligatory Marxism-Leninism and Russian language classes, its main goal was to give recruits a working knowledge of the law and procedures around political crime. Although tradecraft and operational techniques were still mostly learned in the field, taught by Soviet advisers and pre-war KPD members, the school and its subject matters grew rather impressively. In 1956 it was renamed the MfS College (Hochschule des MfS), and in time it came to issue doctorates of law. After the fall of East Germany, former Stasi officers facing accusations of wrongdoing sometimes claimed they couldn't possibly have been working for an abusive or illegal organisation, because they had been so well-trained in the law.

During 1952 Stasi personnel switched from holding police ranks to military ones. Everyone at the Stasi had a rank; for example, cleaners, drivers, waitresses and washer-uppers might hold the rank of Feldwebel, roughly equivalent to a sergeant.[32] In the GDR, as in the Soviet Union, state security ranks denoted more seniority than their army equivalents; a lieutenant in the MGB or Stasi was equivalent to a captain in the army. The Stasi's switch to military ranks served several purposes. Everyone knew where they stood in the hierarchy; everyone had a uniform to wear on special bonding occasions; everyone was assured of the importance of their work; everyone was subject to military discipline. It reminded Stasi personnel they were a martial elite: first class comrades.

Other changes mark the Stasi's steady evolution. From 1950 to 1952 about 30,000 new GI and GM were recruited, although government agencies, National Front parties, civil organisations and sensitive industries, and not the public at large, remained the main targets for informers. In 1952 the Stasi office for the Frankfurt an der Oder area had 533 informers on its books; this was probably a typical number (as was the 2,986 it had in 1965).[33]

Several Stasi departments were growing busier and more significant all the time. By the end of 1953, most of those at headquarters level had been renamed Main Departments (Hauptabteilungen) and given the prefix 'HA'. The personnel of Main Department II (HA II, 'Spionageabwehr') were the Stasi's counter-espionage specialists. Under the leadership of Josef Kiefel, they hunted for and tackled spies throughout East German institutions and society, as well as at the Soviets' Karlshorst facilities. They also conducted counter-intelligence operations in West Germany with a view to penetrating and disrupting the police forces, émigré organisations, and Western intelligence services based there.[34]

Like some of his fellow Stasi executives, Kiefel, a Bavarian and the former chief of K5 in Saxony-Anhalt, had charisma and stories to tell. After plying almost every manual trade under the sun as a youth, he had become an expert furrier while exiled in the Soviet Union during the Nazi era, and was awarded the honour of 'Stakhanovite worker'. He had also denounced at least one Austrian communist to the NKVD, which he continued to serve during the war as an intelligence officer in a partisan group operating in occupied Poland.[35]

Main Department V, an amalgamation of the previous Departments V and VI, was led in its first years by the old warhorse Bruno Beater, with former K5 boss Erich Jamin as his deputy. It had the broad remit of fighting political opposition. This meant tackling any covert oppositional activity in government ministries, state institutions and the leading bodies of National Front parties; safeguarding the SED's activities in culture and sport; invigilating the country's youth and religious believers; neutralising former social democrats and Trotskyists; and thwarting the activities of right-wing extremists and other opposition groups, from the KgU and UfJ to the Ostbüros of West Germany's political parties.[36] Its main weapon, of course, was the use of informers. The department had well-placed collaborators inside East Germany's 'bourgeois' parties, exemplified by the likes of Kurt Wünsche (recruited as GI 'Wendler' in 1954) and Hans-Joachim Heusinger (recruited as GI 'Knebel' in 1955), both of whom sat on the central board of the LDPD.[37]

The work of Main Department III, responsible for securing the economy, intensified with the Aufbau. As well as tackling all the newly criminalised farmers, small business owners and workplace pilferers said to be impeding East Germany's economic rise, the department was a notable deployer of undercover officers at farms and, especially, at Machine Tractor Stations. The latter, copied from the Soviet Union, were politicised storage depots for farming equipment; and HA III was mandated to have an employee working covertly at each one. In a different vein, the early months of 1953 saw the department taking part in Aktion Rose, in which the state confiscated holidaymaking assets on the Baltic coast. More than 400 hotels and 180 restaurants and shops were sequestered, and hundreds of their former owners, cleaners and catering employees were convicted of 'economic' offences. While this was hardly the brutality of other revolutions – there were no piles of skulls like those in Cambodia or Africa or Latin America – this government bullying, particularly in the leisure sector, caused a surprising amount of public resentment.[38]

Department VII, not upgraded to a Main Department until the late 1950s, invigilated the interior ministry and police. Its work increased with the subordination of the border and transport police to the Stasi. Officially the department wasn't allowed to recruit senior police officers as informers, but most were already known quantities and close colleagues of the Stasi. The political loyalty of the police, and officers' knowledge of Marxism-Leninism and Bolshevik history, continued to receive attention, with an expansion of the Politkultur school at Biesenthal. While the Stasi 'took precedence over the interests of the criminal police [and] could at any time override an intended recruitment [of an informer and] take over the case',[39] Stasi personnel and police detectives had a close working relationship. The police helped the Stasi to conduct many of the mass operations of the Aufbau. The next constituents to feel the blows of this two-fisted security force were religious believers.

In at least one matter, Nazi and SED opinion was unanimous: Jehovah's Witnesses were seditious agents of American capitalism. Despite their official status as victims of Nazism – some 5,000 Witnesses had died in concentration camps – in 1950 the organisation was proscribed in East Germany. The SED didn't care for the Witnesses' regular contact with their headquarters in Brooklyn and at Wiesbaden in West Germany – the latter ran the movement within the GDR. In August 1950 the Stasi launched a campaign in which 500 Witnesses were arrested; seven were subsequently convicted as spies in a show trial.[40] In a Stasi instruction of the following year, Erich Mielke wrote that it 'is only possible to uncover the top functionaries and most dangerous agents of the Witnesses sect by targeting our work and recruiting GM and informers with the right potential'.[41] This view of Jehovah's Witnesses as fifth columnists never really changed in East Germany – over the next five years, almost 3,000 did prison time.

Jehovah's Witnesses were among the first victims of systematic Zersetzung (decomposition) operations by the Stasi. In later decades such operations became notorious for unsettling the members of dissident groups. At least one Zersetzung measure was copied straight from the earliest days of the Cheka. A targeted person would be summoned to the nearest offices of the Stasi or interior ministry, kept waiting around aimlessly for hours in a corridor or reception room, and then dismissed and sent back to work without explanation. Unable to explain to colleagues their reason for visiting the government office, these unfortunates would fall under suspicion of being an informer, besmirching their reputation.[42] Furthermore, the Stasi infiltrated Witnesses' schools and study groups, as well as the Wiesbaden site. In later years, one Stasi officer wrote that good ways to weaken the movement included 'defamation of officials', 'denigrating the intellectual and psychological capabilities of group members', 'blaming them for criminal offences' and 'spreading malicious rumours about marital infidelity'.[43] Cross-border operations saw couriers prevented from distributing the publications *Watchtower* and *Awake!*, and Witnesses faced discrimination, such as youths being refused apprenticeships.

After the war the Protestant churches of Germany, including those in the Soviet zone, had been federated in a new organisation, the EKD (Evangelische

Kirche in Deutschland). Around eighty percent of the East German population identified itself as Protestant, eleven percent as Catholic, although a minority were active churchgoers; ancient laws gave the churches the right to levy taxes, and these figures come from the compulsory tax registration in which all citizens had to choose which church their money should go to. In one of their first actions towards the churches, SED officials harangued clerics to vote, and to encourage voting, in the October 1950 election. Over time, participation in elections became a focal point of compliance or defiance among East German church officials, with around sixty percent voting and forty percent abstaining, sometimes vocally.

As the Aufbau got underway, the East German leadership swung its sights on the churches. Their right to exist was enshrined in the GDR constitution. Realistically this couldn't be revoked; so, as with the Jehovah's Witnesses, the Stasi decided the best approach was to penetrate the churches with GI and GM. There were some notable successes. Friedrich-Wilhelm Krummacher, a Bishop of Greifswald and former Nazi party member, worked for the Soviets and the Stasi.[44] At the same time, great pressure was exerted on the eastern Protestant churches to break with those in West Germany. Although these efforts were ultimately successful, they took the best part of twenty years to achieve their goal.

The objective of Main Department V was to penetrate the churches so deeply that the Stasi could steer their policies and activities. So began the complex process of infiltrating and controlling a potential opposition movement; an art in itself, for any security service.[45] One Stasi tactic was to nurture clerics and groups who were amenable to SED rule, in the hope they would come to dominate the opposition. At universities and colleges, pro-SED theology students were urged to besmirch members of the Protestant youth organisation, Junge Gemeinde, as 'totalitarians'.[46] Before long the Junge Gemeinde was declared illegal, despite a barrage of complaints. Then a new rule was brought in that children must be allowed a two-hour break after school before any organised social activity could commence. Cunningly, this prevented many church youth groups from convening, as by that time their members were ready for bed. The Stasi also took action against those who tried to perpetuate the Junge Gemeinde. Fifty clerics were arrested, and 300 children expelled from schools.[47]

At the end of 1952 an MGB report praised the Stasi's operational work over the previous year. It had arrested more than 2,500 people, including 599 alleged spies; established coverage of thirty-five 'enemy centres' and underground organisations based in West Berlin and West Germany, arresting more than 600 of their agents; and helped to conduct sixteen show trials of 'enemy spies, diversionists, and terrorists'. The report also complimented the Stasi's kidnapping skills.[48]

But the Chekist tradition of greedy repression decreed that this wasn't enough; more was required. By the start of 1953, encouraged by events in the Soviet Union, the steely eyes of the SED and Stasi had fixed on East Germany's Jews. At that moment Joseph Stalin was capping off a lifetime of malign fantasies with a fixation on the alleged treachery of Soviet Jews. A wave of officially tolerated anti-Semitism had already swept Moscow and the USSR, and now was rippling through the Soviet Bloc.

Self-identified Jews in East Germany were organised into official communities (gemeinden). The gemeinden claimed 8,000 members in 1950, but the SED's hostility towards religion meant that many Jews, such as the Politbüro members Albert Norden and Hermann Axen, didn't join a community. Other Jews simply left the GDR, and the numbers in the gemeinden declined steeply over time. It didn't help that the SED, aping Moscow, adopted a view of the Holocaust that cast communists as the most important victims. The trauma experienced by surviving Jews was never properly recognised or addressed, and blame was transferred to West Germany – capitalist and therefore 'fascist' – as the guilty party.

As early as August 1952, the Stasi was making plans for the large-scale arrest of Jews.[49] These were averted by the actions of a Jewish state functionary who had been co-opted by the Stasi to help in the coming purge. He had been ordered to infiltrate the upper echelons of the Jewish community and to find – or fabricate – evidence that Zionism was a growing threat to the socialist order; that East German Jews were loyal not to the GDR but to the Jewish Agency and other bodies. Horrified by the task, he told others about it, including a Jewish lawyer from Leipzig. The lawyer, in turn, was able to get word of the imminent arrests to two prominent Jews, Helmut Looser of the Leipzig gemeinde and Julius Meyer, an SED deputy in the Volkskammer and nominal head of East German Jewry. Looser and Meyer then tipped off the gemeinden and the Jewish community of West Berlin, which prepared to receive refugees. A code phrase was agreed upon which, if needed, would trigger the flight from the GDR. On 10 January 1953, in a rapid series of telephone calls, the signal was given. Among the 400 Jews who escaped East Germany were Meyer and five of the country's eight gemeinde leaders.

However, 'anti-Zionism' remained a pillar of Stasi ideology until the end of East Germany. With so many prominent Jews gone, the Stasi made sure it had good coverage of the remainder. One example was the recruitment of

Helmut Aris, president of the Dresden gemeinde, as an informer.[50] When repressing its own executives, the SED conflated Jewishness with ideological deviation. In December 1952 the former Politüro member Paul Merker was arrested, having been implicated in the earlier Slánský trial held in Prague. During his spell in Stasi detention he was threatened with death, deprived of sleep for days and nights on end, and insulted by his interrogators as a 'Jew lackey' ('Judenknecht'). Other disgraced 'bourgeois' politicians were arrested at the same time, including the previously mentioned Georg Dertinger and the former minister for trade, Karl Hamann of the LDPD, who was alleged to be a 'liaison for the American secret service'.

Merker was sentenced to eight years in prison for his alleged connections with hostile Western forces. In itself, communist excommunication could be ruinous. After immersing oneself in an elaborate belief system, full of standards and rules, the observance of which are a matter of personal honour; having conformed to such a system and based one's entire life around it, to be thrown out of the fold was devastating. In Merker's case he was pardoned and released early, but his rehabilitation came at a price. He was made to testify against former friends during yet another wave of show trials in the late 1950s.

To temper the upheavals of the Aufbau, the SED again made some token efforts to lift the public mood. In the early 1950s, culture and the arts weren't really on the Stasi's radar. They didn't need to be – historians have noted that the first generation of GDR writers and artists were pretty loyal to the SED. Like artists in the Soviet Union, they could be flattered with the sensation of being close to political power. Some relished the chance to express their disgust at fascism and their admiration for Marx, Lenin and Stalin.

In the cinema, the DEFA film production monopoly did its best to entertain while glorifying the Aufbau. Its studios churned out hagiographical documentaries on KPD martyrs such as Ernst Thälmann, encouraged public vigilance in spy dramas and exposés of Nazi crimes, and celebrated Germany's benign heritage in bucolic costume dramas.[51] Elsewhere, the German College for Physical Culture, established in 1950, was to gain a reputation for developing world-class coaches – although, from the 1960s onwards, many of their pupils would go through Stasi-run doping programmes – and in August 1952 the important Association for Sport and Technology (GST) was founded. Like a paramilitary Scouts and Guides for grown-ups, the GST rewarded loyal workers with a range of improving activities, from parachute jumps to amateur electronics.

But Moscow was never comfortable with Ulbricht's Aufbau. Throughout it all, the Soviet leadership was receiving accurate information, from Soviet and Stasi inquiries, about the worsening public mood in East Germany. The population was bleeding out; half a million people had fled the GDR since 1951, and 120,000 in the first four months of 1953. In April that year, Moscow officially warned Ulbricht to soften his policies.[52] When he prevaricated he was summoned to the Kremlin for a talking-to; yet upon returning home, he continued to drag his heels on introducing reform. This led to another summons to Moscow, on 2 June. At this encounter Lavrenti Beria was openly aggressive to the SED delegation, insisting that Ulbricht relax his approach to the economy.[53]

Joseph Stalin had died in March, and the nervousness of the battling leaders who had replaced him – Beria, Molotov, Nikita Khrushchev, Georgy Malenkov – was palpable. They were afraid of losing their postwar empire, afraid of being toppled themselves. They foresaw not just public unrest in East Germany but the possible overthrow of the SED, a potential calamity for Soviet communism and for the Cold War defence of Russia. At around this time, the Soviet High Commissioner for Germany, Vladimir Semyonov, commented to *Neues Deutschland* editor Rudolf Herrnstadt that 'maybe in fourteen days you won't have a state any more.'[54]

Official statements were put out, in which the Soviets acknowledged 'serious dissatisfaction in the majority of the [East German] population, including the workers, farmers and intellectuals, regarding the economic and political measures which have been introduced'. Secretly, the SED's mishandling of the churches was also criticised: 'It should be kept in mind that repression of the church [can] only contribute to strengthening religious fanaticism in residual sections of the population, and to increasing their dissatisfaction.'[55]

Finally, on 9 June 1953, the SED issued a communiqué announcing a partial relaxation. This initiative was known as 'the New Course'. There was to be a softening in the collectivisation of agriculture, an end to the persecution of church members and the Junge Gemeinde. Some of the restrictions on private business owners were to be lifted.[56] Ration cards confiscated from the supposed bourgeoisie were largely to be returned. Prisoners sentenced to less than three years under the Law on the Protection of National Property were to be released, as were the inmates of the Stasi's pretrial detention centres. Behind the scenes, it was planned to reduce the number of Soviet military advisers in East Germany from roughly 1,000 to around 250, and to downsize the personnel of the paramilitary police, the KVP, from 117,000 to 93,000.

But all of this was too little too late. As we shall see in a few chapters' time, the Soviet nightmares came true. On 17 June 1953, the people of the 'people's democracy' revolted.

32

Spy Wars

One of the finest British film noirs ever made, directed by Carol Reed, is set in the night-time shadows of a bomb-damaged European capital. It portrays the crime and immorality running wild in the city's alleyways and grimy plazas, revealing the nasty side effects of an infestation of spies. This is not *The Third Man* of 1949. It is *The Man Between* of 1953, set in Berlin; and it is an astute depiction of the spy wars that were raging in Germany and rocking the rest of Europe.

In the film James Mason portrays a man with a guilty Nazi past who wants to live in the West, but has been blackmailed into working for the communist authorities of East Berlin. He, in turn, is blackmailing his former wife, played by German film star Hildegard Knef; she is vulnerable, as the war has obliterated the paper trail of her past.* Claire Bloom plays a young ingenue visiting the city to see her brother, a British officer. In a case of mistaken identity, she is kidnapped by communist agents. The whole tangle ends in tragedy when her escape is arranged by an anti-communist West Berlin smuggler, who enjoys a close relationship with the Western powers and is battled every step of the way by underworld criminals in the pay of the East German secret police.

The Man Between bursts with evocative details. Berlin is largely still in ruins, but monolithic apartment blocks are going up, slowly, thanks to the grudging toil of ill-equipped workers. Groups of women break bricks in the street. The west of the city is full of refugees; typhoid has broken out in one of the resettlement camps. Eastern marks are exchanged, with difficulty, into deutschmarks. West Berlin is starting to glitter; one of its flagship avenues, the Kurfürstendamm, is flowering with shops, nightclubs and life. West Berliners shop for cheap essentials in East Berlin, where their money goes five times farther. The city's sector borders are porous, with only cursory checks of vehicles and hand

---

* Knef herself went through a string of experiences worthy of *The Man Between*. She was, successively, the teenaged lover of a Nazi filmmaker executed by the Soviets; imprisoned in a camp from which she escaped; safeguarded by marriage to an American officer; and rehabilitated by the communists in DEFA productions.

luggage, but innocent visitors are advised against 'wandering into the east' or speaking English within earshot of the border guards.

The details keep coming: men working as labourers near a border crossing are really undercover cops. A kid owns a bicycle thanks to the money he's been paid to assist Western agents. A people-smuggler specialises in helping Volkspolizei officers to defect. The gangsters of East Berlin are seen living well on their earnings from the (unnamed) Stasi; some of them work in a garage packed with Opels, Volkswagens and Mercedes. At one point, the night is split by the noise of gunned engines and screaming tires; spikes are thrown onto the road to prevent pursuit. The incident is put down to the snatching of 'probably someone wanted in the east'. James Mason's character says to the shocked visitor in his care: 'I wanted to protect you from all this dirt.' Surveying East Berlin, she asks him plaintively: 'Why do people stay?'

Clearly there was considerable public awareness of the supposedly covert war being waged in Berlin at the time. It is estimated that up to 100 intelligence services were active in the city, 'masquerading as everything from plumbing companies and jam exporters to academic and research bureaus', in the words of Stasi spymaster Markus Wolf. Every Soviet Bloc intelligence agency operated there, with the Soviets as top dog. The East Berlin embassies of Poland, Czechoslovakia, Hungary, Romania, Bulgaria and Albania were used as espionage residencies. Not only was Berlin a gateway to the West, but many employees of Czechoslovakia's StB, Poland's MBP or Bulgaria's DS could pass for German, making them less conspicuous and better able to penetrate targets. (For the same reason, both sides in the Cold War favoured Balts and Scandinavians, especially Danes, for intelligence work in Germany.) As well as carrying out security operations that targeted political opponents and defectors, often at the behest of Moscow, the Bloc's intelligence services were greatly concerned with the remilitarisation of West Germany.

Spying for Britain were MI6 and the military intelligence branches, the latter declared to the government of West Germany, the former not. By the early 1950s the Intelligence Division of the British occupying authorities, under which cover MI6 officers had been operating, had been renamed the British Intelligence Organization (Germany), although this short-lived body was soon overtaken by events and dissolved. In the meantime, MI6 had moved its German headquarters from Bad Salzuflen to Britain's embassy at Bonn; its West Berlin office, adjacent to the Nazi-era Olympiastadion, was Britain's biggest intelligence outstation in the world. Eschewing the scatter-gun approach taken by others, MI6 now focused on collecting high-grade scientific and political information. Increasingly, it took to interviewing businesspeople and academics who travelled behind the Iron Curtain. The quest for military information steadily became the preserve of the Berlin Intelligence Staff, a forces unit which by mid-decade was feeding two agencies under the British Army of the Rhine – the British Services Intelligence Organization and the British Services Security Organization.[1] To the Stasi, these various intelligence-gatherers were simply 'the English secret service'.

Unfortunately, British military intelligence in Germany harboured at least one Soviet asset – Leonard 'Leo' Long, alias Moscow's agent 'Elli'. Recruited by the bewitching aesthete and arch traitor Anthony Blunt in the 1930s, Long worked for Britain's Control Commission, where he rose to the position of deputy director of intelligence. His enthusiasm for spying for Moscow was on the wane after the war, however, which may have limited the damage done.

The CIA was undergoing the biggest expansion in its history at this time, making use of individuals and front organisations from a variety of European nations. Some of its subtler penetrations of East Germany were especially useful. For example, it gained agents who worked at post offices in East Berlin, able to provide information on which telephone lines were assigned to which customers; thus the US learned details of the cable system and of the lines used by the Soviet and East German authorities.[2] Another recruit was the dentist who treated SED Central Committee members. Other assets occupied perhaps more likely positions, like 'Marianne', who worked in the secretariat of the LDPD.[3] The CIA's resolve was stiffened in these years by the report of a special committee authored by, among others, ex-president Herbert Hoover. Part of it read:

> It is now clear that we are facing an implacable enemy whose avowed objective is world domination by whatever means and at whatever cost. There are no rules in such a game. If the U.S. is to survive, long-standing American concepts of 'fair play' must be reconsidered. We must develop effective espionage and counter-espionage services. We must learn to subvert, sabotage and destroy our enemies by more clever, more sophisticated and more effective measures than those used against us.[4]

Berlin also hosted the military intelligence branches of other NATO countries, some of which, such as The Netherlands and Norway, were engaging in serious modern espionage for the first time. Spies for the Danish foreign ministry were at large in the city.[5] So too were representatives of Asian and Latin American secret services, testing the winds and making deals, mostly for the sake of their economies. West Germany's Organisation Gehlen, closely linked with the CIA and anti-communist political groups, was highly active. Smaller but still significant was the Dienststelle Blank. Known to the communists as the Amt

Blank ('Blank Office'), this was a military planning department that was to evolve into the West German Ministry of Defence. It was named for its chief, Theodor Blank, holder of the snappily titled post of 'Plenipotentiary for the Federal Chancellor for Questions Connected with the Augmentation of Allied Troops'.

France, whose principal foreign intelligence agency was the SDECE,[*] deployed a hydra of competing secret services. Some of the country's leading intelligence officers in Berlin, such as Paul Lombard and Commandant Léon Müller, had arrived in Germany as prisoners during the war. Now, they 'threw all their experience of underground warfare into secret operations against the communist bloc'.[6] And against their western European allies; one French asset was, in fact, the head of intelligence questions at the Amt Blank, Friedrich Heinz.[7] Much of the SDECE's work was carried out by its Research Directorate for Germany, which gathered political, economic and military information. It had at least one well-placed source inside the SED who reported regularly on the political mood.[8]

The main concern for most of these Western actors was the strength, disposition and weaponry of the Soviet forces in Germany. Berlin also offered the chance to infiltrate agents into the wider Soviet Bloc and even – although it was something of a holy grail – into the USSR, about which the West knew remarkably little.

As for counter-espionage in Berlin, the Western spy-catchers notably included West Germany's Federal criminal police, the Bundeskriminalamt (BKA), and the country's new security service, the BfV (Bundesamt für Verfassungsschutz, or Federal Office for the Protection of the Constitution). Federal politicians such as Hans Ritter von Lex consulted with Britain's MI5 over the planned work of these agencies,[9] an interaction that went some way to alleviating British fears about the potential power and independence of a German security service. In its turn MI5, which relied on MI6 for much of its counter-espionage information, kept a close eye on developments in Berlin; it had an agreement with the Air Ministry that its officers could wear Royal Air Force uniform when operating there. France's domestic security service, the DST,[†] and the police detectives of its Sûreté Nationale, both had offices in the city. The security services of Switzerland and Denmark – the Bundespolizei and Police Intelligence Service or PET, founded in 1951 – were considered useful partners of the wartime Allies. And besides the CIA, whose officers operated under military and, later, diplomatic cover, there was the US army's Counter Intelligence Corps (CIC) and the counter-espionage service of the US air force.

---

*   Service de documentation extérieure et de contre-espionnage.

†   Direction de la surveillance du territoire.

The CIC was an avid intelligence-gatherer. One of its most productive informants was future West German chancellor Willy Brandt. In meetings held at a CIC safe house on Hagenstrasse, Brandt would report on developments inside the SED and Free German Youth, and on East Germany's railway system, industrial sites and police force. He even gave details of the Soviet army's telephony equipment, and recommended to CIC potential sources inside the Volkspolizei and interior ministry. The CIA wanted some of this action – in October 1951 it asked Brandt for a survey of East German industrial machinery.[10]

Berlin had its share of pleasures and distractions – many intelligence professionals considered it a plum posting – but the skies remained dark. A British former intelligence officer recalled that there 'was always the imminent threat of another [sic] Russian invasion... a disaster waiting to happen at any moment'.[11] The outbreak of the Korean War in 1950 spurred fears of a similar conflict erupting in Europe. The fear of war, and the opacity of the competing powers' intentions, led to twin obsessions: the Soviets were obsessed with gaining intelligence on the rearming of West Germany, and the West was obsessed with gaining intelligence on a possible Soviet attack.

Steadily, the Cold War divisions hardened. Britain and America were unenthusiastic about a proposal for German reunification made by GDR prime minister Otto Grotewohl, which insisted – they thought dishonestly – on demilitarisation and the withdrawal of all occupying forces.[12] In March 1952 the Western powers, convinced their security was hanging in the balance, reacted coolly to a similar, but more cynical, proposal from Joseph Stalin. In the following months, the signing by six countries of the unratified European Defence Community treaty, and the related Bonn Conventions, brought the Federal Republic more firmly into the Western alliance. Even so, the powers continually rejigged their views on signing a decisive German peace treaty, always unsure of which version of Germany they were prepared to ordain. In the same period, calls from both German republics to roll out their own concept of a 'free election' throughout the whole country led nowhere. Perhaps this was because Soviet spies had learned of the Federal Republic's undeclared bottom line: 'incorporating East Germany within the structure of West Germany [and its] principles and institutions'.[13]

Today it is easy to forget that Western decision-makers varied greatly in how they perceived the conditions and requirements of the Cold War. When he became British prime minister for the second time, Winston Churchill met with Konrad Adenauer. According to a third party, at this meeting Churchill opined that:

a situation might arise, as the West gets stronger, where Russia might be willing to recede and agree to a united Germany, but in that event it would be for the German Government and the German people, in the first instance, to express a view; and Great Britain would not move except in close consultation with the German Government. [Churchill] went on to explain that he ardently desired to restore a tolerable relationship with Russia, but he often asked himself why the Russians had deliberately antagonised the West. They might have easily fooled the Western democracies with small concessions and valueless assurances. Why had they not done so? It was, he was convinced, because they feared our friendship more than they feared our enmity. Friendship would bring contacts between Russia and the West; and this, in turn, would lead to the disintegration of the wicked regime which now ruled in the Kremlin.[14]

Although a discomfiting prospect for many observers, the need to re-arm West Germany was growing increasingly pressing. British decision-makers aired their fears that Western military secrets would leak egregiously to the communists if West Germany were admitted to the West's alliances. France opposed West German entry to NATO. Not that West Germany was clamouring for admission: 'Adenauer makes a great show of saying that he does not want an Army, at any rate for the present,' wrote MI5's Guy Liddell in 1950. He noted that 'this is, of course, a great advantage to Germany: it saves them a good many millions and gives them their young men to work on the land and in the factories. The effect of this has already been considerable; the land is cultivated to the last inch and the shops are full of manufactured goods.'[15]

The fear of war also varied widely among Western decision-makers. So did estimates of when the Soviets might be in a position to wage war. British executives had their nervous moments; in 1952 Liddell wrote timorously that 'there is nothing in the nature of a European Army which could stop the Russians if they chose to get on their feet'.[16] In the face of this threat, the first task of Western rearmament was to reach some kind of parity with the Soviets' conventional forces, but the ball and chain of postwar debt made this difficult for western European governments to countenance, never mind achieve. All were heavily reliant on the US. Liddell wrote of:

an important deserter from the Soviet Air Force, who is under American control, [who] states that the tactical Air Force in Germany has 800 fighters, 300 of which are jet-propelled, and 250 light bombers – probably twin jets. The photographs of these planes, taken in the air, have been submitted to aerodynamic experts in our principal factories here; they say that the planes are more advanced than anything that we even have on the drawing board. It is, however, difficult to say this with any degree of certainty without knowing more about the aircrafts' performance.[17]

At other times, however, the likes of Liddell and Britain's Director of Naval Intelligence, Vice Admiral Eric Longley-Cook, found their American counterparts alarmist, too ready to fight fire with fire. Liddell believed that:

> the Russians show no immediate signs of deliberately provoking a war. They have devastated their own zone and must be feeling the draught. Having been wholly obstructive on all matters of quadripartite control, they lose no opportunity of distorting the facts and arranging matters so that it shall appear to the Germans that we are responsible for their sufferings. At the moment I think the German people are with us, but they are clearly ready to play off one against the other in order to hasten the withdrawal of all forces from Germany. The Russians [show] signs of pressing in the not far distant future for the withdrawal of all Allied forces. This would leave them free to spread Communism throughout the whole of Germany. If we refuse to withdraw, they will make us appear to the Germans as the oppressors.[18]

In these conditions, spies were doing a roaring trade. The situation in Berlin allowed both sides to heavily penetrate the other. The borders of East Berlin ran for some forty-five kilometres, and were easily breached. In the words of one Stasi historian:

> Until 1961, Berlin was a relatively open city in which [it] was possible to move around largely unhindered. Some Berliners lived in the east and worked in the west, some the other way around. For the people in the GDR, Berlin was the open door [to] the opportunities of a prosperous market economy. West Berliners took advantage of the favourable shopping conditions in the east. S-Bahn and U-Bahn trains ran through the entire city.[19]

So did waterways and tramlines. Matters were complicated further by the city-wide electricity and telecoms systems, with telephone and telex connections running through all districts. A few months after the Stasi was founded, its Main Department S (technical security) was created to monitor East Germany's telephone, telegraph and radio communications. Small and under-resourced at first, one of its branches was to develop into the rather formidable Department 26, which would wiretap and video-film the East German population until the fall of the Berlin Wall.

In the early 1950s, 'enemy' radio broadcasters were one of the most serious concerns for Department S. This meant propagandisers such as Radio in the

American Sector (RIAS), Sender Freies Berlin (SFB) and Nordwestdeutscher Rundfunk (NWDR). Although it was feared that communist agents had penetrated NWDR,[20] the station was licensed to beam BBC programmes into East Germany. At least twice per week a BBC show would try to entice defectors by celebrating the successful flight of an important refugee, or pointing out that 'deserters from the Soviet armed forces who sought political asylum in the British Zone of Occupation would not be handed back.'[21]

These radio stations came to play an unlikely but important role in the emerging spy wars. The Soviet and East German authorities hated RIAS with a passion. The station had been set up partly because German communists, as early as May 1945, had commandeered Berlin's best surviving broadcasting facilities on Masurenallee. RIAS sprang up, from very humble beginnings, to express wider, non-communist views. Its objectivity was valuable for East Germans, for the SED was always trying to corrupt the flow of information they received, for example by refusing to print the speeches made by Western politicians at international conferences. In due course, the music and entertainment programmes on RIAS were interspersed with largely accurate features on the hardships of life under the Soviets and SED. Much of the station's information came from voluntary contributors living in East Germany. In the Leninist-Stalinist mindset of the Stasi, these people's behaviour equalled espionage, pure and simple. The Stasi's Department M did its best to prevent postal correspondence between RIAS and its East German audience, and listening to the station was branded a 'hostile activity'.

The hostility was reciprocal. Supporters of RIAS heralded it as a 'Kampfsender' – a combat station. Its first director, William Heimlich, had first entered Berlin as a senior intelligence officer with the American forces. He and his successor Gordon Ewing, who had a similar background, rose naturally to the challenge posed by the communist authorities. To expose communist agents, Heimlich and the SPD's Willy Brandt initiated the broadcast of 'snitch reports' ('Spitzelsendungen') on RIAS every Thursday evening.[22] Following a portentous drum roll, the citizens of an East German town would be told to watch out for a particular individual, whose name, address and covert activity would then be recited. These broadcasts disgraced and impoverished some of those they targeted. They were paid back, with interest, by similar broadcasts on East German radio.

Stasi informers overlooked by the 'snitch reports' were able to do considerable damage. Wolfgang Stiehl, a nineteen-year-old student, was one of those who learned the hard way that contact with RIAS wouldn't be tolerated. In autumn 1952, together with a friend he visited the station's editorial offices in West

Berlin to dish the dirt on the terrible conditions at his place of education, the Workers' and Farmers' Faculty at Halle. Stiehl didn't know that his friend was a Stasi collaborator. One night a few months later, on his way home from a party, Stiehl was walking across the deserted market square in his hometown of Schönebeck when two men grabbed him, slapped on handcuffs, and dragged him into a waiting car. The dénouement was four years in prison.[23]

Certainly RIAS was capable of getting ordinary East Germans into hot water. In another case, the Stasi in Neubrandenburg arrested a bunch of middle-aged acquaintances, some of whom were in possession of a scrap of paper with an odd-looking telephone number scribbled vertically on it. It transpired that one of the group had heard a RIAS broadcast urging East Germans to fiddle the tax system as a way of undermining their government. He mentioned the broadcast to his brother, the owner of a flower wholesalers in Dresden, who sensed a chance to save some money. Word went around the brothers' social circle, although no one fancied making the trip to West Berlin to seek more information on how to dodge taxes. Eventually one of the group persuaded his partner to go. The woman went to the RIAS office, asked about the tax evasion scheme, and was promptly sent to the UfJ offices on Limastrasse. She emerged with a brochure ('no. 17') on tax evasion, together with the mysterious telephone number, which was to be used by anyone who wanted help with emigrating. This explanation, given by the arrestees, is plausible. Human motives being what they are, they were not interested in bringing down the evil empire of communism; they just wanted to save a few marks. They ended up in Stasi cells regardless.[24]

As far as their Western handlers were concerned, the Germans and other nationals who spied and plotted within the Soviet Bloc were freedom fighters battling communist oppression. As far as the SED and Stasi were concerned, they were treacherous spies giving military and political information to hostile foreign powers. While it is true that the Western agencies were trying to tackle a harsh regime unwanted by many of those living under it, and backed by the dreadful Stalin, their operations gave some legitimacy to the SED's complaints of foreign aggression, and encouraged the party and the Stasi to stir up some spy fever in the GDR.

As for the Federal Republic of Germany, it was, in the words of historian Christopher Andrew, 'easier to penetrate than any other Western state'. Not only could Germans and other Europeans intermingle there, but the flow of refugees from the east meant that 'it was not difficult to hide hundreds, even thousands, of East German and Soviet agents among them'.[25]

West Germany also had its homegrown spies. When Germany's political parties were reconstituted after the war, most of them created intelligence units to gather political information. The western KPD was no exception. One task for its 'Party Reconnaissance' service was to watch all commercial travellers around the four occupation zones, then give tip-offs to the Soviet authorities to arrest 'dangerous' former Nazis.[26] In 1946 the SED had taken over some fifty undercover agents of KPD Party Reconnaissance, who offered strong possibilities for spying on rival parties in western Germany. Some of these early agents went on to play important roles in East German security, like Ernst Haberland, a former prisoner at Buchenwald who by the 1960s was leader of the Stasi's guerrilla warfare outfit.

Infiltrating the western CDU and SPD was a primary goal for communist agents. These penetrations proved significant, as the moles inside these parties went on to hold important positions in the West German state. Thus some of the most prized assets of the HVA, the Stasi's mature foreign intelligence service, were ideologically motivated agents planted in western parties in the late 1940s. One example is Kurt Wand, codenamed 'Hülse', who infiltrated the Hamburg social democrats during 1948. Another is Adolf Kanter, codenamed 'Fichtel', who has achieved some historical fame as the Stasi's longest serving spy in West Germany.

Kanter's career shows the vicissitudes of life as a long-term penetration agent. In 1949 the KPD intelligence service ordered Kanter – at that point an open communist and Free German Youth activist – to become its agent 'ck3'.[27] Under this codename he joined the Christian democrat youth organisation Junge Union in the western state of Rhineland-Palatinate. Kanter's political career developed in tandem with that of his associate Helmut Kohl, giving him crucial ties with the CDU leadership. In the late 1960s Kanter's work as both a CDU official and a Stasi spy suffered a serious setback when he was accused of misappropriating party funds. But within a few years he had been resurrected as a Stasi asset thanks to his new job as a lobbyist for an industrial concern, the Flick group. The role gave him exceptional access to government circles in Bonn. It also happened that Egon Bahr, a leading social democrat who was urging warmer relations with the GDR, rented a property from Kanter; this residence was then bugged by the Stasi, providing crucial information on West Germany's negotiating positions.[28] At the height of his spying career Kanter was reporting an item of information every three days.[29] It wasn't until 1981 that various upsets caused the HVA to make less use of him. Despite submitting some 1,200 reports to the Stasi over the decades, Kanter received only a two-year suspended sentence when tried for his activities in the 1990s.[30]

After the war another KPD member, Josef Braun, was ordered to join the western SPD as a mole. His case was eventually taken over by the HVA, for which Braun, codenamed 'Freddy', spied until the mid-1960s.[31] At first Braun was run by Paul Laufer, who went on to have an illustrious career as an HVA agent-runner and was valued highly by Markus Wolf. But Wolf considered 'Freddy' so important that he took over the case personally, supervising not just Braun's information-gathering but also his role as an agent of influence on social democrat policy. Wolf made a big effort to nurture Braun. When their meetings at a safe house got too dull, he changed the venue to a lakeside villa owned by the HVA at Rauchfangswerder, and the agenda became a drinking spree interspersed with lively political chat. Nevertheless, the intense intelligence relationship between Wolf and Braun went through some turbulent times – not least when Braun's communist faith waned and he began calling Walter Ulbricht 'a Stalinist idiot'.[32]

Ludwig Pauli, codenamed 'Adler', was another late 1940s infiltrator who spied in West Germany for decades. Pauli joined the SPD in 1948 at the age of eighteen, working as a minor clerk for the party in Berlin. At the same time, he was a covert SED member reporting to the SED's small intelligence department. The party's patience was rewarded when Pauli, on the orders of the nascent East German foreign intelligence service, applied successfully for a job in the economic administration of the West Berlin senate. As a spy he was judged 'very willing to cooperate' and full of initiative, and was paid twenty deutschmarks a month for the 'relatively important materials' he provided. Better still, Pauli showed potential for 'getting into important positions later on'.[33] He did – at West Germany's Foreign Office. By the 1970s 'Adler' was being run personally by Werner Grossmann, the final chief of the HVA.

Although the Soviets relied on East German intelligence for much high-grade information, they also ran their own discrete assets in the West German political sphere, and had agents inside the SPD and CDU. These penetrations, similarly, began straight after the war. In a case that is likely characteristic, one Soviet agent in the Free Democrats, codenamed 'Mark', a native of eastern Germany, was blackmailed into working for Moscow in 1946 due to 'compromising circumstances' around his wartime service in the Wehrmacht. After a few years 'Mark' managed to flee to West Germany. There he embarked on a successful political career, only to be tracked down and reactivated by the KGB in 1956, a full ten years after his initial unwelcome recruitment.[34]

It wasn't just potential moles who were available for employment. From the mid-1940s onwards, communist secret services were well-stocked with counterfeit currency, thanks largely to what became a major Stasi forging operation under Kurt Lewinsky. During the war Lewinsky, a veteran Berlin forger, had worked for the SS, producing faultless British pound notes and other monies. He had also been incarcerated at Sachsenhausen, from which he escaped in 1945 only to be re-employed by the advancing Soviets. Like so much in the Stasi's world, Lewinsky's counterfeiting efforts were a far-sighted, long-term activity. He was still at it in the 1970s, when South African rands produced at his counterfeiting workshop were donated in their millions to the African National Congress.[35]

In October 1950 an internal guideline drafted by Erich Mielke summarised the information on enemy espionage gained thus far by the various departments of the young Stasi. Mielke intended his document, and the ongoing work of Soviet instructors, to 'elevate the working style and working methods' of Department IV, the Stasi's first counter-espionage branch.[36]

Department IV was divided into four sections to cover American, British, French and West German intelligence services; in some respects, the latter were considered the most problematic and dangerous. In time, intense suspicion of foreigners led to the creation of a fifth section that hunted for spies among the West Germans who had work or residence permits for the GDR. This section also covered border commuters and travellers, and the released prisoners returning to East Germany from other Soviet Bloc countries.

Catching Western spies in the early 1950s was undoubtedly difficult and thankless work. The first three heads of Department IV had brief tenures. For a start, the department was small – three years after the Stasi was founded it had just thirty-two employees at headquarters and about 120 in the regions. The first two chiefs, Werner Kukelski and Paul Rumpelt, were former locksmiths who had joined the reconstituted police forces after the war. Kukelski, who had headed the Kripo in Torgau and served in the Directorate for the Protection of the National Economy before the Stasi was founded, resigned his post within a year. Rumpelt was moved to the less cerebral role of head of Department XIV, which ran Stasi prisons. For the final year of Department IV's existence, before its absorption into the expanded Main Department II at the end of 1953, its chief was Rolf Markert, the former head of K5 in Saxony and latterly responsible for security in the paramilitary police.

In the course of 1951, the Stasi administrations in the Länder and Greater Berlin charged 827 people for espionage-related crimes (figures for Berlin itself are unavailable). Although this was more than were charged with 'underground activity' for the likes of the KgU and UfJ,[37] the work of Department IV was not improving to Mielke's satisfaction. In June 1952 he told the Länder offices that 'despite intensive work, in which considerable individual successes were achieved', the department had been unable to 'penetrate the imperialist espionage organisations'.[38] He blamed uncoordinated work and faulty evaluation, and insisted that better files on every enemy intelligence agency be maintained at the districts and duplicated regularly for headquarters. One section, IVa, staffed largely by former undercover agents of the KPD and SED intelligence services, was hived off as Department II under the leadership of Josef Kiefel. It was mandated to plant or recruit moles inside the intelligence services based in West Germany. This created some overlap with the work of the budding East German foreign intelligence service, but Kiefel clearly relished the task. He went on to lead Main Department II (counter-espionage), which would play a leading role in the Stasi's spy-catching 'spectaculars' of the mid-1950s.

At the same time, the ongoing Soviet oversight of East Germany's spy wars is demonstrated by a decision taken in Moscow by Stalin's Politburo on 23 October 1950. It shows how the spy warfare of the period tended to be conducted over the heads of the Germans themselves. It is also proof that the Soviet authorities arranged predetermined sentences for espionage. On the recommendation of Abakumov of the MGB and Chuikov of the Soviet Control Commission, the Politburo ordered three trials to be conducted against 'American and English agents' for 'carrying out espionage and subversive work against Soviet occupation troops in the German Democratic Republic'. The defendants were to appear before Soviet military tribunals in closed sessions, and everything was to be concluded by the end of the year. Chuikov was notified in advance to 'publish short press releases about the sentences of the convicted Anglo-American spies in the German press'.[39]

33

Gehlen

For the US authorities, the identification of hundreds of infiltrators in just one counter-espionage sweep during summer 1946 was sufficient reason to support the establishment of the Organisation Gehlen (OG), a prototype intelligence service for western Germany.

In the Second World War, General Reinhard Gehlen had led the Wehrmacht's intelligence operations against the Soviet Union, including those conducted by Germany's Slovakian, Hungarian and Romanian partners. Having made sure that he fell into American and not Russian hands at the end of the war, Gehlen was brought to Washington, where he argued forcefully for vigorous action against the Soviet takeover of eastern Europe. He predicted that Stalin would not honour his agreements in respect of Polish sovereignty, and that puppet Soviet regimes would be installed in Bulgaria, Czechoslovakia, Hungary and Romania. The Americans were impressed, and by July 1946 Gehlen was back in Germany as the head of a fifty-strong intelligence outfit. Along with a similar group under Colonel Hermann Baun, it worked at first under the US army's intelligence department, G-2. One of its first jobs, known as Operation Rusty, was to collect information on Soviet forces for the American military. Before long, Gehlen and Baun's units were merged as the Organisation Gehlen. In December 1947 the OG moved to its famous headquarters on a former SS estate at Pullach, near Munich; 'Pullach' would become a standard way of referring to German intelligence. Its head office was disguised as a firm for scientific instruments. Its branches, like those of so many secret services, adopted the cover of small companies, 'registered under commercial and tax law' and conducting 'sham business'.[1]

Responsibility for funding the Organisation Gehlen was soon taken on by the newly founded CIA, which encouraged financial contributions from the American business community.[2] It took the British longer to acknowledge the OG and develop connections with it, mostly due to fears that it was vulnerable to Soviet penetration.[3] The US authorities were to oversee the OG until 1956, when it was subsumed by the West German chancellor's office and renamed the Bundesnachrichtendienst (BND), Germany's foreign intelligence service to this day. In the earlier years, OG employees commonly saw their organisation as 'by its nature an American secret service with German people'.[4] In some respects its relationship with Washington mirrored the Stasi's relationship with Moscow. Among other things, American sponsorship brought a measure of protection. Gehlen personnel and paperwork travelled between West Berlin and Frankfurt am Main on American military aircraft. If picked up by German police, a Gehlen operative could demand to be taken to the nearest US authorities who, having checked a list of 'emergency' personnel numbers, were able to secure the suspect's release and even confiscate any notes taken by the arresting officers.

Although CIA money meant tighter procedures and better security, the organisation's early activities were somewhat loose and unpredictable. Reinhard Gehlen made use of his existing sources inside the USSR and Soviet Bloc, allowing the OG's networks to expand incautiously with the unsupervised recruitment of unknown sub-agents. Transcending its original focus, the organisation began to involve itself with Austria, Czechoslovakia, China, France.[5] Such proliferation and lack of caution were inadvisable with the MGB as an adversary. To pay for information, Gehlen operatives were loaded with gold coins, dollars, and American cigarettes; thus the intelligence they acquired was often unreliable, and the traces to its source almost luminous. Gehlen employed a considerable number of the politically dubious Russian and Ukrainian nationalists who had fought with the Germans against the Red Army. The fact that around one third of the organisation's personnel were former Gestapo and SS officers also left an unpleasant taste in the mouth.[6]

Despite these issues, the OG achieved some valuable high-level penetrations of East German institutions. It was able to draw not just on the General's 'abundant prior knowledge' from the Nazi era, but also from the Wehrmacht's index cards containing information on the personnel of the Red Army and other communist bodies. These cards were still being referred to – in fact, added to – in the mid-1960s.[7] The organisation's operations fired up quickly. From 1946 to 1948, for instance, the director of the railway system in Schwerin, Hanns Jess, reported information and acted as a go-between for other Gehlen sources. This penetration, always under threat, was summarily abandoned when Jess fled to western Germany, where he became a senior police officer and briefly led the Federal security service, the BfV.[8]

One Gehlen spy able to provide high-grade political, military and economic information was Hermann Kastner, an LDPD executive and East Germany's deputy prime minister. Kastner was recruited as an informer by the US in the late 1940s, reporting to case handler Carol Tarney; subsequently he was transferred to the Organisation Gehlen as its agent 'Helwig'. In fear of arrest, Kastner and his wife would flee East Germany in 1956, although his work for Gehlen remained a well-kept secret. There was also Dr Hilde Halm, a wartime logistics administrator for the Wehrmacht who subsequently worked for K5, the GDR Ministry of Finance, and finally the Stasi, which hired her in 1954. Halm didn't survive long in the latter role; the Stasi unmasked her, and she was sentenced to life imprisonment.[9] As we shall see, the cases of Karl Laurenz and Elli Barczatis, who provided Gehlen with information from the office of prime minister Otto Grotewohl, were to end even more calamitously.

Although Halm's case is on record, it is difficult to assess the extent to which the OG penetrated the Stasi. Until the mid-1950s the ultimate responsibility for tackling the organisation lay with the MGB and then the KGB, which often made use of their own German operatives and bypassed the Stasi completely. The facts were also obscured by Reinhard Gehlen's legendary discretion, and by the Stasi's sensible habit of moving suspected Western moles to innocuous jobs in lesser departments, rather than exposing them as it did Halm. By reassigning its suspect employees internally, the Stasi denied them access to usable information and made it less likely they would defect. In turn, fewer defections meant fewer opportunities for the Western intelligence services to bask in a media triumph.

Gehlen's task of spying inside the GDR was made easier by several factors: the unpopularity of the Soviets and communism, the presence of former Wehrmacht personnel in some areas of the East German government, and the large number of East Germans who eagerly sought recruitment.[10] These volunteers had an array of ideological motives – residual Nazism, fears for the future of Germany and Europe, Christian faith, or a belief in genuine, rather than sham, democracy. Some had more personal motives – a close connection with West Germans, the desire to migrate, abject poverty, abject greed. Before and after the Organisation Gehlen became the BND, many of its West German employees had personal and family ties with East Germans, not to mention a shared language, history and culture. Only in divided Germany could spying be made so easy.

The OG's effectiveness came with a price, however. Undoubtedly, the organisation was one place where the Federal Republic had 'an unbroken line of continuity with the Nazi era'. Its objectives were 'rooted in the Third Reich's anti-communism'.[11] Gehlen personnel tended to be hostile to social democrats and trade unionists, and the organisation kept hundreds of files on personalities in the labour movement. Despite representing the properly democratic Germany, it randomly monitored post and telephone contact between West and East Germans; it is estimated that by the 1970s the BND was being sent 10,000 letters per day for evaluation.[12] (It is worth noting that after the war, the requirements of censorship gave the Western occupying powers in Germany the right to intercept any communication they wished to, thus rendering every German letter-writer or phone caller a potential informant. This censorship ended in West Germany in 1952; thereafter, only private communications in Berlin or those emanating from the Soviet Bloc could rightfully be intercepted by the British, French or Americans.)

Intercepting communications was considered something of a Gehlen speciality. The organisation quickly developed a signals intelligence (SIGINT) capability.[13] This effort was headed by Leo Hepp, a veteran of Wehrmacht signals operations whom the Americans had produced as a witness at the Nuremberg trials. During the Berlin airlift, Hepp's team of eighteen SIGINT experts earned praise from their American mentors for discerning the intentions of the Soviet air force, partly by listening to the radio comms of Soviet pilots. Soon Hepp was leading a staff of fifty working at four sites; the 'Dustbin' base at the Baumholder drill ground, and intercept platforms at Bremen, Butzbach and the Chiemsee, a lake near the Austrian border. These sites were able to eavesdrop on the emissions of every Soviet early warning radar station in eastern Germany. Another site, tasked with monitoring radio traffic emanating from the GDR, was set up at Tutzing near Munich. According to James Critchfield, US liaison officer at Pullach, Gehlen's SIGINT capabilities were especially prized during the Korean War.[14] By this time the organisation had taken over a US intercept station at Lauf an der Pegnitz, which monitored Czech border control and security service networks.[15] The organisation also trained radio operators, known as AFU for Aussenfunker, who were intended to operate in other countries. Initially, nine AFU were deployed in East Germany. By the end of 1950, five had been arrested, and more arrests followed in the succeeding years. A later BND report blamed the arrests on 'mistakes unconnected with their radio transmissions', likely meaning they were shopped by informers or by those already held in custody.

West Germany was well-stocked with listeners. Gehlen's interception activities ran parallel with those of the BfV, the Federal criminal police (BKA) and the US, which began to deploy mobile listening posts from its Field Station Berlin in 1951. When enlarged and made more permanent during the 1960s, the latter became the well-known American SIGINT station of Teufelsberg.

These developments weren't lost on the Stasi. Although it didn't equip a proactive radio defence department until the mid-1950s, from 1951 onwards its Main Department S/2 was patrolling frequencies, examining captured codes and ciphers, and logging call signs and regular messages. Other Stasi departments supplied S/2 with Western materials obtained in the course of their operations – transmitters, receivers, converters, crystals, even the diverse packaging used to camouflage radio equipment.[16] The department's expertise would reach its zenith some thirty years later. By then, the successor to S/2, Main Department III, responsible for 'radio reconnaissance and defence',* was working jointly with other Soviet Bloc intelligence services to make the airwaves a highly contested and hostile environment.

Intelligence services are notorious for overburdening their spies. They can demand a prodigious, perhaps ridiculous, amount of information. Throughout the twentieth century, spies were given questionnaires so lengthy, so full of finicky technical detail, that gathering all the required data looked a near-impossible task.

Thanks to its infiltration of the Organisation Gehlen, the Stasi's files give an accurate picture of what Gehlen spies were seeking in East Germany. Even given the stiff tasking common to intelligence services, the OG's demands seem almost ludicrously ambitious.[17] When considering them, a couple of points should be kept in mind. The OG was overseen by the CIA. Therefore its intelligence wish-list represents, to an extent, America's attempt to get information for itself, using German people. Secondly, it was the Stasi's job to prevent any of this information leaving East Germany.

It had little hope of success. The OG stole information throughout East Germany's military, economic, industrial and political spheres, and on the Soviet authorities stationed there. This was stipulated by the 'General Order' given to all OG spies. It set out such universal tasks as reporting the 'current level of performance of the military industry (defence concerns, energy-producing concerns, concerns in the chemical and raw materials industries, and hydrogenation plants)'; and making a 'determination of the police and the internal and external political measures of the GDR and the occupying power', along with the 'resulting actual and psychological effects on the population' and their 'nutritional situation'.[18] Gehlen networks constantly were urged to seek 'P-Quellen' – penetration sources – in an astonishing variety of locations, installations and activities. The organisation's orders have a confident tone, as if such spies were easily found and activated.

Information was expected on hundreds of Volkspolizei and KVP barracks, flak batteries, depots, uniform stores and training grounds, with details of units, vehicles, weapons, supplies and routines, and with the names of all significant officers thrown in for good measure. When it came to the Soviet forces, the OG wanted not just an identification of units and the names

---

*   Hauptabteilung III, 'Funkaufklärung und Funkabwehr'.

of officers but precise data on bomb stores, airfields, ammunition dumps, fuel storage; on jet aircraft – the MiG-9, 15 and 17, their engines and flight controls, their spare parts and armament, their tactics, and what was done with the empty packing crates once they had been delivered to an airfield. Data was sought on radar and radios, including a chronological history of the development of one model at the Zeiss works in Jena; on the new 57mm and 100mm flak guns; on heavy tanks, and the new machine guns with barrel combustion; on the new 160mm grenade launcher, the new 152mm howitzer, the new cargo glider.

This was the start of the Cold War steeplechase – a breathless, compulsive race to better the equipment, and the knowledge, possessed by the other side. Overshadowed by the prospect of war, everyone concerned with European and global politics wanted to know the extent of rearmament taking place in Germany, and the capabilities of the armed forces there. The OG launched Projekt Hermes, a drive to recruit or debrief former prisoners of war, and experts who had worked at aircraft factories and other key sites in the Soviet Union, upon their return to Germany. On a different note, it wanted to know about the Soviet forces' medical supplies in East Germany: the stocks of blood plasma, penicillin, sulphonamides, morphine, of 'all medicinal drugs in easily dilutable form'; the number of bandages, first aid kits, stretchers, ambulances and hospital trains. Gehlen spies were told to report on the Soviet Bloc's reactions to exercises held in the Baltic region by 'Atlantic pact' forces. They were to report the slightest early warning sign of a communist attack: the sudden recruitment of female personnel; the appointment of Soviet officials to key positions; curfews at Soviet barracks; stricter guard routines at sensitive sites; the 'distribution of sealed envelopes to heads of department'.

Neither were the East German government, economy or industry spared this intense examination. The OG called for recruits in important leadership positions at the Ministry of Transport, the Ministry of Machine Building, the Directorate of Motor Transport and Roads, the Secretariat for Materials Supply. It wanted specific data on steel works, brass works, electricity works, coal (black and brown); on machine tools (forge machines, heavy duty lathes, milling and shaping machines, pneumatic and electric drop hammers, 'hydraulic presses of all types and performance'); on the transporting of uranium, on infrared technology, on particle accelerators (betatron and cyclotron); on every aspect of the railway system, its goods carriages, loading platforms and repair yards; on magnetite mining, nickel deposits, the production of high-quality polyvinyl chloride; on high-voltage technology in transformers and x-rays; on economic investments made around the Soviet Bloc; on the Soviet Bloc's circumvention of the West's economic control measures; on the latest discoveries made in the laboratories of factories, technical colleges, universities; and on the latest figures achieved in annual margarine production.

Some of the OG's demands went beyond information. One Gehlen order required 'samples of fuels, lubricants and similar products' of 'between 2 and 22 litres' to be 'taken from fuel depots, tanks, vehicles, weapons, aircraft, etc.' These were to be submitted 'in such a way that processing in a laboratory is possible, if possible in a container with a metal screw cap'; a container protected from the elements and not made of glass, and accompanied by a 'secret report' about the sample. Agents were warned that the substance was not to be 'smelled, touched or tasted', especially if found in jars marked with a skull and crossbones.

Furthermore, it is not exaggerating to say that the Organisation Gehlen was as well-informed as the Stasi about individuals living in East Germany. For example, the OG tasked its spies with acquiring the 'total and individual' results of the 1950 census. Like the Stasi, it fixated on individuals. It requested information, for instance, about a Lieutenant Colonel Amm, the head of a police station, who lived at number 11 Stalinallee. It requested information about a sociable group of taxi drivers in Erfurt, who were known to meet at a café 'opposite the main train station between a cigar shop and a hotel', or sometimes 'at the Quartier Bohème restaurant'. A series of OG orders focused on the female interpreter of Georgy Pushkin, the Soviet High Commissioner; on a certain lawyer from Weimar who was reporting on a trial of CDU members; on a certain customs officer working at Kietz on the Polish border; on a host of named individuals at the Ministry of the Interior, the Bau-Union Nord, the research department of Rostock University. When the GDR's National Democratic Party proposed an initiative to redeem former Wehrmacht officers by employing them in responsible positions, the Organisation Gehlen alerted its spies to take advantage of the move.

Sometimes Gehlen spies were given international assignments, like getting hold of the full range of identity cards issued in Poland. When the Chinese government opened an office in Berlin in the hope of recruiting German engineers, Gehlen personnel were told to recruit spies there. The Stasi's attempt to monitor these recruitments may have been its first brush with a security issue that wasn't exclusively European. The OG also circulated lists of suspected persons believed to be working for the Stasi or Soviets. These lists were detailed and peppery in their language. Those denounced included a Bulgarian known to make 'black market visits to Russian Jews'; 'a snitch from the Democratic Women's League'; a person identifiable by his 'arrogant bearing'; a person reputed to have smuggled socialist youths into East Germany during the World Youth Festival; an official of the Bau-Union Berlin known as 'a very dangerous informer'; a Czech employed at a reception camp in West Germany, whose job was to impede the interrogation of newly arrived refugees. So confident was the OG of its standing within the Volkspolizei that when suspicions arose about a particular police administrator, he was described in a Gehlen report as 'a possible defector' – to the communists. These suspicions made the OG check all its Volkspolizei sources.

Gehlen's penetration of East Germany raises some intriguing points. For a start, there was great erudition at work in its intelligence questionnaires. The wish-list of information reveals very thorough knowledge, not just of the topics concerned but of important places, developments, and people in the GDR. Supposedly this was a time when the Western powers were struggling to gain any knowledge from inside the Soviet Union and the Soviet Bloc, about much of which, reportedly, they were totally ignorant. Clearly, East Germany was an exception.

Then there is the question of how this vast platter of knowledge was acquired. One explanation is that it resulted from the local knowledge and interconnections of ordinary Germans hired by the OG. Hermann Kastner was a likely source of high-grade intelligence, although there must have been others in similar positions. But then, effective espionage is often about the location, and not the number, of one's spies. Just a few well-placed sources inside government departments or economic bodies can go a long way. This is also true of spies at a communications hub – say, a telephony or telegraph office, in the Cold War context – or those who work in any kind of archival or record-keeping capacity. It is astonishing to realise just how much information – especially technical information – can be available to an adversary.

34

Sabotage and Kidnappings

Espionage was just one aspect of the unfolding secret war. There was also an apparent upsurge in sabotage and other dirty tricks. Ernst Wollweber, future leader of the Stasi, was given a senior role in the Soviet zone's directorate of shipping in 1947. In the following years he was suspected of using the position as cover for reviving his pre-war maritime sabotage network.[1]

In 1953 a Gehlen agent codenamed 'Brutus' – actually Walter Gramsch, an official in the government of Saxony-Anhalt – defected to the West. Gramsch, who had also worked for the Administration for Trade and Supplies, brought with him details of Wollweber's alleged activities. Wollweber had set up schools for sailors at the Baltic peninsula town of Wustrow and at two lakeside spots, Goldberg and Ladebow. Gramsch claimed that around ten percent of the trainees at these schools – about twenty pupils per year – were selected for clandestine training. They were taught how to plant explosives and to sabotage ships' engines and navigational equipment. Foreign nationals were among them; Swedes and, reportedly, ninety-six sailors and eighteen dockers from Britain. Wollweber's reborn organisation was said to have sections responsible for seaports, river ports and railways, and to be ready to make attacks on the supply lines of the Western powers.

It was hard to corroborate Gramsch's information. For their part, the Swedish and Norwegian authorities were convinced that Wollweber was active again, and ordered their security agencies to observe suspected East German operatives. In Britain, MI5 investigated the matter, sceptically and inconclusively.[2] Nevertheless, from 1948 to 1953 a string of shipping accidents and sabotage cases seemed to point the finger at Wollweber's group. The most serious incidents appeared to be connected with the Korean War. In April 1950, as the conflict loomed, it was discovered that flares had been placed around the main boiler of the British aircraft carrier *HMS Illustrious*; these would have ignited had the boiler grown hotter. In February 1953 *HMS Indomitable*, an aircraft carrier of the same class, was damaged by fire while sailing for Korea. Explosive devices were found on board. At Swansea docks there was an explosion and fire aboard a tanker destined for Korea. There were explosions at several British arsenals and at French ports, and at least three further cases of suspected sabotage on British warships. Commercial shipping was also affected. Sabotage was the definite cause of fires on three passenger liners – the *Empress of Canada* at Liverpool, the *Queen Elizabeth* and the *Queen Mary*.

Forgotten today, these incidents were a press sensation in the early 1950s. No diplomatic protests were lodged, however, and the issue wasn't raised after the Korean War ended. Although the matter has been hyped-up in other Stasi histories, it is unlikely that Ernst Wollweber was involved. There is no direct evidence for it. The MGB briefly considered carrying out sabotage actions in the West in connection with Korea, but apparently decided they would cause more trouble than they were worth, and had refrained. Thus it is likely that the Soviets had told the East Germans to refrain as well. Perhaps the perpetrators, if they weren't simply disgruntled members of the ships' crews, were Western communist militants acting on their own initiative.

Either way, at least one authority knew where to place the blame. Under the headline 'Crooner Named as Contact for Red Ship Saboteurs', a Canadian newspaper reported: 'Known by the codename of 'Joan', a dance band crooner in a dancehall in London's dock area has been named as secret contact for Red sabotage agents in Britain.'[3] The story also ran in Britain's *Sunday Graphic*, which outed Joan as 'a frequenter of entertainment haunts'.[4]

Then there was kidnapping. The statistics are horrible: from 1945 until the early 1960s a person was snatched from West Berlin or western Germany by communist secret agents at the rate of almost once per week. It is likely the Stasi was responsible for more than 400 of these kidnappings.[5] All intelligence and security services kidnap persons of interest sometimes, usually in wartime or in conflict zones. But the inter-German kidnappings occurred in peacetime, with the victims snatched from the streets of a major, burgeoning European democracy.

The Stasi's culture of kidnapping was probably influenced by the experiences of German communists in the Spanish Civil War. A cult of 'gangsterismo' grew up in Spain, where communist and anarchist militias modelled themselves on America's prohibition-era criminals. Julius Ruiz, a historian of the Spanish war, writes that Madrid cinemas were full to bursting when showing early 1930s crime classics such as *Little Caesar* and *City Streets*. In contrast, the worthy Soviet films that were expected to attract the Spanish proletariat flopped, with *The Battleship Potemkin* deemed too uninteresting to be screened. Photographs survive of gun-toting Republican security squads kicking back among empty bottles of booze, looking for all the world like Chicago hoodlums. One anarchist militia even called itself the 'Gangster Gang'.

In the terminology of America's underworld, the victims of criminal gangs were doomed to 'go for a ride'. This meant being driven by mobsters to a forlorn place to face bloody interrogation, or execution, or both. The same term was adopted in Spain – captured fascists and suspected fifth columnists were 'taken for a ride' and, in Ruiz's words:

> gangsterismo became the dominant killing style... in a grim paradox, the daily 'rides' during that bloody summer [of 1936] did not deter madrileños from watching violent gangster movies. Thus *Scarface* returned to cinema screens in September 1936 and ran until the end of October. With movie theatres like the Cinema Europa being used as bases for revolutionary gangsterismo, life was imitating art.[6]

There were many German volunteers in these Spanish hit squads, and they were implicated in several infamous murders and disappearances. Given that some of these volunteers later re-emerged as high-ranking Stasi officers, their experiences may well have fed into the Stasi's kidnapping practices. As in Spain, those practices relied on powerful cars, underworld muscle, and an almost childlike glee in getting away with it.

During the 1950s, the Stasi perfected a number of methods for kidnapping, an activity it referred to dismissively as 'retrieval' or 'transfer'.* The aim was usually to get victims across the urban borders into East Berlin, or over a secluded rural frontier into East Germany, where Stasi or Volkspolizei personnel could then take possession of them. When the frontiers were fortified more heavily in 1952, a series of covert 'border locks' (Grenzschleusen) were reserved as places for Stasi operatives to cross secretly to and from West Germany. Most victims were kidnapped either to be grilled for information, recruited, or punished. The kidnappings also served other purposes – deterring refugees and defectors, instilling fear, providing material for press campaigns, and demonstrating the power and reach of the East German state.

There were crude kidnappings, like the snatching of Walter Linse from a pavement by thugs. Violent abductions were not uncommon – the Stasi used physical force in at least 100 of its kidnapping operations – and some victims were simply overpowered by armed agents after being manoeuvred towards the borders.[7] In time, subtler methods came to the fore; notably the use of drink, drugs, honey traps, false friends, and bogus invitations.

---

* 'Rückholung', 'Überführung'.

Thus, some victims were encouraged to drink themselves silly before being hustled unexpectedly onto GDR territory. Others were rendered compliant with big doses of such drugs as scopolamine, perhaps concealed in chocolates, cigarettes or drinks. Some were seduced into vulnerability, usually by women in heterosexual encounters. Others were manipulated into crossing the borders by supposed friends who were secret Stasi collaborators. Some entered East Germany of their own accord, after receiving an offer they couldn't refuse – perhaps the chance to visit a relative in prison, or to see the children they had left behind when fleeing the GDR. A variation of this method saw victims tricked by faked letters or telegrams purporting to come from family or old acquaintances. It was common to combine two or more of these methods; thus an operation might involve the use of drugs as well as treacherous friends, or alcohol together with a honey trap.

The Stasi carried out some of its kidnappings on Soviet orders. In the mid-1990s Berlin police re-examined 500 cases of Cold War kidnapping. Many of the victims had disappeared without a trace.[8] This indicates that a Moscow prison or the Gulag may have been their final destination. But unlike MGB personnel, German operatives had local knowledge and could blend in with their surroundings. A kidnapping needed many hands; watchers to observe the victim's movements and habits, helpers to create diversions, drivers, look-outs, back-up teams. Co-opted Volkspolizei or border police officers, sometimes working undercover, would expedite border crossings. The occasional doctor or nurse might also be on hand, in case of emergencies arising from the over-application of knockout drugs. All of this was German-on-German work; but once they had been snatched, important prizes, like Linse, were taken by the Soviets – he was just one example of a kidnap to order.

Another was the abduction of Kurt Koblitz. A social democrat, Koblitz had joined the SED and served in the Land parliament of Brandenburg before his escape to West Berlin in January 1950. He was suspected of setting up a spy network on behalf of an American intelligence service. To get him, the Stasi assigned a collaborator to watch his movements. It was noted that Koblitz often travelled on the U-Bahn from Kreuzberg to Wedding, a route that passed through the East Berlin district of Mitte. On one such journey, six Stasi officers got on his train, arrested him as it went through Mitte, and brought him out to a car waiting on Jägerstrasse. Handed over to the Soviets, Koblitz was sentenced to the Gulag. Meanwhile, with profound creepiness, a Stasi collaborator moved in as a tenant with Koblitz's wife in West Berlin, in order to prolong the Stasi's observations. Unlike many others, though, Koblitz was able to put his life back together; released early from Vorkuta in a mid-1950s amnesty, he would spend much of the 1970s as an SPD member of the Bundestag.[9]

Who carried out the Stasi's kidnappings? Stasi snatch squads usually consisted of employees from Department VIII (observations), Department IV (counter-espionage, later Main Department II), Main Department V (political opposition), or obscure units for dirty operations. Two of the latter, the Department for Special Duties under Joseph Gutsche and the Special Tasks Group under Josef Kiefel,* employed small gangs of Berlin criminals. As will be seen, they were especially active during the big spy-catching operations of the mid-1950s.

The Stasi also made intensive use of secret co-workers (GM) in its kidnapping operations. In later years they would acquire their own designation of Entführer-IM, or 'Kidnapper collaborator'. The participation of these shadowy helpers, especially in West Berlin and West Germany, was another way of demonstrating the apparent omnipotence of the GDR authorities. Often a stranger to the intended kidnapping victim, they would observe the targeted person at work and play, scope out transport routes, and test possibilities. In other cases, it was collaborators who would build up a trusting relationship with victims, and so be able to get them to a certain place at a certain time.

Almost everyone involved in Stasi kidnappings got away with it. The historian Susanne Muhle, who specialises in the subject, has determined that only thirteen former Stasi collaborators, and three so-called contact persons, went on trial after German reunification for the parts they had played in abductions. Seven were given short probationary sentences.[10]

Who were the victims? Some were refugees who had worked in state institutions before fleeing East Germany. Others were opponents of the Soviet Union or SED who had got involved with the likes of the KgU, UfJ, or Western intelligence services. Their kidnappings were intended to discredit these organisations, reduce the number of volunteers they enjoyed, and expose the powerlessness and lack of protection offered by West German police and politicians. Also targeted were journalists whose criticisms of East Germany had grown too resounding, including one who made the near-fatal mistake of deriding Erich Mielke by name.

Deserters from the police and Stasi were also kidnapped, for it is a habit of authoritarian regimes to reserve some of their most belligerent security operations for traitors from within their own ranks. After the collapse of East Germany, records came to light of 484 cases of desertion from the Stasi, dating from 1950 to 1988. Of this number, 120 deserters had been seized in the West and returned to the GDR. Seven were executed during the 1950s.[11] Given the Volkspolizei's problem with desertions, there is no doubt that police escapees were also top targets.

---

* Abteilung zur besonderen Verwendung, abbreviated to Abt. z.b. V.; and Gruppe für Sonderaufgaben.

Besides the fact that deserters might spill official secrets, there was also the risk that they would reveal details of the SED's repression of the East German public – details the party kept a tightly-guarded secret from the West.[12] Thus kidnappings, and other hostile measures such as threatening phone calls to refugees in the middle of the night, or damage to their property in mysterious attacks,[13] were even extended to those who had left the service of the Stasi or police before fleeing the GDR.

Most of the Stasi's kidnapping victims were dealt with harshly once brought to East Germany. Twenty-four were executed, including sixteen convicted by Soviet military tribunals. Around half of the abductees spent between one and ten years incarcerated in East Germany; at least ten of these prisoners died of illness, maltreatment or suicide.[14] Legal appeals about the kidnappings were brushed aside. This happened in the case of the journalist Alfred Weiland who, on the grounds of his 'Trotskyism', was kidnapped violently from West Berlin in November 1950. His abduction was facilitated by an undercover member of the western KPD, agent 'Sergeyev', who had penetrated Trotskyist circles, and another German codenamed 'Wagner'. Both worked for the Soviets.[15] Weiland repeatedly appealed his fifteen-year sentence for alleged spying, including on the grounds that he had been kidnapped. He claimed he had never been a spy and had only signed a confession under the 'intense pressure' of his interrogation. Moreover, he insisted his sentence was null and void because he was a citizen of West Germany, not East Germany. Conveniently for the East German authorities, this tricky argument was dismissed by SED lawyers.

With a malevolent cynicism, most of the kidnapping victims who survived their prison sentences were returned to West Germany, there to serve as living examples of the vengeful power of the GDR. As for the Stasi deserters, their executions were given much in-house publicity. At a staff conference of November 1953, Ernst Wollweber, referring to a former colleague who had been snatched from the West and sentenced to death, warned that it 'doesn't matter where such traitors from the ranks of state security go, they will be brought back in every instance and delivered the punishment they deserve. Because they are among the worst enemies we have to deal with'.

35

The Institute: The Birth of East German Foreign Intelligence

Four types of officer are discernible among the first twelve staff members of the East German foreign intelligence service.

There were a few ardent and well-educated SED members, the offspring of trusted communist parents who themselves had known struggle and clandestineness. Also present were a couple of older, grizzled communist guerrilla fighters, with long experience of armed combat and tough security operations. There was at least one representative of type number three: the more erudite breed of communist secret operative, a thinker who could study, write, plan and persuade. Making up the complement were four longstanding Soviet intelligence officers – Chekists with experience of illegal work around Europe – to steer the ship and ensure it stayed afloat. This was the staff of the Institute for Economic and Scientific Research (Institut für wirtschaftswissenschaftliche Forschung, IWF), founded during 1951 – although, in later years, none of these officers could quite remember the exact date.

One of the eager SED members invited to join the new outfit was Markus Johannes Wolf, relatively young at twenty-eight. He would go on to lead the East German foreign intelligence service for thirty-four of the thirty-nine years of its existence. The scion of a German Jewish communist family who had saved their lives by escaping to the USSR in 1933, latterly Wolf had been back in Moscow as a member of the GDR's diplomatic mission. Having been schooled in Russia, including by the Comintern, Wolf was well-liked by Soviet officials, who knew him by the Russian diminutive 'Mischa' and influenced him in many ways; including, reputedly, the way Wolf lit his Russian cigarettes with their long paper filters.

If Wolf had a technical specialism upon joining the Institute, it was radio propaganda. During the war he had written and presented German-language broadcasts on the Moscow station Deutsche Volkssender. He later admitted that one of his biggest influences in this work was Sefton Delmer, who had devised much of the British 'black' propaganda designed to sap the morale of Axis troops. Wolf's regard for Delmer would become significant many years later, when the Stasi's black propaganda specialists were given lectures on Delmer's pioneering techniques.

When Wolf returned to Germany in 1945 he had been installed in a luxurious apartment on Bayernallee in western Berlin. He had continued to work in radio, chairing pro-Soviet talks on the Berliner Rundfunk station under the dashing-sounding alias of Michael Storm. He also covered the Nuremberg trials as a journalist, a role that brings up a quirky footnote to his career. For decades Wolf was referred to by Western intelligence services and newspapers as 'The Man Without a Face'. He was famously unphotographed, and only his name and position as East Germany's top spymaster were known. When he was finally photographed on a covert mission to Sweden in the late 1970s there was a near-ecstatic reaction among counter-espionage officers and West German media editors alike. But Wolf's photograph had been possessed by the CIA all along. For a start, it had appeared on his Nuremberg trials' identity card: pass number 3657 for 'Mark F. Wolf' of Soviet press room 110. The CIA probably knew more about Wolf than it did other Soviet Bloc intelligence chiefs.[1]

The Institute for Economic and Scientific Research was a viable front; behind closed doors the IWF came to be referred to as the Foreign Political Intelligence Service or APN.* It was not part of the Stasi. After being subordinated briefly to the GDR Council of Ministers it was transferred to the portfolio of the Ministry for Foreign Affairs, where it remained until the autumn of 1953. Nevertheless, it was Walter Ulbricht, Wilhelm Zaisser, Erich Mielke and the SED Politbüro who undoubtedly were its most important clients and taskers.

The Soviet authorities were deeply wary of granting East Germany a foreign intelligence capability. Such a move brought the prospect of losing German spies who thus far had been run by the KI and MGB. The creation of the IWF-APN was approved on the understanding that spying on the 'Main Enemy', the United States, would remain the preserve of the Soviets. With this caveat in place, a founding directive was drafted with the input of senior officers at Moscow and Karlshorst, including Colonel Ivan Fadeikin and Lieutenant Colonel Grigori Slavin, MGB and MVD deputies for Germany. The directive made it explicit that the IWF was to focus its spying on the Federal Republic, covering the 'internal political and economic situation in West Germany' and 'the activities of the Bonn government and its departments, the Bundestag [and] Bundesrat'. Further targets included 'the leading organs of the bourgeois and social democratic parties, scientific-technical centres and laboratories, and also churches and other public organisations'. The IWF was also to shed light on 'the policies of the Western occupation powers'.[2]

---

* Aussenpolitischer Nachrichtendienst. The name APN was never used widely, and the first written evidence of it dates from early 1953.

Besides the Stasi's short-lived Department II, which aimed to recruit agents in West Berlin, East German foreign intelligence before the IWF had consisted of a few secret sections of the SED. As well as the previously mentioned Transport Department under Richard Stahlmann, there was another with responsibility for industrial espionage. This was headed by Kurt Stoph, brother of the future GDR prime minister Willi Stoph. These were modest outfits, with no more than 100 agents.

Like the Stasi, the IWF began life as little more than an auxiliary of Soviet intelligence. In time the service was to transcend these second-string beginnings and, in the words of the historians (and former intelligence officers) David Murphy and Sergei Kondrashev, 'surpass its Soviet tutors in the depth and breadth of agent penetrations of the government of the Federal Republic'.[3]

In a way, this is an understatement. By some measures, the mature version of the IWF, the Stasi's HVA, was the most successful espionage service in history; surely no other can lay claim to having 20,000 spies at work within its main target country, riddling its government, military, media, intelligence services, businesses, and scientific and academic communities. But perhaps it was harder for Wolf's intelligence service to fail than to succeed. Divided Germany presented unique opportunities for espionage, and the game was heavily loaded in the HVA's favour.

The nominal head of the new intelligence service was deputy foreign minister Anton Ackermann, a leading ideologue and graduate of the Lenin School who had been performing important functions for the German communist movement since the 1920s. A month after the Soviet directive was issued, Ackermann summoned Markus Wolf to the SED Central Committee building and told him he was to contribute to the 'enlightenment of the young state' by working at the IWF. Another appointee was Richard Stahlmann, who relinquished leadership of the Transport Department to fellow Spanish Civil War veteran Adolf Baier.

On the pair's first day of work together, Stahlmann picked up Wolf, with shades of 'gangsterismo', in a capacious eight-cylinder Tatra limousine. Stahlmann was renowned for his pull; he was the type who could meet with the finance minister and come away with a satchel full of bank notes. Stahlmann used that clout to procure twelve Tatras from a Czech shipment to the East German government, and they became the vehicle of choice for the otherwise cash-strapped new intelligence service.[4] Its first headquarters was a spartan former school building on Tschaikowskistrasse in Berlin's Pankow district, an area favoured by the SED leadership for their homes. In the following years, no one could remember the precise date on which the IWF's dozen officers held their inaugural meeting. They decided to settle on 1 September 1951 as the official birthday of East German foreign intelligence.

The leading Soviet officer at the IWF was 'Comrade Akimov', actually Andrei Grauer. 'We sat at his feet,' wrote Wolf of this veteran of NKVD operations, 'wide-eyed at his accounts of moles unearthed, services penetrated, and heroic agents.' Wolf credits Grauer with putting in place a workable structure at the IWF, but Grauer's career was to end badly as he suffered worsening bouts of psychosis. One of his fixations centred on Anton Ackermann, whom Grauer believed was untrustworthy and out to get him. Weary of being undermined, Ackermann resigned as head of the service; he was replaced briefly as chief by Richard Stahlmann before Markus Wolf took over. For Wolf, Grauer's delusions were caused by spending too many years in the snakepit of the Stalinist secret services, although he was told that Grauer had been diagnosed with schizophrenia. The diagnosis is questionable; the Soviet authorities institutionalised many falsely diagnosed 'schizophrenics'.

Back in Berlin to assist Grauer was Aleksandr Korotkov, the MGB's top German specialist. Together they set about creating an intelligence service that was, according to Wolf, an exact mirror of the Soviet version, with internal guidelines that betrayed their original Russian text. The IWF had four main departments, each of which started life with two German officers under a Soviet instructor. These were responsible for (1) espionage within West German parties and government bodies; (2) espionage within the West German economy and industry; (3) evaluation and analysis; and (4) technical and administrative support. Several operational departments (Operative Abteilungen) were added over time. The first was a counter-espionage department tasked with infiltrating the West Berlin and West German police and intelligence services. The second had responsibility for collecting scientific and technical intelligence.

Although the structure and naming of IWF departments went through convoluted changes in its short life, it is possible to put together an outline of the organisation and its key players. The first Main Department (I Hauptabteilung), responsible for political intelligence, was led by thirty-two-year-old Herbert Hentschke under the supervision of Ivan Susenkov.[5] When the Nazis seized power Hentschke's communist father had moved the fifteen-year-old Herbert to Czechoslovakia, where he had promptly become an activist for the Czech communist party. He had then moved on to Moscow, but was arrested in 1937 and survived Stalin's purges only by a fluke. After a wilderness period spent working as a locksmith, Hentschke was brought back into the fold with a spell of Comintern clandestine training, where he likely became friendly with

Markus Wolf; he then served as a partisan with Soviet forces in Belorussia. Before joining the IWF he had been a Volkspolizei officer in Thuringia.

In time, Hentschke's department came to be staffed by several officers who went on to enjoy notable careers. They included Horst Jänicke, who later ran a special tasks department as a deputy chief of the HVA, and Alfred Schönherr, who became a powerful SED secretary within the Stasi. As well as gaining agents inside 'bourgeois' parties and West German government offices – especially the foreign ministry – the department was expected to infiltrate the Catholic and Protestant churches, civil organisations, and the administrative bodies of the Western powers in Berlin. At first, however, it took on the existing agents of the western KPD's 'Party Reconnaissance' service – agents which, as we have seen, were soon judged by Markus Wolf to be thoroughly compromised. It took several years for political espionage within the Federal Republic to be put on the right footing.

II Hauptabteilung, responsible for economic intelligence, was led by Walter Muth under the Soviet adviser Vasily Morgachev. Wolf served in the analysis department, III Hauptabteilung, under Robert Korb, with whom he had worked in Moscow; their Soviet instructor was Dmitri Bronski. Wolf looked up to Korb, an experienced propaganda brain who had edited the KPD newspaper *Red Flag* in the 1930s while exiled in Prague. Born in Bohemia and a member of the Czech communist party, Korb had been through the characteristic baptisms of the interwar years, including a spell in prison and service in the Spanish Civil War. In 1946 he became chief editor of the SED press service, then head of the Central Committee's agitational propaganda department. Throughout his service in the IWF Korb maintained his cover as an official of party agitprop. Other IWF officers, after initially using SED Central Committee IDs, were given Stasi IDs to flash whenever necessary – the party didn't want too obvious a connection with the intelligence service.

Robert Korb exemplifies the connections between writing and spying. He was the kind of polymath so essential to foreign intelligence services, tutoring Wolf in such diverse subjects as Islam, the complexities of founding Israel, and the ethno-religious tensions of India. It was from Korb that Wolf learned to treat intelligence reports with scepticism, to cross-reference their claims with other sources, and the pair adopted a maxim – that a careful reading of the foreign press can produce better intelligence than the reports of secret agents.[6]

The administrative and support department at the IWF was led by thirty-five-year-old Gerhard Heidenreich, who previously had held a trustworthy position in the personnel department of the SED Central Committee. He too was an alumnus of a Comintern training school.[7] Heidenreich was joined in IV Hauptabteilung by thirty-one-year-old Helmut Hartwig, who was to enjoy a lengthy career providing HVA agents with technical support and gadgetry. Their department forged passports, devised radio transmission procedures, and manufactured secret containers for hiding reports or microfilm. In time they created a small laboratory, Haus II, in which worked an engraver, a photographer, an offset printer and a chemist.

The first 'operational department', 1. Abteilung, responsible for counter-espionage, was at first led by the veteran communist streetfighter Gustav Szinda. Although the department aimed to penetrate West German intelligence and security services, it spent most of its time trying to ascertain the damage done by British and American penetration of the western KPD. Szinda, a merciless interrogator, had been used by the NKVD to ferret out traitors in civil war Spain and late 1930s Moscow. For the IWF, however, he was less successful, and his work was taken over by Markus Wolf for a while.

The first head of scientific and technological spying at the IWF was the leader of 2. Abteilung, Heinrich Weiberg, a chemist and former Wehrmacht soldier who had spent most of the war in Soviet captivity.[8] Liked by subordinates for his mild, professorial demeanour,[9] Weiberg was to spend decades building up East Germany's considerable scientific espionage capability. His department had a grandiose remit to acquire information on patents, nuclear and rocket weaponry, nuclear energy, chemical research, electronics, electrical engineering, and aircraft design. Under-resourced and thinly staffed, it couldn't possibly achieve much; but Weiberg did make the sensible decision to rely on the services of Robert Rompe, a physicist with connections to Soviet intelligence who had been an industrial spy for the KPD in the 1920s and 1930s. Despite an almost obligatory period of disfavour with the communist authorities – he was interrogated over his alleged connections with Noel Field – Rompe became an influential figure in East German science, and ultimately was run as an agent by the Stasi's deputy head of scientific espionage, Willi Neumann.[10]

Of the other operational departments, 3. Abteilung (later Abteilung K) vetted candidate pupils for the school of foreign intelligence founded in April 1952, most of whom were student members of the SED and Free German Youth; 4. Abteilung was the registry and archive, and was led, exceptionally, by a woman, Emmi Becker; and the Abteilung Verwaltung und Wirtschaft was a back-office admin team that managed the IWF's money, paperwork and supporting services such as drivers.

Among the first intake of pupils at the IWF intelligence school was Werner Grossmann. He would cap his espionage career as head of Stasi foreign intelligence in the late 1980s. In April 1952 Grossmann left his wife and daughter in Dresden and went to Berlin, there to 'attend a school run by the Central Committee' as preparation for 'a responsible position in the state or the party'. Upon arriving at the school he was told to surrender his identity papers; in return he was given new papers in the name of 'Olldorf', and advised never to reveal his real name. He caused amusement by asking if he could write to his wife; he was told to hand every letter he wrote to the school office, and never to write anything about the school, its teachers or its pupils. He only realised he was training to be a spy when he attended 'the first lectures on intelligence theory and practice'. He and his fellow pupils warmed to the task: 'We are to set up a functioning, effective intelligence service,' wrote Grossmann excitedly, 'while at the same time penetrating enemy headquarters and gaining information.'[11]

This all looked fine on paper, but almost from the start, and despite the presence of such stalwarts as Stahlmann, Szinda and Wolf, the IWF had a killer weakness, a festering sore that was destined to lame it. His name was Gotthold Krauss; he worked in the department for economic espionage; and from late 1951 onwards he was reporting everything he knew about the IWF to Walter O'Brien at the CIA's Berlin Operations Base.

The IWF was not a roaring success. One of its many flaws was adopting Stalin's louche habit, widely copied throughout the Soviet world, of working at night. It began its endeavors with around 100 agents inherited from the KPD and SED intelligence units, which were soon found to be riddled with Western moles. One of its sources in Hamburg, codenamed 'Mertens', was arrested by the Stasi at the IWF's own request.

Although the IWF was supposed to provide intelligence that allowed the SED to make 'correct decisions' and pursue 'correct policies', another of its agents, a journalist codenamed 'Kornbrenner', embarrassed the service by supplying false information that badly misled the party leadership. Other agents were busted. The head of the GDR's office for inter-German trade at Frankfurt am Main, Ludwig Weis, was uncovered rather quickly as an IWF spy and sentenced to four years in prison.[12] And important targets such as the Amt Blank, the prototype West German defence ministry, proved more challenging to infiltrate than first imagined. One of the IWF's only known successes from this period was its acquisition of a copy of the unratified European Defence Community treaty.[13]

One IWF recruitment that did pay dividends was that of Hannsheinz Porst of West Germany's Free Democratic Party. Signed up as agent 'Wiese' in February 1953, by the following decade the millionaire Porst was using 'his position to establish high-level political and business contacts'.[14] One of those contacts, Erich Mende, was urged by Porst to take the position of minister for German affairs in West Germany's CDU government, thus giving East German foreign intelligence a source in this crucial area. Porst, a covert SED member, was betrayed by his secretary in 1967 and spent two years in prison.[15]

The social democrat Otto Graf was also significant. Graf was one of the first of East Germany's spies to serve in West Germany's parliament, the Bundestag. He had begun to report secretly to the western KPD before the two republics were founded. In this work he would be visited on Sundays by one Rudolf Wörsching, aka 'Georg', a twenty-seven-year-old KPD official from Bavaria, who would photograph documents purloined by Graf and then speedily returned to their proper place. A 'particular highlight' received from Graf was a report on discussions with a French delegation about 'the creation of a European army'. But the IWF was never sure of Graf, who was suspected of being friendly with 'Trotskyists and Titoists', and even known to the US intelligence services. The relationship waned when 'Georg', in an attempt to have Graf assessed, arranged a meeting in East Berlin to which Graf didn't turn up.[16]

There was high turnover among the forty-odd staff at the IWF. Many of its employees simply weren't up to the job. The organisation was peripatetic, moving from Pankow to Rolandufer in Berlin's Mitte district, and with other scattered premises – buildings on Segelfliegerdamm, timbered villas in Schulzendorf and by the Langer See. The authority of its leaders was trumped by that of Wilhelm Zaisser and especially Walter Ulbricht. When the Western penetration of the IWF's early networks was discovered, Ulbricht characteristically used the scandal to besmirch party rivals such as Franz Dahlem, who had had some formal responsibility for the security of the western KPD. And while the Soviets were provided with every scrap of intelligence gained by the IWF, however faulty, it was the East German government that was footing the bill.

The IWF's cause wasn't helped by the fact that the Stasi's domestic departments – especially the counter-espionage branches, Departments II and IV – were running their own spies outside the GDR with some success. The records of Department II in Leipzig show the recruitment of a West German communist in his mid-twenties who was given the cover name 'Josef Brandl'. The Stasi assessed him throughout 1952 as he studied journalism at the University of Leipzig. He was distrusted by the West German authorities, who at one point denied him a permit to return home to Regensburg in Bavaria. On other occasions he was allowed to visit his family, and he made one such trip to attend his brother's wedding.

Department II told 'Brandl' to gather reams of information on this trip: information on the location and personnel of American intelligence services in the area; on military sites, airfields and training grounds; on troop units, their numbers and equipment; and on Federal police and security services based near the Czech border. He was expected to get this data from casual conversations with family and friends. If he did approach sensitive sites, he was told to act naturally, and if questioned to insist that he was only back in Bavaria to see his brother get married.

It seems 'Brandl' did a good job of gathering this information. He noted the controls carried out on his railway journey by the Volkspolizei and Federal customs officers. He reported a debate with a customs officer about the validity of his interzonal pass. After the wedding, he and his brother went out on motorcycles; 'Brandl' noted fenced-off arms depots in the woods and twin-engine planes at a local airfield, apparently a training ground for American jet pilots. He noticed that new track had been laid at local railway stations, and that American soldiers were loading freight trains; that some local bridges had been reinforced; that US soldiers in full combat gear would ride in train carriages with a white stripe and 'RC120' painted on the side; that twenty tanks had arrived on a freight train at Lichtenfels station. He also called on a young communist friend, who told him about the Counter Intelligence Corps and BfV offices on Dachauplatz in Regensburg; about the locations of American barracks and officers' homes on Prufingerstrasse; and about the area's Federal riot police, armed with machine guns and water cannon.[17] 'Brandl' was quite the spy, but his reliance on West German communists for information counted against him, and Department II curtailed his employment.

In general, it wasn't too difficult to find people who were prepared to spy for East Germany. Markus Wolf remarked that in the early days, the West Germans who were amenable to recruitment were not communists but rather well-wishers who wanted to bring the two republics closer together, or who disliked the Western powers' presence in Germany. Finding the right people was a different matter. One IWF asset claimed by Wolf fitted the bill: Andrew Thorndike, a feted filmmaker from a wealthy Hanseatic family whose father had been on the board of Krupp before the war.

Thorndike had been captured by the Red Army in 1945, and subsequently had lived in eastern Germany, but he remained on friendly terms with the industrial magnates and champagne socialists of Hamburg. Suspected of espionage, and disliked for his Stalinist films in which he lambasted the Federal Republic, Thorndike was arrested in West Berlin after he had been fooled into travelling there by a telegram claiming that his aunt was ill – clearly a favoured trick of the Western authorities, as well as the Stasi. Fortunately for the IWF, there was a sufficient outcry to secure his quick release.[18]

Well-connected spies like Thorndike were a rarity, however. It took time to find, foster and train talented spies with the right skills and the right kind of access to desirable information. Wolf's subsequent Stasi intelligence service managed this feat; the IWF did not.

In spring 1953, the defection of the IWF traitor Gotthold Krauss led to the staging of operation Vulkan (Volcano) by the West German security service, the BfV. Vulkan effectively blew apart the IWF.

For more than a year Krauss had been reporting on meetings and handing over IWF documents, but he was under increasing strain. A memo written by Richard Helms, future CIA chief, noted that Krauss had provided 'voluminous documentary information on [the IWF's] aims, staffing, methods, training, and agent personnel', and that, 'for security reasons, none of this data was given to other Allied or German agencies'.[19] As an employee of the economic branch, much of Krauss's information concerned industrial negotiations between the two republics, and attempts by the IWF to 'exploit the German interzonal trade system both for cover and for access to targets'.[20]

It wasn't just the CIA that was apprised of the IWF's secrets. Organisation Gehlen documents from the same period suggest a remarkably accurate knowledge of the IWF's leadership.[21] Most of their home addresses were known – Markus Wolf at number 16 Thomas Mann Strasse, Robert Korb at 92 Kuckhoffstrasse 'or one house beyond it'. The OG knew that Anton Ackermann's secretary was called Erna; that IWF employees went about their business under cover roles at government ministries such as the Ministry of Machine Building and the Ministry of National Education; that Richard Stahlmann only appeared in the office 'two or three times per week'. None of this augured well for the future of East Germany's foreign espionage.

The IWF materials provided to the CIA by Gotthold Krauss, especially his minutes of staff meetings chaired by Markus Wolf, suggest a rather unhappy place. On 7 February 1953 Wolf moaned to his senior officers that they didn't yet 'understand how to properly mobilise all the forces of our department... many employees get bogged down in their daily work and completely forget about the measures needed to achieve the goals they've been set'. Wolf believed 'the work of departments and employees must be made more systematic'. 'Currently,' he said, 'the IWF has little political intelligence and almost no economic intelligence. The little information we have isn't enough to inform our government and leadership.' Walter Ulbricht had complained to him about IWF personnel travelling on the budget, and with the identity papers, of the SED Central Committee; henceforward this was 'strictly forbidden'. It wasn't the only error. Wolf pointed out that 'a mistake was made, in that when training residents [who were to serve in West Germany] it was said that the required sources [i.e., spies] would be provided to them by headquarters. This should be avoided in future. The residents should actively search for sources themselves.'[22] There were security fears too:

All recruited agents, residents, couriers, drop-off points, conspiratorial apartments, cover addresses, etc., must be checked extremely carefully and precisely. Don't just do a surface check, go into it deeply. Relatives, environment, wives and children especially, vehicles and travel, etc., have to be ascertained scientifically. If we go through all of this scientifically, we'll certainly experience far fewer setbacks. Setbacks are predominantly caused by careless work.

Wolf then gave the floor to Emmi Becker of the files department, who lectured on the correct ways to archive data and share information with 'the friends' (the Soviets). It seems much of her audience had closed their ears; Krauss noted for the CIA that Gustav Szinda, in particular, was 'very anti-Emmi Becker'.

A meeting chaired by Wolf the day after Stalin's death was even more wracked.[23] In his write-up of it, Krauss documented a great fear that the West would seize this moment to unsettle, even topple, the governments of the Soviet Bloc. 'The women personnel appeared in black clothing and behaved as if their own mother had died,' Krauss wrote. Wolf was flanked by nine 'advisers' from Karlshorst. He announced that all 'operational employees', 'with the help of their agents', were to determine Western reactions to Stalin's death, Western views of the reshuffle in Moscow that had seen Georgy Malenkov briefly emerge as leader, and, most importantly, 'the real reason' why the Western powers had decided to move East German refugees from Berlin to West Germany in military aircraft. 'The friends urgently need this intelligence,' Wolf said: 'a shock operation [Stossaktion] must be initiated immediately.' The required information had to 'come from Bonn government circles, business circles and the circles of West German parties. Special attempts should be made to get such intelligence from the circles of the High Commissioners in West Germany'.

The mystery of the military aircraft portended war. Wolf stressed that:

the legitimate assumption [is] that the departure of refugees from West Berlin in military aircraft is just a cover. It is therefore necessary, particularly in this area, to carry out very rapid and systematic espionage work in West Berlin and the Federal Republic. This intelligence work is very, very urgent and very important.

Wolf suggested that spies broach the subject of Stalin's death in conversations, as a way of segueing into the more important matter of the aircraft. Moreover, 'the Tempelhof airfield and the West German airfields in particular must be monitored to see whether the aircraft are flying empty to Berlin or are transporting troops and military equipment. A precise description of any loads must be given in messages.' IWF agents who travelled routinely to West Germany were to ascertain:

> what Allied troop movements are taking place [and the] form of these troop movements, i.e., by rail or road, etc. What types of weapons are involved. Observers should also be sent to the harbours of Kiel, Hamburg, Bremen, etc., to determine what material is being loaded and which warships are at anchor.

Krauss concluded this report with a list of the major IWF assets expected to take part in the 'shock operation'. Included were two executives of East Germany's central bank, the Deutsche Notenbank; the head of foreign exchange at the Ministry of Internal and Foreign Trade; two leading economists; senior staff from the Directorate of Shipping and the DEFA film studios; and 'recruited sailors' working the inland waterways between Magdeburg and Hamburg.

Fortunately, Europe survived Stalin's death. So did the IWF, just, with no thanks due to Markus Wolf. When Gotthold Krauss escaped from East Germany on 4 April, together with his immediate family and eight other relatives – Krauss had feared greatly for their lives – it is said that Wolf, vaunted as the new IWF chief, was nowhere to be seen. The storm broke, but Wolf, absent and uncontactable, showed his bureaucratic talent by managing to fly above it.[24] (Perhaps the Soviets had known about the coming disaster, and for strategic reasons had spirited Wolf away.) A couple of weeks before Krauss's flight, the CIA had shared the secret of his cooperation with the West German government, and had helped the BfV to prepare arrest operations. On 6 April the BfV swooped, detaining nearly forty alleged agents of the GDR. This was less than half of the possible tally, as Krauss, who had arrived laden with documents, had named at least fifty more suspects.

The West German authorities then ran straight to the media, which proclaimed this counter-espionage coup from the rooftops. An article in *Der Spiegel* even named Markus Wolf as chief of the busted outfit. The problem, however, was that most of the arrested agents had been establishing their cover and sniffing the air. Few had done any real spying. As a result, it was possible to charge only three with an offence. Lenient sentences were handed to two of them, Hans Bogenhagen and Josef Gebhardt.[25] Wolf later claimed that only six of the arrestees were IWF agents anyway, and that most of the remainder were 'innocent businessmen who did deals in the East'.[26] Either way, the majority were swiftly released, and so both sides lost something – the East Germans their budding networks, the West Germans the chance to watch those networks and gain a thorough understanding of them before moving in.

36

'A Fascist Putsch': The Uprising of 1953

June 1953 witnessed the first mass revolt inside a Soviet Bloc country. Demonstrations flared up in Berlin and throughout East Germany. The Stasi failed to prevent the uprising, although some of its senior officers, and some SED executives, had been aware of the worsening public mood. The Soviet leadership, especially Lavrenti Beria, who had temporarily become ruler after the death of Stalin, were nervous in the months before the uprising. They recognised that Walter Ulbricht's hardline Aufbau policies were deeply, angrily resented. Even so, the Soviet intelligence services at Karlshorst, disorganised by Beria's tampering, were caught unawares by the uprising. So too were Western intelligence services.

From the start of 1951 until the middle of 1953, more than 300,000 people left the GDR for a new life in West Berlin or West Germany. Among them were some 4,000 SED and Free German Youth members, and an estimated 8,000 police officers.[1] The majority made their exit through the sector borders of Berlin.[2] The leakage of its population was always a major Achilles heel of the GDR. It couldn't get on its feet, or make itself appealing to West Germans as intended, without workers and educated professionals. Yet for decades there was a chronic shortfall in certain occupations, especially those that in other countries tended to be independent and lucrative – dentistry, for example. Public discontent and flight to the West – known as *Republikflucht* – increased considerably as a result of Ulbricht's acceleration of socialism. In May 1953, 30,000 citizens fled; in the first half of June, another 30,000.[3] An MGB report, based on the opinions of a senior French official, came to the fair conclusion that the GDR no longer held 'any attraction for citizens of West Germany'.[4]

In his short spell as Soviet leader, Lavrenti Beria exhibited a cautious, if not fearful, attitude towards maintaining Moscow's empire. Like all empires, it was considered vital for his country's defence. Moreover, the Soviet military considered East Germany to be hard-won territory gained through blood and sacrifice. Nevertheless, Beria inherited Stalin's complex interest in German reunification. His long-term plans revolved around a neutral, demilitarised Germany which could be swayed into the Soviet, and not the Western, camp. In the short term, this entailed showing a friendlier face to the West. In anticipation of the GDR's expected sovereignty, the Soviet Control Commission was closed down and replaced by the Office of the High Commissioner of the USSR, who initially was Vladimir Semyonov.

But diplomatic tinkering didn't soothe the population. In a report prepared for his Kremlin colleagues, Beria agonised that 'the number of refugees cannot be explained only by the hostile propaganda directed by West German organs at the population of the GDR'. For Beria, the exodus reflected:

[the] unwillingness of individual groups of peasants to enter the agricultural production cooperatives... the fear on the part of small and middle-level businessmen of the abolition of private property and the confiscation of their goods, the desire of youth to avoid military service, and the difficulties experienced in the GDR in supplying the population with foodstuffs and consumer goods.[5]

Beria's proposed solutions were standard Bolshevik fare, like strengthening political indoctrination in the police and at workplaces. As has been seen, however, he was sufficiently worried to harangue Ulbricht personally to retract some of his stricter socio-economic measures. Unfortunately for Beria, he didn't get to see the results. He was arrested at the end of June, only to become a droplet in the tidal wave of executions he had for so long presided over.

Meanwhile, some SED executives had seen the writing on the wall. Karl Schirdewan, head of the party's mood reporting agency, the LOPM, demanded urgent situation reports from key industrial sites – important factories at Leuna, Buna, Bitterfeld, Karl-Marx-Stadt, the border regions, Berlin. These reports no doubt reflected the workforce's resentment towards Stalinisation, which seemed only to be intensifying, not mellowing.

For wherever the East German people chose to look, there was no sign of the changes they wished to see. Stalin's death in March, rather than auguring greater freedom, had prompted weeping black-clad grief among SED members throughout the land. On 5 March, at a special Central Committee commemoration, Stalin was eulogised as 'a great friend of Germany who was always an adviser of and help to our people'. The dissonant commemorations continued thereafter. The 135th anniversary of Karl Marx's birth in May was marked by a celebratory raising of work quotas at industrial sites, as well as the renaming of Chemnitz as Karl-Marx-Stadt and the creation of a supposedly encouraging state award, the Order of Karl Marx. Just over a week later, the

13th conference of the SED Central Committee concluded that productivity had to increase by at least ten percent. A steep rise in production quotas was announced.

After all the hardships of the Aufbau, the rise in production quotas proved a tipping point. For some workers they amounted to a thirty percent cut in wages.[6] There were immediate signs of unrest, the most serious being a walkout of 900 labourers from the metal works in Leipzig on 16 May. In the second week of June, the SED Politbüro reacted to Beria's reproaches and retracted some of the Aufbau measures with the party's 'New Course'. But Politbüro members still insisted that productivity needed to rise. The battle lines were drawn.

On 15 June the construction workers building a new hospital on Stalinallee, in the Friedrichshain district of East Berlin, insisted that their party delegate deliver a resolution to prime minister Otto Grotewohl. Part of the resolution read, 'We believe that the 10 percent norm increase is a great hardship for us. We demand that our construction site be exempted.'[7] The following morning, fifteen SED agitators were sent to Stalinallee to deliver the response. They explained that while Grotewohl was prepared to raise the matter of the norms in forthcoming meetings, at this point they wouldn't be retracted.

The 600 or so workers in attendance had been locked into the site to listen to this address. With the help of some labourers who had arrived from other workplaces, they pushed through the gates and began to march to the GDR's seat of government, the House of Ministries. The raucous crowd passed Alexanderplatz, crossed the Spree, headed along Unter den Linden, and made a turn at the Brandenburg Gate. By the time they reached the House of Ministries on Leipziger Strasse, they were 5,000 strong.

For five hours the crowd chanted protests. There were calls for a general strike, calls to overthrow the government. Volkspolizei and KVP personnel were on hand, but were nervous and didn't intervene. Finally, a beleaguered government representative appeared; Fritz Selbmann, minister for mining. He tried to placate the crowd but was shouted down. Nevertheless, the protest lacked focus and the day was stinkingly hot. Gradually, the crowd drifted away.

Starting at 4.30 p.m., however, RIAS began to broadcast news of the disturbances. A ninety-second news flash went on rotation, publicising the occurrence of a 'mass demonstration' which the Volkspolizei hadn't dared to break up. There were disturbances throughout the rest of the evening, now under torrential rain. At one point, a driver was dragged from a Free German Youth truck; its loudspeaker was then used for shouts of 'Down With The

SED!' and 'Overthrow The Government!'[8] Another crowd formed, ultimately of around 3,000 people; on Bersarinplatz these protesters attacked a monument to Stalin, overturned a government truck, and tried to break into the houses of SED officials.[9]

Volkspolizei leaders understood that the police were in the firing line. Reinforcements were called in from Potsdam, Magdeburg and Leipzig, and 200 officers were assigned to protect the police presidium on Alexanderplatz. At an emergency meeting held overnight, the Politbüro decided to make the higher production quotas voluntary rather than compulsory. But this concession didn't prevent what happened next.

Strikes started at 6.30 a.m. on 17 June. Columns of strikers began to march on the centre of Berlin. One large column of factory and railway workers headed for Stalinallee. Another formed at factories in Hennigsdorf, northwest of the city. These marchers set out on a twenty-seven-kilometre tramp which took them past the 'Walter Ulbricht' stadium, inaugurated for the World Youth Festival, where they paused to tear down the giant letters of Ulbricht's name. Crowds of demonstrators converged on the House of Ministries, breaking through lines of Volkspolizei and blue-shirted Free German Youth activists. Alerted by broadcasts on RIAS, people began travelling to the city centre on the U-Bahn to join the protests.

What did the demonstrators want? After the event, the deputy head of the Volkspolizei reported on the eight demands that were most discernible among the protesters: a reduction of the work quotas, a reduction of prices in state-run shops, the removal of agricultural quotas, the release of prisoners, free elections, the deprecation of the SED, the resignation of the government, and the removal of Germany's zonal boundaries.[10]

Two popular demands were noticeably absent from this list – the reconstitution of the SPD and the expulsion of Russians. This must have been due to nervousness on the part of the report writer, for the social democratic bent to the demonstrations was painfully obvious, as were the anti-Russian slogans which appeared on many walls. There were also calls for an improvement in living standards, for the privacy of post to be respected, and for the disbandment of state paramilitaries like the KVP.[11] Another prevalent demand was the licensing of all political parties. Presumably this included the far-right parties of West Germany, such as the Socialist Reich Party; for many Germans were not pro-democratic in a Western sense, and continued to crave the chauvinistic, nationalistic hierarchies of Nazism and Prussian imperialism. Moreover, a dull-minded self-interest was apparent among some demonstrators; those who complained, for example, that their taxes had been miscalculated. However, in a characteristic incident, employees of the Zeiss works in Jena put forward to the authorities a considered programme of thirty-three political and material demands. Number one on their list was free elections.[12]

As the number of demonstrators on Berlin's streets swelled, the mood got uglier. Volkspolizei cars were damaged and there were attacks on Free German Youth members. In one incident, demonstrators tried to throw some FDJ activists into the Spree but were stopped by fellow protesters.[13] A police officer was stabbed when a crowd of some 5,000 attempted to storm the police presidium. Here as elsewhere, Soviet forces arrived to put down the disorder.[14] In the early morning, some troops had been deployed at such nerve centres as post offices, railway stations and bridges.[15] By 11 a.m., police officers and Soviet tanks were stationed at the Brandenburg Gate, from where they fanned out to disperse the crowds. Public transport had already been shut down. A state of emergency was declared by the Soviet commandant of Berlin, Major General Dibrova. The sector borders were then sealed by Soviet troops, the Volkspolizei, and the KVP, in what was 'the most complete isolation of West Berlin from Soviet-controlled areas yet seen'.[16] Eventually, despite an afternoon of unfettered political expression and contagious rioting, the tanks won.

Walter Ulbricht's cluelessness in the face of the revolt is evinced in a comment he reportedly made upon hearing of the first strikes: 'It's raining and people will go home.'[17] The penny soon dropped, however, for Ulbricht and Otto Grotewohl promptly retreated behind the walls of Karlshorst to sit out the emergency in safety.[18] At least 100,000 demonstrators came out on the streets of Berlin that day. Some 400,000 people demonstrated throughout the rest of East Germany, in rural areas and in hundreds of towns, despite the numerous declarations of a state of emergency. (Only in the north, in such places as Rostock and Neubrandenburg, were the Stasi and other local authorities better prepared; the rebellion was quieter there.) Among the demonstrators were more than 250,000 workers from state-owned industrial concerns. The task of confronting them fell mostly to deeply shocked officials of party, state, and industry, and to hastily formed groups of SED agitators, all of whom were exposed as relatively powerless. After all, many of the striking workers they were supposed to pacify were living in unheated barracks without light, water or toilets. They were unlikely to be halted by a group of trembling communist students.

Thus the revolt in the regions was as full-blooded as that in Berlin. Almost anything flammable went up – trucks, trams, station waiting rooms, poster columns. In Magdeburg, the police chief and his officers stationed at the 'Karl Liebknecht' factory were attacked during the first work stoppages. Some 8,000 striking workers were then joined by members of the public; at 10.15 a.m. this combined force stormed the offices of the city council and the trade union federation, the FDGB, where they battered some union officials. The city's police prison was stormed next; a police officer was beaten up there. Twenty prisoners were then released from the court prison in the Sudenburg district. A Stasi sergeant, Hans Waldbach, was shot dead while guarding a building; his corpse was pelted with rocks. Soon after midday Soviet troops arrived. They went into action in at least one district, Neustadt, where it was claimed that police and the machine-gunners in Soviet tanks fired into the crowds. Besides Waldbach, two police officers and four demonstrators were killed at Magdeburg, while forty-two people were injured.[19]

Similar scenes played out elsewhere. An SED member was shot by protesters at the railway station of Herzfelde, near Frankfurt an der Oder. Demonstrators stormed the SED building in Niesky, east of Dresden; a party secretary was hospitalised by a beating. The town's Volkspolizei officers were attacked with rocks and beer bottles before retreating to their main station, which they defended with the help of fifteen border guards. A crowd then stormed the Stasi office, disarming and locking up in dog cages the personnel they found there.

In nearby Görlitz the remand prison was overrun, its inmates freed. Demonstrators then stormed the city hall and the offices of the Stasi and the local Soviet commander. Axe-wielding protesters forced the SED mayor to sign the release of all inmates at the court prison; in a subsequent report by the Stasi's Dresden office, he was castigated for 'sinking so low'.[20] A short-lived alternative government was proclaimed in the town, with social democrats as its driving force.[21] In Leipzig there were attacks on the police station, the prison, the FDGB and FDJ buildings, a radio station, and the offices of the SED's *Volksstimme* newspaper. The members of an impromptu 'task force' led by Major Kaul of the Stasi's Department XIV resorted to firing warning shots to repel rioters armed with crowbars and whips.[22] In Brandenburg, 15,000 demonstrators gathered; when they assaulted the SED headquarters, a party secretary narrowly escaped being thrown from a third-floor window. This was followed by the storming of the FDGB building and police station; forty prisoners were freed, several police officers stripped and beaten, and an SED activist's head split open with a blow from a stick. The violence was so unbridled that the local police thought the government had fallen. Only the arrival of Soviet troops persuaded them otherwise.

Prisoners were also freed from two jails in Halle, where several police officers and a judge were beaten up. There were more attacks on police officers in the streets, and an eight-metre-high portrait of Stalin was trampled gleefully by thousands of demonstrators. (After an agitated debate, a portrait of Karl Marx was left alone because 'he was a German'.)[23] A crowd of 1,000 protesters then headed for a nearby work camp, intent on freeing the inmates; they were dispersed by Soviet troops who, along with local police officers, fired their weapons. There was a striking ideological twist to the events in Halle. Erna Dorn, a former Gestapo and concentration camp employee, was freed from prison to address the crowds.

At Merseburg, the police station, prison, and Stasi office were all stormed, their interiors demolished and prisoners freed. At Bitterfeld, 10,000 striking workers marched on the police station; SED members were attacked along the way, and a party secretary was dragged along by the crowd as a trophy. Demonstrators who announced themselves as repressed SPD members then freed the inmates of the town's police prison before attacking the Stasi and FDJ buildings. At Jena, 20,000 demonstrators stormed the offices of the National Front, as well as the buildings of the German-Soviet friendship society, the SED, and the Stasi. Sixty prisoners were freed, while four injured police officers were refused treatment at the local hospital; they had to be tended by the Soviet military. At Cottbus, a prison and pretrial detention centre were targeted; here, Soviet tanks arrived only to be attacked by the demonstrators. Protests were especially animated in rural areas with a high number of collective farms. Incendiary crowds gathered to demand the release of all imprisoned farmers, the return of private ownership, and the creation of a properly democratic farmers' union.[24]

Despite the fame of 17 June, a report by the Soviet army estimated that even more workers went on strike the next day.[25] Even with Soviet tanks and troops deployed in every hotspot, the disturbances continued. The SED, hitherto remarkably quiet, published notices urging 'workers and all honest citizens' to 'seize the provocateurs and hand them over'.[26] A planned demonstration at Stalinstadt, a new town being built near Frankfurt an der Oder, was foiled by the arrest of its organisers; the East German authorities thus averted the unthinkable prospect of popular anger being turned, visibly, towards the Kremlin. At Drewitz, it took a company of KVP troopers and tanks to prevent the storming of a penal camp. The KVP was also deployed at Halle, where a bystander was shot as demonstrators were dispersed.[27] In all, around one million people in more than 700 locations are thought to have taken part in the rebellion.[28]

It is estimated that almost 100 people lost their lives during and after the East German uprising. More than fifty were killed during the demonstrations, including at least twenty who were shot by Soviet forces under the conditions of martial law.[29] In addition to the tanks, two divisions of Soviet troops, some of them MVD paramilitaries, had been deployed across more than 100 towns and cities.

These forces had to maintain readiness for several weeks, as sporadic strikes and unrest fizzled on. In July, 2,000 workers at Zeiss went on strike over the imprisonment of a popular union official, Eberhard Norkus. Workers at an engineering plant in Netzschkau walked out when the local Stasi chief turned up to arrest a suspected troublemaker and loudly threatened to shoot the man 'between the ribs' if he didn't come quietly. The strikers told mediating officials that they would no longer accept such 'Gestapo methods'.[30]

The Stasi's performance in the uprising was unimpressive; more a rubber sword than the 'shield and sword of the party'. Wilhelm Zaisser had rendered Stasi officers powerless by giving an order not to shoot at demonstrators, although some did. At the time Zaisser was judged harshly for this decision; in retrospect it seems sensible, even – just possibly – humane. Worse still for the authorities, hundreds of police officers had swapped sides during the disturbances, while much of the SED leadership had shirked their duty by scurrying to the relative safety of the party's domestic settlement at Pankow. Along with the Stasi offices at Bitterfeld, Görlitz, Jena, Niesky and Merseburg, at least twelve prisons and thirteen police stations had ended up in the hands of protesters, and as many as 3,000 prisoners freed. The government, always loath to admit the truth, had to face facts and announce publicly that 'a member of the MfS and three members of the Volkspolizei lost their lives'.

Another authority figure who died at the hands of demonstrators was a resident of Rathenow called Wilhelm Hagedorn. Before his age-related retirement from the police, Hagedorn had served in K5. He had then worked as head of security for the state-run shops in Rathenow. Well-known in the town, he had once boasted of exposing and imprisoning '300 fascists and agents'. He had also been targeted by RIAS broadcasts. During the disturbances he was spotted, chased, and apprehended. Then he was lynched. He died from his injuries soon afterwards.[31]

It is tempting to think that Wilhelm Zaisser, having spent a lifetime steeped in clandestine struggle and revolutionary bloodshed, was a little too old, and a little too tired, to commit fully to the aggressive defence of the young republic. Before the uprising there were signs of his fatigue, his ambivalence. He hadn't wanted the job of security minister. His deputy, Erich Mielke, was far more vociferous and active in running the Stasi. Markus Wolf commented that in their meetings Zaisser seemed more interested in discussing his translation of the collected works of Lenin than intelligence reports.[32]

Behind closed doors Yevgeny Pitovranov, chief of the Karlshorst apparat, slammed Zaisser's Stasi as being 'in no condition to cope with hostile underground forces'. The Soviets promptly appointed an imposing Ukrainian counter-intelligence officer, Vasily Bulda, as a top-level adviser to the Stasi,[33] and created forty operational groups to investigate the uprising. Each was staffed by around sixty officers from MGB military counter-intelligence – the heirs of SMERSH – and from the MVD. More than forty officers were assigned to the Stasi's Greater Berlin administration, and smaller MVD groups were placed at more than 100 district offices. Together they guided the Stasi in uncovering the revolt's 'organisers, ringleaders, and instigators'. Soviet counter-intelligence wisdom dictated that some of the suspects should be recruited as agents during 'the screening and interrogation process', as having such people under the thumb might prove highly useful.[34] And before June had ended, the Soviets had devised plans for strengthening 'MfS organs, reinforcing the frontier guards, and ensuring reliable guarding of MfS installations and GDR prisons' in the future.[35]

The arrest of 'ringleaders' – the main organisers of strikes, the instigators of violence and prison breaks – began on the evening of 18 June. In the following days the arrests broadened to encompass anyone who had addressed crowds, rioted, shouted anti-government slogans or broken the curfew. The Stasi's arrest teams worked quickly: 3,791 persons arrested by 22 June, with more than 2,200 still in custody three days later;[36] almost 5,000 arrested by 7 July, and an ultimate tally of 6,000.[37] The Volkspolizei arrested another 7,000.[38] Represented among them were thousands of small acts of defiance: a former state functionary who had pushed empty tram cars into the path of Soviet tanks in Jena; a pastor who had called for the resignation of the government he 'hated like the plague'.[39] Subsequently a relatively modest number of people – around 1,600 – were put on trial for their part in the uprising. Besides public order offences, convictions for 'defamation of the state' and 'boycotting of democratic institutions' predominated. Lengthy prison sentences were handed to those thought to have been the worst offenders, but most sentences were determined by the provisions of Allied Control Council Directive 38. Although not too stiff – around one and a half years, mostly – they had repercussions in the countryside, where badly needed workers spent the harvest and sowing seasons in jail.[40]

There were worse repercussions. Although CDU and LDPD members had not played a prominent role in the demonstrations, the former chairman of a CDU group at Rudolstadt was summarily executed, probably by Soviet personnel, for his actions during the uprising.[41] Willy Göttling, an unemployed father of two, was killed in Soviet custody, accused of fomenting riots in the service of an unnamed Western intelligence service.[42] More executions followed. A Soviet tribunal decreed the death by shooting of locksmith Alfred Diener, who was said to have led the assault on the SED office in Jena.[43] Erna Dorn, the former concentration camp employee freed from prison by demonstrators in Halle, was beheaded at Dresden on 1 October. There is ongoing debate about whether Dorn had been doing time for common crimes or crimes against humanity. Either way, the mere fact she had once worked at Ravensbrück concentration camp was, for the SED, proof that the uprising had been a fascist project. A worker from Magdeburg, Ernst Jennrich, suffered the same fate. Although he admitted using an old rifle to shoot through the window of a police station, he denied killing a building guard.[44] Despite these measures, the disorder continued into the autumn. SED members were attacked and speakers at public events beaten up. At its fiercest the resistance was deadly. Several chairmen of collective farms were shot dead.[45]

In a series of pronouncements and *Neues Deutschland* articles, mostly originating from Walter Ulbricht and the newspaper's chief editor Rudolf Herrnstadt, the SED labelled the June uprising a 'fascist putsch' organised by the Western powers. This was a Soviet conception, endorsed by the MGB and MVD in part to discredit Lavrenti Beria; and it was adopted, not devised, by the SED and the Stasi. Nevertheless, they enthusiastically toed the line that, in the words of one Stasi report, the 'tense domestic political situation was exploited by the enemy and his agent apparatus in order to push through the long-planned X-Day'.[46]

Although the communist authorities were gripped by notions of fascism and Western orchestration, there was far greater proof that the rising had been spontaneous and social democratic in tone. Swastikas had been chalked here and there, and impromptu choruses of the *Deutschlandlied* belted out; at that time it was the anthem of neither East nor West Germany. Plenty of letters containing threats of psychotic violence had been sent to regime loyalists,[47] and there were other hints of right-wing malevolence. When strikers in Dresden had fixated on springing prisoners from a city jail, an SED factory official had asked if they intended to release 'the Nazis who beat our people to death'; he was ignored, and the prisoners freed anyway.[48] One Karl-Heinz Pahling, arrested as an alleged leader of strikers in Brandenburg, admitted he had served in the Waffen-SS during the final months of the war.[49] And Lothar Markwith, the main culprit in locking the Stasi officers of Görlitz inside a dog cage – he had also threatened to force-feed them dogfood – was a former SA Brownshirt.[50] Moreover, after the rising the KgU had published a leaflet in which the SED regime was described as 'many times worse than that of the Nazis' – a view which, according to reliable surveys of the time, was shared by a majority of West Germans.[51] But none of this amounted to evidence of a conspiracy.

One of the more serious incidents to implicate fascists and Westerners was a physical attack on Lieutenant Colonel Rudolf Gutsche, the son of Stasi stalwart Joseph and formerly a youthful wartime partisan. On the morning of 17 June, Gutsche junior, chief of Department VIII for Greater Berlin, had been driving through the disorder in a BMW with two colleagues. Upon reaching Alexanderplatz the BMW was recognised as a government car; it was rammed by a Bedford truck driven by a protester, bringing it to a halt. The driver of the truck and four others then dragged out the car's occupants and beat them viciously. One of the Stasi officers lost his pistol to an assailant, and a shot was fired.

Subsequently five East Berliners were put on trial for their part in this attack. Significantly, they were unworthy 'anti-social' types, petty criminals who had done plenty of prison time between them; their prior convictions included stealing the ration card of a five-year-old child. One seventeen-year-old defendant told the Berlin City Court how he enjoyed hanging out in American-themed cinemas and clubs in West Berlin. He and a fellow teenaged defendant had, in the words of a Stasi report, been 'mostly concerned with the products of American unculture'.[52] It hadn't escaped the Stasi that nicknames like 'Capone' and 'Dillinger' had become popular among Berlin's more robust youths. It was established that in late 1952, these two teenagers, who were said to hold regressive 'fascist' views, had joined a League of German Youth (BDJ) cell based on Potsdamer Strasse, its premises adorned by the Stars-and-Stripes and portraits of Konrad Adenauer. The same Stasi report described their BDJ activities: some minor, like scrawling graffiti and handing out leaflets; some martial, like weapons and unarmed combat training; and some rather odd, like being treated to women's mud wrestling matches as a morale booster – 'events that appealed to the lowest instincts', as the Stasi put it.

Another defendant admitted he had been hired by 'the English secret service' after going on a three-day binge with a West Berlin prostitute earlier in the year. A fourth, the driver of the Bedford truck, was an active supporter of the KgU. On 17 June, he and the rest had been directed to Alexanderplatz, so they said, by RIAS broadcasts, which were indicating the best spots for rioting. It was perhaps the misfortune of these five that they had assaulted a senior Stasi officer. The incident allowed the Stasi and judiciary to tie in a number of enemies – BDJ, KgU, RIAS, British intelligence, the United States – with the notion of planned violence against East German officials, to be inflicted by young Nazis; a fascist putsch, no less. The defendants received prison sentences of between six and twelve years. The Bedford truck was added to the state-owned fleet.

As for other signs of Western orchestration, during the disturbances some leaflets printed in Reinickendorf in the French sector of Berlin had appeared, urging the workers of two factories to strike and push for a return to private ownership. Soviet personnel had noted the presence in East Berlin of vehicles with American and West Berlin number plates. This was taken as evidence that Western agencies were marshalling the revolt, but such vehicles had a right to be in East Berlin if driven by military personnel, for at this time only civilian vehicles were subject to Volkspolizei checks.

Despite the paucity of proof, an analysis by the SED Central Committee concluded that hundreds of thousands of East German workers had been made the tools of the fascist-imperialist West. The cover of a propaganda brochure issued later by the Stasi showed the faces of four hate-figures said to be especially culpable for the 'fascist war provocation' of 17 June: West German chancellor Konrad Adenauer, US secretary of state John Foster Dulles, West Berlin mayor Ernst Reuter, and the Federal minister for all-German affairs, Jakob Kaiser. The Stasi cited as evidence the Western radio broadcasts that had accompanied the disturbances. Some Soviet officials opined that the uniformity of the demonstrators' demands was proof of Western orchestration.

But the West hadn't lent substantive support to the uprising, never mind instigated it. By all reliable accounts, the CIA was taken by surprise and didn't consider arming the demonstrators, as has been claimed.[53] Winston Churchill expressed the view that 'it would indeed [have been] a poor service to the German people, with whom I have the deepest sympathy, to provoke them into revolt against overwhelming power.' In fact, behind closed doors Churchill 'certainly thought the Russians could not have been expected to remain inactive' and reportedly '"had the impression that they acted with considerable restraint in the face of mounting disorder".'[54]

This is an important point, for it exposes mistaken historical perspectives on the Cold War. Although in the early 1950s America was embarked on its anti-communist crusade, in which it had co-opted Konrad Adenauer and his burgeoning West Germany, for all their horror of communism many Europeans – including Winston Churchill – continued to see Germany as a problem land and Germans as a problem people. The Second World War was not forgiven or forgotten – indeed, why should it have been? So while the deployment of Soviet tanks may have signified a threat to European order, so too did an uprising of Germans. It is anachronistic nonsense to think that Britain might have stepped in to foster a rebellion in Germany. This truth has been obscured by our US-centric views of the Cold War, and by the inability of some Germans to understand that Nazism and the world war had generated a degree of resentment, and wariness towards German empowerment.

How, then, had the uprising really started, and spread? Radio reports played a large part; this was a revolt spread by word of airwave, as well as word of mouth. It is likely that radio stations, above all RIAS and NWDR, had galvanised communities into holding their own strikes and demonstrations. Egon Bahr, at that time a RIAS employee, said later that 'RIAS had – without knowing it and without wanting it – triggered the uprising. The enormous power of the electronic medium was proven for the first time in history.'[55]

The CIA's analysis of the uprising was fair enough: that it demonstrated the widespread resentment felt towards Moscow and the SED, was proof of Soviet distrust of East Germany's police and security forces, had embarrassed the SED, and was generally bad for the image of Soviet communism.[56] But perhaps the only Western agency to respond to the revolt with some alacrity – apart from radio stations – was the Organisation Gehlen.

At about 8 p.m. on 16 June – long after RIAS and Bayerischer Rundfunk had started to run newsflashes on the disturbances – reports from Gehlen agents began to reach Pullach. They arrived when the working day was over, however, and there was no one on duty to respond to them. It wasn't until the following afternoon that the Organisation Gehlen began to formulate its response. For several weeks thereafter Pullach mobilised more than 500 agents in the GDR, who generated almost 1,300 reports on the situation, including on the actions taken by the Soviet military.[57] Revealing its lack of knowledge about the rising, the OG posed set questions to its sources: 'Was the date of the action [uprising] controlled from above? In what recognisable form was it controlled? How did the demonstrations spread?'[58] The resulting reports, and the difficulties around receiving and checking them, were to influence the spy wars of the coming years; for they showed the OG that links with spies in East Germany could be severed rather easily, and that it was necessary to prepare better means of communication between the two republics – especially radio contact.

In fact, the OG was pretty disgusted with its performance during the rising. The Stasi got hold of an internal report in which a senior OG officer complained that 'a real intelligence service reports on the enemy's intentions and allows assessments and measures to be taken in advance', something the Gehlen networks had singularly failed to do. The OG was overly reliant on 'frontline reconnaissance' sources, who could describe events just after they had happened but not anticipate them. This condemned the OG to fail 'as an adviser to the state leadership at exactly the decisive moment'. It had had 'no secure means of smuggling, secret telephone lines or other means of communication that could not be prevented by cordons of barriers'. Thus it received substantive information only in July, 'after the lifting of the postal blockade'; altogether, a 'grotesque picture', in which 'sources who lived far away from Berlin in the provinces were more likely to report than those stationed in Berlin and the surrounding area'. The only positive was that OG spies, as ordered, had refrained from taking part in the demonstrations.

The report suggested a range of improvements. More training in the use of morse keys and secret inks; more training for spies on when to stop and when to continue reporting; the preparation of better places to smuggle people and materials across the sector borders; the establishment of new cover addresses in East Berlin, to be served by a new courier system; and the laying of secret telephone cables in Berlin's waterways. The latter step came with a warning: 'Note that water bodies where dredging work takes place should be avoided!'[59]

The June 1953 uprising brought home the terrible vulnerability of the SED. The historian Roger Engelmann has written that the events:

> gave rise to a double trauma: that of the functionaries who were confronted with a 'working class' revolting against them and whose power had already slipped away, and that of the opponents of the regime, who had to realise that the Soviet Union would never give up its German satellite state.[60]

Stasi personnel were made to feel vulnerable too. Some officers grew fearful over their likely fate in any future revolt.[61] One senior officer shot himself. And Soviet personnel were also punished; the MVD replaced several hundred of its staff members in East Germany.

As the dust settled, the accusations started to fly. Most flew towards Wilhelm Zaisser and the Stasi. At a party meeting, Otto Grotewohl, with something of a brass neck, called it unacceptable that 'all of us' were able to understand and stay abreast of the rising while 'only our state security was not able to ascertain what was happening'.[62] Soviet criticisms were lacerating. The Stasi was dismissed as amateur, the SED leadership belittled like guilty infants. Even as the revolt was raging, the Politbüro had been summoned to Karlshorst, where Vasily Sokolovsky had excoriated Zaisser for his criminal negligence, for not recognising that 'a complete enemy network' had organised the strikes.[63] Even Erich Mielke was judged to have 'underestimated the seriousness of the developing situation' and not taken 'the tough, punitive measures necessary to identify and arrest the instigators'.[64] Perhaps worst of all, about 100 Stasi employees studying at the Potsdam school were known to have joined the demonstrators.[65] Thirty Stasi officers were arrested for their actions, or inaction, during the revolt.[66]

Behind closed doors the SED acknowledged that repressed social democrats had been highly active in the uprising. This prompted Horst Sindermann, leader of the Central Committee's agitprop department, to comment, 'We should examine how it is that agents of the SPD Ostbüro have a relatively large influence with the working masses compared to other agents.'[67] In essence, Sindermann was asking, 'Why do they prefer social democracy to us or the Nazis?' It was obvious that social democracy remained a sleeping giant in East Germany.

Regardless of the claiming and blaming, the June 1953 revolt chiefly reflected the demand for improvements and German unity; not the demand for an end to the socialist experiment itself, which was largely absent.[68] Almost seventy percent of those arrested were classified as a 'worker'. Government employees and the intelligentsia made up just over thirteen percent. Apart from the disturbances around collective farms, every other social class – farmers, tradespeople, businesspeople – had much lower representation.[69] This, then, was a revolt of the workers and of educated, state-employed professionals over specific economic, political and material grievances. Short of revolting, these people had had nowhere else to go, for the SPD no longer existed and the CDU and LDPD had become thoroughgoing 'instruments of the SED'.[70]

Moreover, besides venting their spleen at the SED and its arms like the FDGB and FDJ, the demonstrators had focused above all on freeing prisoners. Clearly, the perceived wrongful imprisonment of friends, family, colleagues and neighbours had incensed the East German public; imprisonment which resulted largely from the draconian laws of the Aufbau. Arrests under these laws were carried out by the Stasi and Volkspolizei. Thus, great anger had been directed specifically towards those two agencies. The KVP, too, had faced popular fury. Afraid of civil war and the firmer division of Germany, many citizens didn't want rearmed military forces in the GDR – the notion was anathema.

In the wake of the rising, the CDU asked its members in the districts to gather information on what had just happened, and why. They reported that citizens mostly wanted an end to the 'lies' of the SED press; disapproved of the government leadership; didn't like Germany's separation into zones; and wanted improvements in agriculture, and freer access to West Berlin. Their most important grievance was said to be the lack of 'legal security'. Again, this captures the public anger about arrests and incarcerations for new crimes around collectivisation and state-owned property, but also about the way that arrests, trials and incarcerations were conducted, with little regard for proper procedures. For many citizens, the thousands imprisoned under these laws were wholly innocent victims, arrested and tried in a lawless manner. In its summary the CDU report noted that 'people demand over and over that every person arrested must be informed as to the reason for the arrest. The next of kin must also be informed'.[71] It is obvious that, as in the late 1940s, people were continuing to disappear from workplaces, homes and communities, with no explanation of the charges they faced and no news given out.

The SED's reaction to the revolt took a form that would be repeated in the coming decades: an apparent public softening accompanied by a secret, behind-the-scenes toughening up. As early as 25 June the Politbüro announced planned improvements in living standards. Extra foodstuffs were to be brought in from the Soviet Union, prices lowered on public transport, funds made available to repair accommodation, and factories made more hygienic.[72] Rudolf Herrnstadt drafted a Central Committee resolution, 'The New Course and the Renewal of the Party', part of which read, 'It is important to create a GDR whose prosperity, social justice, legal security, national traits, and atmosphere of freedom will meet with the approval of all honest Germans.'[73] The party showed it had eyes and ears. By the end of July, ten percent of LPGs had been dissolved, with the relaxation prompting a mass exodus of workers from remaining collective farms;[74] and from June to October nearly 24,000 prisoners were released. As noted, a relatively low number of prison sentences were handed to the 13,000 June demonstrators who had been arrested.

Yet the party's two-faced response is illustrated by the simultaneous introduction of House and Court Societies.* These residential cooperatives were set up ostensibly to provide more and better accommodation, and to increase public security; they were promoted in cinema adverts as 'centres in the fight against agents, spies and provocateurs'.[75] They proved unpopular, for the public came to see them as nests of state surveillance.[76] This view was not far-fetched. At the 15th plenum of the SED in late July, party functionaries had called for 'a more complete system of monitoring and controlling the population'.[77]

In the spaces the public couldn't see into, the SED's leaders dropped the caring act. The apparent lenience shown towards arrested demonstrators was tempered by the fact that the Stasi and Volkspolizei secretly handed over more than 400 arrestees to the Soviet authorities.[78] The Stasi was instructed to interfere with an American programme to provide East Germans with food packages, mostly by subtly threatening the intended recipients; for the US authorities had disguised this disruptive act of psychological warfare as a caring display of international amity, and it could not be tolerated by the SED. (It proved so difficult to stop people from travelling into West Berlin to pick up the packages that train tickets to the west of the city were temporarily withdrawn from sale.) Another move saw party luminaries such as Max Fechner, minister of justice, placed under arrest. He had supported the workers' right to strike in a *Neues Deutschland* article, and had admitted that unlawful arrests were being made.

---

* Haus- und Hofgemeinschaften.

Fechner was sentenced to eight years in prison, and spent nearly three in the 'Yellow Misery' at Bautzen; he was, however, amnestied in 1956. Meanwhile, the fearsome Hilde Benjamin, who by this time had acquired the nickname of 'the Red Guillotine' to complement 'Red Hilde', replaced Fechner as justice minister.

The revolt accelerated the SED's preparations for war and civil unrest. The Soviets called for strengthened forces to protect government buildings, industrial sites and radio stations. A motorised police unit some 4,000-strong was created,[79] as well as the Combat Groups of the Working Class (Kampfgruppen der Arbeiterklasse, KdA). At its height this workers' militia boasted more than 200,000 members; its first intake marched proudly in the May Day parades of 1954. The Stasi had already become an acknowledged paramilitary force earlier that year, with the reclassification of its guard units as 'interior troops' along Soviet lines. The revolt's most significant outcome was the ousting of Wilhelm Zaisser and the Stasi's demotion from a government ministry to an agency under the Ministry of the Interior.

Zaisser was relieved of his duties on 26 July 1953. As well as his failings around the revolt, he had fallen foul of his Politbüro colleagues by intriguing against Walter Ulbricht, who accused him of making the Stasi unaccountable to the party and of forming a faction with Rudolf Herrnstadt, who was also purged. Zaisser's pre-eminent role in the twentieth century German communist movement came to an abject end. At his final Politbüro meeting he accused himself of defeatism and social democratic tendencies, voted for his own expulsion, burst into tears, and swept from the room.[80] Not long afterwards he was forced out of the party altogether. He spent what remained of his life buried in his books and the quandaries of translation from Russian to German.

These events coincided with a corruption scandal in which Zaisser, Erich Mielke and several other Stasi high-ups were accused of stealing some 230,000 marks in unauthorised payments and loans. Some of this booty was said to have been spent on maintaining a luxurious hunting lodge, formerly owned by Hermann Göring, by the Wolletzsee in Brandenburg. But it was only Wilhelm Zaisser whose face didn't fit; the rest were all kept in a job thanks to Walter Ulbricht's support.

Thus the Ministerium für Staatssicherheit was no more. By September 1953 the Stasi had become the State Secretariat for State Security (Staatssekretariat für Staatssicherheit, SfS) under the interior ministry. This aligned its status with the security services of other Soviet Bloc countries. Only in November 1955 would it become a ministry again. The new Stasi chief, Ernst Wollweber, was appointed to the SED Central Committee but, unlike Zaisser, not to the Politbüro. In the words of Jens Gieseke, henceforward 'Ulbricht personally took over competence for the SSD [state security service] in the Politbüro'.[81] Yet despite the Stasi being subordinated more firmly to Ulbricht and the party, the Soviets still played a key role: in the event of any doubt about a security matter, Karlshorst had the final say.

None of the adjustments made after the revolt stemmed the leakage of the GDR's population. The year 1953 saw 331,390 people flee to the west, including 2,718 SED members.[82] So on the orders of the Politbüro, the Stasi devised two initiatives for tackling the problems with subversion and unrest.

One of them, beginning in autumn 1953, was a series of concerted counter-espionage arrest campaigns targeting 'the organisers and people behind the fascist putsch attempt'. This was the start of the Stasi's 'big operations' or *Grossaktionen*; large-scale, purposefully 'spectacular' round-ups of spies and agents, in operations that made great newspaper copy.

The other initiative, with ominous portent, was an effort to put the East German public under wider and closer surveillance. One of Ernst Wollweber's first acts as chief was to establish new 'information groups' within the Stasi. Those at district level were to send situation reports on the public mood to their district chief and to Stasi headquarters, which would then collate the findings for Wollweber, the SED Politbüro, and the Council of Ministers.[83] The head of the new Information Service (Informationsdienst), Heinz Tilch, formerly a teenaged communist activist and then long-serving Wehrmacht soldier, wrote that informers should be part of the general population – not the likes of SED functionaries or factory managers. The ideal informer was 'a mechanic in a factory, for example... Because nobody will know that he has contact with the SfS, workers will talk to him exactly how they talk to other colleagues'.[84] This, then, was the pre-dawn of the surveillance state: the methodology that came to underpin the biggest snooping exercise on a population in history.

A new category of Stasi collaborator was introduced, the Lead Secret Informer or GHI (Geheimer Hauptinformator). Politically reliable and personally capable, GHI were tasked with recruiting and managing other collaborators. Their first goal was to expand the web of informers at important worksites and industrial concerns; the places where the rebellion had kicked off.[85] Wollweber made it clear in his founding order that the Information Service was to be faster and less cumbersome than previous Stasi reporting channels. Parts of it read:

> In order to acquire better, verified information in the future, I order:
> 1. In the State Secretariat for State Security, reporting directly to the State Secretary, an information group with a strength of 4 employees is to be formed.
> 2. In the district administrations, directly subordinate to the head of the district administration will be an information group of 3 employees in the larger

district administrations, 2 employees in the other district administrations...
[The groups'] information will include:

a) Mood reports with 2-3 characteristic examples, regardless of whether positive or negative;

b) Questions asked by dissatisfied members of staff;

c) Characteristics of the political aims of hostile and provocative elements;

d) Arguments made in support of the policy of the Central Committee and the government powers...

The information group of the Secretary of State is open daily until 10:00 a.m. [to collate information from] the heads of the district administrations, from the situation reports of the main administration of the Volkspolizei, the head office of the German border police, the transport police, the situation report from the President of the Berlin Volkspolizei, the wiretapping report of RIAS, and the most important reports in the Western press that reveal political aims, [all to be extracted in a daily report] on a maximum of 5-6 typewritten pages...

All information given must as a rule be verified. Rumours are to be reported but marked as such...

The Information Service has meaning only when it works quickly and [delivers] for the previous day [a] written summary for the information of the Politbüro, the Prime Minister, the Minister of the Interior, the State Secretary for State Security and the Deputy of the Secretary of State [Erich Mielke]...

Regularly, twice a month, [there will be] an analysis of the development of the situation, with its characteristic features, over the last 14 days.[86]

37

Main Department XV:
Foreign Intelligence Joins the Stasi

The defection of Gotthold Krauss triggered a root-and-branch reorganisation of the East German foreign intelligence service. It was renamed Main Department XV (Hauptabteilung or HA XV) and by autumn 1953 had been integrated into the Stasi. Markus Wolf now reported to Ernst Wollweber, although the Stasi's number two, Erich Mielke, remained an unignorable presence in much of Wolf's affairs.

Wolf beat Richard Stahlmann and Gerhard Heidenreich to the job of foreign intelligence chief. At the end of 1952 he was summoned by Walter Ulbricht to the Central Committee building near Alexanderplatz, where Ulbricht had pronounced, 'We are of the opinion that you should take over the service.' Wolf was still in his twenties. It isn't clear why he was appointed chief, though his popularity in Moscow must have counted. He had a good brain and his loyalty was considered as solid as anyone's possibly could be, in the Stalinist milieu. The historians Childs and Popplewell give a persuasive description of Wolf's worldview in the early 1950s; a worldview that would have recommended him to the SED hierarchy. It was one that saw West Germany as:

> a state in which Nazis were tolerated, the industrialists and civil servants who had supported or served them were restored to their property and influence, and the generals who had carried out Hitler's murderous plans were being looked after until they could once again wear uniforms. 'Mistakes', roughness, dictatorial methods in the Soviet zone could be explained by Soviet war losses [and] the belief that the majority of Germans needed long re-education before they could be trusted to run a democracy.[1]

Wolf was to attract professional admiration from all quarters, including his opponents in Western intelligence services. He showed 'undoubted skill at engendering loyalty',[2] and his intelligence service proved unusually successful in terms of fidelity, suffering only one very serious defection, that of Werner Stiller at the end of the 1970s. Werner Grossmann, who took over the leadership from Wolf in 1986, was recruited in 1952. Another officer close to Wolf, Klaus Rösler, was not untypical; he too served from 1952 until the fall of the Berlin Wall. Like other associates of Wolf, Rösler later claimed he was proud to have worked for such a progressive and noble organisation, although he conceded that he and other fellow officers had had their private doubts about East Germany's 'moral integrity'. Rösler admitted ruefully that the Stasi's hellhole prison at Bautzen 'cannot be thought out of existence'.[3]

Like all driven Alpha humans, Markus Wolf had his routine. He would rise by 7 a.m., jog, do back exercises, then get to the office at 8.15. He allowed himself the luxury of a driver, two secretaries and a personal assistant. In another demonstration of the loyalty he inspired, Wolf's principal secretary, who started work in 1954, served him for thirty-two years. To break the deskbound routine of intelligence work, Wolf insisted throughout his career on running a dozen or so agents personally, which gave him welcome trips to Dresden and other places.

Wolf encouraged *esprit de corps* by building up the stories of his intelligence service, celebrating its heroes and hallowed operations. This was 'Traditionspflege', the preservation of tradition. It was a practice copied from the KGB, which had its own 'Memory Room' at Moscow headquarters, a hall of fame containing spot-lit portraits, historical texts and glass cases filled with revered objects. Wolf and other Stasi high-ups insisted that similar little shrines be erected in every Stasi office. He recalled:

From our very beginnings, we in East Germany presented intelligence as an honourable profession. We were able to build on the experience and on the legends instilled by great spies who had worked against the Nazis – Richard Sorge and his famous assistants, such as Ruth Werner, alias Sonya, who spied in China, Danzig, Switzerland, and Britain for the Soviets during the War; Ilse Stöbe who spied from the heart of Hitler's foreign ministry… Our own apparat featured many veterans of the Communist movement during the Third Reich, like my first bosses, Wilhelm Zaisser, Richard Stahlmann, Robert Korb, and Ernst Wollweber. I was personally enthralled by their stories and saw the value of presenting them to our recruits as models for the role of spycraft in underpinning socialism. I put great effort into building up a sense of tradition and belonging within my service by having the lives and deeds of great spies memorialized in films and books.[4]

But how honourable was Wolf's service? When Main Department XV was incorporated into the Stasi, it signalled the start of a conceptual unification: the blending of foreign espionage with internal security. There was a symbiosis between foreign and domestic spying. This was embodied in a phrase used widely at the Stasi, 'reconnaissance and defence' (Aufklärung und Abwehr). All oppositional behaviour in East German society was said to result from subversive interference (Wühlarbeit, or 'undermining work') organised by secret Western agencies in the service of capitalist-fascist-imperialist enemy states. In the face of this threat, foreign espionage was a form of self-protection, and self-protection entailed domestic espionage – attack and defence, thrust and counter-thrust, working in harmony.

Thus Wolf's foreign intelligence service became an intrinsic part of the SED's political repression and belligerence. Its role wasn't restricted to gathering intelligence; it was another 'fighting organ' with which the SED could bolster its contested rule. Foreign intelligence officers performed important liaison roles at the Stasi's domestic security departments. Contrary to Wolf's later claims, his service didn't merely support the operations of Main Department II and other branches of the Stasi that harassed the East German population; it, too, was directly responsible for the surveillance of ordinary citizens and the disruption of domestic political opposition.

This crossover is exemplified in the person of Hans Fruck, one of Wolf's notable deputies. Fruck had wide experience of repressive security measures and dirty operations, as well as espionage.[5] In 1950, shortly after he had joined the Stasi, he was involved in a plan to kidnap West Berlin police officers from the 'extraordinarily complicated' border junction at the corner of Chausseestrasse and Liesenstrasse. This plan, intended to prompt the release of some GDR transport police officers who were being detained in West Berlin, called for plainclothes provocateurs from the Volkspolizei to publicly broach the western sector and start painting graffiti, thus drawing the wrath of the West Berlin police and luring them across the borderline. It failed, but the East German officers were released anyway.[6]

Before he retired, Markus Wolf inadvertently confirmed for all time his service's role in domestic repression in a document he sent to Erich Mielke. Titled 'Report on the HVA's contribution to guaranteeing the interior security of the GDR', it detailed the ways his personnel had disrupted the emigration movement (referred to as 'human trafficking') and a range of political opponents, and its success in carrying out 'hostile activities in church circles'.[7] This was the grubby work of political repression that Wolf subsequently claimed he had had nothing to do with.

Wolf's Main Department XV went through constant baffling rounds of reorganisation until its relaunch in summer 1956 as the more famous HVA. One of the only constants was its registry and archive, which remained firmly in the hands of Emmi Becker. The logic behind the changes is all but impossible to follow. Often, departments kept their usual workload while swapping designations with one another. In essence, HA XV had six main departments and a few smaller ones. Its staff count, after a couple of years, was 430 full-time employees.

Among the more notable branches was Hauptabteilung I, led by the old hand Herbert Hentschke and responsible for political espionage in West Germany. Its sub-departments were devoted to government ministries, the Bundestag, parties and trade unions. One of its top sources was the Federal Foreign Office's Ludwig Pauli, aka agent 'Adler'. It also dealt with émigrés and the handling of confidential contacts, and even had a smuggling capability in the form of Günther Neefe's 'Special Unit' (Spezialreferat).

Hauptabteilung II spied mostly on the Western powers in Germany. It was organised into 'lines' for the US, Britain and France, while a sub-department under Werner Steinführer targeted the NATO liaison sections of the Amt Blank and its successor, the West German defence ministry; reputedly, Steinführer personally recruited at least one source there who provided high-grade information 'for several years'.

The evaluation department, Hauptabteilung V, was joined in January 1954 by Colonel Erwin Koletzki, a close associate of Erich Mielke who previously had run the Stasi school at Potsdam. Koletzki was no academic; he was a watchdog whose probable role at the school had been to slaver at the pupils and maul transgressors. The esteemed Robert Korb was one of the first to feel Koletzki's presence. Although on paper Koletzki was supposed to be evaluating intelligence on West Germany's nascent armed forces and 'bourgeois parties' such as the CDU, he instigated nocturnal visits to Korb's office that revealed several security lapses, including a key left in a safe door and another key left in a coat pocket. Markus Wolf then had the awkward task of reprimanding Korb, his beloved mentor.[8]

Korb and Koletzki jointly led the evaluation effort, including the analysis of information from the Federal Foreign Office, Chancellery, and Ministry of the Interior. Close attention was paid to the Chancellery's press office and its liaison section with the Organisation Gehlen. One analyst, Walter Freiberg, who started in September 1952, evaluated information on West German parties and ministries until the 1980s, becoming a font of knowledge on the Free Democrats. Another, Kurt Müller, performed 'special work' (sonderarbeit), assessing the signs of preparation for a nuclear war. Korb, meanwhile, used his expertise to develop standard questionnaires for gathering information on military targets, which were distributed around the Stasi and, reportedly, appreciated greatly by Ernst Wollweber.

At the suggestion of Ivan Agayants, a highly experienced Soviet security officer whose successful career spanned decades, an 'operational component' was introduced to the evaluation department in the form of a small unit under Richard Stumpf, which sought to secure the western KPD. It was firmly believed that West Germany would ban the communist party – which it did, in 1956 – and Stumpf's team sought information and assets that might help the KPD to delay or circumvent the ban. Stumpf ran a number of agents in the media; a West Berlin writer for *Der Spiegel*, an editor at the West Berlin economic newssheet *Wirtschaftsblatt*, a university professor from Mainz. Given that Stumpf's boss, Robert Korb, had a background in press and propaganda, these and other assets were used for 'active measures' – influence and disinformation campaigns that anticipated the work of the HVA active measures department, which was only founded officially more than a decade later.

Another development was the rolling-out of HA XV around the Stasi's regional offices, in the form of corresponding Department XV branches at local level. These were overseen by Soviet liaison officers and sometimes coordinated their work with the GRU. Each department was given responsibility for a patch of West Germany – so Department XV in Cottbus gathered information from the Saarland, that of Rostock covered Hamburg, and so on.

Main Department XV was stiffened by the steady arrival of hardened personnel from around the Stasi. Joining Wolf, now a deputy head of the SfS, and his deputies Stahlmann, Heidenreich and Fruck, were the likes of Alfred Scholz, who after the war had terrorised Rostock as its twenty-five-year-old police chief before leading the infamous investigators of the Stasi's Main Department IX; and Otto Knye, fresh from his kidnapping operations against KgU members. Scholz and Knye took over the branches that spied on the Western powers and West German military.

The Soviets maintained close oversight. The work of HA XV was directed by a clutch of luminaries from the MVD and MGB – the latter became the KGB in March 1954 – including Maria Kirina, Dmitri Bronski, Vasily Morgachev, Ivan Fadeikin and Alexander Panyushkin. Also imparting their expertise were the teachers at the foreign intelligence school, which was now known, with tantalising obliqueness, as Objekt VII. The school ran half-year courses of up to thirty pupils – if they were lucky they got to study at a site located among the pretty vernacular villas of Gransee in Brandenburg. Along with their basic political and spycraft training, students could specialise in foreign languages and get additional tutoring in military and economic subjects.

Despite these endeavours, Markus Wolf wrote of the difficulties in recruiting suitable HA XV personnel, who now were joining an organisation with a military hierarchy and ethos. Staff numbers remained low, partly because 'the security requirements in our own apparatus imposed by the Soviets were extremely strict. Thousands of recommended candidates had to be screened in order to come up with a handful who were acceptable. Those with Western relatives were ruled out, as were most who had spent the war years as refugees or prisoners of war in the West.'[9] The scattered work locations of HA XV also made life difficult. It was yet to be accommodated at the Stasi's Normannenstrasse headquarters, and worked from offices dotted around East Berlin; at Johannisthal, Karolinenhof, Karlshorst, Schulzendorf and Hohenschönhausen, and with its headquarters on Klosterstrasse in the Mitte district.

Even with its challenges, Wolf's service was able to unearth the odd jewel. Although at this point the Stasi's vaunted scientific espionage capability wasn't well developed, one of its stars, Horst Vogel, was recruited by HA XV in 1955. After political and operational training, he took a degree in chemical engineering; and he was destined to lead the HVA's scientific spying effort from the mid-1970s until the collapse of East Germany.

Stung by the mauling of the IWF, Markus Wolf and his officers were determined not to make the same mistakes again. Although an ambitious plan known as 'Aktion 100' was formulated, with the aim of infiltrating 100 new resident spies into the Federal Republic, caution won the day. Werner Grossmann recalled that only fifteen 'Aktion 100' agents were despatched. Mostly they were couples – spy duos – who hailed from the GDR but had a connection or some familiarity with western Germany. They included 'Vera' and 'Rolf', who embedded themselves in Cologne; the 'Grützner' couple, also based in Cologne, where the male partner secured a job with Ford; a couple called 'Forster'; and another pair known as 'Isabella Wilken' and 'Rolf Bergmann'.[10]

In his memoirs Grossmann recalled the difficulties of finding suitable spy material, even among dedicated SED activists. Along with 'commitment, courage and determination', candidates needed 'the ability to learn, patience and perseverance'. As every intelligence service knows, it is rare to find in any person the right combination of qualities in the right doses. Grossmann also noted that most of the 'Aktion 100' agents were given the identity of a 'live double' – a real person whose personal papers had, for one reason or another, become available to HA XV. This error-prone approach required agents to internalise 'a second biography' and 'be able to live it', perhaps learning new skills to perform a new type of work. Not every recruit was up to it. And the lives of the spy couples as they underwent training were 'completely turned upside down'. None of their friends or family members could understand why their politics and routines seemed to have changed beyond recognition.[11]

The GDR enjoyed a number of advantages when infiltrating spies. For a start, East German agents could use the identities of people killed in the bombing of Dresden. But when faced with creating cover identities for a real or purported married couple, Markus Wolf, like Grossmann, found it difficult to develop two false identities that interwove plausibly with one another. The next hurdle was getting through the Federal Republic's camps for re-settlers, such as at Marienfelde in West Berlin, where refugees could expect to be screened and debriefed thoroughly by Western agencies. Some of Wolf's agents tried to bypass these camps altogether, using various workarounds to move straight into rented accommodation and get jobs, often as manual labourers, before attempting to move on to better things. If anyone asked, the couples could choose a story to tell: they had relocated in order to reunite with relatives, or they had lied to the East German authorities about their Nazi past, or they had criticised the government and were afraid of retribution. To fool any Federal official who might pry into their stories, invented misdemeanours were sometimes put on their records at East German ministries.

One example of the early missions assigned to HA XV spies is an order from 1953 to collect and analyse the communications equipment used by Western police and security services.[12] And just as in the late 1940s, some spies were planted or recruited who paid dividends many years later. They included 'Kruger' from Dresden, recruited in 1953, who took more than twenty years to reach his potential; it was in the 1970s that he was able to supply information on the Federal Republic's banking system, revealing otherwise unknowable details concerning West Germany's relationship with Poland.

HA XV got creative in the hunt for assets. Wolf recalled targeting the summit of foreign ministers held in Berlin in 1954. His department set up a brothel with the aim of luring delegates. Women were sent to the press centre and nightspots near the meeting venue, and would invite interested parties to accompany them to Wolf's bordello. Despite laying on drinks, snacks, sex workers, and pornographic films provided by the former head of the Berlin vice squad, there was only one taker for the brothel, and he soon made his apologies and sloped off. A contact was made, however, with a West German journalist, Heinz Losecaat van Nouhuys, who in time ended up as editor of *Quick*, a mass market right-wing magazine. Despite the anti-communist slant of *Quick*, van Nouhuys, codenamed 'Nante', proved a good source of inside information on affairs in Bonn for some years.[13]

The recruitment and deployment of Susanne Sievers also took a roundabout route. Sievers is best remembered in Germany as the 'other woman' in an infidelity scandal that beset the election campaign of Willy Brandt, then mayor of West Berlin, for the chancellorship in 1961. Besides its misogyny, this view of Sievers is pathetically narrow given the obvious depth of her personality and experiences.

Sievers was arrested by the Stasi in 1951 after travelling from West Berlin to the Leipzig trade fair. Although she claimed to be a mere freelance journalist, she was sentenced to eight years for spying: reportedly she was already working for intelligence agencies in both republics.[14] A few years later Markus Wolf, on the hunt for potential spies, spotted her profile when rifling through the records of prisoners who were about to be released in an amnesty. According to Wolf, when visited in prison by a colonel of HA XV, this 'tall, slender' woman in her mid-thirties, with a 'strong and self-confident personality', denied ever being a spy and didn't hide her resentment at being imprisoned. At the same time, she pricked up Wolf's ears by criticising the pro-American policies of Konrad Adenauer. At a second meeting, by which time Sievers knew of her coming release, she agreed to become agent 'Lydia', a spy for East Germany.

Once freed, Sievers ran a salon in Bonn where influential people came to discuss politics and business – especially right-wingers and nationalists, dubbed 'Ultras' by the SED. At one point, Sievers supplied promising news of a secret meeting between Willy Brandt and Franz Josef Strauss of the Christian Social Union. It appeared to herald a coalition that might bring Brandt's SPD into government for the first time since the war. The SED was gripped by this momentous prospect, as the social democrats were likely to encourage a degree of international recognition for East Germany. The SPD did not enter government at this time, however, and in 1961, with the laying of the Berlin Wall, the Stasi's contact with Sievers waned.

Her subsequent experiences, though mysterious, look like the stuff of box-set spy drama. Sievers left for the Far East in the company of a Bundeswehr major who served as military attaché at several embassies. By the late 1960s she was working for a spy network under Hans Langemann, a German operator with CIA connections. She ended up as chief of a BND residency in Hong Kong, codenamed '150', running sub-stations in Tokyo, Manila, Jakarta and Singapore. Reportedly, Sievers was retired with a payment of hush-money: 300,000 deutschmarks to keep quiet about the BND's interference in West German politics.[15]

Given the painstaking trouble of planting and recruiting spies, Wolf was angered whenever their cases were blown for the sake of a triumphalist media campaign. After all, boasting about the intelligence one has acquired is a good way to ruin effective spying. Yet it happened. Main Department XV liked to recruit conservative West German politicians who were opposed to the pro-American path taken by Adenauer. One such recruit, Günther Gereke, was expelled from the CDU after meeting publicly with Walter Ulbricht. After his expulsion, it was found that his assistant had been working for British intelligence. Gereke began to suspect that his own exposure as a spy was imminent. At the Stasi's suggestion he relocated to East Berlin, where Wolf hoped in time to revive his intelligence role. Instead Gereke was paraded before the media as a true German patriot who had rejected the Federal Republic, ending any prospect of his future use.

Wolf recalled that the incident 'awakened an unhealthy appetite for classy defections' regardless of the costs to intelligence-gathering.[16] The same thing happened with Karlfranz Schmidt-Wittmack, codenamed 'Timm', a CDU member of the Bundestag who, among other valuable items, had been able to provide crucial materials on the negotiations for West Germany to join NATO. With a view to a propaganda triumph, Schmidt-Wittmack was told, wrongly, that he was under suspicion, and urged to relocate to East Germany. He obeyed, and was duly shown-off at a press conference. With the help of further information provided by GRU spies, Schmidt-Wittmack was able to expose Konrad Adenauer's dishonesty in secretly organising the creation of a West German army while publicly denying it. After his exposure Schmidt-Wittmack did well enough, living in 'a pretty lakeside house' and serving as vice president of the GDR's foreign trade organisation. But Wolf was left to wonder if East German intelligence had lost 'a future [Federal] defence minister for the sake of a headline'.[17]

In 1955 the Department for Special Duties, Joseph Gutsche's dirty operations unit that had begun life two years previously, was transferred to Wolf's Main Department XV as its Department III. Gutsche now concentrated on internal communications and 'control' for the Stasi's domestic departments, spot-checking their work and suggesting improvements. Major Richard Schmeing, who had worked under Gutsche, took over the leadership of Department III, reporting directly to Wolf's deputy, Hans Fruck. The unit was to remain under Wolf's aegis for four years. During this time, from its office at Gross-Berliner Damm 101, it made extensive preparations to carry out sabotage in the Federal Republic, ostensibly if war should come.

To formulate its plans for causing mayhem, Department III was tasked with spying on the weak points of West Germany's infrastructure. It procured safe houses and cover addresses there, identified and recruited saboteurs, and found suitable spots to cache arms or to serve as operational bases. It is unclear why it was allocated, albeit temporarily, to Wolf's foreign espionage service. It may have been confidence in Wolf himself, a trusted young Stalinist spymaster. Equally, it might have been a punitive reaction to a botched operation; for the

Department for Special Duties had tried to send a letter bomb to the prime minister of the Saar Protectorate.

In 1955 the inhabitants of the Saar Protectorate, an area of southwest Germany with a history of disputed ownership and occupation by France, were due to vote in a referendum over the territory's future. Reportedly, an agent of the Department for Special Duties in the area, codenamed 'Wenig' (Little), was given an instruction to cause 'political nervousness' among the circle of Johannes Hoffmann, the protectorate's prime minister. Hoffmann was urging the electorate to vote in favour of the Saarland becoming an autonomous member of the Western Union, the military alliance that was then causing great concern in East Germany.

So 'Wenig' prepared a letter bomb for the personal attention of Hoffmann. The operation failed only because a postal worker spotted the contents of the badly sealed package. Whether the device had the strength to kill or merely alarm Hoffmann is unclear. Either way, the department was transferred to Wolf's portfolio, and Wolf reassigned 'Wenig' to Hamburg, there to build up another dirty ops cell. The Hoffmann operation was a farce, but it had an unpleasant symbolism that has gone unremarked. In targeting Hoffmann, the Stasi was choosing to attack a politician who during the 1930s had bravely criticised the Nazis in the Saarland's press, had been forced into hiding in a monastery in Provence early in the war, and finally had been hounded from Vichy France into exile in South America under a false identity. Apparently the Stasi felt no compunction about murdering or maiming this particular anti-fascist resister.

Department III had a number of sites (Objekte) at its disposal. Many of its saboteurs were West German communists who had renounced or concealed their party membership. East Germans who were to be resettled in the West as 'sleeper saboteurs' were trained at Objekt A, situated in the Brandenburg countryside east of Berlin. Objekt D hosted radio training. Collaborators in the Federal Republic who played supporting roles, such as the owners of safe houses or land where weapons were concealed, were not made aware of the department's work. By 1956 its regional responsibilities were well established. The 'North' section, for example, planned sabotage acts in Hamburg and Bremen, employing such collaborators as the carpenter codenamed 'Hammer I', who sought out vulnerable points in the military shipping yards, and the metalworker 'Hammer II', who planned for the destruction of bridges. If anything, the department's role was considered more important as time went by. In February 1959 it left Wolf's portfolio and was reorganised as a standalone Stasi department, Department IV, as East Germany's preparations for sabotage and guerrilla warfare intensified.

*

Following the abortive four-power conference in Berlin in early 1954, to which Markus Wolf had contributed as a brothel owner, the Western powers reconvened in Paris in the autumn to agree upon West Germany's future as a sovereign state. Even before these discussions came to fruition the following May, when the Allied occupations formally ended and a sovereign Federal Republic joined NATO, they had triggered a 'turn to the west' within the Stasi. This new direction was announced by Stasi chief Ernst Wollweber, and it signified an increased focus on espionage in West Germany.

Other international events influenced Wollweber's 'turn to the west'. The expansion of NATO prompted the signing of the Warsaw Pact by the USSR and seven countries of the Soviet Bloc. The two military alliances further cemented the rupture of Europe, and saw East Germany create a Ministry of National Defence and its new National People's Army (Nationale Volksarmee, NVA). In the same period West Germany adopted the Hallstein Doctrine, named after one of its architects in the Foreign Office, Walter Hallstein. The doctrine decreed that West Germany would not maintain diplomatic or trade relations with any state that recognised the GDR. It succeeded in warding off countries from dealing with East Germany, including those in Africa which sought West German aid and investment. It also meant that Markus Wolf's intelligence service was denied the use of GDR embassies as a base for espionage – they didn't exist. According to Wolf, his service responded by making greater use of 'illegals'.[18]

Within the Stasi it was made explicit that foreign espionage was a new priority. At an SfS conference in January 1955, Wolf emphasised that spy networks in West Germany had to be improved and expanded; he mentioned scientific institutions and the SPD as top targets. He also asked the Stasi's domestic departments to pass on to him any information they acquired on political conflicts within the Federal Republic, or on discord among the NATO members.[19]

Two months later Wolf's message was reiterated by Ernst Wollweber at a meeting of the security services of the Soviet Union, Czechoslovakia, East Germany and Poland. They should, he said, focus on obtaining intelligence in the 'political centres' of Western countries, prioritising information on the equipping of armies, mobilisation plans, and the secret clauses of official treaties.[20] In addition to HA XV establishing a presence in district Stasi offices, Wolf and Wollweber's appeals resulted in the Stasi's economic branch, Main Department III, setting up working groups with a mission to penetrate and plunder Western manufacturers, especially of military technology. There was a drive to recruit more informers in the West German refugee camps at Emden, Borkum and Aurich, and increasing efforts were made to assess the espionage potential of all West German citizens visiting relatives in the GDR.

There were great hopes for the four-power Geneva summit of July 1955, the first such gathering of national leaders since the Potsdam conference ten years earlier. But no agreements were reached; the only result was a brief and slight reduction of tension. Soon afterwards, the Cold War's divisions were deepened further. In a speech given in East Berlin on his way home from Geneva, Nikita Khrushchev expressed doubt that Germany would be reunified. This was followed quickly by the USSR's first explosion of a hydrogen bomb (or its Soviet equivalent), and its recognition of the GDR's full sovereignty. Gary Bruce opines that the 'American administration interpreted Soviet interest in disarmament [expressed at Geneva] as a sign of weakness, and hoped that continuing the arms race would quickly bring the Soviet Union to its knees'.[21]

It was in the wake of Geneva that Ernst Wollweber gave the pivotal speech in which he urged for fifty percent of the Stasi's resources to be 'turned to the west'.[22] Bruce has analysed and quoted Wollweber's speech at length, noting that Wollweber's call was rooted in the increased threat of both nuclear and conventional war. In the light of West Germany joining NATO and developing its army, the Bundeswehr, Wollweber believed the Stasi's 'first and most important task' was to provide warning of a Western attack. He warned that failure to predict the use of nuclear weapons would result in near-instant annihilation, as 'an atomic war will likely be decided on the first day'.[23] Wollweber dwelt on such frightening developments as the proliferation of long-range bomber aircraft and the USSR's new hydrogen bomb capability. He also spoke of the growing likelihood of peace activism in the West, and its potential for providing the Stasi with willing agents. It mattered little that the motivation of such recruits – a desire to 'avoid a war for [the sake of the] special interests of certain capitalist groups or individual countries' – were not strictly Marxist.

Key parts of Wollweber's address, as translated and quoted by Bruce, include the following:

World peace depends above all on whether America refrains from starting a war. Everything else is an aside... The air raid manoeuvres in America demonstrated that, theoretically, 5 million people would die in the first few hours... to protect us from a surprise attack from the enemy, it is most important to know who is planning what against whom and when. This can only be achieved through information-gathering... 75% of the expansion of the information-gathering branch must work in the enemy camp...

Nothing should happen in West Berlin that we do not know about... we must achieve a situation where every [hostile] agent in West Berlin must expect that in a short time he could be with us... amongst agents in West Berlin, we must produce such a psychosis that they believe they are fighting a losing battle...

We have been successful in creating this powerful instrument. But now new tasks lie before us. We must now work on preventing war... We need precise information, we need documentary material. Special groups must be established. We need the information in time, because if we receive the information that we need in time, then the element of surprise is of no use to the enemy... enormous damage and destruction and many victims [will be] avoided. We therefore fulfil a great task. That is our duty.[24]

In pronouncing the 'turn to the west', and carrying out the mass counter-espionage operations, the *Grossaktionen*, Ernst Wollweber was orienting the Stasi towards the two functions he considered necessary for East Germany's survival, and for which he, personally, had an appetite: acquiring defensive military intelligence, and catching real enemy spies. These were classic spy and secret police functions, embodying 'reconnaissance and defence'. Later, Walter Ulbricht was to use Wollweber's shift in emphasis to make the cynical claim that surveillance of the population had been abandoned in the GDR – it certainly had not. But Wollweber was to lose his job, among other reasons, for his relative reluctance to persecute ordinary members of the East German public.

In the 1990s, prosecutors in the reunified Germany had a tricky time levelling charges at Markus Wolf. The Stasi's foreign intelligence records had been destroyed. By his own boastful admission, much of Wolf's operational knowledge had never made it onto paper. 'Nowhere in my directorate did there exist a single record of all our spies,' he wrote. 'I was determined that no card index or computer disc should ever hold all our operational details... I and my senior officers kept the names of most important agents in our heads.'[25] But one historical charge against Wolf, dating from the time of Main Department XV, was made to stick: his involvement in the kidnapping of Christa Trapp from West Berlin in 1955.

Trapp worked as secretary to the head of eastern affairs at the US High Commission for Germany. She was identified as a potential asset by Heinz Bielke, a Stasi informer in the High Commission's personnel section.* Her abduction was organised by the HA XV officers Major Horst Jänicke and Captain Werner Prosetzky. Their eight-page plan was signed off, in his own hand and with suggested changes, by Markus Wolf. Two secret collaborators in West Berlin were chosen to play key roles.

---

* A couple of years earlier, Bielke had reported the sensational information that Allen Dulles, CIA chief, had visited Berlin a week before the June 1953 uprising, thus fuelling the communists' conviction that the uprising was organised by the Western powers.

First, Trapp's neighbour Hildegard Diskowski – the GM 'Gisela' – was to introduce Trapp to a charming potential suitor called Henry Gerlach, a merchant seeking lessons in 'business English', for Trapp taught English in her spare time. After getting acquainted, Gerlach was to pick up Trapp one evening in a chauffeur-driven car – to be supplied from the Stasi's motor pool, complete with West Berlin numberplates – ostensibly for a dinner date. She would be driven to a checkpoint, where East German border police officers – one of them portrayed by an undercover Captain Prosetzky – would arrest Gerlach on charges of illegal trading across the Berlin frontiers. (This staged arrest would keep Gerlach's reputation intact in the western sectors of Berlin, and thus prevent him being blown.) Trapp would then be invited to go along with the police to provide information on her arrested companion. Once ensconced with Prozetsky and Jänicke, she would be persuaded or bullied into spying for the Stasi. If she happened to protest while at the border crossing, Gerlach – alias GM 'Stein' – was to subdue her physically.

All went well on the chosen night – 16 June 1955 – except that Trapp insisted to Gerlach that her mother accompany them to dinner. Afterwards, with the three of them seated in the chauffeured car, Gerlach said he had forgotten something from his office and so needed to make a detour. Only when Trapp saw a sign saying 'You are leaving the American sector' did she realise she was being kidnapped; she screamed for the car to stop, but it didn't. Once on Bouchéstrasse in East Berlin, Trapp was separated from her mother and driven in another car to a Volkspolizei station.[26]

There she was joined by Jänicke and Prosetzky, who tried various means to secure her cooperation as a spy. These ranged from 'good cop' offers – a monthly salary, to be followed by help with emigrating for the United States – to 'bad cop' threats of harm to her mother. The 'bad cop' technique persuaded Trapp to play ball, at least temporarily. She agreed to provide the Stasi with information on the structure and personnel of the US High Commission and, most importantly, with copies of its monthly reports on the political situation in Germany. After signing a receipt for an advance payment of 100 deutschmarks, she and her mother were set free. The pair returned to the American zone on the U-Bahn, disturbed and dazed in the harsh morning light.[27] Trapp promptly told her employers what had happened, and handed over the unwanted money.[28]

Oddly, Trapp's abduction echoed a similar incident endured by one of her colleagues, Elizabeth Erdmann, two months earlier. Erdmann, a secretary in the High Commission's political affairs department, had been pulled off a bus by border police when travelling from East Berlin into the American zone; during a sleepless night at a Stasi office in Potsdam she was pressurised into becoming a spy. Like Trapp, Erdmann reported her recruitment immediately to her superiors in West Berlin, who chose to hush up the matter. Had Trapp known about Erdmann's ordeal, she might never have associated with 'Henry Gerlach' – whoever he was.

In the weeks and months after her abduction, Trapp received telephone calls reminding her that she had promised to get copies of the High Commission's reports. The calls stopped when the Americans belatedly went to the newspapers with both women's kidnapping stories.[29] After that, the pair were left alone. Trapp and her mother moved to America, without the Stasi's help; and in 1997 Wolf was convicted for his role in the affair. Charged with four instances of kidnapping, deprivation of liberty and bodily mistreatment, he avoided the maximum possible sentence of fifteen years and was given a probationary sentence of two years.

Part IV

Grossaktionen:
Spy-catching with the Stasi

'We have to hit hard and ruthlessly. There is no room in our ranks for weak-kneed pacifists and dreamers… We must make the GDR into a hell for enemy agents. Comrades, that is your primary duty.'

Hermann Matern, head of the SED Control Commission, 1953

38

A Crisis of Spies

When Ernst Wollweber became chief of the Stasi – now placed under the Ministry of the Interior as its Staatssekretariat für Staatssicherheit or SfS – he was ordered to find the enemy spies and saboteurs deemed responsible for inciting the June 1953 uprising. The Soviet and SED authorities wanted to create an impression of strength and solidity, and hit back at the Western enemies interfering with their state-building. The result was a wave of mass counter-espionage operations. The most significant were Operation Firework (Aktion Feuerwerk) of autumn 1953, Operation Arrow (Pfeil) in August 1954, and Operation Lightning (Blitz) over winter and spring 1954-55. These were the so-called *Grossaktionen* – the 'big operations'. The media in East Germany trumpeted the successes of these spy-catching 'spectaculars', in which more than 1,000 alleged Western agents were arrested.

Wollweber's demonstrative leadership contrasted sharply with Wilhelm Zaisser's diffidence. Like Zaisser, though, for much of his career Wollweber had been able to win over the right people. 'Wollweber impressed me,' wrote Pavel Sudoplatov, one of Stalin's top security officers. Sudoplatov admired Wollweber's background as a diehard revolutionary and bombmaker. The pair had met in the late 1930s, when Wollweber's maritime sabotage cells were sending shipments of arms destined for the Spanish Nationalists to the bottom of harbours around Europe. Sudoplatov was then working undercover as a ship's radio operator, on a mission that had culminated in him assassinating the Ukrainian nationalist Yevhen Konovalets in Rotterdam. Sudoplatov's admiration was shared by others in Moscow, who trusted Wollweber to run his sabotage networks with great independence for a lengthy period. He was also granted Soviet citizenship during the war, in order to secure his release from a Swedish prison. According to Sudoplatov, Wollweber had arrived in the USSR 'in time to recruit German prisoners of war for NKVD operations'.[1]

Wollweber made capital of his gruff, seadog demeanour. A cigar clamped permanently between his teeth, he was coarse, short, and wide; his nickname within the Stasi was 'the walking pancake'.[2] He was a bullish orator and he got a kick out of hectoring crowds; 'Wollweber hurled his words like rocks into the masses' is how his speaking style of 1918 was described by one audience member.[3] Aware of the Stasi's failure to avert the June rising, Wollweber did something unthinkable for Wilhelm Zaisser and most other intelligence professionals: he went on a rabble-rousing tour of East Germany to whip up public support for state security. He barked at school pupils; he yelled at rallies, public meetings, the Society for German-Soviet Friendship; he admonished and consoled the workers at factories where spies had been arrested. Sometimes these lectures veered into communist panto, with rehearsed audience members joining in, or catcalling whenever Wollweber described the disgraceful behaviour of Western spies. The *Tägliche Rundschau* recorded a typical interjection:

> [After the speech] the grey-haired worker Svenson stood up. "Colleagues," he said, "how often have we heard the careless words at work: 'Oh, let's put an end to all this talk of agents.' Today we've been convinced that we need to talk about it even more. Now we understand why RIAS and the Western press are supporting this espionage rabble. Because all the warmongering plays into their hands…"[4]

Wollweber's proselytising may even have taught the Soviets something, for the 1960s were to see a big increase in the KGB's use of media and public comment. Whatever Wollweber's audiences really thought, there was a sharp rise in the number of Stasi informers. The network doubled in size from 1953 to 1955.[5]

During Wollweber's tenure there was, however, no let-up in the acute tensions racking the Stasi; tensions between its secrecy and its legal rectitude, its boldness and its caution, between force and restraint. These tensions would, in fact, play out until 1990, in an exaggerated version of the balancing act required of all security services. Having been ordered by the Politbüro in September 1953 to find at all costs 'the organisers and people behind the fascist putsch', Wollweber immediately felt compelled to make a show of the Stasi's probity. At one meeting he stressed that 'if anyone treats a prisoner unlawfully to reach his goal more easily, he will be punished. If anyone puts a person in prison only to show he's getting results, he will be punished.'[6] At least, that was the aspiration. The fact that Wollweber was making these comments suggests that malpractice was still rife.

In theory, Wollweber's Stasi was to be a precision instrument, sparing the innocent. In autumn 1953, while hunting down the alleged inciters of the uprising, Wollweber appealed for 'no shock effect for the population. People should not feel that a wave of arrests is moving through the GDR, or that we are at the beginning of such a wave… The population must believe that the instruments of state security aim for, and hit, the right targets'.[7] In an address on the radio he insisted that a 'wave of arrests is not taking place. There are carefully targeted strikes against important sites of enemy activity'.[8] Of course, what this really meant was that a wave of arrests was indeed taking place, many of them handled behind closed doors with little or no accountability.

Yet the Stasi continued to publish internal manuals on the correct procedures for working with judicial organs.[9] For its own sake it remained wary of making disputable arrests, acknowledging at one conference that 'wrongful arrests create enemies'.[10] In 1954 Wollweber issued a directive in which he addressed the criticisms of a recently formed body, the Politbüro's Security Commission (Sicherheitskommission). He pledged his employees to greater diligence in their investigations and stricter compliance with the law. Among the commission's complaints were numerous instances of 'confusion over names, unverified one-page GM reports [and the investigation of] unverified acts that do not constitute a state crime'.[11] But even now Wollweber took a vague approach in his orders, phrasing his words in such a way that the Stasi wasn't strictly required to get external sign-off for an arrest warrant, and could issue its own. This meant business as usual.

The uprising of 1953 was not organised by Anglo-American secret services, as charged by the SED regime. Nevertheless, from the early 1950s until the building of the Berlin Wall, the GDR went through what the historian Paul Maddrell has called 'an intense spying crisis', with its 'government institutions, armed forces, factories and research laboratories... more deeply penetrated by spies than those of any other state in the Soviet Bloc'. Ernst Wollweber freely admitted that East Germany had become the base from which the West tried to spy on the entire communist world.[12] For Maddrell, 'The open border between the Soviet and Western sectors of Berlin in the years 1945-61 enabled the Western secret services to undertake mass espionage and very threatening subversion throughout East Berlin and East Germany. These operations depended largely on freedom of movement over the sectoral border.'[13] Once the smoke of the June rising had cleared, the streets running between West and East Berlin remained open, many with no barriers or identity checks; and there were still no formalised identity checks on the underground and overground railways running throughout the city.

The most common method for recruiting agents in East Germany was for refugees who had fled the GDR to write letters on behalf of the Western intelligence services to acquaintances still living there. These letters, suggesting innocuous-looking meetings or further correspondence, were delivered by couriers or posted within East Germany by Berliners crossing the city's borders. The results could be impressive. For example, Western agencies even managed to equip some newly recruited amateur spies in East Germany with radar detection devices, which could locate the sites of surface-to-air missiles.

At the same time, political activists of the anti-communist and humanitarian organisations based in West Berlin and the Federal Republic, many of them funded by Western intelligence services, were also able to cross into East Berlin with impunity. The dovetailing of political opposition with espionage and subversion gave the SED and Stasi a severe headache, but it also gave them an opportunity.

For in some respects, the fight against spies and saboteurs *was* the fight against political opponents. After the uprising, in which the demonstrators had made clear their preference for the SPD, and even loudly demanded its reconstitution, the Stasi targeted the SPD Ostbüro with increased venom. Its personnel, agents, and admirers alike were deemed dangerous enemies of the state. The problem was that while some Ostbüro activists indeed spied on military sites, or tried to subvert the work of East German institutions, others identified with the Ostbüro merely to keep alive their faith in social democracy; even in the mistaken hope that social democracy might return to play a role in the GDR, to which they were not implacably opposed.

Yet for the Stasi, with its simplistic 'friend-enemy' worldview and grounding in Leninism-Stalinism, this layered situation meant a straight fight between Chekist and 'enemy agent'. The Stasi used the word Agenten (agents) as a blanket term for all opponents: spies, saboteurs, subversives, disrupters, terrorists, propagandists, even cultural dissidents.[14] Arguably, as a state security service it had reason to take seriously even peripheral forms of oppositional activity. Nor could it avoid conflating West German political opposition with wider Western hostility.

One of the major forms of Western subversion was to encourage East German citizens to leave for the Federal Republic. The BBC liked to broadcast the stories of successful refugees. Voice of America and RIAS exhorted well-qualified people to head west, making it little wonder these stations were so despised by the SED and Stasi. In summer 1953 the US National Security Council (NSC) ordered American agencies to 'intensify defection programs' aimed at 'police leaders and military personnel', and to 'launch black radio intruder operations to encourage defection'.[15] Already the 'Engross' operation of 1952, a programme of psychological warfare, had used propaganda to prompt the defection not just of military personnel but of scientists and technicians, all of whom were offered guaranteed jobs in West Germany. German scientists and engineers who had been taken to the USSR after the war were highly prized, and an increasing number defected thanks to 'Engross'.[16] Such activities benefited West Germany and the United States in equal measure. The Stasi saw these interests as interwoven because they were.

In fact, the handling of defectors had turned out to be a major Cold War specialism, for which the Western powers had gone through a steep learning curve. Defectors, in the words of intelligence historian Kevin Riehle, compelled Western countries 'to address a series of thorny issues: how to ensure a defector was genuine; how to protect defectors from Soviet retaliation; what to do with them when interrogations ended; what types of people to accept; and how to handle demanding, disgruntled, and difficult people'.[17] In Britain criteria were put in place, according to which a defector was someone of 'considerable intelligence value' rather than a simple deserter. In an NSC memo, defectors were described as participants in 'a battle for civilisation'.[18]

The same view applied to officials and members of the GDR's non-Marxist parties, which for some years had been considered prime intelligence targets by the Western powers. After the rising, the Stasi responded with its Operation Citizen (Aktion Bürger), a thorough campaign to gain regular information from inside every party of the National Front. The Stasi now prepared detailed monthly reports on developments within the CDU, LDPD and other Front organisations, keeping an even sharper lookout for traitors among them. Moreover, in an example of 'the unity of reconnaissance and defence', Aktion Bürger also entailed penetrating the offices of the CDU Ostbüro in West Germany, to determine the whereabouts of 'enemy' Christian democrats living in the GDR.

This, then, was a morally nuanced situation. But the period continued to see more straightforward forms of great power espionage and Cold War tit-for-tat. One example is the activity around the Western powers' Military Liaison Missions, based largely in Potsdam, which were allowed to carry out chaperoned inspections of military sites. The SED encouraged the Stasi and Volkspolizei to disrupt the missions' work and prevent the agreed tours of inspection, if only with bureaucratic shenanigans. Restricted areas seemed to spring up at random, access roads were inexplicably blocked. The Stasi's Department VIII, responsible for observations, set up a new branch to watch the three missions. Its seventy-five staff members learned their trade from the ubiquitous Soviet advisers. Surveillance cars, each containing three Stasi employees and a Soviet officer, would shadow all Western vehicles setting out from Potsdam. They did so conspicuously, to increase unease. Field telephones were installed at staggered observation posts, to spread news of the imminent arrival of a Western delegation. In late 1953 the job of watching the missions was given to a new Department Z under Captain Wilhelm Schwerdtfeger. This arrangement lasted a couple of years before the unit was returned to its original home at Department VIII.

To better equip the Stasi for its coming showdown with enemy agents, the SED Politbüro put the SfS on a statutory footing. First, a secret resolution issued on 23 September 1953 defined the Stasi's role:

a) Carrying out active reconnaissance work in West Germany and West Berlin with the aim of penetrating the most important institutions of the occupation powers, of the Bonn government, in the central party committee of the Social Democratic Party and the bourgeois parties and in particular their eastern offices, among West German industrialists and in other monopolistic organisations, in military and scientific research offices and institutions.

b) Carrying out active counter-espionage in West Germany and West Berlin as well as within the territory of the German Democratic Republic. Penetration of informers into espionage organs, schools, and headquarters of espionage and subversion organisations, for the purpose of uncovering the enemy's plans and intentions as well as uncovering agents of enemy espionage services, and of West German and West Berlin espionage, subversion and terrorist organisations who have infiltrated the GDR, the USSR and the People's Democracies.

c) Carrying out agent work in the German Democratic Republic within the bourgeois political parties, socio-political mass organisations and the church organisations, among the intelligentsia and the youth, for the purpose of uncovering illegal, anti-democratic organisations and groups and eliminating their undermining activity.

d) Carrying out the battle against destructive activity, sabotage and subversion in the national economy, the timely uncovering and stopping of undermining activities of foreign espionage services and their underground organisations [to] ensure the execution of the New Course, which is directed towards a definite improvement in the material situation of the GDR population.

e) Carrying out defensive activity in the garrisoned, sea, air, transport and other Volkspolizei forces, including the criminal investigation department, with the aim of protecting these organs from penetration by agents of imperialistic espionage services and the West German underground headquarters.

The most senior woman officer in the Stasi's first decade,
and still in her twenties, **Lieutenant Colonel Isolde Sobeck**.

Erich Mielke – from Berlin streetfighter to security minister.

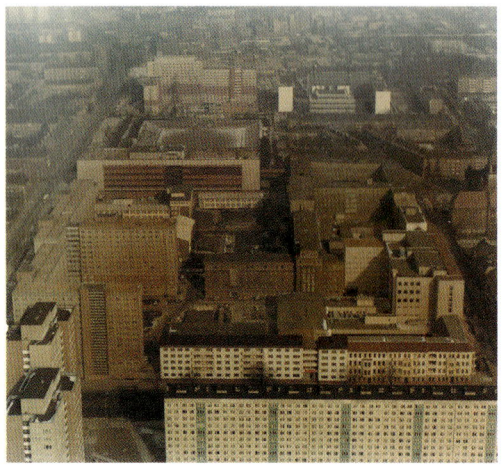

Stasi offices. From the sprawling headquarters in Berlin…

© Barch, MfS, HA II, Fo. 32, Bild 13

…to vernacular villas in the smallest of districts, here Arnstadt.

© Barch, MfS, BV Eft, Abt RD, 23, Seite 0002

All Stasi offices were identified with a name plaque.

© Barch, MfS, ZAIG, Fo. 61, Bild 0005

Stasi propaganda brochure. Dissolute Western agents and their Nazi backers.

Founder Members

Joseph Gutsche,
first Stasi chief in Saxony.

Karl Kleinjung,
first chief for Greater Berlin,
pictured in his later years.

Otto Last,
SED golden boy and first
chief in Mecklenburg.

Martin Weikert,
first chief in Saxony-Anhalt.

Banquet at Stasi HQ.
Raising a toast, l-r, are Markus Wolf, Erich Mielke, and the KGB's Aleksandr Korotkov.

© Barch, MfS, ZAIG, Fo. 3663, Bild 0018

The 'brother organs'.
Stasi and KGB officers in festive mood, 1957.

© Barch, MfS, ZAIG, Fo. 3663, Bild 0020

Stasi sergeant Hans Waldbach, killed by demonstrators on 17 June 1953.

© Barch, MfS, BV Mgb, Abt IX, 6 Foto Seite 42

Poster displayed in a Stasi office:
'The founding of the MfS – a prerequisite for ensuring state security'.

NVA troops lay the Berlin Wall between Mitte and Kreuzberg, August 1961.

From Erich Mielke's Wall scrapbook:
a triumphant Walter Ulbricht addresses the workers' militia, Karl-Marx-Allee.

More First Class Comrades

Josef Kiefel,
counter-espionage specialist.

Paul Rumpelt,
head of Stasi prisons.

Richard Stahlmann,
Stasi legend, around the time of his retirement.

K5 and Stasi executive **Erich Jamin**, alumnus of an SS penal brigade.

f) Ensuring reliable protection of responsible functionaries of the party and government.

g) Ensuring the exact co-operation of the state security organs with the police organs in central and subordinate offices.

The Central Committee of the SED steers the attention of the state security organs particularly to the need for fundamental reinforcement of the work in the districts and regions where there is a concentration of former social democrats, former fascists and bourgeois specialists who have connections to concerns in West Germany and West Berlin.

The Central Committee requires of the state security organs that they expose and unmask the underground organisations of the West German and West Berlin [agencies] in Magdeburg, Halle, Leipzig, Dresden, Jena and other towns where most fascist activity was recorded during the provocations of 17 June 1953.[19]

Accordingly, in an internal directive the Stasi reformulated its task as the 'establishment and maintenance of effective agent centres in West Germany, West Berlin, and in East Germany in equal measure': again, the concept of reconnaissance and defence.

Then, on 6 October 1953, a secret statute for the SfS was issued. Supposedly, it was approved by a decision of the Politbüro. In reality, it was signed off by a small hand-picked committee around Walter Ulbricht. It set out the Stasi's right 'to arrest enemy spies, agents and criminals if, on the basis of acquired documents of hostile activity, there is a reasonable suspicion or evidence'. The Stasi had the authority to 'carry out all necessary investigations up to the final report to the organs of justice' and was expected to work collaboratively, making use of 'the possibilities that police organs or other institutions have for successfully fighting hostile activity'.[20]

Rather than thinking ahead or blazing a trail, the statute tried to address the burning issues of the moment: who does the Stasi answer to, who counsels its leader, how does the party exercise its control, and what rights does the Stasi have to intervene in citizens' lives? Consequently, the statute established that the Stasi's tasks flowed from the decisions of the SED Politbüro and Central Committee, from resultant laws and regulations, and from the orders of the prime minister and interior minister. Based on these resolutions and orders, it was 'to create the conditions and to take the measures that ensure the security of the state, the consolidation of state power and the maintenance of public order'. This was a partial admission that the Stasi was expected to be one of the load-bearing pillars on which East Germany would stand. By monitoring and intervening in communications, it would also carry out 'censorship for the detection, suppression and unmasking of hostile activities', and it had the 'use of technical means (eavesdropping)' to perform these duties.

According to the statute, 'all police stations and other institutions' were obliged 'to support the organs of state security'. A newly formed Kollegium of senior officers would advise the Stasi chief, while the cadre department of the SED Central Committee would approve all high-level appointments. To 'constantly improve operational work [the] technical and political training of employees' was considered a top priority.[21] The 'strict observance of discipline and strict conspiracy' were deemed essential for all Stasi personnel, whose military ranks were then set out. They ranged from two grades of junior employees (Soldat, Gefreiter) through various NCO positions (Unteroffizier, Feldwebel, Oberfeldwebel and Hauptfeldwebel, the latter only for office staff) up to the officer ranks: Unterleutnant, Leutnant, Oberleutnant, Hauptmann (captain), Major, Oberstleutnant (lieutenant colonel), Oberst, Generalmajor, Generalleutnant, Generaloberst (colonel general).

In another development that anticipated the forthcoming spy-catching operations, the Stasi created its primary counter-espionage branch, Main Department II (Hauptabteilung II or HA II). It did this by merging Department IV (counter-espionage) with Department II, which had been trying to acquire agents inside Western police and intelligence services. HA II operated inside the GDR and in the so-called Operational Area (Operationsgebiet) of West Berlin and West Germany. Its personnel carried out a mix of defensive and offensive spying to thwart the efforts of Western intelligence services.* Hostile intelligence services were defined broadly: they included the likes of RIAS which, although a radio station, was deemed a key component of the West's espionage onslaught against East Germany. From 1953 until 1960, HA II was led by the formidable Josef Kiefel, who at first reported to deputy state secretary Erich Mielke and then, from 1955, to the no less imposing Bruno Beater, who was by that time a deputy minister of security.

Until his promotion to a deputy minister position, Beater led another department that was to play a prominent role in the *Grossaktionen*. This was Main Department V, responsible for fighting political opposition. As well as securing state institutions, National Front parties, unions, mass organisations, and the churches, HA V tackled the UfJ, KgU and 'bourgeois' Ostbüros. When it had the time, it cracked down on such misfits as alleged Trotskyists and Titoists.

---

* The Stasi, and those in Germany who have studied it, tended to make a bureaucratic and semantic distinction between 'defending' against foreign spies (Spionageabwehr) and the disruptive penetration of enemy spy agencies on foreign soil (Gegenspionage). This distinction is not reflected in the English term 'counter-espionage'.

Beater was succeeded as HA V chief by Fritz Schröder, a former butcher from East Prussia. Having joined the Wehrmacht as early as 1936, Schröder had been captured by the Red Army and politically re-educated in Soviet camps, emerging as a frontline evangelist for the National Committee for Free Germany. Schröder epitomised those former servants of the Nazi regime who, after learning the error of their ways, had in Erich Mielke's words 'put their lives on the line' for communism. He had joined the police in 1945, progressed smoothly to the Directorate for the Protection of the National Economy, and in February 1950 was a founding officer of the Stasi in Brandenburg. Schröder's deputy at HA V continued to be Erich Jamin, former K5 boss and wartime soldier of the hideous Dirlewanger SS penal brigade, who now led the Stasi's crusade against social democrats.

39

'Concentrated Blows'

Despite being under intense pressure, Ernst Wollweber struggled to find the foreign-directed, fascist-imperialist agents thought to be responsible for the June uprising. In September 1953, when no conspirators had been unearthed, the SED Politbüro rebuked the Stasi, asking how it was possible that 'the state security organs have not yet unmasked the organisers of the provocations'.[1]

Erich Mielke, especially, was stung. Speaking to the Politbüro on Mielke's behalf – and covering his own back in the process – interior minister Willi Stoph announced a few recent successes: the arrest of twenty-nine enemy agents, the rolling-up of a spy network operating from West Berlin under the cover of the 'Institute for Industrial Hygiene', and the arrest of eight youths from Potsdam who had been conspiring with the KgU to blow up a railway bridge. Mielke added that activists of the UfJ, and the SPD and CDU Ostbüros, had recently been arrested. And he complained that some of these arrestees were state officials and SED members, compelling the Stasi to 'take care of people' who were 'hiding behind a party card'. Mielke grumbled that 'responsible comrades' in state institutions should at least be able to spot such unreliable party members.[2]

These small achievements were not what the Soviets and Politbüro had in mind. Where were the American spymasters, pulling the strings of their minions in Europe? Where were the former landowners and Nazis, their faith unextinguished, intent on restoring capitalism to eastern Germany? Where were the threads linking all the rank-and-file spies, their various nerve centres, their organisations? And who was to be blamed and – it was hoped – executed for steering the June revolt? The Leninist-Stalinist mindset demanded the existence of an immense conspiracy, with seemingly unconnected enemy organisations all working in tandem towards a shared goal. Seen in this light, the Stasi's piecemeal arrests weren't cutting it.

So, in the absence of clear culprits for the June insurrection, it was decided to remove a great haul of enemy agents from the streets and workplaces of East Germany. This was to be done in a series of 'concentrated blows' ('konzentrierte

Schläge'), to use the words of the SED and Stasi. These hard, clean hits on enemy organisations were intended not only to leave untouched any blameless members of the East German public, but to earn their admiration and gratitude. The strategy was devised by Walter Ulbricht and Volkskammer vice president Hermann Matern – both intent on using the Stasi surgically, avoiding any suggestion of undue oppressiveness on the part of the SED – in collaboration with Yevgeny Pitovranov at Karlshorst.

It would seem that the 'concentrated blows' were not foreseen by Western intelligence services – there is no apparent prediction of them in CIA documents, for example – which suggests the concept was devised in great secrecy and among a small number of people.[3] Western intelligence services had accurately defined the dilemma facing the Soviets after the June rising: Moscow could not admit fault for a failed political and economic system, or easily dismantle the SED, or blame the East German populace. In this respect, the 'concentrated blows' strategy was a clever way out of the predicament: blame the Western powers and their manipulation of a minority of misguided Germans.

Soviet oversight of the *Grossaktionen* was a given, and Soviet assistance crucial to their success. Moscow's moles in the West – notably Kim Philby and then George Blake at MI6, Sasha Kopatzky at the CIA, and Heinz Felfe and others at the Organisation Gehlen – were providing bucketloads of information on Western spies in East Germany. But to conduct the operations smoothly, and to avoid any blame for 'excesses' landing at their own door, the Soviets wanted German spy-catchers to carry out the arrests on the ground. Thus Ernst Wollweber oversaw the operations while his deputy Mielke saw they were implemented robustly enough to achieve their twin goals: demolishing the enemy spy networks operating in East Germany, and proving the June events had been orchestrated by the West.

In a new twist, each round of mass arrests was to be accompanied by a dynamic media campaign. The *Grossaktionen* were about publicity – the kind of publicity that would shame capitalist countries, unnerve West Germans, subdue dissenters within the GDR, and dazzle the remainder of the population into dumbfounded reverence. The Soviet Union, SED and East German population would be cast as a trinity of innocents. The arrests would allow the SED to blame its failures – especially East Germany's poor material conditions, so obviously lagging behind those of the Federal Republic – on outside interference: on the enemy saboteurs, terrorists and 'diversionists' who were impeding production and sapping the resolve of East German workers; on the Western spies whose information was fuelling the fascist-imperialist war machine that was set to crash eastwards. These revelations were expected to rally the public into greater vigilance and inspire even stronger feelings of socialist patriotism, for they would show that the Western world was intent on strangling at birth the first truly socialist German state.

The *Grossaktionen* were linked so closely with propaganda that the form and timing of many of the arrests were decided by the needs of the media. It was planned to use particular operations to make specific polemical points. Different types of arrested agent were to illustrate different facets of the West's aggression and interference. Some German historians have made much of the fact that these operations were organised with the media in mind, as if this serves as another example of Stasi perfidiousness and suggests the innocence of the arrestees.[4] In reality, spy arrests in all countries tend to be coordinated with government messaging, if only via leaks to the odd sympathetic journalist.

As well as being loud and visible, the *Grossaktionen* were to be harsh. In December 1953, when the first of the arrestees were being interrogated, Alfred Scholz, head of Department IX (investigations), cautioned his staff that 'implacability towards all prisoners [is] an important prerequisite for a political interrogation'; and that any Stasi employee 'subject to hesitancy' was 'halfway to making concessions to the prisoner'. Scholz's personnel were not to waver from their 'belief in the victory of the working class'.[5] This was all, of course, time-honoured Stalinist talk.

It was acknowledged in advance that many targets of the *Grossaktionen* would have to be kidnapped from West Berlin and West Germany in order to stand trial in the GDR. It was intended to do this covertly; once in court, the accused were to be prevented from referring to their abduction. However, Stasi kidnappings were already common knowledge and continued to be so. One article in the Western press told of how:

> when he became SSD chief, Wollweber expanded his criminal repertoire to another Soviet secret police speciality – political kidnapping...
>
> Through evidence obtained by Western counter-intelligence, the SSD has been linked again and again to terrorist kidnappings... Although ambush and physical assault are their favourite tactics, Wollweber's terrorists employ gangsterdom's gamut of ruses and treacheries. Drinks are 'doctored' with narcotics, victims are lured by 'friends', male and female.[6]

All the same, the SED's loyal judges and prosecutors were forewarned to stifle, refute or dismiss any mentions of kidnapping by defendants.

Of all Western intelligence services, the Organisation Gehlen was at this point considered the Hauptfeind – the main enemy. The Stasi's successful infiltration of the OG was epitomised by the likes of Gerhard Prather and Hans-Joachim Geyer, the latter a Gehlen courier turned by the Stasi after his capture. For its part, the OG was now extending its operations into Poland, Hungary and the Soviet Union, no doubt helped greatly by Reinhard Gehlen's wartime intelligence archives. In East Germany it still enjoyed the services of the highly useful Hermann Kastner, sitting near the top of government. The OG's steady acquisition of data on the Soviet Bloc was helped by the fact that it opted to refrain from blowing things up – unlike the anti-communist hotheads of the KgU – and instead concentrated on expanding its massive index of names and details.

The Stasi, of course, didn't care. Gehlen and KgU operatives alike were heavily represented among the arrestees of the *Grossaktionen*. These operations would see the arrest of some 1,200 people – every one deemed a hostile 'agent' of the West. They resulted in many lengthy prison sentences and at least ten executions. But how guilty were the guilty?

Unsurprisingly, and with solid justification, German historians see no legitimacy whatsoever in the *Grossaktionen*. Karl Wilhelm Fricke, himself a victim of Stasi kidnapping and one of the first authors to shed light on the Stasi for a Western audience, has written that:

> Even if actual espionage or other acts were involved, which essentially are punishable in every state, the cases concerned political resistance and political persecution. It was about resistance and persecution in the context of the still unrestrained Stalinist terror and the division of Germany in the harshest phase of the Cold War.[7]

Yet considering the wider perspective of Cold War intelligence activity, and some of the barely distinguishable tit-for-tat operations and self-justifications indulged in by both sides, the naiveté of some of the arrestees is at least as striking as their innocence. It cannot be expected of any state security service to ignore real, armed opposition to the state it serves, however justified such opposition may be. And armed opposition to the SED regime certainly existed. It was heavily funded by the Western powers, above all the United States, and it broke the rules that apply almost anywhere on the planet.

Of course, people who had fled from East Germany should have had the right to explain, publicly and in safety, their reasons for fleeing. They should have had the right to advocate elections that weren't fixed, or to complain that the East German press was biased and untruthful. They should have had the right to compile inventories of the legal malpractice occuring in the GDR. Disapproving socialists should have had the right to assert that East German socialism was a travesty. Journalists should have been at liberty to write critically of the East German government and its key personalities, or to disclose the GDR's economic failings. Moreover, some things the Stasi did were so horrific that it hardly matters if there was a law for them or not.

But at this moment in its history the Stasi was carrying out 'classic' spy and secret police functions. Its job was to defend against criminal opponents of the government and state. Of course, properly democratic countries do not practice the laws that made such people 'criminals' in East Germany (though it should be noted that some of these laws reflected distinctly German concepts of the primacy of the state, which play a part in German judicial practices to this day). Neither did Western countries persist in the cynical use of Allied Control Council directives, or Soviet Russian law, as an easy way to prosecute undesirables. (In fact, ACC Law No. 10 was repealed in West Germany, to the benefit of some former Nazis.)

Nevertheless, to quote Susanne Muhle, 'the lines between political activity and intelligence work were blurred' for many of the people who were targeted by the Stasi. Western political groups and intelligence services were almost running riot with espionage and subversion in East Germany. The Western powers were continuing to launch quixotic operations, making use of ordinary members of the German public, aware that these incursions would be tackled by Soviet Bloc security services renowned for their violence and arbitrariness. And these operations were not really analogous with, say, the French resistance of the Second World War, for they occurred in what was ostensibly a Europe at peace, and in a more contentious political environment.

At the hands of the SED, the Stasi, and the East German judiciary, arrested agents were prosecuted with a stunning harshness. In so doing, the SED regime criminalised many highly moral and personally decent social and Christian democrats. In some cases, people were arrested and incarcerated for doing nothing, or next to nothing. Others were branded a hostile 'agent' or enemy of the state when they were not even fundamentally opposed to the GDR; as they saw it, their political opposition was aimed at reforming East Germany's government, not overthrowing it as charged.

But for as long as there were real spies and real saboteurs operating within and against East Germany – gathering intelligence on military sites or government departments, sharing this information with Western governments or intelligence services, plotting to blow up Soviet troop trains – the Stasi had to detect and prosecute them. That was the Stasi's job. It went about it with some ardour.

40

The First *Grossaktion*:
Feuerwerk, October–December 1953

In January 1953 the counter-espionage department of the Stasi in Dresden arrested a minor courier for the Organisation Gehlen called Hans-Joachim Geyer. Under interrogation Geyer agreed to work as a Stasi mole within the OG. He was released to return home to West Berlin.

At the time of his arrest, Geyer was a small cog in a Gehlen cell referred to as X9592, run from number 19 Apostel-Paulus-Strasse in the Schöneberg district of West Berlin. Little was expected of him. But to the Stasi's surprise, over a few months he rose to be second-in-command of X9592. Suddenly, Geyer was able to supply weighty information on the cell's agents, contacts and couriers. The Stasi learned of the cell's group leaders, each responsible for a different aspect of its espionage and designated by a number and codename: 9880 Ahrens, 9890 Hermann, 9980 Möser, 9995 Oertel, 9592 Kreuder. Deferentially, the Stasi handed over one of the cell's main sources on the Soviet military to the MGB, which then ran him as a double.[1] Geyer was also in a position to provide general information on the rest of the OG. His intelligence was considered so valuable that in September 1953 the Stasi paid him an eye-popping reward of 10,000 deutschmarks.

That same month, however, concerns arose that Geyer may have been 'de-conspired'. There were indications that his Gehlen colleagues were growing suspicious of him. Perhaps Geyer had been too free with his reward money. Either way, it was decided to pull him out of West Berlin and relocate him to East Germany; and to use him, and his information, as the bedrock of Aktion Feuerwerk, a mass round-up of the Gehlen agents he had identified.

The plan for Feuerwerk was approved by Erich Mielke on 20 October 1953.[2] To oversee the operation he placed himself at the head of an Einsatzstab, or special operational staff, based in room 2282 of Stasi headquarters. He was joined by Rolf Markert of Department IV (counter-espionage, soon to be merged into the upgraded Main Department II), Alfred Scholz of Department IX (investigations), and Bruno Beater of Main Department V (political opposition). Corresponding Einsatzstabes were founded at regional level, with Mielke stressing that everything was 'to be coordinated with the Soviet instructors'.

On the appointed day, Mielke personally triggered Feuerwerk by telephoning every regional Stasi chief and announcing the codeword 'Angel'. Most of the arrests took place over two days – 31 October and 1 November – with 109 alleged agents arrested. On the latter date, the first press item heralding the operation appeared in *Neues Deutschland*, in an article headlined 'Hostile espionage agencies smashed in the GDR'. The paper claimed that it was the vigilance of members of the East German public that had led to the arrests. As well as being an important propaganda message, this claim reflected the Stasi's use of a large-scale ruse when making arrests, one that it would continue to employ in the following years. After a suspect had been investigated and an arrest decided upon, the Stasi would discreetly instruct the likes of work colleagues, party officials or the local police to go through a charade of denouncing the suspect or calling for an arrest. This helped to disguise the Stasi's own investigations and keep its profile low, and to protect the identities of KGB and Stasi spies who had infiltrated enemy organisations. A subsequent string of newspaper articles about Aktion Feuerwerk described the liquidation of a number of 'espionage, sabotage and terror groups', exposing 'a network of agents of the West German espionage apparatus in the service of the Americans, under the direction of former Hitler general Gehlen, as well as groups of agents from the American Counter Intelligence Corps'.

It was true that not every arrestee worked for the Organisation Gehlen – 'the Org', as the Stasi knew it. Prior to the operation it was decided that district Stasi offices, on being telephoned the codeword 'Nachslag', should extend the arrests to other known or suspected agents, especially those thought to be working directly for the United States. The high number of arrested agents could then be blamed on America, seen to be running its own spies as well as exploiting its German sidekicks at the OG. The codeword was telephoned around, and the net duly widened.

Mielke's operational plan had stipulated that the Feuerwerk arrests be 'well prepared and, if possible, carried out conspiratorially', requiring the 'responsible employees to determine the exact location and draw up an arrest plan'. Soviet experience lay behind the instruction to conduct 'conspiratorial' arrests. Secret arrests, 'organised in such a way that neither accomplices nor family members or other acquaintances find out', and underpinned by paragraph 141 of the code of criminal procedure, were considered appropriate whenever 'the public interest of our workers' and peasants' power demands it'.[3] As well as sowing confusion and fear, they were deemed necessary when overt arrests might cause accomplices to flee or evidence to be destroyed. And by using secrecy and deceit to bring people in, thus keeping others in the dark about who had been arrested and why, the Stasi kept open the possibility of releasing arrestees to work as double agents or prosecution witnesses. This was the old adage of counter-espionage once again: you only expose an enemy agent when it suits your purposes.

To ensure the arrests were carried out with sufficient cunning, Department IV 'instructors' were assigned to the Stasi offices in major cities.* Mielke also gave 'special instructions' in advance – delivered in his distracted, impulsive style – on such topics as the spouses of arrestees. 'It should be noted,' he dictated, that an agent's wife could be 'aware of her husband's espionage activities' and act 'as a courier or serve as protection'. So too could 'other family members if he doesn't have a wife'. Thus it was necessary 'to know the family circumstances' of arrestees and 'consider carefully whether the wife or any other family member must be held in custody', especially as they might be 'tasked with immediately destroying material (radios, etc.) that may incriminate the spy'.

Mielke reminded his staff that radio operators were known to 'procure alternative quarters for their radios, the owners of which also have knowledge of the radio operator's espionage activities or are co-opted'. There was likely to be plenty of evidence to unearth, as some operators were known to have '2 or 3 radios', '6 code books', 'secret ink' and a range of accessories: 'antenna wire, headphones, accumulators, crystals, Morse key, spare tubes'. In some cases, Mielke's exhortations paid off. During the Feuerwerk raids, Hildegard Schmidt from Luckenwalde was caught red-handed when being trained in radio work and morse code by the Gehlen 'espionage instructor' Horst Pelzer, in the apartment of Hans and Myla Fuhrmann. All four were arrested.[4]

Mielke also stressed that every arrestee was to be assessed for 'the extent to which there are prospects of recruitment'. And for the sake of uniformity, and to coax the most vital information, an interrogation brief was attached to his order for Feuerwerk. It is worth quoting at length, for it illustrates the Stasi's preoccupations:

1. With which people from West Berlin is the arrested person connected, what kind of connections are they, how long have they existed, and how did they come about (possibly through a 3rd person)?
   When was he [sic] last in West Berlin?
   How often was he in West Berlin overall, and at what intervals?

---

* Mielke himself chose these instructors: Oberstleutnant Karl Heine for Halle; Oberstleutnant Werner Kukelski (Leipzig); Major Werner Grünert (Magdeburg); Hauptmann Krusch (Dresden); Hauptmann Hans Schneider (Potsdam); Hauptmann Helmut Bauer (Cottbus); Hauptmann Staudte (Schwerin); Oberleutnant Sonntag (Frankfurt an der Oder); Major Helmut Träger (Greater Berlin).

Why are connections to West Berlin maintained?

Where did he meet people in West Berlin?

2. For which secret service did he carry out hostile activities against the GDR, and since when did he carry out this activity?

How did he get in touch with the secret service?

3. Which other people does he know who are engaged in hostile activities against the Soviet Union, the GDR and the people's democracies?

When, how and where did he meet these people?

How do these people carry out their hostile activity?

What tasks did he himself receive to carry out hostile activity, and who helped him to carry out the assignments?

Did he receive money?

Did he write or sign a commitment?

When did he pledge his commitment?

What codename was he given, or what code number or emergency number?

4. If it is a courier:

What was his task? When and from whom did he receive orders? Were his orders to deliver or collect messages?

What journeys has he made so far, and where did he set out on them?

What means did he use to make these journeys (train, bicycle, motorbike, car, etc.)?

To which persons did he hand over material or from which persons did he collect material? Get him to describe exactly when, how and where. Get a precise description of the persons. What material did he hand over or pick up?

5. If it is an information-gatherer:

On whose behalf and about which people has he sought information so far?

Which people does he know who were approached and recruited by the secret service?

6. If it is a radio operator:

How long has he been in service?

Which agency (radio centre) is he in contact with?

Has he received training, between which dates and where?

Who was the radio instructor?

Is he used as an emergency radio operator?

Who is the resident?

How many spies does the resident handle, and how many does [the arrestee] serve as radio operator?

Where is his dead letter box located?

How many radios does he own?

How many code books does he have, and how many crystals?

What is the transmission frequency?

What is the alias of the station in West Germany, and what is the actual station?

With whom did he set up his alternative quarters?

What functions does his wife or other family members have?

Does he have secret ink? What accessories does the radio have?

7. All spies and agents must conform to a security system.

This includes cover addresses that the spy or agent uses to report to headquarters, and where he will receive a message [or] warning from the espionage centre.

To what extent are the owners of these cover premises informed of the activity of the spy or agent?

The Feuerwerk arrests went well. With the cells at pretrial detention centres heaving with suspects, Ernst Wollweber wrote to every Stasi office to extend his 'personal thanks' for their 'strike against the enemies of our working people'. He invited regional chiefs to 'submit proposals, with appropriate justification, for promotions, awards and personal commendations' for 'outstanding and special achievements' by employees.[5] The captives were grilled, with Alfred Scholz instructing his Department IX interrogators to concentrate on unearthing preparations for another uprising or 'X-Day' ('Tag X'). Thus Feuerwerk crackled on for another month or so, as more leads were discovered and more material accrued that could be used to make connections between individuals, networks, and organisations.

Sub-operations of the time included Fuchs and Schlag, and there was renewed activity under Aktion Ungeziefer (Vermin), in which more undesirables were removed from border areas. This included twelve members of a group called the '17 June Committee', which had been helping June demonstrators to escape from East Germany. Four of its members were put through a show trial, which set out to prove the group's connections with Western intelligence services.

Although the OG's Hans-Joachim Geyer had been recruited by the Stasi when Wilhelm Zaisser was chief, it was Ernst Wollweber who got to bask in the glory of Geyer's collaboration. On 9 November Geyer appeared at a press conference in East Berlin hosted by three senior officials: SED propaganda chief Albert Norden, Fritz Beyling of the prime minister's press office, and Colonel Gustav Borrmann of the Stasi. With captured spy gadgets such as radio converters on show, Geyer told Germany and the world about the Organisation Gehlen's nefarious activities, so shockingly illustrated by Aktion Feuerwerk. 'We're sending the idea of German understanding and peace from East to West Germany,' Norden pleaded in his closing remarks. 'But you, the Washington and Bonn governments, are sending spies, assassins, murderers.'[6]

At the conference, and in the piles of paperwork he had given to the Stasi, Geyer was able to explain the OG's complicated, many-handed system for delivering clandestine mail, designed to cope with border closures and crackdowns in postal censorship.[7] He revealed the names of the fake companies under which the OG's branches operated (Herzog, Hase, Schlosser, Nordland); the backgrounds of senior personnel, such as the cell leader 'Westphal, alias Donner', a former Luftwaffe lieutenant colonel, and Gärtner, a former Luftwaffe major and the head of cell X8970. He had provided documents describing the Gehlen procedure for meeting an unknown courier:

> The location must be precise. This means that it must be possible from the description to determine it with an accuracy of a few metres ('the meeting point at Bahnhofsplatz' is not acceptable). The place should be as close to passing traffic as possible...
> An alternative location must always be decided...
> Repeated meetings should be held at irregular times...
> The recognition process has three parts:
> i.   Sentence (spoken by courier) that makes sense in the circumstances.
> ii. Sentence (spoken by agent) that still makes sense, but is unexpected.
> iii. Sentence (confirmation by courier) that is meaningless, unrelated to the previous sentences.[8]

The East German press also published Geyer's 'declaration', in which he admitted his errors and warned others not to follow his example. Written mostly by the Stasi, it aimed to persuade readers not with ideology but with patriotic feeling:

> I realised that the entire activity was criminal and had an adverse effect on the German people and my fatherland... my actions were helping to bring about an even greater disaster for my fatherland than the Hitler War... [my Gehlen colleagues] pursue their shameful craft without scruples, without morals and without a shred of national feeling [and] drive every person they pull into their networks onto the path of betraying our own people, [creating the prospect] of genocide and fratricide... I dare to ask you to give me the opportunity to start a new life because, like all true German people, I love peace.[9]

In fact, the Stasi received solid information that Aktion Feuerwerk had shaken the Organisation Gehlen to its core. It purloined a document in which the OG leadership wrote of a 'very serious incident' that had brought the 'previously safe conditions' to an end.[10] To avoid being drugged and abducted, its operatives were warned not to accept cigarettes from East Berlin friends or to finish any half-drunk drinks. A Stasi report noted that the OG was ousting 'senior employees who have family ties to the GDR', and had banned the employment of refugees as agents. The same report claimed that Feuerwerk had damaged the OG's constitutional status: 'Another effect of the blows against the OG is that its legalisation, which was supposed to take place on 1 January 1954 under the Bonn puppet government, has had to be postponed indefinitely.'[11]

Hans-Joachim Geyer wasn't the only Gehlen employee to be used for propaganda after Feuerwerk. The Stasi sucked the marrow out of another case, that of Werner Haase. A former Wehrmacht major, Haase headed the Gehlen branch '120A' in West Berlin using the alias 'Fritz Heister'. He was captured thanks to information prised from previous Feuerwerk arrestees, with help from yet another Stasi collaborator; and he became the central figure in a trial of seven Gehlen agents that kicked up a media storm.

Haase was caught red-handed while attempting to lay a telephone cable across the border between Kreuzberg, in the American zone of Berlin, and Treptow in the east. The cable, some of which was intended to run beneath the surface of an old city moat, the Heidekampgraben, was supposed to enable secure communications with Gehlen agents, removing the need for risky courier runs across the sector borders. Haase's plan was to fix the cable to a small model boat with an electric motor, propel the boat for some distance along the moat, and then detach and sink the cable. On the night of 13 November Haase and an assistant called Heinze had set about this work. They sneaked onto Kiefholzstrasse, just across the sector border, where they were relying on a local resident to help them unfurl the cable to its destination. But the local had already been co-opted by the Stasi. It was probably he who gave the signal for two Stasi teams to pounce on Haase and Heinze. They were arrested within fifty metres of the American zone.[12]

Within a month Haase was on trial at the Supreme Court together with six alleged Gehlen agents captured during Feuerwerk, all East Germans.* Despite being unknown to one another, they were said to make up an experienced spy ring. Much of the testimony against them came from Wolfgang Paul Höher, another Gehlen operative who had been kidnapped from West Berlin some months earlier.

Höher was to appear at several trials as an expert witness on the OG, which had recruited him in 1951. During the war he had worked for the SS security

---

* Siegfried Altkruger and Helmut Schwenk, both teachers; Rolf Oestereich, electrician; Walter Rennert, farmer; Karl-Heinz Schmidt, lathe operator; Walter Schneider, merchant.

forces, and he was taken to the Soviet Union during denazification. He had returned to Berlin in 1949, apparently the owner of a small business. Höher's abduction involved two of the regular methods of communist kidnappings – the use of knockout drugs and the deceit of a supposed friend. At a meeting in the Moselstuben restaurant on Wittenbergplatz, Höher's drink was spiked by a pal whom he knew as a fellow Gehlen operative, but who really worked for the MVD. Höher became so ill that it was possible to manoeuvre him, near-catatonic, onto an underground train. At Potsdamer Platz he was handed over to the care of the Volkspolizei.

Once Höher was in the GDR, the prime minister's office distributed a propaganda tract with 'excerpts from the authentic minutes of the interrogation of Wolfgang Paul Höher [of] Adalbertstrasse 5'. Among other things, Höher admitted being commissioned by the OG 'to activate espionage activities against France, so that the West German secret service could be informed about the measures taken by France on the German question'.

At Haase's trial, Höher asserted that the United States provided ninety-nine percent of the Organisation Gehlen's funds. The court and the press were given some details of Gehlen cells, each led by a V-Mannführer and consisting of about ten operatives, and based usually in West Berlin for ease of access to the GDR. For the East German authorities, the trial was a thumping success. The defendants were found guilty, variously, of gathering and transmitting military, economic and political intelligence, working as couriers, managing dead letter drops, and in one case maintaining a radio for emergency broadcasts to a West Berlin 'alarm centre' in case of war. A conspiracy was woven successfully into these charges, establishing that the OG was indeed planning for a new insurrection or 'Tag X'. This was due to take place in spring 1954, preceded by 'decomposition work' within the Stasi, KVP and Soviet army, 'in order to prevent the members of these institutions from taking action against the putschists'.[13]

The GDR authorities didn't have it all their own way, however. While in the dock, Werner Haase went seriously off-script on the matter of culpability for the June uprising, stating that:

> As far as I know, we were completely surprised by the putsch in the GDR on the 17 June. We were also not involved in its implementation. Since we no longer had any contact with our agents in the GDR for about four weeks after 17 June, 1953, we were given the task of ensuring that agents could transmit messages in the event of any new incidents similar to 17 June. Therefore, the laying of telephone connections, that is secret telephone connections between the American and the democratic sectors of Berlin, was demanded with the utmost priority.

Nevertheless, in sentencing Haase to life imprisonment and the six others to lengthy terms, the chief judges delivered a blistering assault on the evil designs of Western conspirators, venting every ounce of their righteous bitterness:

> In the former Soviet zone of occupation, now the GDR, the principles of the Potsdam Agreement were implemented, and the monopolies were smashed, the corporate bosses and Junkers were disempowered and the war criminals were punished. The GDR is determined to continue on the path of peace and peaceful reconstruction…
>
> In West Germany, on the other hand, the Junkers and corporate bosses have been left in their positions and the Nazi and military war criminals have been released, violating the Potsdam Agreement. The Adenauer government, on the instructions and with the support of American imperialism, is pursuing a policy of division contrary to the principles laid down in the Potsdam Agreement. America has not only allowed the emergence of a new German imperialism but demanded it. All efforts by the governments of the Soviet Union and the GDR to create a unified Germany have therefore been unsuccessful. Instead, in West Germany, remilitarisation is being carried out with a large-scale nurturing of the spirit of revenge. The aim of the ruling powers in West Germany is to unleash a new world war, through which the old capitalist conditions are to be restored… With all its institutions the Adenauer state serves this goal of American and German imperialism.

Remembering the presence of the convicts, the judges' summary added:

> In accordance with the policy of remilitarisation pursued by the USA and the Adenauer government, and the inclusion of West Germany in the so-called European Defence Community… the OG, as a tool of American imperialism and the West German militarists, pursued the aim of preparing a new war, a civil war between Germans in the east and west of our fatherland, through extensive espionage activities directed primarily against the GDR.

It has been noted that the wording of this judgement was almost identical to that of the indictments against the seven defendants, drafted earlier by the Stasi.[14]

Although it was followed by even larger operations, the lessons and polemics of Aktion Feuerwerk had a long shelf life. The protagonists had mixed fortunes. The six Gehlen agents convicted for their membership of Haase's network had to spend between eight and eleven years in prison before the efforts of the Bonn government wrested them free – the last was released in 1964. Haase himself served only three years of his life term; he was exchanged in a spy swap for the alleged East German agent Ule Lammert, an old pal of Markus Wolf who had been arrested in West Berlin some years before. Wolfgang Paul Höher put his name to a propaganda publication called *Agent 2996 Revealed*, and continued to work for the Soviets until he died, before his time, in 1959.

In the months after Feuerwerk, an unsurprising bout of *Republikflucht* compelled Ernst Wollweber to do some backtracking. In a service instruction of December 1953 he urged restraint on his no-doubt confused personnel, so as not to induce a 'psychosis of flight' from East Germany.[15] He then issued a weighty guideline on the correct procedures for paperwork. This is a significant document: in effect, a comprehensive summary of what the Stasi was, who its enemies were, how it defined its own operations, and how its personnel were expected to record its swelling data.[16]

In defining the Stasi's individual enemies, the guideline listed 'all persons who carry out active anti-democratic activity' or who were 'suspected of doing so; spies, terrorists, diversionists, saboteurs, wreckers, provocateurs, former leading employees of the Gestapo, the SD and the NSDAP, former officers of the Wehrmacht, functionaries of the SPD, expellees from the SED, all Trotskyists, sectarians'. The Stasi's corporate enemies were 'all parties, associations, organisations and groups that actively engage in anti-democratic activity; centres and schools of enemy secret services, rendezvous and conspiratorial apartments, as well as companies, institutions and other sites which are used by the secret services of capitalist countries to camouflage their demoralisation work'.

Instructions then followed on how to file and index the subjects of operations and investigations, 'according to the type of crime committed or contemplated'. The main enemy secret services were considered to be those of the US, 'England', France and 'the Bonn government'. These were followed by 'the Blank service', 'the Gehlen secret service', the BfV ('Amt für Verfassungsschutz'), the Federal press office ('Informationsbüro 'West"'), the Vatican, 'other secret services' – which were 'to be specified' – and 'unknown' secret services. Also considered dangerous were former members of the Abwehr, the police, and other 'German punitive bodies' from the Nazi era.

The Stasi's political opponents were growing in number. The list now included 'participants in the right-wing social democratic underground movement and other anti-democratic organisations'; the Ostbüros of the SPD, CDU and FDP; the League of German Youth (BDJ); the Stahlhelm and German Patriots (Deutsche Patrioten); the Union of Deportees (Bund der Heimatvertriebenen) and the Association for the Victims of Stalinism (VOS); and a further four organisations whose names were all miswritten or misspelled in Wollweber's document – the KgU, UfJ, the Association of Political Refugees from the East (VPO), and the League for Peace and Freedom (Volksbund für Frieden und Freiheit).

Stasi personnel were reminded not to neglect Trotskyists, anarchists, and members of other political movements 'to be specified'; holders of public office during the Third Reich; clergy, and 'dangerous members' of churches and sects, including Catholics, Unitarians, Lutherans, Jehovah's Witnesses, rabbis, and the Orthodox church. Finally, persons who had committed any other anti-state crime, including leaving East Germany without authorisation or helping someone else to leave, were also considered 'enemies'. Every one of these people and groups was to be 'processed' ('bearbeitet') – a direct translation of the word used in the Soviet Union for any kind of intervention by state security, from distant observation to assassination.

41

An Outbreak of Kidnapping

At the time of the *Grossaktionen* the Stasi had two detachments for special tasks – mostly kidnapping – under the leadership of two senior officers who had cut their teeth in irregular warfare before and during the Second World War: Joseph Gutsche and Josef Kiefel. These detachments, it was hoped, would improve on the hit-and-miss performance of other Stasi employees, mostly from Department VIII, who had previously carried out dirty operations outside East Germany.

As has been seen, Joseph Gutsche's Department for Special Duties, founded in 1953, was transferred to Markus Wolf's portfolio after its fluffed attempt to send a letter bomb to the prime minister of the Saarland. Before its transfer, its operatives took part in many of the kidnappings that brought the victims of the *Grossaktionen* onto East German soil. Its proficiency was outmatched, however, by Josef Kiefel's Special Tasks Group, which became operational early in 1954 and spent the following years kidnapping victims to order.

Kiefel's wartime service as a partisan in Poland, and his instinctive bent for counter-espionage, have already been mentioned. By the time he came to lead the Stasi's spy-catchers of Main Department II, he had suffered further for the cause; it was recorded that Kiefel received '120 serious head injuries' in 'the fight against provocateurs' on 17 June 1953.[1] A key member of his Special Tasks Group was the Berlin wideboy Hans Wax, a major Stasi collaborator of whom more will be seen. Another commissioner of kidnappings was Bruno Beater of Main Department V. Upon his death in 1982, Beater's role in abductions prompted the *Berliner Morgenpost* headline, 'SSD kidnapper Beater dies in East Berlin'.[2]

The outbreak of kidnapping that flared up with the *Grossaktionen* is illustrated by a show trial held at the Supreme Court in June 1954, timed to mark the first anniversary of the uprising. All four defendants – Hans Füldner, Horst Gassa, Wolfgang Silgradt and Werner Mangelsdorf – had been abducted and brought onto East German soil.

Hans Füldner of the FDP Ostbüro was kidnapped from West Berlin in October 1953 as part of Aktion Schlag. He had been fooled into thinking that two Stasi operatives were actually employees of the West German security service, the BfV, who wanted to recruit him. Under that misapprehension he got into a BMW with British number plates, which proceeded to convey him smoothly to East Berlin.

Füldner had been on the Stasi's radar for some time. Originally a member of the LDPD in Erfurt, he had fled west, under threat of arrest, in September 1949. Throwing in his lot with West Berlin's Free Democrats, he had made a nuisance of himself by organising mass leafletting campaigns aimed at GDR citizens. Once brought into East Berlin, his arrest was made by Colonel Werner Kukelski who, as the former chief of Department IV, and now a section head in Main Department II, was already a seasoned spy-catcher. It transpired that Hans Füldner hadn't been completely unprepared for this event. A report of his arrest noted that he had concealed a gas-fired pistol under a floormat in the back of the BMW, but hadn't had the chance to use it.

Following Füldner's abduction, the FDP Ostbüro received warnings that the Stasi intended to kidnap more of its members. Sure enough, four months later Horst Gassa was abducted in almost identical circumstances: driven into East Berlin, apparently compliant, by two acquaintances – probably the same pair who had tricked Füldner. For what it was worth, Gassa had been on his guard. He had left a note for his wife before leaving their home, telling her he was heading to a meeting near Potsdamer Platz and expressing doubts about his two associates. 'Should something happen to me,' he wrote, 'I have the feeling that G. and V. could be there – they both live at Mommsenstrasse 56.' When Gassa was arrested at East Berlin's Gendarmenmarkt, again by Colonel Kukelski, a blank-firing pistol was confiscated from him.[3]

The abduction of Wolfgang Silgradt in February 1954 was more complex. Silgradt was a former administrator for Leipzig city council who had begun to collaborate with the CDU Ostbüro in autumn 1950. After fleeing East Germany the following year, Silgradt got involved with the Free Democrats and a couple of campaigning organisations, the Research Advisory Board for Questions of Reunification and the League for Human Rights. For the latter he organised 'political refugee' status for others who had fled from East Germany. The Stasi chose to exploit this role in order to get hold of him.

Silgradt was befriended in West Berlin by a false refugee – a Stasi GM codenamed 'Meier'. The pair became drinking buddies, spending long evenings together in pubs and bars. 'Meier' reported back to the Stasi, among other things, about Silgradt's taste in women. So it was that one night, 'Meier' was able to introduce to Silgradt a woman – another GM – who was guaranteed to attract him. The trio got steaming drunk, and she invited the men to her apartment. They piled into a taxi and headed off. Silgradt was so drunk that he didn't even realise he was in East Berlin when he barrelled out of the taxi.

Silgradt's interrogation soon ran into difficulties, for there was a lack of documentary evidence proving his 'anti-state' activities. This was remedied when the Stasi sent two more collaborators to Silgradt's Charlottenburg apartment. After gaining access by posing as detectives investigating Silgradt's absence, they ransacked the place and managed to come away with incriminating materials.[4]

Werner Mangelsdorf was tricked into captivity too. The main instigator of a strike in his hometown of Gommern on 17 June 1953, Mangelsdorf had run to West Berlin, where he had set up the detested '17 June Committee'. He had also collaborated with Western intelligence services, for whom the likes of Mangelsdorf were a priority for debriefing.

To get him, the Stasi put Mangelsdorf's brother in prison. Mangelsdorf's estranged fiancée was then sent to West Berlin to see him. She convinced Mangelsdorf that he could come safely to East Berlin and secure concessions from the authorities that would ease his brother's plight. Reassured, Mangelsdorf accompanied her eastwards on the train, and was arrested at Friedrichstrasse station.

After several months of interrogations, the show trial commenced. Mangelsdorf was the only defendant who had played any role in the June uprising. But the Stasi and SED were so desperate to prosecute masterminds of the 'fascist putsch' that all four were framed as 'leaders and instigators' who had 'played a key role in the years of preparation and the triggering of the fascist coup attempt'. Füldner, under who knows what pressure from the Stasi, made the obliging statement that:

> Yes, 17 June 1953 was a clear expression of the preparations planned by the West for Tag X. On this day, the putschists tried to put the preparatory work they had done up to that point into practice... the espionage and agent centres in West Berlin and their backers went over to terrorise progressive people on the territory of the GDR and in the democratic sector of Berlin, using fascist means by setting fires, looting people's property and committing other crimes to overthrow the government of the GDR.[5]

Although the Western press didn't swallow this Stasi-penned rubbish, there was certainly confusion over who the defendants really were and how they came to be on trial. *Die Welt* described the accused as 'double agents who the Soviet zone state security service has been preparing for this show trial in the past few weeks'.[6] The terrible doubt that could be sown by a Stasi kidnapping is clear in a diary entry made by Wolfgang Schollwer, head of the FDP Ostbüro, on 12 October 1953: 'Füldner has disappeared! There has been no trace of him since Friday evening. However, the circumstances of his disappearance augur evil. Everything suggests our colleague has been transported to the eastern sector.'[7] Despite these misgivings, Schollwer and other Free Democrat officials came to suspect that Füldner had gone to East Berlin of his own accord. The FDP even filed a criminal complaint against him. It took some time for investigations by the West Berlin police to establish that he had been kidnapped.

These abductions, like so many others, resulted in long, lost years of prison. All four convicts served their terms at either Brandenburg-Görden or Bautzen; dismal, harrowing places. Gassa got out in 1959 and Füldner was pardoned for propaganda purposes the following year. Silgradt and Mangelsdorf served more than ten years. Bought out of jail by the West German government in 1964, they were finally able to set the record straight about their ordeal.

Other Stasi kidnapping victims fared even worse. Karl-Albrecht Tiemann, a lecturer in philology who had fled to West Germany in 1950, was kidnapped by one of the special ops units with some help from a cousin of Tiemann's wife. Tiemann had been working variously for American and British intelligence and the BfV. Sentenced to death in a secret trial at Cottbus district court, he was beheaded at the Stasi's Dresden detention centre.[8] And in April 1954 a Stasi officer called Heinz Gleske, who was operating undercover in West Berlin, was ordered by the KGB to lure Alexander Trushnovich of the anti-communist NTS to his home in the British sector. There Trushnovich was kidnapped; neighbours saw an unconscious man 'being carried downstairs on another man's shoulders'. Communist newspapers claimed that Trushnovich had repented his NTS activities and resettled in the Soviet Bloc of his own volition. In reality, he died at Karlshorst while struggling with his KGB captors, a rag shoved down his throat.[9] Heinz Gleske profited all the same. He was awarded a prestigious Soviet decoration, the Order of the Red Star.[10]

42

The Second *Grossaktion*: Pfeil, August 1954

Operation Arrow (Aktion Pfeil) saw the arrest of 547 alleged agents. Most were apprehended over a two-day period in the first week of August, a round-up triggered by the codeword 'Echo' being telephoned around every Stasi office. Interrogations then revealed more suspects who were arrested in the following weeks and months.

Pfeil was aimed chiefly at three enemy intelligence targets – the Organisation Gehlen (277 arrests) and the intelligence services of the United States (176 arrests) and France (94 arrests). Erich Mielke boasted to the Central Committee that the arrestees included members of two major networks, four Gehlen 'residencies', four residencies of the US, and two of France. Delighted with this haul, the Stasi was able to vaunt its success through its new propaganda unit, the Agitation Department (Abteilung Agitation). This was led by Gustav Borrmann, an old soldier of security who had first produced inflammatory leaflets for the KPD more than thirty years previously. To generate the right content, the Politbüro's Security Commission ruled that Ernst Wollweber was to be trailed for a while by 'two qualified, reliable comrade journalists'.[1]

Erich Mielke had big ambitions for Aktion Pfeil. He placed himself at the head of another operational staff, where he was joined by Main Department II leader Josef Kiefel and two of Kiefel's deputies – Helmut Träger, responsible for counter-espionage against West Germany, and Karl-Heinz Böde, responsible for counter-espionage against the US. Two sub-operations that preceded Pfeil, codenamed Anton and Raket (Rocket), were said to have revealed 'active war preparations by American imperialism' against East Germany, the USSR and the Soviet Bloc.[2] In addition to foiling these aggressive plans, Mielke wanted Pfeil to sow discord among the Western powers. Big strides towards these goals had already been taken by Feuerwerk, which according to Mielke had 'contributed to ensuring peace. We were able to mobilise even such capitalist countries as France against the Organisation Gehlen'. Now, Mielke believed the 'political impact' of Pfeil could 'inflict such a blow [that] under certain circumstances, the Organisation Gehlen may even be dissolved'.[3]

An interrogation brief was sent out with the orders for Pfeil. The investigators of Department IX were 'to convict the agents of their criminal activity and to find out about their sources of help'. They were also to focus on 'the recruitment of agents with prospects of penetrating enemy headquarters'. A note from Major Träger to the Stasi office at Karl-Marx-Stadt suggested one way of doing this. He wrote that 'due to the cooperation of the GM 'Andreas' of the Schwerin district administration,' the East German parents of a Gehlen 'head agent' had been identified. 'Due to his current economic hardship and depression, there is a possibility that he can be persuaded by speaking to his parents... It is therefore intended to approach the parents in Zwickau with the aim of persuading their son to contact us.' The employees at Karl-Marx-Stadt were to devise 'a corresponding legend' for getting in touch with the parents.[4]

As always, the plans for Pfeil were hatched under Soviet eyes. An initial list of arrestees was drawn up at Stasi headquarters in collaboration with the recently founded KGB. The names were then given to district Stasi offices. Some of the suspects were wanted exclusively by the Soviets – on the paperwork these arrestees were marked 'fr', for 'friends'. As with Feuerwerk, Stasi offices were encouraged to use the coming operation to pounce on sundry other undesirables. Thus the Stasi in Dresden reported it would 'liquidate several cases that are ready for closure... These are Jehovah's Witnesses and other enemy groups'.[5] For the Stasi this was perfectly coherent, as any troublesome Witness was considered an 'agent' of the United States.

Main Department II distributed planning documents, which outlined the roles to be played by named Stasi collaborators in the coming operation.[6] One 'network manager' for the OG was to be brought onto East German soil by his girlfriend, the Stasi's GM 'Nannte', with whom he was having an 'intimate love affair' and wished to marry. Long before the Stasi's so-called Romeo spies became famous for coercing women in the West, the Stasi was making good use of their female equivalents. They are less discussed than the Romeos, and should be researched further. It is likely that some were recruited once they were known to be the partner of an enemy agent, but there is evidence that others underwent training in East Germany before being sent westwards to dupe the Stasi's intended victims.[7]

According to the plans, another enemy agent was to be 'put under pressure by his mother, who lives in Dresden, by presenting compromising material' to him. In one case, following an arrest scheduled to take place at a 'conspiratorial apartment' run by the Stasi in West Berlin, evidential documents were to be retrieved and brought to East Berlin by the GM 'Melita Sommer'; in another case, the arrested person's in-laws from Cottbus were to fetch the evidential documents. Some collaborators were praised for being especially well-placed, such as GM 'Jürgen', whose 'father has a good relationship with employees of the Amt Blank and might be employed there himself, since he was a major in the fascist Wehrmacht'; and GM 'Ingeborg', as 'the father of her child is an agent of the German intelligence service [and] her sister probably also works for an intelligence service.'

Potential collaborators who had hitherto rejected the Stasi's advances were to be hassled again. One, who had 'already been approached by us, made positive statements, and later declined', was 'to be approached again by relatives who live in the GDR'. Another attempted recruitment, carried out by an existing collaborator, had failed because 'it is suspected that GM 'Arzt' did not act as instructed and therefore no positive result was achieved'. The candidate was now to be 'addressed through the sister'.

These, then, were some of the people who would help the Stasi, willingly or unwillingly, to implement Aktion Pfeil. As for those targeted for arrest, it must be said: the Stasi records of Pfeil reveal the extraordinary number and diversity of East Germans who were prepared to connect with a Western intelligence service in order to do something, anything, to counter the SED regime.

An analysis by Main Department II of the first two days of arrests, written just after they had occurred, detailed the responsible positions held by some of the detainees. There were 'agents' hidden in the ministries of heavy industry, post and telecommunications, and agriculture and forestry; there were senior employees from the government departments for food distribution, waterways, metals and minerals, and fuel. There was an editor from the East German press agency, ADN; a registrar in a local prosecutor's office; two KVP officers; a senior Volkspolizei officer; ten teachers; twenty railway employees; twenty-nine businesspeople; eleven scientists, six engineers, and three doctors; and, for good measure, three students, six pensioners, and twenty-three 'housewives'.[8]

The report gave a breakdown of the arrestees' former party affiliations, Wehrmacht ranks, and social class. Thirty-three arrestees had been members of the Nazi party, and forty had served in the Wehrmacht. Worryingly, forty-eight were members of the SED, perhaps the only part of East German society where the Stasi had to tread carefully; this high tally suggested that yet more vigilance, and possibly more purges, were required. Another problem was that most of the arrestees were deemed to be working class. A pencilled-in correction on the report reduced that number from 154 to 121, moving the shortfall over to the 'petty bourgeois' category.

Pfeil saw some 'excesses and events', to use the Soviet phrase. It was recorded that one arrestee, fifty-two-year-old Ottomar Naunapper from the village of Tröglitz in Saxony-Anhalt, had committed suicide 'by hanging himself in the detention centre of the S.f.S. in Halle'. There was at least one Stasi casualty too.

While making an arrest at Hennigsdorf, Generalleutnant Heinz Krause had struck the struggling suspect with a pistol with its safety catch off. 'Shielding his face from the blows,' the suspect had grabbed the pistol, and a 'shot was fired that hit Gen. Lt. Krause in the abdomen'. The suspect had then escaped as Krause's fellow officers tended to him.

Other Pfeil documents reveal the Stasi's unceasing interest in arrestees' friends and family members. A memo from HA II in Berlin to its employees at Halle/Saale stipulated that each arrestee should be grilled for information on their 'relatives and acquaintances… who are they, and where do they live?' Curiously, in the same memo, scepticism was expressed about the release of a suspect who had been 'allegedly recruited'. This person's interrogation was deemed inadequate. Head office demanded he be re-interviewed and give the address, personal description and known 'relatives and acquaintances' of another person of interest who had cropped up in his interrogation, and admit to the relationship between the two of them.[9] Here, despite the regular exhortations to recruit arrestees, the Stasi seems suspicious of its own employees and their motives for recruiting someone instead of punishing them.

The main thrust of the HA II analysis was that Gehlen and the United States were preparing for war and establishing a fifth column to serve in it. This applied not just in East Germany but in other Soviet Bloc countries; Poland and Czechoslovakia were mentioned. (The GDR and Soviet Union were, of course, making similar preparations in Western countries.) Some of the Pfeil arrestees had been spying egregiously on military sites. Others had orders to make contact with the West in time of war, and were equipped to do so with radio sets, dead drops, secret writing materials, and emergency telephone numbers, 'through which they can contact any branch of the imperialist powers'. It was noted that this effort was well-resourced; one Gehlen agent was said to have been paid 15,000 deutschmarks over three years, a massive sum. But Main Department II was reasonably satisfied with the results of Pfeil. While acknowledging that further operations were necessary, Stasi and KGB moles inside the Organisation Gehlen were already reporting 'differences and distrust' among Gehlen employees, some of whom had been 'banned from going out' and withdrawn from duty.

Most damningly, the HA II report claimed that the West was preparing for bacteriological warfare. This was a semi-permanent claim in the GDR; there was, for example, a long-running accusation that cattle were being poisoned with toxins at the behest of America. In this instance, the claim derived mostly from the capture, from 'clever hiding places, such as in light switches and under roof tiles', of the 'General Order' of the Organisation Gehlen. Printed on a piece of silver foil just a few centimetres square, the order was said to include instructions 'to determine how the "allied air raids" affect railway systems, roads, bridges, larger telegraph offices and the like, what losses occur among the German population, and where epidemics occur among the civilian population'. For the Stasi report writers, the latter phrase 'obviously means the effects of bacterial weapons'.

Armed with this and other propaganda gems, the SED and Stasi publicity machine kicked into life. A terse article in *Neues Deutschland* revealed the harsh sentences given to some of the ordinary and working-class East Germans who had been arrested:

'Verdict in the Gehlen trial'
The Potsdam district court has announced the verdicts against nine agents of the Gehlen espionage organisation, which is financed with American money.

The following were sentenced for crimes against Article 6 of the Constitution: the pensioner Erwin Hesse from Brandenburg to 13 years in prison, the former clerk Hartmut Schuppenhauer from Berlin and the car mechanic Wolfgang Hesse from Ziesar to 12 years each, the teacher Ernst Braun from Borgsdorf and the pharmacist Walter Ulfert from Brandenburg to eight years in prison each, the student Klaus Hennig from Borgsdorf to four years in prison, the secretary Annelies Schuppenhauer from Borgsdorf and the pub landlord Helmut Löbert from Dörnitz to two years in prison each, and the locksmith Helmut Schenke from Ziesar to one year in prison.[10]

An infamous show trial resulting from Pfeil, held in November 1954, revolved around the Gehlen agents Karli Bandelow and Ewald Misera. Bandelow, an engineer for the State Secretariat for Road Transport, was recruited for the OG by his girlfriend Käthe Dorn, a secretary from Berlin. He provided information designed to assist a military advance through the Soviet Bloc, detailing bridges and highways, and describing engineering work across the border in Poland. He was joined in this effort by Misera, a clerk for the East German railways. Bandelow, Misera and Dorn, all apprehended in the initial two days of Pfeil, were accused of sabotaging the East German transport system.

The trio were tried at the Supreme Court along with four more Gehlen agents: clerk Vitalis Dalchau from Berlin, accountant Gottfried Schrör from Altenburg, fisherman Christoph Komorek from Wesenberg, and lathe operator Werner Laux from Leipzig.[11] Erich Mielke led the planning of a media campaign, giving himself the task of 'using concrete material to elaborate an argument for speakers and agitators about the complex Gehlen organisation'. Newspapers and the ADN press agency were to report developments in real time, and radio stations were to broadcast important moments from court; furthermore, DEFA was 'to film particularly effective parts of the trial'. Former colleagues of the three defendants were invited to attend, along with favoured workers from the 'J.W. Stalin' works in Treptow, National Front agitators from factories, and 'other employees from the ministries', for a total of some 130 spectators. The Stasi's new agitprop department was to 'guarantee that the participants' would go on to 'use the results in agitation operations within their workplaces.'

Before the trial began, the Soviet High Commissioner, Georgy Pushkin, wrote to the American official James Conant with a taste of what would follow in court. Pushkin protested that:

> GDR state security organs have uncovered numerous cases of illegal work against the GDR by espionage and diversion organisations located in West Berlin and West Germany. As the material shows, more than 400 spies and criminals of these organisations have recently been arrested… In addition, more than 100 agents turned themselves in voluntarily because they regret their criminal activities…
>
> Karl Bandelow, Ewald Misera and Käthe Dorn [all] sabotaged railway traffic in the GDR. They all confessed that they were preparing diversionary acts on important railway objects (railway junctions, bridges, depots, water towers). Secret texts, codes, instructions and other means for carrying out criminal tasks were confiscated.

As it happened, all seven defendants had indeed set up dead letter drops and trained as radio operators for use in wartime. This was a gift for the propaganda campaign. The corridors around the courtroom were hung with photographs of radio gadgetry and copies of secret instructions, illustrating the OG's methods. *Neues Deutschland* published full-page excerpts from the indictments and a stream of vituperative articles as the trial progressed: sample titles included 'Gehlen criminals in court', 'Crimes against Germany', and 'Dishonourable crooks – the tools of the USA'. As with Soviet show trials, the disgust of loyal workers became daily news in itself. It was reported that the likes of '2,000 miners from Muchel' and '900 telecommunications workers from Dresden' were demanding 'the severest punishment'. Another to express his contempt was one Arno Lehmann, shunter in a Schwerin freight yard, who told newspapers that the court should 'pronounce a sentence that will render these parasites harmless forever'.

Three double agents were brought in as witnesses. One was Wolfgang Paul Höher, whose testimony had already sunk Werner Haase. The others were the well-placed infiltrators Gerhard Prather and Gerhard Kapahnke, both of whom had allegedly defected to the GDR in the months beforehand. Prather had worked for the Gehlen branch '60/80' in Berlin, all the while reporting to Department V of the Stasi. Kapahnke, a former SS telegraphist, had been a Soviet agent since 1946, and over the years had risen to be deputy chief of the OG's 'Branch K' in West Berlin. Prather and Kapahnke also appeared at a press conference hosted by Albert Norden, the SED's head of propaganda.

In court these witnesses were joined by Friedrich Karl Bauer, who was brought to the witness stand from Brandenburg-Görden prison. An employee of the BfV, Bauer had been kidnapped some months previously, lured into an ambush by a Stasi double agent. Snatched at a secluded border location in the Harz mountains, he had been beaten up by his abductors and held in custody without trial ever since. It would be another year before Bauer received a life sentence; his appearance in court at this juncture was probably a vain attempt to win favour with his captors. Of course, not one of these witnesses was acquainted with the cases of the defendants. They were there to provide general information on the Organisation Gehlen, which could then be applied to those on trial.

The SED Politbüro demanded, and secured, harsh punishments for the 'Gehlen seven'. Four of the convicts received prison sentences of between twelve years and life. Bandelow and Misera were sentenced to death. Bandelow, hoping for clemency – or perhaps promised it – recited pitiable closing remarks written by the Stasi:

> My judges... In view of the proposed death penalty, I would like to use my concluding remarks to appeal to those who, like me, have become guilty towards the people and the state, to have confidence in our government, to put an end to their criminal activities and [not] unleash a crazy new war... to believe the assurances of our government that they are promised immunity from punishment if they voluntarily submit their documents to investigative bodies. I want to shout out to them, accept this generous offer from our government so that you don't end up in the same situation.

But there was to be no mercy. Bandelow and Misera were beheaded on 10 November 1954 at the Stasi's Dresden detention centre. The executions were resolute and rushed; uninformed of them, Bandelow's defence lawyer, Friedrich Wolff, appealed for a reprieve four days after his client had been decapitated. Before being guillotined Misera asked for, and was refused, a Catholic priest. Nor did the deaths end there, for within two years Werner Laux had died in prison. In 1992 the Berlin regional court overturned all seven sentences, on the grounds that they were based 'on a serious violation of the law'.

43

New Friends: The KGB

In March 1954 the Soviet intelligence and security service adopted its most famous form, becoming the Committee for State Security or KGB. Placed in charge was Ivan Serov, who had presided over the pre-war subjugation of western Ukraine, and the postwar subjugation of Poland and eastern Germany, in his role as NKVD plenipotentiary. Although his escapades weren't as lurid as those of a Yezhov or Yagoda, Serov was to continue the venerable tradition of dissolution among Soviet security chiefs; worryingly, even Lavrenti Beria saw fit to criticise Serov as a 'petty womaniser'.[1]

Every pertinent department of the KGB was represented at Karlshorst: branches for espionage against Western intelligence services and the West German military, counter-intelligence against Western spies, logistical support for agents, and sections for gathering economic, scientific and technical intelligence. Unfortunately for the KGB, however, its founding year proved something of an *annus horribilis*. Soviet intelligence was rocked by a spate of defections: Yuri Rastvorov in Japan, Peter Deriabin in Vienna, Nikolai Khokhlov in Frankfurt, and Evdokia and Vladimir Petrov in Canberra. Between them, these escapees 'haemorrhaged their inside knowledge of Soviet operations on a hitherto unprecedented scale'.[2]

Moreover, Moscow considered its foreign intelligence capabilities to be inadequate. Georgy Malenkov, who briefly led the USSR after Stalin's death, complained of 'low standards', and published a decree on 'measures for improving the intelligence work of the State Security organs abroad'. In some respects, the KGB was suffering from its precursors' excessive focus on punitive operations against expatriates and defectors. It was now to intensify its espionage activities against the main enemies, America and Britain, and all 'those countries used by them in their fight against the Soviet Union, above all West Germany, France, Austria, Turkey, Iran, Pakistan and Japan'.[3]

In due course the KGB managed to stem the exodus of its staff. Several would-be defectors were liquidated. Feliks Krutikov, a government minister's son who was spying under trade cover in Paris, was recalled to Moscow halfway through negotiating his defection with representatives of Britain and France. Colonel Mikhail Fedorov, a GRU officer, vanished in Paris in 1958 after offering himself to the CIA. Two years later, also in Paris, a Polish KGB illegal, Wladislaw Mroz, was found dead on the back seat of a Peugeot 403 with a bullet in his head. These operations probably resulted from tip-offs by KGB moles inside Western intelligence services.

The KGB also strove to address Malenkov's criticisms around foreign intelligence-gathering. When in late 1961 Anatoli Golitsyn defected from the KGB after fourteen years' service, he 'provided tantalising clues to penetration of the CIA, British intelligence and [France's] SDECE in which an entire network, codenamed SAPPHIRES, had flourished'.[4] The intelligence historian Nigel West has given a breakdown of some of the KGB's successful recruitments in its first decade, based on spies who were captured or identified:

> Senior long-term spies were caught in Paris (George Pâques), Bonn (Heinz Felfe and Hans Clemens), London (George Blake) and Oslo (Ingeborg Lygren). Those who fell victim to [KGB] entrapments in Moscow included British (Geoffrey Harrison), Canadian (John Watkins) and French (Maurice Dejean) ambassadors, a cipher clerk (Roy Rhodes), defense attaché staff (John Vassall, Gunvor Haavik, Louis Guibaud)... and numerous diplomats. Similar ensnarements were conducted in Prague (Edward Scott and John Stonehouse) and Warsaw (Harry Houghton and Irwin Scarbeck).[5]

The KGB's modus operandi of the mid-1950s, and its relationship with East Germany, are illustrated by the cases of Nikolai Khokhlov and the previously mentioned Otto John. The disappearance and resurfacing of John remains one of the enduring mysteries of the Cold War. At the time, the KGB's German department was led by Aleksandr Korotkov, already mentioned as a long-standing Chekist, not to say murderer. Korotkov infuriated Ernst Wollweber by not informing the Stasi about the Otto John operation.

John was the first chief of the BfV, the West German security service, established in 1950 with its headquarters in Cologne. His anti-Nazi credentials were decisive in his appointment. As a Lufthansa employee in 1944, John had been on the fringes of the military plot to kill Hitler. When it failed he had fled to neutral Portugal and then Britain, where he joined the Allied propaganda effort against the Third Reich. Although he had little intelligence experience, the British – who took a close interest in the creation of the BfV – were especially keen on his appointment.

On 20 July 1954 – the tenth anniversary of the attempt on Hitler's life – John disappeared. He turned up at a press conference in East Berlin, where he praised the Soviet approach to the German question. He denounced the Federal Republic as a cushy refuge for former SS officers, rearming in order to shatter the peace of Europe once again. By December 1955, however, it seemed John was repenting his decision to flee to East Germany. After being driven into West Berlin by a Danish journalist, supposedly to regain his freedom, he was arrested by the Federal authorities and sentenced to four years in prison.

For the KGB, John's defection, though temporary, was a major coup. It proved to be the first of many embarrassments for the West German intelligence services. The Soviets had been able to watch John in West Germany thanks to sources inside the BfV, and the affair played into the hands of Reinhard Gehlen and others who were arguing that former Nazis should be fast-tracked into the Federal intelligence services. Old Nazis were reliable and expert; compared to the likes of former SD officers, Otto John was an untrustworthy amateur. Yet John was to spend the rest of his life claiming that his vanishing act had been a kidnapping and not a defection. After many years of press coverage and investigation, John was partially vindicated. It appears that on the night of his disappearance, John was drugged by one Wolfgang Wohlgemuth, a medical practitioner with whom he was acquainted, and then held against his will by the KGB and, later, the Stasi. Various ruses were used to put pressure on him; for instance, it was arranged for him to hear a fake radio news broadcast in which his defection was celebrated by the communists.

The Nikolai Khokhlov affair showed another side to Soviet security operations. Khokhlov was an assassin sent into West Germany to carry out political killings.[6] He had undergone years of training and acclimatisation as an operative. Attractive and artistic, Khokhlov had begun his career as an NKVD snitch among Moscow's cultural intelligentsia. Later, using the false identity of a 'Herr Hofbauer' and with Romania as a base, he took numerous trips to western Europe to accustom himself to the life there. His usefulness as an intelligence agent was ruined, however, by a daft slip-up: he tried to smuggle an accordion bought in Switzerland into Austria, was detained by customs for several hours, and had his papers and false passport thoroughly examined.

Despite being blown as a spy, Khokhlov was deemed useful for other work, and was assigned to Karlshorst as an interpreter. He was performing this innocuous role when he was selected to kill Georgi Okolovich, a prominent anti-communist who had settled in West Germany. On 18 February 1954, equipped with a weapon developed in the MVD-MGB laboratory – an electrically operated gun with silencer, concealed inside a cigarette packet, firing cyanide-tipped bullets – Khokhlov turned up at Okolovich's apartment in Frankfurt am Main. Instead of killing him, Khokhlov proceeded to warn Okolovich of the danger he was in, before turning himself in to the West German police.

Khokhlov ended up with the Americans. At a triumphal press conference, he showed off the intended murder weapon, berated the newly formed KGB, and professed his undying loyalty to the West. The debate about Khokhlov's true motives for defecting, and the part played by both the CIA and Soviet intelligence, rumbled on for decades – the affair cropped up in the European parliament in the early 1990s. One fact is certain: despite the Khokhlov affair, the KGB and its toxic weapons laboratory continued their efforts to silence Moscow's defectors and detractors.

The Stasi continued to learn and adopt Chekist methods from the KGB. Such methods played a part in the East German general election held on 17 October 1954. Despite the experiences of the preceding years, some voters were still capable of open resistance to the SED. A party member and a Free German Youth activist were beaten up when campaigning in Schwerin. In another incident, three representatives of the National Front were beaten up at a pre-election debate.[7] One response by the authorities was to spread news of the Aktion Pfeil arrests and convictions, in an attempt to sway the voting public.

Much publicity was given to the case of four employees at the Ministry of Machine Building, who publicly challenged their convictions, unsuccessfully, at the Court of Appeal. According to one newspaper article, 'Dealing a heavy blow to these incorrigible warmongers is the opportunity and welcome duty of all good and decent Germans on 17 October.'[8] The piece went on to describe how the convict Rudolf Klare had been trained as a radio operator by the CIC, but it was mostly economic woes that were blamed on the group.

It was claimed that Klare's main task had been 'to deliver production figures, reports on material shortages and export orders from 80 foundries' to the Organisation Gehlen. He was said to have 'impeded the production of turbines by Leipzig factories, needed for the 1953 energy programme', and to have blocked imports. Another convict, a 'former specialist in the optics and precision engineering department' called Karl Richter, had sold himself 'for a few Westmarks' to reveal 'the 15-year development plan of the Zeiss works in Jena to the CIC agent Ilse Becker. This made it possible for the pseudo-Zeiss factories in Württemberg to recreate our devices and optics, and thus put our trade at a disadvantage'. An admonishment was added: 'If his colleagues had been more vigilant, major damage could have been prevented in good time.' A third agent, Riedel, was said to have sabotaged industrial production 'as ordered' by misdirecting supplies and delaying the delivery of raw materials: 'At VEB Fraureuth, for example, large amounts of copper, which was urgently needed elsewhere, remained lying around.' Riedel's activities were said to have become worse 'since the New Course was announced'.

The last of the four agents, Fraulein Büttner, as a 'senior consultant in the mass consumer goods department [had] a precise overview of production. With almost pedantic precision, she delivered all the documents about production conditions, meetings, ministerial exchanges, telephone conversations, and the ministry's bulk goods planning' to the OG. Büttner claimed she had been bullied and threatened into becoming a spy. She got no sympathy; hers was 'the familiar fate of all agents once they have sold themselves. Instead of voluntarily surrendering to the GDR's organs as a sign of atonement, she allowed herself to be abused to the bitter end'. The article concluded that the 'total damage these four inflicted on our national economy, and thus on every single citizen of the GDR, exceeded the million mark'.

Meanwhile, Stasi vetting of electoral candidates was growing ever tighter, for there had been obvious failures in the election four years earlier. As part of Aktion Bastion, the Stasi's effort to secure the elections, Erich Mielke wrote to Hermann Matern of the Politbüro about some seriously doubtful cases. Ruth Fabisch of the LDPD, state secretary at the Ministry of Food, was known to have flouted the rules by getting her driver to change eastern marks into 'Westmarks' at a Berlin bank. 'In the summer of 1951,' Mielke continued, 'she visited an exhibition in West Berlin, which she glorified upon her return and expressed that [it] was a real pleasure.' Ernst Lorenz, deputy chair of Magdeburg district council, was known to have 'an immoral lifestyle' (he was gay). Volkskammer member Josef Wujciak had told fellow Christian democrats that prisoners of the Stasi were made to stand naked in waist-deep water (which some of them had been). A car belonging to the 'US forces in Germany', its number plate with 'yellow lettering on a green background', had been seen outside the home of CDU candidate Heinrich Toeplitz 'on several occasions' during 1952. Gerald Götting, Volkskammer vice president, had criticised the press; Mielke quoted him saying that 'in *Neues Deutschland*, Walter Ulbricht's visit to the Leuna factory got only positive reports – the negative side, that the workforce went on a five-hour strike, was kept quiet'. Moreover, wrote Mielke, Götting's wife was financed by a rich uncle in West Berlin and her sister worked in 'an English office' there. Mielke deemed these and other misfits to be 'unsuitable for re-election'.[9]

Simple Chekist tricks helped to skew the results on polling day. Once again, voting took the form of submitting an unmarked ballot paper to signify a 'yes' vote for the pre-selected candidates on the SED-controlled 'unity list'. Stasi collaborators made sure that polling stations experienced a distinct lack of pencils and pens, needed to write a 'no' vote. If the word 'no' did appear somewhere on the ballot paper, this was counted as disapproval of the particular candidate it sat next to, not as a 'no' for the unity list as a whole. Again, pressure was applied to the electorate; if the Stasi learned of an abstainer who happened to work in a responsible position, that person was highly likely to be sacked or demoted.[10] Although Ernst Wollweber's information groups recorded a barrage of complaints about such abuses, the election results stood, with the SED all-conquering.

44

The Third *Grossaktion*:
Blitz, December 1954-April 1955

The final big operation, Blitz, which unfolded over some months, resulted in the arrest of 521 suspects. It was the broadest swipe yet against the enemies of Moscow, the SED and the Stasi.

Led by Bruno Beater's Main Department V, the chief aim of Blitz was to tackle political resisters by tying in their activities for anti-communist and humanitarian organisations with the work of foreign intelligence services, which were providing much of those organisations' funding and direction. The message of Blitz, intended to influence West and East Germans alike, carried a threat and a patriotic appeal: You might think you are a political activist, but you are actually an agent of hostile foreign powers, and it is fellow Germans who suffer from your actions.

Main Department V defined four goals for Blitz:

1. To liquidate a large number of networks of the underground movements.
2. To further penetrate the apparatuses of the enemy underground movements, disrupt existing connections and introduce uncertainty.
3. To expose publicly the criminal activities of the underground movements and thus generate hatred and increased vigilance among all decent German people.
4. Provide evidence of the unity and cohesion of the party by proving that the 'SED opposition' does not exist, but is simply the work of the enemy agent headquarters.[1]

Targeted were the alleged spies and agents of the American, British, French and West German intelligence services; activists for campaigning organisations, mostly the KgU, UfJ, the Association of Political Refugees from the East (VPO), and the League for Human Rights; governmental functionaries, such as employees of the Western high commissions and the Amt Blank; and people connected with a range of political entities, especially the Ostbüros of the SPD, CDU, FDP and the right-wing Deutsche Partei, as well as West Germany's trade union federation, the DGB. As always, and with some justification, the Stasi conflated these political opponents with espionage and sabotage, seeing each one as a direct or indirect tool of Western intelligence services.

In the operation's second phase, Aktion Frühling (Spring), some of the focus shifted to Britain's penetration of East Germany. Reputedly, five MI6 networks were demolished with information provided by George Blake, newly arrived in Berlin, and Kim Philby.[2] Although Philby had ostensibly lost his job at MI6 some years previously, it appears now that he had continued to work informally for British intelligence, and thus remained capable of identifying its agents to the KGB. One result, according to the Stasi, was the arrest in Halle of a 'large number of agents of the English 'Secret Service',' led by a former Wehrmacht soldier known as the 'Gruppenleiter Ost'.[3] Erich Mielke said that Aktion Frühling netted '105 agents of the British secret service',[4] as well as thirteen radio sets, secret writing materials and weapons.[5] According to one account, at least one person accused of spying for Britain, Heinz Friedemann, was executed the following year.[6]

A further sub-operation conducted towards the end of 1955, Aktion Wespennest (Wasps' Nest), brought in forty-two suspected CIA spies involved in scientific espionage. It was made possible by the Stasi's infiltration of their network. Altogether, operations in the closing months of the year, including Main Department II actions such as Gärtner (Gardener) and Anweisung (Instruction), saw the arrest of a further 200 alleged spies and agents.[7]

In its preamble, the order for Aktion Blitz recalled 'the work meeting of 11 November 1954, in the presence of the comrade department heads of HA V [and] the district administrations,' where 'the decision was taken unanimously, [after] a thorough discussion, for a concentrated blow against the underground movement.' It was planned for Blitz to 'be completed by the 5th anniversary of the SfS' – that is, by 8 February 1955, although this deadline wasn't met.[8]

As before, Stasi offices throughout East Germany submitted their action plans. Blitz was enabled to a large extent by the Stasi's remarkable penetration of enemy organisations. Stasi moles were inside their offices, inside the lives and homes of their leaders. Counter-espionage operations tend to start with a targeting of the small fry, with arrests moving higher up the food chain until the most senior figures are caught. The Stasi took rather the opposite approach. Helped by KGB information, it targeted those it called 'residents' and 'main agents', surrounding them with collaborators. The arrest of these high-ups then led to the identification and arrest of their subordinate networks; sometimes twenty agents, sometimes forty, and so on.

To this end, intensive efforts were made to recruit informers and collaborators to expedite the arrest operations. In an example of 'the unity of reconnaissance and defence', it was planned to create 'new agencies', or networks of informers, 'in the West to further penetrate enemy headquarters'. The Blitz order stated that 'if necessary, signed recruitments are to be made with great haste – but nevertheless, of course – with the utmost conscientiousness'. Presumably this was one reason why the informer network swelled during Ernst Wollweber's time as Stasi chief – it was enlarged for special arrest actions.

Some GI and GM were notably well-placed. According to the Stasi's records, the GM 'Kurt Hartmann', a former leader of 'the notorious Trotskyist "Schneeweiss Group"', had been 'personally acquainted with Trotsky and his son. Hartmann was solicited as a GM with the prospect of penetrating the leading Trotskyist circles in West Germany and the Fourth International in Paris'. The GM 'Ruth Becker' had been manoeuvred into the orbit of 'a full-time functionary of the DGB main board'; when Blitz was in the planning stages, she was due to start working for the DGB in Frankfurt am Main. A GM codenamed 'Miller' was employed by 'the main board of the SPD in Bonn', while another, 'Hengst', who had 'fled to West Germany on the advice of the personal secretary' of an SPD executive, was expected imminently to begin working for the party's leadership.[9] In contrast, other informers were considered expendable, like the GM 'Fredi', a trooper in the KVP. Because he had 'recently been under a lot of pressure from the American secret service to obtain important secret documents', and because he 'has no special prospects as a GM', it was decided to blow 'Fredi' by transparently using his information to make arrests.[10]

Along with the use of collaborators, kidnapping was the main means of conducting Aktion Blitz. The operation was an exercise in mass abduction. These 'transfers', to use the Stasi term, were a built-in component of the whole thing. They used endlessly tweaked forms of deceit – 'variants', as the KGB and Stasi liked to call them. For example, the plan to get a secretary of the VPO into East Germany called for:

a group of three people to be deployed under the following disguise: two people (French) as members of a French administration, one as an interpreter for the [West Berlin] police. This group will contact [the secretary] for clarification on a matter. She will be informed that the French authorities have arrested a person known to her (GM 'Kasner'), so she will be asked to go with them to a French office in West Berlin. She will be invited into a waiting car, which will head towards the French office at a place on the sector border [and] will get into the democratic sector without being checked… In the car they will show her a picture of 'Kasner' and start a conversation with her about him. This will distract her from observing the route, which will undoubtedly contribute to the success of the transfer.[11]

Another variant was devised for the abduction of Paul Cunow, a deputy leader of the FDP Ostbüro. First, the Stasi deployed his mother against him.[12] Like other security services, the Stasi often planned to have a secret meeting with targeted persons, in the hope of recruiting or somehow influencing them without resort to more dramatic measures. Only if such a meeting proved impossible or unsuccessful would it escalate its actions to an arrest. In this case, the mother was sent to West Berlin to appeal for her son's return to East Germany. Cunow refused and reported her visit to the Federal authorities. Based on information from its GM 'Radeberg', whom Cunow considered his best friend, the Stasi then planned for:

> a group of operatives, disguised as [West Berlin] police, to contact [Cunow] with the explanation that his mother, who was allegedly sent to him on behalf of the state security organs, has been arrested. [Cunow] will be asked to go to a police station to clarify the matter, and to get into a car… If this operation is successful, [Cunow's] appearance in the GDR will be presented as a voluntary conversion, with his own confession.

'Radeberg' was Werner Hähn, a liberal democrat who had fled East Germany in 1953. The following year, aware of the kidnapping operations that were targeting FDP Ostbüro personnel, Hähn had warned Paul Cunow, at that time still living in the GDR, that he was in danger of imminent arrest. Cunow had been able to escape to West Berlin. Thereafter he felt he owed his freedom to Hähn. Not long after this, however, Hähn had noticed a Stasi watcher on his own tail around West Berlin – a GM codenamed 'Erika'. He told the West Berlin police, who arrested her. But the Stasi's interest didn't stop. In the end it proved rather easy to recruit Hähn as a collaborator, with money and promises of care for the two children he had left behind in East Germany. In his first act as 'Radeberg', he shopped an East German friend who was working for the FDP Ostbüro. The friend was promptly arrested. Hähn then made himself useful by presenting the Stasi with complete visitor lists, and details of personnel and refugees, from the Ostbüro's office in West Berlin. He secured the job of picking up letters to and from the Ostbüro, which he gave to the Stasi for perusal before they made their way onwards. Thus the Stasi learned of every Ostbüro cover address, activist, and sympathiser.[13]

Another enemy agent was to be abducted through the efforts of GM 'Geier', a fruitful Stasi collaborator. The target, described in the Blitz plans as 'the resident of an American secret service' – he was also said to be working for the BfV and Amt Blank – had recently ordered 'Geier', his supposed agent, to recruit an employee of the East German railways. The Stasi planned for 'Geier' to introduce to the resident another Stasi collaborator, 'Walther', who would pose as the recruited railway worker. Then an 'active group' led by 'Walther' was to abduct the resident using the latter's own car, an Opel P4, 'with which he always drives to meetings'. To ensure all went smoothly, the plan noted that the resident's movements were 'currently being ascertained in detail by the GM "Mecki Faber" and an observation group'.

The Stasi wrung a lot from GM 'Geier', an employee of the VPO who had been recruited after his own abduction. According to a Stasi assessment, 'Geier' had given details of the VPO's headquarters 'in such a way that we can use an operational group to steal the files that are in the room of [a] manager'. He provided documents that raised the possibility of 'compromising the West through propaganda' and 'arousing mutual distrust among [VPO] employees'. 'Geier' was also said to have attended 'an American agent school' in 1953, and 'named 47 people who had connections to the Organisation Gehlen... Of these, 13 people were arrested with the consent of "Geier"'. These arrests had been a success, for 'during the interrogations they confirmed that they were agents.' 'Geier' had even begun 'an intimate relationship' with the secretary mentioned above, who was to be fooled by the bogus French officials. As well as grooming her for her planned kidnapping, 'Geier' was aware of a back-up plan to 'violently transfer' the secretary, should the Stasi's ruse not work.

This and other operations against the Ostbüros and VPO were dreamt up by section 3 of Main Department V. (The SPD Ostbüro had a section to itself, HA V/1 under Erich Jamin.) Captain Rahnsch of HA V/3 reported that his GM 'Adler' was acquainted with a Berliner who:

> works for a coffee warehouse in the democratic sector, owns a Kübelwagen and has had his driving license revoked by a Volkspolizei patrol for drunk driving. 'Adler' has promised [this person] to get his driving license back, since he has the opportunity to do so, but set some conditions, e.g., making the vehicle available to him for his own use. 'Adler' [wants] to use this vehicle to approach [a VPO employee] in the guise of a criminal police officer and ask her to come along. He wants to carry out this measure without the help of another person.

Already the Stasi was keenly focused on woman secretaries. In a way, the 'Romeo' cases of later years, where West German secretaries were seduced by

Stasi spies, were nothing new. In the 1950s, however, secretaries working at Western organisations were targeted mostly for security operations rather than intelligence-gathering. One example is an HA V/3 plan to 'transfer the former secretary of the head of the FDP Ostbüro'. The woman's father, a resident of Halle, was to visit her in West Berlin, soften her up, and discover where she now worked. Once brought to the GDR by 'the group of the GM "Schwarz"', it was hoped that her information would enable 'the group of the GM "Jawo"' to steal 'agent files' from the offices of the FDP Ostbüro.

Perhaps by these means, an 'active group' did manage to break into the FDP Ostbüro building on the night of 13 February 1955. The documents they stole named 957 members of the LDPD who had been identified by refugees as hostile to East Germany and 'useful for espionage'. According to the Stasi's follow-up investigations, 100 of them were already 'FDP Ostbüro agents'. Their number included a district chairperson of the LDPD and an employee of the Ministry of Agriculture.

As head of the CDU Ostbüro in Berlin and chair of the VPO, the Tempelhof resident Werner Jöhren was a prime target for the Stasi. Through a collaborator it was discovered that Jöhren's driver, Kurt Weiss, was 'in financial difficulties' and 'very dissatisfied'. Stasi investigations then unearthed Weiss's brother Walter, a locksmith in Dresden. Walter was sent to West Berlin with a sum of money for Kurt, who reportedly said that it would be easy for him to kidnap his boss – he would just have to 'press the accelerator at the Brandenburg Gate'. At this point, however, Kurt requested direct contact with a Stasi officer, as his brother Walter 'did not have the mental qualifications' to negotiate such a task.

As was often the case, the Stasi developed several parallel operations against Jöhren. One involved a KP, or contact person, who had served with Jöhren on a CDU committee before the latter's flight from East Germany. The Stasi ordered the KP to rekindle the pair's friendship. At the same time, he was instructed 'to study all of [Jöhren's] characteristics and thereby determine further measures that might make it possible to penetrate his agency'. On a different note, there was a failed attempt to kidnap an Ostbüro employee, Hanna Hermann, who worked closely with Jöhren.[14] A fourth 'variant' involved another pair of brothers. One worked under Jöhren at the CDU Ostbüro, the other was an SED functionary in the GDR's Ministry of Light Industry. First, the Ostbüro employee was approached and asked to return to East Germany, presumably to be recruited. Upon learning that he had rejected this appeal, his brother told the Stasi that 'as a comrade' he 'would feel guilty' if his sibling wasn't brought to heel, and so 'declared his willingness to forcibly bring his brother here'. The

Stasi noted this offer, but wanted to try something else. It was thought possible to put pressure on the Ostbüro employee with the fact that he had visited his brother, the SED official, in 1952 – that is, to threaten him with exposure in West Berlin as an alleged Stasi collaborator.

The industrious Captain Rahnsch of HA V/3 also planned actions against the Ostbüro of the Deutsche Partei. A battery of collaborators was deployed against its West Berlin leader, who went by the name 'Walter Brandt'. One such GM, 'Jäger', had been recruited when the Stasi's Magdeburg office had 'developed enough bargaining chips against him'; he had, perhaps unwittingly, 'helped to expose some enemies of the GDR who were convicted'. At first the Stasi tested 'Jäger' with small tasks, such as checking personal backgrounds and reporting on the mood within the Deutsche Partei. But as the DP Ostbüro began to make more use of 'Jäger', so too did the Stasi. The Ostbüro gave 'Jäger' a film camera with which to shoot military sites and the traffic system around Magdeburg. Then he was given 2,000 deutschmarks to buy an Exakta Varex 35mm camera and deliver it to another Ostbüro agent. All of this provided solid evidence for the Stasi; and all the while, 'Jäger' intensified his friendship with Walter Brandt to the point where he was a frequent visitor to his home.

This was also true of GM 'Iltri', another supposed friend of Brandt who notified the Stasi that he 'takes his files home in his briefcase every evening. He probably keeps them in his study'. Two more collaborators, 'Schmidt' and 'Klotz', then 'observed him on his way home [and] discovered that he really was carrying a briefcase and was constantly carrying it towards the walls of the houses'. So Captain Rahnsch refined his plans, noting that:

> after leaving the Ostbüro [Brandt] crosses the road after about 50 metres. Here he passes a ruin that is unlit. After crossing the road, he still has to walk about 200 metres to his apartment, passing a coal and lumber yard, which is also poorly lit. It is intended to snatch the briefcase containing the files and bring it here. Further observations are intended to determine the extent to which it is possible to overpower [Brandt] and transfer him to the democratic sector.

Another GM, 'Panter', had been planted close to a Deutsche Partei executive known as Segel. According to a Stasi interim report on Aktion Blitz:

> SEGEL, who is also a resident of the American secret service, vetted the GM 'Panter' thoroughly and then sent him to a radio school in West Berlin, which the GM completed successfully. 'Panter' will expect to receive a radio from there in the near future. 'Panter' has received the order from the West to nominate candidates from the GDR for the radio operator school. [Also] the GM learned

from SEGEL that the DP Ostbüro wants to start a large-scale operation to create unrest in the ranks of the KVP by sending fake letters of promotion to officers. There are also plans to send conscription letters to members of the FDJ (young people).

The biggest and most troublesome Ostbüro remained that of the SPD, but by the time of Aktion Blitz it had been thoroughly penetrated by Erich Jamin's personnel. The co-option of its employees took various forms. An Ostbüro functionary using the alias 'Kramer' had twice been given money by the Stasi GI 'Amicus'. In return he had written reports on such events as a rally addressed by Konrad Adenauer. 'Amicus' used the variant of working for a think-tank on German reunification; 'Kramer' saw through the ruse but apparently didn't care – as noted in a report by HA V/1, 'it can be seen that "Kramer" is not averse to working for us.'

While preparing for Blitz, Jamin's officers wanted to recruit another SPD Ostbüro employee codenamed 'Köhler'. This planned operation was yet another family affair. The man's father, who lived in East Germany, was a supporter of the Ostbüro and had recommended several acquaintances as potential activists. His brother was a Stasi GI in Magdeburg with the codename 'Michael II'. It was planned to arrest the father and several old friends of 'Köhler'. 'Michael II' would then visit his brother in West Berlin and insist that 'Köhler' was to blame for these arrests. He would offer 'Köhler' redemption and 'a big amount' in deutschmarks if he agreed to collaborate with the Stasi. If he refused, he was to be threatened with ruin: 'Michael II' would explain to his brother that the arrests would render him 'compromised, fired from the Ostbüro and [with] no chance of taking up any other work in West Berlin or West Germany'.

Some measures planned by HA V/1 were much simpler. One kidnapping scheme saw GM 'Bier' tasked with visiting West Berlin to do his Christmas shopping. He was to meet his old friend, an SPD Ostbüro activist, for 'a drinking party, as it is known that [the activist] likes to drink more than he can hold. After this drinking spree, GM "Bier" will bring [him] on the S-Bahn to the democratic sector'.

Main Department V plotted more insidious methods to tackle the leadership of the UfJ. According to its plans:

Documents show that the head of the UfJ [Horst Erdmann, alias 'Theo Friedenau'], his deputy [Walther Rosenthal], as well as one of the residents and a driver for the headquarters, were former agents of the Soviet services. Because of their double-dealing [i.e., their simultaneous work for the West], all connections with them were broken off and they fled to the West. There are ways to give certain people the impression that they still have connections to and work for the Soviet agency.

The Stasi's planned 'combination' called for patient deceit:

A recently 'sacked' employee of BV Potsdam [the Stasi's office in the city] will decide to send his wife to the political department of the West Berlin police because of his resentment towards the state security organs. She will explain that her husband has material of interest to the police. First, the police will be handed a duplicate of the personal file of a useless GM of BV Potsdam, who lives in West Berlin, in exchange for the appropriate fee. When this file is handed over, it will be explained that the sacked employee possesses much more important documents. It is believed that in order to check the matter, the police will arrest the said GM.

A little later, doctored material will be handed to the West Berlin police [that looks like] instructions from the BV Potsdam [for] the GM... This 'letter' will also indicate that [Walther Rosenthal] was handed over [as an agent] to the state security organs by the Soviet authorities, but that [Horst Erdmann] still works with the Soviet friends.

Similar skulduggery was planned against the KgU, to 'create distrust, intrigue and disinformation' inside it. As with the UfJ, it was important for the Stasi to highlight the organisation's links with Western intelligence services and how it impacted the German public. By revealing 'the production and distribution of counterfeits and other hostile measures' which prevented 'the adequate supply of the population', the Stasi hoped to stoke 'hatred and disgust towards [the KgU] underground groups and contempt for the American and other imperialist secret services'.

Caution was to be exercised in the arrest operations, as in the case of the GM 'Karl':

In order to ensure the security of this GM, the KgU network he described will not be arrested as part of operation 'Blitz'. There are serious indications that GM 'Karl' will soon be appointed as deputy head of the KgU's intelligence service and thereby have access to the entire agency and all the enemy headquarters' documents. The GM fully understands our intentions and intends to prepare an action that will lead to the definitive exposure of the KgU.

The KgU also figured heavily in the Stasi's propaganda plans. This reflects several factors – its level of threat to the SED and Moscow, its appeal for some of the East German public, and the relative ease of besmirching it. Newspapers, radio stations and DEFA productions were to attack the KgU's 'sabotage, espionage, diversion and terror'. Much of the responsibility for compiling this propaganda lay with two senior HA V officers, Major Tresselt and Otto Knye, the latter first encountered when leading an anti-KgU task force soon after the Stasi's foundation.

Tresselt and Knye's plans covered several themes. One called for a contrite public statement from a former KgU agent, GM 'Emma', who supposedly had surrendered herself voluntarily to the Stasi and had 'already been spoken to. She agreed and will submit a manuscript for planned publication'. Her admission would be trailed by press and radio, then followed by detailed articles. These would describe her orders from the KgU, her smuggling of subversive literature, her sending of threatening letters to party and government officials, her search for new agents, and her collection of military intelligence. All of this was to demonstrate the 'low morals' and 'corruption' of KgU employees. Also planned was propaganda to expose KgU forgery, as one of the organisation's professional forgers was a priority target for arrest. The public would be shown examples of fake petrol and grocery stamps, coal ration cards and discount vouchers, and made aware of the 'administrative disruptions' caused by fake letters sent to state-owned companies and collective farms.

The propaganda plan also called for a new 'central public trial' of KgU suspects. This was to include 'arrested agents from Berlin, Cottbus and possibly Erfurt', augmented by some new, as yet unidentified arrestees – ideally 'a female KgU agent with a connection to a main KgU agent' and, it was hoped, some students: 'The goal is to include these students in the trial if they are suitable.'

The testimonies of Stasi collaborators who, like GM 'Emma', had been 'withdrawn' from their positions in enemy organisations, were considered a good way to 'corroborate the trials'. GM 'Schmidt' was to coordinate his resignation from the KgU headquarters with the Stasi's Greater Berlin office, which would then help to bring him to East Germany. GM 'Hans', 'a former volunteer at the FDP Ostbüro', had in 'his short stint gained insight into the criminal work of this agent headquarters [and] knows the connections between the residents and their backers'. GM 'Blume', who was recruited by the Stasi after fleeing East Germany, had good knowledge of Werner Jöhren and could 'make important revelations about the criminal activities of the CDU Ostbüro'. A similar role would be played by an infiltrator at the VPO, GM 'Christian'.

Despite the exhaustive planning, Aktion Blitz didn't run smoothly. A progress report of 17 January 1955 complained about the Stasi office in Dresden, which had reported on:

the 'Nest' operation, for which 12 arrests are planned. However, review has shown that the material is based on the information provided by a single GI and cannot be viewed as concrete evidence. BV Schwerin has also planned 15 arrests, but these are only based on information from a GM and no concrete evidence has been produced so far.

In fact, because of its reasonably high requirements for documentary evidence, the Stasi had to plan actions to acquire documents from West Berlin and West Germany almost as assiduously as it planned to acquire people. The report went on to criticise 'too much focus on accumulations [of suspects] and less on qualified recruitments in order to penetrate deeper, or at all, into the agent headquarters'. Moreover, 'all district administrations have ignored the important factor that material is being developed for propaganda purposes.' At this point only a few cases were considered viable for propaganda. One was 'the case of the Evangelical Church of Magdeburg'. Another concerned 'a young person from Schwerin who became a victim of listening to current Western broadcasts', while a third was suitable for demonstrating 'the insidiousness and depravity' of the UfJ.

In another report, Erich Jamin asked for more time to make arrests, as 'it should be borne in mind that further operational work will decline during the Christmas holidays and we will probably encounter difficulties in requesting assistance from departments VIII, IX and XII, as these departments only have a Sunday service during the festive season.' That most maddening of all Stasi difficulties – not knowing which Western agency a suspect worked for – was illustrated in a communication from the Wismut office about its case codenamed Zentrale Kurier. Several arrestees had given addresses where they had met with their handlers – a meeting room in the 'Bonn Ministry of the Interior', an apartment in Berlin-Lichterfelde, a house at 'Johann Sigesmundstrasse 136, 130 or 146'. Wismut asked HA V to 'determine whether these locations are [known] and [therefore] which enemy intelligence agencies these agents work for'.

When all else failed, Stasi departments could always resort to coercion and blackmail. An employee of the Amt Blank was signed up by the Cottbus office having 'lost the trust of his clients due to his immoral and depraved actions'. Another report contained information from the GM 'Kropf' that a 'former resident of the CDU Ostbüro' had been 'removed from his position without notice because of immoral offences'. Such people were vulnerable. So too were refugees who had once served the SED or the Stasi. At least one Stasi defector was to be brought back into the fold as a collaborator.

This case began when the Stasi heard from its GM 'Schwarz' that a former employee of the economic branch, Main Department III, who had been briefly imprisoned in East Germany, was now living with a girlfriend in a sublet in Berlin's French sector and 'probably' working for the BfV. 'After consultation with the comrade advisers,' Main Department V deployed 'Schwarz' to 'persuade [the former employee] to come to the democratic sector to consult with us'. Starting in February 1955, the pair met several times at restaurants, with the refugee changing the venue each time. Finally, he opened up, reportedly saying:

> 'Schwarz', I trust you and that's why I can tell you that I've expected for a long time that someone from the SfS would approach me. I made the move to West Berlin because no one cared about me after I was released from prison... Please inform your client that I have now collected good documents and also have good connections with Bonn. You don't need to know the details because I'd like to talk about them myself.

Another meeting was scheduled, at which 'Schwarz' was to give the refugee some money and a requested bottle of 'Hungarian brandy'. Before he would return to East Germany, however, the refugee had a condition: 'As reassurance I would like a certificate with the signature of Comrade Generalleutnant Mielke or Reinhold Knoppe so that nothing happens to me over there.'

It is highly unlikely that a pledge from Erich Mielke would guarantee anyone's safety. As for Reinhold Knoppe, he had once led HA III and now ran the Stasi in Magdeburg. He was a first class comrade – a young communist who had escaped to Czechoslovakia in 1933, served in Spain for two years, was interned by the French, handed over to the Gestapo, and then sent to Sachsenhausen, from where he was released to serve in the Soviet zone's police force. He was a founding officer of the Stasi. It was perilous being a Stasi defector. Knoppe, just maybe, might offer the kind of protection one needed.

45

The Holes and Corners of Blitz

Like the other big operations, Blitz was seen as a chance to wrap up outstanding cases, especially those 'whose liquidation must start in West Berlin and West Germany'. It was time to tidy up loose ends. 'Reports and tip-offs that have not yet been checked [are] to be checked immediately for their authenticity,' read the Blitz order. On paper the operation had a coherent concept, but combing through the back files in Stasi offices led to curiosities among the arrests. In Frankfurt an der Oder, a suspected war criminal was brought in for crimes against humanity. In Dresden, a GI was arrested for dishonesty in his interactions with the Stasi. One case, codenamed 'Illegale', targeted a ring of twelve 'Trotskyists'; it seems the Stasi was determined to continue Stalin's great schismatic battle, almost thirty years after it had first flared up.[1]

At the time of Blitz, some KPD members were on trial in the Federal Republic. One Blitz arrest, of 'an agent provocateur' for the BfV who had 'penetrated a district headquarters of the party', was intended to help these West German communists by securing 'valuable documents for the defence lawyer'. A case run by the Stasi in Erfurt, codenamed 'Fanal', targeted the former head of personnel for the Essen police, who was suspected of collaborating with 'the Yugoslav secret service': 'It is known from GM reports that he has a connection to a Yugoslavian officer with the first name Alexander, from whom he once received 3,000 DM. At the same time, he worked with the British secret service while working for the West German police.' Given the links forged in wartime between British intelligence officers and their Yugoslavian counterparts, such a connection is plausible. An odder operation saw plans to recruit 'the head of the balloon launch base in Philippsthal', just across the border in Hesse, 'through his son-in-law'. This was an attempt to subvert the dropping of Western propaganda leaflets, for a person on the inside might be able to engineer any number of mishaps.

One especially problematic pamphlet, which may have originated from the staff of a Western high commission and was discovered in big numbers during Blitz, was called 'The SED Opposition'. It encouraged party members to query Walter Ulbricht's policies and strive for a more benign social democracy. In response, some Stasi measures were intended to spread a quasi-patriotic message, that 'disunity among party members only helps American imperialism and the destruction of the German nation'. In classic communist style, much of the inner-party dissent was blamed on followers of Georg Dertinger, the disgraced former foreign minister. One of Dertinger's secretaries who had fled East Germany, now deemed 'an American agent' who 'works in the CDU Ostbüro', was to be 'transferred' to East Berlin in order to reveal 'further hostile connections and as yet undiscovered threads [leading] from Dertinger' to the Christian democrat opposition in the GDR.

The Stasi arrested lots of women during Blitz. Their alleged roles varied greatly. One was a cleaning woman in the Potsdam council offices, whom an unnamed Western agency had codenamed 'Luise' and tasked with gathering scraps of paper from wastebaskets. Another had been told to join the Volkspolizei: 'She turned down this assignment for personal reasons and instead took a job with the Treptow district council. In the period that followed, she provided verbal information about the structural make-up of the council.' An arrestee called Johanna Kotschate, who had received 'big payments' to work for a Western service under the codename 'Klinge', was considered a major courier. The Stasi was satisfied that 'an explanatory drawing' found in her apartment was proof of her espionage activity. Made on 'Japanese rice paper', it showed 'a spider within a spider's web' and 'some numbers', each of which 'must correspond to a person receiving deliveries'.

Serious allegations were developed around an arrestee called Katarina Kutow. Said to be the lover of one Western espionage 'resident' and acquainted with at least two more, Kutow had recruited her own sub-agents. One of them, Martin Wagner, was a self-employed electrician who worked in the 'restricted area' of Hohenschönhausen. Wagner had 'ascertained the exact addresses of individual employees [of the East German state], provided a map of the prison in Hohenschönhausen, and was specially responsible for reconnoitring the apartment of the Comrade State Secretary [of security, Ernst Wollweber]'. Having done so, Wagner had given Kutow 'a precise map' of Wollweber's home. Under interrogation, she claimed that Wagner 'had offered to install an explosive charge in the hot water tank' there. Wagner denied this, but it was a gift for the Stasi, which always struggled to provide evidence for its regular claim that East German officials were threatened with assassination.

Although Blitz was led by Bruno Beater's department, as always it was Erich Mielke who granted himself the pleasure of breaking down its successes to the SED Central Committee. According to his announcement, 393 of the 521 arrestees were deemed to be agents of Western intelligence services: 188 of

America, 105 of Britain, and 100 of West Germany. These numbers included many people who ostensibly were working for the Ostbüros or other political agencies. The remainder were said to be solely in the service of political organisations: fifty-six the KgU, thirty-two the UfJ, twenty-seven the SPD Ostbüro and seventeen the FDP Ostbüro.[2] Mielke's figures added up to 525 arrestees but, as Nikolai Yezhov had once said, 'better to do too much than not enough'.

Exactly how Mielke apportioned the arrestees to specific organisations will be forever a mystery. In the case of arrestees working directly for Western intelligence services – and there were many – it was fairly straightforward. No doubt it was much harder to establish corporate connections for those arrested on the grounds of being an undeclared former Nazi or SA member, or listening to Western radio, or disrupting their workplace or collective farm, or owning 'fascist and militaristic literature'. Usually, contact with one of the Ostbüros was invoked to make such a connection. Sometimes house searches yielded weapons, as there were still plenty of wartime firearms around. Although Mielke applied the blanket term 'agent' to most of those apprehended, their number included unfortunate eccentrics and individuals who merely had doubtful connections with West Germany or with other arrestees. Many arrests were prompted by the writing or sharing of Western propaganda ('Hetzmaterial'), much of which criticised the Soviet Union rather than the GDR. Those arrested for this offence weren't necessarily political activists of any description.

More seriously, there were genuine guerrilla 'sleepers' among the arrestees, especially workers in industry and on the railways. In his pronouncements Mielke made much of this; in the event of war, it seemed the East German transport system was to be paralysed by Western saboteurs. Given the political sensitivities of divided Germany, and the delicate balancing act being maintained by the world powers, all of which professed to want peace but were preparing avidly for war, these were potentially damning revelations.

Hostile agents could be found in unlikely places. Mielke told the Central Committee that the radio stations RIAS and NWDR, while gathering news and working up their propaganda, also tipped off Western intelligence services about promising-looking recruits. So too did West Germany's political parties. The US Counter Intelligence Corps was judged to be exploiting the virulently anti-communist membership of the Deutsche Partei. The Organisation Gehlen was said to recruit heavily from within the 'bourgeois' parties of the National Front: CDU, LDPD and NDPD. East German suspicions of the League for Human Rights intensified when it was established that several of its members, arrested by the Stasi office in Potsdam, were former members of the Nazi party and SA.[3] All of these overlaps show how the Stasi was able to conflate spying, sabotage, hostile propaganda and oppositional politics as 'merely different manifestations of Western malice'.[4]

Summer and autumn 1955 saw a wave of post-Blitz show trials, with Ernst Wollweber luxuriating in the publicity. These trials were probably successful in dissuading many Germans from offering their services as agents to the Western powers. They were preceded and accompanied by a cloudburst of propaganda about the Blitz arrests. Much of it attempted to hit the East German public where it hurt: in the wallet and the belly. Shortages and economic chaos were blamed squarely on Western interference. Enemy intelligence services and the Ostbüros were accused of coercing officials to prevent the arrival of necessary imports, and arranging the delivery of 'superfluous' ones. 'A gang of counterfeiters' headed by a 'CIC agent' was said to be forging letters to disrupt trade relations with West Germany. Some of these letters terminated contracts or claimed that the GDR was unable to deliver goods as promised. To 'slow down the fulfilment of the economic plan in industry and agriculture', East German companies were given fake orders to cease or change production, and farms 'false instructions about cultivation, harvesting and delivery'. Furthermore, to 'damage the state budget and to worry the middle class in particular', local tax offices were induced by forgeries to overcharge 'companies, craftsmen [and] members of the liberal professions'.[5] When making these allegations, the Stasi always took care to back up the testimonies of informers and arrestees with some form of documentary evidence. Much of the economic disruption was said to emanate from 'the CIC office at Clayallee 99'. This was actually the compound that housed the US military headquarters for West Berlin, and the site of the CIA's Berlin Operations Base.

While in its pronouncements the East German government branded refugees, dissatisfied SED members and critical journalists as 'traitors' and 'renegades', it had to tread more carefully around the fact that, once again, a majority of the Blitz arrestees were working class. The occupations of a group of arrestees in the town of Wernigerode, as recorded in a Stasi file, are entirely typical: chicken farmer, self-employed farmer, trainee farmer; carpenter, machinist, wheelwright; goldsmith, baker, housewife, pensioner; and, for good measure, a worker in a cheese-making factory.[6] These were hardly the gilded toffs of fascist Junkerdom.

Moreover, at least fifty Blitz arrestees were SED members, and some worked for banks, councils, government bodies or the Volkspolizei. These were infiltrations that must have caused much righteous exasperation at the Stasi. One case, codenamed 'Deserteur', targeted a ring of Volkspolizei spies around the refugee Paul Drzewiecki. Before fleeing to West Berlin in the spring of 1953, Drzewiecki, a blacksmith by trade, had been employed at two police prisons. He gave information on the conditions there to an editor at the *Telegraf* newspaper – a person described by the Stasi as the paper's 'Resident' for East Berlin, as if the *Telegraf* itself were a spy agency.[7] Drzewiecki stayed in touch with former colleagues, including a senior woman officer and an employee of the police presidium on Alexanderplatz, reporting their information to the SPD Ostbüro; in the run-up to the Blitz arrests, the Stasi noted that Drzewiecki's two friends were 'still constantly travelling to the western sectors'. By the time of his arrest, the evidence against Drzewiecki included denunciations by a Stasi informer inserted into his circle, and a letter from a department of the Bonn government to the West Berlin senate, which gauchely revealed Drzewiecki's role as a source of Western information. After his arrest Drzewiecki saved his skin by taking part in at least one Stasi kidnapping.

Drzewiecki's arrest wasn't the only one to play into the hands of the East German authorities. It was known that the OG had already obtained expertly drawn diagrams of the layout, industrial processes and personnel structure at the Wismut mining complex.[8] During Blitz, thirty-two suspects, including two alleged arsonists, were arrested at the site, justifying the introduction of ever-harsher controls there.[9] And a suspected arson attack on the studios of the State Broadcasting Committee on 17 February 1955, carried out by an engineer and allegedly prepared 'down to the last detail' by an American secret service,[10] may have been viewed as justification for a reciprocal attack on a radio station in West Germany, which occurred a few years later.

The arrest of some middle-class journalists living in West Berlin – an aspect of Blitz that has been over-emphasised in the German historiography – reinforced the message that humanitarian or polemical activities were punishable, if they tarnished the GDR. At an international press conference held on 5 May 1955, a stark warning was sent out: journalists and do-gooders beware. Referring to the likes of RIAS and the VPO, it was stated that 'anyone who continues to provide help to these agent centres or who works for them will be brought to justice'. A pinch of sugar was sprinkled into this medicine with the claim that the government had chosen not to punish eighty 'agents' who had given themselves up voluntarily in the preceding weeks.

The elections to the West Berlin senate in December 1954 were another factor in Aktion Blitz. The Stasi considered them 'of great national and international importance',[11] and Blitz seems to have been planned in the expectation that West Berliners might be influenced by the arrests. Presumably the Stasi hoped to damage the reputation of the social and Christian democrats who dominated West Berlin's political scene.

Here there arises another side to Blitz, beyond the mass arrests – the gathering of compromising information on West Berlin's churches and religious organisations.[12] Given the delicacies around arresting clerics, Main Department V contented itself with working up a secret case against the likes of the hated Bishop Dibelius. Stasi investigators were tasked with determining Dibelius's 'attitudes during fascism and after 1945'; his 'functions and how he acquired them', his 'glorification of the US imperialists', his 'anti-Soviet and warmongering' views, and 'how Dibelius supports the remilitarisation of West Germany'. This was a reference to the bishop's willingness to provide pastoral care in the nascent Federal armed forces.

Stasi documents also contain allegations against the Kolping Society, a Catholic social organisation. The Stasi decried the society's alleged connections with the Vatican and the Bonn government, as well as its desire 'to make pastoral care of the armed forces its own, and to procure the pastor's position as an officer'. Given that the Bundeswehr was yet to be created, the Stasi was gathering material that had the potential to shock and disgust both West and East Germans – material that showed how avidly West Germany was rearming, and how this was being rubber-stamped by the church.

Other Stasi accusations against the religious were of a more practical nature. A pastor from Jessen in Saxony-Anhalt, influenced by the preaching of Dibelius, was said to have forged documents to help refugees escape East Germany. The Jehovah's Witnesses were branded as murderers of their own flock. The Karitasverband (Charity Association) was believed to be engaged in 'the smuggling of diversionists and saboteurs' between the Soviet Bloc and West Berlin, and 'the smuggling of hate material' concealed, for example, in baked bread – the Stasi had photographic evidence of this. Stasi reports also claimed that the leader of the organisation Arbeitswerk für christliche Kultur, who regularly propagandised against the Soviet Union and GDR, had escaped justice after abusing children at a Catholic orphanage in Görlitz, only to reestablish himself in West Berlin.

The Stasi intended to deploy this information, and more, in newspaper articles. Towards the end of Blitz, it also made plans to arrest almost fifty 'reactionary church leaders' in East Germany. This was an organisation-wide effort. All sixteen regional administrations of the Stasi, as well as Main Department V at headquarters, put forward between one and six candidates for arrest within their jurisdictions.[13] In the event, it would be several years before the Stasi realised these plans by indulging in vigorous anti-church campaigns. Its ferocity was, as ever, watchful, and of a depthless patience.

46

Wrath

Aktion Blitz saw the Stasi make intensive use of its three favourite tricks: kidnapping, the infiltration of enemy organisations, and lengthy, complex entrapments. For some of those who were targeted, the outcome was death. In October 1955, forty-three-year-old Elli Barczatis and her fifty-year-old partner Karl Laurenz were guillotined, deemed guilty of espionage. Their deaths were the result of four years of Stasi suspicion and surveillance.[1]

Elli Barczatis had once enjoyed the position of chief secretary in the office of prime minister Otto Grotewohl, who valued her greatly. A committed SED member, she began working for Grotewohl in 1950, one year into her relationship with Karl Laurenz. The couple had met when working for the coal department at the Ministry of Industry. At first, their prospects in East Germany had looked good. But as Barczatis advanced, Laurenz had fallen victim to the period's Stalinist viciousness. A former SPD member, in 1950 he was expelled from the SED for 'lack of vigilance and petty-bourgeois ideological deviation' – basically, he had remained too much of a social democrat. By this point he was working for a Berlin law firm, but the expulsion rendered his doctorate of law virtually unusable in East Germany. Worse was to follow. In 1951, now trying to scrape a living with low-paid journalism, Laurenz served a short prison sentence for the offence of 'favouring prisoners'* in his previous legal work. After his release he returned to journalism; and Barczatis continued to help him, by supplying papers and other information from Grotewohl's office.

At his trial Karl Laurenz claimed that enforced unemployment and poverty had pushed him into the arms of 'the opposition'. By 1952 his opposition was taking the form of giving the Organisation Gehlen every confidential document supplied to him by Barczatis. It had happened that Laurenz had run into Clemens Laby, a former colleague at the coal administration and now an organiser of industrial espionage for Gehlen. Laby didn't have to do much persuading. Laurenz jumped at the chance to strike back at the SED and earn some proper money in the process, and agreed to become the OG's agent 'Daisies' ('Gänseblümchen').

---

* Gefangenenbegünstigung.

This was an odd case of espionage as a self-fulfilling prophecy, for the Stasi had begun to investigate Laurenz and Barczatis before the Organisation Gehlen had even entered the picture. On New Year's Eve 1950 an old acquaintance had happened to see the couple at a café, and had watched as Barczatis slipped Laurenz a bundle of files. The woman's observations were reported to Department III, the Stasi's economic branch. The report then made its way to Department VI, which monitored state institutions. To look into the matter, the Stasi hired the acquaintance as a GI with the cover name 'Grünspan'. This was the first step in what became years of wary, probing investigation.

At first the Stasi proceeded with caution, attempting to deal with the matter discreetly and off-record. After all, Barczatis was a favourite of Otto Grotewohl. Only in June 1951 did Erich Mielke order the start of Aktion Sylvester (New Year's Eve) – the 'group operation' (Gruppenvorgang) designed to catch Barczatis and Laurenz in the act of spying.

From then onwards the pair were subject to round-the-clock surveillance organised by Department VIII – a costly and many-handed activity – and to postal and telephone interception. The operation was overseen by the MGB and its successor, the KGB, for Laurenz was briefly suspected of collaborating with the NTS, the anti-communist organisation for Russian émigrés. The whole of 1953, and most of 1954, were consumed by this watching.

At least five secret informers were cultivated or inserted into the couple's lives. Laurenz was observed meeting American intelligence officers in the café at the Hotel Kempinski;[2] one wonders if the place had any customers other than American intelligence officers at this time. Stasi reports describe the system adopted by one GI for signalling to collaborators when watching the pair in a café:

1. Glove is on the table: Barczatis is sitting in the restaurant.
2. Cigarette is in ashtray: [an acquaintance of the couple] is sitting in the restaurant.
3. Matchbox is placed on top of cigarette packet: Laurenz is in the restaurant.
4. Newspaper 'Neues Deutschland' is on the table with the front page facing up: Laurenz has received material.
5. Newspaper 'Neues Deutschland' is on the table with the front page facing down: Barczatis still has the material.[3]

These observations fuelled suspicions without providing concrete evidence. To reduce her access to confidential information, Barczatis was sent on a training course. She was then transferred to a position more distant from Grotewohl, becoming head clerk in the prime minister's economics department. One GI,

'Lina', was a fellow administrator there. Although she and other informers considered Barczatis's behaviour suspect, by now Barczatis was mostly passing information to Laurenz orally, and several attempts to catch her red-handed failed.

One attempt occurred in November 1954, when an envelope containing innocuous documents was left in a tempting spot in Barczatis's office. 'Lina' placed two tiny hairs on the envelope and inserted a black dot within the address on its front. Some days later she noticed the envelope had been tampered with and readdressed, complete with two typos which weren't in the original text. By testing the ribbon and keys of Barczatis's typewriter, 'Lina' discovered that the new address on the envelope had been typed on the machine. Inspired by this incident, the Stasi hatched a plan to arrest Barczatis in possession of documents taken from Grotewohl's safe. Subtly she was provided with a duplicate key and plenty of opportunity to raid it; but the two Stasi officers who went to her office to check the safe's contents and make the arrest found everything untouched.

The breakthrough came in March 1955 when 'Lina' saw Barczatis hide papers about the upcoming Leipzig trade fair within the pages of a magazine before leaving the office for home. The next day, forty officers surrounded Barczatis's apartment in the Berlin suburb of Köpenick. At the same time, Laurenz was observed meeting two known Gehlen operatives in West Berlin. The pair's arrests were carried out as part of Aktion Blitz; they then underwent three months of aggressive interrogation at Hohenschönhausen.

Their trial was held in secret at the Supreme Court, with only Stasi officers permitted to attend. The court vice president, Walter Ziegler, and attorney general Ernst Melsheimer, who delivered the indictment, had both practiced under the Nazis. Sensing the pointlessness of making a case, the couple defended themselves. Barczatis insisted she had no idea that her partner was using the stolen information for espionage purposes. Laurenz supported her in this claim. No one knows if it is true or not; nor if Laurenz's connections with American intelligence predated 1952. Either way, in his closing plea Laurenz blamed the SED for ruining his life, but called upon the judges to observe the 'magnificent principles' of East German law and sentence the pair humanely. After short deliberations they were sentenced to death. Grotewohl personally turned down pleas for clemency, and they were beheaded at the Stasi's detention centre in Dresden.

The couple's families were not informed of their fate. The following year, Barczatis's sister was still trying to send letters to her via Otto Grotewohl's office. Ever since the details of the case were clarified in the 1990s, the executions, and that of Barczatis in particular, have caused great shock and anger. This is understandable and right, but to lament that Barczatis was merely an accessory who unwittingly provided harmless information, none of it pertaining to military or defence matters, is to misconceive the conditions and spirit of the SED regime and its executive arm, the Stasi; and to misconceive the behaviours of the Cold War. Otto Grotewohl was prime minister in a party dictatorship with no legitimate right to rule, engaged in what it saw as an existential struggle for the future of humanity; a ruling elite that was viciously wary about its own unpopularity. Given that news of the executions was bound to spread in whispers around East Germany's state institutions, these death sentences were intended to send out a very severe warning. Disloyal activity was unacceptable in a schoolteacher, a machinist, a farm labourer; in a state servant working at the heart of government it was unthinkable, and was punished as such.

The kidnappings carried out for Aktion Blitz raise many questions, relatively few of which can be answered by studying the Stasi's files, others only with guesswork or deduction. How did the Stasi and KGB select their kidnap victims? Why were some political opponents left alone? Why did the Stasi kidnap some people brazenly, knowing their disappearance would be noticed and protested, and others secretly? Why did the potential victims in West Berlin and West Germany continue to leave themselves vulnerable, and not take the prospect of kidnapping seriously?

The West Berliner Carola Stern, born Erika Assmus and a writer and refugee from East Germany, was the subject of two failed kidnapping attempts. Stern was, in fact, up to her neck in the political and espionage complexities of the time. In 1947 she had been approached in East Berlin by 'a certain Mr Becker', who wanted information and promised to secure cancer treatment for her mother if Stern provided him with it. On his urging she joined the SED which, with high hopes for her political future, groomed her attentively. All the while, she reported back to the employers of 'Mr Becker' – reputedly, the US Counter Intelligence Corps.

In 1951, with Stern working as a history teacher at the SED's 'Karl Marx' party school, an old letter she had written came into the hands of the East German authorities. In it Stern admitted to a friend her contacts with the Americans. As it happened, that summer she was due to go through a standard vetting interview before a party commission. Twice she was asked by the commission if she had contact with Americans. She said 'no' the first time and nothing the second. Adding insult to injury, the commission's report complained that Stern 'did not shake hands or say goodbye' when leaving the room.[4]

In the days after the review, it became obvious that Stern had run away. Her partner, an FDGB official, was arrested and grilled over her disappearance. So began an archetypally thankless Stasi inquiry, with suspicions running high and evidence at rock bottom; this was one of many occasions when the Stasi's wrath was blunted. Stern's partner piqued the Stasi's interest when it transpired that he had given conflicting accounts of his Wehrmacht service in different questionnaires for the party, government, and FDGB. A report by Department VI noted:

> In a questionnaire from 19 May 1947 he states that he was sentenced by court martial to 9 months in prison because of making repeated statements against the SS in a circle of comrades. On 3 April 1948 he stated that he had been sentenced to only 3 months for talk that undermined military strength. In a questionnaire from 1946 he states that he was sentenced to 3 months in prison for making a public statement against the SS, and in a questionnaire dated 15 February 1949 he states that he was sentenced to 3 months in prison for actively supporting the Slovak civilian population with stolen army property. He also concealed the fact that he was a member of the NSDAP in all of his questionnaires. There is a further contradiction in that he writes that he was forced to join the Hitler Youth and yet he became [the leader] of a group.

As well as showing the Stasi's keen interest in former Wehrmacht personnel – which undoubtedly could pay dividends in its counter-espionage work – this passage highlights the young state's assiduous record-keeping in what was otherwise a chaotic eastern Germany. It was decided to interrogate six of the man's passing acquaintances from his Wehrmacht days. It was anticipated that this might prove pointless, but it was precisely the kind of thing the Stasi was compelled to do; its investigations thus expanded geometrically, with a life of their own. The interrogees opined that the man had a weakness for sex and alcohol – tastes which always made the Stasi's ears prick up – but otherwise yielded nothing.

With no evidence that he had helped Stern to flee, the man was recruited as the GM 'André', and took part in the attempts to abduct Stern during Aktion Blitz.[5] She survived these attempts, going on to become one of West Germany's most celebrated political commentators. One can almost feel the Stasi seething, just across the border. Department VI was left with the consolation of discovering who had been responsible for allowing Stern (Assmus) to hold responsible positions in the GDR state. As an officer noted, 'Assmus comes from a family that was dispossessed after 1945. Without doing much party work, she attended a history teacher's course, the state party school and the "Karl Marx" party school. In further processing of the Assmus case, it will be necessary to determine who made this rapid rise possible.'

*

There are other examples of the Stasi's slow-burning interest in its targets; of the years it would spend circling people in the darkness beyond the firelight. Lisa Stein, an employee of RIAS, was singled out for attention a long time before her attempted kidnapping in March 1955.[6] 'Stein works in room 27 at RIAS, Kufsteiner Strasse,' read a Stasi report of the previous year. Ominously, 'information from 1953' described the entrance to room 27 as being situated 'directly from the corridor, as well as through the side-room number 24'. At around the same time, a detainee under interrogation gave a possible description of Stein: 'She doesn't speak with a pronounced Berlin dialect, more High German... All I know is that before leaving the apartment, she put on an ocelot coat that seemed almost new to me.'[7] Above all, it was the real-time RIAS coverage of the June 1953 uprising that made the SED and Stasi so determined to act against her. It wasn't difficult to connect the station with the labour unrest, for on 16 June a delegation of striking workers from Stalinallee had turned up at the RIAS offices, asking to broadcast an appeal for a general strike.[8]

To get Lisa Stein the Stasi made use of a GM, twenty-nine-year-old Gerhard Beck from Teltow, who was a regular visitor to the RIAS offices. At an after-work drink in the Wilmersdorfer café on Fehrbelliner Platz, Beck offered Stein some pralines laced with scopolamine. Having eaten one or two, she was supposed to lose consciousness and be spirited away, apparently to hospital, by Beck and the concerned occupants of a passing car. At least, that was the Stasi plan. But Stein didn't pass out. Beck panicked and abandoned her in her groggy state. Stein made it back to the doorstep of her apartment, where she collapsed. Neighbours then rushed her to hospital, where she lay unconscious for forty-eight hours as experts pored over the contents of her stomach.

A few days later, a chastened Beck made another attempt to kidnap a RIAS employee. He tried to lure one Franz S out of his apartment and into a waiting car full of Stasi operatives. Beck didn't know that he had been under surveillance since poisoning Stein, and he was arrested on the pavement by West Berlin police. At his trial on 29 May he was unrepentant, despite the prosecutor asserting that his actions towards Stein amounted to attempted murder. 'I was forced to do this,' Beck claimed. 'I have a large family that I was not prepared to endanger.'

Beck was one of very few Stasi kidnappers to see the inside of a prison, with a sentence of twelve years. Meanwhile, the director of political programming at RIAS, Eberhard Schütz, broadcast a talk on the attempted kidnappings of Stein and Franz S. He detailed other cases of blackmail and threats to RIAS employees. The East German media scoffed. 'This employee of the special

RIAS Hate Department was obviously struck down by the political poison pumped out there at all hours,' ran one article on Stein. 'They should let the lady go. She can't stomach anything anymore.'

Another Blitz victim, the journalist Karl Wilhelm Fricke, was to become a pioneering expert on the Stasi. After fleeing East Germany, Fricke had devoted himself to attacking the SED regime in print. His resentment was personal as well as political. His father, a supposedly 'exonerated' Nazi party member, had died in prison after being sentenced at the Waldheim trials. Fricke himself was once dragged out of a college classroom by a Volkspolizei officer, having been reported for making a disparaging remark about the SED.[9] His abduction, possibly carried out on Soviet orders, was prompted by a specific incident. Fricke had published a personal attack, in a West Berlin newspaper, on a named Stasi executive: Erich Mielke, deputy chief.

Fricke's article ridiculed Mielke as a 'new type of gunslinger'.* Worse, Fricke had mentioned Mielke's involvement in the murder of two police officers back in 1931. For Moscow and East Berlin, enough was enough. Mielke was important in the Soviet Union's plans for East Germany, and neither his role nor his past crimes could be broadcast in this way. Moreover, when capturing Fricke there was a chance the Stasi could lay hands on the 'Trotskyist archive' of names and writings that Fricke was known to keep in his West Berlin flat. This paperwork became another target of the operation. Above all, the objective of the kidnapping was to silence Fricke. It did – for a while.

The Stasi used a false friend to carry out the kidnapping. This was Kurt Rittwagen, alias its GM 'Fritz', a supposed pal of Fricke's who had been actively suggesting ways to abduct him for some time. Rittwagen knew that Fricke wanted to review a particular East German book that was hard to obtain. Miraculously Rittwagen acquired a copy, and on the evening of 1 April 1955 he invited Fricke to come and pick it up. Fricke joined Rittwagen and his wife, Anne-Maria – the Stasi's GM 'Peter' – in an apartment rented for the couple by the Stasi. The three friends tucked into coffee, brandy and cigarettes. It was probably Anne-Maria who trickled a mixture of scopolamine and atropine into Fricke's glass. At first, he noticed that his brandy was 'soapy tasting'. He then broke into a sweat, ran to the toilet, and started pleading with Rittwagen to call a taxi. After that he passed out.

The Stasi's so-called 'Paket Fricke' ('Fricke package') was bundled up in a sleeping bag, shoved into a car boot, and driven across the sector border. He

---

* 'Revolverheld neuen Typus'.

awoke, hours later, in a harshly lit room. Immediately he was shouted at by the four or five men present, some in uniform and some civilian clothes, who called him a 'scumbag' and 'arse fucker' before beating him unconscious.* He next awoke naked under a freezing shower. This was Hohenschönhausen.

Neues Deutschland mocked the articles about Fricke's disappearance that appeared in West German papers: 'Since the beginning of this week the West Berlin press has been making a noise because a certain Fricke is said to have made off unannounced.'[10] Fricke was held for 467 days before going to trial, interrogated usually in two shifts: 7 a.m. to 1 p.m., and 11 p.m. to 6.30 a.m. He wasn't a spy and so was accused, under the old legal instruments, of inciting war and the boycotting of GDR institutions. In July 1956 he was sentenced at the Supreme Court to four years in prison. The Stasi got his mother, too. Although a trumped-up charge of being a courier for her son's seditious writings couldn't be made to stick, she was accused of defaming the state and, for good measure, a foreign exchange irregularity.

After his release Fricke struck back at the Stasi with information. For many years, much of what the world knew about the Stasi came from his research. His kidnappers were not imprisoned, however. Asked about his role by a TV crew in 1991, Kurt Rittwagen responded with 'I don't remember it,' and died shortly afterwards. His ex-wife Anne-Maria was given seven months' probation in 1997, although she never admitted her culpability. 'I was more of a country girl,' she said in court. 'I never met this Fricke.'

---

* 'Drecksack', 'Arschficker'.

47

Liquidating the Müller network in Aktion Frühling

One afternoon in February 1953, a party meeting was convened by the planning department of Deutsche Reichsbahn in the north-eastern town of Greifswald.[1] The assembled railway workers discussed a number of issues at the gathering, among them the need for vigilance. It was deemed imperative that they play their part in detecting spies and saboteurs on the railway system. One of those present went home that night and thought about it. In his mind he started churning over an incident that had occurred the week before.

At lunchtime on the previous Wednesday or Thursday, his wife had answered a knock at the couple's front door. She found an unfamiliar man standing before her. He asked to see her husband. Curiously, her husband was indeed supposed to be home at that moment. It was his routine to eat lunch with his wife on those days. By chance, however, he wasn't there; he had been roped into doing something at work. Disappointed, the stranger handed the woman a sealed envelope. He told her to give it to her husband, and to tell him to make plans to come to West Berlin. He would be reimbursed for his travel expenses.

That night the man read the stranger's letter. It turned out the stranger was a former resident of Greifswald who was now living in West Berlin. There he had met an old acquaintance of the railway employee, who wished to make contact with him again. The letter explained that this acquaintance was in the railway worker's 'old line of business'. This could only refer to being a radio technician – the railway worker was a former radio operator for Lufthansa and the Luftwaffe.

Although unsettled, the couple had ignored the incident and the letter, but the discussion on vigilance prompted the railway employee to go to Comrade Keller, the SED secretary at work, and let him know what had happened. Keller wasted no time in informing the Greifswald branch of the Stasi's Department XIII, responsible for the security of the transport system.

At this point of the 1950s, between thirty and fifty percent of major Stasi investigations into political opponents originated in anonymous tip-offs from members of the public.[2] In this instance, the Stasi had even more to work with

– a known and trusted citizen, alert to the dangers of espionage, had brought news of a potential spy case. The railway employee was swiftly recruited as a GM under the cover name 'Karl Walter'. He was instructed to go to West Berlin to meet with those soliciting him.

At a café on Savignyplatz in Charlottenburg, 'Karl Walter' met the two individuals aiming to recruit him for the West – the head of a spy network and his immediate subordinate. The latter, one of three brothers called Hopf who had connections with Rostock, served as a radio operator and recruiter for the network. It was he who had organised the unknown courier's visit to Greifswald. It transpired that Hopf lived at number 73 Fasanenstrasse, a wearingly long street that bisects the Kurfürstendamm. As well as housing his radio apparatus, this address served as a makeshift headquarters for his boss, defined by the Stasi as the network's 'Resident': a citizen of Hamburg known in the Stasi files as Willi Müller, alias 'Bauman', 'Paul', 'Erwin Schulz' and 'Fritz Weber'.

Müller – whom the Stasi recorded as working variously for the Organisation Gehlen and the British and American 'secret services' – was busy putting together an espionage ring to cover the north-east of the GDR. He had agents in Rostock, Neubrandenburg, Frankfurt an der Oder and Potsdam. As well as gathering intelligence on the region's transport infrastructure, and on the Soviet and East German armed forces there, his ultimate aim was to organise emergency 'radio centres' that could transmit real-time information to NATO commanders in the event of war. In this capacity Müller had recruited the so-called 'Nord/Ost' radio team led by Wilhelm Lehmann, whose show trial is discussed in the next chapter.

'Karl Walter' signed up to work for Müller. One of his first tasks was to deliver a new radio set to Lehmann – all under the eyes of the Stasi, of course. His infiltration soon led to the capture of a woman courier who was responsible for much of the network's communications. Following her arrest, the Stasi recruited her as its GM 'Wiek'. She soon proved to be pure gold. As she made her rounds carrying Müller's messages throughout the north-east, 'Wiek' steadily identified most of the Müller agents who would be arrested when the Stasi finally decided to strike.

Although he may have started out as a Gehlen agent, Müller's most likely employers were the British military – he was said to report to 'an English officer' in Hamburg, whose intelligence was forwarded to the NATO staffs at Frankfurt and Paris. It was this reporting chain that led to the Stasi's subsequent claim that Müller worked for 'the NATO secret service', an organisation that didn't exist. Whatever these ambiguities, the Stasi was in no doubt about Müller's personal attributes. 'Müller has 9 siblings, was a member of the NSDAP, is extremely reactionary and a brutal person,' read one report. He was someone who 'carries weapons, is morally inferior, drinks, goes a lot with other women, probably has venereal disease, and will stop at nothing for his own gain'. The report writer added that, understandably, 'his relationship with his wife is not the best'. In the morally superior world of the SED and Stasi, Müller's dissolution went hand-in-hand with his commitment to fascist imperialism.

The Stasi spent two years watching the Müller network. Its investigation was given the cover name Anwerbung (Recruitment). As the case grew in importance, responsibility for it passed from Department XIII in Greifswald to Department II (counter-espionage) in Rostock, then all the way to Main Department II at Stasi headquarters. On 23 March 1955, during Aktion Frühling – the final phase of Blitz – Erich Mielke signed off on a plan, drawn up by Colonel Werner Kukelski of HA II, to liquidate the case. Most of the suspects were rounded up on the morning of 2 April. Some thirty arrests were made, leading to seventeen convictions.

Müller's accomplices were a mixed bag. Wilhelm Lehmann's 'Nord/Ost' radio team was considered the prime catch. Almost as important were Karl Tunn and Karl-August Hormann. They first fell under suspicion when another Stasi GM engaged in the operation, 'Retlaw', had watched the pair emptying a dead drop at the Zum Immendiek restaurant in Rostock. They had made this pick-up after leaving a tell-tale 'all is well' sign in the display booth of the nearby People's Theatre. As friends and travelling sales reps – one for a brush factory, the other for a cosmetics firm – Tunn and Hormann were especially useful to Müller. Using Hormann's van, they would scour the highways and lanes of Mecklenburg, building up a remarkably detailed picture of the road system. They both knew that their mapping efforts were intended for the use of NATO tanks and heavy guns.

For the Stasi, Tunn and Hormann epitomised the dangers of the petit bourgeoisie. Although his membership of Nazi organisations was unclear, Tunn was believed to have joined the SA in 1933 and the Nazi party during the war. Hormann's family had for generations owned a toy factory, precisely the kind of business the SED wanted for the state. During the war he had been a field telephone operator in a cavalry unit. Captured by the Americans in 1944, he had been put to work as a labourer in France for a couple of years.

The pair's story unfolded in interrogations. Hormann had been introduced to Willi Müller in December 1953. Given the codename 'Dose', he had then brought Karl Tunn into the fold – the latter was codenamed 'Siegel'. Convinced opponents of the SED regime, their espionage career had proved lucrative; Hormann had earned more than 5,000 deutschmarks for his trouble. Meetings in West Berlin were held at the café on Savignyplatz, apparently a home-from-home for Müller. One of the pair's earliest tasks was to service a dead drop underneath a gents' toilet in a pub at Koitenhagen near Greifswald. Once they had started to reconnoitre the road system, Müller gave Hormann a Praktiflex camera with a long-range lens to photograph the road surfaces, hazardous stretches and topographical features; Hormann found it ineffective, and soon reverted to his trusty Taxona model. These and other items were found when the pair were arrested. Tunn had written Müller's telephone number in a pocketbook, in the form of an invoice. He also possessed a cigarette packet covered with his scribbled 'spy notes'.

Karl Tunn wasn't the only Müller agent to have a National Socialist background. Another arrestee, Erich Oberländer, was deemed an 'old, die-hard fascist' who had worked as a fitter for the Arado and Junkers aircraft factories during the war. He had been a Nazi party member from the mid-1930s until 1945, and had reached the rank of Oberscharführer in the SA. In light of this past, he had been interned by the Soviets until 1948.

It is possible that Oberländer's enthusiasm as an agent stemmed from his resentment and latent Nazism. Under the codename 'Schröder', and employed as a mechanic, Oberländer had gathered information on the KVP vehicles under repair at his workshop, helping to build an inventory of their vehicle numbers. Without being asked, he gave Müller information on a range of other matters – the strength and features of the Zecheriner bridge leading to the Baltic island of Usedom, the Volkspolizei's new diesel vehicles, the torpedo testing facility at the Tollensesee. Spotting this keenness, Müller had offered him 1,000 deutschmarks to recruit an employee of the German Shipping & Handling Company who might be able to smuggle agents along the Baltic coast into Poland. Oberländer was arrested before he could carry out this task.

Significantly, Oberländer had disguised himself in East German society by joining National Front organisations – the FDGB and the Society for German-Soviet Friendship (DSF).* In fact, many of Müller's agents were DSF members; the Anwerbung case suggests that Western intelligence services encouraged their agents to join the society as a way of camouflaging themselves and gaining information on the Soviets, although membership could also bring personal and professional advantages. Perhaps membership of the DSF was vetted less stringently than for other East German bodies. A Müller agent called Enders, who had served as a radio operator for the Kriegsmarine throughout the war and then spent two years in French captivity, had joined the society in 1951. Two more of Müller's agents, employees of the Deutsche Reichsbahn with the codenames 'Schneider' and 'Köhnke', who had stolen classified documents on

---

*   Gesellschaft für Deutsch-Sowjetische Freundschaft.

the railway system and Soviet military rail traffic, were both members. Enders had even served the Free German Youth as a radio instructor at the Stralsund maritime school.

Another alleged Müller agent, a secretary at the meat products factory in Stalinstadt, had a similar background to Oberländer. During the Third Reich she had progressed from the League of German Girls to the National Socialist Women's League, to which she had belonged until 1945. By the time East Germany was created, these affiliations had been superseded by membership of the National Democratic Party and FDGB. A confirmed Müller spy, Hans Hübner, codenamed 'Schlicker', who gathered information on the goods traffic between East Germany and Poland from his position as restaurant manager at Tantow railway station, had been in the Nazi party during the war. By 1947 he was the second secretary of his local SED group. Both of the previously mentioned Deutsche Reichsbahn employees had also joined the SED, although one had already been expelled. Understandably, in its reports the Stasi lamented all of these infiltrations, but such incidents strengthened the hand of the authorities when demanding greater vigilance and the purging of East German institutions.

Other Müller agents were more easily spotted. Otto Zirzow, who lived in Wieck near Greifswald, was well-known locally as an 'enemy' of the GDR and an 'avid listener and disseminator of the hate broadcasts of Western radio stations'. Assigned the codename 'Kruger', he had set up two dead drops – one under the armrest of a sofa in his local pub, the other in a courtyard toilet. Müller had also tasked him with surveying the road system, partly as a way of checking the information received from Karl Tunn and Karl-August Hormann. Like other Müller agents Zirzow was well paid, receiving some 5,000 deutschmarks over the course of a year or so.

Worryingly for the authorities, at least one Volkspolizei officer and two Stasi employees were connected with Müller's network. The former, a captain in the maritime police at Kühlungsborn, was once observed by the GM 'Retlaw' meeting with a suspect person at Rostock railway station, although he later denied any wrongdoing. The maritime police (VP-See) were of great interest to Müller, who gave several agents the task of watching and sketching their facilities, boats and movements.

The two Stasi employees worked at Stendal. One of them, Lötsch, was a cousin of the Hopf brothers, one of whom was Müller's second-in-command. The Stasi believed that Lötsch had tipped off a different Hopf brother that he was under investigation, prompting his flight from East Germany. But it was decided not to arrest Lötsch or the other in-house suspect. Instead, with heavy patience, they were to be transferred quietly to the Stasi office at Magdeburg and 'kept under constant control'.

In an action plan, the Stasi described its intention to lure one of Müller's accomplices into East Berlin by using the man's girlfriend, the GM 'Dagmar Lorm'. Sex and purported romance played a notable role in Müller's espionage network. A young woman from Greifswald, who had already been arrested and convicted for spying, was known to have had an affair with Müller, whom she knew as 'Baumann'. It was discovered that Müller programmatically used marriage proposals as a method of recruiting women in East Germany. Having identified a suitable candidate for his network, Müller would write to the woman with an offer of marriage, flaunting his solvency by putting a fifty-deutschmark note into the envelope. If interested, the woman would meet with him in West Berlin. This was a simple way of identifying women who were uncommitted to the SED regime. At their first or a subsequent meeting, the woman would be told that marriage would have to wait. Instead, Müller would offer her a salary – perhaps even 800 or 1,000 deutschmarks per month – to be a courier or to report any information available to her. She didn't have to be highly placed – at least two of Müller's agents were recorded by the Stasi as being 'housewives'. It was thought that Müller had recruited the secretary from Stalinstadt in this manner for, in a classic case of Germany's postwar upheaval, the woman's first husband, a Wehrmacht sergeant, had gone missing in 1944, never to be seen again. Although Western commentators criticise the Stasi's so-called Romeo spies, here was a Western spy behaving comparably.

Not everything had run smoothly for Müller. On one occasion, the Stasi's GM 'Wiek', his top courier, had reported a troubling incident to him. It had occurred when she had handed a letter from Müller to a lapsed woman agent who was staying at an FDGB holiday home in the Baltic resort of Heringsdorf. The former agent's aunt, who was present, had commented that this was 'a rotten thing', and told her niece to take the letter to the local Volkspolizei. When 'Wiek' informed Müller of the incident, she realised that he must have had another source close to the lapsed agent, as Müller already knew what had happened, and that the letter had ended up with the police. He told 'Wiek' she was not to return to Heringsdorf. Thus, when 'Wiek' told the Stasi about this train of events, her information prompted yet another investigation: to find the unidentified Müller agent in the trade union holiday home. The Stasi planned to question the lapsed agent, who was not a German, asking her the following questions:

a) Who did she tell that she had received the letter?
b) Who from her homeland is employed at the FDGB home?
c) Who knows that they used to have a captain of the KVP staying there?
d) Who left the home and travelled away after the letter was handed in?
e) With whom is she particularly good friends in the home?

The redoubtable 'Wiek' survived another unsettling incident. In December 1954, at a meeting in West Berlin with Müller's subordinate Hopf, she was told that one of Müller's agents had complained about her opening a letter before giving it to him. Actually it was the Stasi's Department M that had opened the letter, an intervention that was supposed to be undetectable. As it happened, the agent hadn't been home when 'Wiek' had called for him, and she had handed the letter to his father. So she used this as an excuse, insisting to Hopf that the man's father must have opened the letter. Hopf seemed unconvinced.

With 'Wiek' due back in West Berlin soon, she and her Stasi handlers worked out her approach to the problem. She would insist that Hopf arrange a meeting with Müller, to whom she would protest her innocence in person. Then she would attack. She would assert that she had always worked honestly, that she couldn't continue working if distrusted. If Hopf happened to advise her against meeting Müller, she would defer to Hopf's judgement. 'This covers GM 'Wiek' in the event of a later query, since she can always refer to that conversation,' wrote a Stasi officer in the file. 'At the same time, it gives us material against Hopf.' The suspicions came to nothing, anyway.

Stasi officers were palpably disgusted by the Müller network's espionage. Some of the arrestees' methods were annoyingly simple. One was found to have smuggled sensitive documents from his workplace by hiding them in the football boots he sometimes carried for after-work games. Another had got into the habit of hanging his overcoat some distance away, wherever he found himself, so that he could disown it if it were searched and stolen documents found. The Stasi's reports stressed certain aspects of the spying, like the fact that the Deutsche Reichsbahn employees had indicated where explosives could be planted on railway bridges for maximum destructive effect. For the Stasi, this was evidence that these lackeys of NATO had intended 'catastrophic consequences' for civilian travellers, in line with their 'despicable and inhumane strategy of total annihilation' of the GDR.

Throughout the Stasi documents, and in public pronouncements about the affair, the arrestees were cast as warmongers, 'traitors to the interests of the German nation' who were 'threatening the peace of the peoples of Europe'. For much of the East and West German public this was probably quite powerful stuff. At the time, few things were considered more reprehensible than stirring up a German-on-German conflict. The defensive argument that the arrestees had been preparing for a theoretical future war didn't cut much ice. For a start, at least one arrestee admitted that he had believed the war to be imminent: he said that Müller had given him to understand that NATO forces were 'preparing for the planned invasion of the GDR in a hurry'. Either way, activities such as plotting the road network, which could be 'decisive in the strategic planning of aggressive actions', were taken with an outraged seriousness in East Germany. Karl-August Hormann received a life sentence for doing it. Karl Tunn got fifteen years. Like the other convicts, they were prosecuted under Article 6 of the GDR constitution in conjunction with Directive 38 of the Allied Control Council.

48

Treacherous Trials

A string of carefully arranged trials – some highly publicised, some held in secret – made the most of the Blitz arrests by tying in suspects' alleged activities with every polemical point that the SED and Stasi wished to make. Thus some defendants were cast as organisers of the fascist putsch, some as slaves of the United States; some were said to have been duped into opposition by such prominent anti-communist campaigners as Margarete Buber-Neumann; some were guilty of political apathy, having joined National Front organisations for selfish career reasons; some had consumed too much RIAS hate propaganda; others had wished to reinstate capitalism, or shatter the pledges made at Potsdam, or start a new war. In this way, a range of current political sins was covered, with arrested agents serving as an example of each one.

There were Blitz arrestees who were condemned before they ever went to trial, denounced at the international press conference held on 5 May. In his prepared statement to the media, Gustav Borrmann, head of the Stasi's agitprop department, named Wilhelm Lehmann, Erich Eich and Martin Schneising as 'a three-person agent group of the NATO secret service'.[1] A few weeks earlier, the Council of Ministers had announced publicly that the arrestee Wilhelm van Ackern, whom the Stasi had kidnapped from West Berlin, was the leader of a Gehlen cell, and that the arrestee Benedykt Szuminski was a long-serving agent of the United States. This was before the pair had even been charged. These five suspects went on trial six weeks after the press conference, alongside two more Blitz arrestees, Johann Baumgart and Hans-Joachim Koch.

During their interrogations, the Stasi draped layers of conspiracy over all seven defendants. Erich Mielke personally threatened Wilhelm van Ackern with the death penalty if he mentioned in court that he had been kidnapped. To get van Ackern, the Stasi had used the combination of a deceitful friend, alcohol, and knockout drugs. The abduction was organised by Main Department II, with Major Helmut Träger given overall responsibility, Major Pompe in charge of the snatch squad, and Lieutenant General Janz overseeing arrangements at the sector border. When van Ackern had paid a visit to a supposed friend, actually the Stasi's GM 'Schutte', the pair got drunk and then took coffee; van Ackern's was spiked by his companion. He became so torpid he could barely see. His friend shepherded him to the street and the pair set out for van Ackern's home. At a prearranged spot, a three-man team grabbed van Ackern, delivered him a left and right hook to the jaw, and dragged him into their waiting Opel Kapitän. He was then driven along a pre-tested route from Neukölln in the American sector to Hohenschönhausen. To cause further disorientation, his first interrogation lasted almost seventeen hours.

Van Ackern didn't deny working for the Organisation Gehlen, nor that he had recruited one of his fellow defendants, Johann Baumgart. The latter, a steward on passenger trains, had been given considerable espionage tasks. Baumgart was to gather details of the track, points and signals from Frankfurt an der Oder to Brest in the Soviet Union; assess the weight capacity of bridges; record the movements of Soviet troop trains in Poland and East Germany; and map the locations of factories, barracks and airfields along the route.

Hans-Joachim Koch was another avowed Gehlen operative. The Stasi had missed him – it was a tip-off from the Soviet 'comrade advisers' that had brought Koch to light. He had become a 'radio agent' for the OG in 1952, and was supposed to be activated in wartime, when he was to broadcast information twice a day, at set times, to radio 'control centres' in Munich and Frankfurt. Koch had already made a number of test calls to the Federal Republic, and had even transmitted information on five occasions during the June 1953 uprising. When revealed in court, this fact caused near-apoplexy in attorney general Ernst Melsheimer.

During the preparations for the trial, Koch revealed many details of life as a Gehlen agent.[2] He had been recruited when an anonymous letter was handed to his mother, telling him that 'an old war comrade' wanted to meet him on the corner of Seestrasse and Müllerstrasse in the French sector of Berlin. Once signed up, he had been given the cover name 'Rudolf Schubert' and was run by two handlers he knew as Burger and Hochberg, whom he met every week in an apartment near Tempelhof airfield. Alongside his radio work, he was expected to gather military information and to service dead letter drops. He had set up two of these drops inside the railings of old bridges in Bürgerpark and Schlosspark. He had been instructed 'to always behave passively and not take part in any political actions or riots'. He possessed key books for two radio codes, called 'Bär' and 'Bärenfang', and cheat-sheets that allowed him to transliterate Cyrillic texts. When transmitting, he was reminded to 'make sure that I used an indoor antenna if possible, and that doors and windows were always locked'. His radio apparatus was installed in a garden shed with one small window; he would draw the little curtain when on the air.

Koch also explained Gehlen's warning system for its agents – sending them telegrams with an innocuous text containing a number. Number 1 meant, 'Watch out, stop work and hide your equipment'; number 2, 'Hide your equipment, immediately go elsewhere in the GDR, and wait'; number 3, 'Get to the West for resettlement'; and number 4, 'Restart work'. Koch's handlers had praised him for managing to transmit during the June uprising, and given him a bonus of 150 deutschmarks.

Koch spoke plainly in response to Stasi questioning. He refused to play ball with the conspiracy theory about a new insurrection: 'I have not heard anything from conversations or any suggestions that a similar coup is being prepared.' He was straightforward about his motivation: 'I was hostile to the social conditions and developments in the GDR, and recognised the system prevailing in West Germany as correct.' And he had always understood the bigger picture:

> It was clear to me from the beginning that my work... served directly to prepare for and carry out a war. This was clearly and unequivocally expressed in my general brief. I consciously decided on this activity, and carried it out because I wanted to support the system that prevailed in West Germany in every way.

Another defendant at the trial, Benedykt Szuminski, was similarly uninterested in denying his involvement in espionage. He had been arrested late one evening in December 1954, apparently by chance, when walking across a railway bridge near the border with Poland. Detained by watchful transport police officers, he was found to be in possession of three sets of false identity papers, a 7.65mm pistol, a camera and a knife; also Polish and German cash, wristwatches, stockings, and chiffon scarves with which to reward those who might help him. He was loaded with this finery, he admitted in his first interrogation, because he was trying to reach Poland on behalf of the US Counter Intelligence Corps.

The trio accused of spying for 'the NATO secret service' – Wilhelm Lehmann, Erich Eich and Martin Schneising – also admitted their part in clandestine operations. Eich, who came from Greifswald, and Lehmann, owner of an anchor-winding workshop in the Baltic coastal town of Anklam, had both been recruited by British intelligence during 1952. Lehmann had agreed to work for the British after being contacted by a former business partner who had fled to West Germany. He was tasked with collecting any information on the KVP which might be of interest to NATO. After a while Lehmann had brought local taxi driver Martin Schneising into the set-up.

Before the onset of Blitz, the three had attended a meeting in West Berlin with their V-Mannführer – the leader of their cell – whom they knew as a resident of Hamburg. There they had agreed to become the 'Nord/Ost' radio signalling team, a communications unit to be activated in wartime. Lehmann was to be the leader and collator of reports, Eich the radio operator, and Schneising the courier and manager of dead drops. They were provided with three American-made radio sets, which they never got to use.

As part of the propaganda campaign for the trial, it was decided to film dramatised reconstructions of Lehmann's cell at work. This was becoming a common practice on both sides of the Cold War; West Berlin news services had filmed reconstructions of such events as the kidnapping of Walter Linse. During its planning stage, suggested scenes for the film included Lehmann and Eich practising radio operations at Lehmann's apartment, Schneising picking up two radio sets from Lehmann, and Schneising servicing a dead drop.

Compared to some other trials in East Germany, where sinewy reasoning was needed to make the charges stick, this trial of avowed secret agents was relatively straightforward. Ernst Melsheimer had no compunction in denouncing these 'hardcore', 'outrageous' enemies. Moreover, the moral compromises of espionage were plain for all to see in the person of Hans-Joachim Koch. Although a proud supporter of the West German system, committed to fighting the iniquities of communism, there was more to him than met the eye.

Koch had spent almost his entire war serving in the SS Police Division. This had entailed crushing resisters in France, carrying out reprisals on Greek and Russian villagers, and taking part in the infamous barbarism of the anti-partisan war in Serbia. When the Stasi arrested him, Koch was in possession of 'atrocity' photographs he had bought from a fellow member of his unit. One showed the hanging of a Russian peasant. Koch had written a sarcastic note on the back of another, which showed enslaved Jewish women washing an SS car. He also possessed some brass knuckles from his time in the Hitler Youth; a letter he had written to the Gestapo, in which he denounced a personal rival; and wartime diaries recording his participation in punitive operations, including 'a court martial and the subsequent shooting of a Wehrmacht soldier'. It could be argued that Koch was just the type sought by Reinhard Gehlen for his burgeoning intelligence service. When questioned, he didn't deny it. 'My fascist upbringing had a significant influence on my political views,' he said. 'After 1945 there was no fundamental change in my attitude.'

Another trial held in the summer of 1955, of several legal practitioners, provides a sharp contrast. It shows how the spy trials of the period tended to be underpinned by a conflation of elements and associations.

In 1953 Dr Rudolf Reinartz, a former head of department at the Ministry of Justice, left East Germany in disgust to begin a new life in the Federal Republic. A few months after leaving, however, he made the mistake of popping back into East Berlin, where he was promptly arrested. Reinartz was put on trial alongside Lothar Cetti, a Leipzig lawyer and liberal democrat, and Cetti's wife. The couple were arrested on Christmas Eve 1954, an operation timed to cause maximum disorientation and the maximum distress to their two young children. Soon after their arrest, the Stasi spotted an opportunity. A report writer from Main Department V noted 'the possibility of connecting the Cetti couple, who were also hostile in the field of justice, to this trial [of Reinartz]'.[3]

The truth was that Reinartz, disillusioned by developments in East Germany and especially by the persecution of his former boss, the disgraced justice minister Max Fechner, had had contact with the SPD Ostbüro, the UfJ, the Federal Ministry for All-German Affairs and, possibly, an American intelligence service. The Stasi wished to portray him as an exploited dupe, his case illustrating the regrettable path 'that agents have to take after being grabbed by the imperialist secret services'.

The Cettis, meanwhile, had developed connections with a West German campaigning organisation called the Liberation Committee for the Victims of Totalitarian Despotism.* Lothar Cetti had continued to be a friend and admirer of Hans Lindemann, a Leipzig public prosecutor who had left the GDR in 1951 and was involved in the work of the Liberation Committee and the UfJ.

The Cettis' actual crime, committed possibly at the behest of two West Berlin students who were connected with the KgU and acquainted with Lindemann, was issuing paperwork that secured the release of prisoners held in East Germany. In a search of the couple's home the Stasi found 'a fake instruction to prepare for release from prison' and a form for 'false release from prison, with the signature of the attorney general' – documents that, in the Stasi's words, 'serve to free white-collar criminals'.[4] This was considered so serious an activity that Erich Mielke told the SED Central Committee about the couple and their efforts to help 'agents imprisoned in Bautzen to escape'. By the time the three defendants came to trial, their separate and, in Reinartz's case, rather minor activities had been stirred into a thick stew of conspiracy.

Thrown into the pot were the anti-communist writer and campaigner Margarete Buber-Neumann – said to have provided funding and recruited at least one of the defendants for the American intelligence services – and several other figures: Hans Lindemann, the deposed justice minister Max Fechner, and his replacement Hilde Benjamin, said to be the victim of a seditious campaign.

---

* Befreiungskomitee für die Opfer totalitärer Willkür.

The defendants were prosecuted under Article 6 of the GDR constitution and Control Council Directive 38, instruments which rested on the notion that they were guilty of 'fascist' and warmongering deeds. The Cettis were bought out of prison by the Bonn government in 1964. Reinartz, who spent more than a decade in jail, never recovered from his experience and committed suicide in 1972.

The arbitrariness and severity of SED justice surfaced again in a trial of KgU activists held in June 1955. The main defendants were the schoolteacher Gerhard Benkowitz and his friend Hans-Dietrich Kogel. Benkowitz had first contacted the KgU when seeking information on the whereabouts of his father, who had disappeared after being arrested by the Soviets in 1945.[5] The KgU had ignored him. Then, in 1949, the KgU had suddenly got in touch, suggesting that Benkowitz start reporting on the mood in eastern Germany as payment for its efforts to locate his father. Despite this somewhat exploitative approach, Benkowitz jumped at the chance. A convinced opponent of the SED, by the following year, under the codename 'Dietz', he had built up a spy network of like-minded acquaintances. The group provided wide-ranging information to Benkowitz's contact at the KgU. This was 'Wolf', the KgU resident for Thuringia.

Unfortunately for the network, 'Wolf' had been turned by the Stasi. This had occurred when one of his acquaintances, the Stasi's GM 'Gottlieb', had noted that 'Wolf' was 'very materialistic'.[6] By early 1955 'Wolf' was being paid by 'Gottlieb' for information about the KgU. He revealed a KgU plan to subvert East Germany's petrol supply by introducing more than a million litres of fake petrol. He reported that forged letters had been sent to sixty foreign companies in the name of the GDR Office for Foreign Trade, cancelling contracts or reneging on commitments. He told 'Gottlieb' that the Americans were setting up a 'psychological warfare' department in Munich, where he hoped to get a job. He also named twelve KgU agents, ten of whom were arrested.

Unaware of the treachery of 'Wolf', Gerhard Benkowitz had come to specialise in spying on KVP and Soviet army units. He had also made preparations for sabotage in the event of war, photographing electricity stations, pylons, and the Saale dam. It was in this connection that he had invited his friend Hans-Dietrich Kogel into the fold. The pair had got acquainted when working as administrators at the Weimar city council, where Kogel was still employed. Kogel agreed to his apartment being used as a store for explosives, and to serve as an emergency rendezvous for Benkowitz's posse of saboteurs. Beyond donating his property – which in the end was never used for stashing explosives – Kogel was relatively uninvolved.

When Benkowitz wasn't reconnoitring targets for sabotage he took to venting his spleen in threatening letters which he scatter-gunned to East German officials. He also indulged in the kind of shenanigans that would have been familiar to any Anglo-American 'black' propagandist from the war, circulating counterfeit products made by the KgU, such as fake postage stamps and trade union brochures with mocking portrayals of SED leaders snuck into them. Similarly, a third defendant at the same trial, a trainee vet from Berlin called Christian Busch, had been distributing adulterated petrol and inedible muck disguised as genuine East German meat products, and disrupting coal supplies with forged ration cards. The Stasi also established that Busch was in contact with the overall head of the KgU's underground resistance campaign, Gerd Baitz. Although Benkowitz and Busch were strangers, the similarity of their 'diversionist' activities saw them tried as familiar collaborators in the same network.

Benkowitz was a genuine acquaintance of the remaining two defendants at the KgU trial, Willibald Schuster and Gerhard Kammacher. Both railway workers, they were said to have been 'systematically organising train delays through the deliberately inadequate implementation of existing service regulations'. They were also accused of spying, which was news to Benkowitz; as far as he was concerned, the pair were simply couriers.

As the Stasi investigation unfolded, an opportunity was spotted to make an example of these arrestees. Alfred Scholz, chief of Main Department IX (investigations), wrote to the public prosecutor's office to insist that his investigators be given more time. The final report by Scholz's staff was used as the group's indictment, with only minor changes. It declared:

> The accused are agents of the West Berlin criminal organisation 'KgU' who, under the guidance and with the support of the US secret service, the offices of the Bonn government, and the administrative offices of West Berlin, carried out acts of diversion, explosions, arson, the destruction of power plants, industrial facilities, bridges, transport and planning, organising and carrying out the assassination of progressive, democratic public figures.

In reality, the defendants hadn't destroyed anything, never mind assassinated anyone, but they were duped into making incontinent admissions as their trial was being prepared. Partly through the use of planted cellmates, the defendants were given to understand that the fuller their confessions were, the lighter their sentences would be. This led to plenty of revelations for the East and West German press, and apparently stoked the indignation of the many GDR citizens who were quoted in newspapers on the need for harsh punishment.

Among those to express their disgust were Benkowitz's fellow schoolteachers, workers at the VEB Leipziger Werke, students of the Workers' and Farmers' Faculty at Halle, and employees in the wages department of the VEB Optima factory in Erfurt. Some of the latter were reported as wondering whether those 'who volunteer to prepare for such crimes still count as human beings'. The promise of lenience wasn't met. Benkowitz was sentenced to death, the four others to prison terms of between ten and fifteen years.

Walter Ulbricht personally ensured that more than one person died. When given a report of the trial which detailed the convicts' sentences, he underlined a description of Kogel's role: 'Kogel also declared his willingness to take part in the planned demolitions, to hide the demolition squad and the explosives in his apartment.' Having added an exclamation mark next to this passage, Ulbricht changed Kogel's sentence from imprisonment to death. He didn't bother to write it; he just crossed out Kogel's prison term and added 'ditto' marks underneath Benkowitz's death sentence. Both were executed on 29 June at Dresden.

The Benkowitz trial serves as a textbook example of the era's spy trials: seeds of truth buried under mounds of political invective and hysterical exaggeration, judged in corrupt legal processes planned by the political leadership, with a marked discrepancy between what the accused persons actually did – acts which might indeed be crimes in any country – and what they were convicted of doing; and all of this capped with jaw-dropping sentences, sometimes to death.

The trial also shows how Stasi investigations tended to spread as months and even years went by, spilling over into the lives of widening circles of conscious and unconscious participants. In the 1990s many people would experience a string of revelations by studying their own Stasi files, gaining a behind-the-scenes view of their own lives.

49

'His Trench Coat Was Splattered With Blood'

Throughout the 1950s the Stasi ran with gangsters. The world of intelligence services was entwined with the world of criminal Berlin. Intelligence officers hired crooks to buy and sell things, steal and smuggle things, cache things; to introduce people, persuade people, threaten and beat people; to make money, spend money, exchange money; to watch and shadow and tip-off and trick; to drive and deliver, abduct and imprison.

Every operational Stasi department recruited secret collaborators, and a good number of those collaborators were villains. Some of the officers at Departments II and V, concerned as they were with snatching wanted persons from West Berlin, were in thick with the *gangsterbanden*. And so into the Stasi's orbit came all the components of underworld thuggery: reputations, threats, and boasts; cars, guns, knives, coshes; debts, favours, swindles; childlike schemes for self-enrichment; adolescent protests of innocence.

It isn't surprising that intelligence services were able to recruit so many civilian bystanders, bent or straight, in divided Berlin. Life in the city was hard. The atmosphere remained uncertain. The postwar crime wave took time to abate; Europe was still sick with the black market. Jobs could be scarce and were often temporary. Even so, they were fought over by furious widows and scruffy kids, by hundreds of thousands of dazed refugees. People ended up doing all sorts of work they had never planned for or wanted. And yet here were the secret people, American and British and French, Russian and German, or of obscure pan-continental origin, offering five deutschmarks to jot down a phone message, twenty deutschmarks to stand on a street corner. There were always takers.

Intelligence services were feeding Berlin's criminal underworld, in more ways than one. They bought the things that black marketeers had to offer. They paid well for trifling tasks. In an incident that is probably typical, the Stasi forced one of its criminal helpers to take a job as night porter at a Berlin restaurant, just to have some visible explanation for his earnings. A report from a court case in West Berlin noted that one career criminal, 'although not entirely through no fault of his own,' had:

found himself in an unfortunate situation, because he had not received a permit to live either in the western sectors of Berlin nor in the Soviet occupation sector, and thus had to live from hand to mouth. So he succumbed to the temptations of the SSD, which spends money on petty activities that bears no relation to the small scope of the activity, and therefore offers great temptation for people of weak character and those in need.[1]

Nevertheless, crooks and intelligence officers had a tempestuous relationship. Criminals could cause problems for the Stasi; the Stasi could cause even bigger problems for the criminals. This can be seen in the Stasi's involvement with a couple of criminal gangs which, between them, made heavy weather of a pair of kidnappings towards the end of the *Grossaktionen*.

The weak link in these two abductions was Hans Eichhorn, a fifty-seven-year-old spiv who got caught. As a young man Eichhorn had been trained in banking by the Potsdamer Creditbank. Later he had got involved in imports and exports. According to the story he retailed, which wasn't much credited, he had been arrested by the Gestapo in 1940. Supposedly he had refused to transfer ownership of some engineering patents to the Nazi state. Later he would claim to have spent several years in prison for this 'political' crime, but no documents about this period in his life survived the war. All that survived was a note in a file from a Berlin court, recording that Eichhorn was being prosecuted for 'fraud, etc.'

In 1945 the victorious Americans had freed Eichhorn from prison in Leipzig. He was set to work reorganising the city's tax office. When the Soviet occupation zone was established he was kicked out of this role, apparently at the instigation of the KPD. He ran a restaurant for a while, but fled to West Berlin in 1949 under threat of arrest for 'an economic crime'.

Eichhorn considered himself a political refugee, but he didn't apply for formal recognition. Instead he married a childhood friend and lived off her earnings for a bit. When they divorced in 1952 he tried to apply for political refugee status and thus gain compensation for being persecuted by the communists. He was rejected. So he moved in with a new partner, whose small textile shop in the Schöneberg district kept him afloat. Gradually he established himself as a player in the black market. At the same time, he was hired for piecemeal work by an American intelligence service. This was a steady earner, bringing in some eighty marks per month. He started to dress well, took a room at a guesthouse called the Astor. But the MGB and Stasi were watching.

Eichhorn had a black-market friend called Stahlberg. Badly wounded in the war, Stahlberg made his living selling glassware and optical goods – cameras, binoculars – on the streets around Zoo station. He also worked for a US intelligence service, with whom he was in pretty deep. Among other things, Stahlberg sold stolen Russian military gear to his American employers – helmets, gas masks, uniforms. He was wanted by the Soviets and the Stasi. However, Stahlberg was known to be wary. Unhelpfully for the communist secret services, he had even been denounced as a spy on Soviet-sponsored radio. It was obvious that he could only be brought into a vulnerable position by a person he trusted.

Stahlberg trusted Eichhorn, the enterprising refugee who had run away from the communists. One spring day in 1955, Eichhorn visited the offices of the Ministry for Inner-German Trade in East Berlin. He was doing a favour for some friends, whose truck had been impounded by border police; Eichhorn believed he had the pull to get it released. He was received in an office, but had barely made it back onto the street after this meeting when he was arrested and taken into custody by plainclothes officers. They accused him of recruiting an East German woman friend for the Americans – which was true – and probably brought up his 'economic crime' of 1949 as well. At a certain point they were joined by a person with whom Eichhorn was already friendly – a mysterious Berlin character called Lindström. The arresting officers then got down to business. A plan was hatched. Eichhorn agreed to participate in it, and was released. He went home to West Berlin.

A few days later, Stahlberg wasn't unduly suspicious when Eichhorn invited him to a promising-looking meeting. Eichhorn told Stahlberg that three representatives of Carl Zeiss in Jena wanted to do large-scale illegal business with a suitable salesman in West Berlin. They were willing to purloin the latest Zeiss models from the laboratories and production lines, the kind of world-beating optical goods that Stahlberg promised his customers around Zoo station. Eichhorn wanted to make introductions, as Stahlberg was perfect for the salesman job. So on the evening of 6 May 1955, they all got together at the Café Rütli on Kantstrasse, in Charlottenburg.

It was a friendly, boisterous, optimistic night. Everyone got along. The beer and schnapps flowed. Stahlberg liked the Zeiss people – a manager, a foreman, and a worker. The manager had his Mercedes 180 saloon parked outside the café. They all got into it – the manager driving, with Eichhorn beside him; Stahlberg on the back seat sandwiched between the foreman and the worker. The new friends made their way from venue to venue, visiting a small restaurant on the corner of Potsdamer Strasse and Bulowstrasse, where they drank and ate meatballs, and a dance hall near Moritzplatz. By now it was the small hours. Eichhorn said he knew a decent night café not far away. So they drove down Luckauer Strasse and crossed the sector border into East Berlin. They ended up on Neanderstrasse, where the manager stopped the Mercedes.

At that point they were blinded by the headlights of an oncoming car. It pulled up and three figures sprang out. In an instant, these three and the Zeiss representatives were trying to grapple Stahlberg, with great violence, into the second car. Even with six to one, it was a nasty struggle. Stahlberg punched, kicked, thrashed around. Eichhorn just sat there in horror. Someone started dealing out blows with a cosh. Someone else fired a gun. Stahlberg was dragged into the second car, which sped away.

In reality, the three Zeiss representatives were Eichhorn's friend Lindström, a dodgy pub landlord from East Berlin called August Tresp, and a young drifter called Bachmann. All three were criminal employees of the Stasi. Lindström had got an acquaintance to rent the Mercedes from a hire firm in West Berlin. The owners weren't pleased when informed by phone that their car had been left on a quiet street with the Mercedes emblem torn off the bonnet and a bullet hole in the front bumper. At the heart of this little group was August Tresp, known in the underworld as 'Big Fritz'. His pub on Strelitzer Strasse had become a magnet for thieves and trick-turners, who had recognised a place where they could drink, scheme, sing. For the Stasi, these unfortunates were ripe for the plucking – people whose lives had already been broken by war, hardship, and the callous commands of survival.

The second car was driven by the most senior Stasi collaborator involved in the incident – a Yugoslavian operator called Jovan Holec. He was one of the Stasi's main recruiters of underworld types. With him in the second car were two fellow East Berliners, one of them a Stasi GM codenamed 'Schubert'. Holec liked to hang out in August Tresp's pub, and at an inn called the Wappenklause, and at the Alt-Düsseldorf restaurant on Wilhelm-Pieckstrasse. He was often accompanied by a clutch of sidekicks – a fellow Yugoslavian called Toni, a blonde German youth called Kalli, and a petty criminal called Willi Eggert, who was able to cause all sorts of confusion simply by being the namesake of a respectable employee at Siemens in West Berlin.

During investigations by the West Berlin police, some details on Holec were provided by his reluctant acquaintances. His former housekeeper said Holec had been a colonel in the Yugoslavian army, and had 'an officer's demeanour'. He employed a chauffeur and owned three cars, including an American model and a new Opel Kapitän with West Berlin number plates, tokens of the security aristocracy that tends to arise in authoritarian states. The housekeeper had been horrified to learn that Holec had bullied her son-in-law into working for 'the SSD'. When the young man had fled to West Berlin to escape Holec, taking his wife and child with him, Holec had badgered the housekeeper into persuading her daughter to return to East Berlin, as a means of luring back the son-in-law. Pretending to carry out this order, the housekeeper had entered West Berlin and never returned.

Another refugee couple, the Münsters, described their brush with Holec. When he had entered their lives they were temporarily living apart, Otto in West Berlin, Martha at her hairdressing salon on Alte Schönhauser Strasse in the east. Otto Münster had met Holec on a chance visit to the Wappenklause inn. On discovering that Münster lived in West Berlin, Holec had plied him with beers. He told Münster he could get him a fake residence card for East Berlin, which would enable Münster to spend more time with his wife, who was in the process of closing down her business prior to emigrating from East Germany. Instead of being paid for this favour, Holec had given Münster a string of espionage tasks, at least one of which was distinctly dangerous – observing meetings of the nationalist veterans' society, the Stahlhelm, at the Pasewalker Hof restaurant. Otto Münster had fudged his way around these missions before the couple had run for their lives.

Jovan Holec, complacent, noticeable and full of drink, clearly was a risk for his employers, the Stasi. He was blown yet further when Bachmann, who had played the part of the young Zeiss worker in Stahlberg's kidnapping, handed himself in to the West Berlin Kripo and confessed. He and Eichhorn were then put on trial along with Willi Barner, a longtime jailbird and grifter who, although not implicated in the kidnapping, had been arrested while performing a similar dirty job on the streets of West Berlin.

In detention Bachmann described his induction into Holec's gang. First he had befriended Lindström and Tresp at the latter's pub. Then he had been introduced to Holec, who made his customary offer of obtaining false papers. This appealed to Bachmann, who was living in East Berlin without authorisation. His first jobs for Holec were innocuous enough. He earned twenty deutschmarks for providing some muscle on a trip to buy a car in the Dreilinden woods, near the Drelitz border checkpoint. On another occasion he was given five deutschmarks to drink in the Cafe Schäfer on Potsdamer Strasse, where he was to take a telephone call for one 'Günter'. Having done so, he relayed to Holec the message he had heard on the phone: 'The car with the CD number plate arrived. Four men got out.' He was then asked to perform this task a second time, making sure to learn 'how many men got into and out of the car'. For this, Holec gave him an impromptu pay rise – twenty deutschmarks.

When it happened, Bachmann wasn't surprised to find himself taking part in a Stasi kidnapping. According to a court report, it was 'completely clear to the defendant that he was carrying out orders for the SSD. He knew this not only from Tresp, who is himself an SSD agent, but also from Holec, and he recognised it from the type of tasks assigned to him'. A few days after the kidnapping, Holec gave Bachmann the keys to Stahlberg's West Berlin apartment and offered him 500 deutschmarks to fetch some papers from Stahlberg's desk, evidence required by the Stasi.

Bachmann thought this job too dangerous. Instead of doing it, on three occasions he drank in a bar near Stahlberg's home, keeping receipts for the drinks to prove he had been there, and giving Holec a different excuse each time: the lights were on in Stahlberg's flat; he had sent up a child to knock, and a woman had answered the door; two ominous-looking cars were parked on the street outside. Meanwhile, Bachmann had learned that Tresp had cheated him on the reward money for Stahlberg's kidnapping, giving him 200 deutschmarks instead of the 400 that Holec had allocated; the first in a string of bad breaks that had led Bachmann to present himself to the West Berlin police.

The Stasi's employment of Willi Barner, Bachmann's fellow defendant at trial, had been equally casual. It was August Tresp who had recruited Barner, explicitly, for 'the SSD'. First he was given a dummy task – travelling to Munich to distribute leaflets, using an interzonal pass in the name of Blaschke and in possession of the telephone number of a Stasi employee, to call in an emergency. Barner admitted that he had simply gone on a jolly in Munich, drinking the 250 deutschmarks expenses and dumping the leaflets.

With a little thought, the Stasi could have anticipated this behaviour. Barner had been imprisoned ten times since the early 1930s – for theft, false representation, aiding and abetting forgery – with sentences ranging from a few months to several years. None of this had put off his recruiter, August Tresp. He next tasked Barner with observing houses, mostly in West Berlin's Zehlendorf and Dahlem districts, where Barner assumed 'American spy organisations' were based. He reported his observations to two Stasi handlers he knew as 'Kreinke' and 'Nückel'. It was on one such reconnaissance that Barner had been arrested, outside the home of a RIAS employee who was being protected by West Berlin detectives. Barner claimed he had only been looking for a local restaurant called Knoke. It was noted that Knoke was a name on the building's plate of apartment numbers.

The investigation and trial saw Hans Eichhorn come apart at the seams. A bedsheet was found knotted into a noose in his cell, but he denied suicidal thoughts; he claimed not to know Bachmann when presented with him; he insisted that the American secret service would vouch for him. It didn't. An American officer called Grund from Public Security said that Eichhorn had been hired by a US agency but never given any work, as they had been warned he was untrustworthy. Eichhorn told how, after Stahlberg was driven away on the night of the kidnapping, he and the 'Zeiss representatives' had repaired to August Tresp's pub. After a while, the man he now knew to be Jovan Holec had turned up. 'His trench coat was splattered with blood,' recalled Eichhorn, all the while claiming ignorance of any kidnapping. He had even gone to Tresp's pub again a few days later, only to be thrown out by the irate owner, who warned him to stay out of East Berlin.

The big problem for Eichhorn was that he was accused of a second kidnapping. This one, of an agent for France, had occurred a month after Stahlberg's. Eichhorn had received instructions – he never admitted from whom – to seek out a couple called the Bergemanns, who had left East Germany and now lived at the Zastrow guesthouse in West Berlin. Herr Bergemann had formerly worked in food distribution for the East German government. Eichhorn was told to introduce himself as a wholesale trader in fruit and vegetables, looking to recruit a new executive for a company called Cerbados from Barcelona.

Having successfully got acquainted, Eichhorn said he could introduce Bergemann to a top Cerbados executive in Germany, a certain 'Herr Stein'. Although Bergemann had been spying for France for some time, money was short and the future uncertain. He agreed to go along with Eichhorn to meet Herr Stein. What followed was a series of typically drunken get-togethers, with Bergemann, Eichhorn and 'Herr Stein' plotting ways to make their fortune.

Bergemann's wife, deeply suspicious of the whole scenario, had shadowed her husband to these appointments. She would wait in cafés near the meeting venue, ready to raise the alarm if her husband didn't join her. Her suspicions were largely confirmed when she was visited by an old acquaintance of her husband, who told her a chilling story. He had recently been detained by Stasi officers in East Berlin, one of whom had commented, 'We'll get Bergemann back here, even if we have to bring him over in a box.'

On the evening of 20 June 1955 Frau Bergemann accompanied her husband to a meeting with 'Stein' at the Zum Kuchenmeister restaurant in Charlottenburg. After food and drink, it was decided to repair to Nikolassee in south-west Berlin where, it was said, the head of Cerbados in Germany lived. The couple joined 'Stein' in his black Mercedes, driven by an unknown youth. On the way, it was decided that Frau Bergemann needn't come along after all. Intending to follow surreptitiously, she asked to be dropped off at a taxi rank on the corner of Wilmersdorfer and Kantstrasse. 'Stein' overrode this suggestion, and instead had her deposited in the middle of nowhere.

That night, Bergemann vanished. A few days later, two Volkspolizei officers called at the home of Frau Bergemann's parents in East Germany. Her father was told that Bergemann had been arrested for his part in a drunken traffic accident. Although she made enquiries of every conceivable authority – including the SPD Ostbüro, with which the Bergemanns were otherwise unconnected – Frau Bergemann received no news until the following January, when a letter from her husband arrived. Written in Brandenburg-Görden prison, it briefly repeated the story of the traffic accident.

The West Berlin authorities rightly recognised this as a kidnapping. In the legal formulation of the time, Eichhorn was convicted of:

> taking a person by cunning to an area outside the scope of the court constitution in force in Berlin [i.e., into the GDR], or causing him to go there, and thereby of being exposed to the danger of being persecuted and of suffering damage to life or limb through violence or arbitrary measures, in contradiction to the principles of the rule of law, or of being deprived of freedom or of having one's assets, professional, or economic position seriously impaired, and at the same time that he intentionally and illegally imprisoned a person or otherwise deprived him of the use of his personal freedom... acting on behalf of the SSD.

He was sentenced to four years in prison. Bachmann got two years for helping to kidnap Stahlberg, with lenience shown for his confession and relative youth.

The Stasi obtained the police and court documents on the Stahlberg and Bergemann investigations. It must have been a shock to see how shoddy their kidnappers' work had been. Holec, in particular, was a problem. Before the 'Zeiss' ruse was devised to kidnap Stahlberg, Holec had even asked a random acquaintance to lure Stahlberg into East Berlin by promising to sell him a glass prism.

The Stasi's reactions are revealed in the paper trail. In the period before he handed himself in to the West Berlin police, Bachmann had been ushered into a reception camp for returnees to the GDR at Fürstenwalde, then pressed into a job he didn't want in Cottbus. Holec was arrested and brought to book for being a long-term employee of the Americans, which was true; he had worked for the US as well as the Stasi. Tresp's pub was raided by the Volkspolizei, with its owner, staff and customers all placed under arrest. Officially, Tresp was accused of a currency violation – serving drinks to known West Berliners without demanding payment in western marks. Although released, he was destitute; in ruinous health, he took up with a sixteen-year-old prostitute. The whole business probably influenced the Stasi's decision to do two things: give Markus Wolf more ownership of such activities, by transferring the Special Duties Group to his portfolio; and create a new, more professional dirty ops outfit, with a seasoned Berlin operator, Hans Wax, at its heart.

Yet just as Eichhorn, Holec and Tresp were being ground under the wheels, the high-ups in Moscow and East Berlin were showing their satisfaction with the Stasi's performance during Aktion Blitz. Its temporary period as the

SfS, a mere secretariat, was brought to an end. In November 1955 the Stasi was returned to the status of a government ministry – the Ministerium für Staatssicherheit – with Ernst Wollweber, now a member of the SED Central Committee, promoted from state secretary to security minister. Erich Mielke was by his side as deputy, again.

Josef Keifel's Special Tasks Group (Gruppe für Sonderaufgaben) became operational during Aktion Blitz. It was built around two units of collaborators, one codenamed Blitz and the other Donner. Both were led by tough characters from Berlin's underworld: Blitz by the GM 'Neuhaus' and Donner by the garage owner and mechanic Hans Wax.

These units spent the remainder of the 1950s carrying out kidnappings, burglaries, the procurement of cars and other desirables – like the Walther pistols now made under licence in France – and even the occasional bomb attack. In 1960, with Kiefel still in charge, the Special Tasks Group was given a veneer of respectability when designated as the Stasi's Department XXI. Its kidnappings of defectors – now termed 'the supervision of dismissed or unreliable staff' – continued.*

Details about Hans Wax's employment by the Stasi began to emerge in the mid-1990s.[2] Until then Wax had remained in the shadows, a secret legend who probably relished his whispered notoriety. Born in the Saarland in 1927, Wax was boorish, muscled and flash. He chain-smoked and cared about his haircut. He was good at making and fixing things. By his mid-twenties he had done time twice, including a three-year stretch for black marketeering.

Once he was free, Wax opened his garage on Kantstrasse in West Berlin. Amid the growing glamour and excess of the western sectors, he and his employees fixed up and resold sports cars, mostly Alfa Romeos. Wax did illegal business on the side, trading in luxury goods such as coffee and stockings. The Stasi encountered him in 1954, when he tried to sell a stolen truck in East Berlin. This transaction brought him to the attention of Paul Nitsch, a thirty-five-year-old butcher and boxing fanatic who worked at a slaughterhouse on Leninallee. Nitsch was well-acquainted with the criminal underworld then swelling in the city. Under the cover name 'Fred Thornau', he talent-spotted for Josef Kiefel's dirty ops squads. When, decades later, a journalist asked him why he had recruited criminals for the East German secret police, Nitsch replied,

---

* The official descriptor for Abteilung XXI was 'Department for special tasks against "hostile" centres working against the MfS' (Abteilung für spezielle Aufgaben gegen "feindliche" Zentralen, die gegen das MfS arbeiten). In 1980 its duties were dispersed around other departments.

'I was convinced of our cause... I thought bandits had to be fought with bandits.'

Nitsch was impressed with Wax, whom he sensed 'had no fear'. Taking the codename 'Donner', the name by which his unit became known, Wax headed a trio of hard-drinking operatives. One was the GM 'Teddy', a young East Berlin greengrocer who was lucky enough to own an Opel car; he had come to Nitsch's attention when selling petrol as a sideline. The other was panel beater Walter Jacobs, alias 'Blitz'.

This three-man unit became what *Der Spiegel* has called 'probably the most successful terror and kidnapping squad that the Stasi ever deployed'. In operations that ranged throughout West Germany – in Munich, Bremen, Hanover – the trio hunted down and snatched wanted persons, including some of the 120 Stasi defectors who were brought back to East Germany.

One of Wax's first triumphs was the kidnapping of a suspected Gehlen agent known as Werner Rieker. In the months before Rieker was seized, a Stasi collaborator called Gerhard Bernatzki, codenamed 'Herbert', had observed him at length. Unaware that Bernatzki worked for the Stasi, Rieker had recruited him as his own sub-agent. Steadily Bernatzki had learned about Rieker's home, his pet Alsatian, his drinking sessions at the Eva bar in Schöneberg – and about the pistol Rieker always carried in his briefcase. There were several failed attempts to kidnap him. On one occasion, Rieker was ushered away from a drinks party by his wife after an acquaintance from East Berlin handed him an unusual-looking liqueur. The Stasi persisted; and one morning in November 1955, Rieker and Bernatzki set out from West Berlin for a reception camp for East German refugees near Kassel in the Federal Republic, where they planned to recruit more anti-communist agents. Once on the autobahn their car was rammed by a Mercedes 220 driven by Hans Wax; the vehicle had been specially outfitted for kidnapping, including with bulletproof tyres. In the ensuing melee at the roadside Rieker drew his pistol and shots were fired, but he was severely beaten before being driven away in the soundproofed boot of Wax's Mercedes. Rieker's wife hadn't been expecting him home for a while, and it was some time before his disappearance was noted.

A few months later an East German court sentenced Rieker to fifteen years. Besides his activities for Gehlen, he had been an agent of the Danish foreign ministry.[3] He served nine years at Bautzen before the Bonn government bought him free. In 1994 Gerhard Bernatzki was given a two-year probationary sentence for his role in the kidnapping. Two years after that, a journalist tracked down GM 'Teddy' in Berlin and asked him about his time as a henchman in Hans Wax's snatch squad. He replied that he had 'never had anything to do with all that'.

*

Not content with kidnapping suspected OG operatives, at one point the Stasi had advanced plans to kidnap Reinhard Gehlen himself. For almost two years, a Stasi employee called Otto Freitag observed Gehlen, whom the Stasi codenamed 'Jäger', at his Bavarian home in Berg am Starnberger See. Freitag rented a house not far from the general's, big enough to accommodate a snatch squad. He bought an 8mm camera with which to film Gehlen's journey to work, doing so from a moving open-topped Volkswagen. The potential kidnapping was a challenge, for Gehlen's Mercedes, when making journeys to and from Pullach, was invariably followed by a clutch of bodyguards in a second car. Nevertheless, Freitag extensively photographed possible abduction sites and escape routes to East Germany. The Stasi archives still contain his images of roadsides, secluded spots, and village houses overlooking the road. No doubt to Freitag's chagrin, the operation was cancelled after Konrad Adenauer's heralded visit to Moscow in September 1955.[4]

50

The Stasi of the *Grossaktionen* Years

By the end of the *Grossaktionen*, the Stasi was starting to embody its leaders' concept of 'the unity of reconnaissance and defence'. Foreign intelligence-gathering and internal security operations were symbiotic means of fighting 'class enemies'. In terms of its internal logic, the Stasi's conflation of political resisters and reformers with hostile Western governments and intelligence services was proving a success. Ernst Wollweber himself had expressed the Stasi's tasks in this respect, telling a meeting of subordinates that 'we must eliminate the impression that a person is only an enemy when he is a genuine agent, when he belongs to an enemy organisation. We must overcome the view that only agents are of concern to us, and not enemies.'[1]

Certain operations of Main Department III, responsible for securing the economy, exemplify the 'reconnaissance and defence' concept. In December 1954 Major General Otto Last, Wollweber's deputy for economic affairs, ordered the creation of a special task force to infiltrate West German industry. This was a response to reports received by Last describing attempts by US agencies to disrupt East Germany's coal supply.[2] To deal with the matter, espionage in the Federal Republic became the GDR's first line of defence. The staff of Department III in district offices set up working groups, each of which was given responsibility for procuring scientific and technical information from a selected West German company.[3]

At the same time, Ernst Wollweber urged HA III to intensify its fight against sabotage inside the GDR. He believed that the next 'fascist putsch' was most likely to originate in the construction sector or supply system. His suggestions included placing a GI next to the minister for food, 'so that hostile elements can't plant anything on him'. HA III stepped up its checks on executives in the economic bureaucracy. More than 500 were vetted, their details embedded in the Stasi's archives. Some HA III officers were so intent on providing information that they 'de-conspired', or blew, their informers in a number of companies and organisations. It transpired, for example, that four of the sixteen heads of department at the State Planning Commission were Stasi collaborators.[4]

Another strand to the 'reconnaissance and defence' of HA III arose when Wollweber tightened the supervision of agriculture, an area in which the Stasi tended to struggle. Wollweber's 'fight against hostile underground activity in the village', announced in September 1954, saw changes at the Machine Tractor Stations, the state-run depots of agricultural equipment. Every station had a political department, of which the deputy head was always an undercover Stasi delegate. Unusually, these deputies now shed their disguises and began to work openly as Stasi employees. Concurrently, Wollweber demanded the recruitment of more informers where they really counted, among such 'hostile elements' as wealthier farmers and agricultural merchants with connections to West Germany. Finally, HA III boosted its coverage of the Leipzig trade fairs. Here it had a dual 'reconnaissance and defence' role – to ensure a trouble-free event, and to spy on the foreign companies taking part. Although Erich Mielke warned against the 'mass soliciting' of collaborators and 'double and triple work [by Stasi departments] with one and the same person', Wollweber wanted GI and GM 'of real quality' to be recruited before and during Leipzig. He stressed the need for collaborators who could help improve East Germany's energy supply, always vulnerable due to its weather-dependent mining of low-grade brown coal.[5]

Wollweber reorganised the Stasi's departments in 1954. He oversaw a steep rise in the number of employees, from 4,000 in 1953 to 10,000 two years later; one source puts the figure at 16,000 employees by early 1956.[6] This was perhaps deemed overkill, for the Stasi went through a recruitment freeze in 1957 and 1958, experiencing a slight drop in the number of its employees for the only time in its history.

There was a similar refining of the informer network. Although there were some 30,000 collaborators in the mid-1950s, the quality of their information was low. To initiate investigations, the Stasi remained reliant on denouncements from members of the public, tip-offs from party officials, and information shared by the KGB. Thus by 1957 the informer network had been rationalised to around 15,000 persons.[7]

Wollweber's tenure saw a slight relaxation in prison conditions and interrogation methods.[8] It was during the *Grossaktionen* that the Stasi acquired its full complement of pretrial detention centres (Untersuchungshaftanstalten). They were to become notorious – two in Berlin (at Hohenschönhausen and on Magdalenenstrasse in Lichtenberg), and one in each of the fifteen regions. Wollweber made some efforts to encourage a culture of probity at these centres. In an internal order of August 1955 he complained that pretrial detainees in Potsdam 'were ill-treated, including one person who then had to be released a short time later due to lack of evidence'. His concern wasn't motivated by humanitarianism – it was that 'such actions are capable of damaging the public image of the state security organs'.[9]

Gradually, violent interrogators began to be censured. The head of Department IX in Potsdam was demoted and transferred, partly for failing to punish a transgressor on his staff. The Stasi office in Weimar expressed disapproval and contrition when one of its employees put an arrestee against a wall at the point of a pistol. The office in Neubrandenburg detained an employee who had threatened an arrestee with burning cigarette ends and by organising a mock execution in an adjacent cell. The employee then spent a year and a half in prison at Bautzen.[10] Of course, arrestees could still expect a rough time in Stasi custody. A service instruction of 1955 decreed that Stasi detainees were to be isolated from society and treated as 'criminals and enemies of peace and progress', whether convicted or not.[11]

Understandably, many developments of the mid-1950s were prompted by the June 1953 uprising. This included the creation of Operational Leaderships (Einsatzleitungen) at central, regional and district levels of the East German state. These were emergency command centres that would spring into action in a crisis or war. As well as the local Stasi chief, their membership included local party secretaries, the leaders of the local police and armed forces, and the chairperson of the district council. The interior minister, Willi Stoph, defined their role as 'suppressing hostile provocations such as strikes, demonstrations, riots and revolts'. In a later directive, the Leaderships were given full responsibility for 'protecting the socialist achievements of the district'; they were to assume power during 'counter-revolutionary actions', and decide on 'measures to smash enemy action and restore order and safety'. To this end, isolation camps were prepared for holding rioters and other political enemies in preventive detention.[12]

In a straight copy of the KGB, the Stasi Kollegium, ostensibly an advisory body for the Stasi chief composed of senior officers, came into being in July 1954. According to its founding order, at its meetings the state secretary (or later, the minister) had to 'hear from every member of the Kollegium', each of whom had 'the right and the obligation to express his opinion openly'.[13] During Ernst Wollweber's tenure this was unlikely; by the time Erich Mielke was chief the idea was a nonsense. The year 1954 also saw the emergence of the Security Commission of the SED Politbüro. Its nine founding members included Walter Ulbricht, Ernst Wollweber, and 'more high-ranking SED members than any other' party body.[14] One of its first acts was to formally forbid the Stasi from operating inside the highest bodies of the SED. This was a reaction to the accusations of intriguing levelled at Wilhelm Zaisser. The ruling meant that any SED member who entered a full-time job in the Central Committee or higher party apparatus had to stop working as a Stasi informer. Exceptions had to be approved by the chair of the Security Commission or, after 1961, by the chair of the National Defence Council which had superceded it. In both cases, this was Walter Ulbricht.

Main Department II profited from its leading role in the *Grossaktionen*. It retained its original four departments, responsible for counter-espionage against the American, British, French and West German intelligence services. They were augmented by new departments that reflected the evolution of East Germany and the Soviet Bloc. East Germans studying in or returning from the USSR were made the responsibility of HA II/6. Large numbers of workers were now being imported from other Soviet Bloc countries, especially for such enterprises as the chemical industry in Halle. Despite their 'socialist' origins, these people were not eastern Germans and thus aroused Stasi suspicions. Therefore, HA II intensified its coverage of such incomers, especially from Poland and Czechoslovakia. Another move saw Karl-Heinz Böde, latterly directing counter-espionage against the US, given command of HA II/7, which tackled the spies of any 'non-socialist' country other than the big four. (Notably, this branch was soon transferred to Markus Wolf's foreign intelligence service as its 'Third Countries' department.)[15]

Main Department II also boosted its efforts against the espionage activities instigated by Western radio stations. This tied in with the creation in 1956 of the 'Coordinating Apparatus', a combined 'radio counter-intelligence' service for the USSR, East Germany, Czechoslovakia, Hungary, Romania, Bulgaria and Albania. Based in Warsaw, this agency shared technical knowledge, equipment, training facilities and joint listening stations, especially on the Czech-East German border.

Stasi departments that had played a lesser role in the *Grossaktionen* continued to toil and learn. Department VII, responsible for the security of the interior ministry and police, was still pretty tiny – just twenty-four employees at headquarters at the end of 1954. Gustav Szinda, veteran of the Spanish Civil War and the Moscow purges, and latterly carrying out counter-espionage duties under Markus Wolf, was transferred to Department VII as its new chief. He scored immediate successes, busting 'a big gang of smugglers' and uncovering agents in the printing works of the Volkspolizei.[16] Thereafter, an 'operational group of unofficial employees' was embedded in the main administration of the Volkspolizei as a 'protective residency' (Abwehr Residentur). Szinda's department was then instructed to secure the personnel offices of the KVP, believed – rightly – to be hotbeds of Western spying. A little later, it acquired responsibility for monitoring refugee camps, returnees and asylum seekers.

In June 1955 Department VII joined with Main Department I, which invigilated the border and standby police, in Aktion Bumerang, an operation to secure East German institutions over the second anniversary of the uprising. (A similar operation, Aktion Bollwerk (Bulwark), had been conducted the previous year.) As discreetly as possible, added protection was given to government offices, the homes and travel routes of SED officials, and to buildings used by the party, Stasi and police.[17] More than 100 informers were mobilised within government ministries and universities, while around sixty units of specially mobilised collaborators performed 'reconnaissance of agent centres and underground organisations' in the West.

The launch of the Stasi's propaganda department, the Abteilung Agitation, was one of the period's innovations. The Stasi already had much experience of public communications. It had, for example, steered the publicity around its fifth anniversary in February 1955, showing celebratory documentaries in cinemas and sending speakers into workplaces. The task of Gustav Borrmann's new department was the 'systematic informing of the GDR population on the activities of the SfS', so that the 'vigilance of all workers [and their] willingness to work for the instruments of state security will be increased'.[18] Its work was coordinated with the SED propaganda department, publisher of the 'Agitator's Notebook'. One aim of this publication, which was updated regularly, was to feed party workers with lines they could use in arguments. It demonstrates the tone expected of Borrmann's copywriters at the Stasi. 'Leaving the GDR is an act of political and moral depravity', thundered the November 1955 edition. Flight to the West was posited as 'recruitment' by the enemy classes and capitalist system, and 'those who let themselves be recruited serve West German reaction and militarism, whether they know it or not'. Contempt was heaped on those seeking material comfort or professional advancement:

> Is it not despicable when for the sake of a few alluring job offers or other false promises about a 'guaranteed future' one leaves the country in which the seed of a new and more beautiful life is sprouting, and is already showing the first fruits, for a place that favours a new war and destruction... Does not leaving the land of progress for the morass of a historically outmoded social order demonstrate political backwardness and blindness?[19]

Similar outrage is discernible in early Agitation Department publications like *In the Spy Jungles of West Berlin*.

The department's deputy chief, Major Gerhard Kehl, became something of a familiar spokesperson. He was master-of-ceremonies at such Stasi-hosted exhibitions as 'Protection and Security for Peaceful Reconstruction', which attracted more than 40,000 visitors in a two-week run at Leipzig. In a glowing review of its own event, the Stasi purred that there had been 'universal praise' for the 'comprehensibility and presentation of evidence on the criminal activity of our enemies'.[20]

There was a problem with the Stasi's new responsibilities around public interaction: it continued to suffer from a poorly educated workforce. A report by Department IX (investigations) complained that around fifty percent of its staff, including captains and senior lieutenants, were ignorant of Walter Ulbricht's policies, of which they were 'unable to explain the nature'. They lacked initiative in their work. For example, people arrested for demonstrating on 17 June 1953 were 'only formally questioned about what they themselves had done'. Investigators didn't conduct 'any intensive inquiry into the organisers and enemy connections', which was precisely what they had been instructed to do.[21]

There were various attempts to remedy the situation. In 1955 the Stasi school at Potsdam-Eiche was upgraded to the status of Hochschule, a technical or vocational college. The observation branch, Department VIII, set up its own training facility, with courses catering for fifty employees at a time. It was intended to become a 'central educational institution' of the Stasi, 'with international standards'. Undertrained staff and a shortage of teachers saw it closed after two courses, although it was later resurrected.[22]

The struggles at the Stasi reflected the ongoing struggles in East German society. The first six months of 1955 saw acute shortages. There was little sugar or fat to be had; bread was of poor quality. The Stasi's mood reporters, working in Wollweber's vaunted Information Service, told of hundreds of people queuing for butter and fistfights in shops.[23] On the political front, the demand for free all-German elections was stoked by the Geneva conference of July 1955 and its short-lived hopes of achieving German reunification. The SED responded with a public message that contained a kind of backhanded honesty: free elections throughout Germany were undesirable because they would play into the hands of rich farmers and the bourgeoisie. Ernst Wollweber made the point more bluntly at a Stasi conference: 'We are democrats, but not idiots. We support free elections, if at these elections the working class and its leading party play the decisive role. We support free elections, where those who do not deserve freedom do not have freedom.'[24] Clearly it was proving difficult to stoke class war among East Germany's citizens.

Wollweber made another statement in the wake of Geneva – that 'it is self-evident that there is no solution [to the German question] which would see the German Democratic Republic in any way integrated into the Federal

Republic.' Maybe it was such pronouncements by SED executives, maybe it was the *Grossaktionen*, but a growing resignation among East Germans becomes apparent at around this time. Although the public could tell that free elections were unlikely, arrests now seemed to be less random and there were occasional releases of prisoners, which placated people somewhat. Regrettably the Soviets continued to dominate the picture, and couldn't be argued with, but neither were the Western powers so impressive; they seemed incapable of agreeing on how to reunite Germany. After years of shock and confusion caused by the division of their country, some East Germans now tried to acclimatise to the split, instead of expecting it to be mended.

Throughout the *Grossaktionen*, the Stasi honed its operational methods. Securing evidence was one of the most important factors in its work. The Stasi wanted to prove, to itself and to its SED and Soviet taskers, that it was tackling East Germany's spy infestation. It needed evidence for propaganda too. In many cases, it wasn't overly challenging for Main Department IX to find the evidence it longed for.

In these earlier years of divided Germany, Western intelligence services preferred their spies to meet handlers or couriers in person. Personal meetings meant that more information could be passed, with more accuracy. In return the handler could offer advice and encouragement, and give clearer instructions. In time, however, the majority of significant Western spies in East Germany received instructions by radio and sent their information with secret writing in letters. (A few of the more important spies for the US and France were an exception; they were given two-way radios and tape recorders that allowed them to transmit secret messages at high speed.) Usually, spies in the GDR would listen out for their call number and take down and decode their instructions. They were provided with converters that could be plugged into radio sets to receive shortwave transmissions from the West. Those who sent back letters and paperwork tended to make use of a complicated relay system of couriers, as with the Organisation Gehlen. Alternatively, letters were simply posted to the Federal Republic or third countries such as Denmark and Greece, always with innocuous-looking cover addresses.

Every one of these practices generated evidence. Spies working directly for the US, Britain, France and West Germany routinely were provided with radios, codebooks, invisible inks and other secret writing equipment. HA IX found that searches of homes, buildings and public spaces often revealed stashes of this gear, or clear signs of a dead drop; incontrovertible evidence that it was onto a spy.[25] KgU agents had to make carbon copies of all their reports for the US Counter Intelligence Corps, which could be something of a giveaway.[26] From 1953 to 1961, at least 200 spies were discovered as a result of their radio transmissions to the West. This was despite the fact that the BND, successor to the Organisation Gehlen, had got its agents' transmission times down to forty-five seconds using 'quartz and a cranking device attached to a mini-transmitter small enough to fit into a cigarette packet'.[27]

The upshot of all this was that the Stasi tended not to manufacture evidence. It didn't need to. Studies by Paul Maddrell suggest that the practice of making a suspicion 'come true' – that is, investigating relentlessly until something, anything, could be pinned on a suspect – was more common in the 1970s and 1980s, when the Stasi was more focused on political opposition among ordinary citizens.

It was difficult for the Stasi to present its informers or their testimonies in court. So it found ways to make arrests, and bag proof, without implicating its collaborators. The staged break-in was a favourite method. A Stasi operative would burgle a property known to contain compromising materials or evidence; another operative would happen to witness the crime and call the police; the police would arrive at the scene and 'discover' the evidence while dealing with the burglary.[28] To clear the way for a surreptitious house search, residents could be removed from the scene by a bogus gas leak, or a compulsory medical appointment for the whole community, or an unexploded bomb scare.[29] Searches took in furniture, vacuum cleaners, musical instruments, door and window frames, panelling, objets d'arts, barns, dung heaps, animal feed, pipes, drains.[30] The searchers' job was made easier by Western organisations' use of ordinary East German citizens, who tended to pick obvious places to hide things. Few knew that an indistinguishable spot on a riverbank, or an unmarked spot in a large field, were better places to conceal compromising items than in furniture or other objects.

Once a suspect was incarcerated, the usual purpose of a Stasi interrogation was to prove guilt, ideally by deploying strong evidence and obtaining a confession.[31] Every interrogee had to sign the record of an interrogation, the Erlebnisbericht. In a land where state security wanted ultimately to know everything about everyone, any interrogation was worthwhile. Even if the accused wasn't proven guilty as charged, all manner of valuable or compromising information might be elicited. Suspects could be charged with something else instead, or implicate others – it was all good for a department's statistics.

Unsurprisingly, Stasi jails were harsh. Prisoners were disorientated from the moment of their arrest. Even when using words that looked polite on paper, the Stasi's arresting officers were hard-faced and hard-voiced: strong, fast, and invasive. A person of reasonable strength and temper was likely to become frightened and compliant in a heartbeat. Well into the 1960s, it was common practice to keep suspects in the dark as to why they were under arrest and where they were being taken.[32] They might be told they were needed to 'clear up something'. By any suitable means, they were prevented from seeing the route they were travelling.

The spouses and children of prisoners who had attempted to flee East Germany were often arrested too, with all family members then incarcerated separately. Parents could be threatened with the institutionalising of their children. Although the use of outright violence declined during the 1950s, incarceration was still distressing enough to cause lifelong problems with physical and mental health in survivors. And all released prisoners had to sign a pledge of silence (Schweigeverpflichtung), agreeing not to talk 'to anyone about the matters that have come to my knowledge during my imprisonment'. Breaches were punishable under section 353c of the code of criminal procedure.

Once prisoners were in custody, the guards of Department XIV kept them isolated whenever possible, restricting any access to people or news.[33] The Stasi's pretrial detention centres were dark and dirty places, their corridors dotted with barred or opaque windows. Prisoners were stripped naked and searched, sometimes several times over. They were given a number, and thereafter not referred to by their names. Lying down in cells was prohibited in daytime, and standing promptly to attention was mandatory when officials entered. Regularly, silent guards would study the occupants of cells through peepholes in the doors, and it was common for lights to be flashed on and off at night, causing further discomfort and confusion.[34]

While it became unusual for prisoners to be beaten, interrogees were still subject to intimidation and forms of torture – sleep deprivation, threats. To prompt confessions, they might be deceived with bogus evidence or forged letters from loved ones.[35] They might be shown the faked confession of a co-conspirator. They might be duped into opening up to a friendly doctor or nurse. As in police forces the world over, one technique was for an interrogator to reconstruct the alleged offence but to exaggerate the prisoner's role in it, in order to prompt the truth; or to omit certain details when reconstructing the offence, then ask the prisoner to describe it. If the prisoner included an unmentioned detail about the incident, there was evidence.

It became Stasi practice to record prisoners' conversations with lawyers, who were usually given scanty documentation to work with.[36] But it wasn't until the 1970s that cells were routinely bugged and filmed. Before this, cell informers were used. It was a simple matter to recruit prisoners as informers by offering better treatment or early release, or by suggesting it was a way to atone for their crimes.

Manuals issued by Department IX defined the role of cell informers as 'the complete unmasking of imprisoned persons', revealing 'other persons active in the enemy camp' and acquiring information on 'planned and implemented crimes'. Informers could help in the 'examination of the statements and political attitudes of imprisoned persons' and their 'reaction to interrogations'; and in the 'control of imprisoned persons against whom public trials are to be carried out'. They could also check the reliability of other potential Stasi recruits.[37]

A code of practice reminded Department IX staff that 'under no circumstances' were the words of cell informers to be used in interrogations, unless they had been 'checked for their correctness by statements from other suspects or witnesses, by expert opinions, or when legitimised by operational work'.[38] When recruiting cell informers, on paper it wasn't permitted to use 'promises regarding the length of punishment or early release from prison', but this regulation was ignored. Secretly but officially, informers were to be offered perks: extra meals, permission to smoke or read, additional free time, more visits, sometimes money.

Walter Linse, kidnapped in 1952 and executed the following year, was a prominent victim of cell informers. He trusted his cellmates. He told one that he intended to delay the disclosure of names for as long as possible and to muddy the investigation with disinformation. The cellmate put this and other revelations into twenty-five reports he made to the Stasi. Linse's next cellmate was tasked by the Stasi with wearing down Linse's hopes of a prisoner exchange with West Germany. This informer reported that Linse was indeed becoming exhausted, partly through 'constant nightly interrogations' but also 'due to my influence'. Such tasks were not uncommon for cell informers, who might also put pressure on arrestees by feigning mental illness or behaving violently.

Professional spies were trained to cope with capture and interrogation. They would prepare in advance a sequence of information, ranging from the most innocuous to the most precious, to be revealed incrementally under interrogation. To counter this, interrogators needed to disrupt the planned sequence.[39] The interrogators' real interest would be hidden in a welter of unrelated, banal questions. Interrogees would be thrown off their stride with pedantic demands to clarify unimportant details – addresses, dates, spellings.

The Stasi's common practice of isolating prisoners for weeks or months meant that interrogators were prisoners' only contact with the world, the only source of news on their spouses or children. This was a powerful and persuasive position. Interrogators could then choose, at turns, to be distant, threatening, supportive or helpful. They might sympathise with the prisoner and muse on their own moral shortcomings. They might tell suspects in confidence that their partners were sleeping with someone else. Flattering interrogees could get results. So could insulting them by voicing condescending views of their work, or implying that they or their intelligence service were amateurish or inconsequential.[40]

The Stasi learned old techniques from the Cheka and its successors: detain suspects for an unspecified length of time, impose inactivity upon them, be vague about the accusations they face. Often, Stasi investigators had the advantage of the exhaustive inquiries already made about a person's life and activities. Nevertheless, in the first interrogations, suspects might be told to guess, and comment upon, the reason for their arrest. They were told that this would save everyone's time. This approach was especially likely when evidence was lacking. As they roamed around trying to answer, suspects could incriminate themselves or bring up the names of other persons of interest.[41]

There is no doubt that Departments IX and XIV employed plenty of thugs, but even their officers realised that, in such a hostile environment, a prisoner was likely to be disarmed by an interrogator who was friendly, reasonable and eloquent. An unexpected meeting with an educated and affable person could lower all defences (especially after a string of beatings). One former prisoner explained that he was 'thrown' when, to his surprise, he was interviewed by a Stasi major who was 'not in a bad mood but polite and obliging... His manner was conciliatory and unexpectedly displayed the characteristics of a normal human being'.[42] Markus Wolf wrote that the purpose of an interrogation was to extract useful information, not inflict pain and misery. 'Our techniques,' he claimed, 'depended on isolation and warnings, not gross physical punishment or sheer fright.' On one occasion, Wolf had:

> decided that our best tactic [with an uncooperative detainee] was to use a personal touch in dealing with him. We managed to secure from his Algerian wife their wedding photo album and to arrange for some of his relatives to send letters. This gesture softened [him] and prompted him to start talking more freely.[43]

Interrogation is considered an art, and seasoned interrogators are loath to admit defeat, even when confronted with stony-faced silence. The British crime writer and MI5 officer John Bingham, who spent much of the Second World War interrogating suspected spies, claimed that any person is breakable provided the interrogator ascertains what that person most wants, or most fears, in life – anyone can be opened up with the use of one or both of those pieces of information. Failing that, there was always the method described by Mark Lynton, a German-born British intelligence officer who interrogated suspected war criminals in defeated Germany. The Stasi was known to adopt this method: 'continuous interrogation', whereby 'a team of three or four interrogators' hammer at a suspect 'around the clock' in 'six or eight hour' shifts, while the interrogee 'gets no sleep'; an approach likely to 'break anyone within forty-eight hours'.[44]

Away from the frontlines of interrogation were the Stasi's departments for intercepting communications. Western intelligence services continued to favour letters as a means of communication because they were cheap, anonymous, and stood a chance of getting through. Letters and postcards could be used to give instructions, relay information, arrange a meeting, impart a warning, or confirm that all was well.[45]

Although agents used tell-tale signs to prove their identity and show they weren't under enemy control – a hair in the envelope, a missing comma in text – the Stasi quickly became skilled at recognising these methods and spotting the traffic between individuals. The Organisation Gehlen and BND proved poor users of cover text. They tended to employ stock phrases with discernible meanings, and didn't take the trouble to draft natural, believable padding around messages.[46] Cover addresses were concentrated in particular locations and remained in use for too long, sometimes even when the Stasi had arrested one of the recipients. Envelopes that looked too clean and orderly gave the game away; the exact postage, an unblemished appearance, a single sheet of paper inside. Another clue was when addressees' names were written vaguely or in less noticeable print.

It was the job of Department M (post control) to do something about this clandestine correspondence. Political censorship was as important for the department as counter-espionage and, of course, the two fields were conflated. The Stasi's authority to monitor post and carry out wiretapping was established in the secret statute of late 1953. From that point on, Department M was subordinated to Martin Weikert, who tended to oversee task-specific service units: Main Department S (technical security), and Departments VIII (observations and arrests), XI (codes and ciphers), and XII (card files, statistics and archive).

The Stasi's checkers of post were organised into a five-step work process.[47] There was sorting, which was sub-divided into broad, filtered and task-specific sections; technical processing; reading; recording/writing; and finally, the staff 'on the lamp' ('an der Lampe'). The sorters of the 'broad' section forwarded 'all suspicious shipments' – letters or packages – to the groups for filtered and task-specific items. They would then classify items according to districts, towns and streets, and then according to persons or organisations under postal control. Sorters were forbidden to open any envelope or package; that was not their job. Department M's headquarters staff were notified immediately of any items suspected of having an espionage or security connection.

Items then were opened by the 'technical processing' personnel, using special apparatus and steam. Of course, this was supposed to be undetectable, as was the replacing of any adhesive materials – it was mandatory for every item up to 1,000 grams to re-enter the postal system and be delivered. Once opened, items were given to the readers, who had to empty envelopes over a white-topped table, give any money or valuables to superiors, and ascertain if letters had any suspect content. Every day they reported the number of letters checked and any relevant pieces of text. Their honesty was tested regularly with dummy letters containing money or suspect contents.

Any indications of espionage or sabotage, such as arranging a conspiratorial meeting, had to be copied, exactly, by the 'recording/writing' staff, and forwarded immediately to the relevant Stasi department. The close examination of intelligence and security material was performed by the staff 'on the lamp'. In a dark room, beneath a quartz lamp, each piece of correspondence was scrutinised. If further technical examination was required, the item was forwarded to Department K, the forerunner of the Stasi's scientific branch, OTS.

This attempt at systematic proficiency was undermined by a shortage of staff and a rule of three minutes for each initial check of an item. The Stasi recognised that Department M's personnel were unmotivated and unsure of what they were seeking. Its headquarters staff fluctuated from around 100 to 150 employees, most of them women, which was unusual. They were paid less than their male colleagues and, in terms of the Stasi's culture and *esprit de corps*, disparaged.

This was unfortunate. The Information Service created by Ernst Wollweber considered postal monitoring a vital means of assessing the population's mood. In theory, Department M could play a key role in unmasking enemy agents, and by the mid-1950s it was expected to perform a foreign intelligence function too. It created a giant index, the Auslandskartei, of the correspondence between East Germans and Western citizens and organisations. On one occasion, when major political unrest had broken out among medical students in Greifswald, the department launched a campaign to collect information from the letters and telegrams sent to every East German university. When the East German army, the NVA, was created, the department systematically gathered information on the topic. It was tasked with capturing the mood among soldiers and their families, determining foreign reactions, and indicating the sources of 'hate material' that might sap NVA morale. In a campaign around *Republikflucht* in 1960-61, the department tried to gain information about refugee organisations, the porous Berlin borders, and other escape routes from the GDR.

The department's work improved when it was moved to a Stasi complex on Freienwalder Strasse. This site housed the HQ of Main Department IX, a pretrial detention centre run by Department XIV, and the Stasi's increasingly important scientific and technical units. The location allowed for more space and more secrecy. At around the same time, Ernst Wollweber installed Colonel Willi Schläwicke as the new chief of Department M. Schläwicke had trained as an accountant before being drafted into the Wehrmacht late in the war. In 1945 he was commissioned into the Berlin detective police, the Kripo. Later he was the first head of the Stasi's finance department. He then performed a run of shadowy roles where conspiracy was of the essence: head of the Stasi's 'wanted persons' unit, Department X (which was dissolved in 1954); head of Department M until 1957; then undercover Stasi delegate in the passport office of the Ministry of the Interior.

Markus Wolf's foreign intelligence service, which founded its own section for processing mail, became a major client of Department M. Once the Berlin Wall existed, the department achieved its mature efficiency and ubiquity. Special courses for its staff were set up at the Stasi school in Potsdam-Eiche. Reflecting fears about Western intelligence services making greater use of post because of the Wall, its training materials focused on counter-espionage. Lieutenant Colonel Walter Mehrbach, who had a proven track record of postal spy-catching, became its deputy head. The department concentrated on speeding up its work, so that enemy spies weren't alerted by delays in delivery. There was closer collaboration with the customs service. Most impressively, its staff were blended into East German society. Their Stasi role was hidden; they were employed by the postal service, sharing its uniform, salary and benefits, and had no contact with other Stasi employees apart from the occasional SED invigilator.

In the *Grossaktionen* years, the job of tapping telephones was simplified by the fact that most East Germans didn't have one. Instead, people used phones at work, communal phones in buildings, or street phone boxes. Everyone knew that calls on the latter weren't private and might be monitored, if only randomly. Until 1955 this job was performed by Main Department S/I, 'observation and interception technology'. It consisted of Major Adolf Viehmann and some twenty employees trained to install the wiretaps.[48] Stasi personnel, sometimes seconded from district offices, would listen to calls in twenty-four-hour shifts, transcribing every word. On paper, every phone tap had to be ordered by Wollweber or Mielke, and could run from twenty to thirty days. In practice, district chiefs and their deputies, and local heads of Departments II, V and IX, commissioned much of the tapping, and ran it for as long they liked.

When Main Department S was dissolved in 1955, the wiretapping branch became Department O. Its headquarters' staff trebled to sixty-five employees. One of its first major acts was the 'Cable Disconnection Operation' (Kabeltrennaktion), instituted in 1956 and maintained for more than a decade. It helped to ensure that telephone traffic was routed mostly though Berlin. As well as locating and, if necessary, cutting all cables that crossed the German borders or ran near them, the operation also sought to identify disused ducts that might be used for border-crossing.

American agencies in West Germany had long since realised that the overhead phone lines used by senior personnel of the MGB and Soviet authorities were a hard target. New voice-scrambling technology was in place, and there were frequent patrols along the routes taken by telephone poles. Underground lines were more vulnerable.[49] Gradually, the Stasi found, checked, and catalogued subterranean cables throughout East Germany. There were surprises. For example, two underground cables were discovered running from the Alexandershall potash mine in Thuringia to Wintershall in West Germany. They had been laid before the war by a mining company. The Stasi rendered them harmless.

Again, Department O was chronically understaffed. It took hours to listen to recordings and pick out any 'valuable political-operational information'.* The department was shaken when Major Viehmann was demoted for having an affair with a junior colleague – he spent the remainder of his Stasi career as head of the fire investigation committee. In 1960 it became Department 26, the Stasi's mature wiretapping service, which was to achieve an altogether more complete and efficient overage.

The Stasi's radio interception service, Department F (for Funkabwehr, radio defence), also emerged from Main Department S in 1955. At the end of the following year, the Soviet radio specialists who thus far had performed radio interception duties in the GDR returned home. It fell to the all-German staff of Department F, operating on behalf of East Germany and the wider Soviet Bloc, to search for spy transmissions and illegal stations, control the transmissions of captured spies, analyse the methods of the Western services, and invigilate the broadcasts of overt and covert senders in East Germany.

At this point radio counter-intelligence began in earnest, and the department worked closely with the spy-catchers of Main Department II. It had a listening centre at Hessenwinkel near Berlin, where twenty listening posts were staffed

---

* 'Wertvolle politisch-operative Informationen'.

in shifts by eighty operators. Another listening centre at Hohen Luckow outside Rostock was camouflaged as an army intelligence site. Four direction-finding facilities, each with a manager, four radio direction finders, a technician and a driver, were located at Bautzen, Gotha, Leipzig and Magdeburg. The fifty-odd employees of its search department (Fahndung, or 'manhunt') were equipped with direction finders to be carried in cars and suitcases, and on belts. In 1957 the department began to construct its nerve centre at Gosen, where all of its units came to be housed; to East Germans, a site of impenetrable mystery.

51

Investigations, Observations, Arrests

In March 1956, deputy security minister Martin Weikert authorised a set of instructions for conducting undercover investigations in the field. In the same period, the old Red Army partisan Joseph Gutsche, in his capacity as head of internal information, and drawing on all his experience as president of Saxony's detectives after the war, distributed a couple of manuals for the staff of Department VIII. Taken together, these three documents show how Stasi personnel were expected to investigate, observe, and arrest suspects.

These tasks were underpinned by two practices familiar to all security services, foundation stones of state security. One was the use of official-looking cover – that is, pretending to be an employee of a ministry, agency or organisation other than the Stasi. The second was the use of informers: grasses. It is notable that Weikert and Gutsche's guides don't often go into the nitty-gritty of observing or investigating; such arcane details were still learned on the job and not written down. The documents are general and offer more 'don'ts' than 'do's'. But the 'don'ts' are illuminating, because they reveal the mistakes being made on the job by the Stasi's personnel, most of them young and drawn straight from manual trades or elementary schooling.

Investigation was defined as the 'gathering of materials about specific persons or sites, by the use of conspiratorial documents, legends pertaining to these documents [i.e., false identities for the investigators], by secret informers or by means of other sources'.[1] The Stasi usually sought 'biographical information' on a targeted person, and details of 'professional activity, political activity, political attitude'; and wanted to know the person's 'place of residence, place of work, social background, social situation', along with 'implicating and compromising material' and 'the circle and character of [their personal] connections'. As well as responding to the modus operandi of Western intelligence services, whose spies often relied on some form of family support, this approach meant the Stasi gained a broader view of the surrounding population with every investigation.

Stasi investigators were political fighters. The preamble to these documents stressed that employees were to be 'imbued with love' for 'the working class and its party, and for the unwavering defence of the workers' and peasants' government'.[2] They were to have 'constant and unbreakable trust in the great Soviet people' and their 'glorious and invincible party', to 'systematically study the works of Marx, Engels, Lenin and Stalin', and 'understand the domestic and foreign policies of the GDR government' in order to 'be an active fighter for the realisation of the idea of Marxism-Leninism'.

They also had to meet high personal standards, for 'the investigative worker must be optimistic, fresh and full of life' and 'always appear disciplined in the office, at work, as well as in his free time'. A blend of working-class hero and knight of old, they should 'always be friendly and accommodating to the collective' and 'help the weaker', but 'not allow a pally relationship' with fellow citizens. They 'must be distinguished by modesty, vigilance and honesty' and 'not allow any contradictions between word and deed'. Any employee who made mistakes 'must openly admit to them so that the mistakes are eliminated'.

An investigator – who would usually be an employee of Department VIII or IX but might, in theory, work for any branch of the Stasi – had to live a semi-permanent double life. Each was 'responsible for ensuring that his [or her] affiliation with the MfS does not become known to the public. For this reason, he is camouflaged in public life by an invented employment relationship, receives corresponding conspiratorial documents, and has to adapt his behaviour to the cover'. Armed with their 'conspiratorial documents', investigators were to register 'with the police in their area of residence' using 'identity papers for various public administrations and institutions or organisations'. Suggested as cover were 'insurance concerns, state administrations, city or district council agencies – housing, social affairs, health care – or papers for social security, journalists, building inspectors'. Every legend was to be chosen 'in such a way that it corresponds to the assignment, the place of implementation' and 'personal skills and knowledge'. Like all the best spies and agents, investigators were to make a decent fist of their cover occupation. This meant knowing not just the 'opportunities' and 'rights' afforded by their cover jobs but their 'obligations' when performing them; as well as knowing the addresses, building layouts, telephone numbers and senior staff of their pretended places of work.

Confident that they could pass as the person they claimed to be, investigators were to 'thoroughly study the district assigned' and set up 'an agency' – a network of 'secret informers and conspiratorial apartments'. The latter had to be sought and rented 'conspiratorially', be situated on a ground floor, have at least two exits preferably on different streets, be in an area where 'the residents of the house in question or the neighbouring houses will not notice', and be presented and furnished according to their cover (e.g., massage equipment in a pretend massage parlour). If used by a team of investigators, premises could 'only be exited or entered by one or two employees at a time'; furthermore, Stasi colleagues were not allowed to 'take pictures of each other or to visit public events, pubs, or sports facilities in groups, or go on group excursions'.

It was prohibited to talk about any secret matter over the telephone, or to possess written notes about it – the investigator must 'only make notes that correspond to his legend'. When gathering information, investigators were to 'speak politely and correctly [in order] to gain the source's trust'. As well as talking to people who may have lived or worked with the targeted person, investigators were encouraged, under the guise of their cover roles, to recruit sources – not necessarily signed up as a GI or GM – who could be called on for help whenever needed. It was useful to have sources whose job gave them access to information on members of the public – 'union files', 'wage and salary records, personnel files, files of employment concerns, the land registry office' – provided that the investigator check to 'determine whether [the source has] any connection with the person to be investigated'. Investigators also had to find out if there were any 'compromising material' on a potential informer, or if they were known to be 'talkative'.

It was made clear that investigators should recruit such casual informers 'from circles of progressively minded citizens – members of the SED, patriots… honest people who are connected to the population'. They might be 'cashiers or organisation managers, street wardens, helpers and chairmen of social and housing commissions'; or 'pensioners, housewives, chairmen of allotment gardens'; or employees of state concerns such as the 'city or district council, chamber of commerce, light and gas company, post or newspaper deliverers'. Especially useful were informers who, 'because of their professional or social position, can issue orders to their subordinate colleagues without the MfS appearing to give the order'. This meant the likes of 'department heads of local industry, the tax administration [or] the Democratic Women's League'.

Although it isn't mentioned in these documents, problems arose from the Stasi's recruitment of apparently loyal state servants. For a start, much of the organised opposition to the SED, including spying, took place among state employees – such a job was no guarantee of loyalty. Another, bigger, problem, which manifested itself from the 1960s onwards, was that the Stasi found itself unable to get information on the SED's political opponents. Its informers, drawn from this 'loyal' section of the population, were precisely the type of people whom dissidents avoided.

This issue was less present in the 1950s, when such helpers could 'be used to carry out investigations in the residential area and at the workplace or to obtain recorded information', and if 'used in the right place make the investigator's work easier by relieving the difficulties of creating the right legend'. However, these enquirers were to be given oblique tasks and unspecific briefs; never was the investigator to 'reveal the person who is directly of interest to us'.

It was not permitted to report unchecked information; all information had 'to be verified from talking to other sources'. In larger workplaces it was possible under one's legend to consult managers for information and records, and to select sources around the targeted person. For this the instructions suggested active SED members, 'progressive functionaries of the FDGB', employees of cadre and personnel departments, or 'executives such as directors, colliery managers, etc.' To camouflage interest in a worksite, an investigator had to 'visit several similar establishments in addition to the actual establishment to be investigated, with the same legend'.

Smaller workplaces were to be handled with care: 'In factories, workshops, offices and other administrations with a small number of employees, direct investigation is not recommended if no source is available.' Similar difficulties arose with investigations in the countryside: 'In the villages and farms, the people who live there are usually more closely connected to each other, which can be an advantage but also a disadvantage for conducting investigations.' Investigators were to work with 'conspiratorial documents from administrations and concerns that maintain contact with the villages'. Suitable informers might be 'employees of the machine tractor stations, postal workers, officials of social organisations, foresters, veterinarians, livestock inspectors, municipal clerks' or, in 'special cases', local police officers.

Despite its complexities, Stasi investigators could certainly enjoy their work. Whenever a new lead is described in a report, the pages emit a keen sense of blood-scenting. 'Through testimonies from a prison inmate,' reads one report from Blitz, 'we learned that [the detainee] has set up a dead letter box in Leipzig [on] Geschwister-Scholl-Strasse.' This box was housed 'in a display case of the street community or the street peace committee'; to its right was 'a chalked sign', below it 'two circles, each with a cross'. Main Department V in Berlin told its Leipzig investigators to 'photograph this display case' and to 'carry out the following investigations: 1) How long has this box been there? 2) Who is responsible for the contents of the display case? 3) What is known about this person?' The answers and photographs were to be sent to 'Hauptabteilung V/3/1 immediately'.

The manual for investigators ends with a section on the need for clarity, objectiveness and accuracy in written reports. They were to include the name and address of all sources and 'the persons from whom the source [received] information'. All such persons were to be 'registered on the special index to enable further use'. Here compartmentalisation came into play, for details of these informers were not to be shared outside of the investigative team; when reporting to whichever Stasi department had commissioned the investigation, 'statements about the sources are categorically forbidden'. If that department wanted to interrogate the sources, special permission was needed from the head of the investigative team, to avoid blowing 'the investigative method and the investigator'. The document ended with a warning: investigators' work would be checked periodically by the control inspectorate to 'determine how the behaviour of the investigator went down in the residential location, whether he used the right legend, the right identity papers and the right conversation'.

Much of the Stasi's advice for investigations was standard fare for all police detectives and private investigators. The same is true of the instructions for Department VIII on conducting observations. The motivation was different, however: for the Stasi, observation was described as 'the most active instrument in the fight to uncover and destroy agencies of the hostile powers, fascist underground organisations and other hostile elements that were and are created in the GDR on behalf of the Adenauer clique'.

The ideal observer was said to be mentally and physically gifted. Of a technical turn of mind, observers were to 'study the nature of models of secret camera, the processes of laboratory work, and the methods of secret photography'; a driver was 'to have complete command of the technology and driving of his work car, to know the individual technical parts of the car and to keep them in operational condition at all times'. Because of the 'great physical endurance' and 'patience and perseverance' required, an observer was 'to systematically work on his [or her] physical fitness'. And they were encouraged to take their work home with them: 'If an observer discovers a suspect person in his free time, he is obliged to monitor them, determine their personal details, address and connections, study their behaviour and immediately report these observations to superiors.'

As in the previous manual, employees of Department VIII were, in 'their area of residence', to be 'disguised as employees of other administrations or institutions'. They were to have expert local knowledge, 'well informed about the location of the train stations and their surroundings, as well as about the timetables of S-Bahn, U-Bahn and long-distance trains, and tram and bus lines'; and be 'well acquainted with the location and surroundings of the airfields and the inland and sea ports, the individual airlines and their timetables'. Employees in Berlin needed 'a good knowledge of the route of the sector borders and a good knowledge of the S-Bahn and U-Bahn lines that go into the West Berlin sectors and their final stations within the democratic sector', and to know 'very well about the entry and exit roads as well as about the individual checkpoints'.

All observers were to know the location of local 'businesses, factories, companies, hotels, restaurants, theatres, cinemas, department stores, administrations, police stations'. They were to study the 'profiles of the streets, the density of pedestrian and motor traffic'; and 'know the national flags of their country and those of other countries, as well as the uniforms, rank insignia and colours of the individual units of the KVP, the Volkspolizei and all other uniformed administrations – such as railway workers, tram workers, miners, customs officials'.

Units of Department VIII were divided into 'brigades' of four to six observers under a 'brigadier', who would instruct subordinates in all areas of their craft. This included the visual signals 'of mutual understanding', unnoticeable to bystanders, to be used on the job. Observations were planned meticulously and usually involved setting up covert observation posts. These were to 'correspond to local conditions', give the 'opportunity to properly observe the object [i.e., the targeted person] as soon as they leave their home or place of work', but not be visible 'from the windows of the object's home'. Employees could occupy such posts after being 'given covert identification papers, an appropriate sum of money and the means of personal disguise'. Most were armed, although automatic pistols and revolvers were to be 'used in such a way that the object or attacker has no chance of escaping or attacking, but is not killed' – shoot to wound, basically.

Observers were 'obliged to behave at the observation post in the same way as the people around them' and 'not draw the attention of these people through their behaviour or clothing'. If observers were disguised as a delivery service, they were to deliver things. If an observation post was a hut for municipal gardeners, the observers were to garden, all the while remaining alert to signs of 'counter-observation'. Much detail was given on how to change shifts. Members of the relief team were not to approach the post directly. Instead, one brigadier would walk or drive past the observation post, paying it no attention, and then be followed at a distance by the brigadier of the shift to be relieved. After a quick debrief on the work, the new brigadier would take to the observation post while the old shift would 'conspiratorially leave'; the new shift would then 'appear conspiratorially', although if the post was inside a building it could 'only be entered and exited individually at certain time intervals'.

Usually, targeted persons on the move would be followed by a number of observers, 'distributed in such a way that they do not immediately come into the field of view of the object' and using 'the conditions of the street' – 'the public, vehicles, trees' – 'to mask themselves'. Observers in cars were to keep at least one vehicle between themselves and the target's vehicle. There were established routines for what to do at an intersection, whether on foot or in cars. For example, if a target turned left at an intersection, one observer was to go straight ahead at the same junction, pause, and then keep the target in sight while the remaining observers followed the target at a distance.

Observers were reminded that targeted persons 'look for passage courtyards, ruined sites, corridors of apartments, open spaces, and streets with little traffic' as places to spot or evade watchers. In a section on pursuing targets into bars and restaurants, it was deemed 'imperative to wait a few minutes until this restaurant has been entered by some other people'. Once inside, an observer was to choose a place 'from which he can see the entire room'; it was 'forbidden to walk through this room to find the object'. Food was to be paid for straight away, and the observer was reminded to order wisely, for 'if the observer orders more than the object and thus takes longer than the object to eat', the uneaten food may 'lead to de-conspiring'. The observer should pause before following someone out of a restaurant, and leave the place 'together with one or two strangers'. It was emphasised that 'ordering or consuming any spirits is categorically forbidden'.

If a target got into a car, observers were to note its type, 'engine performance, colour and police identification number', and followers must remember to 'not all get into their car at the same time'. If a target took a train, plane or boat, observers were to notify the Stasi office at the destination. If they also got on board, and found themselves 'drawn into a conversation by the object', they should 'not behave negatively towards them' but give 'very well thought out' answers: 'The observer must appear absolutely composed and calm towards the object. The observer's legend must be believable.' Given that it 'cannot be ruled out that the object will ask the observer about the reason for and destination of his journey', the observer should 'always name the terminus of the train, ship or plane'.

If a targeted person posted a letter, observers were to post a similar-looking item into the same postbox to make the target's letter easier to find. For this contingency, an observer was 'obliged to have envelopes of various sizes and colours with him during working hours'. The 'exact number and location of the postbox' should be noted 'so that Department M can then arrange for immediate removal of post and initiate a search for the letter'. If necessary, observers could 'address the postman under the legend of the criminal police, find out the name of the postman, and forbid him to take mail from this box until further notice'.

Other contingencies were covered. If the target sent a telegram, the observer was to send one too, making it possible to identify the target's telegram from the sequence of the reference numbers. When taking secret photographs, the target should be approached 'in such a way that it appears random and natural.

The moment of photographing must be chosen in such a way that the object is focused on something else'. To spot counter-observation, observers were always to 'study the crowd in the vicinity of the object'; if counter-observation was detected, the observation was to stop at once. They were to have a sharp eye and memory, for personal descriptions in written reports had to cover a person's 'physical size, age, figure', the 'shape and colour of the face, hair, eyes, eyebrows, ears', the 'shape of the nose and lips', the 'type and colour of clothing', any 'peculiarities and tendencies', and 'special features' such as 'lame gait, missing fingers, metallic and gold teeth, scar or mole on the face or neck'.

What if the targeted person noticed the observation, and confronted the observer? Then an observer was to 'convince the object that he has no interest' and 'complain about the object's improper behaviour', then stop work without approaching any other observer, 'lest they be de-conspired'. Blown observers only had 'the right to return to base' once certain there was no counter-observation in place. They were then to report the incident immediately to superiors.

If observers lost their target, there was to be 'no panic, because the object can hide and the public can watch and thus the observers will be noticed by their nervous behaviour'. One observer 'stays in place and observes the area where the object was lost', since there was 'a possibility that the object entered a building, shop or office'. Other observers were to hunt around.

Whenever a target met someone else, there was a priority question to answer: 'Was this meeting accidental or prearranged?' To answer it, observers were 'obliged to remember and describe it in detail', noting 'when the meeting took place' and how the parties behaved before, during and after it. Sometimes it was easy to spot someone heading for an espionage meeting, as that person 'behaves restlessly before the act and will take various measures to spot observation'. It was important to pay attention to 'the end of a cinema or theatre programme', as the spilling out of an audience was a chance for targets to 'make connections, to hand something over, or to disappear from view'. A target's family members were always suspect: there were 'many examples from which it can be seen that the hostile elements use their wives, parents, grown-up and even underage children to maintain contact with their accomplices'.

The Stasi set high reporting standards for observers. When the Potsdam school began to host training courses for Department VIII personnel, they were taught how to make oral reports, final written reports, and an 'observation analysis', the latter a kind of quality control. It had five sections:

1. What goal was achieved during the observation?
2. Which connections and addresses were discovered?

3. Which employees determined the connections and addresses?
4. Which employees did a particularly good job during the observation?
5. Where and when did any de-conspiring take place?[3]

A dedicated file was created for each observation, containing the various reports and any photographs and their negatives. From these files the head office of Department VIII made indexes of significant people, buildings, hotels, streets and houses. It also indexed relevant connections with the Stasi's 'operational partners', such as the Volkspolizei.

So much for the paperwork. At Potsdam and a departmental school in Eberswalde, Department VIII employees practised car chases, actions from a moving car, and silent killing with knives. Steady professionalisation saw the department receive Soviet-made Neywa radios, and new secret inks, miniature cameras and secret containers. In due course, another training element was introduced – living undiscovered in the western sectors of Berlin for a set period of time.[4]

It is in the third manual, the instructions for Department VIII 'on the arrest, detention, investigation and securing of wanted persons', that differences really start to show between the Stasi and other law enforcement or investigative agencies. The preamble asserts that an 'arrest is of great political importance'. Personnel were expected to be highly skilled, as always: 'The staff assigned to an arrest unit must have courage, prudence, dedication, a sense of responsibility and determination. They must also be adept at inventing legends and nimble in applying them.' They had to cope with staying 'in a certain place while performing their day and night duties, no matter what the weather', requiring 'perseverance, adaptability and iron discipline' and ruling out 'conspicuous behaviour such as speaking loudly, coughing, smoking'. To 'cope with the requirements', employees were to 'systematically work on their physical fitness through sporting activities such as judo, etc., and be trained in the use of firearms'.

Arrest teams were to have a minimum of three employees, and base their work on East Germany's criminal code and code of criminal procedure. Both instruments are quoted throughout the manual. One of the first references is in a section on circumventing the need for an arrest warrant. Stasi personnel could invoke article 152 of the code of criminal procedure: 'The public prosecutor and investigative bodies are also authorised to make provisional arrests if the prerequisites for an arrest warrant or a detention order are met.' Similarly, and usefully for the *Grossaktionen*, if 'immediate arrest actions' were ordered by a deputy minister (Mielke) or any head of department, the paperwork could be done after the arrests were made.

The next sections cover the differences between an 'official' and a 'conspiratorial' arrest. An official arrest could be made whenever 'the course of the investigation is not jeopardised'; when 'the crime has been cleared up', 'all accomplices are known and their escape is impossible', and 'evidence cannot be removed from the person concerned or concealed from the investigative bodies by other people'. Such arrests 'can be carried out in the home of the person concerned, at his place of work, in a bar or in the presence of family members or acquaintances', and were followed usually by a search of the arrestee's home or workplace. A conspiratorial arrest was made when 'the criminal act itself has not been fully clarified', and 'any accomplices are unknown and could be warned by an official arrest', or 'given the opportunity to destroy evidence'. Conspiratorial arrests also served to 'keep the public temporarily unaware'. Propaganda, and the presentability of an arrestee, were kept in mind: 'If this arrest [will result in] publicity, this must be noted in the order, otherwise firearms might be used in the event of an escape.'

Before making an arrest, employees were to 'conduct conspiratorial investigations' of the targeted person and make sketches of the arrest location, the layout of apartments, and possible escape routes. Arrestees in vehicles were to be stopped at bends in the road or spots where movement was limited. Arrest teams, especially 'when using a car', were to be equipped with 'a flashlight, ratchet, toggle chain, handcuffs, rubber gloves, bandages, sealing strips, search logs of the MfS and the Volkspolizei, [and] tools of various kinds... screwdrivers, pliers, wire cutters'. Automatics and revolvers were to be 'ready to fire', 'kept in the pocket or at the ready'. Cars were to have curtained windows, their door handles 'unscrewed on the inside so that the doors can only be opened from the outside'. Arrest teams could be enlarged with personnel from other departments if arrests were to be made 'in unfamiliar areas, forested areas, streets with a bad reputation, or pubs', although it was considered best practice to wait until a target had left a pub before moving in. It was acknowledged that there might be 'disturbances from the population', in which case the members of a support team could step in to help, 'under the cover of passers-by'.

Preferably, an arrest site was to be surrounded by the members of a support team before the core unit moved in; the latter were to 'act vigorously, quickly and precisely'. One employee would determine if the arrestee was present while other team members kept out of sight; this was 'necessary so that the action can be repeated at another time if the person to be arrested is not there'. If an arrestee wasn't present but the arrest team had entered a premises using the cover of police detectives, things got awkward: 'You are not allowed to leave the apartment until the person to be arrested arrives, to avoid any possibility that the person to be arrested will be warned ahead of time. However, if, after a long wait, it is assumed that the person to be arrested will not visit the apartment [then] two employees will continue to keep the apartment under surveillance.' Anyone else present, or who arrived at the scene, was to be detained while their 'personal details' were checked at the nearest Volkspolizei station. This was to be done quickly, 'in order not to violate the legal provisions regarding personal freedom'. Some people could be let go, such as 'employees of authorities, building supervisors and street wardens', provided 'their presence has nothing to do with the person to be arrested, from a criminal point of view'. Persons from West Germany or West Berlin could be 'dismissed after consultation with the department issuing the [arrest] order'. Clearly things had gone wrong during arrests in the past, for it was stressed that 'an arrest operation will fail if the employees of the arrest team move noisily in the apartment, stay at the windows, illuminate the apartment brightly when darkness falls, or behave in a way that is conspicuous. The vehicle used for the arrest may not be parked in front of the house'.

Requests by an arrestee to change clothes or go to the toilet were to 'always be treated with suspicion. If this cannot be avoided, a container (bucket) is fetched in which the arrested person has to defecate'. If arrested in 'a scant state of clothing, the clothing [put on by the arrestee] must be searched beforehand'. Under article 113 of the criminal code, 'all necessary measures' could be taken 'to break passive or active resistance': 'physical force', 'judo grips, rubber truncheons, toggle chains, handcuffs'. Arrestees were to be 'advised that firearms will be used in the event of an attack or attempted escape'. They were taken to vehicles with a Stasi employee on either side and one behind them, and seated between two Stasi employees once on the road. Conversation was banned, including 'among the employees'.

Searches of persons and property, and the compulsory inventorying of an arrested person's possessions, were to be handled with care. Body searches of women could only be done by female employees. No doubt because of prior tragedies, caution was to be exercised with diabetic or unwell arrestees, for whom 'a Volkspolizei or other doctor must be consulted'. Bedridden sickness didn't rule out a room-search, however, for after such a room had 'been searched, relatives or witnesses are asked to move the sick person so that this bed can also be searched'. Searches could extend to an arrestee's family and friends – there were legal mandates to search persons, and their rooms and belongings, if suspected of 'taking part in a crime' as a 'facilitator or go-between', or if it might reveal evidence.

Each search team was to consist of at least three employees under a supervisor. Instead of taking part, the supervisor would gather two 'impartial witnesses' ('house warden, caretaker or resident') to observe the search, and would answer any questions as the search was carried out. 'The following principles apply to every search,' reads the instruction: '1. Search everything! 2. Leave nothing untouched! 3. Work thoroughly!'

Before commencing, a search team was to be given 'indications of what to look for first and foremost, such as Western correspondence, hate literature, addresses, telephone numbers, sketches and drawings, carbon papers, weapons, etc.' They were reminded that a search 'may not be aborted when the specified items [have] been found'. Items that were always to be seized and logged included 'photos, fountain pens, propelling pencils, all identity documents, pieces of paper with and without notes, telephone numbers [and] cinema and theatre tickets or other evidence that can be used to determine where the prisoner has been'; plus any 'slips of paper or writing that employees cannot decipher'.

Evidence might be found anywhere: in 'switches, sockets, chandeliers, curtain rods, clocks, pictures, door and window hangings, safes built into the wall, hollow tables and chair legs, toilet cisterns, bicycle parts, blankets, loose floorboards, or parts of a parquet floor'. Windowsills were to be checked inside and out, walls and floors tapped, beams and rafters sounded, fireplaces dragged. The inner and outer dimensions of walls and furniture were to be checked, to see if they agreed. The inner and outer components of an oven or burner were to be taken apart. Searchers were to take 'precautions and safety measures' if encountering any 'vessels, containers, canisters, bottles and the like which emit strong acrid and foul odours. As well as excrement, it can be acids, chemical substances, powder or explosives' which must be 'checked by specialists'. Garden plots were 'also to be searched thoroughly', although searching was not an exact science: 'In general, the success of a search depends on the resourcefulness of individual employees', who were also to 'pay attention to how an arrested person behaves during the search – facial expressions, etc.' Signs of relief could be more damning than signs of nervousness.

Which personal quality was deemed most important for a Stasi searcher? 'Incorruptibility', for temptation was everywhere. An employee who accepted 'cigarettes or coffee' on the job, never mind 'gifts or luxury items', could face five years in prison for bribery under paragraph 332 of the criminal code. (A similar prison sentence hung over anyone who allowed an arrestee to escape.) Here too, the instructions indicate the things that hitherto had been going awry. 'All items of jewellery' were to be recorded specifically as 'gold or yellow metal, silver or white metal'; in 'the case of gemstones, the colours of the stones are given'. The makers and serial numbers of clocks were to be recorded, so too the engine and chassis numbers of vehicles. Responsibility for pets and livestock was to be signed over to the Volkspolizei or the nearest collective farm. The manual gives more instructions on the process for animals than it does for any children present, who were to go to a children's home 'with the consent of those arrested'.

Presumably Stasi employees had been pinching arrestees' food, for this matter was addressed. 'Perishable foodstuffs are not recorded in the seizure report, but are specifically noted to inform the ordering department', which would then make a decision about them: 'No employee of the arrest unit has the right to make decisions about this themselves.' During a search, employees were to 'avoid speaking as much as possible'. Smoking was 'absolutely not permitted', and it was 'the duty of every employee to behave politely and correctly towards witnesses and relatives'. A forlorn request was added: 'If possible, leave the apartment as you found it.'

Such calls for rectitude and politeness in these documents are significant. They illustrate the noble role that the East German authorities were trying to play, and the prim, citizenly atmosphere intended for the GDR. This wasn't to be a land of louts (however many had been employed by the Stasi); it was to be a land of conscientious self-restraining Marxists. As in other areas of life, East Germans arguably were better off than the citizens of other Soviet Bloc countries, where making an inventory of a detainee's valuables was the last thing on the minds of security police. Nevertheless, these documents dehumanised persons of interest with the term 'object'. This was a reminder to Stasi personnel that arrestees were the enemies in a vicious class war.

The documents show a clear desire – or need – to imbue professionalism in the Stasi's employees, to whom it may not have come naturally. The constant exhortations to maintain conspiracy, in everything an employee did and said, reflect the fact that a blown observer or investigator is worse than useless to a security service. Conspiracy had another aspect: it helped to shield the public from the presence and activities of a secret police. This clashes with the common depiction of the Stasi as a Stalinist terror machine, oppressing the people with outright fear. These documents express rather the opposite aim – to limit fear, to avoid alarm. The motive was not humanitarian. The motive was to govern with a minimum of unnecessary trouble.

52

Reflections on the *Grossaktionen*

The German and European spy wars of the mid-1950s were won by the communists. As the Stasi's older, wiser brother, the KGB was satisfied with the *Grossaktionen*. The Stasi had acted efficiently and decisively on information derived from Soviet moles. As well as the likes of George Blake and Heinz Felfe, there were similar penetrations in France; penetrations that in the following decade were to rock the French secret services, which all but dissolved in a whirlpool of accusation and counter-accusation. As early as 1953 the MGB had boasted of recruiting:

four officials in the SDECE (codenamed NOSENKO, SHIRAKOV, KORABLEV and DUBRAVIN) and one each in the domestic security service DST (GORYACHEV), the Renseignements Généraux (GIZ), the foreign ministry (IZVEKOV), the defence ministry (LAVROV) [and] the naval ministry (PIZHO).[1]

The recruitment of agents in more humble jobs could also pay off. A KGB source in the French military mission at Bad Godesberg near Bonn, a waiter codenamed 'Arnold', did great damage. He was able to steal secret documents for his handlers, the spy couple Yevgeny and Valentina Runge, who had settled as Soviet 'illegals' in Cologne.[2] Another source for the couple was a waiter at diplomatic receptions.[3]

For its part, the Stasi counted on innumerable collaborators inside the Ostbüros, UfJ, KgU and other organisations. Some of them opened up proxy penetrations of these organisations' sponsors, such as the CIA. In the words of an internal KGB history,[4] it was this massive penetration that enabled 'the elimination of the adversary's agent network in the GDR 1953-55'.

Some senior KGB officers had been opposed to the *Grossaktionen*, considering it bad counter-espionage practice to reveal one's hand in such show-boating fashion. Then again, never in history had the KGB and its 'brother organs' faced such an onslaught of professional (and amateur) opposition. In previous eras, the KGB and its forerunners had wiped the floor with adversaries – for instance, the likes of the Poles, British and White Russians after the Bolshevik Revolution. The *Grossaktionen* were a response to the fact that the KGB now had an enlarged and threatening new enemy: a Western world that was at last taking communist espionage seriously.

The *Grossaktionen* made it obvious that Western countries, spearheaded by the US, were using mass-scale espionage to prepare for a land war in Europe. This war, so the West believed, would arise from a Soviet attack. The Western counter-attack was to draw on the experiences of the Second World War, when the likes of French resistance fighters had helped the Western Allies to advance towards Germany. It was hoped that a similar advance, now helped by the likes of KgU activists, could be made towards the frontiers of the Soviet Union.

All governments of the time were duty bound to prepare for this possibility. Plans for stay-behind partisans to operate behind Soviet lines had been discussed by the members of the Western Union as early as 1947, and were subsequently refined by NATO. Bridges in western Germany had been rebuilt with hollow supports, where explosives could be inserted to blow them in case of a Soviet attack. In 1949 MI6 had published its 'S.O. [Special Operations] Handbook', with 'detailed instructions, for example, on 'Clandestine Air Operations', primarily intended for use in the event of another war and clearly drawing on the experience of 1939-1945'.[5] And for most of the 1950s the French government had a secret plan, codenamed Arc de Ciel (Rainbow), to leave stay-behind guerrillas in a Soviet-occupied France and move the administration to north Africa. Service Action, the paramilitary branch of the SDECE, had 'drawn up a list of all the key points in [East and West] Germany that it would be necessary to sabotage in order to halt an invasion by the Red Army'.[6] The French had even taken the battle to the communists, recruiting nationalist partisans from émigré circles of Bulgarians and Romanians and parachuting them into the Soviet Bloc, in an operation called MINOS.[7] All things considered, it was really no surprise that the *Grossaktionen* exposed plans for Western forces to make a counter-thrust through eastern Europe.

It is generally true that Cold War espionage and counter-espionage were easier for the communists, thanks to their closed authoritarian systems and the sundry vulnerabilities of the West. The *Grossaktionen* offer a somewhat different view. Western intelligence services, and the political organisations they endorsed, were helped in diverse ways by a great variety of German people, from both republics. As revealed by the *Grossaktionen*, these people came from all walks of life. Interrogations by the Stasi confirmed that the Western services had successfully recruited large numbers of East Germans by letter, or by having refugees contact acquaintances back home. Such recruits might be motivated by hardship, or affront at the behaviour of Moscow and the SED, or by ideologies that ranged from reformist socialism through to outright nostalgia for Hitler. Some thought they were helping to avoid a German-on-German war, a noble motivation claimed by Western spies and communist spy-catchers alike. Some just did it for the money.

Either way, spying was relatively easy while the Berlin borders remained open. But was it appropriate for the Western powers to, for example, hire so many ordinary Germans to assess the capacity of East German roads for bearing columns of tanks and guns? Partly, this had been deemed necessary because Soviet and East German barracks and other military sites were placed in obscure locations, where privileged local knowledge was essential for spotting and monitoring them. But the SED regime was insecure, and spying of this kind was taken with a grim seriousness in the GDR. The many Germans caught doing it suffered terribly. In 1955 East German courts convicted 2,272 people on the basis of Stasi investigations. Over forty percent were given prison sentences of longer than five years, and twenty-two death sentences were pronounced.[8] Some West German newspapers picked up on the ethical uncertainty of these activities. An article in the *Fuldaer Zeitung* opined that, 'Ultimately, the Gehlen office is jointly responsible if the courts of the Soviet zone impose severe prison sentences on saboteurs and informers from West Germany.'[9] From a Western perspective, it is perhaps a shame that many of those arrested during the *Grossaktionen* were, in the words of historians David Childs and Richard Popplewell, 'not wholly innocent victims'.[10]

As early as 1952, MI5's deputy chief, Guy Liddell, had criticised what he saw as the excessive, unfocused Western intelligence activity being aimed at East Germany and the Soviet Bloc. 'I wondered whether the many projects which were put on foot were in fact profitable,' Liddell wrote in his diary. He had spoken to a senior American colleague, who had told Liddell that the prevailing view in the US was that:

Russia was a tough target, but that everything must be tried, from which it followed that the most hare-brained operations were carried out without anybody sitting down and asking whether if successful they were worthwhile. He agreed with me [Liddell] that to push agents across the various frontiers was by and large a wholly unprofitable operation, which could not really result in telling us what Russian intentions and capabilities were. We might learn that a harvest in a certain place had not been good, or that some village had a section of anti-aircraft guns, etc., but such information is really of little or no value. It did,

however, enable [intelligence officers] to say that they had put so many agents
into Russia or a satellite country...

Liddell continued:

> In my view there were roughly three profitable operations. Firstly, it was desirable
> to get as much overt information [as possible], on an exchange basis, which gave
> a frame into which to put any piece of hot information that might come in, and to
> assess it against the background of the picture. In our particular line we wanted
> to get as broad a picture as we could of the enemy's Intelligence organisation,
> wherever it manifested itself. Secondly, one should have feelers out which would
> enable one to encourage a possible defector who could give information of real
> value. Thirdly, one could decide that one wished to obtain a particular type
> of information, that such information was available in a particular place, and
> that such and such individuals had access to it. One could then sit down and
> endeavour to plan a careful operation. I doubted whether there was much else
> that was really profitable.[11]

In a similar vein, British High Commissioner Ivone Kirkpatrick once
complained that 'there are too many Americans [who] think that annoying the
Russians is an end in itself, and who are zealous to play with fire in Berlin.'[12]
It is worth noting that very few of the Western agents arrested during the
Grossaktionen had been in a position to provide information on the workings of
the Stasi or KGB, identified by Liddell as a priority.

Yet it should also be remembered that Aktion Blitz, in particular, evolved into
a *de facto* purge of East German society. Its original scope was widened by local
Stasi offices, which took the opportunity to arrest every kind of undesirable. As
in the USSR in the late 1930s, at certain points the headquarters staff demanded
a higher number of arrests from local offices, which then overfulfilled these
demands in order to win favour with their bosses.

For the SED and Stasi, newspaper and radio propaganda had been a crucial
factor in the *Grossaktionen*. How effective was it? Did the German population
really come to hate the likes of the KgU for disrupting supplies? Were people
put off becoming Western agents or political reformers? Even protracted
study of the Stasi's own mood reports might lead to wrong answers to these
questions, but we can surmise. For obvious reasons, most German people were
intensely interested in international peace, and might have been swayed by
arguments that invoked it. Thus, when the SED or Stasi claimed in the media
that the Western powers were a threat to peace, this message may well have
resonated.

However, the covert side to the *Grossaktionen* – the disappearances and executions – were probably much more frightening than the righteous propaganda. It is possible that millions of East Germans already resented the SED regime and were engaged in at least mild forms of resistance to it, such as reading and passing on leaflets. Then came the *Grossaktionen*, with their outcomes proclaimed in the media but with the Stasi operating in a world of implied threats, shadows and whispers. When East German households got to hear these whispers – that educated professionals were being guillotined for helping organisations like the KgU – it must have been highly disturbing, and certainly a disincentive to political opposition.

The *Grossaktionen* spy cases were intensified by the personal relationships concerned in so many of them – the involvement of best friends, lovers, siblings, mothers. Even the kidnapping of a Stasi deserter, Major Sylvester Murau, had been aided and abetted by Murau's daughter, acting as the Stasi's agent 'Honett'. Here we see the uniqueness of divided Germany. Often, the involvement of a family member was crucial for making an arrest, or was the deal-maker or deal-breaker in whether or not someone was recruited, by the Stasi or by the West. All security services know the value of acquiring information on the family members of persons of interest. The *Grossaktionen* show why.

They also show what a thankless slugfest Cold War espionage could be. It was an activity that the protagonists, try as they might, could never quite make pay off, and never quite bring themselves to temper. The horrible truth for the Soviet and SED regimes was that, from the moment the *Grossaktionen* ended, the West's dismantled spy networks began to rise again. One Stasi report detailed Western efforts to repair the damage. It noted that a new agent had been sent into East Germany to recruit three people, including a (presumably Soviet) interpreter, who worked at an industrial facility in Dresden. The agent was under orders to then do the same thing at the Wismut mining complex and in Karl-Marx-Stadt. An agent for France had been tasked with 'ascertaining all the structural changes and guarding' at an industrial site in the same city. An American agent working from Clayallee had been 'instructed to recruit a student from the "Free University" in West Berlin' who was to be sent to 'a nuclear physics institute in the United States' before being deployed against East Germany. In a different vein, 'a bricklayer' was to be 'smuggled' into a new construction site in Dresden. Large advertising signs had appeared on roads around West Berlin, encouraging informants and defectors. The Stasi judged that they were installed by the US military, and were 'presumably intended to cause unrest among the population, to attract the attention of the MfS and divert attention from their main agents, and to create a certain network of agents on which the enemy can call to cause provocations'.[13]

Thus the *Grossaktionen* brought a brief pause in the mass-scale spying inside East Germany, not an end to it. It wasn't long before KGB chief Ivan Serov was talking once again of the 'total espionage' being conducted against the Soviet Bloc by the US and Britain.[14] And while the *Grossaktionen* had terminated plenty of important Western penetrations, they had missed others.

A valuable Danish spy in East Berlin codenamed 'Standfuss' remained at large. Another important Danish source, at the home of Soviet military intelligence in Wünsdorf, was recruited just after the *Grossaktionen* had died down.[15] A woman called Anna Kubiak was a prominent survivor. She had been recruited by the CIA in 1952 when working as a housekeeper for Yevgeny Pitovranov and other Soviet high-ups at Karlshorst. Although she had fallen under suspicion and been sacked, bizarrely she had found work as a housekeeper for Karl Linke, one of the early chiefs of East German military intelligence. Linke was an alcoholic and his wife a reputed tyrant, but the CIA persuaded Kubiak to stay in the job until spring 1957. She helped to bug Linke's home and acquired some precious secret documents, including the minutes of a GRU conference held in Moscow, and a list of the names and phone numbers of 150 military intelligence officers.[16]

The CIA continued to run sources who held innocuous jobs at Karlshorst – cleaners in the hotel where visiting officials stayed, an administrator who dealt with freight shipments to and from the compound, a postal clerk who handled undeveloped films from the cameras of Soviet officers.[17] One of the Agency's best known Cold War sources, the GRU officer Pyotr Popov, survived the *Grossaktionen*; it was probably George Blake who did for him a few years later. Likewise, an Agency asset in the Volkspolizei, Fritz Fehrmann, continued to operate, and was even able to get hold of secret Stasi documents.[18] And some time in 1955, the CIA gained a source on the periphery of the SED Central Committee who was to provide for more than a decade.

Recruited on her leisure trips into West Berlin, Gertrud Liebing was a telephone and radio operator in the committee's communications section. From this crucial position, she supplied whatever she could lay hands on – documents, names, functions, telephone numbers. She also identified more than forty individuals who might be open to recruitment by the CIA. Some were enlisted, including Harry Wierschke, one of her colleagues in the telecoms team. It took the Stasi almost a decade to discover these penetrations.[19]

At the end of May 1955, in an address to the Society for German-Soviet Friendship, Erich Mielke gave his personal verdict on the *Grossaktionen*. His audience comprised both West and East Berliners.[20] The state security organs had, Mielke said, 'rendered harmless a large number of espionage and terrorist groups' whose crimes had harmed 'the lives and property of the peace-loving citizens' of East Germany. These groups had disrupted supplies to the public, sabotaged trade through organised counterfeiting, harmed industry and agriculture, and created a host of 'armed gangs'. Mielke didn't point out that the Soviet communist movement had been indulging in this stuff since the early 1920s. Instead, he stressed that the Western services 'do not shy away from abusing young people and taking advantage of the physically disabled, pensioners, women and the elderly'. He played the patriotic card, insisting that scientists and engineers were being lured to West Germany 'to get hold of their patents and inventions, and to entice them to commit national betrayal'. And he lamented that these problems also beset Poland, Czechoslovakia and the USSR, 'the leading force in maintaining peace, which through its efforts [supports] the German people in the struggle for the reunification of their fatherland'.

Mielke urged 'all peace-loving citizens' to 'recognise that these criminals benefit no one'; they were 'only a detriment to everyone, including the citizens of West Berlin and West Germany... their criminal activities endanger peace and make the reunification of Germany more difficult'. He couldn't resist some Stalinist pomp: 'Berlin was not liberated by the glorious Soviet army so that the same fascist criminals can today, disguised with a different mask, continue their plans of conquest and their policy of aggression.' And he almost apologised for the actions of the Stasi:

> One must understand that the GDR has to take measures to prevent further harm being caused... These measures naturally result in difficulties and hardships for the population of West Berlin, which are unwanted by the government of the GDR, but are forced upon it. All citizens who are dissatisfied with these measures must help to eliminate the main evil and, through their efforts, ensure that decent conditions are restored in all relationships in Berlin, in questions of transport, the economy, and in social and cultural life.

There was another twist to the *Grossaktionen*: the Stasi released a surprising number of the people it arrested. Most releases were decided after Department IX had investigated and interrogated suspects. For example, from 1 January to 31 August 1954 – a period covering arrests under Feuerwerk and Pfeil – 251 people were released from custody by Department IX. Public prosecutors' offices ended the criminal proceedings against a further eighty-eight people, and eighty-five defendants were acquitted in court. The highest percentages of release and acquittal occurred in the Stasi administrations of Dresden (twenty percent of the 247 arrestees), Potsdam (twenty-five percent of the 273 arrestees) and Suhl (thirty-two percent of the 87 arrestees).[21]

Besides recruitment as a Stasi collaborator, or an existing role as one, which no doubt applied in many cases, the main reason given for releases was lack of evidence. Although it contradicts certain notions of an 'evil empire', the Stasi didn't want to concoct unproven cases against innocents and loyalists. The Stasi wanted real evidence because East Germany had a real problem with real spies. Here, perhaps, was the biggest difference between state security operations in the GDR and those in Stalin's USSR. In the latter, thousands upon thousands of loyal Stalinists were executed or sent to prison camps, their loyalty counting for nothing. In East Germany, when no proof could be found against a person who seemed, under interrogation, to have a favourable attitude to the SED, that person was quite likely to be released. The SED could not afford, and did not want, to persecute its own supporters. It wanted the Stasi to concentrate on those who might really aim to topple the SED regime – although, of course, a security service in a properly democratic country would not have hauled in so many suspects on the grounds of suspicion alone.

A Department IX report from late 1954 gives explanations for the release of hundreds of suspects. The reasons were varied and sometimes surprising. Cases of mistaken identity were quite common. So were malicious denunciations. Once discovered, they were recorded by the Stasi as 'personal differences' between accuser and accused. The Stasi had to watch for collaborators who were 'not upright', as some informers were known to frame innocents for their own gain, a practice that was stamped on. The Stasi regularly checked the honesty of its collaborators by giving them dummy missions, having them shadowed, or giving the same task to two informers in order to compare their reports.

Some of those released were known to have received a letter or other solicitation to become a Western spy, and provably had not responded. There were cases where decent working-class folk had been misled by those in authority, as with some farmers arrested for heckling at a production meeting ('During the investigation it was determined that those heckling were incited by the incorrect behaviour of the district council of the Peasants' Mutual Aid Association [and as] working farmers, they were released from custody'). Sometimes a person's connection with a known transgressor was deemed to be 'not of a criminal nature', as in the case of unknowing family members. If a case was in any way borderline, release might be expedited if the arrestee had 'progressive' relatives. Some suspects were saved by forensics, as the work of the Criminal Technical Institute in East Berlin improved; they were found innocent of writing seditious texts or damaging machines in the workplace. There were cases of vaguely politicised misbehaviour that were considered too minor to be pursued. And according to the report, one elderly arrestee, against whom there was scanty evidence, was released partly because he was the sole carer for his grandchildren.

Public prosecutors were responsible for a small minority of these releases. Mostly they intervened in cases of mental illness or disability, for intelligence services weren't above preying upon people with learning disabilities to perform their tasks. Some suspects were released because the Stasi couldn't 'de-conspire' an existing collaborator in order to push ahead with a prosecution. At least one release, of a former Volkspolizei officer who regretted fleeing East Germany and had returned, was politically motivated:

> Since the prevailing opinion in West Germany is that every returnee will be arrested, and a worker from Zwickau [is known to be] waiting at his workplace in Essen for news that this rumour is untrue, in order to then return himself, and given that the parents [of the accused] and the accused himself were informed by the Volkspolizei that impunity was guaranteed, it was necessary for political reasons to show generosity on our part in this case, so as not to give rise to such rumours, especially since [the accused] does not give the impression of being an enemy of our state, and has promised to make amends for his guilt through good cooperation.

Contrary to his usual form, Erich Mielke personally authorised the release of several spouses of arrested spies, whom he deemed to be unaware of their partners' activities. There were other anomalies of this kind, like the case of four workers in the coal industry arrested by the Stasi's economic branch, Main Department III. By falsifying the water content in briquettes of brown coal, which were made heavier with water, they had hit their production targets and earned themselves small bonuses. At first, the authorities wanted their blood. But an investigation found that 'increasing the water content does not have to mean a reduction in quality, and the bonuses received were very small'; there was, therefore, 'no question of any damage to the national wealth'. The four were released from custody by order of the SED Central Committee. One wonders why, exactly.

Part V

Up to the Wall

It would be extremely difficult for the East Germans to seal off the Western sectors completely. The border passes through streets, squares, woodlands, fields, and lakes, and along canals. There are also several Western enclaves in East Zone territory. The East German police, border guards, and workers' militiamen could be posted at strategic points, but it would be impossible to seal the dividing line effectively.

CIA weekly intelligence summary, February 1959[1]

53

Spies, Again

The *Grossaktionen* were supposed to strike a once-and-for-all blow against Western espionage in the GDR, but the Stasi's counter-espionage hauls of 1956 and 1957 were even bigger: 679 and 582 arrests.[1] East Germany's spy problem wasn't going away. The former CIA officer Harry Rositzke, among others, later claimed that after the *Grossaktionen* the CIA was still able to maintain big networks gathering large amounts of military, economic, political and scientific intelligence.[2] It is perhaps unsurprising that Erich Mielke and top SED leaders began to look for other solutions to the spy crisis, like building walls.

Still, the *Grossaktionen* prompted the sponsors of the KgU to look long and hard at the organisation's worth. A CIA report admitted that:

> in the summer of 1955, when the KgU received large-scale unfavorable publicity as an alleged U.S. spy center in East and West German newspapers, CIA increased its attempts to reach a cooperative understanding with West German-West Berlin governments regarding the future of the KgU. A joint commission was formed consisting of representatives of CIA, the West German Ministry for All German Affairs and the Berlin Senate in order to evaluate past and current activities of the KgU and to make recommendations for the future. At the present time the results of the reevaluation and the recommendations are still outstanding... Operations against the East German economy, particularly those involving third countries, have been deemphasized.[3]

The Organisation Gehlen undoubtedly was lamed by the *Grossaktionen*. At the start of 1953 it had moles inside the Stasi; by the end of 1955 these appear to have been lost. Meanwhile the Stasi's penetration of the organisation continued. Just one Stasi infiltrator of this period was Ernst Schwartzwäller, who had joined the OG on the recommendation of wartime SD colleagues, and who was able to supply information and identify other potential recruits.[4]

On 1 April 1956 the OG was finally integrated into the West German administration as the Bundesnachrichtendienst or BND, although its officers continued to be issued with false papers as American citizens as a protective measure.[5] Reinhard Gehlen was to remain as chief until 1968. Having clarified and secured his agency's status, Gehlen had great ambitions for it. He had pull with Konrad Adenauer, winning from him impressive funding and resources. Gehlen wanted his BND to become a global presence rivalling the intelligence world's big hitters – CIA, KGB, MI6, Mossad. Within a year the BND employed 1,245 people.[6] Like its predecessor it specialised in SIGINT, for which purpose it built a new facility inside the Stöberhai, a peak in the Harz. Its codebreaking effort under Erich Hüttenhain, former head of cryptanalysis for the Wehrmacht, was conducted by the Central Cryptography Office, a semi-independent body. In general, the West German authorities were soon satisfied with the BND's work. Early in its lifetime a senior officer, Hans Langemann, pulled off a coup by arranging the defection of a Stasi officer, Heinz Kupfer.[7] And the BND's main customers – the Chancellery and Foreign Office, the Bundeswehr – usually received timely information on East Germany's economy and on the Soviet military presence. Much of this came from the BND's SIGINT, however. Its HUMINT in East Germany continued to experience setbacks, just as the OG had.[8]

Vague estimates suggest that around 10,000 East and West Germans spied for the BND inside East Germany in the course of the republic's history. Reportedly, as many as 4,000 – many of them minor agents in low-level positions – were identified and arrested. Some areas of BND espionage were better than others. One of its well-placed spies was a National Democratic Party member codenamed 'Lena', who worked in the NDPD's publishing branch. 'Lena' had either been missed by the Grossaktionen or was recruited just after they had finished; or, perhaps, he had been arrested and offered the reprieve of working for the KGB. Either way, when 'Lena' told the BND that he had agreed to become a KGB double agent, the BND decided to continue running him as a triple. 'Lena' was now in a good position to provide information on Karlshorst and the KGB's modus operandi. The BND assigned a specialist officer in West Berlin to concentrate on affairs at Karlshorst; he was liked by the Americans, who gifted him a set of false number plates for his vehicle.[9]

Soviet garrisons continued to be watched by a reformed legion of BND spies, some of whom delivered information well into the 1960s.[10] This was detailed reporting, with data on every unit adding to the overall picture of Soviet strength. Often it was conducted by cleaners, mechanics or electricians working at Soviet sites. The CIA urged the BND to expand its coverage by recruiting the likes of street cleaners working in the Karlshorst compound.

It was probably they who reported a tightening of security there. Many low-level German workers were dismissed, there was increased patrolling in the area by Stasi paramilitaries, and a 'well integrated system of MfS informers [was] established among the remaining German employees'.[11] These were the results of a Stasi operation codenamed Partisan, in which more than 250 domestic workers and tradespeople were investigated.[12] Some were arrested, including an electrician who had tried to install a CIA bug in a chandelier.[13]

One morsel of information passed to the CIA at this time was the news that the drama society at the Soviet embassy on Unter den Linden had ordered an expensive new film projector, suggesting that Soviet officials weren't intending to leave East Berlin any time soon. Such intelligence could be useful for determining the locations, roles and habits of Soviet personnel and, to an extent, their plans for the near future. Better still was the reporting by BND sources of the arrival of SS-3 'Shyster' medium-range missiles at Soviet bases, a coup that delighted and impressed the Americans.[14] Moreover, the East German railway system, seen as 'an impeccable barometer of Russian troop movements',[15] continued to be watched closely.

Despite its built-in aversion to social democrats, the BND also worked quite productively with the SPD Ostbüro. The Ostbüro's leaders, 'Stephan Thomas' and Helmut Bärwald, were always open to collaborating with Western intelligence services against the hated SED which, after all, had destroyed their party in eastern Germany. It is possible the BND contributed to new programmes for inducting East German refugees as Ostbüro activists. New arrivals would undergo coaching at Hanover to remove 'the dead weight of pseudo-Marxism' they had been saddled with in the GDR. If it was planned to return them there as a spy, they would be spirited to such locations as Wieda in the Harz mountains, where they were taught how to gather and transmit intelligence, and learned about 'the functioning of the MfS'.[16]

Cooperation with the BND did not improve the Ostbüro's security, however. The Stasi's moles were busily collecting information on such Ostbüro luminaries as Konstantin Pritzel ('Dr Reinhardt'), Eberhard Zachmann ('Müller') and Alfred Weber ('Peter Wandel'). All three ran secret Ostbüro cells in Berlin and had propaganda connections with such American publications as *Time* and the military paper *Stars and Stripes*. However, in its study of internal Ostbüro materials, the Stasi struggled to find evidence of calls for terror and sabotage. The Ostbüro tended to urge East Germany's repressed social democrats to make gentle suggestions for free all-German elections, or simply to refrain from endorsing the SED. But the Ostbüro did carry out more lively actions. One was to post parcels containing nothing but a length of rope to East German executives.[17]

*

No one knows the full extent to which the BND was penetrated by communist agents. Once exposed, the trio of Heinz Felfe, Hans Clemens and Erwin Tiebel became famous in their own lifetimes in Germany. Another mole to make the newspapers was Ludwig Albert, a former Gestapo officer who supplied information to the Soviets from his successive posts as a Gehlen cut-out in Hesse, an executive of its Darmstadt office, and finally an officer based in Frankfurt. Albert was arrested in Bonn in 1955 and killed himself in Bruchsal prison, not the kind of publicity desired by Reinhard Gehlen's new agency.[18] Moreover, from 1954 onwards the Stasi's agent 'Rumland' – Hans Sommer, another former SS officer who at first worked for Gehlen's office in Hamburg – delivered more than 2,000 documents and 800 items of information on OG and BND agents and cover addresses.

Another important Soviet mole was discovered after his suicide in 1960. During the war, Willi Kriechbaum had been an SS officer, sometime assistant to Gestapo chief Heinrich Müller, and ultimately head of the Wehrmacht secret field police. He was unquestionably connected with war crimes, but his appearance as a witness at Nuremberg, and his professional qualifications, were enough to convince Gehlen and the Americans that he should be nurtured. Kriechbaum began working for the OG as a personnel officer in 1946; by the late 1950s he was a regional chief of the BND. Throughout this period he was reporting to the Soviets. It is likely that Kriechbaum was a major source of the tip-offs which saw so many Gehlen and BND agents arrested or turned.[19]

Reviewing the arrests carried out in one year, a Stasi counter-espionage officer once broke down the factors responsible for the Stasi's spy-catching achievements. Tip-offs from 'brother organisations' had led to three percent of successful arrests. Investigations of suspects spotted by the Stasi accounted for six percent. Information from collaborators within East Germany, and routine operational measures – postal surveillance, border controls, security practices at important sites – were responsible for seventeen percent. It is possible that almost a quarter of arrests resulted from denunciations by members of the public. But the Stasi's most significant counter-espionage tool by far was the penetration, by itself and the KGB, of agencies and organisations in West Berlin and West Germany. 'Initial tips from the operational area' accounted for half of all successful spy arrests.[20] While this analysis applied to a later period of Stasi history, it is likely that Ernst Wollweber's 'turn to the west' – an initiative requiring every major Stasi department to recruit or place 'defensive' spies in West Germany – lay behind these figures.

In later years, the Stasi virtually took over BND spying in East Germany. It is believed that by the 1980s some ninety percent of the BND's sources in the GDR served as double agents for the Stasi which, in a triumph of counter-espionage practice, had recruited instead of arresting them. The Berlin Wall helped in these recruitments, for it prevented BND spies from running away. If found, they were cornered.

Following the suppression of the 1953 revolt and the skittling of spy networks in the *Grossaktionen*, the Western powers had to reassess their priorities. Inciting resistance, and spying on the East German political scene, had lost some of their appeal and purpose. Although further economic spying was prompted by fears that the Soviet Union's economic potential might surpass that of the United States,[21] the West's main interest in East Germany remained the Soviet military presence there. Reflecting this, and the dire fate suffered by some of their agents, for the remainder of the 1950s and throughout the 1960s, Western intelligence services generally preferred to make use of East Germans already on the spot, rather than sending agents into the GDR.[22]

Moreover, interviews with commercial and academic travellers, and intelligence collection programmes such as Britain's 'Dragon Return' – the long-term debriefing of scientific workers who had returned from deportation to the USSR – helped to secure information on Soviet science and technology. Of most interest were developments in atomic energy, guided missiles, electronics, torpedoes and mines, artificial fibres, radio technology, optical glass, armaments design, and fuels.[23] Many 'Dragon Returners' managed to resettle in West Germany, having been 'evacuated' from the GDR by the British authorities. (If they stayed in the GDR, these returnees, though sometimes pampered by the state, faced being watched by the Stasi. According to one report, the Stasi was suspicious of their potential for 'espionage, anti-Soviet feeling, [former] connection with the Gestapo and anti-Communism'.)[24]

Subversive activity under the CIA's DTLINEN workstream, in which the Agency utilised the KgU, continued. In a renewal of the campaign for the fiscal year 1957, the objective was described as 'to harass and weaken the Soviet administration of East Germany (including East Berlin) and the East German puppet regime, to help retard East German economic development, to help promote and sustain popular anti-communist resistance within East Germany, and to help expose conditions within the Soviet zone to the Western world.' It was acknowledged that 'the U.S. faces the difficult task of sustaining, increasing and exploiting East German popular resistance over a relatively long period of time [in order to] demonstrate that the East Germans have not been forgotten or abandoned by the West, and persuade them that they have the power to alleviate their condition to some extent through their own current resistance actions.'

Thus far there was no evidence whatsoever that conditions for East Germans had been substantively improved by resistance actions – rather the opposite. Still, the document revealed that the KgU, acting partly on behalf of the CIA, at this time boasted 'approximately 80 covert Soviet Zone [sic] contacts,' and each month 'debriefs approximately 20 members of the People's Police [and] turns over an average of approximately 200 intelligence reports'. The document then gave a list of planned activities for the coming year. Most were unlikely to put German activists in any great danger – the likes of funding print runs of leaflets, or debriefing refugees. An exception was the 'preparation and execution of administrative harassment operations designed to ridicule, confuse and undermine the efficiency [of] East German governmental and Communist Party offices,' an activity that was far from safe. It was noted that the 'impact of KgU administrative harassment operations has been reflected by reports of KgU co-workers or other CIA agents, reports of counter-measures which the GDR government has been forced to take, and numerous accounts in the East German press warning the population to be on their guard against KgU activities'. So much for the impact; achievements, on the other hand, were not noted. And although the CIA deemed the KgU to be 'engaged in a basically humanitarian and anti-Communist program', it was admitted that there remained a 'continuing risk [of] the kidnapping of key personnel by agents of the East German or Russian security services'.[25]

By this time the KgU had stopped carrying out incendiary sabotage. But there were still instances of it, leaving the Stasi with the difficult task of discovering who was responsible. It was relatively straightforward to determine whether an incident had, in fact, been sabotage or a deadly industrial accident (they were frequent). The tricky part was determining the motive for sabotage, and if the damage had been done on behalf of a Western organisation. Some events remained a mystery. When, in spring 1956, repairs were made to a water tower at Aue, part of the Wismut AG operation, a stash was found containing three bottles of petrol, a packet of cotton wool and a blanket: sabotage gear. Despite a spirited investigation, the Stasi couldn't work out who it belonged to, or why exactly it was there.[26]

In other areas, the spy wars were losing some of their face-to-face intimacy. Reconnaissance overflights and technological sources of intelligence were growing in importance. The most famous example was one of the biggest espionage endeavours of the decade: Operation Gold, the Berlin tunnel. This involved the tapping of phone cables used by the Soviet military, including the high frequency line linking Moscow with the military intelligence hub at

Wünsdorf. The dig site in the American sector was disguised as a depot, the fences around it laced with microphones so that guards stationed at a listening post could hear intruders or East German patrols.[27] Despite these precautions, and the skill of the British engineers who rigged hundreds of tiny amplifiers to the telephone wires, in April 1956 the tunnel was busted before the world in a gala press day organised by the Soviet and East German authorities. First to be photographed entering the tunnel, complete with disgusted expressions on their faces, were Ernst Wollweber and Adolf Viehmann, the head of the Stasi's wiretappers at Department O. Thereafter, queues of curious Berliners flocked to see the tunnel.

Operation Gold had been suggested partly by the CIA's penetration of the East German telecommunications system. For years there had been CIA sources at East Berlin post and telegraph offices, at the Ministry of Post and Telecommunications, at switching offices in Erfurt, Dresden and Magdeburg.[28] Among other contributions, these sources made the first identifications of sensitive cables. But from the start, the KGB knew of the tunnel's existence thanks to George Blake at MI6.

Debate still rages about why the KGB allowed the tunnel to function for a while. It was probably a combination of factors: best practice in counter-espionage (that is, hold your fire and observe the espionage as it unfolds); a reluctance to implicate Blake; perhaps a desire to belittle, and spy upon, the GRU – one of the main users of the telephone lines, and a not-so-friendly rival. The intelligence gained by the CIA was far from worthless. Markus Wolf admitted the value for the West of hearing conversations between Karlshorst and Moscow about 'weapons acquisitions, shortages, technical deficiencies, and code names for newly developed weapons'.[29] Special teams of analysts spent years ploughing through recordings of the traffic, gaining useful detail on the personnel and practices of the Soviet armed forces.

But this was still the 1950s, still a world of print and parochialism. In the month of April 1956, according to the Stasi, a total of 1,684,363 propaganda leaflets were dropped on East Germany from Western-launched balloons, and 124,219 leaflets entered the GDR by post. These were typical monthly figures.

UfJ leaflets were denouncing the Stasi's interception of communications. Under the heading 'The State Security Service reads and listens!', the text of one informed readers that:

the systematic violation of postal secrecy continues. Recently, the network of letter control points at main post offices and at other important post offices has been expanded. Day and night, employees of the State Security Service are busy opening letters, reading through them and submitting 'incriminating' political statements to the responsible operational department of the State Security Service for further action. Nor have the activities of the parcel control offices been restricted in any way… seizures continue to take place today, if the contents of the parcels do not comply with the complicated and vexing regulations. Finally, it should be noted that the surveillance of private telephone traffic also continues – the large interception centre at East Berlin's long-distance office at Dottistrasse 4 is in full operation. At other large telephone offices in the zone, postal workers are permanently assigned to monitor private telephone lines.[30]

It was pushing it to describe the Dottistrasse operation as 'large' – the beleaguered Department O had just a few employees there. And in West Germany the duty of monitoring post had merely been passed by the occupying authorities to the BND. But the propaganda was the point. Judging by the leaflets it spread in East Germany, summer 1956 found the FDP Ostbüro in ebullient mood:

If each of you would send a letter to the state organs just once a month, with sharp criticism of the supply situation and other 'non-political' phenomena, the whole place would very soon be thrown into such confusion that regular activity in the administrations and authorities would no longer be possible… Or write to the newspaper, to the National Front, to the authorities or parties! Shower the organs of this criminal state with criticisms, don't give the bigwigs a moment's peace. The time is ripe, for the comrades have become uncertain.[31]

54

Special Tasks

The growth of technical espionage did not retire the Stasi's dirty ops squads. The group known as Blitz led by the GM 'Neuhaus', and the Donner group under Hans Wax, continued to refine their kidnappings and special actions.

Not every dirty operation of the time involved hired hands, however. Regular Stasi officers were quite capable of violence and skulduggery. At some point in 1956, in an incident that is still debated, the defector Robert Bialek, formerly the SED's functionary for police affairs and a vocal apostate of the regime, died in Stasi custody.

Under the Nazis, Bialek had spent six years in prisons and camps. After the war he was a natural for promotion, prospering in the Free German Youth and the SED. Worryingly, however, two party colleagues in particular rubbed Bialek the wrong way: Erich Mielke and Walter Ulbricht. In October 1948, in a screaming office row, Bialek and Mielke had drawn their service pistols when the former had accused the latter of careerism and excessive harshness. In another aggravated confab some time later, Bialek reputedly threw his police uniform jacket at Walter Ulbricht. Thus disgraced, he went through the customary downward slides of a leisurely purge until, successively demoted and starkly unimportant, he put an end to his descent by defecting to the West.

Arriving in West Berlin in August 1953, Bialek worked as a vehement propagandist for the BBC and, under the alias 'Bruno Wallmann', the SPD Ostbüro. After listening to an especially mocking episode of Bialek's Saturday night BBC radio show, 'We Speak to the Zone', Walter Ulbricht is said to have telephoned Erich Mielke to ask why this 'renegade' was still on two feet. Mielke replied that he would deal with the matter.

The operation to 'retrieve' Bialek was led by Erich Jamin, stalker of social democrats for Main Department V. At least six collaborators were deployed to observe and manoeuvre him to his fate. Worse still for Bialek, he lived in the same building as MI6 traitor George Blake. Although Bialek reportedly lived 'in great secrecy', 'protected by steel shutters and a siren alarm', it is quite possible that Blake kept a glinting eye on him.[1] On the evening of 4 February

1956 Bialek was invited by two friends to a pretend birthday party in a flat on Jenaer Strasse in the Wilmersdorf district. One of these friends was named Herbert Hellwig. The other was former Volkspolizei officer Paul Drzewiecki, last seen under Stasi arrest during the *Grossaktionen*. Once set free Drzewiecki had rekindled a supportive-looking friendship with Bialek, as the pair were old acquaintances from their police days.

Either Hellwig or Drzewiecki slipped knockout drugs into Bialek's beer. He got woozy and staggered from the room. At around 9.30 p.m. he was discovered in the toilet by the owner of the apartment, who knew nothing of the kidnapping scheme. Hellwig and Drzewiecki apologised for their drunk friend and manhandled him outside and into a taxi.

For decades there was no further trace of Robert Bialek. His disappearance was protested from West Berlin to Britain's House of Commons.[2] It was assumed he had been put to death or otherwise silenced in the Soviet Bloc. In the twenty-first century, a striking entry was discovered in the prisoner log at Hohenschönhausen. At 11 p.m. on 4 February, prisoner number 2357 was admitted, although a name and date of birth were not recorded, as was usual. A few days later 2357 was logged as no longer present.[3] It must have been Bialek, and the mystery seemed to be solved – as suspected, he had died at Hohenschönhausen shortly after his abduction. However, new testimonies came to light in 2010, including from a prison doctor who claimed to remember treating Bialek, near death from torture and tuberculosis, at Bautzen prison in summer 1956.[4] Whatever the details, Bialek's life was ended by Stasi violence or maltreatment, payback for once pulling a gun on Erich Mielke. And at some point he had talked. Soon after Bialek's disappearance, nineteen SPD Ostbüro activists in East Germany were arrested in one swoop.[5]

In the late spring of 1956, Hans Wax and a Stasi collaborator called Horst Hesse, codenamed 'Jürgen', carried out an audacious operation for Main Department II. It led to the arrest in East Germany of 140 alleged agents of the US Military Intelligence Department (MID).

At a press conference held in East Berlin in July, the Stasi boasted of Horst Hesse's brilliant penetration of MID.[6] After more than a year working for the 522nd Military Intelligence Battalion at Würzburg in Bavaria, one May morning Hesse had jumped into the passenger seat of a white Mercedes Benz convertible, which then made a beeline for the East German border. Before leaving, however, Hesse had grabbed two military-issue safes from the office of his commander, Captain James Campbell.

The safes contained documents giving crucial information on the MID effort in East Germany – most importantly, the details of its agents. Most were railway employees tasked with reporting any tank and troop movements. Upon realising that the safes had been stolen, MID broadcast a radio alarm signal, which was picked up by some of these agents. Several fled in terror to prearranged locations in West Germany, where they later demanded steep compensation from the American authorities for the danger they had faced. Others were less fortunate.

The US army had recruited Horst Hesse by letter. In January 1954 a former neighbour who had fled to West Berlin had written to him in Magdeburg suggesting they meet. Hesse had immediately informed the Magdeburg office of the Stasi. He was told to meet with his old neighbour and become an American agent.

Hesse had personal reasons for alerting the Stasi to this approach. A former KPD member and Volkspolizei sergeant, he had been dismissed from the police in 1951 during wholesale discharges of 'Western' prisoners of war; Hesse had been captured by the British when serving as a Wehrmacht corporal. By the time he received his neighbour's letter he was working in a machine factory, looking for ways to prove himself a loyal GDR citizen. Ironically, his dismissal from the Volkspolizei was probably the reason he was targeted for recruitment by the Americans, who probably banked on Hesse holding a grudge.

Josef Kiefel masterminded Hesse's service to the United States. His first order from the Americans was to get a job as a mechanic with the Soviet army. Kiefel duly arranged with the KGB that Hesse be employed at the Soviet garrison in Magdeburg. At meetings in West Berlin, Hesse began to supply photographs, technical data and building plans of the base, all generated by the KGB. The Americans bought it, however, and were then duped by a staged defection. Hesse had told Kiefel that his old neighbour kept written records of all the East German agents he had recruited, including Hesse, in his West Berlin apartment. One night a Stasi burglar broke in and stole these papers, enabling a string of deceptions.

Apparently suspected by the East German authorities, Hesse was visibly marched off for questioning by the police in Magdeburg and dismissed from the SED. This charade reportedly fooled not only the Americans but Hesse's wife and son, who considered him a traitor to East Germany. When he was temporarily released from custody Hesse ran to West Berlin, feigning panic and demanding shelter in the Federal Republic. By these means he had ended up employed at Würzburg, in a vital intelligence station responsible for observing Soviet military movements in the west of Thuringia, near the Fulda Gap. Together with the Cheb Gap on the Czech border, this pass was considered the likeliest route for a Soviet tank offensive on western Europe. Ostensibly an employee of the 522nd Battalion's Public Opinion Research Detachment, Hesse – agent 'Lux' to the Americans – was tasked with maintaining radio contact with East German agents, and recruiting new ones.[7]

The plan to steal the safes, blow Hesse's cover, and expose the US army networks in East Germany, was part of Aktion Schlag, an ongoing HA II operation. The Mercedes 190 SL that spirited Hesse out of West Germany was driven by Hans Wax. It was probably one of Wax's comrades who burgled the apartment of Hesse's old friend. Hesse and Wax had no bother when they reached the GDR border with the stolen safes. Wax was well known to the East German border officials, whom he had befriended in the course of his shifty career. When they commented that his Mercedes looked lower to the ground than usual, he told them it was laden with Italian engine parts for his car business. He then proceeded to hand out free tickets for car races at the Nürburgring and to pass around a box of cigars, which were grabbed readily by the border and customs officers.

From the start, then, the KGB and Stasi were in control of Horst Hesse's employment by the US army. This was enough of a coup that it required no embellishment. Nevertheless, embellishments typical of Wollweber and Mielke were tacked onto it at the July 1956 press conference; like Soviet propaganda, the GDR's media pronouncements never knew when to stop. In this case, it was claimed that Hesse and hundreds of others had been threatened into cooperating with the Americans, whose policy was to shoot any who refused.

This silly claim raises a cardinal point about propaganda: unwise exaggerations reduce its impact and damage the legitimacy of those who issue it. Overstating the viciousness of the American intelligence services probably played into Western hands. Although the effects of SED and Stasi propaganda are mysterious, it is likely that East Germans of the 1950s could tell when they were being hoodwinked by their own authorities.

Still, Hesse's penetration of US army intelligence was an achievement; one that 'exposed the weaknesses of the US military and pointed to future possibilities'.[8] These possibilities weren't lost on Markus Wolf. Neither was the chance to produce further propaganda about the operation, including Hesse's autobiography and a 1962 feature film, *For Eyes Only: Streng Geheim* (strictly secret). The exaggerations continued in these party-made productions. As partial justification for the Berlin Wall, the film depicted – without any basis in known facts – the NATO armies gearing up for a mass assault on East Germany.[9]

The special ops group under GM 'Neuhaus' was not to be outdone. In March 1956, having been told to temporarily curb their operations, 'Neuhaus' and a fellow criminal, the Stasi's GM 'Bär', kidnapped a random West Berliner after a night out in a pub, in order to prove their skills and commitment. Having brought the hapless victim into East Berlin, they were warned that such measures must only be carried out with express permission, but received a bonus of 200 deutschmarks anyway.[10] In September the pair were back in action, kidnapping a suspected US agent who they got blind drunk in a bar near the Berlin sector border. This man, known in the literature as Siegfried Wenzel, had been watched by the Stasi for at least two years. The Stasi's first plan had called for a woman collaborator to seduce and recruit him. When this didn't bring Wenzel to East Berlin, new acquaintances – 'Neuhaus' and 'Bär' – worked their way into his social circle. The three began to indulge in heavy drinking sessions, on the pretext of discussing a lucrative potential job for Wenzel. When he regained consciousness in Stasi custody after the latest drinking session, Wenzel's reaction, like that of certain other kidnap victims, was apoplectic fury. He refused to play ball when told not to speak of his kidnapping, raising it for the record on several occasions during the preparations for his trial. Interrogators from Department IX complained that he was 'constantly trying, with challenging and provocative behaviour, to prevent MfS investigators from completely unmasking him'.[11]

Other drunken spies of the time were more obliging. In 1957 the KGB and Stasi penetrated the US air force when a hungover Airman First Class, Robert Glenn Thompson, appeared in East Berlin after a night of drinking and offered his services to the Soviets. Thompson had already been court-martialled, demoted and fined for his alcohol abuse. Yet for some reason, his access to secret information hadn't been withdrawn.[12] In an era when hard drinking was considered standard, this laxity wasn't so rare. Thompson spent a year betraying the identities of agents in East Germany who reported to the Office of Special Investigation, the US air force counter-espionage service based in West Berlin. His treachery was discovered only when he was back in America in the 1960s; sentenced to thirty years in prison, he was exchanged in a spy swap at the end of the following decade. Erich Mielke trumpeted this example of the Stasi's caring attitude. In an internal letter, he told his staff to use Thompson's case as encouragement for all the Stasi's spies: 'The liberation of Thompson proves anew that all of our patriotic and unofficial workers, even those in difficult situations… can rely at all times on the active support and welfare of the MfS.'[13] Contrary to the cliché of spies being 'on their own' once arrested, the Stasi, like most intelligence services, considered it vital to reassure agents that they wouldn't be sacrificed or abandoned.

Another spy case of the period, the arrest of three CIC agents, was given great publicity in the GDR. A major public trial was conducted against Friedrich

Weihe, Alfred Fritsche and Werner Chrobock,[14] who had been arrested after Weihe was kidnapped from West Berlin – or rather, 'induced to enter the Democratic Sector by operational measures and arrested there in a drunken state'.[15] Weihe had form in East Germany. He had been prosecuted in 1952 for 'an economic crime', his guilt compounded by the fact that he had concealed his former service in the Kriegsmarine. His fellow defendants were former Nazis. Shortly before the trial, which was held in September 1957, the Stasi's Agitation Department drew up a publicity plan. There was to be pretrial build-up from the ADN press agency, public displays of the evidence, a special brochure, and a Stasi exhibition called 'Breaking Through the Secret Front' ('Geheime Front Durchbrochen'). The audience in court, some 300-strong, would comprise specially checked officials from government ministries, eighty Stasi employees, functionaries from the Ministry of Justice and Public Prosecutor's Office, and some fifty journalists.

The participation of Europe's press was closely managed. Besides ADN, East German media attendees included the State Broadcasting Committee, DEFA, *Neues Deutschland* and other papers with big circulations – *Bauern Echo, Junge Zeit*. From the Soviet Bloc came *Pravda, Izvestia*, the Hungarian and Bulgarian press agencies. There were communist reporters from Britain's *Daily Worker* and France's *L'Humanité*; 'bourgeois' reporters from *Die Welt, Frankfurter Rundschau, Der Spiegel, Stern*. All were briefed carefully in the days before the trial.[16]

The trial was considered a success in presenting Friedrich Weihe as a helpless, poverty-stricken victim of the American secret services. Weihe played ball and publicly repented, praising the 'decent and generous treatment' he had received from the Stasi and urging former associates who had fled the GDR to 'return to the security organs [and] lead a decent life'. He was given a life sentence under Article 6 of the GDR constitution, while Chrobock, who had also been kidnapped to East Germany, got fifteen years.

Despite such bad publicity, US military intelligence had its successes. Once the *Grossaktionen* were over, MID recruited a woman from Dresden called Hella Zickmann. Until the advent of the Berlin Wall she was able to report personally by entering West Berlin and flying from there to Hamburg to visit her son.[17] Zickmann worked in a food supply depot, and by assessing the food orders which came in from the Soviet army she could ascertain if VIPs were visiting or if troop numbers were changing. It took almost thirty years for the Stasi to bust her.

55

Changing Times

On 20 September 1955 East Germany was accorded full sovereignty by the Soviet Union. The Soviets made their presence felt until the very last – the final sentence imposed by a Soviet tribunal was passed just four days earlier.[1] Sovereignty was accompanied by two interconnected developments: a slight relaxation in the policies of Walter Ulbricht, and a behind-the-scenes militarisation. The mild political thaw lasted little more than a year. Throughout, the public mood was monitored by the Stasi's Information Service, although its reports were always a sensitive matter. At this stage, they tended to quote verbatim much raw comment and opinion, gathered straight from the streets and factory floors. Walter Ulbricht, in particular, grew wary of this 'warts and all' approach, finally losing his temper with the department and accusing it of 'legally spreading enemy hate propaganda'.[2] After its subsequent relaunch as the Central Information Group, more attention was paid to editing.

Like all communist societies, East Germany experienced a policy pendulum. In true Bolshevik fashion, Ulbricht's policies, based on fixed principles and centrally planned, had regularly to be reversed, then reinstated, in a jagged pattern of about-turns. So it was that in the mid-1950s, the policy pendulum swung towards a less harsh, more democratic-looking approach. Censorship was loosened. Cultural activity became somewhat freer. Not to be outdone by West Berlin's zoo, the SED created a zoo in Friedrichsfelde Park, urging party members to contribute to its upkeep. And the party tried to win favour by releasing some 25,000 prisoners. Included were nearly 700 social democrats, 400 functionaries of National Front parties, several hundred prisoners convicted by Soviet military tribunals, and such disgraced SED notables as Paul Merker and Max Fechner.

The prison population of this era tells an oblique story. In the first quarter of 1956 there were 48,747 prisoners in East Germany, of whom 13,014 had committed crimes against the state. Thus, almost one third were political prisoners, although that term wasn't used. By the end of 1958 there were 22,343 prisoners, with 8,115 sentenced for anti-state crimes; the total had fallen but the political share had increased. It increased again to almost forty percent in 1960 (18,198 prisoners),[3] reflecting a rise in sentences around *Republikflucht* and a new burst of agricultural collectivisation, which proved every bit as unpopular as the last.

Moreover, even as the atmosphere seemed to relax, death sentences were passed which appeared flagrantly spiteful. During 1955 they included the director of a power plant who had attempted to flee the GDR and a railway worker who had thrown a wrong switch and been convicted of sabotage.[4] A RIAS listener called Joachim Wiebach was guillotined, reportedly on the insistence of Walter Ulbricht, for leading a clandestine circle guilty of the 'fabrication and circulation of rumours that put peace at risk'.[5] And on 14 September that year, Bruno and Susanne Krüger, both defectors from the Stasi who had fled to West Berlin two years previously, were executed at Dresden. Bruno Krüger had been abducted by a Stasi snatch squad after leaving a restaurant near the Berlin sector border. The information that enabled the kidnapping was provided by his mistress, who had taken custody of the Krügers' two-year-old son when the couple escaped the GDR. In a separate operation, Susanne Krüger, desperate to see her child again, was tricked by a former Stasi colleague who turned up in West Berlin in the guise of a fellow refugee. Thinking the man had news of her son, Susanne had accompanied him into East Berlin in a taxi; it pulled up near Potsdamer Platz and she was arrested. These executions, in Stasi jargon, were a part of 'repatriating traitors' ('Zurückführung der Verräter').

Yet for a while Walter Ulbricht seemed almost to regret the *Grossaktionen* policy of mass arrests and convictions, despite the fact that they were supposed to have been carried out discerningly; Ernst Wollweber had even told radio listeners that the number of confessions obtained from arrestees proved that the Stasi was tackling 'the right people', and that 'every honest person can be reassured'.[6] Ulbricht wasn't. At a Stasi party meeting in May 1956 he urged personnel to 'establish normal relations with public prosecutors', and resist the temptation to 'press a bit' on prosecutors and judges. Evidence, he said, and not pressure on the judiciary, should be the deciding factor in convictions. Taking Ulbricht's lead, other SED high-ups, including deputy chief public prosecutor Bruno Haid, started to complain about the secret connivance between the Stasi and prosecutors, and of the Stasi's over-involvement in judicial appointments. Some legal professionals blew the whistle on Stasi officers who had flouted 'democratic legality', pointing out that confessions were unreliable if obtained after months of night-time interrogation.

Sensing the mood of thaw, Main Department IX investigated just 1,500 suspects in 1956 – one of its lighter years.[7] Then the policy pendulum swung. Within a few months, both the Stasi and the judiciary were under the cosh for being too lenient. At a Central Committee plenum in February 1957 Ulbricht moaned that the Stasi had 'not arrested anyone at all for a long time', and in the previous year had been 'only concerned with the release of prisoners'. Erich Honecker of the Politbüro's Security Commission reckoned the Stasi was being 'prevented from punishing violations of the law by the unhelpful attitude of public prosecutors'.[8] Bruno Haid lost his job.

Policies that swing wildly from place to place, or that create unnecessary problems which are then addressed by militant mass campaigns, are a feature of ideologically driven states. It happens when governance is based on ideological fanaticisms rather than on more empirical approaches. It is a cycle that East Germany inherited from the Soviet Union – the phenomenon is visible throughout Soviet history. In the 1920s and 1930s, ideological policies formulated in Moscow led to grievous problems with the likes of food supplies. Sometimes such a policy was reversed sharply; sometimes it was addressed by campaign-style policing or industrial activity. Usually, the population was mobilised to deal with the problem caused by the leadership's mistaken policy.

Having sought to soothe and enthuse the public by launching the SED's 'New Course' in 1953, Walter Ulbricht was insisting as early as summer 1955 that the initiative had been misunderstood. Contrary to previous pronouncements, consumer goods were less important than heavy industry, for which the plans had to be fulfilled. Above all, developments in the Soviet Bloc caused a return to stiff discipline and authority. Although Nikita Khrushchev famously criticised Stalin in his 'secret speech' of February 1956, sending reformist ripples through the communist world, the unrest in Poland in June, and the Hungarian uprising in the autumn, badly shook Ulbricht, Mielke, and everyone else invested in the SED regime.

One result was the total subjugation of the National Front. Having seen the dangers of political free-thinking, the SED made sure that the other block parties became its virtual satellites. At its seventh congress in July 1957 the LDPD confounded its original raison d'être by supporting the nationalisation of remaining private businesses. The following year the CDU announced its desire to reconcile the Christian population with 'the construction of socialism'; in 1960 its tenth congress declared abjectly that 'the members of the CDU recognise the working class and its party as the destined leaders of our nation'.[9]

Some international developments also led to a hardening of political attitudes. In spring 1955 the Federal Republic joined NATO, East Germany the Warsaw Pact. A new West German army, the Bundeswehr, was formally established, together with its military intelligence service, the Militärischer Abschirmdienst or MAD, which quickly got into an unhealthy rivalry with the BND and BfV. From the start the Stasi had spies inside the West German armed forces, like Horst Ludwig, a naval officer who was passing information to Main Department II from at least 1954, before the Bundesmarine officially existed. Ludwig agreed to spy for the Stasi to prevent further harm coming to his family in East Germany, where his father had been arrested and his sister harassed. His arrest in West Germany in October 1958 was one of the first spy scandals to hit the Federal armed forces; he was sentenced to five years in prison for treason and aggravated bribery.[10]

Meanwhile, representatives of the 'brother organs' – the security services of the USSR, East Germany, Czechoslovakia and Poland – had convened at a pivotal meeting in Moscow, where they had agreed to make their cooperation more explicit. With the Stasi now formally accepted into the fold, there was talk of 'uniting the strength of the intelligence services [of the Soviet Bloc] against the "principal aggressor governments of the United States and England",' and of conducting 'joint measures' against them.[11] It was agreed to share information on individuals and investigations.

It is notable that Walter Ulbricht and Erich Mielke both reacted badly to Khrushchev's 'secret speech'. Mielke remained a lifelong Stalinist, wont to toast Stalin (with soft drinks) and belt out 1930s Soviet chain gang songs. Ulbricht claimed that the abuses described by Khrushchev hadn't occurred in East Germany. Two months after Khrushchev's speech, the SED Politbüro voted to stop commenting on the topic of Stalin's crimes, as the revelations were feeding anti-communist sentiment. The movement was faring badly in West Germany; in August 1956 the KPD was banned by the Federal government. This led to criminal investigations of almost 200,000 West German communists and sympathisers, of whom some 9,000 were convicted.[12]

The SED did what it could to help them. The Transport Department of the Central Committee, still responsible for secret inter-German communications, ran the Phoenix printing works and a motor pool in West Germany. A radio station, Freiheitssender 904, began to beam communist news into the Federal Republic; its base, a cluster of buildings in the Brandenburg woods known as Objekt 'Valentin', was disguised as a boring warehouse. But the SED was more concerned with issues closer to home; above all, optimising the GDR's new Ministry for National Defence and its National People's Army (Nationale Volksarmee, NVA).

The Stasi's Main Department I had the job of securing the new ministry and army. The chief of HA I, Karl Kleinjung, brought to this task all his experience of enforcing discipline and catching spies in the International Brigades during the Spanish Civil War. His personnel were responsible for rooting out traitors and Western infiltrators, monitoring or halting soldiers' contacts with Western countries, and protecting weaponry and military technology.

They also thwarted desertions and anti-state agitation, vetted personnel, and reported on the mood among soldiers and defence ministry employees.[13] A side project for Kleinjung's department was to chaperone the Wehrmacht's famous Field Marshal von Paulus, defeated at Stalingrad and a resident of East Germany, whose household staff and driver were supplied by the Stasi. Among the department's prime sources was Bernhard Bechler, another former Wehrmacht officer captured at Stalingrad and the postwar interior minister of Brandenburg. As deputy chief of staff of the KVP and then the NVA, Bechler worked steadily as the Stasi's GI 'Wölfi'. In contrast, Vincenz Müller, NVA chief of staff, was ultimately dropped as an HA I informer due to his suspect contacts with Western agencies. He subsequently committed suicide.[14]

Death had already marked the department. One Christmas, a Stasi NCO called Paul Köppe had gone into West Berlin, passed information to a Western agency, and agreed to recruit Stasi and KVP friends as spies. Köppe was driver to Lieutenant Colonel Kurt Schneider, head of HA I for the GDR's southern region. The Stasi arrested Köppe as he attempted to make a recruitment. He was executed in May 1955, after a trial held at Cottbus district court in front of hundreds of Stasi colleagues. Other Western incursions ended similarly. Christian Lange-Werner, teacher at a police flying school, was unearthed as a spy for America. *Neues Deutschland* published a spirited celebration of his death sentence. This was followed by the execution in 1956 of Werner Flach, who had been spying on the NVA for the Organisation Gehlen.[15] There was a lesson here: it was fatally dangerous to betray the East German armed forces.

Despite this bloodthirstiness, the NVA was conceived as 'the ultimate defensive force for protecting workers' and peasants' power'.[16] A flagship national army, it was only to be deployed in exceptional circumstances. As the Hungarian revolt was being suppressed, the Politbüro approved a plan to use the Volkspolizei, armed Stasi units, and the workers' militia – the Combat Groups of the Working Class – to put down any similar disturbances in East Germany. Erich Mielke wrote to regional Stasi chiefs with blunt instructions on what to do in a Budapest-style emergency: 'Control the guarding of the most vital sites'; 'Broadcasters' offices must be controlled'; 'Deploy GM and GI for reconnaissance in West Berlin'; 'Counter all rumours and agitation; Smear [Western] broadcasters, the smuggling of leaflets.'[17]

In a related development, Erich Honecker, in his capacity as the SED's security watchdog, wrote to the party organisation within the Stasi, urging a 'more lively' campaign of education and vigilance. Any GDR officials attempting to restore 'international monopoly capitalism' to East Germany by calling for 'softening' were to be identified and silenced. 'It must be emphatically pointed out,' wrote Honecker, 'that any doubts and wavering by individual employees of the Ministry for State Security, caused by insufficient knowledge of the policy of the Party and Government, of the laws and legal norms of our state, or by an incorrect attitude towards democracy, helps the enemies of our republic.'[18]

The aftershocks of Hungary continued to rattle communist governments for several years. There was something in the communist claims that the rising was fomented by the CIA. James Angleton, the Agency's head of counter-espionage, liked to claim that American propaganda had touched off the revolt. Moreover, 'According to Angleton, the CIA had been training Hungarian exiles at a secret base in Germany for just such an uprising, but the appearance of the Khrushchev speech in the *New York Times* prematurely ignited the revolution before the Agency-trained forces were ready to enter the fray.'[19]

Realising the worst fears of the SED and Stasi, the Hungarian discontent indeed did spread to East Germany. Sympathisers ran up black flags to mourn the suppression of the revolt, including at an NVA facility; Main Department I arrested the three perpetrators there for 'warmongering'.[20] Even as Soviet tanks crushed the disturbances in Budapest, cities such as Magdeburg experienced an upsurge in cases of sabotage, arson and *Republikflucht*. Anti-SED leaflets proliferated. The state construction firm, VEB Bau-Union, received a big supply of bricks branded with swastikas and SS runes. Elsewhere, the slogan 'Hitler awake!' was scrawled on walls. Drunken youths 'singing fascist songs' beat up SED activists.[21] Although Walter Ulbricht's policies and the GDR's poor material conditions were the most common causes of public anger, some of the political dissent expressed in East Germany at this moment was, with its visceral hatred of Russians, 'quite consistent with Nazi and indeed long-standing, pre-Nazi sentiments about the alleged "inferiority" of the Germans' eastern neighbours'.[22] Maybe such sentiments came spontaneously from the public, maybe they didn't. The CIA, for one, had form in fuelling such 'Nazi' expressions of opposition.

Towards the end of 1956 some of East Germany's most prominent socialist ideologues were arrested as state enemies. They included the author and commentator Walter Janka and a professor of philosophy at Berlin's Humboldt University, Wolfgang Harich, who was charged with the 'formation of a group hostile to the state'. On 5 November Ulbricht wrote to Central Committee members and Stasi high-ups, urging them to 'heighten your revolutionary vigilance and combat readiness. Allow no wavering in your ranks and strike the enemy wherever he dares to raise his head'.[23] He was referring to a newly dangerous, if not new, enemy: the independent Marxist.

Ulbricht's half-hearted de-Stalinisation was ending. As far as he and other Stalinists were concerned, the events in Hungary showed that outright rebellion began with thoughtful divergences of opinion and an excess of cultural freedom, not to mention the machinations of Western intelligence services. This was not to happen in East Germany.

Encouraged by the twentieth congress of the Soviet communist party, at which Nikita Khrushchev had denounced Stalin, Wolfgang Harich had started to believe that a truer and more democratic socialism could be realised in the Soviet Bloc. He formed a discussion group that formulated a new programme: the replacement of Walter Ulbricht, free elections, cultural freedom, economic reforms, and a revived relationship with the West German SPD to bring about a reunified, demilitarised socialist Germany. In an act of almost idiotic hopefulness, Harich gave a copy of this manifesto to Soviet ambassador Georgy Pushkin, thinking that it would then make its way, with Pushkin's endorsement, to Ulbricht himself. Walter Janka, too, had his own ideas for the SED, and took part in Harich's discussion circles. Janka was somebody in the GDR – writer, broadcaster, thinker and International Brigade veteran, and head of an important state publishing concern.

The Stasi's Main Department V delivered a mortal blow to this little hub of reformists. Harich was arrested on 29 November together with Manfred Hertwig – like Harich, the editor of a philosophy journal – and the economist Bernhard Steinberger. The arrest of Janka followed on 6 December. Janka's trial was conducted in an intimidatory Stalinist atmosphere, before an audience vetted, and probably constituted, by the Stasi. Young 'rowdies' yelled abuse throughout: 'Down with the traitors!', 'To prison with the criminals!'. This behaviour recalled the earlier Moscow show trials, where planted crowds had chanted 'Shoot them, shoot them!', as Karl Radek and other revolutionary heroes had shuffled abjectly to and from the dock. The presiding judge at Janka's trial didn't comment on the shouting. Members of the prosecution, it was reported, 'drummed on the tabletops with their fists like students gone wild after a fascinating lecture'. Janka noticed that fellow writers in the audience – Anna Seghers, Bodo Uhse – 'remained mute' and 'grew pale'.[24]

Questions arise about the reporting or broadcasting of such audience anger. Was the East German public impressed by this vitriol? Deceived by it? Frightened by it? Perhaps it had a similar effect to that discernible in Stalin's USSR – the inculcation, throughout society, of a dual passivity and viciousness. People grew cowed and enervated, but prone to interpersonal suspicion, envy and malice. This, presumably, was not what Karl Marx had had in mind.

Tried alongside Janka were the journalist Richard Wolf and the editors Gustav Just and Heinz Zöger. All worked for *Sonntag*, a journal for politics and the arts published by the Kulturbund der DDR, a National Front organisation. In the indictment they were accused of trying to 'liquidate workers' and peasants' power' by destroying 'socialist achievements in the political, economic and cultural fields'. Janka, their intellectual leader, had 'called for the removal of leading figures from the party and government'. Wolf had 'demanded the withdrawal of Soviet forces from the GDR and the release of all people convicted under Article 6 of the constitution'.[25] Janka was sentenced to five years, the others to slightly shorter terms.

Wolfgang Harich, tried before attorney general Ernst Melsheimer, got ten years. Perhaps hoping for clemency, he joined the ranks of those prepared to trot out a dismal Stasi-penned apology in court. 'I have now had experience with the state security of the GDR,' he said, and 'they are very correct and decent.' Moreover, the Stasi was 'to be thanked', for Harich believed himself to have been 'unstoppable. I was like a runaway horse that can't be stopped by shouting... if they hadn't arrested me, I wouldn't be facing the ten years that the attorney general has requested, but the gallows'.[26] Humboldt University was then classified by the Stasi as an Objekt – a site of security interest – and more of Harich's academic associates were arrested. After protracted investigations, the lecturers Heinrich Saar and Herbert Crüger were sentenced to eight years for treason – a newly defined crime in the GDR – although they were released in a 1961 amnesty.[27]

The assault on academe demonstrates that dissenting Marxists, perhaps more than fascists or capitalists, were an enemy the SED and Stasi really feared. Such dissenters offered the populace a potentially wiser and more efficient version of the party's own creed. From the public's point of view, 'humanistic' socialism was familiar enough to be comprehensible and different enough to inspire. But any tinkering with the party's tenets – not to discard them but to reconfigure them, as if they were common property, objective and up for grabs – caused immense distress at the top of the SED. It made party leaders feel vulnerable and, quite possibly, it made them feel stupid.

This dynamic can be seen in the case of Robert Havemann, an academic chemist. Havemann's life took a complicated course from anti-Nazi resister to GDR functionary to, ultimately, Marxist dissident.[28] In 1953 he was recruited by the Stasi's Department III as a contact person, becoming a full-blown informer, GI 'Leitz', three years later. At first he was unswervingly loyal. Having been imprisoned by the Nazis, Havemann felt he owed his freedom – his life, in fact – to Joseph Stalin. After the war he was sufficiently confident and motivated to work for the MGB, on whose behalf he got acquainted with officers of the American and British military administrations. He also reported on groups of West Berlin social democrats and Trotskyists. Havemann's intellectual brilliance saw him established at Humboldt University and other seats of learning, but he retained his ideological fire. In 1950 he published an article in *Neues Deutschland*, 'Truman's great theatrical thunder', in which he criticised America's development of the hydrogen bomb. For this he was summarily dismissed from a senior position at West Berlin's Kaiser Wilhelm Institute.

Still, Havemann remained well-connected in scientific and cultural circles across the two Germanys. He caught the Stasi's eye with his friendships with West German physicists and chemists, among them three Nobel Prize winners. An early Department III report on Havemann's potential noted he had 'interesting connections to West Germany and through him it is possible to attract scientists [to the GDR] and penetrate objects'. Once signed up as a collaborator, Havemann 'brought valuable tips and information'.[29] In December 1954 he introduced a West Berlin scientist from the Max Planck Society to the Stasi, who recruited him. Havemann also strove to secure the return of refugees to the GDR and, in one case, prevented the flight from East Germany of a professor from Leipzig, notifying the Stasi of the professor's planned escape. Remarkably, and initially unknown to Main Department III, Havemann was simultaneously cooperating with both NVA intelligence and the Stasi's Main Department I. These relationships had come about through a family connection with one Heinz Hofmann, an intelligence officer and secret HA I invigilator inside the army.

Havemann was notably vicious in his informer reports. He excoriated scientists who were 'old fascists', accused several professors and doctors of being former Gestapo spies, and abused other colleagues for their alleged shady business deals or professional inadequacies. Yet Havemann, it seems, was of a certain type – a person prone to entering grateful allegiances and fulsome enthusiasms which then go cold and are replaced. Gradually his informer reports to the Stasi began to deviate from the party line. He began to air spiky opinions around the standard discontents of regime loyalists – Khrushchev's revelations about Stalin, the heavy-handed suppression in Poland and Hungary, the lack of freedom of expression in East Germany, and Walter Ulbricht's self-serving, snakelike leadership. Havemann, perhaps, was a prime example of a person who tried to improve the SED regime by collaborating with its security service. It backfired, of course. So did his quixotic lectures to students and frank discussions with state officials, all of whom reported everything he said. German authors make much of Havemann's bravery at this moment. They overlook his tremendous egotism. His was the kind of ego, not coincidentally, possessed by many of those who interact with intelligence services; the likes of double agents and attention-seeking defectors. Havemann apparently was convinced that his own brand of Marxism would resonate and even be adopted in East Germany. For a while the Stasi stuck with him as a collaborator, but his 'undiscipline' and 'shortcomings' soon saw him cast as an enemy, and his status shifted from that of Stasi helper to Stasi victim.

Havemann was gradually excluded from the Humboldt party leadership, then the party itself. He went on to endure long years of postal and telephone interception, Stasi burglaries of his home, periods of house arrest, and convenient convictions for apparently 'unpolitical' offences such as foreign exchange irregularities. In a word, Havemann had been fooled. He had completely misread the character of his own party and government.

A similar blind spot affected some of East Germany's literary stars. In the early 1950s the Stasi had 'viewed neither "cultural workers" nor "members of the intelligentsia" as a group that particularly needed to be monitored'. Now, fearing 'Hungarian conditions', it set up a permanent case file on the German Writers' Association, and 'concentrated on [the] press, radio, television and film', with 'technical areas such as transmitters, studios, production rooms and broadcast vans... subject to particularly strict controls'.[30] Although few East German writers were actively opposed to the SED, and none were opposed to socialism, they were hit hard by the toughening of policy from 1957. Erich Loest spent seven years in prison at Bautzen for treason. Uwe Johnson left the GDR, only to be secretly watched in exile for the next two decades.[31] Others tried to stay on the right side of authority by becoming informers. The award-winning novelist Hermann Kant, codenamed 'Martin', was said by his Stasi handler to derive 'amusement' from their meetings.[32] And in the late 1950s Christa Wolf, East Germany's preeminent woman writer, was hired as GI 'Margarete'. Her exposure in the 1990s was devastating for those who still hailed the GDR's literature as one of its untainted socialist achievements.

Having dealt with some of their professors and role models, the Stasi turned to stamping on students. By the end of 1957 cogent student opposition in East Germany – much of it triggered by Khrushchev's de-Stalinisation and events in Poland and Hungary – had been almost obliterated. Main Department V was given fresh orders to recruit more informers in such 'objects' as student dorms and clubhouses, and at the pubs and restaurants of 'all university towns'. It was made clear that professors, preferably from 'the middle teaching staff', didn't have to sign the usual declaration of commitment as an informer, although 'under no circumstances' were conspiratorial meetings to be held in universities, only in safe houses. The same order mentioned 'the use of all the possibilities of operational technology', as in cameras and bugging. All of this was to provide 'a complete overview of the focus of hostile activity'.[33] Before long, undercover 'operational groups' had been created at universities in Berlin, Leipzig, Jena, Dresden, Greifswald, Rostock and Potsdam.

The authorities responded to students' dissent in a variety of ways. Sometimes teaching staff, the local party or Free German Youth would step in to arrange corrective discussions. This was done, for example, in the wake of the problematic seminars for young Berliners organised regularly by the Federal Ministry for All-German Affairs. At other times Stasi infiltrators would try to exert influence, steering groups of students back onto the right ideological path. Sometimes ringleaders were arrested.

There wasn't always the opportunity to do so. In one celebrated incident, sixteen teenaged students from Storkow secondary school in Brandenburg ran from the GDR, after one of their parents shopped them for holding a minute's silence in honour of Hungary. Their flight was prompted partly by a furious visit to the school by education minister Fritz Lange, demanding to know who had instigated the action. He then accused the students of being the type who 'not only applaud when a minister like himself is hanged, but tighten the rope'.[34] After entering West Berlin by riding the S-Bahn 'with little luggage', at least one of the students subsequently received a telegram, probably sent by the Stasi, claiming falsely that his mother was terminally ill back in East Germany and he should return. Some of the students' parents were visited by Stasi employees, likely in the guise of education officials, urging them to retrieve their teenagers from the Federal Republic. There were no takers.

Stasi reports sometimes reveal a thoughtful, reformist attitude among students. Many of them quite liked socialism; they just didn't like Walter Ulbricht or rule from Moscow. One Stasi informer described a group at Dresden's technical college trying, poignantly, to understand the deceits of the SED's newspapers. They wondered aloud why it had been necessary for the Soviet army to intervene in Hungary, if the rising there were merely the work of 'fascist gangs', as reported. 'Is it possible to incite people to such acts of violence,' asked one student, 'just with demands from fascists?' The group expressed the wish to form a more independent students' association, and complained about their compulsory Russian language lessons, asking 'How can we best serve socialism? By speaking Russian well, or becoming good chemists?' This conversation was deemed 'particularly aggressive and hostile' by the Stasi's informer.[35]

Other students formed bona fide resistance organisations. One of them tried to soothe the authorities with a beguiling name, the National Communist Student League; the Stasi arrested its leaders anyway. Better known is the Eisenberger Circle from Thuringia, founded by students who resented the

'Stalinisation' of their curriculum and the expulsion of overtly religious pupils. While its first actions were modest – tearing down SED posters and distributing anti-communist literature – the circle developed contacts with the SPD Ostbüro and, more dangerously, the KgU. The tone of its actions changed accordingly. First a museum was burgled in the hunt for old firearms, then an army shooting range was burned down. In February 1958 the circle's leaders were arrested after a patient infiltration by the Stasi. After this, the wind fell from its sails.[36] A total of 116 years' prison time was handed to the arrestees. Once out of prison the circle's leader, Thomas Ammer, moved to West Germany, where he was watched by the Stasi for more than a quarter of a century.

For tricky operations against possible dissidence in the church, the Stasi recruited theologians as collaborators, especially at the University of Leipzig. These were long-term sources who continued reporting as their academic careers ascended. Kurt Meier, a professor of church history at Leipzig, was a notable recruit of 1957. Like others, he was tasked with informing on fellow theologians, talent-spotting students for the Stasi, influencing church opinion in favour of the SED, and attending conferences in West Germany, where he could propagandise about the GDR's religious freedom and gather information on church matters in the West. In a similar vein, Hans-Joachim Seidowsky, an employee of the SED department for church affairs, worked for the Stasi under the codenames 'Gerhard' and 'Jochen', infiltrating both Protestant and Catholic churches in the guise of an unorthodox Marxist disillusioned with the GDR.[37]

The return to hardline policies saw renewed attacks on the church. The SED mocked the decision of Germany's Protestant church organisation, the EKD, to assign West German chaplains to the Bundeswehr. For the East German authorities this was tantamount to the church joining NATO. Ernst Wollweber closed the chapels at railway stations, complaining that they were being used as dead drops by Western agents. Seminaries and cloisters were termed 'objects', and so came under more intense Stasi scrutiny. A secular confirmation ceremony, the Jugendweihe, had already been introduced in schools; clerics who complained about it became Stasi targets. One such was Otto Spülbeck, Catholic bishop of the diocese of Meissen, who recorded on tape a speech in which he ridiculed the ceremony's atheism. The tape was played at many churches; Stasi informers were particularly outraged by Spülbeck's sarcastic delivery of the Jugendweihe text, which aroused laughter every time.[38] The Stasi's counterattack didn't require much imagination. In an instruction for the branch of Main Department V with responsibility for churches,[39] Erich Mielke urged officers to gather compromising information about clergymen – usually their sexual transgressions or crimes, which didn't have to be fabricated – in order to have leverage over them.

There were subtler forms of manipulation. Walter Ulbricht recognised the propaganda value of church ministers, especially at conferences in the Federal Republic. He pushed clerics to join the Prague Christian Peace Conference, a Marx-friendly international society founded in 1958. The SED also launched a front organisation, the Association of Protestant Pastors, though it was so obviously a sham that it was dissolved after a while. Moreover, the SED saw the church as a valuable provider of social welfare. Church money, much of it pumped in from the West, was useful for taking care of the elderly, the mentally ill and disabled; care that the SED regime itself couldn't afford.[40]

In 1956 the Stasi was involved in an operation that contributed to the church's emergence as a cash cow.[41] On the basis of trumped-up advice from the Ministry of Justice, the government halved the subsidies paid to churches and stopped collecting the religious taxes which are traditional in Germany. As predicted, the EKD stepped in with hard currency transfers to East German churches. On the advice of banking specialists, some of them Stasi collaborators, these Western donations were made using a complex system of counter-trade bartering with the Ministry for Foreign Trade.

The SED regime benefited in every way from the crisis it had prompted. It acquired desperately needed hard currency and goods that usually were unavailable – from the late 1950s onwards, the Lutheran church alone sent more than two billion deutschmarks into the GDR. The situation also caused embarrassment to the churches of both republics. In early 1957 the homes of some prominent East German clerics were raided. Large sums of foreign currency were discovered, feeding the SED's claims that the churches were secret agencies of the Bonn government.

Even so, it proved surprisingly difficult to inculcate the required hatred of religion in Stasi personnel. Willi Butter, head of the anti-church branch of Main Department V, complained at a service conference that his young employees, for reasons of ingrained respect, were 'afraid of talking to clergy'. Worse still, noted Butter, 'employees of the MfS had had their children married in church or had their children baptised and confirmed.' These problems were addressed by a three-week crash course for all employees, at which Willi Barth, head of church affairs at the SED Central Committee, gave lectures on the party's policy towards religionists. Attendees also took 'Chekist lessons' in psychology and 'special methods for educating, recruiting and processing clergy'.

Willi Butter's days were numbered. He was replaced as HA V section chief by Hans Ludwig, a former furniture maker who had begun his state security career in 1949 as a political instructor with the Directorate for the Protection of the National Economy. Within a couple of years his section boasted 122 informers in key positions: forty-eight in the Protestant church, forty-four in the Catholic, twenty-three in the Jehovah's Witnesses, and nineteen in West German churches. Ludwig, like any true-red SED member, despised believers and their faiths. He was to lead the Stasi's anti-church efforts for more than a decade.[42]

56

Mielke Wins

In his final year as Stasi chief, Ernst Wollweber was an organisational ghost: unwell, often absent, barely relevant to his subordinates. Erich Mielke was *de facto* chief long before his official appointment as security minister on 1 November 1957. By this time the Soviets had fallen out of love with Wollweber. He was less obedient than other SED executives, and Moscow detected in him a brooding German nationalism with which it was uncomfortable. An equally big problem was his mistress, Clara Vater. As a KPD member she had spent much of the 1930s in Soviet exile; typically, she had fallen foul of the purges and received a Gulag sentence. Although the SED admitted Vater, the KGB considered her untrustworthy and kept her and her daughter under surveillance. Aleksandr Korotkov, head of the KGB's Germany department, wasn't the type to tolerate a former Gulag inmate sharing a bed with a Soviet Bloc security minister.

Wollweber's troubles were worsened by his toxic relationship with Walter Ulbricht. The main issue was perceived faction-forming within the SED, at a time when Ulbricht was acutely aware of his own unpopularity in the party. Wollweber was associated politically with Karl Schirdewan, a prominent potential successor to Ulbricht who became something of an East German Trotsky. Some of Ulbricht's unease about Schirdewan had a rational basis, for the CIA indeed had sources in Schirdewan's circle, as suspected. When reporting to the CIA's Berlin Operations Base, these informants exaggerated the potential of an opposition movement within the GDR.[1] American money then paid for a lengthy campaign of leafletting, emanating from the purported 'SED Opposition'. This tendency, while it may have existed in the safety of party member's minds, was certainly not overt or organised.

The antipathy between Ulbricht and Wollweber surfaced during the operations against the dissident communist intellectuals around Wolfgang Harich. For Ulbricht, Harich was a dangerous counter-revolutionary. For Wollweber, he was an irritating boffin. It was Ulbricht who had acquired the killer evidence against Harich – the manifesto and other papers setting out Harich's alternative programme – without Wollweber's knowledge or involvement. This brought the very workings of the Stasi into question. In retaliation for being sidelined in the Harich affair, Wollweber ordered his staff to notify him of all contacts between the Stasi and members of the Central Committee. For Ulbricht, this suggested that Wollweber was trying to usurp the party's leadership.

Ulbricht embarked on a systematic campaign to oust Wollweber and several other executives. He told the Central Committee that Wollweber's 'focus on external enemy agents' had 'led to the neglect of vigilance': as a result, political opponents had become 'cheeky'.[2] Although Wollweber had not ignored political dissidence to the extent alleged by Ulbricht, such signalling prompted a change of focus within the Stasi. In April 1957, following a review overseen by the Politbüro Security Commission, Ulbricht told a decisive conference of top Stasi officers that the SED was now to have a stronger presence in the ministry. Furthermore, the Stasi was to boost its security operations at lower, local levels, in closer collaboration with local party secretaries, and to develop more sources inside important workplaces and state institutions.[3] 'If we give local [state] bodies more rights,' said Ulbricht, referring to his own recent 'thaw' policies, 'if we encourage the working masses to participate more [then] at the same time we must also take security measures, so that our opponents do not find divisions.'[4] This, then, was an admission that any apparent public softening was always to be accompanied with a behind-the-scenes hardening.

With Wollweber off sick, Erich Mielke's obsequious response to Ulbricht's hints was to rush out Stasi order 16/57: 'Measures to improve operational work in factories, ministries and main administrations, universities, colleges and scientific institutes, as well as at agricultural sites'.* The order called for networks of informers, each led by a Lead Secret Informer, to be set up inside workplaces while also permeating the residential areas around them. At every workplace the informers were to have good channels of communication with managers and party officials. As well as 'processing' each 'object' to neutralise security threats, the new informer networks were to ascertain how SED policies were going down, and to watch out for dangerously sloppy work or bad conditions. There was to be increased informer coverage at local councils, post offices and railway stations.† At educational institutions, the likes of rectors and chief librarians were to be signed up as collaborators (if they weren't already). Full-time Stasi staffs were to be established at more than fifty key industrial

---

*   Massnahmen zur Verbesserung der operative Arbeit in den Betrieben, Ministerien und Hauptverwaltungen, Universitäten, Hochschulen und wissenschaftlichen Instituten sowie in den Objekten der Landwirtschaft.

†   Trusted and capable officers of Department XIII were made responsible for the security of key train stations: Berlin Ostbahnhof, Berlin Friedrichstrasse, Dresden Neustadt, Leipzig, Erfurt, Magdeburg, Frankfurt/Oder, Bad Schandau, Wittenberge, Karl-Marx-Stadt, Halle.

sites, with employees or collaborators working undercover in useful roles such as personal secretaries or heads of department.[5]

Ulbricht did not desist from feuding even when Mielke was appointed chief of the Stasi. In February 1958, at the thirty-fifth plenum of the Central Committee, Wollweber, Schirdewan and Fred Oelssner were charged with 'repeated infractions of Politbüro discipline' and removed from all their remaining positions. Another alleged member of the Schirdewan faction, the SED secretary for economic affairs Gerhart Ziller, was already out of the way – he had committed suicide after turning up drunk at a Wismut AG meeting. Ernst Wollweber – once the proud revolutionary sailor who had hoisted red flags over mutinous German ships, bossed the Comintern with a click of his fingers, and spent years cosseted as a prize asset of Moscow – drifted off into ailing obscurity. Even so, Walter Ulbricht enjoyed kicking a person who was down. He threatened Wollweber with legal action and with eviction from his home at Karlshorst, and cancelled his access to a superior Soviet-run hospital.[6] Given that Wollweber had suffered a heart attack, this was unhelpful.

Once Erich Mielke was chief, Ulbricht and the SED exercised a political control over the Stasi that never wavered and was never challenged. Ulbricht had cowed the ministry; from this point onwards, the Stasi would never consider itself to be above the party or attempt to decide East Germany's strategic policies. Its reporting to party and state officials duly was affected. Whatever it really knew, henceforth the Stasi began to sweeten-up any unpalatable assessments for the consumption of SED executives. Much of the baldness and rawness was lost from its coverage of citizens' comments, for it was safer to speak untruth to power. Mielke also restricted the dissemination of Stasi reports, which were shared with an ever-shrinking number of party high-ups.[7]

The Stasi inherited by Erich Mielke had grown to 17,400 full-time employees. Like all intelligence and security services of the period it was largely male, despite relying on women in important areas such as party work and the curation of organisational memory. This imbalance reflected the somewhat double-edged position of women in the republic. On the one hand, the GDR could boast in 1970 that thirty-four percent of its doctors and fifty-three percent of its judges were women; it had also achieved the world's highest female representation in an industrialised workforce. Even Erich Mielke announced that in a socialist society, women were equal to men.[8] On the other hand, traditional chauvinism was rampant throughout East German life, and nowhere more so than in the pumped-up military environment of the Stasi. The SED itself advocated domestic roles for women and a higher birth rate, which were considered more valuable than women's work.

Mielke tried to set a standard at his ministry by working usually from 7 a.m. to 10 p.m., although the daybed he kept in his private office suggests that he wasn't always vertical during these hours. He was enthusiastic about Ulbricht's demands to focus less on foreign espionage and more on domestic political enemies. To help in this fight, Mielke began to use a new term for oppositional thought – 'political-ideological diversion' or PiD.* This term was to become central to the Stasi's mindset and behaviour. Above all, Mielke, in the words of historian Mike Dennis, continued to attribute 'all forms of domestic opposition in socialist countries back to the influence of "imperialistic enemy headquarters", whether there were direct, provable intelligence incursions or only intellectual influence'.[9]

Although Mielke never stopped celebrating the 'fighting alliance' (kampfbündnis) between Stasi and KGB, once he was installed as chief the Soviets relinquished some of their control. Mirroring the relationship between the Soviet Union and the GDR, it was noted that Stasi officers were growing in confidence and were less inclined to follow KGB orders 'without question'.[10] KGB liaison officers, most with the rank of colonel and their own rooms at the Lichtenberg complex, remained with the Stasi's main departments. As well as its 1,000 or so employees at Karlshorst, including an important residency of its Third Chief Directorate (counter-intelligence), the KGB maintained its own informer networks and some thirty offices around East Germany, with one at each of the Stasi's fifteen regional headquarters.

The KGB continued to receive the bulk of the intelligence gathered by the Stasi, for a vague signed agreement entitled it 'to be provided all information pertaining to the general and operational situation in the GDR, West Germany and other capitalist countries'.[11] And the Stasi's information flow continued to run upwards and inwards from its outposts towards its centre. It was virtually impossible for Stasi departments or officers to act independently, whether of their own leadership or the KGB. Whenever an officer at regional or district level received an order from Berlin, he was to tell a superior what the order was, who had issued it, and how he planned to implement it. When not conducted by the main departments in Berlin, Stasi operations were mounted, and information gathered, at the lowest and smallest level – the district or Kreis office – often in consultation with local SED secretaries. Information was then passed upwards to the regional, or Bezirk, office. It then made its way to Stasi HQ at Lichtenberg, where after scrutiny and grading by the analysts of the new Central Information Group, it ended up on the desk of one person: the Stasi chief. In theory, it was possible to filter or adulterate the information at every

---

* Politisch-Ideologischen Diversion.

step of this journey. By the time it made it to Mielke, and from him to the top brass of the SED and KGB, information that might discomfit the party or Moscow had doubtless gone through a sanitising wash.[12]

The Stasi continued to work in an evolving legal environment. To keep abreast of the changes, it relied on its three-person 'advice centre' for legal matters; only in the mid-1960s was this expanded into a proper legal department. It was led by Hans-Georg Filin, formerly of the Stasi's Information Service, who in fact had dropped out of his law course at Rostock University. Filin had Stasi interests at heart, drafting proposals, for instance, on how to prevent 'disruptions to operational (conspiratorial) work caused by the improper intervention of public prosecutors'.[13]

Developments in the law tended to favour the Stasi anyway. In February 1958, paragraph 14 of the Criminal Law Supplementary Act saw the specific crime of espionage instated, at last. In response to the judicial mish-mash thrown up by the *Grossaktionen*, and the GDR's overreliance on vague and ageing legal instruments, the Act formalised the punishments for a range of offences. These included 'propaganda and hate speech that endanger the state', 'inducement to leave the republic' and 'connection with criminal organisations'.[14] Lobbying by Mielke and others saw the 'collection and transmission of non-secret information' criminalised as well. It was hoped this might stop refugees and would-be refugees from briefing the Western authorities about the GDR.

Although influenced by Soviet criminal law, especially Article 58, the Act employed the traditional German concept of 'endangerment of the state', and mirrored elements of the Criminal Law Amendment Act passed in West Germany in 1951.[15] But its enshrining of concepts around the Stasi's new catchphrase – 'political-ideological diversion' – was distinctly East German. PiD came to underpin 'not only the operational activities of the state security service, but indirectly also the political criminal justice system'. The Act was a weapon in the fight against 'ideological decomposition' caused by 'revisionist, opportunistic and liberalising views'.[16] This was considered a priority after the mistakes of Poland and Hungary.

Now, meeting people 'for the purpose of devising, developing or realising a treasonable concept' was considered a preparatory act for the newly defined crime of treason. This innovation, influenced by the trials of Wolfgang Harich and Walter Janka, was useful for prosecuting independent thinkers; people who, in the words of historians Engelmann and Joestel, might otherwise have been 'fundamentally loyal to the GDR'. The investigators of Main Department IX – which was transferred to Erich Mielke's personal portfolio – quickly applied this law to the 'so-called literature evenings and poetry readings' which they believed were masking seditious gatherings. The likes of choral societies and equestrian clubs were also fair game for investigation. The participants could now face a minimum of five years in prison.[17]

Mielke tried to further professionalise Main Department IX by creating its Murder and Fire Commission (Mord-und Brandkommission), represented at every district Stasi office. Staffed by forensic science specialists, and including trackers, fire experts and a doctor, the commission was supposed to improve the Stasi's performance around forensics, lessening its reliance on the Volkspolizei. The Stasi knew that incidents of sabotage, for example, had diverse causes, and it wanted to clarify them. In June 1957 an oil-soaked rag and burnt matches were discovered at the site of an extinguished fire in a shaft of the Wismut mines; six suspected perpetrators were arrested. This was sabotage. But the very next day, a fire in a fruit and veg warehouse in Rostock, which caused 100,000 marks-worth of damage, was traced to the distinctly apolitical antics of a drunken Finnish sailor.[18] The Stasi wanted to get these incidents right – it didn't want to cry 'sabotage' when there was none.

Throughout his life as a communist operative, Erich Mielke had had to carry out difficult orders and shoulder tough responsibilities. He now expected the same of his subordinates. He demanded more vigour and conscientiousness from regional and district Stasi chiefs. It helped that the Stasi, temporarily, was shedding some duties. Focused on purifying East German society, Mielke wasn't sorry that in Wollweber's dying days as boss, responsibility for the border, standby and transport police had been transferred to the Ministry of the Interior. The Stasi's Department VII continued to invigilate the security of these forces, however, making use of such long-term assets as Major General Rudolf Bamler, who had served in the Abwehr in the 1930s and latterly held a senior post in the KVP. The chief of these forces at the interior ministry was Hermann Gartmann who, although transferred out of the Stasi, undoubtedly continued to be its eyes and ears.

While it is true that one person doesn't make a system, the Stasi came to be moulded so faithfully in the image of its leader, and became so intrinsic to East Germany's makeup, that Erich Mielke, the Berlin street brawler, ended up with an unlikely historical significance as one of the shapers of Europe. Wilhelm Zaisser, and even more so Ernst Wollweber, had been important figures in the interwar communist movement. Compared to them, Mielke was an ideological nobody. So what can be made of his vision, his political commitment?

Mielke's communism – that is, his Stalinism – was not insincere. Imbibed from childhood and versed in doctrinal texts, his beliefs ran through his veins. But communists of Mielke's generation tended to be idealists. Mielke never was. He did not embody the intellectual and visceral faith of the clever communist, observed by Fitzroy Maclean in Edo Kardelj, a wartime partisan who later served as Yugoslavia's foreign minister:

> Kardelj knew all the answers. He was a fascinating man to talk to. You could never catch him out or make him angry. He was perfectly frank, perfectly logical, perfectly calm and unruffled. Muddle; murder; distortion; deception. It was quite true. Such things happened under Communism, might even be an intentional part of Communist policy. But it would be worth it in the long run. The end would justify the means. Some day they would get their way; some day their difficulties would disappear; their enemies would be eliminated; the people educated; and a Communist millennium make the world a happier and a better place. Then the need for strong measures would disappear. He might not live to see this happen. But he was quite ready, as they all were, not only to die himself, but to sacrifice everybody and everything that was near and dear to him to the cause which he had chosen, to liquidate anybody who stood in his way. Such sacrifices, such liquidations, would be for the greater good of humanity. What worthier cause could there be.[19]

The ruthlessness and purportedly noble motives described by Maclean are discernible in Erich Mielke, but the idealism – especially its tone of self-sacrifice and its far horizon of universal happiness – bypassed him completely. Mielke didn't argue that the end justified the means. For him, the means *were* the end. For other communists, the 'dictatorship of the proletariat' was a temporary necessity when establishing true socialism. A passing phase, it would be replaced by the full flower of proper communist equality. For Mielke, the dictatorship of the proletariat was the highpoint and endpoint. He thrived on it; perfect already, it didn't need to be superseded. Seen in this light, his veneration of Joseph Stalin is unsurprising: after all, Stalin had, in the words of Donald Rayfield, 'made revolutionary socialism a container for his own fascism – he was no more a communist than a Borgia pope was a Catholic'.[20] Mielke never accepted Nikita Khrushchev's criticisms of Stalin, and he spent the rest of his life glowering at anyone who did.

From the time of his appointment onwards, the Volkskammer repeatedly re-elected Mielke as minister for state security. In 1958 he was 'elected' as a Volkskammer deputy, and thereafter was re-elected every time East Germans went to the polls. He was also a member of the Council of Ministers, ostensibly the government cabinet. Although he didn't become a full member of the Politbüro until the 1970s, his role as head of security appears never to have been threatened, and his conduct in that role was never seriously scrutinised.[21]

In terms of his political morality, Mielke could, perhaps, play one winning card: his anti-fascism. The fight against fascism had been the great battle of Mielke's era. By the time he became Stasi chief, the East German authorities were recognising that anti-fascism was one of their major strengths in the propaganda war. Not only did anti-fascism provide the GDR with a reason to exist, it became the stated reason for most of the KGB and Soviet Bloc intelligence activity of the period. The presence of former Nazis in influential positions in West Germany – the illegitimate 'State of Bonn', according to the SED – gave East German propagandists a field day. The GDR wasted no opportunity in proclaiming its own rectitude and denouncing the fatal corruption of the Federal Republic. Whenever there were calls to discuss reunification, the GDR authorities always expressed their unease about the 'revival of militarism and fascism in West Germany'.[22]

'Hitler's followers again hold positions of power and attempt to draw the nations of Western Europe into atomic war to advance their revanchist plans,' wrote GDR president Wilhelm Pieck in a government publication.[23] He continued:

> They see West Germany as a staging point and advance base for atomic war. Under the leadership of Hitler's criminal generals, they seek to build the strongest military power in Western Europe and are beginning to arm themselves with atomic rockets. They reject any agreement with our republic to reunify Germany, seek to annex the German Democratic Republic, [and] are preparing a new war...

At this time the GDR had numerous producers of propaganda: the party's efforts under Albert Norden, the prime minister's press office, the council of the National Front and the Stasi's Agitation Department, to name just four. From 1957 to 1974 the Agitation Department was led by Günter Halle, a key figure in East German propaganda. Also influential as a propagandist was Gerhart Eisler, whose deportation from America, and alleged mishandling by British police officers while en route to Europe, had been another fleeting, long-forgotten press sensation of the early Cold War. All East German propagandists pushed the idea that West Germany was 're-Nazifying', in material that sometimes was overt (so-called white propaganda), sometimes unattributed (grey propaganda), and sometimes falsely attributed (black propaganda). Albert Norden directed the besmirching of West Germany from his official position at the Committee for German Unity, a pleasant-sounding government body formed in 1954. He went on to head the SED Westkommission, which continued to investigate and expose Nazi criminals in the Federal Republic during the 1960s. On occasion Norden's public messages were backed up by John Peet, an oddball British expatriate who had settled in East Germany in 1950 and then spent decades trying to convince Western journalists that he had made a good decision.

A rich seam of propaganda material lay in the Nazi archives that had fallen into communist hands at the end of the war. Their contents turned up in a string of so-called 'exposure films' – documentaries offering proof that Nazism was thriving in West Germany. These included *Der Fall Heusinger* (The Heusinger Case, 1959), *Mord In Lwow* (Murder in Lvov, 1960) and *Aktion J* (1961), but the most notorious was *Unternehmen Teutonenschwert* (Operation Teutonic Sword) of 1958. It alleged that Hans Speidel, commander-in-chief of NATO's central European land forces, had been involved in the assassinations of King Alexander I of Yugoslavia and the French foreign minister, Louis Barthou, in 1934, acting on Nazi orders. The film backfired somewhat; it was banned as defamation in some countries, including Sweden and Britain, where legal action was taken against its distributor.[24] In general, the effectiveness of these efforts was hampered by that perennial flaw of propaganda: exaggeration. While the GDR authorities tried to popularise slogans like 'Hitler to Adenauer', suggesting continuity from the Nazi era to the Federal Republic – which existed, in many walks of life – their messages tended to be undermined by wild or tenuous claims.

This wasn't always the case. One major propaganda attack begun in the late 1950s, the 'Bloody Judges' campaign, was based squarely on truth, for the West German judiciary was a bastion of former Nazis. At the end of the war, the majority of German judges and prosecutors had been members of the Nazi party, and most had continued to practice uninterrupted.[25] This was one reason for the SED's drive to train a new generation of socialist legal professionals in East Germany. It may also explain some of the anomalous behaviour of West German courts after the war. Field Marshal Erich von Manstein, for example, convicted of war crimes, served only four years of an eighteen-year sentence. The diplomat Franz Rademacher, who had attended the Wannsee conference at which the Final Solution was agreed upon, and who was convicted of complicity in war crimes in Yugoslavia and the deportation of Jews from western Europe, was given three years in prison and immediately granted bail, which he skipped before heading to safety in Syria.

Albert Norden launched the 'Bloody Judges' campaign at an East Berlin press conference on 23 May 1957. He presented to the assembled reporters a booklet, co-produced by the Stasi and titled 'Yesterday Hitler's blood-judge – Today Bonn's judicial elite'. It named 118 Nazi legal professionals still practising in West Germany. Understanding the reluctance in the Federal Republic to hear anything about the Nazi past, the SED and Stasi planned for a long-term, drip-feeding campaign. A new edition of the booklet was published every six months, with the names of 200 more 'Bloody Judges' added each time, until by the end of 1959 the total had reached 1,000.[26]

This campaign caused problems for the Federal authorities. A decade later, protests by West Germany's left-wing students were still focused on the issue. The press got excited. Death sentences from the Nazi era were reviewed. The point was made in Britain's House of Commons that the employment of Nazi lawyers violated the Potsdam Agreement. A few Nazi judges and prosecutors were investigated and proceeded against; others moaned that they were being 'vilified'. Wartime resistance fighters, from western Europe as well as Poland and Czechoslovakia, backed up the SED's statements. In February 1959 resisters from France, Belgium and The Netherlands appeared at another East Berlin press conference, titled 'We accuse – 800 Nazi blood-judges – pillars of the Adenauer regime'.

The campaign was all the more forceful because the Stasi and its fellow propagandists did their best to be accurate about the Bloody Judges. When mistakes were made in reciting a former Nazi's biography, they were subsequently admitted and corrected. It was rightly believed that falsifications 'would have done more harm than good'.[27] To prove they cared, the Federal Association of Judges and other West German bodies embarked on a campaign of 'self-purification' of former Nazis, which didn't get far. They explained that it wasn't feasible to use evidential documents provided by East Germany's Committee for German Unity, as it was the agency of a government they didn't recognise. Arguably, justice in this area was never done. In the 1990s there was a judicial stampede to prosecute East German judges and prosecutors who were connected with the 200 or so death sentences passed on Germans in the GDR. In West Germany, there was not a single criminal conviction of a judge or prosecutor involved in the 20,000 death sentences passed on Germans during the Third Reich. It is a stark and meaningful disparity.

Even as Mielke's Stasi played its part in anti-fascist propaganda campaigns, Western organisations continued to balloon-drop hundreds of thousands of propaganda leaflets onto the heads of East Germans. During 1957 the Stasi hit on a new way to stop them – interrupting the supply of gas which floated the small balloons. At the end of June the SPD Ostbüro admitted that its balloon operations had been halted 'due to a concentrated attack by the Stasi'.[28] Balloon-launching sites in West Berlin were shut down by the arrest or intimidation of their personnel. Trucks containing hydrogen bottles, manufactured at the Salzgitter works in Lower Saxony and destined for West Berlin, were confiscated at the border by East German customs officers. Erich Mielke issued an order stating that 'active measures will be initiated against the Linde company regarding gas cylinders'. It isn't clear what kinds of pressure were applied to the West Berlin employees of Linde, manufacturers of industrial gases; but by October 1957, high-ranking Linde executives were attending meetings with GDR customs officials and the Stasi's Erich Jamin, who was no doubt appearing undercover, to give assurance that 'all precautions had been taken' to prevent the SPD Ostbüro from obtaining Linde gases. In return the company was awarded free access to and from West Berlin for its goods.

The stoppage was short-lived, however. Within six months the SPD was obtaining gas from a small company outside Nuremberg, while the CDU Ostbüro had made new arrangements to be supplied via the Federal Ministry for All-German Affairs.

57

More Dirty Operations

Erich Mielke's reign meant business as usual for the dirty ops groups led by Hans Wax and GM 'Neuhaus'. In 1958, undoubtedly at the instigation of the KGB, Wax was paid 15,000 deutschmarks to blow up the radio transmitter of the anti-communist Russian émigré organisation, the NTS, near Offenbach in the Federal Republic. When the igniter given to him by the Stasi failed, Wax hurriedly bought two watches and made a new ignition device. His explosives destroyed the transmitter and the building housing it, temporarily halting NTS propaganda broadcasts, although the US soon paid for replacements.[1]

Despite his high earnings from dirty ops, Wax still managed to run up whopping tax debts, prompting the closure of his garage and a Stasi-sponsored move to East Berlin. True to form, Wax summarily abandoned his first wife and powered into the east behind the wheel of a distinctly undemocratic Lancia. Soon he was making a good living repairing the vehicles used by the Stasi for its operations in West Germany. His workshop expanded to make speedboats, several of which were commissioned by Bruno Beater and other Stasi high-ups for their private use.

Wax liked to call himself a Bolshevik, and he kept inventing things to improve the GDR economy – heated rearview mirrors for cars, for example, and a streamlined windscreen to improve the performance of lorries. None of his designs were taken up by the state, however, which instead nationalised Wax's business. He continued to do an illegal trade in goods that were scarce in East Germany – not even the Stasi knew where he obtained some of them. And he still did odd jobs for The Firm. One night a lorryload of boats arrived at his workshop; Wax made plaster casts of them, to be used as manufacturing models for production in the GDR. By the following morning, the vessels had all been returned safely to the West.

Although he remained on the Stasi's books as a special operative, things eventually took a darker turn for Wax. In the early 1970s he got into trouble with his old crony 'Teddy' when the pair somehow stole a computer from West Germany, which they claimed had Mossad information on it, and tried to sell it. By this point the Stasi was deeply suspicious of its former servant, a maverick who knew too much. Wax was detained and spent a couple of years in a penal psychiatric institution; he claimed to have been force fed mind-altering drugs there. Thereafter, the Stasi carried out a massive surveillance operation of Wax, stopping only when he died of lung cancer in 1984.

The dirty ops squad around GM 'Neuhaus' continued to specialise in kidnappings, especially of deserters from the Stasi, Volkspolizei and NVA, although some escaped their clutches. One who got away was Siegfried Dombrowski, a military intelligence officer who was spying for the West from at least the mid-1950s. As a youth Dombrowksi had performed undercover work for the KPD. The Nazis arrested him in 1937; reportedly he was liberated as a Kapo from the Majdanek concentration camp, and politically re-educated in the USSR. He ended up working directly under the early chiefs of East German military intelligence, Karl Linke and Willy Sägebrecht.

The Stasi suspected Dombrowski and warned his employers against him. Department VII initiated an investigation that encompassed relatives and neighbours, postal monitoring, and the recruitment of Dombrowski's driver as a collaborator. Nevertheless, Dombrowski kept his job, and continued to make hard-to-explain visits to West Germany.

Aware of the suspicions, in August 1958 Dombrowski fled to West Berlin with his wife and two sons. He was in possession of 71,000 deutschmarks taken from a safe at his office. He was debriefed thoroughly by US intelligence at the Oberursel interrogation camp, then by the CIA at Langley.[2] As well as securing information on East Germany's growing military establishment, these debriefings led to recruitment letters being sent – some friendly, some threatening – to former colleagues of Dombrowski in the GDR. In time, Dombrowski was given a job at a US special forces base, located in former SS premises at Bad Tölz in Bavaria.

Five months after his defection Dombrowski appeared at a press conference, where he read out a seventeen-page statement on the GDR's espionage activities against the Federal Republic; the kind of activities he himself had been conducting on behalf of the West for some years. 'I spent eight years in Nazi concentration camps,' he told the assembled reporters. He had fled because he 'did not want another dose of it'. But the newspaper coverage of the conference indicated the growing weariness of press and public. A correspondent for *Time* noted that, 'While applauding the Western underground's previous services against the Reds – which include everything from smuggling out scientists to sending anonymous warnings to East German authorities that their misdeeds are being recorded – Berlin officials and newspapers have begun to suggest that some of the spook groups are overdoing it.' Willy Brandt, mayor of West Berlin, was said to regard 'much of the underground activities as "grownups playing cowboys and Indians"', and was determined to rid the city of '"certain undesirable activities in the twilight zone of political propaganda"'.[3] Once out of the spotlight Dombrowski and family took the name Hersch and began new lives under heavy police protection – no doubt the reason that 'Neuhaus' and other Stasi collaborators never got him, though they tried.

The Stasi showed typical persistence in other, successful operations. In August 1958 Erwin Neumann, who had succeeded Walter Linse as head of the UfJ economics section, was also kidnapped.[4] Neumann was snatched while sailing on the lakes at the south-west tip of Berlin, across which ran one of the sector borders. Like other publications, *Time* magazine subsequently reported that Neumann had been abducted 'when he went for a sail alone'. The truth is that he was taking pornographic photographs and partying with a woman and a male friend. She was Erika Scharfschwerdt, the Stasi's GM 'Sylvia'.[5] The friend was Wolfgang Weidhaas, alias the Stasi GM 'Weitzel'.

'Weitzel' worked as an assistant at the UfJ. He spent a long time observing and softening up Neumann, reporting his every word to his handlers at Main Department V. The latter were amazed by Neumann's talkativeness, remarking in one report that, 'We have not yet had such an example [of indiscretion] in the processing of the UfJ.' Neumann and 'Weitzel' went to cinemas, went on drinking sprees, spent time at one another's apartments. In due course 'Weitzel' reported that Neumann was over-fond of booze and porn.

At first there was a plan for 'Weitzel' to carry out a straightforward drunken abduction – get Neumann legless and drive him into East Berlin. Neumann had already mentioned the fact that he no longer carried a pistol, as he considered the period of Stasi kidnappings to be over. With this plan in mind, 'Weitzel' took lessons in handling an Opel Kapitän. Then, as he and Neumann developed a shared passion for sailing, the kidnap plan took a new direction. It was based on what the Stasi knew of Neumann's weaknesses.

The Stasi had a copy of a Volkspolizei report in which the border with the American sector on the Jungfernsee was described as insecure. So, on the suggestion of 'Weitzel', the two friends began to take sailing trips there. 'Weitzel' tested Neumann by plying him with drinks and sailing close to the sector border. Neumann was unconcerned. The Stasi hoped to embed 'Weitzel' yet further into the UfJ after Neumann's kidnapping; thus 'Weitzel' had to appear innocent, and make it back to West Berlin after the deed was done. He would then visit Neumann's young daughter and deposit some sensitive documents with her, and seek help from the West Berlin police to be resettled as an endangered refugee.

Meanwhile Neumann had been introduced to GM 'Sylvia', and was smitten. On the morning of Wednesday 20 August, the three friends set out. The photography and debauchery began on the islet of Kälberwerder. Once re-embarked, the beers flowed again, but Neumann noticed that his friend 'Weitzel' was dropping pills into the bottles he was handing him.

What followed was surely one of the strangest moments of the Cold War: Neumann, growing sluggish, realising his friends were trying to knock him out with pills in the middle of a lake; his friends, at least one of them naked, realising that Neumann had realised it. Struggling against the anaesthetic, Neumann began to accidentally drop his beers overboard and make disguised attempts to mess with the sailing gear. His friends tried ever subtler ways of getting the pills down him. Despite Neumann's best efforts, they took effect. He stayed conscious but was immobilised. 'Sylvia' and 'Weitzel' managed to get their vessel across the watery border, where a motorboat was waiting to tow them to the shore.

Once in the Stasi's hands, there was little Neumann could do. He was arrested drunk, drugged, and arguably a pornographer. Most of his subsequent daily interrogations lasted from 9.30 a.m. to 2.30 a.m. After fourteen months of this he was charged with a serious case of espionage; he received a life sentence at the district court in Frankfurt an der Oder. He spent most of it in solitary confinement at Hohenschönhausen. Unlike some of his contemporaries he wasn't bought out of jail by the West German government, and he died of heart failure in a prison hospital in 1967.

By the time of Neumann's abduction things had begun to unravel for the UfJ. The intrigue and kidnappings saw it accused of naiveté and 'dilettantism'. The residents of West Berlin were growing increasingly resentful towards the geopolitical machinations which were seeing their beloved city bartered over by scheming foreign powers. They objected to their unwanted image of secret fighters in a shadowy war. In March 1959 an article in the *Spandauer Volksblatt* asserted that 'West Berlin is not a "sabotage and spy centre". Its more than two million inhabitants are honest, hard-working and politically clear-thinking people... the handful who work in various organisations and groups wanting to lead the "struggle for freedom" do not represent our city.'[6]

The Stasi's penetration of the UfJ grew painfully obvious. Stasi documents from as early as 1951 suggest that it was systematically recruiting legal professionals to infiltrate the UfJ, and already possessed a list of the employees at UfJ headquarters, with personal details and character notes recorded for each one.[7] Such information likely came from one of the earliest infiltrators, Heinz Zickler, planted at the UfJ as an administrator when the organisation was founded.[8] The infestation lasted. In 1958 huge press coverage was triggered by the arrest of a senior UfJ employee, Dr Kurt Werner, as a Stasi spy. Three years earlier, the organisation's deputy head, Walther Rosenthal, had been detained by West Berlin police on suspicion of being a communist agent. The incident followed the unearthing of a signed document dating from January 1950, in which Rosenthal had pledged to 'perform for the Soviet authorities the required intelligence tasks' under the cover name 'Schmidt', and confirmed that he understood the consequences should he break his vow of secrecy.[9] Supporters of the UfJ claimed the document was a forgery – certainly the Stasi had made plans to besmirch Rosenthal – and he was released for lack of further evidence.

By the end of the decade, Rosenthal was head of the UfJ. He tried to curb some of its more dangerous and controversial activities. If he was a communist agent, he certainly suffered for the subterfuge. When informers revealed that Rosenthal and an associate were making the same daily car journey in West Berlin, taking in 'winding streets and alleys, and along a railway embankment in a desolate area', the Stasi arranged for a Zersetzung measure in which 'two honest and verified GI' would throw stones and bricks at the car, in order to 'frighten the occupants'.[10] The Stasi's GM 'Norge' even suggested leaving a grenade on Rosenthal's car seat, purely to scare him. (This idea was rejected, interestingly, because the grenade might cause harm to the driver.)[11] Although Rosenthal was clearly in some danger, doubts about him festered on; the German press was still debating his loyalty in the early 1990s.[12]

More generally, the UfJ was beset by pestilential Zersetzung operations. The Stasi arranged for UfJ employees to receive fake invitations to non-existent birthday parties, to be harassed with threatening night-time phone calls, to have funeral wreaths delivered to their apartments, and to be defamed in fake 'wanted' posters plastered all over West Berlin. Marshalled by a pair of imaginative officers, Lieutenants Sommer and Reimann, the personnel of Main Department V booked pest exterminators to visit UfJ premises, signed fake contracts on the UfJ's behalf with air freight companies and central heating installers, and placed fake adverts for the sale of the UfJ's office furniture. On one occasion the department ordered the construction of an entire prefab garage for UfJ vehicles, at great and unnecessary cost. The organisation's property was targeted – cockroaches let loose in waiting rooms, toilets blocked, water pipes cracked. Using a supply of West Berlin police summonses and official seals, Stasi collaborators sealed up the apartments of UfJ employees who were known to be on holiday.[13]

Perhaps even more disruptive was the Stasi's Aktion Wiedersehen, initiated back in 1955. Aimed at discrediting UfJ officials, the campaign revealed that founder Horst Erdmann was not the person he claimed to be. For this operation the Soviets had released Nazi party records to the Stasi which, unlike in some other cases, were genuine and un-doctored. Far from being a victim of the Nazi regime, Erdmann had been a participant in it – a party member, Hitler Youth leader, and senior official of the German Labour Front, the Nazi replacement for trade unions. Moreover, he had falsified his birth date and place, and contrary to his claims had studied law only briefly, without graduating. Erdmann resigned in July 1958. Within two years the CIA had withdrawn its funding.

The UfJ struggled on for another decade, although Stasi moles such as Götz Schlicht, recruited as GM 'Lutter' after his own arrest and imprisonment in the GDR, continued to do harm. Another important figure in the later work of the UfJ, Wolfgang Vogel, an East German representative in negotiations for prisoner releases, had been talent-spotting ('tipping') and reporting to the Stasi as its agent 'Georg' since at least 1956.[14] Overall, the UfJ's story in the 1950s highlights some of the perennial problems that arise when intelligence services make use of proxy organisations. For a start, UfJ activities were reputedly overseen by Henry Hecksher, the CIA loose cannon who unnerved some of his colleagues. When intelligence services do not exercise due diligence, such unbalanced personalities can carve out little fiefdoms for themselves, where they can play fast and loose with the lives of well-meaning but ill-equipped volunteers.

The UfJ is overshadowed, above all, by an almost unbearable claim – that it was created and run by the Soviet secret police. The Soviets had form for doing this. For decades they had created 'enemy' organisations to attract unsuspecting traitors and opponents of communism, thereby identifying and supervising them. The practice dated back to the Cheka's celebrated Trust operation of the early 1920s.* The CIA, even as it was funding the Free Jurists, was also funding WIN, an anti-communist network in Poland. WIN subsequently was discovered to be a large-scale deception masterminded by the Polish security service under Soviet direction.[15] In his book *Stasi*, John Koehler gives full vent to the theory that the UfJ was Soviet-controlled. He states that the organisation was the brainchild of General Nikolai Melnikov of the MGB, and that Horst Erdmann was in on it from the start. Yet Koehler's claim is not repeated by others, and in German-language publications appears to be completely taboo – it is avoided even by those who admit the Stasi's thorough penetration of the organisation. This silence helps to preserve the honour of the UfJ's employees and helpers, who were sincere in their efforts to address the injustices of the SED regime. It also avoids embarrassing the high-profile legal professionals

---

*   The Trust was a false anti-communist organisation created by Cheka officers, which fooled numerous opponents of the Bolsheviks. It enabled many counter-espionage successes for the Cheka, and for the rest of the century was used as training material for KGB personnel.

who endorsed the organisation. Moreover, the Stasi's alarm at the UfJ's activities was undoubtedly real. If the UfJ *was* a Soviet deception, the extent to which it was shared with the Stasi is unclear; possibly it wasn't. Either way, the mystery stresses the fact that making use of proxy intelligence services means rolling the dice, every time.

In internal documents the Stasi described GM 'Neuhaus', its criminal collaborator, as 'very cold-blooded and courageous'.[16] 'Neuhaus' and his gang proved it when they kidnapped an employee of the French intelligence service, the SDECE, in October 1958. Their victim is known in the literature as Friedrich Böhm. He had fled from East Germany in 1950 and was recruited by France three years later. Typically, the Stasi watched him for years. During that time Böhm recruited some fifty sub-agents in the GDR and Poland, illustrating how the porous Berlin borders could facilitate spying in the wider Soviet Bloc.

When the time came to halt Böhm's activities, the Stasi developed a kidnap plan in which its GM 'Consul', a Berlin criminal, would lure Böhm to an isolated rendezvous with a supposed informer and then drug him with chloroform or knock him out with a cosh. This plan was then superseded by another. By early 1957 Böhm's personal and professional circles had been infested; he was surrounded by no less than fifteen Stasi collaborators. Among them were the GM 'Tell' and his wife, both of whom Böhm had recruited into his espionage network. The couple and their children lived in West Berlin as political refugees. 'Tell' was a trainee forester who, Böhm knew, spent much time in the Gatower woods of south-west Berlin.

On the day of the kidnap, Böhm and 'Tell' took a walk in these woods. At a certain point, their path was blocked by a fallen birch tree. Out of the woods came another forester, who appeared to be acquainted with 'Tell'. He told the walkers that a young boar was lying dead nearby, and offered to show them.

This second forester was 'Neuhaus'. When the party reached the dead boar and began to examine it, he pulled a pistol and told Böhm to come along. Two more Stasi collaborators then sprang from the trees. A fierce struggle ensued. Böhm was beaten with coshes, then shot in the shoulder. 'Neuhaus' told the Stasi his pistol had gone off when he struck Böhm with it; one of the other collaborators claimed 'Neuhaus' had taken deliberate aim. Either way, Böhm was overpowered, tied up, carried from the woods and thrown into the back of a Volkswagen camper.

There was plenty of evidence left at the scene for West Berlin investigators: blood, Böhm's broken glasses and comb, a dead pig. But the gang's border crossing had been simple enough. The Stasi's Main Department I, which invigilated the border police, had arranged for the barbed wire strewn across the Potsdamer Chaussee to be removed, and the placing of a temporary wooden bridge across a trench. At Frankfurt an der Oder district court, Böhm was sentenced to life for serious espionage. He was lucky. After fourteen years, he was bought out of prison by the West German government.

58

The Informer Age: The 1958 Guideline on Collaborators and Stasi Reporting

Erich Mielke's appointment as Stasi chief saw the true dawn of the informer age. The 1958 guideline for handling collaborators, a major internal document, was a further attempt to systematise the Stasi's use of unofficial help, to try to bring some science to the thing. Compared to previous guidelines it was neater, wordier and better printed. Informers were defined as the Hauptmittel, or main means, of battling internal and external 'class enemies' – a phrase now preferred over the previous 'agents, saboteurs and terrorists'. The priority now was to secure and defend important institutions, and important ideological tenets, inside the GDR. Thus the guideline contained an updated mission statement: 'The Ministry for State Security is entrusted with the task of preventing or throttling at the earliest stages – using whatever means and methods may be necessary – all attempts to delay or to hinder the victory of socialism.'[1]

By now the Stasi's unofficial helpers were subdivided into five categories. There were GI and GM, contact persons (KP – 'trusted citizens approached to perform specific tasks') and owners of conspiratorial apartments (KW). Lead Secret Informers (GHI), of whom the Stasi had some 2,300 on its books, were reliable comrades who recruited and ran other informers on the Stasi's behalf.

Some of the basics for running informers, laid down in earlier documents, still held:

All operational employees [are expected to] spend the majority of their working time searching for and finding GM and GI and employing them.

In general each operational employee should have at least ten informers and three Lead Informers. As a rule, each of these should have four informers. Particular attention should be paid to the ability of [Lead Informers] to judge informers...

Senior employees (Main Department heads, heads of district administrations) should have fewer, but more valuable, informers.[2]

It was important to communicate with collaborators 'at specified time intervals', and to conduct 'constant systematic review of both GM and GI', covering 'their curriculum vitae and way of life', and the value of their reports.

The guideline stressed that the ideal informer was recruited on the basis of political convictions. This helped to avoid the 'damaging' failures and inconsequential data that came from coercive or commercial recruitments.[3] In their write-ups, Stasi officers began to emphasise their informers' 'high level of commitment, reliability, and ideological solidarity' with the SED regime.[4] Previously this hadn't been considered necessary. Another option was to recruit former Volkspolizei and Stasi personnel, provided their service hadn't ended in disgrace. This was the case with one Richard Fiolka, whose son had disappeared to West Germany. He wasn't deemed responsible for the youth's errant behaviour, and although sacked from Department VIII over the incident he then spent fifteen years working as GI 'Richard' in Erfurt, receiving 500 marks per month and several decorations for his trouble.[5]

The guideline clarified that informers who blew the whistle or tried to walk away could be charged with betraying state secrets. Ideally they wouldn't want to, for the guideline also emphasised the power of atonement – Wiedergutmachung, or 'making amends' – as a motive for becoming an informer. This was an important concept in the communist world, evident in the 'self-criticism' sessions held in Soviet workplaces and schools, known in Russian as Chistka, or cleansing. People who had fallen foul of the authorities could show their contrition by admitting their faults and collaborating. It was also a good way to avoid the term 'blackmail', although the Stasi certainly continued to recruit people with compromising materials on their sexual activity or unpunished crimes. If no such material existed, it could be faked.

Mielke stipulated that the running of informers was to be professionalised. Tighter security was to be observed around meetings, which were 'normally' to be held in safe apartments and nowhere else. It was inadvisable to meet with an informer more than once per week, or to see more than four informers at one apartment. Furthermore, every handler was to give ongoing political coaching to informers, developing their convictions to the point where they 'would be prepared to give [their] life for the cause'.[6] To expedite recruitment, Mielke wrote that sensitive souls such as writers and scientists didn't have to sign the declaration of engagement usually required of an informer. But writers were less important than members of the growing armed forces.

Wary of a military coup, the SED was always concerned about the armed forces as a power base. Informers within the NVA were crucial. The Stasi targeted former Wehrmacht personnel for recruitment as informers, for on paper they were politically untrustworthy, and so might have good access to oppositional individuals and groups. Karl Kleinjung boasted that from 1956 onwards his Main Department I recruited one informer for every ten NVA soldiers.[7] Informer penetration of the Volkspolizei was even higher, with up to twenty percent of personnel reporting to the Stasi.

How, in practice, were recruitments carried out in accordance with the 1958 guidelines? Recollections of later periods shed some light on this. A woman who was recruited as a sixteen-year-old schoolgirl recalled that she was summoned to the school office and introduced to a man who looked 'like a builder in Sunday clothes'.[8] She assumed he was a Free German Youth official; he said he wanted to chat about the town's young people. 'Nobody would tell him anything because he was an adult,' the man had told her, and 'that meant he couldn't change anything for us'. At the end of their conversation the man admitted he was from the Ministry for State Security. He told the girl she was:

> not allowed to talk with anybody, not even my parents, about our meeting and conversation. If I had questions, I could contact him...
>
> My feelings were on a roller-coaster... I already knew at age 16 what state security was. People spread rumours about it with their hands in front of their mouths... They were there to stop people running to the West, they were responsible for stamping visas, that's all I knew... The building where they had their offices was protected like a fortress... they were important.
>
> On the one hand this conversation made me feel queasy, on the other hand I was curious.

The girl met the man again, in a car behind a railway station, and they drove out of town. She was nervous about being seen:

> After we'd talked about this and that for a while, he asked me the first concrete questions about our youth club in the church hall and about the pastor and his wife... what kind of literature the pastor gave us, if anything happened that was hostile to the state. I was absolutely not conscious of what he was getting at with all this.

Despite the girl's confusion, she was signed up. Other youthful informers were volunteers. A long-running investigation codenamed 'Postman', aimed at busting a Western spy network, started when two trainee teachers in East Berlin contacted the authorities.[9] They had been approached in a bar by an unknown West Berliner who offered them money to pick up and deliver letters. The Stasi was fortunate that these two were persistent, for after mentioning the incident to the FDJ secretary at their school – 'a class-conscious childhood friend' – the school's party secretary had tried:

> to contact an employee of the state security service. Unfortunately, we didn't get anyone, so we asked two SED officials at the Ministry of the Interior for advice. They promised to support us and tried to phone the state security service. However, they didn't get a connection either so advised us to go and [meet the West Berliner].

Eventually the Stasi answered the phone and then recruited the pair as GI 'Schutte' and GI 'Stern'. They began to journey throughout Berlin and East Germany, meeting Western handlers, servicing dead drops, and observing cut-outs. Their reports to the Stasi were eager and comprehensive, for this was clearly the most exciting thing that had ever happened to them. Suddenly their lives were full of intrigue, sworn loyalty, travel, cunning, risk. No other form of state-sponsored entertainment could possibly compete with this.

When Walter Ulbricht accused the Stasi's mood reporting body, the Information Service, of tacitly spreading anti-SED opinions, it led to a brief hiatus in its work. Already Ernst Wollweber had tried to improve the service, for example by standardising the twice-weekly reports coming in from its outposts. Each report was now divided into five sections: 'The situation in industry and transport', 'The situation in trade and supply', 'The situation in agriculture', 'Events of particular importance', and 'An assessment of the situation'. Hostility directed towards party officials, and activity by Western enemies, were detailed in appendixes. The reports' distribution, which shrank over time, was also categorised. Reports marked 'Ia' were for full members of the Politbüro, 'Ib' the top management of the Stasi, and 'Ic' for candidate members of the Politbüro and section heads in the Central Committee. Note that this was the party hierarchy, not that of the government.

By 1959 the work of the Information Service had been resurrected with the founding of the Stasi's Central Information Group. In later years this was to evolve into the formidable Central Evaluation and Information Group or ZAIG, considered an elite 'control centre' at the heart of the Stasi.[10] In a land where it was impossible to express truthful opinions openly, the SED and Stasi had to know what East Germans were really thinking and saying to one another. So the raw reports received by the Central Information Group are one of the richest sources on the political, economic and social life of the GDR. In their way, like other Stasi documents, they are trustworthy; it wasn't until the 1970s that they became thoroughly bland and orthodox.

It is no exaggeration to say that the Central Information Group, and even the Information Service towards its end, gathered and assessed reports on the minutiae of East German life. In its vulnerability the SED was over-sensitive to discontent, which it thought might arise from the smallest of incidents or the unlikeliest of causes. Furthermore, East German society was a rumour factory, and the SED knew it. The likes of supply problems might swiftly escalate into a grave national security issue. So the Stasi's information reports cover the appearance of heavy frost in the Frankfurt an der Oder area; the 'lively discussions' about a train accident near Oschatz; potential pilfering and fraud at a state-owned Berlin restaurant; a fatal glider accident near Trebbin. For the SED, any one of these events might have presaged the party's overthrow. In the same vein, data and opinions were gathered on the shortage of maternity beds in Königs Wusterhausen; the overproduction of unwanted furniture; cases of scarlet fever at a children's holiday camp; the percentages of cancelled trains and delayed passengers; damage caused by wild boar; and the printing of erroneous desk calendars. There were reports devoted to named individuals – local mayors and newspaper editors, sports coaches, physics teachers and church ministers; reports on student communities, specific factories, entire fields of industry; on planned strikes, assaults on police officers, the interminable workplace accidents; on ticket-touting at football matches, and the mood 'among the fishermen on the island of Poel'.[11] Through it all, East Germany in the late 1950s comes across as cold, unwell, bad-tempered, and irremediably dilapidated. Yet the Stasi had to know about this microcosmos because the SED had to know where the danger might come from. In a sign of the changing times, only a small minority of these reports dealt with Stasi business proper – the presence of spies, agents and saboteurs.

Whatever else the Stasi was, it was second to none as a collector of raw data. How did it gather this stupefying volume of facts and utterances? Unlike today, it was done by human and not technological means. Some of the information came from local officials or representatives of state agencies. Doubtless most of it came from informers. But despite this staggering haul, the high-ups at the Central Information Group poured relentless criticism on their subordinates' use of informers.

'Important areas such as re-settlers, universities, bourgeois parties, the church, and former fascists and officers are dealt with completely inadequately,' read one criticism of the Stasi's district information groups. 'In no district is there a precise overview of the number of people released from prison, visitors from West Germany, asylum seekers [from the West, and] tourist traffic.'

Employees were said to be skipping meetings with informers, not recruiting enough new ones, and not monitoring those they had. In one case the Stasi hadn't known that the owner of a 'conspiratorial apartment' had married a recently released prisoner, an unacceptable transgression.[12]

Certain reports, however, were pertinent for security and policing. Informer coverage of the International Police Exhibition at Essen 'established that the police of the Federal Republic [and] those of foreign countries use extremely sophisticated technology in their work'.[13] A report on the event concluded that the Volkspolizei had 'a lot of catching up to do'. The Western innovations were enumerated:

1) Television Recording Cameras. The size of a flat shoebox. With the help of these television recording devices, traffic is controlled from a central point at busy intersections in Hamburg. This means that the Police Presidium in Hamburg [can] oversee all traffic and thus change the traffic lights according to the needs of the traffic.

2) Speedometer. This device is used to measure the speed of a vehicle on the road... The device records the speed on a strip of paper, similar to a calculating machine.

3) Traffic Accident and Crime Scene Surveying Device. This device contains two cameras at a distance of 2m from each other, with which the scene of an accident is photographed from one point... the three-dimensional image is scanned with a special device.

4) A device for wireless voice communication... particularly well designed... the size of a shoebox with an oversized telephone receiver attached and a pull-out antenna.

5) A so-called robot camera. This is used for a wide variety of purposes. This device can be installed anywhere, camouflaged and triggered automatically. For example in a car, so the car thief convicts himself. When the car door is opened, the camera shutter and its lighting system are activated.

6) The polygraph or lie detector... a registration of expressions, which enable an assessment to be carried out.

The report also mentioned an exhibit on 'capital crimes, with a particular focus on gangsters, smuggling rings, murders, sex murders and abnormalities', which was 'a special attraction for young people'.

It was at election time that the Stasi's information-gatherers really came into their own. A nasty rash of popular resentment broke out with every East German election. For a start, each one was preceded by a burst of Western propaganda, on radio but especially via balloon-dropped leaflets, urging citizens not to participate. At such times the Stasi virtually became a counter-leafletting rather than a counter-espionage service, mobilising police and party activists to gather up the unwelcome windfall, and reporting assiduously on the contents.

Plenty of East German citizens – especially those who had drunk too much – remained capable of expressing dissent at election time. Thousands of SED posters always got torn to shreds. Police officers would get harassed or roughed up, often by groups of youths. Every instance of such behaviour was reported and examined by the Stasi. Thanks to its discreet leadership role on electoral committees, and in the work of counters and returning officers, the Stasi always had the first and best view of the true election results. It reported on them in great secrecy and minute detail; not just breakdowns of the voting statistics but information on individual abstainers or the suspected reasons for poor results in a certain place.

Stasi reports describe incidents of subtle dissent at election time, like a pile of books by Lenin left in a park with a note saying 'unwanted'. Some dissent was garish, like the swastikas that would appear everywhere, without fail. It would seem that daubing swastikas had become a standard way of expressing disgust with the SED regime; it is impossible to say if it represented real National Socialist belief, or was a Western provocation. Occasionally this dissent looked more sinister, like an incident in Cottbus before the 1957 council elections, when fifteen cyclists and the occupants of a car had ridden around singing the Horst Wessel Lied.[14] In Ludwigslust, before the November 1958 general election, posters were torn down by a former POW who had returned to Germany from the Soviet Union in 1955, released early from a twenty-five-year sentence for taking part in mass shootings of partisans. The Stasi believed the man's associates were responsible for more than 300 items of graffiti, with such messages as 'Heil Hitler', 'Hitler is coming back' and 'NSDAP still here', as well as 'numerous swastikas and SS runes'. It linked this behaviour with a move made by the West German government, which tried to mess with the elections by announcing a clashing 'people's holiday' to commemorate fallen German heroes of the Second World War. When children were found to be responsible for daubing swastikas, for the Stasi this suggested a 'fascist influence on the part of the parents'.[15]

When reporting on incidents of 'enemy activity' before the 1957 and 1958 elections, the Stasi's information-gatherers would also indicate which authority would deal with each incident – whether it was to remain a police matter or be 'processed' by the Stasi.[16] The decision-making around this division of work isn't always clear. Sometimes relatively minor incidents would be taken on by the Stasi; sometimes fairly serious ones would remain with the Volkspolizei. Available resources may have played a part.

Some of the election-related incidents to be 'operationally processed' by district Stasi offices included the case of a group of former SPD members who were trying to 'gain influence' before an election, 'especially among older people, by donating clothes and food'; the removal of election announcements on a community noticeboard; a 'handwritten inflammatory slogan' criticising a candidate that was found 'on a forest path'; a threatening letter being sent to the editorial team of a local newspaper; a local chairman of the Democratic Farmers' Party trying 'to disrupt the election preparations' and incite collective farmers to leave the SED; a farmer making 'very derogatory comments' about the election candidates at a meeting, and 'rudely insulting' the hosts; a speaker at an election meeting being constantly interrupted by drunken workers 'with interjections such as "pack of lies", "all talk" and "not true"'; a comment made by a student that instead of voting he would 'take a different route... namely to West Germany'; members of the Democratic Farmers' Party demanding twenty council seats instead of twelve; and the following comments made by a pub landlord: 'I'll be in the West soon. Economically, I can't take any more. Taxes are too high and I can't afford them. But before I go west, I'll burn my property so that no one can use it anymore.'

Cases slated to remain with the Volkspolizei included that of a person who aggressively demanded unavailable goods in a state-run shop before threatening that 'something could happen in the election'; a district councillor being insulted in a pub 'by a young person from Birkenwerder'; election noticeboards in Oranienburg being smeared with manure; an approved candidate from the NDPD being showered with sand after a meeting; six young people disrupting a meeting 'with conversation and loud laughter'; and the following incident:

> During the National Front committee meeting held in the hotel at the train station, those present, mostly SED members, were insulted by two young people who were sitting in the hotel restaurant. When the committee members left the restaurant, the young people incited murder and physically attacked these people. Both were arrested by the Volkspolizei.

Of course, the usual mix of pressure, persuasion and fiddling always led to the safe return of the vast majority of the SED's pre-selected National Front candidates. After the general election, the Stasi concluded that there had been 'no major weaknesses'. Yet there was another curious feature to the Stasi reports: a refusal to accept good news. The Stasi's analysis included comments along the lines of, 'many voters, even those who voted for the National Front openly, were only doing it to look good – really they are against the government'; or, 'serious enemies of the state did not expose themselves by disrupting the elections, so we need to look even harder to find them'.[17] Despite a successful election, the Stasi believed there remained an organised oppositional conspiracy, still needing to be cracked.

59

Enlightenment: The Growth of East German Foreign Intelligence

'Our sins and our mistakes were those of every other intelligence agency.'

Markus Wolf

The Stasi's famed foreign intelligence service, the HVA, came into being in summer 1956. Its initials are said to stand for Hauptverwaltung Aufklärung, meaning Main Intelligence Directorate or, more literally, Main Directorate of Reconnaissance.* But its name was probably a simple echo of the KGB's foreign intelligence branch, the First Chief Directorate; in the Stasi's case, foreign intelligence was Hauptverwaltung A, or Main Directorate A.

The HVA stepped straight into an intelligence war that was continuing to make frontpage news throughout the world. British newspapers, for instance, were contributing to proceedings with such articles as '500 Red spies cross into West Germany every month' and 'Berlin's Spy Jungle', the latter a phrase beloved of Nikita Khrushchev and the SED. 'Most spies cross [into West Germany] in the guise of innocent businessmen, political refugees, students or East Germans visiting relatives in the west,' announced *The Star*. 'Last year 6,200 people were seized [in West Germany] for activities endangering the security of the state' – although this was a reference to the round-up of KPD members rather than spies. 'Recent arrests have included a Bad Godesberg boarding-house keeper,' the article continued, 'whose rooms, occupied by minor diplomats, were wired for sound to a tape recorder in the attic. The tapes were shipped weekly in soup tins to East Berlin... 5,000 spies and counter-spies are believed to be working in the vicinity of the Federal Capital of Bonn.'[1]

A *Sunday Times* article, contributed by that purveyor of fine nonsense Antony Terry, whose reportage is said to have inspired some of the less likely James Bond plots, told of the 'ding-dong battle' between 'Berlin's 47 espionage services'. 'From now on,' wrote Terry, 'it is the experts and not the playboys of dilettante espionage who are going to feed each other with false information, control their secret agents, photo-copy the secret reports, and compile the secret

---

* As well as meaning 'scouting' or 'reconnaissance', Aufklärung is the German word for the historical Enlightenment period, and connotes 'becoming informed'.

blacklists which have made spying between East and West such a profitable blackmailing business in Berlin.'[2]

Some of this reporting was correct and some of it wasn't, but all of it begs the question, once again, of how secret the supposed 'secret war' really was. Press and public were familiar with its characteristics if not its details. When placing spies, Markus Wolf's HVA, as reported, made use of travelling merchants, family ties, and purported refugees; students too, as there was a good chance they would enjoy a subsequent career in West German politics, industry or science.

In time, however, the HVA's penetration of West Germany – always its chief concern – came to outstrip the guesswork of 1950s reporters. Cautious estimates of the total number of spies run in West Germany by the GDR during the Cold War range from 17,000 to 23,000.[3] Benjamin Fischer, a chief historian at the CIA, writes that, 'Five out of every 100,000 West German citizens spied for East German intelligence.'[4] Not all were run by the HVA, although 6,000 West Germans and 20,000 East Germans were catalogued in the HVA's index of assets, acquired by the CIA in the 1990s.[5] These numbers endorse a view of Markus Wolf as 'perhaps the most successful spy chief in intelligence history, certainly the most effective in the Cold War'.[6] And everything he knew about spying was learned on the job.

The HVA was born around the time of the popular unrest in Poznań and Hungary. Later in life Markus Wolf liked to boast that, thanks to his spies, he had been able to radio the Soviets and assure them that NATO wouldn't intervene if tanks were to roll into Budapest. According to his memoirs, at this time Wolf became acutely conscious that the world had been sharply divided into spheres. Hitherto things had looked more fluid, with varying possibilities; perhaps even a reunited and demilitarised Germany, for this continued to be the stated ambition of the SED. The bloody suppression of the Polish workers, the events in Hungary, and America's curtailing of independent action by Britain and France over the Suez crisis, all indicated to Wolf that the superpowers were now bossing an us-and-them planet: two blocs, for or against.[7]

An HVA priority in this stand-off was to penetrate West Germany's intelligence services. Its internal guidelines stressed that the main Federal agencies – the BND, BfV and MAD – were key targets. The HVA's counter-espionage branch – Department IX, later Department IV – had four sections working on West German intelligence. Only one section was devoted to the US, while another covered 'other Western intelligence services'.[8]

As for foreign intelligence-gathering, a department designated HVA/I targeted West German government institutions.[9] This meant penetrating the

Chancellery and president's office, the Federal press office, and government ministries; among the most important were the Foreign Office, the ministries of the interior, defence, and economics, the Ministry for All-German Affairs and, slightly later, the Ministry for Economic Cooperation.

Meanwhile the SED was growing increasingly interested in stealing science and technology to boost East Germany's economy and military strength. By this point, trade was regulated by systems established on both sides of the Iron Curtain. Moscow devised and ran Comecon, which attempted to stimulate and control the economies of the Soviet Bloc. On the Western side, the Consultative Group for Multilateral Export Controls oversaw the embargo of many goods, above all those of military significance. In Germany these rules were overseen by an agency known as CoCom, the Coordinating Committee for East-West Trade. Once called 'the policeman of the West's exports',[10] much of CoCom's work was based on intelligence supplied by the CIA. Although West Germany's leaders considered it important to continue trading with the GDR, especially as a means of gaining political concessions and encouraging reunification, Konrad Adenauer launched a 'Policy of Strength' to restrict exports.[11] Starting in the 1950s, the Stasi devoted decades of effort to circumventing such embargoes and acquiring the goods anyway. Almost as highly prized were blueprints or the materials necessary for making an East German version of a Western product. One Stasi officer, Horst Müller, earned promotion for obtaining new plans for the manufacture of nylon.[12]

Thus the HVA's economic and scientific-technical branch, known in its early years as Main Department IV and then V, targeted sources in industry, research and development, academia, and inter-German trade; every year there were rich pickings to be had at the Leipzig trade fair. To begin with, the department was directed from a villa in Schulzendorf by Willy Hüttner and his two departmental heads, Heinrich Weiberg and Gerhard Franke.

Weiberg's sections were responsible for chemistry, rocket and aircraft technology, electronics and electrical engineering, and atomic energy; the latter branch was led by Willi Neumann, later deputy chief of scientific espionage. Franke's sections dealt with finance and banking, machine building, and vehicle technology. An order of June 1956 from Ernst Wollweber created the Working Group for Scientific-Technical Evaluation under Paul Bilke, which disseminated stolen scientific information around East Germany's scientists, ministries and industries.[13] Over time, this unit became one of the Stasi's most important hubs of analysis, playing a major role in East Germany's efforts to boost its economy with new technology.

The HVA's main evaluation department continued to be led jointly by Erwin Koletzki and Robert Korb. A deputy chief of the HVA from 1956 to 1959,

Korb soon streamlined his evaluators into using five classifications for their sources: 1 stood for secret documents, 2 for secret information from reliable and verified sources, 3 for unverified sources, 4 for opinions and semi-overt information, and 5 for suspected misinformation. Koletzki, on the other hand, was to leave the Stasi in peculiar circumstances in the early 1960s, investigated by police and his health impugned.

The year 1959 saw the first big reorganisation of the HVA, which was rationalised into eight departments plus Objekt 9, its training school. The leadership of its party organisation passed from Alfred Schönherr to the long-serving Otto Ledermann, and its special tasks unit was transferred back to the domestic Stasi, where Erich Mielke could keep a closer eye on it, as Department IV (Diversion).

The HVA school, located first at Tchaikowskistrasse in Berlin, then Belzig and finally Gosen, was headed into the 1960s by Rudolf Bartoneck. It awarded diplomas and offered military, economic, and Marxist-Leninist studies, as well as courses in Russian, Polish, Czech, English, French and Spanish. The students, of whom there were around 100 at a time, learned about imperialism, the history of the German workers' movement, the traditions of 'socialist reconnaissance', and the 'Operational Area Conditions' they would encounter as a spy in the West. The school also boasted sports facilities and an above-average library.

Around twenty teachers lectured in tradecraft at the school, covering technical skills, psychology, methods of penetrating institutions and groups of people, counter-surveillance, and how to subvert or avoid the investigations of Western security services. Potential HVA spies had to be sharp, creative, and flexible. One training exercise borrowed from the KGB saw the students informed about a 'West German businessman' who was said to be working somewhere in the GDR. They had to find, befriend, and recruit this person, who was supposedly connected with valuable sources in the Federal Republic. The role of 'businessman' would be played by an experienced operator, who would wait for each student to find him before attempting to foil his own recruitment with all manner of complications; political arguments, greed, unfriendliness, the distractions of alcohol and sex. If the exercise ended with the 'businessman' agreeing to become an HVA spy, the student had performed exceptionally well. This assignment was conducted in earnest, not as a lesson.

Despite the effort and resource poured into the HVA, its work was paralleled by other Stasi departments and by the National People's Army (NVA). In August 1956 Erich Mielke sent out an instruction titled 'Measures to deal with the Bundeswehr, the Federal Ministry of Defence and its subordinate offices, the NATO staff, and soldiers' associations in the Federal Republic'.[14] As well as drawing attention to emerging military enemies, the instruction aimed to encourage coordination between the branches of Department XV – the foreign intelligence units which still existed at the Stasi's regional offices – and the new HVA. It also trod on Markus Wolf's toes. It can be seen as a bureaucratic shot-across-the-bows from Mielke to Wolf: you might be the head of a new department, but I have a big say in your affairs.

Mielke's instruction called for a new branch of the HVA to 'organise a mass infiltration into the troop units of the Bundeswehr'. It is obvious that he and other Stasi high-ups were trying to thrash out who would be responsible for what. So while 'defensive processing' of West German military institutions remained in the hands of the Stasi main department concerned – say, HA III for a case of economic interference involving West German army officers, or HA V for a case of political influencing – Wolf's HVA was to concentrate on 'penetration into the intelligence and counter-intelligence offices' of the Bundeswehr and Federal defence ministry. This, wrote Mielke, was urgently required by the 'active involvement of the Federal Republic in the aggressive NATO system, the creation of the West German army and the introduction of general conscription in West Germany' – the latter had come into force that year. It was essential for 'the MfS to clarify [the West's] military plans and intentions and to prepare active measures to thwart these plans'. Collaborators were to be recruited or reactivated, their information 'concentrated by the head of the HVA'. West Germany's resettlement camps were considered good places to recruit or plant spies. Meanwhile, Department M was to step up its hunt for military and defence-related correspondence.

The intelligence service of the NVA, established under the cover of the Mathematical-Physics Institute at Köpenick, went through a string of name changes – Verwaltung 19, 12 Verwaltung, Verwaltung Aufklärung. Its main target was the NATO forces stationed in West Germany: their strengths and dispositions, routines and equipment, morale and manoeuvres. Compared to the HVA it was under-resourced. It also had its customary share of scandal. In 1961 one of its officers, Helmut Scheithauer, murdered two of his agents, a pair of Nicaraguan students based in Munich, as he thought they might expose his financial corruption. Following a Stasi investigation Scheithauer was executed, in great secrecy, in 1968.[15] Nevertheless, in the later Cold War some of the most important penetrations of western European institutions, including in Britain, were effected by NVA intelligence rather than the Stasi.[16]

The service got off to a promising start with the recruitment of Reinhold Ginolas, a Federal air force captain. He began to provide information on training programmes and operational efficiency in 1958; he was to continue for more than thirty years.[17] In the early 1960s, Denmark and West Germany formed the NATO command called BALTAP, or Baltic Approaches, with its headquarters at Karup on the Danish mainland. Thereafter, Scandinavia and the Baltic – called the 'Sea of Peace' in sentimental East German propaganda – became a major focus of military intelligence. The NATO order of battle was tracked by the navies of East Germany, Poland and the Soviet Union, and coastal areas were reconnoitred, photographed and mapped. In Denmark itself this work was undertaken by teams of East German agents known as Mark Scouts ('marchaufklärer').[18]

A secret department of the NVA, led initially by Gustav Röbelen and known successively as Dienststelle R and Verwaltung 15, planned for acts of sabotage and guerrilla warfare in West Germany in the event of hostilities. It set up a logistics network, cached arms throughout the Federal Republic, and trained paramilitaries drawn mostly from among West Germany's crypto-communists. In 1959 the Stasi stepped in to arrange Röbelen's removal as chief of the department, despite his status as a legendary underground operative; its Main Department I had discovered numerous examples of Röbelen's laxity, such as hiring drunkards and sabotage specialists who had spent years living unaccounted for in western Europe.[19] A few years later Erich Mielke was able to transfer the department from the NVA to the Stasi, clearly relishing his ownership of this small band of scuba diving, parachuting, bridge-blowing commandos. By that time the department's assets 'stretched from List on the North Sea island of Sylt all the way down to the Black Forest'; its arms dumps housed 700 handguns and rifles, 67 submachine guns, 17 heavy machine guns, over 1,600 grenades and more than 200,000 deutschmarks in cash.[20] Mielke reported that he was confident of its abilities to conduct 'effective partisan activity in the enemy's hinterland when [and not if] the Bundeswehr attacks the GDR'.[21]

Markus Wolf's autobiography, however mendacious, is a treasure trove of tips and tricks. In it Wolf described his profession as 'essentially a banal trade of sifting through huge amounts of random information in a search for a single enlightening gem or illuminating link'.[22] Sceptical about SIGINT, Wolf insisted that 'no technical method can substitute for good human intelligence and judgment'. Technical intelligence, he wrote, provided only 'information without evaluation', whereas a human can give 'information about plans, can analyze the political and military outlook, and can place documents and conversations in context'. Another of Wolf's firm principles was that of 'need to know'. His application of it was submersible-tight: he refused to give either his own staff or other Stasi departments any lists of HVA agents, 'since this would have made us vulnerable to betrayal from officers in departments over which I had no control'; he acknowledged that gossip, 'however fiercely discouraged, always goes on in a large organisation'. Names were never used in internal HVA communications, only employee numbers, and files shared with the Stasi's domestic departments were censored as needed.

Like other Cold Warriors, Wolf learned, or relearned, that a front organisation set up to conceal espionage needs to be run well, as if it were a competitive going concern. It isn't enough to focus on the spying and let the business side muddle on, while unexplained payments pop up in accounts, possibly in full view of a security service. Wolf was reminded of this when his department co-opted one Heinrich Wiedemann, a lobbyist for German reunification, and set up the Office of Economic Aid for Fixed-Salary Earners, a campaign group among Federal civil servants. Wiedemann wasn't much of a manager and the enterprise had to be abandoned, albeit mostly because a defector from the GDR spilled the beans on the whole endeavour.

Wolf's best advice for locating a mole? Look 'for quirks in behaviour'. His best advice for recruiting a source? Don't try to blackmail the well-connected. Recognise that potential sources might 'shy away from a formal commitment and actually prefer an ambiguous relationship'. Sometimes recruitment was unnecessary, for as long as a government minister 'was chatting away with old friends and colleagues who reported to us', the effect was the same. Don't overlook greed and vanity as motive forces: 'the more lavish the welcome' given to a prospective Western recruit, 'the greater the chance they would feel flattered and respond positively.'

Others responded to an inner emptiness. Wolf noted that in the case of 'Westerners from upper-middle-class backgrounds with strong and complex personalities', it paid to offer 'the chance of mixing idealism with personal commitment, something that is missing in many modern societies'. Sometimes HVA recruiters pretended to work for the 'Institute for Policy and Economy', which helped: this way, a recruit 'could gather that he [or she] was talking to the [East German] foreign intelligence service without the need for the embarrassment or fright that would have been engendered by a formal introduction'. Wolf believed his staff to be subtler recruiters than 'the Americans, who always struck me as too ready to admit openly that they came from the CIA or FBI'.

The one-upmanship didn't stop there. 'By simply monitoring casual approaches to our countrymen,' wrote Wolf, 'at cocktail parties, sports clubs, bars and cafés… we were soon able to draw up a list of CIA workers.' Moreover, 'spotting CIA operatives in Bonn was ridiculously easy. Quite unlike my own insistence on careful preparation and slow, almost imperceptible approaches to a potential recruit, they always set off on a frantic round of making contacts.'

Silence, invisibility, the non-explanation: they all seemed to come naturally to Wolf. He disparaged defections: 'a good agent in place is usually worth a dozen defectors', and if 'someone has been turned once, the assumption is that they can be turned again'. He despaired of the open hostility shown to many Western journalists in the GDR; instead of 'making their stay unpleasant' he wanted to 'direct clever disinformation at them, giving them scoops and insights that somehow benefited us rather than drive them away full of resentment'.

Wolf also understood 'how difficult it is to resolve through the methods of the law disputes originating in the complex world of intelligence'. He found this murkiness liberating. While every operational plan acknowledged 'the possibility that things might go awry', with 'the price of failure [calculated] from the beginning', Wolf's agents were trained 'very strictly' on how to conduct themselves if arrested. They were to 'give name, address and date of birth as required by West German law and then say nothing other than to request that contact be taken up with the East German mission in Bonn, which would nominate an experienced lawyer.' This procedure ensured that 'the burden of proof lay entirely on the West Germans'. Wolf's brass neck comes through in other ways in his book. When insisting that 'no intelligence service can afford' a reputation for being 'seedy', Wolf was overlooking an awful lot of his own behaviour, or at least that of his service.

Wolf's skills and knowledge were not unique among intelligence professionals. He was lucky, in more ways than one. He had thirty-five years to perfect his craft, in a stable and well-resourced position. Others were quite capable of spotting the weaknesses exploited by Wolf: the dearth of men in western Germany that led to a preponderance of single women, targeted by Wolf's so-called Romeo spies; the poor pay and unsophistication of US service personnel in Europe; the chance to insert spies in refugee flows; the widespread European interest in peace, pan-German cooperation and anti-nuclear campaigning, all of which helped the HVA. Other things about Wolf were perhaps less typical. His loyalty to his own staff was beyond reproach, and by running a dozen or so agents personally throughout his career, he stayed in touch and understood the problems faced by his subordinates.

Once appointed to a senior role in East German foreign intelligence, Markus Wolf immediately began to practise the Soviet method of long-term agent penetrations.

Wolf's 'long-range agents' (Perspektivagenten) were Stasi sleepers planted in target countries. They were told not to spy, but merely to live: to build up their careers or pursue their studies; to make homes, socialise, meet partners. If, years or even decades later, they could serve a useful espionage purpose, then fine. They would be reactivated by the HVA.

A great many of these long-range agents were recruited or planted in the 1950s, carried out their spying in later decades, and were exposed in the 1990s after the collapse of East Germany. Some important ones were shopped by Werner Roitzsch, a former HVA officer who testified to the Federal authorities. He shone a long-overdue spotlight on the likes of Klaus von Raussendorff, who in 1957 was a youthful history student at West Berlin's Free University. Unusually for a West Berliner, Raussendorff was drawn to communism and fell in with a group of radicals. He was soon spotted by the Stasi. In 1960, now with the codename 'Brede', Raussendorff entered the Foreign Office in Bonn. Initially an embassy attaché, he rose through the ranks: by the time of his arrest at the age of fifty-five, Raussendorff was acting ambassador to UNESCO. He was also reckoned to be one of at least a dozen HVA spies in West Germany's diplomatic corps.[23]

Throughout the 1960s and beyond, Raussendorff would meet twice a year with HVA couriers, to whom he handed reels of microphotographs of Foreign Office documents. He would also deposit items in dead drops in the toilet compartments of trains crossing the inter-German border;[*] the intelligence services of both republics liked to use such dead drops, hidden inside toilet-roll holders or door stops.[24] On two occasions he was received in East Germany by a grateful Markus Wolf, who rewarded him with his habitual gift, the rank of lieutenant colonel.

Similar to Raussendorff's recruitment was that of Hagen Blau, who entered the Federal diplomatic corps in 1961 and spent decades spying from the embassies of Tokyo, Vienna, London and Sri Lanka. Blau was another Free University student, of the Chinese and Japanese languages, recruited in 1960 and given the codename 'Detlev'. Clearly the Stasi had effective talent-spotters at the Free University. This was also true of other institutions; an estimated one quarter of Humboldt University staff, and a similar percentage at the Ministry for Higher Education, worked secretly for the Stasi.[25] Like Raussendorff, Blau used a miniature camera to photograph documents; his was concealed inside a cigarette case. In the later Cold War he was able to inform the Stasi, and thus the KGB, about the Western positions in negotiations over arms reduction, giving the Soviet Bloc a headstart in the international talks. Also like Raussendorff,

---

[*]   Known by the Stasi as Z-TBK for Zug-tote Briefkasten (train dead letter boxes).

Blau was an ideological recruit. At his trial he made a meal of the fact that he was never paid to spy, emphasising his pure political commitment. Raussendorff, too, laid it on thick, opining that, 'All of us had the same motivation – to make a contribution to protecting the first socialist state in Germany and thereby serving peace.'[26] But it can be difficult to tell where political idealism ends and personal neediness and pomposity begin. One former colleague of Blau, retired ambassador Günter Diehl, remarked that Blau's 'muddle-headed' treachery was perhaps due more to his 'complex of self-importance' than his politics.[27] Either way, Blau's ultimate reward, like Raussendorff's, was a six-year prison sentence in middle age.

Another spy to face justice in the 1990s was Armin Hindrichs, codenamed 'Taler', who was recruited by the HVA in 1960 after serving a lengthy prison term in East Berlin. Perhaps for reasons of 'atonement', as the Stasi called it, Hindrichs agreed to relocate to West Germany and infiltrate the SPD. He was highly successful, becoming an SPD speaker on foreign policy in the Bundestag. He ended up as head of the party's documentation and archives; it would be hard to find a better-placed political spy. In 1996 Hindrichs was sentenced to three years in prison.[28]

Some East German spies were revealed by Western intelligence services. The CIA tipped off the Federal authorities about three decades of spying by the famous reporter and radio news anchor Karl-Heinz Maier, whose full exposure came posthumously in the mid-1990s. Three decades earlier Maier had been a respected reporter for a popular paper, *Westfälische Rundschau*, before moving on to head the government radio service Deutsche Welle in Berlin. As chair of a venerable press association, the Berliner Pressekonferenz, Maier spent years hosting and interviewing VIP guests at an annual gala – the likes of François Mitterand and American secretaries of state George Schultz and James Baker. He was decorated by the governments of West Germany, Britain and Austria. All the while he was reporting to the Stasi, which in its records judged him 'an interesting collaborator who delivered important information'.[29]

Another notorious press spy, Diethelm Schröder, may have been recruited as early as the 1940s. As a young teenager in the dying days of the war, Schröder was pressed into a Hitler Youth anti-tank unit that was expected to mount a last-ditch defence against the oncoming Red Army. Most of his comrades were killed in a single battle, but Schröder was captured. It is possible he became a spy for the Soviets soon afterwards. Reportedly, he was ideologically motivated. At some point, the HVA acquired him. In October 1956, now with the codename 'Schrammel', he moved permanently to West Germany in the guise of a refugee. He enjoyed a stellar press career at *Der Spiegel*, *Bild*, and Associated Press. He reported to the Stasi on a range of topics: the opinions of

West German politicians and journalists, news of the Bundeswehr, test flights of Western aircraft and, on two occasions, details of NATO manoeuvres. All of this might have ended in 1963, when the Federal authorities intercepted radio messages – bursts of numbers in the ether – intended for one 'Schrammel'.

Schröder was arrested in Bonn on suspicion of espionage. Investigators found three small texts in a notebook, including a few lines from a nineteenth century poem by Friedrich von Bodenstedt. This, it transpired, was the key to Schröder's radio code. It allowed Federal cryptanalysts to decode fifty-seven messages broadcast to him from East Germany between October 1957 and December 1958. Schröder swore he was simply a poetry fan, however, and was released for lack of evidence.

This moment would come to haunt West Germany's spy-catchers, for they had let a Stasi spy go free. From the mid-1960s, now run by Werner Grossmann, Schröder met with Stasi officers about eight times a year, receiving payments of several hundred deutschmarks per meeting and, eventually, an annual salary of 1,200 deutschmarks. At one of their meetings Grossmann presented him with the Fatherland Order of Merit in Gold.

It all ended disappointingly. The HVA considered Schröder unreliable, and couldn't decide how best to exploit his position at *Der Spiegel*. By the time of his last meeting in 1986, with the HVA Instrukteur (agent handler) 'Weinert' at West Berlin's Zoo station, Schröder had stopped delivering information altogether. That didn't prevent him being prosecuted in the 1990s, when he was charged with 'carrying out intelligence activities against the Federal Republic of Germany for the secret service of a foreign power'. He hadn't helped East Germany much, but the Federal criminal code, like the law in most countries, criminalised any 'communication or delivery of facts, material or findings' to an intelligence service. Many commentators – especially at *Der Spiegel* – were opposed to the prosecution, but prosecutors asserted that spying was a 'permanent crime', ending only with a 'clear and definitive' severing of relations with one's case handlers, which Schröder had never made. He received a suspended sentence of twenty-one months and was fined 30,000 deutschmarks.[30]

Other journalist spy cases were more straightforward. In 1961 the Stasi enlisted Dietrich Staritz, who had escaped from East Berlin as a refugee, while he studied at the Free University. Staritz was to spend some years as a reporter and editor for *Der Spiegel*. His media contacts brought him political information and news of dissidents in East Germany, which he passed to the HVA until the early 1970s. He was rewarded with two medals presented by Erich Mielke.[31]

A smaller number of HVA spies were caught when active. Manfred Rotsch was recruited in 1954, agreeing to work for both the Stasi and the KGB. He was sent west in the refugee flow and, as instructed, found a series of jobs in aircraft factories. KGB and HVA patience paid off in 1969 when Rotsch got a job in space technology at MBB, an important West German defence contractor which was hit hard by communist espionage. Rotsch was able to leak significant and damaging material until his discovery and prosecution in the mid-1980s. In his defence he claimed that he had long since lost his enthusiasm for being a spy, but the KGB had refused to let him stop.[32] Another Perspektivagent, Armin Raufeisen, was caught thanks to the defection of the HVA's Werner Stiller in 1979. Raufeisen had been recruited as a graduate geophysicist in 1957, and after resettling in Hanover had spent years delivering information from his place of work, a large nuclear energy concern.[33]

Sometimes the HVA's spies could cause trouble for innocent bystanders. The political Perspektivagent 'Zady' was recruited by the Stasi in Dresden in 1954, before heading to West Berlin to embark on a long-term infiltration of the CDU. By the end of the 1980s his reports on the party's figures and policies filled sixteen files. At the same time, his infiltration of a political group in West Berlin led to a three-year prison sentence for the Leipzig engineer whose escape from the GDR had been planned by the group.[34]

Other long-range penetrations were a multi-generational family business. Dieter Feuerstein, agent 'Petermann', was a spy at MBB. His parents had been deployed to West Germany as HVA spies in the 1950s. Noticing their son's interest in communism, they had come clean about their identity before proudly steering Feuerstein towards recruitment in the early 1970s.[35]

60

Tradecraft and Technologies

In 1957 an article in *Reader's Digest* announced that a communist spy 'sentenced in Stuttgart was equipped with two micro-cameras, a printing machine, a two-way radio, 22,700 marks (£1,900) in cash and a new Volkswagen!'[1] Espionage was entering its Cold War High Renaissance.

The period saw the HVA refining its tradecraft, including for couriers and for the bread-and-butter activity of the spy world – the clandestine meeting or *treff*. The HVA quickly deemed women to be safer than men as couriers and cut-outs, for which there was evidence: for example, two women who worked for Markus Wolf spent years passing items between changing cubicles at a Munich swimming pool, with never a hint of danger. In general, the safety of a treff was underwritten by a set of principles: alertness, appearance of innocence to any observers, easy means of escape, and constant changes of procedure.[2] The latter principle was captured in the phrase 'Routine is the deadly enemy of conspiracy', used widely at the Stasi and HVA and dating from the interwar communist movement. Moreover, every treff needed a plausible cover story so that participants, if questioned or arrested, could explain what they were doing in a particular place. Well-chosen meeting places enabled the participants to arrive inconspicuously and by different routes, to find each other easily, and to wait innocently for one another if necessary. An 'Instrukteur' – the HVA operative delegated by a case officer to instruct and debrief a spy in-person – might spend up to five hours travelling around on foot and other modes of transport before arriving at the treff. When approaching the spot, it was important to check not just one's own safety but to look for signs of unusual activity around the person one was meeting. Wordless signals were devised to communicate whether the meeting should proceed or be aborted, and to give such information as 'I'm safe' or 'I've got news'.

If the participants hadn't met before, the reconnoitring of the area and the exchanging of mute signals became more elaborate. To impart information in such situations, the KGB and its 'brother organs' favoured the likes of coloured drawing pins stuck into a timetable at a bus stop, or orange peel scattered at a certain spot on the pavement, or a discarded beer bottle pointing in a certain direction, or a telephone call consisting of just a few taps on the speaker. The HVA adopted the KGB technique of participants passing one another on opposite sides of the street for several blocks before actually meeting, in such a way that each could see whether the other was being followed. A pre-arranged fall-back treff could be used if an agent lost contact with handlers for some time, and needed to reopen communications. This might mean waiting at a certain spot at a certain time – say, a pet shop at three o'clock every other Tuesday – to see if contact was made. And treff terminology diversified in HVA hands: a Materialübergabetreff was a wordless exchange of items; a Sichttreff was a dummy run to test agents' proficiency or check if hostile surveillance was in place.

HVA agents drew on the arcane knowledge of such pre-war spies as Leopold Trepper: swallow a spoonful of olive oil before heavy drinking, to lessen the effects of the alcohol; always travel in the last carriage of a train, and be among the last to leave it at a station, in order to observe other passengers; exchange items in the crowded corridors of an underground station; never give the correct day, date or time when arranging a meeting – always add or subtract or cipher such details; use inverted language on the telephone or when in earshot of others – 'I'm leaving Dresden' instead of 'I'm staying in West Berlin', 'I'm leaving on Tuesday' instead of 'I'm arriving on Saturday.'[3]

Similar care was taken over filling and emptying dead letter drops – TBKs, as the Stasi knew them. They had to be sited in places where their users could explain what they were doing in the area. They had to be robust enough to withstand disturbance by other people or animals. Counter-surveillance procedures were used when approaching and leaving the spot. Those depositing items would leave a sign that the TBK had been filled – say, a chalk mark on a nearby stone – and those picking up items would do likewise, to show the TBK had been emptied. The Stasi kept minutely detailed records of its TBKs: their location and surroundings, the schedules of deposit and collection, their every successful or unsuccessful use. Spies' personal files contained sketches or photos of each TBK they used.

Stationary TBKs ran the risk of being placed under fixed surveillance if discovered. Traps could be set to see if anyone had interfered with one. Mobile dead drops could be safer; for example, an item might be thrown from a moving vehicle or bicycle. This method had the benefit of unpredictability, but the drawback that someone had to hunt around for the dropped item. Often, cut-outs were used as surrogate dead drops – people who picked up or deposited items with no knowledge of what they were carrying, to whom, or why.

The HVA used coded radio messages to give warnings to its spies, although it would telephone them at home if necessary, using short and prosaic language and avoiding, as Wolf put it, 'obvious tip-offs like "Your aunt in Dresden is very ill."' There was extra safety in broadcasting messages to spies on public platforms like radio stations: 'Wilhelm, Greta says sorry for leaving early and she'll have the bike repaired.' The recipients of these communications, like SOE and OSS agents of the Second World War, were inactive and hidden in a crowd. Wolf also described a code system based on the serial number of a twenty deutschmark note. Spies were able to contact the HVA on various telephone numbers, which they would work out by listening to 'coded strings of numbers' on short-wave radio and then applying them, in mathematical sums, to the serial number on the banknote. Wolf reckoned it was 'virtually impossible' for anyone else to determine the telephone numbers.[4]

Most HVA spies were trained to use miniature cameras. The HVA's Department K manufactured spy gadgetry. It farmed out some of its work to scientists and workshops, but always with the Stasi's presence concealed. Department E, for Einsatz, was the link between the HVA's technicians and field personnel: it handed out the kit. In 1960 all such functions were absorbed by the Technical Operations Section (Operativ-Technischer Sektor, OTS). Based eventually in premises at Hohenschönhausen, the OTS specialised in chemical and physical technologies, including the manufacture of spyware and forensic science. Its first chief was Colonel Herbert Henschke, who had joined the IWF in 1951 to work in political intelligence. Enthused by the diverse products made at the OTS, which he defined as 'special and secretly created technical instruments', and which were always referred to by codenames, Henschke believed the job of his department was to 'increase conspiracy'.[5] He also developed the forensic services provided by the OTS crime lab, known as Department 32. Its work in 'chemistry, biology, fingerprinting, ballistics, documents, voice analysis, photography [and] explosives' served the HVA and the domestic Stasi departments – especially the investigators of Main Department IX – as well as the customs authorities.[6]

The OTS manufactured secret containers in objets d'art and ornaments; in beer cans, which also contained liquid to make them more authentic; in false teeth, foodstuffs, cigarette packets, clothing, shoes, and household items like brushes. It employed handbag makers and leather workers. It evolved different types of container: those for repeat use, made with stronger materials; disposable and self-destroying containers; and containers that signalled if they had been tampered with. In 1960 a Czech agent was arrested in the West with an OTS container in the form of a jar of baby powder; when opened incorrectly, an interior flash bulb was set off, destroying the film concealed inside. By the 1970s OTS containers were able to thwart the X-ray checks at airports.[7]

Miniature cameras, microphotography and microdots kept improving. By the late 1950s the HVA and Carl Zeiss were collaborating to make cameras the size of small coins, each with fifteen circular negatives and capable of photographing A4 paper. The spy's favourite, the Minox camera, could be concealed inside a glove, with a small hole in one finger for the lens, and a spring rod to release the shutter and wind the film.[8] Operatives would also use commercially available cameras, 35mm or Super 8, which aroused little suspicion. Stasi employees liked Robot cameras from West Germany, some of which came with concealment kits: a holding frame, a battery, a remote shutter switch and a spring-driven motor to wind film automatically. They could be concealed at chest or waist level under a coat. Secret writing also continued to evolve. Department K and then the OTS steadily developed inks and papers from a wide range of materials: shellac, benzyl alcohol, cerium, manganese, hydrogen peroxide, ammonia carbonate and other chemicals, in hundreds of combinations.[9]

Press and public, never mind counter-espionage agencies, cottoned on rather quickly to these innovations. In January 1957 Britain's *Daily Express* reported that 'a new miniature camera is being manufactured in a heavily guarded factory at Hohenschoenhausen, near Berlin, says a refugee scientist from the Russian zone. It is no bigger than a stamp… is completely "clickless" [and] can be disguised as a tiepin, cufflinks or matchbox.'[10] The same newspaper caused consternation at MI5 and the Press and Broadcasting Committee when another article, based on information acquired in Germany, revealed that:

> Soviet engineers have perfected a new 'super hearing aid' which makes it possible for Soviet agents to listen to, and record, a conversation taking place up to a mile away.
>
> The great thing about the new 'Hearing Aid' is that it is operated without the aid of a microphone – which on account of its dependence on cables and wires could always be located in a careful check.
>
> All that is needed for the new device is that an operative – an office cleaner will do – hides a small metal disk somewhere in the target room…
>
> You can imagine the flurry the discovery of this secret apparatus has caused among those in the Western world whose job it is to see that secrets don't leak out.
>
> But the really ironic thing is that the Soviet device has caused an equal anxiety in Moscow. For the Soviet security authorities are assuming that anything developed by their own people may well have also been developed by the Western scientists.[11]

In fact, for years the FBI and MI5 had for counter-espionage purposes been using a 'small wireless set which can go easily into an inside breast pocket with an aerial up the arm'. When tested at MI5 headquarters in 1951, the device had proved able to pick up 'speech quite distinctly from someone walking in the park or in the streets, or anywhere in the building'.[12]

Clearly the race for technological supremacy was on; it has never ended. By the time computer technology came along, some of the HVA's long-term spies were poised to steal it. One of them was Kurt Blaschke, whose parents fled to West Germany in 1956.[13] Blaschke followed them a year later but continued to visit East Berlin, where he socialised with fellow science students. At one meeting his potential was spotted by an undercover Stasi employee, who subsequently suggested to Blaschke that he do something useful 'for securing freedom'. Having expressed interest, Blaschke was sent on an espionage test run, photographing the US listening facility at Teufelsberg. He then signed an agreement to spy for the Stasi but, as in so many cases, it took years before he was able to achieve anything in the West. Only in 1970 did he get a job as a lab assistant at AEG Telefunken. He had no access to classified materials but was active in the trade union movement. This brought potential recruits into his orbit; hence the HVA activated him in a talent-spotting role for its computer technology section. Most of Blaschke's tip-offs came to nothing, but in the late 1970s he was able to recruit an electrical engineer with access to secret information on the conversion of analogue signals to digital. Decades of effort, decades of watching, decades of dead ends, all boiled down to this: one valuable source, an espionage success.

61

Love Rats

In the early 1950s East German foreign intelligence began to make sporadic use of a particular method of acquiring spies. West German women who worked with sensitive political or military information would be seduced by specially selected, well-trained male operatives. Many of the targeted women worked as secretaries or personal assistants in Federal ministries and political parties. Having been courted by the Stasi operative and entered a steady relationship, each woman would be persuaded, tricked or pressurised into supplying secret information from her workplace. The men who carried out these recruitments have acquired the crass term 'Romeo spies', although the connection between Shakespeare's profound lover and these dead-eyed intelligence sex-workers is tenuous indeed.

In his memoirs Markus Wolf recalled his first Romeo, codenamed 'Felix', whose identity he chose never to reveal.[1] Spring 1952 found 'Felix' 'studying engineering in a small town in south-east Germany'. His potential as an undercover operative was spotted by senior Stasi officers, who regularly hunted for talent at universities, in the SED, and in youth and sports clubs. Despite being unenthusiastic when approached by Wolf – 'Felix' didn't want his studies interrupted by espionage – he agreed to enter a training programme. Like every prospective agent he was soon sent on a practice mission, one he believed to be a genuine emergency and not a dummy run.

During his training 'Felix' had been taught how to spot and shake-off followers. As Wolf put it, he had 'studied our diagrams showing the visual angles from which surveillance is possible and how to avoid certain positions in a crowd'. On his dummy mission, 'Felix' was told to travel to Hamburg, make brief contact with a courier near the railway station, and then pick up materials from another contact at the harbourside. Within minutes of arriving in the city, however, 'Felix' managed to convince himself that he was being shadowed by a legion of raincoated watchers. He saw followers everywhere; and as far as he was concerned, these were real Western counter-espionage agents. So he made a panicky decision to shift the angle of the newspaper he was carrying under one arm, thus signalling to the waiting courier that the mission be aborted.

This was an inauspicious start to what became a glittering career as a spy, but on one level Wolf was encouraged, as it suggested that 'Felix' couldn't be accused of over-confidence or complacency. These failings could be the undoing even of experienced agents. For Wolf, there was one 'basic rule, even for the most advanced spy', which was 'never to assume that you are not under surveillance'.

In time 'Felix' was deployed to Bonn under a false identity and with the cover occupation of a sales rep for bathroom products. This was an odd choice as cover, for how might a shampoo seller discover West Germany's political and military secrets? But it paid off. The Stasi was keen to penetrate the office of chancellor Konrad Adenauer, about whom it knew too little. Wolf admitted that he didn't possess 'even the basic tool for understanding any institution, the internal office telephone directory'. By hanging around at a bus stop near the chancellor's office at the end of each working day, 'Felix' managed to befriend a secretary who worked for Adenauer. She was given the codename 'Norma'. The pair's friendship was useful from the start, for at social events she introduced 'Felix' to more of Adenauer's employees, and he began to pick up scraps of information. Before long, a romance developed. 'Felix' and 'Norma' moved in together.

East German foreign intelligence learned well from its Soviet parent. Among other things, it learned that great patience can be rewarded. The casual skimming of information from 'Norma' and her colleagues continued for several years. 'Norma' never knew the true identity of 'Felix'. The affair ended only when the HVA scented disaster; an East German mole inside the West German security service, the BfV, warned that 'Felix' was under investigation. He was summarily withdrawn from Bonn. One day 'Norma' returned home from work to find her partner gone, without explanation. Wolf admitted this must have caused her pain, but there is more than a hint of professional self-satisfaction in his closing remark on the matter: 'in a choice between saving an agent and saving a romance, I had to be ruthless.'

Before his career was wound down, however, 'Felix' gave the HVA a tip-off. He had identified another secretary in Bonn who might be vulnerable to a romantic recruitment. She worked for state secretary Hans Globke – a man whom the Soviets and GDR were keen to expose as a former high-ranking Nazi and symbol of Western hypocrisy. Furthermore, communications between Globke and Reinhard Gehlen routinely passed through the woman's hands. She was given the codename 'Gudrun'. According to Wolf, the Romeo chosen to seduce her was 'an amateur pilot' called Herbert Söhler:* actually he

---

* Wolf's autobiography, like those of most high-ranking spymasters, is deliberately littered with misnomers, misremembered details, and the transposition of facts and events among its stories.

was Hans Stöhler, a Luftwaffe veteran.[2] Although Stöhler had converted to communism as a result of political re-education in a Soviet POW camp, his war service had counted against him in East Germany, limiting his career options. Reputedly he was thrilled to be selected for covert operations abroad.

Codenamed 'Astor', Stöhler moved to the Bonn area under an alias and in the guise of an estate agent. He appealed to 'Gudrun', who fell for him deeply. Stöhler even sensed that 'Gudrun' could be recruited explicitly; that she would not be averse to becoming a conscious spy, provided she sympathised with the recipient of her information. Stöhler realised this wouldn't be the GDR – like many Germans, 'Gudrun' didn't recognise East Germany's right to exist – but it might, he thought, be the Soviet Union. In conversations he often praised the Soviet political officers who had changed his worldview, and emphasised the strong ties between the hard-working, no-nonsense peoples of Germany and Russia. 'Gudrun' seemed impressed, and so, despite Markus Wolf's unease, it was decided that Stöhler would come clean that he was using her as a spy, albeit for the KGB.

Throughout its existence, the information the HVA gave or revealed to those it recruited as agents varied wildly. Some recruitments were made with cards on the table; you are being asked to spy for the East German state security service. Sometimes this was made clear to recruits by inviting them to East Germany, where they were entertained by senior Stasi officers whose role and high position were so obvious that it didn't require comment, never mind explanation. Other recruitments were concealed behind thick coatings of lies. It all depended on the agent in question, the circumstances and, perhaps above all, on the skill and intuition of the recruiter, who was often the person to decide on the best approach.

There were some fixed rules to it, though, one of which was to avoid making a recruitment pitch to West Germans on West German soil, whenever possible. Doing it in a neutral country allowed for a smoother escape if things went wrong. It could also avoid the common practice of counter-espionage agencies 'to shadow a suspected recruiter, prime his [or her] intended target, and then film the recruitment to gain evidence of espionage activity and grounds for immediate arrest'.[3] In the case of 'Gudrun', the attentive Stöhler took her on a lavish trip to Switzerland. As he had predicted, she reacted well to the news that he was a KGB recruiter, and agreed to supply him with secret information.

Reportedly her stint as an agent ended when Stöhler became terminally ill and went home to East Germany to die. It wasn't possible to give her a new handler, romantic or otherwise; she wasn't interested and, to avoid the possibility of her talking to the West German authorities, she was left alone.

The Stasi achieved its aim anyway, acquiring enough information to damn Hans Globke, who resigned in 1963.

Another early Romeo case – and perhaps the first to be exposed – came to light in 1958: the seduction of the secretary of Franz Josef Strauss, Federal defence minister. A staunch Bavarian right-winger who almost became chancellor later in his career, Strauss was instrumental in pushing for West Germany to be equipped with nuclear weapons. The importance of the information acquired from his desk is obvious. The HVA always aimed high. His secretary wasn't the only betrayer of Strauss's secrets; from 1956, a close confidante of Strauss, Gerhard Baumann, who had once worked for the Organisation Gehlen and was intimate with the BND, delivered materials to the Stasi as GI (later IM) 'Schwartz'. Baumann was recruited under a false flag, with his handlers pretending to be French.[4] Meanwhile the West German newspapers had some fun with the case of Strauss's secretary, coining her seducer, Carl Helmers, the 'Red Casanova'.[5]

From the start, the moral details of the Romeo cases were layered, and messy. In 1960 a barmaid at a Bonn nightclub introduced her friend, Marianne Lenzkow, to two Danish men who claimed to be employees of Denmark's military mission in West Germany. Lenzkow, a thirty-one-year-old divorcee, worked as a teletypist at the Federal Ministry of the Interior. The men, who called themselves Kalle Schramm and Kai Petersen, invited her for a weekend away at a Danish diplomatic property. Over that weekend Schramm seduced and recruited Lenzkow. He claimed that Denmark was tired of being overlooked by NATO's senior members, and suggested that Lenzkow could do a good turn for international relations by giving him confidential materials from her office. After all, the information would only be going to a friendly NATO partner. Lenzkow was apparently touched by Denmark's plight. She began to supply Schramm with NATO teletype messages, including bulletins on wanted communist spies. Her couriers were her barmaid friend, Anita Brünger, and Brünger's fiancé, the Danish-born Stasi operative Eric Michaelson, codenamed 'Singer'.

In time, Marianne Lenzkow suggested to her younger sister, Margarete Lubig, that Schramm's friend Kai Petersen was promising boyfriend material. Lubig – single, twenty-five-years-old, and a devout Roman Catholic – worked as a secretary and translator for the Federal Ministry of Defence. Her boss had an office at NATO's European command centre in Fontainebleau, outside Paris.

Margarete was intrigued, and so Schramm and Petersen took the sisters on a romantic trip to Vienna. As hoped, Margarete fell for Kai Petersen there, remarking at one point that she had 'never had such a lovely time with anyone before'.[6] Soon the pair were an item. Margarete then agreed to give secret documents to Petersen, on the same understanding as her sister – that she was helping West Germany's under-informed ally, Denmark.

Kai Petersen's real name was Roland Gandt. He was an East German HVA operative codenamed 'Venske'. 'Kalle Schramm', meanwhile, was the HVA officer Karl-Heinz Schneider. Both worked for Markus Wolf from an HVA sub-office at Karl-Marx-Stadt, a site of feverish activity which became renowned for 'conceiving wild schemes and baroque projects'. Wolf praised Gandt – 'highly intelligent, fine-featured, and with an actor's talent for disguise' – as nothing short of a 'super-Romeo', a 'king of melodrama'.[7] Fittingly, his day job was actor-director at a respected arts theatre. Reputedly, Margarete Lubig had already been targeted unsuccessfully by three HVA suitors; it took Gandt to get the job done. He began to make regular trips to Bonn, where Margarete supplied him with documents on NATO's military exercises and deployment plans.

The HVA didn't have it all their own way. In time Lubig's guilt got the better of her, and she told 'Kai' she would stop cooperating unless she were allowed to confess her behaviour to a priest. This caused a brief panic at the usually unflappable HVA, which couldn't afford the insecurity of Margarete making a real confession. But a sparsely attended church in Jutland was located, where the ritual could be staged. 'Kai' suggested to Margarete that they make a nice trip of it. In Denmark he introduced her to his mother and his boss at Danish military intelligence, the former portrayed by a Stasi agent from Sweden and the latter by a member of the Danish communist party.[8] At the church Margarete duly confessed and received absolution. The priest to whom she unburdened herself was Karl-Heinz Hüppe, a Stasi officer who had taken a crash course in Danish in order to fake the procedure and shed his Saxon ploughman's accent. He had simply snuck into the confessional when no one was looking.[9]

Markus Wolf's account of the Lubig case is probably deceitful; most spy memories are. He claimed that Margarete stopped passing secrets when Gandt, whom the Stasi thought was under suspicion, was withdrawn from the operation. Others are confident that Lubig continued to pass confidential materials, including from the West German military mission in Rome, until 1989.[10] In the mid-1990s she was tried in Düsseldorf and, in view of her cooperation, received an eighteen-month suspended sentence. Her older sister Marianne was never prosecuted – by that time she had died.

The Romeo cases were relatively unusual in their targeting of women. As far as the Stasi was concerned, the world was male. Over the years it recruited relatively few women as high-grade sources. It is notable, though, that when the HVA's scientific and technical section recruited women, it didn't use the

Romeo method. These women, though relatively few – just ten, by the 1980s – were all recruited for their political beliefs or for money. Perhaps it was simply unnecessary to use Romeos; perhaps there were other reasons. Most of these women were administrators and laboratory assistants – only one of them had a PhD, in biology – but they all reported valuable information. Katherina Straub, agent 'Ilona', was an office manager at the defence contractor MBB. A socialist and GDR sympathiser, she was recruited by the HVA's rocket science section in the early 1960s. For twenty years she provided hundreds of high-grade items, including information on Western weapons systems, satellites, and space programmes, and even highly sensitive materials on America's cruise missiles.[11]

The full and horrible possibilities of Romeo spying weren't realised until the 1960s and 1970s, when Markus Wolf began to make large-scale, programmatic use of the method. Often Romeos would make 'false flag' recruitments, hiding their real nationality or true allegiance; in general, false flag approaches are favoured by pariah regimes that don't expect sympathy or cooperation. The HVA had a recurring problem when it came to fooling women from West Germany, who were likely to realise their seducer was a fellow German. So the Romeos adopted false nationalities that allowed for speaking German with a trace of easily-mimicked accent – Denmark, South Africa.

Eventually Wolf's Romeos came undone in public scandals of the late 1970s and 1980s. In later years Wolf was unabashed, irritated by what he saw as the West's hypocritical criticisms. He publicised several examples of Romeo spying carried out by the BND, including in America and Norway. He tended not to mention the fallout for the Romeos' victims. Many were vulnerable to start with, targeted because they had no supportive links with parents or wider family. Although they are often described, or perhaps dismissed, as 'middle-aged', the youngest was nineteen. And lives were lost. In 1967 Leonore Sütterlin, a secretary in the Federal Foreign Office, was convicted for passing 3,500 classified documents to the KGB via her husband, who had married her solely to gain this access. Shattered by the revelation of his motives, she hanged herself in her prison cell.

62

A Torrent of Spies

From the late 1950s onwards, the HVA's deployment of spies begins to augur the scale that would cause such shock after the reunification of Germany. Although most of the HVA archive was destroyed in coordination with the Federal government, copies of index cards with spies' codenames and targets – the so-called Rosenholz files – came to light in the 1990s. Their numbers are almost overwhelming. They show the HVA in spate: a torrent of spies.

What is striking, as well as the extent of the penetration and the secret knowledge that must have been gained, is the longevity of these agents. Sources who were delivering in the 1980s often had been associated with the HVA, or even its predecessors, since the 1950s. Many recruitments of the early 1960s didn't start to pay off until at least the following decade. West Germany was a sitting target, and Markus Wolf was in the enviable position of being a spymaster within a patchily divided country. Nevertheless, his HVA took full advantage of the situation. An astonishing level of commitment and staying-power is apparent among the following selection of spies, some of whom were identified and sentenced.[1]

HVA Department I/2, responsible for operations against the Federal Foreign Office, had the important IM 'Merten': he started reporting in 1959, and by 1989 had delivered 1,450 items of information; ninety-six of these items were graded 'very valuable' and 357 'valuable', and more than 200 reports were based upon his work.

HVA Department II focused on West German parties and political organisations. Among its agents were 'Steiger', recruited in 1960, who worked alongside the chair of the Federal trade union organisation, the DGB; 'Becker', recruited in 1961, an SPD member of the Bavarian parliament; and 'Milli', recruited in 1960, a functionary at IG Metall who reported on the SPD and the peace movement. Department II/1 dealt with the CDU and conservative Christian organisations: its agent 'Iltis', a CDU secretary recruited in 1961, bided her time and began reporting in 1967. Department II/2 covered liberal and nationalist parties, including the Free Democrats and Deutsche Partei. William

Borm, its agent 'Olaf', registered by the HVA in October 1959 after spending years in an East German prison, was a Free Democrat executive and member of the Bundestag who reported until at least the mid-1980s. Department II/4 was responsible for the SPD: its spy couple 'Hans' and 'Marcella' were SPD members of the West Berlin senate, recruited in 1957. Department II/5, which dealt with trade unions, in 1956 recruited the agent 'Wein', who sat on the executive committee of IG Metall.

Details of the HVA's specialisation are everywhere. Its agent 'Jörg', signed up in 1956, contributed analyses of US policy. Department XI/9 focused on US forces and citizens in West Berlin, and the US military mission at Potsdam; its agent 'Stamm' was recruited in 1960. The agent 'Flame', recruited the same year, later worked for Danish military intelligence. He supplied information on the aims, methods and identities of Danish intelligence officers, and was able to give a concrete tip-off that a Soviet correspondent in Bonn was under suspicion.

Scientific and technological espionage only increased in importance. Agent 'Weisskopf', Manfred Wittig, went west as a migrant in 1961 after studying at Dresden's technical college; he then worked as a chemist at Leybold in Cologne and directed three other sources, including employees of Bayer and Hoechst. Peter Stickel, 'Pfeiffer', a physics professor at Bielefeld University, was recruited for ideological reasons in 1955 while studying in East Berlin. He passed information on other physicists and their potential for recruitment. After reunification he was questioned about these activities but not prosecuted for them. Planted in the 1950s at Standard Electric Lorenz (SEL), an important communications technology firm, were 'Otto' (Gerhard Müller) and 'Jürgen' (Andreas Berndt). Both were convicted in the 1990s. Agent 'Alvar', sent west in the late 1950s, became a 'star source' at the European headquarters of IBM in Paris. Markus Wolf referred to the East German company Robotron as 'a sort of illegal subsidiary' of IBM, given the amount of information that was stolen. Another agent there, Gerhard Arnold, who occupied a senior position, arrived as a fake refugee in West Germany in 1957.[2]

No one knows the extent to which Siemens was penetrated by the HVA, but it was certainly highly active there. Its agents included Oswald Cyron, alias 'Rode', who was infiltrated into West Germany in 1957; 'German' (Günter Gerson, who emigrated in 1954); 'Günter' (Eckhard Schlobohm, who emigrated in 1957 and was imprisoned in the 1990s); and 'Gustav' (Charlie C., who emigrated in 1958). The latter, employed at Siemens's biggest site in Munich, was one of the most important 1950s infiltrators to still be operating in 1989. Schlobohm, on the other hand, was considered by the HVA to be something of a disappointment. He was recruited by Dieter Gladitz of the HVA's scientific-technical section, posing as an official of the Ministry for Higher Education seeking information on the Federal education system. Trained in coding, radio operations and secret writing, Schlobohm managed to occupy a useful position in Siemens' data processing department in 1969. While his prosecution was a success story in terms of counter-espionage, most of his information had been judged inconsequential, although some items were passed to Robotron.

One of the HVA's earliest military sources, 'Ingrid' (Rosalie Kunze) was trained for a year in the GDR before being sent west in 1955 under the cover name Roberta König. Her recruitment wasn't pretty; she was blackmailed into becoming a spy with evidence of a recent illegal abortion. But she took to the task, gaining a job as a secretary with the naval operations staff of the Federal Ministry of Defence. Also at the defence ministry was agent 'Gold', working in his retirement for a security company that protected the building. The couple Horst and Evelyn Schötzki, known collectively as source 'Schatz', were also military spies; but they were unmasked together with Kunze in 1960 and received prison terms. The Schötzkis are said to have recruited Norbert Moser (agent 'Hagen'), an air force colonel, whose wife Ruth, codenamed 'Gerlinde', had previously been married to Karl-Heinz Knollmann (agent 'Stein') of the Federal border police. The Mosers delivered voluminous information on West German and NATO capabilities until Norbert's exposure and imprisonment in the mid-1970s.

From 1959 the HVA's military espionage department was designated HVA/IV and led by Otto Knye, who had previously masterminded kidnappings and other dirty operations against the KgU. In due course it was taken over by Wolf's deputy, Werner Grossmann. Its targets in West Germany included the Ministry of Defence; the district and regional commands of the Bundeswehr, including the southern hub at Mannheim and northern hub at Mönchengladbach; the air force and Bundeswehr offices in Cologne; the navy headquarters at Kiel; the Bundeswehr press offices; and the military universities at Hamburg and Munich. Anyone and everyone connected with these institutions attracted unflagging interest.

Another agency in the sights of HVA/IV was the Federal Office for Defence Technology and Procurement. It was infiltrated by, among others, Gerhard Block, agent 'Sänger'. Block, a patriotic East German, was recruited in summer 1957 by Rolf Wagenbreth, who later led the HVA's department for disinformation and active measures. Block adopted the identity of one Herbert Pfeiffer, a mechanic from Halle, who had been a wartime prisoner of the French. He learned the real Pfeiffer's life story and visited the camp and village in southern France where Pfeiffer had spent time. In October 1959, with his family and acquaintances convinced he had gone to work in Bulgaria,

Block registered as Herbert Pfeiffer in Mannheim. He began to get information from 'Waldemar', a civilian employee of the US army, and from nineteen-year-old Christa Gotter; as agent 'Heidi', she got a job at American Express, thus learning the financial details of American service personnel. Although Block's case handler was the experienced Werner Steinführer, it all went wrong in 1962. Block was remanded in custody and, it seems, summarily dropped by the HVA. 'I felt crushed on two sides,' he wrote later. 'On the one hand by the class enemies, on the other hand by my friends, my comrades from the MfS.'[3] Werner Grossmann responded with disparaging remarks about Block, whom he considered 'soft'.

Over the years the HVA acquired a ridiculous number of spies with access to NATO information. In 1957 Werner Bayer, a foreign intelligence officer in the Stasi's Greater Berlin office, filled in a registration card for Peter Kranick, whom he called agent 'Bruno'. In 1950 Kranick had moved out of his mother's home in East Berlin and joined the French Foreign Legion. Injured in combat against Việt Minh forces, he received the Croix de Guerre. He was then given a job as an archivist at the French headquarters for West Berlin, the Quartier Napoléon, where he befriended his future wife and fellow spy, Renée Levine.

Kranick's recruitment paid dividends in 1960, when he was able to report that 290 active nuclear warheads were stored in France; the country detonated its first atomic weapon that year. He also reported on meetings of the NATO council and secretariat, and of the tensions between the Anglo-American representatives at NATO and Paul-Henri Spaak, the organisation's secretary general and 'pro-nuclear' ally of the Federal defence minister Franz Josef Strauss. Meanwhile, having married Kranick, Renée got a job in the NATO press office.

A similar penetration was effected by Ursel Lorenzen, who became a well-known media figure in the late 1970s as the witting accomplice of Romeo spy Dieter Will. Less well-known is the fact that the pair's spy story began much earlier. Lorenzen worked for the HVA as agent 'Mosel' from at least 1961; she was recruited as a sub-source by a businessman codenamed 'Bordeaux', who later lived and worked in Brussels. Dieter Will, her Romeo, was connected with the HVA from at least 1958, and was encouraged to move to Paris and study at the Sorbonne.

Information on the Lockheed U-2 spy plane was provided to the HVA by Major Bruno Winzer, codenamed variously 'Winter', 'Südpol', 'Rebe' and 'Depot', who was recruited in 1957 when working as a Bundeswehr press officer. A year earlier, two junior employees of the Federal Ministry of the Interior, Josef Paul ('Minister') and Wilhelm Knipp ('Zange'), had started to supply such items as the minutes of NATO meetings. Both were arrested and imprisoned in the early 1960s.

Did the HVA ever refuse an agent? It seems unlikely. Other spies with large case files included 'Iris', a secretary in Düsseldorf; 'Weide', a Hamburg lawyer recruited in 1955; and three spies with access to the Ministry for Economic Property in Bonn, which later became the Federal Treasury – 'Bauer', 'Hartzer' and 'Schneider'.

The HVA did have its defectors. In May 1959 Max Heim ran to the West; he had led operations against the western CDU, and he was soon followed by his deputy, Helmut Fleischer. In June 1961 Günter Männel of the US department also fled to West Germany, prompting much criticism of Wolf's service by Erich Mielke and other Stasi high-ups.

Heim's defection triggered more than thirty arrests and hampered the HVA's infiltration of the western CDU for some years. It halted further work by the likes of Jost Biedermann, an East German politician who for some time had been reporting to Heim the contents of his casual chats with West German counterparts. Heim revealed the identities of four Stasi spies, three working for the HVA, who were steadily penetrating the main CDU office in Bonn. Also arrested in Bonn was Julius Dietz, employee of the Bundestag publishing department, who had procured such essential items as telephone directories. Dietz had been recruited for the HVA by one Lothar Noack, agent 'Norden', a resident of Leipzig who had successfully resettled in Bonn as a medical student. Another HVA re-settler, Johannes Müller (agent 'Mahnke'), had reached a senior position in the Ring of Christian Democrat Students and was 'skimming' information from unknowing CDU politicians. A third, Charlotte Respondek, was working as a freelance journalist in West Berlin with a mission to get close to the Federal minister for agriculture, and later prime minister, Heinrich Lübke.

The HVA launched a damage limitation exercise, operation Gegenschlag (Counterstrike), to assess the damage caused by Heim, place him under constant observation and, it was hoped, return him to East Germany, though this wasn't achieved. Gegenschlag didn't prevent the West German government from publishing its newly acquired revelations. It blew the whistle on an HVA active measure that had been running for several years – an attempt to sow discord in the CDU by sending fake letters, purporting to come from Konrad Adenauer and other party high-ups, in which personal and political animosities were given a good stir.[4]

Heim also betrayed an HVA recruit of whom Markus Wolf was especially proud: Wolfram von Hanstein, an aristocrat and writer who, after a chequered experience under the Nazi and Soviet regimes, had done prison time in Moscow before returning to East Germany. Aristocrats usually had a cluster of motives for becoming an HVA spy: guilt about the Nazi period, dismay at Konrad Adenauer's pro-American policies, the feeling of being no longer important or listened to. When von Hanstein and his wife decided to embark on a new life in West Germany, they left a villa outside Dresden to the East German state; it was quickly bagged by the Stasi. Von Hanstein became a leading figure in human rights lobbying. In addition to disrupting the likes of the League for Human Rights, he was able to provide information about a range of anti-communist organisations.[5] His exposure by Heim resulted in six years in prison where, according to Wolf, he continued to serve the HVA by identifying fellow prisoners who were sympathetic to the GDR, three of whom were subsequently recruited.[6] After his release von Hanstein returned to East Germany.

Defectors weren't the only problem. HVA spies were not immune to arrest. Hinrich Zange, recruited while in prison in the GDR for 'irregularities in his law practice', was unmasked by West German counter-intelligence having penetrated CDU and FDP circles in Bonn. In May 1961 he was sentenced to two and a half years in prison, while his wife, owner of a beauty salon, was given six months as his accomplice.[7] Other HVA spies were doubled by Western services, like its resident in the Saarland, who was turned by the CIA.[8] And even Markus Wolf made mistakes. One of them concerned the West German steel magnate Christian Steinrücke. Wolf, posing as a trade official at the Leipzig fair, had befriended Steinrücke, who was very well-connected in West Germany – Steinrücke's brother-in-law was married to Konrad Adenauer's daughter, and another relative was the niece of Cardinal Frings, a leading figure in the Catholic church. The pair's friendship lasted some years. Wolf treated Steinrücke to regular breaks at a luxury villa in East Germany, where a presenter from GDR television would play the role of Wolf's wife.

Wolf learned that Steinrücke was friendly with Walter Bauer, a senior employee of the Flick conglomerate who brokered trade between the two Germanys. Discovering that Bauer was far richer than his day job would explain, and that he was friendly with former OSS agents, Wolf tried to recruit Bauer by insinuating that he was involved with the US secret services. The implacable Bauer batted away Wolf's hints, and the botched recruitment ended Wolf's friendship with Steinrücke. This was costly: as Wolf had predicted, Steinrücke subsequently became a major player in the German-American arms trade. Wolf learned his lesson, henceforward telling his officers not to try blackmailing the glitterati, and to exercise caution when recruiting anyone: 'If you think that the answer is going to be no, don't ask the question.'[9]

Some setbacks were out of Wolf's hands. When supplied with HVA information, executives of the SED, the government, and even the Stasi didn't always comply with Wolf's rule: that a report 'classified as top secret' was 'for the personal information of the recipient. Once acknowledged, it must be returned [to Wolf's department] in a sealed envelope. I ask that you strictly observe this rule in the interest of the safety of informants'.[10] Despite this plea, such information occasionally made its way to the media. In 1957 Wolf complained that East German radio had broadcast figures obtained from a source on the Bundestag's Legal Affairs Committee. This breach had rendered the source 'inactive', although Wolf limited the damage by making a temporary arrangement to get similar information from the Czechoslovakian intelligence service, the StB.[11]

The HVA's attempt to recruit Erich Meyer, an SPD member of the Bundestag, was also scuppered by gauche press reporting. In autumn 1957 Meyer accompanied fellow members to a special Bundestag session held in West Berlin. His brother-in-law, a resident of East Berlin, had already been recruited as an HVA asset. He was told to set up a meeting with Meyer, at which two undercover HVA operatives would engage him in political discussions, with a view to steering him into working for the GDR. The meeting took place, but the discussions had mixed results. The HVA noted that Meyer agreed with such East German policies as banning nuclear weapons, but 'fundamentally disagreed' with others, such as friendship with the Soviet Union. It was all rendered immaterial when Meyer was suddenly assaulted in an East German press campaign, which accused him of debauchery during his stay: Meyer, said the papers, was 'more interested in the West Berlin red light district than in his parliamentary duties'. Given that Meyer had spent the whole trip in the company of his wife and extended family, the accusations were nonsense, but they ruined Markus Wolf's chances of recruiting Meyer as a spy.[12]

Other recruitments were killed by bad luck. Otto Wittenburg served as a Bundestag member for the far-right Deutsche Partei for much of the 1950s. He hailed from Mecklenburg, where in 1945 a close friend, the local mayor, had rescued him from internment at the hands of the conquering Soviets. Years later the mayor had been recruited by the Stasi's Schwerin office as its GI 'Klause'. In this capacity he was told to rekindle his friendship with Wittenburg, who duly received 'Klause' as a guest at his home near Kiel. 'Klause' reciprocated by inviting Wittenburg and his wife for a pleasant break in Schwerin. The Stasi seized the chance to bug rooms at 'Klause''s house, and arranged for potentially compromising photographs of Wittenburg to be taken at local places of interest. But the bugs failed and the photos proved unusable.[13] Wittenburg slipped away.

Another debacle concerned Karl-Heinz Kaerner, the HVA's agent 'Kohle'. He provided the Stasi with documents he had forged himself, purporting to show West German plans to attack the GDR.[14] A great deal of propaganda was based upon Kaerner's forgeries. In 1960 Albert Norden's Committee for German Unity publicised the documents in such newspaper articles as 'German Warmongers At Work Again'. The Stasi weighed in with its operation Straussenei (Ostrich Egg), in which it released facsimiles of the documents. Erich Mielke wrote in *Neues Deutschland* of an 'imminent Blitzkrieg'. Bruno Winzer, a press officer for the Federal armed forces and the HVA's agent 'Rebe', was hurriedly resettled in the GDR in order to confirm publicly the documents' authenticity.

The HVA should have been sceptical about Kaerner. A freelance journalist, in 1949 he had presented himself to British embassy staff in Paris, claiming to be the personal pilot of Hitler's private secretary Martin Bormann, whom Kaerner insisted was still alive. In an article of the same period Kaerner wrote that Hitler, too, was alive and well and living in a Tibetan monastery. Werner Grossmann, Wolf's long-term deputy, claimed to have discovered and recruited Kaerner at the foreign ministers' conference in Berlin in early 1954; either Grossmann lied or he was unaware that Main Department II had already recruited Kaerner at the GDR resettlement camp in Eisenach.

Provided by Grossmann with the false ID of a West German called Claus Zeinig, Kaerner had set about romancing a secretary at the Amt Blank, Gabriele Clairon d'Haussonville. He managed to sign her up as a Stasi collaborator for a stiff price: 600 deutschmarks per month. It was she, Kaerner said, who had procured the West German invasion plans for him, taking them from the personal safe of General Hans Speidel, at that time the inspector general of Federal armed forces. If Grossmann or other HVA officers had looked a bit deeper, they would have known that Clairon d'Haussonville worked nowhere near Speidel and had no conceivable access to his safe, but the biggest problem was that the HVA lacked the expertise to analyse the documents properly. One of them, appearing to date from spring 1955, was labelled 'secret Federal matters' (geheime Bundessache), a security classification that didn't exist. The graphic symbols in its maps and diagrams were wrong, and its text used odd and otherwise unknown terminology for the Kasernierte Volkspolizei and other East German formations.

Despite all this, the HVA was never quite prepared to admit that the so-called 'Deco' documents were a forgery. Behind the scenes, however, the service did come to doubt, and to imprison, Kaerner. He did time in both West and East Germany, latterly at Hohenschönhausen. After his release he moved to Austria for a while, but Wolf's outfit never trusted him again. Kaerner's forgery, and the inadequacies it exposed in the HVA – hopefulness, boastfulness, complacency, analytical deficiencies – were a blot on Markus Wolf's career.

*

By the end of the 1950s the HVA had about 500 full-time employees, plus some 200 working in its regional offices.[15] Other institutions had a sprinkling of HVA officers; for example, two worked at the Ministry of Culture's Office for Literature. The combined efforts of the KGB, GRU, Stasi and other Soviet Bloc services – especially those of Czechoslovakia and Poland – had led to an immense espionage presence in the West. In 1959, 2,802 suspected communist agents were arrested in West Germany alone, thirty percent of whom had been focused on military targets. In 1960 at least 500 more were arrested by Federal agencies,[16] while from January to October that year, US military counter-intelligence arrested 348 people for spying on American forces' sites in Europe, mostly in West Berlin and West Germany. Those arrested included 266 spies for East Germany – some of whom were probably taking a fall for the Soviets – and sixty-six for the KGB and GRU. The remainder worked for other Warsaw Pact countries.

The intelligence historian Matthias Uhl has provided a breakdown of the various, overlapping tasks that had been given to these arrested spies. Sixty percent admitted to gathering order-of-battle information; thirty-one percent were investigating military units and their armaments; twenty percent were working against US counter-intelligence; fourteen percent monitored garrisons; thirteen percent were spying on units armed with nuclear weapons; ten percent were gathering detail on American military personnel; and five percent were tracking military manoeuvres in order to raise an alarm if necessary.[17] These tasks, of course, mirrored those of Western agents operating in the Soviet Bloc, especially in East Germany.

The growing prowess of the GRU at this moment was significant. Western agencies estimated the GRU as running some 400-600 agents in the Federal Republic. As well as its 250 staff members based at Wünsdorf, it ran sub-offices in Erfurt, Schwerin, Leipzig and Magdeburg. It could make use of the Soviet Military Liaison Missions at Baden-Baden and Frankfurt am Main. And it could gather military intelligence at unit level; for example, intelligence officers of the Soviet 20th Guards Division, stationed in Berlin, spied on military facilities and the police forces in the west of the city.[18]

The GRU had especially well-placed sources in West Germany. One example is Edgar Feuchtinger, a former Wehrmacht general whom the GRU blackmailed with compromising materials on his conduct in the closing days of the war, when he had been demoted to the rank of private and deserted. Most of Feuchtinger's old military cronies were unaware of this shame, so he exploited them to obtain secret files from the Federal Ministry of Defence and NATO. Feuchtinger died in strange circumstances in 1960, suffering a heart attack at a meeting with his case handler. By that point he had delivered more than 1,000 pages of secret documents to the GRU.[19]

Meanwhile the HVA had embarked on its lasting and effective use of the Reisekader, those fortunate and strenuously vetted GDR citizens who were allowed to travel internationally. Permission to travel was often granted solely for the Soviet Bloc or other socialist countries – Cuba, Vietnam – but information from such trips could still prove useful. In another development, the HVA realised that its Soviet-derived cipher system for radio messages, in which messages began with an agent's call-sign number, had been cracked by the West German authorities, who were able to tell which agent was being contacted with each message. Accordingly the HVA changed its cipher system and call-sign method, and, in Wolf's words, 'made it a general rule never to make any concrete mention of people, places, or meetings in radio transmissions'.[20] But however much the HVA learned and grew, it never forgot its origins and benefactors. Copies of HVA files, like those of other Stasi departments, routinely were stamped F for 'Friends' and shared with the KGB.

63

Exposing Nazis

Another early priority for the HVA was to dig around for dirt on the former Nazis who were thriving in West Germany. Some of this information was used secretly. Other bits fed the campaigns of the HVA's active measures department. In time, two well-known SED publications, the 'White Book' and the 'Brown Book', programmatically exposed former Nazis in the West German establishment.

Active measures, known in Russian as Aktivka, are covert interventions designed to steer events. Somewhat confusingly, the Soviet meaning of active measures evolved over time. NKVD documents of the 1930s tend to refer to Aktivka, or 'method A', as assassination. Although this meaning remained in use, by the 1950s the term more commonly referred to disinformation or influencing campaigns.

The first active measures carried out by East German foreign intelligence had seen unwitting journalists exploited by Richard Stumpf's small unit in Main Department XV, in an effort to bolster the KPD in West Germany. Behind this endeavour sat the previously mentioned Ivan Agayants, a Soviet adviser who had been spying and subverting for Moscow since the days of the NKVD. In intelligence histories, Agayants comes across as a wise and sophisticated character. He had his tougher side. Having served in Paris for some years, he once described the French secret service as 'that prostitute I put in my pocket'.[1]

Back in March 1955, Ernst Wollweber had called for the 'exploitation of clashes in the enemy camp'. He wanted to go beyond intelligence-gathering and implement 'active measures to deepen the disagreements [and] weaken enemy forces'. Erich Mielke, in his turn, had urged for 'active measures to thwart NATO policy'. In response, Robert Korb and Richard Stumpf, working in the HVA's short-lived Department V/f (later VIIf), had begun to target the 'enemy camp': the Western intelligence officers and journalists who were producing the West's propaganda and influencing campaigns, including from a 'Psychological Defence' agency set up in Bonn. Korb and Stumpf claimed that this 'particularly complicated assignment' enjoyed 'a considerable measure of success' during 1957.[2]

This wasn't enough to satisfy Markus Wolf. He knew and cared about propaganda, having run anti-Hitler radio stations during the war which, in emulation of their British 'black propaganda' counterparts, had pretended to be broadcast inside Nazi Germany. By 1959 Wolf was chairing a small HVA working group for active measures (Aktive Massnahmen), with 'the express purpose of influencing the Western media and confusing and misleading our opponents in Western Europe and America'. Not every group member was deeply committed; Herbert Brehmer, later the architect of major disinformation campaigns, joined the embryonic outfit to get hold of Western magazines. Wolf described the group's work:

> The central focus of its task was not 'lying' or 'deliberately misleading' but a method of disseminating uncomfortable and embarrassing facts... We combined true and false information and disseminated it so as to strengthen our policies, weaken Western policies and organizations, and compromise individuals... The West German media themselves were eager to print political scandal... Whether we were targeting the West German government, big business, a publication, or a political party, the intention was always to undermine the public credibility in the new and largely untested institutions of [West Germany] and thus sow doubts about the Western political order.[3]

Like others before and after him, Wolf noticed that communist propaganda and disinformation were boosted by habits of the Western media which the East Germans, with their one-sided press, only half-understood. Habits that went beyond, say, healthy criticism of government; habits like attempting to puncture and topple an institution from the closeted safety of an editorial office, or relentlessly insisting upon the iniquity and shadiness of Western societies. No one enjoyed a good crawl through the worst of the West more than the Western media did.

In contrast to the budding work at the HVA, much of the SED's propaganda was overt. Albert Norden's Committee for German Unity, and the Council of Ministers' press office under Kurt Blecha, publicised evidenced-backed truths or sponsored newspaper articles by pro-communist authors. But the party also felt the lure of grey and black propaganda: the grey spreading true and false information with no traceable origin, the black spreading true and false information from a deceptive outlet. At a Central Committee meeting in 1960, Norden called for a propaganda line that would inflict 'disturbance and disintegration' on the Federal Republic. West Germany was to be isolated, its international coalitions damaged. This would coincide with increased positive propaganda about the GDR, especially its peace-orientated foreign policy. East Germany was to be positioned as leader of 'the widest masses in all countries in the fight against German militarism and imperialism'.[4]

Like Comintern propaganda of the 1930s, it was important for such SED propaganda to be signed or endorsed by seemingly impartial, non-communist public figures in the West. Norden's employees created 'campaign plans' for each item of propaganda or disinformation, establishing its goals, assigning responsibilities, and arranging any coordination required. Meticulous plans were made for the way the information was to be leaked, especially if it was to have hidden origins. Communist propagandists made full use of the political left, as well. The likes of *Konkret* magazine – fashionable, socialist and, reportedly, subsidised by the Stasi from the late 1950s onwards – were read by such radical German leftists as the Baader-Meinhof group.

Contact persons in the West, such as academics with concealed sympathy for East Germany, were chosen carefully. For the HVA, the term Kontaktperson (KP) had a different meaning to that of the domestic Stasi departments. An HVA KP was a useful idiot: a citizen of 'the operational area' – i.e., another country, usually West Germany – with 'access to operationally significant information or opportunities to exert political influence', but who was not aware of the 'intelligence nature' of their interaction with HVA representatives.[5] An unknowable number of journalists, diplomats and academics fell into this category.

Western and communist active measures were ramped up in 1959 with the creation of the psychological warfare department of the West German Ministry of Defence and the KGB's Department D, for disinformation (disinformatsia). The Soviets had already initiated a publicity campaign to label West Berlin an 'espionage swamp', a phrase taken up by the East German authorities and media. One task for the new KGB department was to boost Soviet active measures in West Germany and support Soviet policy around Berlin and German reunification.

Until the collapse of communism, and beyond, Department D made excessive efforts to bamboozle Western citizens. It thrived on cheek. Reportedly, the department got a British Labour MP to write a satirical book about CIA chief Allen Dulles, published in 1961 as *A Study of a Master Spy*.[6] That year the department also planned to trick the West into believing that the Soviet Union had developed nuclear-powered aircraft.[7]

Department D began its work with characteristic unpleasantness, organising a campaign to have swastikas and anti-Semitic messages daubed on the walls of Cologne's new synagogue, then on walls across West Germany and western

Europe. HVA operatives were roped into this endeavour, with Stasi files recording the 'realisation of graffiti' to 'provoke psychological reactions'.[8] Later the Czech intelligence service got involved. The defector Josef Frolik described an incident at Castlemartin in Wales, when Czech operatives defaced Jewish graves in a cemetery near to where a Bundeswehr unit was in training. This incident, implying latent fascism among West German soldiers, made headlines in the British tabloid press – in the world of active measures, a resounding success.[9] In 1961, during the trial of Adolf Eichmann in Israel, Jewish residents of Munich were sent hate mail, organised by the Stasi as part of its Aktion 'J' but purporting to come from Eichmann sympathisers in West Germany. Anything was permissible if it helped to 'decompose' an enemy society.[10]

These activities were carried out in support of East Germany's campaign to attack former Nazis in the Federal Republic, and to malign the society that was rehabilitating them – the so-called 're-Nazification' of West Germany. As has been seen, anti-fascism was one of the SED's strongest moral tools, and the passionate creed of many party members. It mattered little that, by this time, the Stasi's own relationship with former Nazis had taken a decidedly unidealistic turn. Most of the convicted war criminals who remained alive had been released from prison in post-Stalin amnesties, and the Stasi was now almost solely concerned not with prosecuting but recruiting them as informers. In investigations conducted in 1957 and 1958, for example, the Stasi office in Leipzig identified some 200 former SD and Gestapo employees living in the area. Although their 'negative attitude' towards the GDR was seen as reason to transfer them out of sensitive jobs, the nobler aims of denazification were long-forgotten – Erich Mielke decreed that 'they should be convinced or forced to cooperate unofficially'.[11]

As one of its prime movers, albeit in secret, Markus Wolf insisted that the GDR's anti-Nazi campaign was thoroughly honourable. He opined that, 'Disinformation was not necessary as long as former Nazis moved into high positions in West Germany [and] the Federal Republic pressed its program of rearmament so soon after the nation's catastrophic defeat in Hitler's military adventures.'[12] For Wolf, this noble cause justified the hate mail and swastika graffiti, as well as the use of information from the Nazi archives to blackmail West Germans into working for the HVA.[13]

At least one East German attempt to besmirch a West German politician lacked any reasonable foundation – the active measures aimed at West Berlin mayor Willy Brandt. 'If we succeed in proving Brandt's collaboration with the Gestapo,' read one HVA report, 'this would amount to Brandt's political death warrant.' In the hunt for evidence an HVA agent was dispatched to Norway, where Brandt had spent time during the war. Nothing was found. Markus Wolf then ordered the arrest on trumped-up charges of Georg Angerer, an old acquaintance of Brandt now living in Leipzig. Despite being mentally ravaged by a six-month interrogation in pretrial custody, Angerer provided no useable dirt on Brandt.[14] There wasn't any.

HVA active measures usually mixed falsehoods with accurate information culled from the Nazi records. This potent mixture of eighty percent fact with twenty percent deceit was learned from the British wartime propagandist Sefton Delmer, whose memoirs were translated into German in the 1960s. As noted, Markus Wolf admired Delmer, whose work he had copied in Moscow during the war. And Delmer was virtually hero-worshipped by Rolf Wagenbreth, the most important black propagandist at the HVA. In the mid-1980s, Wagenbreth was still using Delmer's operations as the basis of training sessions at the HVA school. He considered Delmer a 'Godfather' and 'genius' of active measures: a 'creative journalist, creative manipulator, a well-spoken contact person, a cunning fox', someone who 'combined all competencies in himself, which a good employee of the HVA should'.[15]

It is notable that Wagenbreth referred to Delmer's 'well-spoken' presentability. Soviet Bloc agents could struggle to understand the West and to mix in its bourgeois circles; to be approved of by the wealthy was a desirable capability. Mostly Delmer was admired for his style of wartime black propaganda, in which subversive messages were sneaked into largely accurate reportage, delivered in the Nazis' own jargon and street slang. Delmer's dirty warfare was as vicious and corrupting as any in the secret world. Although he was purposely exaggerating, in 1941 Delmer described his unit as being 'up to all the dirty tricks we can devise. No holds are barred. The dirtier the better. Lies, treachery, everything'.[16] With principles like these, it is little wonder he appealed to many Cold Warriors.

The Stasi's campaign against Theodor Oberländer, the Federal minister for refugees, betrays Delmer's part-truth, part-lie approach. Some of the accusations generated and publicised by the Stasi were true. Oberländer had been a diehard Nazi and had violated the Geneva Convention by helping to create some horrifying wartime military formations – the 'Nachtigall' battalion of Ukrainian nationalists, the Vlasov Army. But when in April 1960 the GDR Supreme Court sentenced Oberländer to death in absentia, its verdict was based on fabricated evidence. Oberländer hadn't taken part in the massacre of Jewish civilians in Lvov or the murder of prisoners in the Caucasus, for which he was convicted. Under pressure from Konrad Adenauer, Oberländer resigned a month later, but his career demonstrates the fact that propaganda victories can have a short shelf-life. Two years later he was back in the Bundestag.

As well as the work of Sefton Delmer, HVA officers studied the military propaganda of imperial Germany in the First World War, including the censorship and manipulation of the press. They learned how sympathetic authors and publishers in enemy countries had been provided with unobtrusive funding; how go-betweens were used to plant stories with important editors and news organisations; and how expatriate Germans were taught to produce leaflets and other communications in the style and idiom of their host countries. In 1961 an East German book, Gerhard Zazworka's *Psychological Warfare* (*Psychologische Kriegführung*), analysed the propaganda and disinformation techniques of the First World War and Nazi periods, culminating with the early 'psywar' battles against the CIA and NATO.[17]

Disinformation had a bright future at the HVA. In 1966 Wolf's working group was formally replaced by the larger Department X, which continued to expose former Nazis in West Germany. Its disinformation campaigns also tried to show incompetence and corruption in the Federal government, and to suggest that West Germany had become a neo-imperialist exploiter of developing countries. These campaigns harmed West Germany's international image.[18] To garner information for them, the HVA put phone taps on prominent Federal politicians such as Helmut Kohl. Calls between politicians and bankers were also tapped, to spot any signs of a scandal or cover-up. These conversations were transcribed in documents that found their way to journalists, and allegations were made. It was easy to blame America's National Security Agency as the source of these transcripts; everyone knew the immensity of the US bugging effort. And it was difficult for the victims, caught red-handed by a transcript of a real conversation, to defend themselves against those parts of the allegation that were invented.[19]

Like its KGB mentor, Department X became a hyperactive publisher. Its disinformation crept into letters, articles, reports, studies, books, official documents, fake documents. It pulled off some coups, like forging an entire draft chapter of Reinhard Gehlen's autobiography, in a successful imitation of his handwriting, which caused no end of trouble. It produced new forgeries to endorse the conspiracy theories of the communist *Brown Book*, published thirty years earlier. Sometimes respectable-looking publishing houses were used as cover; one HVA agent, the Bavarian Christian democrat Hans Frederik, set up a publishing firm called Humboldt Verlag using HVA money.[20] The avalanche of print generated by Department X was disseminated by Western journalists, politicians, scientists, academics and civil society organisations.[21] Some of these recipients didn't know they were helping to spread East German propaganda. Others did.

*

Over the years, the work of the HVA training school at Belzig, south-west of Berlin, had started to pay dividends. KGB personnel were based in the town, so were well placed to act as tutors. And in 1955 one of the school's officers, Colonel Paul Laufer, had spotted two especially promising trainees. They were to change the course of European history.

Laufer had a long and illustrious history as a covert operative. In the 1920s, as agent 'Stabil' (Sturdy) of the KPD intelligence service, Laufer had perfected the Trojan Horse technique of distancing himself from the communist movement and infiltrating a rival political organisation. His communism was secret; for much of the interwar period he was, to all appearances, a loyal member of the SPD.

The recruits noticed by Laufer at Belzig were a twenty-seven-year-old woman and her husband, a photographer for the publishing concern Volk und Wissen.[22] Unknown to Laufer – and potentially disastrous for the pair's future espionage career – was the fact that the photographer's colleagues had already noticed something was amiss in his behaviour; that he might be a Stasi spy. One of them told the UfJ in West Berlin that the photographer took long breaks from work, was sent on inexplicable training courses, and that any questions about these absences were shut down by his bosses. The UfJ put these details on record. Fortunately for the photographer – and the Stasi – this information ended up buried and unnoticeable in the heaps of cryptic Cold War data.

After completing their espionage training, in 1956 the photographer and his wife were told to emigrate. Arriving in Frankfurt am Main, the pair bypassed the usual system of registering with a refugee centre, where escapees' bona fides were checked. The woman's mother was a Dutch citizen who ran a tobacconist's shop in the city. She was able to request refugee status for her daughter and son-in-law without them facing the usual enquiries.

Under the code names 'Hansen' and 'Heinze', the couple took over the tobacconist's shop. They also joined the SPD and began to associate themselves with the party's right wing. Their true identity was known neither to the SPD nor to the West German border police, which during this period intercepted several radio messages beginning with the call sign 'Georg 37', intended for a presumed East German agent. This agent was told to observe such matters as 'factional problems' and the doings of the 'club president', but the West German police couldn't determine which 'club' was being referred to. They noted, however, that 'Georg 37' was also sent birthday greetings, and congratulations on the arrival of at least one child.

By 1962 the photographer had become a salaried employee of the SPD, working for its main newspaper *Der Sozialdemokrat*. By the end of the decade he had been elected to the Frankfurt city council. His wife was secretary to an

SPD Bundestag deputy, a role in which she had access to NATO evaluations of its military exercises, and other materials. At this point it was obvious to no one that in a few years' time, the pair would be responsible for wrecking the career of one of Germany's best-loved and most promising national leaders, Willy Brandt, in the biggest spy scandal to hit Europe during the Cold War. The couple were hard-working and amicable, but otherwise unremarkable. Their names were Günther and Christel Guillaume.

64

Securing the Border

From 1958 until 1961, when the construction of the Berlin Wall began, the Stasi's top priority was to tackle illegal border-crossing. The spy wars and international intrigue continued; there were always secrets to be stolen and spies to catch. But the only domestic issue that came close to troubling the Stasi to the same extent as East Germany's porous borders was a renewed campaign to collectivise agriculture.

The events of the period were determined by the peculiar dynamics between East Berlin and Moscow and, even more so, by superpower politics. At the start of the 1960s, having threatened the Western powers with potential expulsion from Berlin, Soviet leader Nikita Khrushchev was shocked to discover the size of the US arsenal of nuclear missiles based in West Germany. This knowledge, acquired through espionage, forced him to change his approach to fighting the Cold War. Khrushchev realised he had lost much of his geopolitical bargaining power, for his armed forces faced likely destruction if they were to engage in western Europe. The Berlin Wall was one outcome of Khrushchev's change of approach. It was also a glaring example of how geopolitics, and the posturing of national leaders, can decide the day-to-day realities of ordinary people's lives.

Towards the end of 1958, Nikita Khrushchev put forward his plans to make Berlin a 'demilitarised free city'. In an ultimatum issued on 27 November, he gave the Western powers six months to enter negotiations for a new peace treaty with Germany, one that would throw into doubt the whole question of access to Berlin. If they did not enter such negotiations, Khrushchev threatened to sign a unilateral treaty with the GDR. This would likely result in the Western powers being denied use of the access routes between West Germany and Berlin. They were also likely to lose any formal right to be in the city. Hitherto, their presence was based more on 'precedent and usage' rather than firm international agreements, although some bits of paper existed.[1] Regardless, the

Western powers had, said Khrushchev, violated the Potsdam Agreement, and forfeited their right to maintain the status quo.

Khrushchev's ultimatum lapsed and wavered more than once in the following years. Ultimately it was superseded, tangentially, by the building of the Berlin Wall. The background to the ultimatum was complex and is still debated. It encompassed such factors as Khrushchev's desire to resolve the German question with the West, Soviet concerns over the prospect of West Germany acquiring nuclear missiles, and fears that the parlous East German economy would only worsen if the country's population continued to bleed westwards. As has been seen, the Soviets and the Western powers had, in the words of Hope M. Harrison, 'been putting forward various incompatible proposals on resolving the German and Berlin issues (whether to be united or divided and in what form) for several years'.[2]

However, an important but less discussed aim of Khrushchev's ultimatum was to stop Western intelligence services from operating in East Germany. In acceding to the ultimatum, they would agree not to undertake 'any hostile subversive activity' against the GDR. But the Western powers did not accede to the ultimatum. Instead, they began to prepare for whatever aggressive actions Khrushchev might take.

Only relatively recently has it been confirmed that the Berlin Wall was largely an East German, and not a Soviet, idea.[3] The SED regime, which detested having parts of its capital city squatted, was always belligerent and provocative when it came to the divided city. In October 1959, on the tenth anniversary of East Germany's founding, thousands of KdA members disguised as railway workers entered West Berlin and ran up GDR flags everywhere. In acknowledgement of the anniversary, the flag had acquired its central roundel showing a hammer and compass bounded by wheatsheaves. For the Western authorities this incident was troubling in more ways than one, for it highlighted the vulnerability of certain sites in West Berlin, especially police and radio stations.

The problem of the leaky Berlin borders dominated proceedings at the SED's fifth party congress of 1958. An open border allowed Western spies and agents to walk into East Germany and its population to walk out. Paul Maddrell writes that the 'police state of the German Democratic Republic did not function properly in the years before 1961 because East Germans could escape it – either for a day or two, or forever'.[4] And the proper economic and civil life of East Germany couldn't be sustained with a haemorrhaging population.

Although workers from all walks of life were choosing to leave, East Germany was harmed especially by the loss of trained professionals. From 1952 to 1962, almost 4,000 medical practitioners and 1,495 dentists left the GDR.[5] Shortages of basic items didn't help; rubber gloves, for example, were so scarce and of such poor quality that expensive personal supplies from West Germany had to be arranged.[6] In general, the Stasi considered doctors to be among the least politically reliable of all professionals. Although collaborators were recruited in every East German hospital, the recruitment rate in the medical profession remained unusually low, at under five percent.[7]

Throughout the 1950s more than 100,000 people per year had headed west. The years 1953, 1956 and 1957 had seen highs of some 300,000.[8] Various state bodies, including the Department for Population Policy, provided suggestions to the Stasi on how to stem the tide. The Stasi's Information Service collated hundreds of these recommendations. They included allowing more time to assess applications to visit West Germany, which were to be submitted to the local mayor; disallowing relatives of refugees to visit West Germany; tighter control of permits for holidaymakers and visiting students; tighter control of official delegations, and scientific and cultural events; tighter control at railway stations, and spot checks of travellers by border police; longer checks by border police – fifteen minutes per traveller, rather than the current average of eight minutes; permits for East Germans to visit Berlin, to be issued by the local Volkspolizei; changes to the timetables of Berlin-bound trains; seizing refugees' assets for the state more quickly and demonstratively; providing school leavers and 'intellectuals' with a 'decent job' more quickly; and compelling refugees' family members to encourage their return to the GDR.[9]

One outcome from this welter of possibilities was an amendment to the passport laws in December 1957. The previous year, the system of permits for leaving the GDR had been replaced by a tighter requirement to get a visa entered in one's passport. Now, the law was tweaked to effectively frame West Germany as a foreign country, and to further criminalise illegal border-crossing. Also punishable was any deviation from one's stated destinations, dates, and routes of travel. Transgressors could now expect up to three years in prison.[10]

The Stasi steadily stepped up its efforts around *Republikflucht*. More collaborators were inserted or recruited at West German resettlement camps; one of their tasks was to 'carry out subversive activities among the refugees [and] thereby cause unrest in the entire refugee system'. West German individuals or groups encouraging *Republikflucht* were defamed in active measures. Local Stasi offices co-opted more East German citizens – ticket sellers, bank tellers, postal workers and pastors – to provide warnings of flight attempts. Stasi officers, in a range of guises, harangued state officials to take *Republikflucht* more seriously. Whispering campaigns spread negative views of life in the West. Collaborators intensified their observation of railway stations and westbound road traffic. A system of 'helper villages' was established along the borders, whereby an entire local community would be rewarded, modestly, for spotting or halting border-crossers. Department M identified the places from where 'poaching' letters were being sent to East German professionals; besides Western intelligence services, the many culprits included West German media outlets, which were offering jobs and three-bedroom apartments to TV and radio technicians.[11] And law enforcement agencies other than the Stasi did their best. From May to October 1960 the police and customs authorities prevented more than 17,000 would-be migrants from entering West Berlin. In the same period, nearly 3,000 flight attempts were pre-empted by Stasi investigations,[12] many of which resulted in face-to-face confrontations with those planning to leave East Germany.

Returnees to the GDR were a less obvious but vexing aspect of *Republikflucht*. In the first half of 1959, for example, more than 21,000 people returned from extended periods in West Germany and West Berlin. It was rare for returnees to be motivated by political conviction; money problems, homelessness and homesickness were the most common reasons. They were greeted as potential spies. Bruno Beater recommended that those held in East Germany's five resettlement camps be processed by the Stasi's Department VII instead of the police and interior ministry, as this would weed out Western agents more effectively.[13]

There were also severe problems with the security of the 'green borders' away from Berlin. A Stasi report from 1960 bemoaned the difficulty of securing the frontier in the Thuringian forests. The border ran through thickly wooded 'mountainous, river and swamp areas' and was 'completely confusing and consequently insufficiently secured'. With border posts spaced at three-kilometre intervals, a crossing could 'easily take place at any time of day or night', and 'without leaving a trace'. In some spots, heavy vehicles were able to approach the Bavarian side of the border unseen. As in other rural areas, it was quite possible for East German farming families to escape together with their livestock, equipment, and a house-load of possessions. 'Ruins and half-ruined objects' gave border-crossers a place to hide. For good measure, the report writer opined that these ruins 'in no way demonstrate the development of our socialist construction', and were 'exploited by the enemy for propaganda purposes, by photographing them'.

The report revealed that the border police units in this crucial area, adjacent to a number of US intelligence and military sites, were chronically understaffed. Most of the local commanders and their Politkultur deputies were assessed favourably: 'no connections with West Germany, West Berlin or capitalist countries', a 'positive attitude towards the party', and 'good cooperation' with the Stasi. They were judged 'open and honest', 'disciplined and correct'. Below these officers, the problems began. Among the other ranks there was heavy drinking, 'pally relationships', and many 'first degree family relationships' with West Germans. The men tended to ignore the signalling devices strewn along the frontier, such as flares on tripwires, as they were often 'triggered by the wind and game'. Sometimes they listened to Western radio broadcasts. One unit's party secretary was belatedly unmasked as a former Waffen-SS soldier and dismissed. The Stasi suggested a range of measures to fix all this laxity, from better political instruction to the replacement of worn-out equipment.[14]

Nothing worked, whether in Thuringia or elsewhere. Still East Germany's population gushed westwards. No amount of Stasi activity could compete with the news that in 1956, according to a statement published by Federal economic minister Ludwig Erhard, western Germans had achieved 'the highest standard of living in their history'. Erhard boasted:

> Mass consumption has increased extraordinarily. Almost 60% of the total national product went to private consumption. The increase in the standard of living is particularly evident in the fact that it has become possible for an increasingly broad stratum of our people to acquire luxury goods and to spend larger parts of their income on travel and recreation.[15]

Contrast this with the GDR. In 1959 a new centralised economic programme, the Seven Year Plan, was initiated. The previous year it had been decided to focus the economy on mechanical engineering, the mining of potash and lignite (brown coal), and the manufacture of chemicals. These were intended to boost the production of fertilisers and plastics, and expedite the making of consumer goods. But like every SED economic measure thus far, the plans proved unrealistic and led to scarcity in goods and supplies. There were shortages in everything from canned fish to salt, matches to light bulbs. By early 1961 basic nutritional needs weren't being met; bread and milk weren't always available.[16] This led to another rise in the number of refugees. In 1959, 143,000 fled; in 1960, almost 200,000. Discontent with the hardships of collectivisation was compounded by the fact that many Germans, by this point, had been made to feel deeply pessimistic about the prospects for reunification. The Geneva conference of summer 1959 had adjourned without any agreements being reached. In September that year, Khrushchev's visit to America ended with, in effect, a 'no change' compromise: he agreed not to enforce a deadline on US troops leaving Berlin, and the US agreed not to perpetuate the occupation. The mood among Germans plummeted yet further when a planned summit between Khrushchev and President Eisenhower was cancelled after the downing of Gary Powers' U-2 spy plane over the USSR.[17]

In the year before the Berlin borders were sealed, even Markus Wolf – who no doubt was eating and drinking well – could sense a grim mood. Supplies of goods were low, demand for labour high; but those who might perform that labour were nowhere to be found.[18] The damage caused to the GDR by its vanishing population was worsened by a feeling of vulnerability to penetration. The Stasi continued to sense that enemies were strolling into the country with impunity. While the Soviets had always baulked at Walter Ulbricht's suggestion to seal off Berlin, it is perhaps surprising that they weren't more enthusiastic about the idea, for the USSR itself – which otherwise was a formidable target, almost hermetically sealed – had an Achilles heel in East Germany. Soviet officials, armed forces, industrial practices, new technologies; all were potentially accessible in a GDR without barricades around it.

Walter Ulbricht tried to put a positive spin on action to remove the Western powers from Berlin. In one speech he asserted:

> The capital of the German Democratic Republic is Berlin. A part of the capital, West Berlin, is currently still being misused as a base for Cold War, espionage and sabotage against the GDR and the other countries in the socialist camp. The task is to change this unnatural situation, which has also been brought about against the interests of the residents of West Berlin, to normalise conditions in Berlin and to make the whole city a city of peace and progress.[19]

The idea of winning over West Berliners was, by this point, sheer fantasy: the SED ran in elections to the West Berlin senate in December 1958 and won less than two percent of the vote, and no seats. Litte by little, officials in East Berlin, and even in Moscow, began to favour 'die Sicherung der Staatsgrenze' – 'the securing of the state border'. Perhaps, among other things, it might compel farmers to stay in East Germany. Something had to.

The SED's unpopular drive to collectivise agriculture had spluttered out as the 1950s progressed. The majority of East German farms remained in private hands. When the party decided on a once-and-for-all campaign to collectivise farming – a campaign referred to merrily as 'Socialist spring in the countryside' – the Stasi was expected to make it happen.

The campaign accompanied the announcement of the new Seven Year Plan, which was timed to coincide with a similar plan initiated in the Soviet Union. Both plans were expected to showcase the superiority of socialism; the USSR was to surpass America's per capita consumption of important foodstuffs and consumer goods, and East Germany was to surpass the Federal Republic.

Stasi personnel were assigned to the brigades of police and party activists sent into the countryside to organise collectivisation. Subtle methods were introduced to penalise private farmers; they were charged higher prices for seed and animal feed, relegated to the bottom of waiting lists for new equipment. Farmers who refused to join collective farms were arrested, interrogated, and sometimes put on trial. Stasi officers oversaw the creation of summary courts. The widespread use of force returned. In a characteristic incident recorded by the Stasi, a Volkspolizei officer from a local collectivisation task force was assaulted by one 'Farmer K'. After two hours in police custody, Farmer K had 'announced his willingness' to join the collective farm.[20] Here, in sharp relief, is the discrepancy between communism's cultural intelligentsia and its (working-class) practitioners. The intellectual spirit of communism may evoke radical paintings and humanist poetry and groundbreaking symphonies; but in practice, communism means punch-ups between farmers and secret policemen.

Just as the OGPU was an intrinsic element of collectivisation in Stalin's USSR, so the Stasi was during the 'Socialist spring'. Main Department III set up training courses for agricultural officials. Some of the Stasi's personnel, perhaps frustrated by the quasi-legal restraints they were now facing in other areas of their work, took to the collectivisation task with relish. Alfred Kraus, leader of the Stasi in Rostock, was decorated for his role in pushing through collectivisation. In a communication with Erich Mielke, Kraus gloated that kicking around stubborn farmers had been 'a lot of fun for us Chekists'.[21]

There were curious moments during the collectivisation campaign. They show the Stasi going beyond its repressive security remit and, in the words of historian Daniela Münkel, trying 'to remedy the situation in order to calm the situation'.[22] At one point the workers at an engineering plant in Hennigsdorf drafted a resolution on food shortages, stating: 'It is with great concern that we note the reintroduction of butter rationing (one-eighth of a kilogram per family according to customer waiting lists) and the inadequate supply of the most important staple foods such as potatoes, bread, fruit, vegetables, meat and sausages.' As well as demanding change, they identified the cause: 'the hasty collectivisation of agriculture'. Six of these workers were arrested and sentenced to prison. At the same time, the Stasi reported that the supply situation was 'indeed not in order'. Münkel writes that it 'arranged for an additional ton of butter and 1,000 loaves of bread to be delivered to the sales outlets in Hennigsdorf just two days after the resolution appeared'.

Mostly, however, there was repression. The winter of 1959-60 saw a sharp rise in the number of arrests and trials. For refusing to collectivise, or arguing against it, farmers usually were charged with 'seditious agitation' under section 19 of the GDR criminal code. There was a similar increase in charges of 'acts of violence endangering the state' (section 17), 'attacks against local organs of state power' (section 18) and 'diversion' (section 22).[23] These were sensitive matters, given that East Germany celebrated the tenth anniversary of its founding in October 1959. The event saw a tremendous drive to galvanise public enthusiasm. The government rolled out slogans for mass use; the GDR was 'The first German state of peace', 'The country Karl Liebknecht and Rosa Luxemburg fought for'. Another phrase, designed to encourage the East German version of feasting, was 'Lay the table for the Republic, everyone!' Despite the anniversary's martial pageantry, the Stasi named its operation to protect it Aktion Friedensfest (Peace Festival). Its task was defined as 'timely reconnaissance and prevention of all enemy interference attempts such as provocations, terror, acts of diversion, arson, inflammatory propaganda'. Working groups to secure the celebrations were set up in Stasi offices, increased protection laid on at important sites, and suspect persons watched and steered carefully.

In the eyes of one of its main architects, Walter Ulbricht, the collectivisation campaign was a success. More than 9,000 new agricultural cooperatives (LPGs) were founded in the space of six months, co-opting half a million previously independent farmers.[24] The new cooperatives were invigilated by at least 400 of the Stasi's elite collaborators, the Lead Secret Informers (GHI), some of whom even tried to be truthful in their reports to district offices. LPGs were described as dilapidated and despairing places, rife with alcoholism, shirking and discord, most of it – according to the Stasi's informers – sowed by former Nazis and landowners.[25] One GHI informed Main Department III of the obvious: that the rules around animal feed, which was only provided to an LPG after it had achieved its production targets, were unworkable. Resentment also arose when LPG officials were arrested in ways that were 'not always sufficiently circumspect'. Yet no one in Ulbricht's Politbüro ever raised an objection to such rules and practices.[26]

So did the socialist spring usher in a bountiful summer? No – even bigger numbers of people chose to leave the GDR, and there was less produce than before. In June 1961, deputy prime minister Willi Stoph was compelled to announce that East Germany had virtually run out of meat, milk and butter.

65

The Western Powers Prepare

One aim of Khrushchev's ultimatum was to stop Western intelligence services operating from West Berlin. Unsurprisingly, these intelligence services weren't inclined to comply. To leave would mean losing their most important frontier strongpoint and base of operations against the entire Soviet Bloc. Given the likelihood of Western governments calling Khrushchev's bluff, a renewed Soviet blockade looked a distinct possibility. Road, rail and air routes into Berlin might be closed once again. 'Control of access to West Berlin would solve two of East Germany's major problems,' acknowledged one CIA report: 'the exodus of refugees to the West and the influx of anti-communist influences.'[1] The worst-case scenario was war, and a Soviet occupation of the city. So the Western intelligence services began to prepare their spies for all such eventualities, as well as the potential inability of East German citizens to reach West Berlin.[2]

Forewarned by the semi-sealed state of Berlin in the crises of 1948, 1952 and 1953, the Western powers had already made military preparations to deal with a similar emergency. One such preparation was instigated by US secretary of state John Foster Dulles, who set up the Live Oak planning group, responsible for devising the military response to another Soviet blockade. The HVA acquired a copy of one such plan from a source in the British military command; according to Markus Wolf it was titled 'Initial Probe of Soviet Intentions'. If the borders were closed, British, French and American units were to make exploratory movements along the main transit road to West Berlin. The very existence of the plan suggested that Khrushchev's gambling over the city might indeed ignite a war, if only by miscalculation.

Using the records of investigations by Main Department IX, Paul Maddrell has assessed the Stasi's awareness of how Western intelligence services were preparing for three possibilities: war, another Berlin blockade, or the total loss of West Berlin as an intelligence hub. By the end of the 1950s, spies were being told that personal meetings with handlers would be replaced by the use of radio, dead drops, and postal correspondence containing secret writing. But in providing their agents with the necessary equipment for these methods, the Western services played into the hands of the Stasi, which was able to detect and prosecute yet more spies who now were caught red-handed with the tools of their trade.

The Stasi learned much from these arrestees. One spy arrested in 1957, a roadworker recruited five years earlier by the Amt Blank, revealed that he had been instructed in the use of dead drops in case the borders were closed.[3] More arrested spies told the same story. Gisela Zurth, whom the Stasi believed to be a BfV agent, had been told in 1957 to create dead letter drops. Franz Brehmer, a CIA spy, had been instructed in April 1958 not to travel into West Berlin anymore; instead, he was to accustom himself to receiving instructions by radio and passing information with dead drops and secret writing in letters. An MI6 spy arrested in 1959 – a housewife in Erfurt who was reporting on military sites, including missile bases – had also been told to switch to secret writing; previously, she had used a shopping bag with a false bottom to deliver photographic negatives to her MI6 handler in West Berlin.[4] A military spy for the BND had unexpectedly been provided with a radio receiver and transmitter; another had been told that if the Berlin borders were to close he was to organise a stay-behind 'BND headquarters' on East German territory.[5]

The Stasi discovered that shortwave converters, which enabled radios to transmit and receive over longer distances, were being issued to Western spies at an increasing rate. One captured spy who had been observing military sites near Dresden for British intelligence was in possession of a converter. More converters were found in the hands of BND agents, including a husband-and-wife team spying on military sites near Frankfurt an der Oder, and another couple reporting on the Wismut mining complex.

Stasi arrests revealed that more dead drops were being created. Shortly before they were caught, a married couple engaged in military spying near Groitzsch had been told that dead drops were being laid for them. The wife had then introduced her brother to their case handler and, for good measure, it had been decided to train him as a radio operator. A married couple from Leipzig who spied on military installations – the husband a wartime Abwehr officer – had also been told that a dead drop had been arranged. A woman whose house sat next to the Berlin border had been given a radiotelephone with a range of 3,000 metres, and told to give warning if the borders were about to close. Other arrested agents had been trained as emergency radio operators (Ernstfallfunker) and given a two-way set to transmit time-critical information. This was understood to be dangerous work, as such transmissions were easy to detect.

Stasi arrests also showed the striking number of spies missed by the *Grossaktionen*. A railway worker who had been reporting to British intelligence for years had been issued with a Geiger counter, to detect transports of uranium. A spy for Britain codenamed 'Gondel', recruited in 1954, had been issued with spy gear concealed in a razor with a hollow handle. In addition to reporting on his work as an electrical engineer, 'Gondel' had been riding his motorbike around military installations in the Dresden area, faking the occasional breakdown in order to stop and take photographs with a telephoto lens. In another case, an engineer at the Institute for Instrument Construction, recruited by Britain in 1955, had been providing copies of technical drawings and making recces to sensitive places such as Vogelsang, temporary site of a Soviet ballistic missile force; MI6 had been sharing his intelligence with the British Services Security Organization and the BND.[6] And MI6 had even recruited a Stasi informer; under arrest, he revealed that his mission was to seduce the daughter of a Stasi officer, thus establishing a channel for the British.[7] Moreover, not every spy in the GDR was European. It transpired that such international figures as the Shah of Iran had spies in East Germany, reporting on dissident Iranians living there.[8]

As the decade closed the BND withdrew some of its head agents and intelligence cells to West Germany and, like the US, created small groups of spies whose members might be able to support one another in a sealed-off East Germany. It also founded a standalone department tasked with preparing for war. Dead drops were positioned along the transit routes from West Berlin to the Federal Republic. Secret paths for smuggling people and materials were laid on the Berlin and inter-German borders. Other intelligence services, in particular those of the US military, tried to increase their spy coverage at the end of the 1950s, recruiting as many agents as possible while the going remained good. Refugees from East Germany were sent back there, some on brief assignments, others for longer periods to cache equipment and identify places where supplies or parachutists might be dropped if war broke out.

One example is a tractor driver from Thuringia who had run to West Germany to escape punishment for his part in a road accident. He was debriefed by US intelligence at three locations (Fulda, Oberursel, and the Giessen refugee camp) before being trained in firearms and smuggled back into the GDR as a saboteur. His instructions were as follows: if he found himself able to stay in East Germany, he was to take a job at a potash mine and look for ways to flood it in the future; if threatened with arrest or deportation, he was promptly to set fire to two offices – one government, one border police – and flee westwards, to be rewarded with a job for US intelligence. His arrest by the Stasi prevented him from implementing either plan.[9]

The Stasi found itself arresting an increasing number of these returnees. One young refugee recruited by the US had been told to go back and get a job on the railways. He was then to listen to West German radio stations and, when among colleagues, 'carry out subversive activities using these broadcasts'; as the Stasi report writer put it, he had been told to 'organise drinking sessions and carry out his demoralisation at the beer table'. Another youth had been sent back to Karl-Marx-Stadt to gather information on East Germans who were permitted to travel to West Germany. He was told to communicate in letters on Astra notepaper, with secret messages written in urine between the lines of normal text – instructions that evoked First World War espionage. Another refugee had been sent back to East Berlin by the CIC, which wanted him to mail information on state-owned companies to one 'Karl Witzki, Berlin-Charlottenburg, Neufertstrasse 16'. Yet another had been recruited by the BfV as its agent 'Adlerhorst' (Eagle's Nest) and told to infiltrate a collective farm. He was to report on the division of labour, equipment, quotas, and crop yields; and on the mood of the farmers, their political activity, earnings, housing, and cultural stimulation.[10]

Meanwhile, concerns about the economic potential of the Soviet Bloc saw ongoing penetrations of East German industry and the economic bureaucracy. A Stasi report from 1960 details the arrests of economic spies in the preceding period: two were caught in the State Planning Commission (one US and one MI6 spy); one in the Ministry for Foreign Trade (for MI6); one in the Ministry for Construction (the BND's woman spy 'Steinberg', secretary to the minister); eight in agencies for foreign trade (one BND, two US, two MI6, two for France and one for the SPD Ostbüro); one at East Germany's biggest textile manufacturer (for MI6); and seven others at various industrial sites (five US and two MI6).[11]

Some Western spies survived this cull, however, if only for a short time. Remaining CIA assets included a 'significant source' at Comecon, a translator; an economist at the State Planning Commission; a telephonist at the Ministry of Post and Telecommunications, equipped with 'a tiny recording device that switched itself on during conversations';[12] an employee of the Central Statistics Administration, who was providing information on stocks of raw materials used by industry and the armed forces; and an economist at the Institute for Trade Technology, who was able to identify Western companies that were supplying embargoed goods to the GDR. Surviving MI6 agents included a government stenographer, the head accountant of the East German state bank, and an official at the State Planning Commission whose work concerned energy supplies. The BND still had spies throughout the East German economy, including 'excellent sources' covering the GDR's attempts to manufacture jet aircraft. One of them, the aeronautical engineer Manfred Gerlach, reported to the BND's Helga Bock, whose husband was a distinguished aeronautical scientist. Before long Gerlach was uncovered and sentenced to life in prison.[13] Meanwhile, East Germany's development of jet aircraft was aborted after a string of calamitous accidents.

In addition to its military relevance, the information gained from these penetrations fed Western debates about trading with, and granting aid and credit to, the GDR. It also shed light on the strengths and weaknesses of the Soviet Bloc economies. The Stasi thought somewhat differently of its purpose, opining in one report that the 'aim of this extensive spying is the preparation of an economic blockade'.[14] It is true that a blockade was favoured by some American decision-makers; the governments of western Europe were more concerned with maintaining the flow of trade.[15]

There continued to be incidents of espionage and counter-espionage that maintained the shadowy traditions of the early Cold War. Western counter-espionage services tended to conflate operations by the KGB and the Stasi, seeing the two services as interchangeable. This tendency is apparent in the case of the Baltic Sea trading ship *Runa*. In 1959 her crew were arrested; they were all Danish communists, the skipper a veteran of Ernst Wollweber's maritime sabotage network of the late 1930s. The vessel had been making courier runs and was involved in military spying, but the Danish security police, the PET, couldn't discern if the *Runa* was carrying out this work for East Berlin or Moscow. At the time, tensions were rising in the region. The Danish authorities were concerned that East Germany, as part of its propaganda, was wooing Danes with cheap summer holidays, and with sporting and cultural festivals known as the Baltic Weeks. Therefore, although the ship's crew had been working directly for the Soviet Union, the case was classified and reported by the Danish press as an example of East German espionage.[16]

In another heated incident, Stasi personnel intercepted a tour through East Germany by members of Britain's Military Liaison Mission, ransacking their vehicles and arresting Brigadier John Packard, the mission chief. At a subsequent press conference, Walter Ulbricht denounced the West's misuse of the missions for espionage, and displayed confiscated maps which he claimed offered proof of Western plans to invade the GDR. Although Packard was released, he was withdrawn from Germany due to fears for his safety.[17]

It was around this time that Bill Harvey, chief of the Berlin Operations Base, began to keep thermite grenades in his safes, to destroy CIA documents should West Berlin be invaded.[18] But self-protection wasn't the only consideration for

Harvey's outfit; there was great reluctance to abandon the two million West Berliners to an uncertain fate. And all the while the treachery of George Blake at MI6 slithered on. A later Stasi report stated that 100 MI6 spies were caught between 1958 and 1961 thanks to Blake.[19] These were high-level penetrations typical of those favoured by Britain: a secretary working for the Council of Ministers, a senior official at the Ministry for Mechanical Engineering, an NVA colonel. The clock was ticking loudly on such Western infiltrations.

66

A Decision is Made

The closing of East Germany's borders was a gradual process that took place from the late 1940s onwards. The process didn't stop even with the construction of the Berlin Wall. The evolution of the permits issued to West Berliners and West Germans from 1960 onwards, the firmer demarcation of the western borders in 1967, and the new fortifications and armaments of the 1970s, all show how the definition and management of the borders occupied the SED regime over time.

Although known in East Germany and the Soviet Bloc as the 'anti-fascist protective barrier' (Antifaschistischer Schutzwall), the Berlin Wall was inherently aggressive. It was thought that the Wall might contribute to a rise in living standards in East Germany. On the other hand, it was understood that civilians would be shot dead by GDR border guards while trying to cross it. Shoot-to-kill incidents were a built-in requirement of the Wall's success. The Wall was also an example of high strategy and geopolitics affecting ordinary people's existence. Military and nuclear espionage persuaded Nikita Khrushchev that armed conflict with the West was undesirable. A wall, on the other hand, was useful, if only as a strong gesture; and so a wall was built, changing people's day-to-day lives for generations. It played a part in their jobs and marriages, their friendships and families. Often, geopolitical machinations can seem remote, as if they are no concern of the humans living far down below. But sometimes they can shape the way that a person experiences an entire life.

Before the SED began the task of walling in its own population, it walled in itself. In May 1960, still unnerved by the fact that party and security officials had been killed in the Hungarian uprising four years earlier, Walter Ulbricht issued a secret directive for the Politbüro and other top executives to relocate to a compound in the countryside north of Berlin, the Wandlitz forest settlement (Waldsiedlung Wandlitz). There, ensconced in pleasant villas and ringed by Stasi guards, the GDR's rulers were served otherwise unavailable goods by Stasi cashiers in special shops, and were tended by Stasi cooks, cleaners and drivers. Erich Mielke lived at Villa No. 8.

From September 1960 West German citizens had to apply for permission to enter East Berlin. One new control measure was a questionnaire to be completed by West Germans at every GDR border, covering their possible Nazi background and wartime conduct. Tensions were ramped up further when West Germany annulled and then renegotiated its interzonal trade agreements with East Germany and the Soviet Union.

The prime minister, Wilhelm Pieck, died that September. Walter Ulbricht seized the chance to create a *faux* collective head of state for the GDR, in the form of its State Council (Staatsrat). Promptly he had himself elected as chairman. Ulbricht was now, officially and unequivocally, at the top of the party and the government. One of the first things he did, in true Ulbrichtian fashion, was try to look nice.

On 4 October Ulbricht issued a declaration in which he trumpeted the GDR's 'socialist democracy'. He proclaimed that 'the remnants of egotistical, misanthropic behaviour from the capitalist era have been overcome'. In most respects this was merely the latest blather to claim East Germany's legitimacy and propriety. However, it triggered a bout of amnesties for prisoners convicted of lesser anti-state crimes, freeing some 16,000 people.[1] In the shadows, Erich Mielke set up working groups to scrutinise the pardons.

The Stasi still faced occasional challenges for not following legal procedures. In February 1961, in a rare example of demonstrative governance by a non-Marxist block party, Volkskammer president Johannes Dieckmann of the LDPD lodged a complaint with minister of justice Hilde Benjamin about arrestees being kept in custody without charge for excessive lengths of time. Indeed, it was a tradition for the Stasi to pay no heed to the forty-eight-hour detention limit. Benjamin notified Mielke who, with impenetrable cynicism, demanded an explanation from Main Department IX (investigations). In his reply, Lieutenant Colonel Walter Heinitz, deputy chief of HA IX, argued that it was often necessary to prolong the initial interrogations for 'crimes with a high degree of social danger'. Heinitz was a founding officer in the Stasi who had been forced into a Wehrmacht penal battalion during the war and afterwards served with K5 in Chemnitz. He considered the forty-eight-hour time limit 'not appropriate', given that a prolonged first interrogation 'for psychological reasons [creates] favourable conditions for clarifying the facts and is the basis for many successes in investigative work'.[2]

Thus the long, circular story of the Stasi's observance or disregard of legal procedures, which had run throughout the 1950s, continued into the 1960s and beyond. As ever the Stasi was locked in a conflict between, on the one hand, its autonomy, secrecy, and arbitrariness, and on the other, its need to conform to ideals of propriety and legal rectitude. It continued to make attempts to regularise itself, for example by ending, or claiming to end, the practice of night-time interrogation. For some SED executives, the Stasi was demonstrably getting better at conforming to Walter Ulbricht's vision of a legalistic socialist society. But internal reports in early 1961 still found grim conditions inside Stasi prisons and detention centres, which were run by its Department XIV. 'Numerous deficiencies' were noted in sanitary conditions, food, medical care, and guards' treatment of prisoners. Prison guards at Karl-Marx-Stadt and Frankfurt an der Oder were observed shouting 'vulgar phrases' at prisoners, and 'arbitrarily' revoking the perks granted to compliant inmates.[3] Again, this was hardly the savagery of, say, Pol Pot's Cambodia. But SED socialism was a prim creed, and screaming filth at a prisoner was considered unworthy.

The brief thaw initiated by Ulbricht's October 1960 declaration, which he endorsed a few months later with a 'liberalising' resolution on the application of justice, was soon regretted. By June 1961, as the Berlin crisis escalated and the number of westward-bound refugees soared, reports by the Ministry of Justice complained that 'unacceptable' sentences were being passed by lenient judges who were interpreting Ulbricht's judicial resolution 'as an instruction for a generally more generous treatment of violators'. Courts and public prosecutors were guilty of 'liberal wavering', manifesting in their 'underestimation of the social danger of state crimes', their 'over-emphasis on subjective factors', their 'refusal to issue arrest warrants and initiate proceedings', and their 'formal and dogmatic [i.e., apolitical] jurisprudence'.[4]

This was no time for the SED regime to go soft. In March 1961 Khrushchev called a meeting of the Warsaw Pact signatories to discuss the chaotic situation in the Soviet Bloc and the flight of its population. In attendance were Ulbricht, Mielke and Erich Honecker, the latter representing the SED Politbüro's Security Commission. Despite the Germans' pleas, however, Khrushchev refused to seal off Berlin. He still wanted the city kept open: partly for economic reasons, as a trade link between East and West Germany; partly as a bargaining chip in negotiations for German reunification, demilitarisation and renewed sovereignty; and partly for continued access to the West, mostly for the purposes of espionage and subversion.

Although the Vienna summit of June 1961 offered some promise of calming the Berlin crisis, Khrushchev and John F. Kennedy's jousting achieved little. Khrushchev repeated his favourite threat: that he would sign a new peace treaty with the GDR which was likely to remove the Western Allies' formal basis for staying in Berlin. Kennedy, however, was inclined to toughness – he had been elected partly on a commitment to it. Visiting London on his way home from Vienna, he agreed with British prime minister Harold Macmillan that the Western powers would remain in the city no matter what.

*

The trouble for Khrushchev was that he had made his first threats at a time when he believed Soviet armed force in Europe to be much stronger than that of the West. This had indeed been the case since the end of the Second World War. But Khrushchev's growing knowledge of the arms race forced a change of mind. He acquired this crucial new knowledge from spies, especially those working for the GRU and the Stasi; and he learned that his threats rang somewhat hollow.

For while Khrushchev had been calculating, the West had been picking up speed in the arms race. When Kennedy was elected president, he stamped on the accelerator. Thus Khrushchev began to receive alarming news. At the start of the crisis in 1958, the US army in West Germany had been equipped with six batteries of short-range nuclear missiles and twenty-one artillery batteries capable of launching nuclear ordnance. By June 1961 this arsenal had increased to twenty-one batteries of short-range missiles, nineteen batteries of nuclear-capable artillery, and a unit of Redstone ballistic missiles, while every American infantry division had been stiffened with a battery of Honest John tactical missiles.[5]

At the same time, Konrad Adenauer was intent on arming the Bundeswehr with Polaris missiles. In theory, this move was prohibited by the signatories of the Western Union. Behind closed doors, Adenauer asked the Vatican, no less, to urge the WU to rescind its ban on West Germany possessing offensive weapons. Moscow knew about Adenauer's approaches to Rome – the KGB reported this nugget in autumn 1960, based on information received from Hungarian intelligence, which had good sources at the Vatican.[6]

Knowledge of America's speed in developing, manufacturing, and deploying tactical nuclear weapons had a profound effect on Nikita Khrushchev, the city of Berlin, and the history of the century. The numerical superiority of the Soviet Union's conventional forces was virtually meaningless given that the US army's short-range nuclear weapons were capable of obliterating Soviet tank columns in a matter of hours. The West was better equipped and prepared than Khrushchev had dared to believe. Furthermore, although the Soviets stepped up the programme to equip their own land forces with tactical nuclear weapons, and enlarged their long-range bomber force, the potential consequences of war had become horribly clear. Any conflict over Berlin was likely to cause grievous harm to the Soviet armed forces, not to mention the living things and landscape of Europe.

Another GRU report of mid-1961, 'Analysis of the changed planning for the structure of American forces and of the US defence budget for 1961-62', demonstrated two things: the GRU's considerable access to America's military and political elite, and Kennedy's ambition to ramp up his country's nuclear arsenal. Kennedy's plan called for a further twenty-nine George Washington-class nuclear submarines, armed with sixteen Polaris missiles, to be in service within three years. By early 1965 there were to be twelve operational squadrons equipped with Atlas and Titan intercontinental ballistic missiles. The rapid development of the Minuteman was another game-changer. Light, precise and relatively inexpensive, this was an intercontinental ballistic missile that could be launched from an infantry dugout.[7]

These developments were on course to achieving a 1:5 ratio of Soviet and American missiles within a few short years. Khrushchev's strategic vision of a winnable European conflict, or even of a winnable showdown, had been mistaken. To his surprise, the Soviets were in an inferior position and the West was readying itself for a deadly response. Building a wall through Berlin now looked a better option than making threats.[8]

East Germany's western borders were growing tenser all the time. Road and rail traffic between West Germany and Berlin was subject to increasingly stiff controls. Soviet guards and GDR border police now routinely searched every passenger of every civilian vehicle. At the border station of Marienborn, adjacent to the Federal border town of Helmstedt, trains were held up for an unending stream of dubious reasons. Some had swastikas written in the dust on the side of their carriages, either an off-colour joke or a disruptive ruse by communist border personnel. The members of the Western Military Liaison Missions in East Germany bore the brunt of the intimidation. The CIA reported that the missions' personnel had been 'physically assaulted, closely watched, restricted in their travel, and subjected to insulting and irritating incidents'.[9]

The Stasi was able to clarify the tactical Western interests of the moment when Main Department II acquired a copy of the questions now being put to East German refugees by the US and West German intelligence services:

- Which military forces of the GDR and Soviet Union are within a 50km radius of Berlin?
- What forms of heightened alert for the military forces can be detected?
- At which points of the railway network to Berlin do checks take place, and by whom are they carried out?
- What additional Volkspolizei controls have been established in places where there are Volkspolizei tents for control measures?
- What movements of military forces, including the Volkspolizei and Bereitschaftspolizei, are taking place in the areas of the western state borders and Berlin?

- What is known about the introduction of identity cards that are said to be issued on a district basis?
- Do you believe in the conclusion of a Soviet peace treaty with the GDR in 1961?
- What ideas and plans exist about the closure of West Berlin?
- Do you believe there will be a hermetic sealing of the borders between
  a) GDR-Federal Republic
  b) GDR-East Berlin
  c) East Berlin-West Berlin?
- What are the signs of a change of currency in the GDR?[10]

The Stasi also noted that the Bundeswehr tended to rush its best units, such as panzer grenadier battalions, straight to the East German frontier. Combined arms exercises were observed taking place from the Baltic to Bavaria. There were increasing violations of airspace. Intensified training programmes saw Federal police and customs officials taking part in dummy manhunts in the trickiest border country; and they now made a point of confiscating great truckloads of GDR literature, such as National Front leaflets, before it could enter West Germany. The Federal Ministry for All-German Affairs, now led by Ernst Lemmer – whom the Stasi detested as much as his predecessor, Jakob Kaiser – was organising educational trips to the border for West German workers and schoolchildren, so they could see the ugly division of their country. In its internal reports the Stasi deplored the way that West German and American border personnel were trying to entice GDR border police to desert their posts. Cigarettes, coffee, chocolate and bottles of beer would be slung across the border obstacles – sometimes to be caught in outstretched tarpaulins on the East German side – only to be followed by friendly attempts 'to hold political talks'.[11] East Germany's border police had always been prone to desertion; the luxury groceries were probably more persuasive than the political talks.

There is evidence that by the middle of July 1961, 'very close coordination' existed between Nikita Khrushchev and Walter Ulbricht on the matter of sealing off Berlin.[12] Ulbricht's most persuasive argument was probably that, regardless of the signing of any kind of peace treaty, East Germany faced economic and political collapse if its population continued to disappear into West Berlin. The decision to construct the Wall was sanctioned formally by the Soviet leadership in a somewhat roundabout way: by approving the protocol (minutes) of a meeting of Soviet Bloc party secretaries held on 5 August which, by implication, meant approving the motion to build a wall. Walter Ulbricht told his Politbüro colleagues about 'Khrushchev's decision' on 7 August. Four days later Erich Mielke obliquely mentioned 'decisive measures' and 'a new phase of Chekist work' to his senior officers. This gave them little time to prepare the

Stasi's part in Aktion Rose, the operation to seal the borders.[13] The task force for overseeing the operation had already been constituted: Erich Mielke and Erich Honecker, interior minister Karl Maron, defence minister Heinz Hoffmann, and transport minister Erwin Kramer, as well as two Soviet officials. Unsure of their objective, heads of department at the Stasi set up live communications with local army commands, intensified informer reports from factories and sensitive sites, and prepared to put down any form of public disturbance.

67

Old Tricks

Even with the coming of the Wall, and the intricate dance it was having to perform around matters of legality, the Stasi didn't lose its appetite for dirty operations. Some of its most notorious kidnappings occurred in the period before the Wall was laid. Dieter Koniecki, 'eastern adviser' for West Berlin's liberal students' association, was especially unfortunate – he was kidnapped six months before the Wall appeared, only to spend five and a half years in an East German prison.[1]

Other attempts failed, including a renewed effort to snatch Paul Cunow of the FDP Ostbüro. Like the attempt made during Aktion Blitz, this one involved Cunow's best friend Werner Hähn, the Stasi's GM 'Radeberg'. In 1958 the Stasi bought Hähn a flashy new car, with which he offered to take Cunow on a beery outing through the western green belt of Berlin. At a certain point the pair's route was expected to pass through GDR territory, for just a couple of hundred metres. Here, an armed squad of Stasi employees would be waiting to lift Cunow. It all came to nothing, however, when Cunow decided to include his secretary and her dog on this day trip, and so chose to drive his own car. In June 1960 Hähn was killed in an accident when driving the Stasi-bought car in which he had planned to abduct his friend.[2]

The Stasi's Soviet mentors were pressing ahead with plenty of dirty operations. In 1957 and 1959 Nikita Khrushchev personally authorised the assassination of two Ukrainian nationalist figures in West Germany. Lev Rebet and Stepan Bandera were killed in Munich by Bogdan Stashinsky, a KGB operative working out of Karlshorst. On both occasions he used spray guns developed at the KGB weapons laboratory, which fired a jet of poison gas from a crushed ampule of potassium cyanide. These killings were lengthy, patient operations in which Stashinsky used false identities to spend time in West Germany and familiarise himself with the locations and his targets. He regretted his actions, however, and defected in August 1961, the day before the Berlin borders were sealed.[3]

France, too, was carrying out deadly operations in Europe. The main targets were German arms dealers who were supplying African nationalists, as well as the nationalists themselves. Otto Schlüter stopped supplying weapons when his mother 'was vaporized by a car bomb' in April 1957.[4] Two years later Georg Puchert, head of Hamburg's Astromar Import-Export, was blown up in his booby-trapped Mercedes in Frankfurt. Another German arms dealer, Marcel Leopold, was killed in Geneva, reputedly by a poisoned dart fired from a blowpipe. Also poisoned in Switzerland was the Cameroonian politician Felix Moumié, who was lured there for medical treatment organised by a French agent posing as a sympathetic journalist. In another incident, an activist of Algeria's National Liberation Front was gunned down on the streets of Bonn.[5] These actions, confidently attributed to the SDECE, rivalled the trail of blood left around Europe by the NKVD in the 1930s. Arguably they are more shocking than any such operation attempted by the Stasi.

Most of the Stasi's late kidnapping operations targeted apostates from the SED and defectors from the security forces. One of them, Manfred Smolka, had fled East Germany after being dismissed from the border police for 'disobeying orders and being ideologically weak'.[6] Having been kidnapped, he was put through a show trial and executed. Erich Mielke fired off an internal order about Smolka's death sentence, which he insisted be publicised at every level of the Stasi. Declaring that there was 'no lenience for traitors to the cause of peace and socialism', Mielke thundered:

> This order on the crime and punishment of Smolka is to be made known to all employees of the Ministry for State Security.
>
> The contents of this order [are] to form the topic of thorough discussion and instruction in service units in order to heighten their vigilance and solidarity and further strengthen the political-moral unity and team spirit in our ranks.
>
> All colleagues in the Ministry are to be trained to hate treachery, to work as Chekists towards overcoming political-moral weakness...[7]

The Stasi files on Manfred Smolka are a rarity, in that they contain details of a kidnapping yet are available for anyone to see on the Bundesarchiv website, albeit in excerpts.[8] They tell the story of a predetermined execution, with an accused who, until the very last, cannot quite believe what is going to happen to him. Like others executed by the SED regime, Smolka was put to death not so much for his wrongdoing as for his guileless, idiosyncratic personality; for his innocence, in a way.

Manfred Smolka had joined the border police in his late teens, in 1948.[9] A keen hunter and hiker, he was attracted to the job because it meant spending time in nature, roaming the woods and hills. (Smolka was not the first or last member of a border force to join up for this reason.) He got married, had a child, and served for ten years in the area of Titschendorf, where Thuringia meets Bavaria. He took part in the aggressive border operations of 1952 and was promoted twice, reaching officer rank. This was not a career path for the fainthearted. On the other hand, Smolka had a record of falling out with superiors and the local party, earning him a reputation for querulousness.

One day in June 1958, with heightened surveillance in place for the fifth anniversary of the 1953 uprising, Smolka allowed farmers to work their fields near the border despite it being prohibited. He was also known to let villagers without the correct permits approach the frontier. Having been demoted already and regularly dressed down, Smolka was summoned to a disciplinary meeting. It proved to be his last; he stormed out, throwing down his service jacket in disgust. Unsurprisingly, he was subsequently notified that he had been sacked from the border police and expelled from the SED.

With nothing to keep him in the GDR, Smolka escaped to West Germany that November, just before his twenty-eighth birthday. His mother and sister lived in the Federal Republic, and Smolka found accommodation in Gummersbach, east of Cologne. His main concern was to get his wife and nine-year-old daughter out of East Germany to join him, but the Stasi learned of his apparently lengthy interrogation by US intelligence. Given that Smolka was in a position to spill many secrets, the Stasi was tasked with retrieving him, and Operation 'Traitor' was launched.[*]

From the start Smolka was defined as a spy. This was stated in the order initiating the operation: 'Smolka conducts espionage against the German Democratic Republic from West Germany.' Smolka's wife and daughter were his weak spot, and the pair became the bait in a Stasi trap. First the Stasi quashed the official application made by Smolka's wife to leave the GDR.[10] Then a former police colleague of Smolka's made contact with him, claiming to be on the verge of defecting himself. This man was a Stasi KP or 'contact person'. The pair exchanged letters in which Smolka agreed to meet his acquaintance at 'the Brandenburg Gate or the Reichstag ruins' in Berlin, despite it being 'an unsuitable place for me'. In one letter Smolka urged his friend to steal a new model of gas mask recently issued to the border police, and bring it with him to West Germany, as this would make his defection more valuable to the authorities there. The friend then offered to smuggle Smolka's wife and daughter across the border with him as he made his escape. Smolka agreed. Accordingly, the Stasi selected a secluded place near Titschendorf where the conditions were right for an attempted crossing and an abduction.

---

[*]   Operativ-Vorgangs 'Verräter'.

Meanwhile, a commission of border police officers had written a report on the secrets Smolka was known or suspected of leaking to the Americans. They pointed out that Smolka's Titschendorf border company was significant as it faced the Bavarian town of Nordhalben, 'where several offices of the Bavarian Border Police and the Customs Border Guard are located'. Subversive leaflets directed at East German citizens were known to emanate from the town. Smolka was able to give 'the American secret service [details] about the structure, armament and equipment of border police units, as well as about the system of border security,' thus enabling 'the enemy to make a genuine assessment of the combat strength and operational readiness of the border police units in the area'.

More serious and specific allegations followed. They reveal vast insecurity on the part of the report writers. Smolka was said to have provided enough information about the local border police for the West to 'quickly eliminate them as a resistance force':

> The complete exposure of the system of border security through Smolka's statements allows the enemy to take advantage of the most favourable conditions for the infiltration of his agents, spies and terrorists, and to evade arrest by bypassing the border posts...
>
> Smolka gave precise information about the patrol routes, places of deployment and duty times of the border posts...[His] statements about the route and locations of communications stations [give] the enemy the opportunity to connect to the network, to listen in on conversations, to disorganise border security through false conversations...
>
> Knowing the names of senior officers allows the enemy to determine personnel changes in the command bodies and to draw conclusions about the quality of the leadership...
>
> By naming the border police helpers [civilian auxiliaries] from Titschendorf, the enemy can intensify agitation against these progressive inhabitants of the border area and isolate them from the broader population. This makes it considerably more difficult to win over the entire border population to actively support the border police in securing the border.

The kidnapping was set for 22 August 1959. Thirteen Stasi officers and NCOs of Main Department I, and two police officers of the 4th Border Brigade, went to the operational area. At 12.15 p.m., two Stasi lieutenants, Hopf and Taubner, observed a light blue Volkswagen approaching the planned 'place of arrest' from the direction of Nordhalben. In it were Smolka and two West German civilians. The three men left the car and scrutinised the area; this was where

Smolka's wife, daughter and 'friend', the Stasi KP, were due to appear later. They then departed, but during the afternoon the blue Volkswagen was spotted making a couple more recces.

At 4.30 p.m., two groups of Stasi abductors concealed themselves in bushes near the planned crossing point. Two more groups, augmented by border police, took up securing positions to the rear.* Just after 6 p.m., the blue Volkswagen returned and parked about 300 metres away. Smolka got out and climbed a tree to survey the landscape. The two West Germans stayed with the car, from which they couldn't see the crossing point or the action that followed.

At around 7.30 p.m., Smolka's wife and daughter, together with Smolka's old police colleague, approached the site from the east. Smolka didn't see them at first. His wife started whistling to get his attention. He then gestured for the three to cross the lines of wire, but they didn't move. So Smolka jumped over a stream and clambered onto GDR territory to help them over. At that moment Captain Volker's group sprang from concealment about ten metres away to grab him. Volker shouted for Smolka to surrender himself. Instead he ran back towards West German ground, so Volker fired a warning shot. When Smolka didn't stop, Volker fired two bursts from his machine pistol, hitting Smolka in the thigh.

Smolka's wife and daughter had retreated and were watching on helplessly. Smolka, lightly wounded, was arrested together with his 'friend', and they were taken to vehicles 800 metres away. Smolka's wife was taken into custody too. That night, Junior Lieutenant Taubner took the Smolkas' daughter to her grandmother's house. Her parents ended up in the detention centre on Magdalenenstrasse in Berlin.

In its report on the affair, Main Department I stressed that Smolka had been shot and captured on East German soil. This was almost certainly untrue.[11] In the documents prepared for his trial, the Stasi alleged that Smolka had spent 'a stay of several weeks with the American secret service on Leibnizstrasse, Bayreuth'. His 'large-scale betrayal' had enabled 'the American secret service to carry out active smuggling activities in the Lobenstein section of the border and to illegally send trained agents'. Three of these agents had been arrested. Smolka's suggestion to his friend to defect with a stolen gas mask was also used as evidence.

---

* The Stasi personnel for the operation were Captain Volker, Senior Lieutenant Sander, Sergeant Winkler and Unteroffizier Görlich in the first kidnapping group; Senior Lieutenant Sobolik, Junior Lieutenant Kutschke and Senior Sergeant Kalisch in the second; and in the supporting groups, Senior Lieutenant Oxfort, Lieutenant Tyra, Senior Lieutenant Hopf, Junior Lieutenant Taubner, Junior Lieutenant Krönke and Senior Sergeant Sarodnik. The two border police participants, Captain Kinder and Lieutenant Neumann, were both Stasi GI (secret informers).

It was decided to make an example of Smolka. Lieutenant Colonel Neumann of the Stasi's Main Department IX/6, which was responsible for especially important political investigations, proposed that Smolka be sentenced to death at a show trial:

> The trial is intended to prove once again that all relatives and former members of the national defence organs who have fled to West Germany are induced to seek out imperialist secret services and to betray all military secrets known to them, as well as to commit other crimes against the German Democratic Republic.
>
> Furthermore, the urgent need to increase the vigilance of the members of the border police on duty at the western state border, as well as the unscrupulous betrayal of the accused Smolka and its dangerous consequences, will be shown.
>
> The participants in the trial should realise that the disclosure of military secrets to the imperialist secret services is exploited ruthlessly for the purposes of enemy action against the GDR.

Erich Mielke wrote that he concurred.

Although they knew that Smolka intended to mention his abduction at trial, the investigators of Main Department IX were still sufficiently confident to propose a large audience in court. Thirty border police officers were invited, as well as Stasi and party personnel. Expecting a 'provocative appearance' by Smolka, HA IX warned and carefully instructed the judge, public prosecutor and witnesses, as well as the lucky eighty spectators.

A recording exists of Smolka making his final plea in court. Smolka is the only person in the room who doesn't realise that he is going to die. He tries to set the record straight, as if there is still time for facts to change the prosecution's mind.

Smolka insisted that he hadn't betrayed secrets to anything like the extent alleged; the charges enumerated things he *might* have said, not what he did say. He denied agreeing to work for the Americans and refuted the idea that he had spent three weeks with them. This allegation was based on the testimony of a Stasi witness – most likely an asset at Bayreuth – but Smolka was able to prove that he had, in fact, spent only five days at Bayreuth, and was interviewed on just three of those days. It was alleged that Smolka had bought a weapon in West Germany; Smolka replied that this was a small antique hunting gun, clearly unsuitable for use in secret service work. He also denied supplying the information that had led to three attempted infiltrations of spies into East Germany. Two of these crossings had occurred in places he didn't know; the third had been made in such an obvious spot that it was 'inevitable' the crosser would run into GDR border posts. 'If I had told the Americans about smuggling points,' Smolka explained, 'it would never have been that place!'

Following this hopeful waste of breath, Smolka was convicted of treason and sentenced to death. His wife received a four-year sentence, and their daughter was raised by the grandmother. Smolka spent what remained of his life writing secret messages in letters to his mother and sister in West Germany, all of which ended up in his Stasi file, undelivered. He was guillotined in Leipzig on 12 July 1960. A Stasi KP called Erwin Röder was paid for his role in the kidnapping. Röder may have been Smolka's former police colleague, or the Stasi's mole at Bayreuth, or a different participant; it isn't clear. But he got 500 marks for his trouble.[12]

Every intolerant community detests an apostate, and Heinz Brandt was a loud one. A former SED official who specialised in writing propaganda, during the 1950s Brandt grew disillusioned with Ulbricht's regime and in 1958 he fled East Germany. Once established in Frankfurt am Main he continued his work in the labour movement, editing the journal of the IG Metall trade union. The Stasi kidnapped him from West Berlin on 16 June 1961, two months before the city's borders were sealed.

Heinz Brandt was a devout Marxist, but he never cared for Stalin. As a child, he and his German Jewish community in Posen (now Poznań) were shaken to bits by the First World War and the Russian Revolution. For the rest of his life Brandt remembered learning, solemnly and at the age of ten, of the deaths of Rosa Luxemburg and Karl Liebknecht.

Brandt fell deeply in love with the writings of Kant and Marx, and grew into the type of German communist guaranteed to steal the hearts of Western fellow travellers; he was immersed in the theatre and cinema of the Weimar years, captivated by the artistic and industrial ideals of the Bauhaus. He joined the KJVD and graduated to the KPD, but he was never much good at toeing the line. This hardly mattered to the SA stormtroopers who got a kick out of beating him bloody.[13] In 1934, having refused a KPD order to leave for Paris, Brandt was arrested. He spent nearly eleven years incarcerated by the Nazis, sometimes at Buchenwald and Auschwitz. He survived only with miraculous luck. On one occasion, the fellow prisoners in Brandt's work detail were summarily executed by their guards; Brandt had been transferred to another job earlier the same day.

Brandt emerged from captivity as an enthusiastic exponent of the KPD-SPD merger. He is a good example of the kind of German left-winger who was energised by the SED's existence, by its early programme and its sudden, unexpected freedom of action. Brandt put his whole weight behind the nationalising of industry and the redistribution of land, and gave full-blooded approval to denazification and the subjugation of landowners. In fact, his main dislike about the GDR was Walter Ulbricht. This proved unfortunate.

Despite working for some time as a propaganda specialist in the Berlin city government, Brandt found himself increasingly marginalised and challenged. He grew even cooler on Stalin when he learned the fate of two of his siblings in the USSR; his sister Lilli sentenced to the Gulag, his brother Richard killed in the purges of the late 1930s. He was criticised for showing sympathy with the striking workers of 1953, and demoted to a job at a publishing house. So he made contact with the SPD Ostbüro – one of its leaders, Siggi Neumann, was an old friend – and started to provide information on conditions inside East Germany. As one historian puts it, Brandt 'did not understand this as espionage for the West, but as socialist and pan-German resistance to the dictatorship of the SED'.[14]

By 1958, having vocally disapproved of Ulbricht's leadership, Brandt was sufficiently convinced of his coming arrest to flee. He left with his wife and children, going first to West Berlin and then on to Frankfurt. There he developed his connections with the SPD Ostbüro, dived back into the purity of Kant and Marx, and in his writings urged for a reunified and socialist Germany, bound to neither side of the Cold War.

Ulbricht and the SED leadership were badly stung by Brandt's defection and his journalism. His criticisms of the East German regime were strengthened by the objectivity and good sense assumed to be present in an apostate. It was decided to get him back into East Germany and make him repent, publicly. Erich Mielke gave the order to do so.

The Stasi observed Brandt for years, as it did many of its kidnapping victims. Brandt's son Stefan said later that:

> it was very surprising and shocking that from 1958 onwards, when we fled to West Berlin, [the Stasi had] photos, materials about the family, about us children, about our family, about our street… obviously, as early as 1958, plans started to be made to bring him back. And this from 1958 to 1961, with a meticulousness that was impressive… every step we took as a family was monitored.[15]

Although Brandt was unaware of it, a small group of acquaintances – all Stasi collaborators – had begun to plot his downfall. On a work trip to Berlin in spring 1961, Brandt went to a bar for a drink with a colleague, Hans Beyerlein of the IG Metall management board.[16] Beyerlein was acquainted with a couple of the barmaids and introduced Brandt to one of them, a woman in her early thirties who called herself Martina Matt. Her real name, however, was Eva Walter. 'Martina Matt' was her cover name as a Stasi GI.

Eva Walter was a half-starved waitress who had been unable to pursue her intended career in pharmacy because of the war. She had been spotted as a potential Stasi asset by a fellow waitress at the bar who was already a GM. Throughout 1960 Walter had been 'put through her paces' as a trainee operative by another Stasi collaborator living in West Berlin, a struggling self-employed photographer. This was Helmuth Ast, alias GM 'Norge'. Ast's wife Helga was also a secret collaborator, codenamed 'Vera'.

Recruited in 1954, 'Norge' had been used on several occasions to test the suitability of potential collaborators. During a failed operation to kidnap a KgU activist, he had been trained to install bugging devices in his photographic lab, so that the Stasi could hear private conversations between the intended victim and a GM called 'Sybille', to assess whether the latter was following her instructions correctly. Now, in his reports to Main Department V, 'Norge' raved about the promise for clandestine operations shown by 'Martina Matt'. He praised her coldness, calculation, and 'superb gift' for dealing with people.

Having been approved as a GI, 'Martina Matt' rented a room in an apartment bought for 'Norge' by the Stasi, for operational purposes, in the Steglitz district of south-west Berlin. The Stasi always kept an eye on its recruits, and 'Norge' bugged her room before she moved in. 'Martina' was told to resume her table-waitressing job, which she had given up during her training. Her main brief, like that of her waitressing colleague, was to look out for suitable contacts for the Stasi. She was soon lined up for a role in the kidnapping of Heinz Brandt.

Brandt was watched, unblinkingly, right up to his arrival in West Berlin in June 1961, to attend a conference of trade unionists and bankers. Then the trap was sprung. The SED was meticulous in its wrath – Brandt's abduction was carried out on the anniversary of the first 1953 disturbances. During the conference, 'Martina Matt' – who probably was already his mistress – invited Brandt to her home for drinks. He said yes. In later years, Brandt was to explain that her apartment happened to lie on the way to a friend's house, where he had intended to spend the night. But this was clearly a honey trap and Brandt hurled himself into it. At her place, 'Martina' spiked his whiskeys with a knockout drug. Some furniture was damaged as Brandt staggered around or tried to defend himself. He made it out to the street but collapsed after fifteen minutes of stumbling. He recalled his 'last perception, while still sinking [to the ground], was the appearance of four large figures, apparently rushing to help, who offered me a hand with the words: "We've been waiting for you."'[17] He wasn't aware of being dragged into a car; it was driven by a Stasi GM called 'Kurt'. In the preceding weeks, 'Norge' had tested the driving route to East Berlin numerous times, noting traffic lights and potential hold-ups, but the drive went smoothly. Brandt awoke the next day in a cell at Hohenschönhausen.

Although Brandt's wife suspected foul play – her first enquiry to the GDR State Council was made nine days after his disappearance – it was months before his family discovered what had happened. This they learned mostly from an article in *Neues Deutschland*. The subsequent court proceedings against Brandt were a mix of secret and show trials. Like so many others, he was made an example of; reporting to the Central Committee during the preparations, Mielke whined, 'I ask you, comrades, how can [the GDR] defend itself when such people as Schirdewan and Wollweber [and] Brandt, who sat in high and important positions, inform the enemy of all the measures taken to strengthen our republic, destroy our defences and behave so deviously?'[18] Brandt's conviction and sentence were decided in advance. Considered an East German citizen, he was found guilty of 'espionage in combination with seditious propaganda and agitation dangerous to the state' and sentenced to thirteen years.

From then on, however, things went less well for the SED. Although Brandt was harangued to repent and admit his errors – some teeth were knocked out in the process – he refused. He was even offered immediate release if he would publicly confess his ideological mistakes, but still Brandt said no. He was thrown into solitary confinement at Bautzen, the 'Yellow Misery', but became the focus of a vociferous international campaign led by Bertrand Russell, himself no stranger to political imprisonment. In 1963 a new organisation, Amnesty International, publicised Brandt as its 'Prisoner of the Year'. The following year, a silent and fuming SED released him, not admitting that the public outcry had made all the difference.

Although they were well rewarded, Brandt's abductors had mixed fortunes. Hans Beyerlein left IG Metall under a cloud. Eva Walter, aka 'Martina Matt', moved back to East Berlin with a payment of 3,500 marks, and the Stasi found her a job in a department store. 'Norge' received a bonus of 3,000 marks, but he and his wife were considered unsafe in West Berlin, and with great reluctance on their part were relocated to East Germany, in a house move that ended up costing the Stasi a whopping 55,000 marks. The relocation was draped in *konspiratsia*. 'Norge' and 'Vera' staged a very public row at their home in West Berlin, and she stormed off. Later, her friends and family began to receive letters written by her, and posted apparently in Munich, in which she claimed to have left her husband and started a new life. Meanwhile, 'Norge' had told his father-in-law that he had been sucked into shady business deals, and in letters posted from Austria he claimed to be migrating overseas. His father-in-law didn't believe him and filed a missing person's report. This put the couple back on the radar of the Federal police, but they were never apprehended. In the 1980s, as pensioners, they were refused permission to take a holiday in West Germany, partly because the driver in the Brandt operation, 'Kurt', had absconded while on a trip there. No one was punished. At the end of the 1990s an indictment against Eva Walter, then in her early seventies, was dropped due to the statute of limitations.

It took the dirty squads led by GM 'Neuhaus' and Hans Wax four years to capture one Stasi defector.[19] This man, known in the literature as Alfred Glaser, had run away from the GDR and shared his knowledge with the British and American intelligence services. He had settled in Heilbronn in south-west Germany, near to US military and intelligence sites. Not uncommonly, he was a heavy drinker.

Starting in February 1958, 'Neuhaus' personally surveyed Glaser's neighbourhood and routines. Based on this reconnaissance he submitted a kidnapping plan, suggesting the time and place, the necessary personnel and vehicles. The plan was signed off by Josef Kiefel and Bruno Beater. 'Neuhaus' proposed to abduct Glaser at 6 a.m., as Glaser usually left his house at this early hour. 'Neuhaus' and two fellow GM, 'Alfons Dietrich' and 'Schubert', would ambush Glaser in a spot near a war memorial and drag him to their car. He would be bound and gagged and driven along a road running alongside the GDR border to a forested place, the Frankenwald. The bundled-up Glaser would then be thrown down a steep embankment onto GDR soil, collected at the bottom by Main Department II employees wearing border police uniform, put onto a tarpaulin, and carried up a fifty-metre slope to a nearby hamlet. 'Neuhaus' would then return the hire car to its West German owners. He listed the items needed: a syringe, knockout drugs and a pistol.

When in March 1958 the kidnappers deployed to carry out this plan, Glaser didn't show up. 'Neuhaus', 'Alfons Dietrich' and 'Schubert' returned the hire car and headed back to East Berlin. Adding insult to injury, 'Schubert' was arrested by Federal police in an identity check on the train. A valuable GM was lost.

A second attempt was planned for the following November. This time 'Neuhaus', 'Alfons Dietrich' and GM 'Bär' were to snatch Glaser, who would be wrapped in blankets to prevent 'screaming, kicking and moaning'. He would be driven to a 'border lock' in the Thuringian forest, where the barbed-wire obstacles would already have been rendered movable. After Glaser had been driven across, Main Department II employees were to return the obstacles to their original state. The kidnappers would then change their car numberplate for an East German one.

'Neuhaus' requested a Mercedes 220 for the job: fast, with a big boot. He also asked for a seven-shot American revolver – a demand probably inspired by cowboy movies – a syringe, drugs, two coshes, handcuffs, rope and blankets. Finally, a Stasi doctor was to be on hand at the Suhl office. But this plan, too, came to nothing. Stasi personnel in Sonneberg spotted an increase in border patrolling by Federal authorities. Presumably, then, the plans were being betrayed.

Undeterred, in spring 1959 the GM 'Bär' took a job as a sales rep for a firm in West Berlin. The job enabled a swift relocation to Heilbronn. Gradually he befriended Glaser, although the latter was known to be wary: the Stasi was intercepting his letters, in which he wrote of concerns for his safety. Nevertheless, a plan was hatched for Glaser and 'Bär' to go on a pub crawl with a supposed business associate, to be portrayed by 'Neuhaus'. Glaser would be overpowered outside his favourite pub. The Stasi duo were to be armed with steel bars. If anything went wrong, they had orders to kill: a Stasi memo noted that, 'Should any serious complications arise an active measure should be carried out and all traces eliminated, the GM will get verbal instructions for this.'*

Glaser's health deteriorated, however, and he was receiving medical treatment when this plan was supposed to be carried out. It was almost two years before the Stasi tried again. By this time, dirty operations against defectors fell under the new Department XXI. On its behalf, a former colleague of Glaser, codenamed 'Busch', turned up in Heilbronn and made contact with him. Although Glaser should have known better, he trusted 'Busch' as he had 'Bär', believing him to be a fellow defector in fear of his life. Presumably, the solace of having a friend in a similar predicament tended to override any caution. It took time, but Glaser was finally kidnapped, violently, in May 1962, probably by Hans Wax, 'Teddy' and 'Busch'. He spent ten years in an East German prison.

'Neuhaus' had always taken his job as a kidnapper seriously. In 1958 he had requested training in firearms and unarmed combat, the use of knockout drugs and explosive devices, and in techniques of surveillance, arrest and interrogation. His later kidnappings were earning him bonuses of 7,000 (GDR) marks, on top of his monthly expenses – by 1962 he had earned around 50,000 marks. Ultimately he was employed as a full-time collaborator by Department XXI. But the market for kidnapping waned. Reportedly, 'Neuhaus' constantly badgered superiors for the chance to snatch suspects again. He was denied. In 1965 Josef Kiefel, head of Department XXI, explained regretfully to 'Neuhaus' that 'today we can no longer use such working methods as we had to use 10

---

* 'Sollten irgendwelche ernste Komplikationen eintreten, so wird eine aktive Massnahme durchgefuhrt und alle Spuren beseitigt, hieruber erhalten die GMs mundliche Hinweise.'

years ago, 8 years, sometimes even 6 years ago, because they were partly forced on us by the enemy.'[20]

The kidnappings of Manfred Smolka, Heinz Brandt and Alfred Glaser were acts of vengeance towards traitors from within the ranks. They were intended to demonstrate the might of the SED and the creepy reach of the Stasi; to dissuade other would-be defectors; to silence criticism and prevent the spread of secret information; to land blows on hated enemies such as the SPD Ostbüro and US intelligence; and to prompt public admissions of regret from their victims. Underlying these motives was the one essential problem: the ability of East Germans to flee to West Germany.

Once the Berlin Wall existed, Stasi kidnappings petered out. They were harder to carry out and there was less need for them. Unlike in the time of Manfred Smolka, the SED regime no longer had to send out the message that runaways were not to make contact with Western intelligence services, for there were hardly any runaways. Along with Glaser, the last known abductions were of rare defectors: Gerd Sommerlatte of the border police, Walter Thräne of the Stasi, the latter kidnapped not in West Germany but in the mountains of Austria. After the Wall, it was safer for members of the East German security forces, just like their civilian compatriots, to come to some kind of accommodation with the regime, and stay put.

68

'The Anti-fascist Protective Barrier'

By the time the Berlin borders were sealed, an estimated three and a half million people had left the east for western Germany.[1] From January to August 1961, 160,000 East Germans registered in West Berlin. At the same time, Nikita Khrushchev realised his armed forces were considerably weaker than his ultimatums; Walter Ulbricht and other SED officials were envisaging a pitiful end to the party's rule; and much of the Stasi's resources were tied up by problems connected with East Germany's porous borders.

Only about twenty of the GDR's top executives knew about the imminence of the Wall. Markus Wolf was later to claim that he and other Stasi high-ups had no idea about it. Those who did included Willi Stoph, deputy chair of the Council of Ministers, Paul Verner, SED first secretary for Berlin, and Alois Pisnik, first secretary for Magdeburg. However, the Western authorities were forewarned by an agent of the SPD Ostbüro. This person had attended a meeting at the East German Ministry of Health, where the border closure had been discussed. The Ostbüro reported the information to Western intelligence services, including the BND; Reinhard Gehlen personally informed the Federal government in Bonn. The BND believed in the possibility of a sealed-off Berlin. The CIA, while preparing for it, did not.[2]

It was the BND who called it right. On the night of 12-13 August 1961, 40,000 NVA soldiers sealed the borders through and around West Berlin, initially using barbed wire. They were backed up by two divisions of the Soviet army, positioned a short distance away. In the event there was relatively little violence. One person was shot – ironically an SED official who failed to respond to shouted warnings – and a young West Berliner was bayonetted to stop him assaulting a Volkspolizei officer, although he survived the stabbing.[3] The 'anti-fascist protective barrier' was a reality.

It came too late to stop the flight of the 2,400 refugees who entered West Berlin the previous day,[4] but quickly enough to block the 1,500 who were held back as the wire was unfurled. In general, Stasi personnel weren't called upon. It was the army, the police, and even the citizen soldiers of the KdA who did the heavy lifting: sealing transport routes, laying barriers, securing locations, and dispersing demonstrators. The deployment of the KdA's part-time paramilitaries, as well as suggesting that ordinary East Germans approved the Wall, may have helped to dissuade the Western powers from responding with force.

As soon as the wire was unfurled, the SED publicly announced the barrier's purpose: to stave off imminent attack by NATO forces and to prevent foreign agents from entering the country. Some of the party and Stasi leaderships were probably convinced of these threats; others probably weren't. Either way, as a declaration by the Council of Ministers put it: 'To prevent enemy activity by the Revanchist and militarist forces of West Germany and West Berlin, controls will be established along the borders of the German Democratic Republic, including the border to the Western sectors of Greater Berlin, as is customary for sovereign states.'[5]

Quickly the CIA estimated that the number of crossing points into West Berlin had been reduced from eighty-seven to thirteen, then to seven.[6] Telephone and telex services were interrupted. In East Berlin there was a run on banks and shops, as well as 'a very lively fear of imminent war'.[7] West Berliners reacted with fury. Thousands spilled onto the streets, protesting not just the barbed wire but the lack of Western response. Some balloons had been released, with anti-SED slogans on them; some loudspeaker vans had yelled disapproval; the US secretary of state Dean Rusk had declared that America was protesting through 'appropriate channels'; and the Stasi alleged that a smoke bomb had been thrown towards the Brandenburg Gate by the crew of a British armoured car.[8] But none of this was likely to impede the final division of Europe.

The powers were distracted by arguments over the Berlin air corridors, which since 1945 had been supervised jointly by Soviet and Western personnel at the Berlin Air Safety Centre: for a while, the Soviets were intent on closing the corridors to commercial airlines. Everywhere else one looked, problem compounded problem, tension fed tension. Khrushchev continued to threaten the signing of a new peace treaty and the consequent expulsion of the Western powers from Berlin. HVA spies in the West Berlin senate reported that the Western powers had no intention of leaving. HVA spies in Bonn reported total confusion among Federal political parties. Armed patrolling increased along every Western border with the GDR. President Kennedy signed a memorandum increasing the size of conventional armed forces based in Europe. And all the while, the SED basked in triumph. The party had sealed off Europe's problem city, and the West had done nothing to stop it. Erich Mielke compiled a scrapbook of his favourite photographs of the Wall being laid. He treasured the book for the rest of his life.

*

Autumn 1961 was a confusing time in East Germany, a period marked by both aggressive consolidation and disarming retreat on the part of the SED regime. For some historians, 'the half year after the Wall was built was one of the most repressive phases in the entire history of the GDR'.[9] 'Throughout the East Zone,' read a CIA report, 'the impression gained from letters, covert sources, and the observations of U.S. Military Mission personnel is one of depression approaching despair. The Military Mission officers report that streets are almost deserted by day and night.'[10] The Stasi arrested many citizens who protested the border closure. It also took the opportunity to seize other suspects who previously had been spared in order to prevent unrest or flight. By 4 September – just three weeks after the borders were sealed – the Stasi and Volkspolizei had made more than 6,000 arrests between them. By the end of the year more than 18,000 people had been sentenced for crimes against the state, including attempted flight.[11]

On 15 September the border police, many of whom remained ill-disciplined and unmotivated, were upgraded to Border Troops (Grenztruppen der DDR) under the Ministry of National Defence. The Stasi's Main Department I continued to invigilate their security. Henceforth, border-crossers would be tackled by trained soldiers primed to pull the trigger. Five days later the Volkskammer passed the Law for the Defence of the GDR, which established the National Defence Council,* thereafter tasked with organising East Germany's defence during a crisis or war. Its membership consisted of Erich Mielke, the chairman of the Council of Ministers (i.e., the head of government – Walter Ulbricht), several Politbüro members, the ministers of defence and the interior, the head of the Central Committee security secretariat (Erich Honecker), and several regional party secretaries. The Council was replicated in the form of a committee in every region and district, and enjoyed a committed membership; once or twice a year it would hold exercises based on dummy emergencies, with its members wearing full uniform and thoroughly inhabiting the roleplay.

The Stasi was tasked with some resettlement duties. Thirty thousand East Berliners who had previously travelled daily to jobs in West Berlin were dispersed around the country and given other work. There was another round of deportations from the border areas in Aktion Festigung (Operation Consolidation). Police, party activists and removal gangs would arrive in each location, hold a meeting to announce the procedure, and begin. In each district they were accompanied by a Stasi team: four operational employees, two administrators and a car. These teams observed the loading and departure of trucks, filming everything in case disputes arose over compensation. And in a

---

* Nationale Verteidigungsrat der DDR.

demonstration of its staggering local knowledge, at the planning stage the Stasi assigned a multitude of named collaborators to keep a similar number of named deportees 'under control' once the clearances started. These collaborators were expected to 'exert active influence to educate the inhabitants [and] prevent panic and escapes'.

Although the Volkspolizei had to tackle some public disorder – in one village an SED agitator was threatened with an axe – the mood during Consolidation was more depressed than angry. About 3,000 people were resettled. Not untypically, the Stasi office in Suhl reported three suicide attempts among deportees. It also reported some approval for the operation among remaining residents, as the deportations were seen to affect 'citizens who did not appeal to the majority of the population'. As well as common criminals, this was a reference to people convicted of anti-state crimes, who were regarded by some of their fellow citizens as troublemakers jeopardising peace, both in the community and in Germany at large.

These resettlements were not conducted with the savagery of their Soviet precursors. The same report from Suhl gave reasons why some of those on the Stasi's lists were not deported as planned. A few of these decisions evince the closest thing to kindness to be found in any Stasi document:

– The person is a good craftsman, there are no negative facts against him.
– The wife is heavily pregnant and about to give birth.
– The person was negatively influenced by his father-in-law, who has since died. Since his death, he has been actively involved in the amalgamation of the 2 existing LPGs in his place of residence. He also has a positive effect on social life in other ways.
– The person is 75% disabled and has to look after school-age children because the wife has been in hospital for a long time.
– The person has 4 children, is seriously mentally ill, does a good job at the communal restaurant.
– The person in question is the chairman of the LPG. In recent times he has considerably improved his work, so that his resettlement would not be understood by the population.[12]

It isn't clear whether these lenient decisions were made by individuals in the local Stasi or were part of a broader policy. Perhaps bribes were involved. Either way they are important, because they show the Stasi taking care around repression, mindful of its image and that of the SED and government. It should be noted, however, that rather more people avoided deportation because they were already in custody or had fled the GDR.

As usual, such stern measures as Aktion Festigung were accompanied by an apparent official softening. Public opinion was recognised, just slightly, with the renaming of Stalinstadt as Eisenhüttenstadt, and Stalinallee as Karl-Marx-Allee. In October Nikita Khrushchev calmed nerves when he withdrew his tanks from the famous stand-off of armoured vehicles at the Friedrichstrasse crossing point in Berlin, soon to be world famous as Checkpoint Charlie. It is possible that Khrushchev's decision to back down was influenced by GRU spying. At the time, he and a few close colleagues were informed of the number of US nuclear submarines operating in the Norwegian Sea, and of Strategic Bomber Command aircraft stationed in Europe; they even knew the exact number that were airborne at any moment.[13] Given that the Soviet use of satellites and airborne reconnaissance was relatively undeveloped, this information likely came from on-the-spot observers.

With the borders closed there was something of a playground atmosphere in the behaviour of Walter Ulbricht and his associates, as if they could now do what they wanted with whomever they chose. The state could assert itself. Hilde Benjamin, minister of justice, urged a new hard line on the judiciary: 'Crimes such as hate speech, defamation of the state, speculation, hooliganism, resistance against state authority, and attempted human trafficking' – i.e., assisting refugees – were to be punished even more severely, especially 'if committed by provocateurs, loafers... smugglers, criminals'.[14]

This steely new mood manifested at the Stasi in, for instance, a new Main Department V work plan directed at the churches, whose flocks were now fenced inside East Germany. The plan called for the 'systematic and continuous compromise of political-clerical forces through the development of verified documentation' – in other words, spreading dirt about disloyal clerics based on firm evidence, much of it to be culled from the old Nazi archives. The 'decomposition of the reactionary centres of political-clerical forces' was to continue 'through increased recruitment and penetration'. To create 'a loyal, Bonn-free church', the department's efforts were to 'achieve a separation of [GDR] churches from the reactionary pan-German church bodies located in West Germany and West Berlin'. And there was to be 'monitoring and assessment' of a range of international religious events, including the meeting of the World Council of Churches in New Delhi.[15]

The Stasi made stupendous efforts to determine how East Germans felt about their newly sealed borders. Exceptionally detailed mood reports came in from even the smallest rural districts. Much approval was reported; a consensus among regime loyalists that it had been high time for such a measure.[16]

Conversely, the Stasi had to deal with newly organised resistance. In November 1961 it recorded activity by twenty-three Wall-related groups. The introduction of national service – five years after West Germany – and a campaign to recruit more young soldiers and police officers, which was judged by the CIA to be a fig leaf for a simple crackdown on youth,[17] caused yet more resentment. But youths who reacted with mockery or unruliness were walking a tightrope. Youth crime was now firmly regarded as a political matter, and convictions of young people for anti-state offences, especially 'seditious agitation', increased sharply. One provincial youth who scattered leaflets headed 'Think about Berlin', in which he advised fellow citizens not to vote in the next election, was imprisoned for almost a year and a half.[18] According to Erich Mielke, the spike in such activity was caused by the desperation of 'enemies' who, now unable to leave the GDR, were venting their pathetic fury inside it.[19]

The construction of the Wall coincided with a shift within the Stasi. Its fight against political opposition began to grow subtler, more insidious. The analysts working under Robert Korb in the Central Information Group concerned themselves increasingly with signs of non-conformity in the public at large. This focus on wider society was underpinned by the key concept of 'political-ideological diversion' or PiD. Erich Mielke, in particular, began to pepper his writings with the term.

Mielke referred often to the events in Poland and Hungary. He believed these rebellions had occurred because ideological free-thinkers, who invariably were the tools of scheming Western governments, hadn't been identified and dealt with early enough by the authorities. Their ideas had thus spread over time and resulted in uprisings. Henceforth, differences of political opinion in East Germany – or even mere questions about policy among the more politically engaged citizens – were to be attributed, secretly but officially, to PiD. It cemented in official terms the notion that ideological disagreements or unenthusiasm were caused by the systematic influencing of enemy countries, always with a view to overthrowing the SED regime.

This tremendous overreaction to independent thought had welcome knock-on effects for the Stasi, greatly expanding the range of its tasks. This meant bigger budgets, a bigger workforce, and an even bigger say in the life of the GDR. In a directive back in February 1960,* the term PiD had for the first time been used in combination with 'underground activity', thus conflating citizens' thoughts with potential actions to subvert the state. In its way this directive had ushered in a new era, both for the Stasi and in the concept of government surveillance.

---

* 'Directive on improving defensive work against political-ideological diversion and underground activity' (Direktive zur Verbesserung der Abwehrarbeit gegen die politisch-ideologische Diversion und Untergrundtätigkeit).

The directive had been issued with attachments, including a new standard form for reporting graffiti and 'inflammatory letters'. The contents of graffiti were to be broken down into 'a) fascist content, b) anti-Semitic character, c) inflammatory slogans against the party and government' – another indication that real Nazi faith, or at least the fear of it, survived in East Germany. Telephoned threats to officials were singled out as a major problem. So was 'decomposition work' in agriculture, industry and officialdom, including 'passivity and neutrality in enforcing decisions and laws of the party'.

'Experience confirms,' ran the directive, 'that the enemy focuses on ideological diversion.' Stasi offices were now to report such activity every quarter, with attention given to 'Revisionism, social democratism [and] nationalist and fascist activities'. Likely culprits were 'groups of former SPD and excluded SED members, former fascists and officers, etc.' The directive ended with Mielke referring to previous cautions against 'the right-wing SPD leadership and Ostbüro'.[20] German communists of the 1930s had insulted social democrats as 'social fascists'. Mielke's Stasi appeared to consider social democratic and neo-Nazi opposition to be two sides of the same coin.

Another directive of the period urged Stasi personnel to 'process' people who 'represent an element of political uncertainty'.[21] This command, broad and vague and unrelated even to the suspicion of a crime, was in its way groundbreaking. It also required political judgement in Stasi officers; Mielke stressed that the personnel of the district information groups were to be 'experienced in political matters', with their own political loyalty an 'absolute given'.[22]

There wasn't much ideology behind the original purpose of Aktion Licht, however, one of the first major Stasi operations to be initiated after the advent of the Wall. With the help of collaborators working at banks and the Ministry of Finance, Stasi officers opened more than 10,000 safes and deposit boxes around the GDR. The action was quickly extended to searches of 'castles, manor houses, villas, and museums', as well as monasteries and what Erich Mielke called 'similar cultist places'.[23] The East German state thus acquired the money and valuables of people known to have fled to the West, to the tune of four million marks. Jewellery, stamps and paintings were sold on the world market; precious metals were added to the GDR's stocks.[24] And Aktion Licht had an unforeseen benefit for the Stasi. The operation unearthed yet more documents confirming the Nazi past of refugees who were now doing very well in West Germany.

The first post-Wall elections held in East Germany were those for local councils in September 1961. Predictably, Stasi officers found plenty of room in their reports to mention that 'the measures of 13 August' contributed to a smooth and successful election. Also useful, they said, was Operation Oxhead (Aktion Ochsenkopf), a state campaign that encouraged citizens to prevent their television sets receiving Western broadcasts. Named after a West German transmitter beaming programmes into the GDR, the operation saw brawling between disgruntled viewers and the Free German Youth activists who were clambering over their homes to remove antennae.

There was widespread apathy for this election.[25] Public events around it were thinly attended. According to the Stasi's reports, the most common demands expressed at meetings included 'Approval of trips to the West and trips to capitalist foreign countries (mainly from representatives of the intelligentsia and the medical profession)'; 'Provision of cars, refrigerators, television sets (particularly among LPG farmers)'; an improvement in 'the supply situation (housewives)'; and 'housing demands'. There was danger, said the Stasi, because 'in some cases the people who expressed such views accompanied them with a threat that they would not take part in the elections if their wishes were not fulfilled'.

Again, the point was made that a successful election didn't mean the state was safe:

> While the perpetrators [of] verbal hate speech are almost always known and the majority have been imprisoned, the majority of perpetrators of the offences of tearing down flags and posters, anonymous telephone calls, and written hate speech could not be identified. When it comes to crimes of hate speech, there is a relatively high incidence of agitation to murder and threats to citizens who are politically active. The level of danger to society has increased.

On the other hand, the Stasi believed that spoiled ballots didn't necessarily mean disloyalty to the regime, for further investigation sometimes revealed that candidates had been rejected for 'sectarian behaviour, arrogance, inactivity, immoral lifestyle and former activity in Nazi organisations'. It also claimed that church ministers, and former landowners and social democrats, were the most likely to agitate against the elections, not forgetting 'old fascists' who were committing 'their crimes based on this still existing ideology'. However, the statistics for incarcerations tell a somewhat different story.

According to the Stasi's records, in August and September 1961 'a total of 130 people were imprisoned by the organs of the Ministry for State Security' for 'criminal acts directed against the preparation and implementation of the elections'. They were broken down by:

Assaults against candidates and election workers – 9

Incitement against candidates – 12

Incitement during election meetings – 6

Daubing inflammatory anti-election slogans – 11

Distributing inflammatory anti-election leaflets – 4

Tearing down flags at polling stations – 2

Damage to election posters – 11

Calling for non-participation in the election – 2

Demanding so-called free elections – 17

Incitement against the Chairman of the State Council of the GDR [Walter Ulbricht] in connection with the elections – 22

Incitement against the elections during work meetings and among work colleagues – 14

Preparation of inflammatory writings based on reports from Western radio stations – 8

Incitement against the elections in pubs and eateries – 12

The largest group, then, was those who had criticised Walter Ulbricht – 'Goatee and Glasses', as he was known. It was also recorded that 'the majority of those imprisoned are workers, while a smaller proportion are made up of cooperative farmers, [state] employees and self-employed traders.' Not former landowners, then. Moreover, most of them were young: 'Around 40% of the perpetrators are between the ages of 18 and 25.'

By the spring of 1962, the cyclical nature of authoritarian state campaigns – the policy pendulum that swings between repression and reward – was showing itself once again. Having built the Wall and locked in its own population, and cracked down hard on dissenting voices, it was incumbent upon the SED to establish some form of renewed contract, in good faith, with East Germany's citizens. If the party were forcing people to stay, then staying had to be made worthwhile.

A new economic policy – yet another – incentivised the production of consumer goods. The number of arrests suddenly plummeted. A decision of the State Council – i.e., Walter Ulbricht – required 'all-round clarification' and the 'exact determination' of facts in every criminal proceeding, especially when young people were involved. There were official calls for the greater use of 'conditional sentences', and for 'public censure' to be preferred over criminal conviction. The issuing of arrest warrants was to be scrutinised more fully, to determine 'whether the suspicion of absconding or the risk of collusion was specifically justified'.[26] The attorney general was given more powers to govern all judicial activity, a move that restricted some of the legal autonomy the Stasi had enjoyed throughout the previous decade.

It is possible that these relatively liberalising moves by Ulbricht were influenced by incidental information he picked up from Stasi reports. The extent to which Stasi officers reported political grievances varied. As has been seen, much bad news was likely filtered out by Erich Mielke when reporting to the SED's high-ups. Nevertheless, some Stasi investigators chose to give detailed breakdowns of political complaints in their reports. An example can be found in the case of Karl Block, a film actor and radio announcer who had been arrested back in June 1960.[27]

Block belonged to a social and professional circle of pre-war anti-fascists, most of whom had met while incarcerated by the Nazis at Sachsenhausen. Many of his friends plied their trade in the GDR's state-run arts scene: actors, singers, musicians. As officially recognised victims of fascism, they received quite generous pensions and were fast-tracked into decent careers; Block won acting parts in some twenty DEFA films. But, typically for all those who wandered into the Stasi's sights, Block and his friends, having fallen under suspicion, were woven into a conspiracy, one that was part of the fallout from the disgracing of Ulbricht's rival, Karl Schirdewan.

Although Block's circle belonged to an esteemed social group in this supposedly anti-fascist state – former concentration camp inmates – the Stasi's initial investigations discovered much that was undesirable about them. Block was friendly with Karl Raddatz, whose social democratic tendencies had already seen him ousted from his job as head of the Association of Victims of the Nazi Regime. The investigation now cast Raddatz as a troublemaker. A Stasi informer, the GM 'Marianne' – Karl Block's live-in partner, with whom he was apparently besotted – reported a comment made by Raddatz that former camp inmates in East Germany were 'reproached' and 'seen as traitors' if they had managed to survive twelve years of incarceration. The Stasi also believed another of Block's acquaintances to be unentitled to his pension, since he had been in a camp for 'criminal offences' rather than anti-fascist idealism. Block had connections with dissidents who had escaped East Germany, such as the kidnap victim Heinz Brandt. Equally suspect was his friendship with West German communists – unknown quantities like an 'old comrade' living in Düsseldorf. Even worse was Block's acquaintance with Walter Schönwetter, who had absconded from the GDR on a medical visit to Norway in 1958. Although more than one 'imperialist secret service' was cited in the Stasi's investigation – some of the suspects were said to be linked with the BND and UfJ – Schönwetter, as a known CIA agent, was deemed the worst spy of all.

Under interrogation Block admitted passing social and political information to Schönwetter, and tipping him off to potential recruits.

The upshot of all this dot-joining was the trial and imprisonment of three of those named in the investigation – Heinz Brandt, Karl Raddatz and Wilhelm Fickenscher. Among other sins, they were viewed as acolytes of the deposed Karl Schirdewan. Walter Ulbricht's eye would certainly have been drawn to the case by its mentions of the hated Schirdewan, who was said to have influenced the opposition programme expounded by Block and his associates. According to the Stasi report writers, they sought the 'replacement of comrade Walter Ulbricht as first secretary of our party'; the 'reversal of the socialist transformation of agriculture'; 'a moderate pause in building socialism'; the excusal 'of the intelligentsia from socio-political work'; 'greater freedoms in the fields of cultural policy and science'; as well as stronger trade with West Germany and the return of some privately owned business. It is striking that in the following years, Ulbricht was to meet several of these demands.

Block's case shows the Stasi's cynicism when it came to suspects who had been in concentration camps. Block's group was said to 'rely on the organisational connections [of] those persecuted by the Nazi regime' for its subversive work, as 'these people have a certain sympathy among the population'. Ill with cancer, and traumatised by his arrest and incarceration at Hohenschönhausen, on 23 May 1962 Block seized upon the casualness of his Stasi guards and threw himself from a window of the Potsdam district court. He died on the way to hospital.

Whatever Ulbricht's attempts at reform, the Berlin Wall proved a bloody creation. When they came, the first deaths at the Wall caused a shock and dismay that resonate in Germany to this day. Crossing the borders had been a potentially deadly activity long before 1961; sixteen people had already been killed trying to escape into West Berlin, and 100 had died along the inter-German frontiers.[28] Nine days after it was erected, the anti-fascist barrier cost its first human life: Ida Siekmann accidentally fell from the window of her apartment on Bernauer Strasse while trying to get out of East Berlin. The next day, transport police shot dead Günter Litfin, a twenty-four-year-old Christian, as he tried to escape across the Spree; after his death, East German newspapers smeared him as a reprobate homosexual with the nickname 'Doll'.[29] On 29 August Roland Hoff tried to swim across the borderline on the Teltow canal, and was fatally wounded by gunfire.[30] The following year, the killing of Peter Fechter, an eighteen-year-old bricklayer who bled to death in the frontier no-man's-land after being shot by border guards, caused a public disgust that remains raw to this day; his death was witnessed by hundreds of spectators and extensively photographed. Earlier, in October 1961, there had been similar outrage at the death of journalist Kurt Lichtenstein, shot near Wolfsburg while on a press trip along the inter-German border. His killing was suspect in more ways than one.

Lichtenstein was another apostate from communism who had thrown in his lot with the social democrats. In his younger life he had been a KPD member and impeccable revolutionary. In 1933 he had fled to the Soviet Union, where he underwent political education before being sent to the Saarland as an underground agitator. He went on to organise communist youth groups in Paris. During the Spanish Civil War he served as a political commissar in the International Brigades and was wounded at the Battle of the Ebro. Having been interned in France in 1939, Lichtenstein was judged to be in danger of arrest by the Gestapo, and the KPD ordered him to escape the internment camp and join the French resistance in Toulouse. He accomplished this feat unquestioningly. In 1944, again on the party's orders, he volunteered to be a foreign labourer in the Reich. He worked under a false name in an armaments factory, explaining his knowledge of the German language by claiming he had lived with grandparents at Strasbourg as a child. Meanwhile, his parents and sister disappeared; they almost certainly died at Auschwitz.

Lichtenstein resumed his communist activities in western Germany after the war, but suspicions about 'western émigrés', and his association with the disgraced KPD leader Kurt Müller, saw him slip ever further from grace. In 1953 he was expelled from the communist party; by 1958 he was an SPD member.

Lichtenstein died on his press assignment when he crossed some border obstacles to reach East German soil, in the hope of talking with a group of workers from the local collective farm. He was hailed by GDR border guards and started running back towards West German ground, but was mortally wounded by fire from their submachine guns. Reportedly, his body fell precisely across the border between the two Germanys. He was carried into the GDR, but endured a long delay before receiving any medical treatment.

In the days before Lichtenstein had arrived in the area, the Stasi had told local border guards to watch out for 'provocations' involving work gangs. The inference is that Lichtenstein – who was known and disliked personally by Mielke and Honecker – was enticed by the work gang to move towards them, thus becoming fair game for the guns of the forewarned border guards. To be successful, this frame-up would have needed ongoing observation and knowledge of Lichtenstein's planned movements, the reporting of his location in real time, and astute forward planning, some of it involving the farm labourers.

All of this was well within the Stasi's capabilities. Lichtenstein's death became yet another passing Cold War cause célèbre. In the West his killing was decried as Soviet-inspired savagery. In East Germany he was scorned as a provocateur and traitor.

By December 1961 most of the barbed wire on the Berlin borders had been augmented or superseded by concrete barriers. Attempts to breach the Wall began. There were tunnels, and vehicles fitted with secret compartments; less subtly, there were cases of reinforced trucks being driven straight at the barriers. Some East Germans tried to fake the uniforms of British, French or American soldiers, who at border crossings were required to present themselves to Soviet military personnel but not to GDR border guards. Other escapees posed as Soviet officers. Successful crossings were made in a homemade hot air balloon, in a miniature submarine in the river Spree, on a high-wire pulley powered by a car on the western side. Markus Wolf enjoyed telling a story about a Spree pleasure boat, upon which the ship's cook and his family got the captain drunk and made him chug into the Neukölln sector of West Berlin, where they waded ashore.[31] Among the most dramatic escape efforts were attempted hijackings of aircraft departing from East Germany. By 1972 the Stasi had prevented fifty-four such attempts.[32]

Less spectacular, but still nervy, was the use of genuine West German passports by GDR citizens, especially at the border with Czechoslovakia or when holidaying in Hungary or Bulgaria.[33] It took a while for the authorities to realise that escapees were using the ferry route from Sassnitz on the island of Rügen to Trelleborg in Sweden. Other departures were impossible to miss. In December 1961 a passenger train smashed through the barriers at Albrechtshof station and thus entered the West Berlin district of Spandau. Its driver and thirty passengers chose to stay; twenty other passengers walked back to East Berlin along the railway line.[34]

It has been written that the Berlin Wall 'inaugurated a greater period both of international stability as far as central Europe was concerned (the attentions of the superpowers turning elsewhere) and of domestic stability in the GDR'.[35] This is no consolation for the 140 people who would lose their lives at the Wall before it was smashed down in November 1989. It is notable that reconnaissance and intelligence-gathering along the western frontiers was entrusted to the Stasi and not to the border troops. These tasks were carried out by Main Department I in the form of three Reconnaissance Border Detachments – North, Central, and South. Some 900 people were killed trying to cross the inter-German borders, and more than 1,000 were seriously injured; 175 drowned while trying to swim or navigate the Baltic Sea.[36] It is also claimed that thirteen would-be escapers committed suicide in the face of capture or prosecution, and that accidental shootings by border troops, or detonations of explosive devices, led to a further 300 deaths in the border areas.[37]

Willy Brandt, mayor of West Berlin in 1961, was determined to see the deaths of wall-crossers recorded officially. To this end, the Central Registry for Political Crimes was set up at Salzgitter in Lower Saxony. When prosecuting members of the GDR's National Defence Council in the early 1990s, this agency alleged that there had been 4,400 actual or attempted killings by the East German state over the course of its history.

69

Spies, Still

Once the Wall was up it was much harder for the West to send spies or sponsor underground groups in the GDR. The stream of refugees from East Germany, which had brought the West new recruits or tip-offs about suitable contacts, was stemmed. No longer could GDR citizens take short trips into West Berlin, where their potential as an agent might be spotted, even in a visit of just a few hours; for the Western services had always been on the lookout for assets, just as the Stasi had been. All that was finished.

The CIA tried to put on a brave face. 'It has been a source of tremendous satisfaction,' read a Berlin Operations Base report, 'that we have been able to continue to maintain contact with more than 25 of our agent assets via previously established alternate communications channels.' The report praised the 'foresight and professional skill' of case officers who had already set up 'two way communications', which 'while slow (and a scant substitute for personal meetings) have permitted us to maintain intelligence collection activities'.[1] Nevertheless, by the time the Wall was a year old, the Berlin Operations Base had renewed contact with just thirty of its 100-plus agents in the GDR.[2] Partly because of advances in technological spying – the Americans' first successful use of a Corona spy satellite had occurred in summer 1960 – the CIA began to focus more on its tangential, 'cultural' activities, like aiming propaganda at East German border guards to dissuade them from shooting border-crossers.

Some of Denmark's spies in East Germany were able to continue their activity, having been provided with radios in 1959.[3] But when it came to making new recruitments, the remaining options for all Western intelligence services were to use West Germans to recruit friends, relatives or acquaintances inside the GDR, or to make use of West Germans who were allowed to go there, like students or professionals working in industry or the media. Partly as a result, the BND emerged during the 1960s as the biggest Western espionage presence in East Germany. Another possibility was to recruit spies from among the Reisekader, the clique of East German citizens able to travel abroad: diplomats, sportspeople, academics. That wasn't easy. Stasi vetting was so stringent that many travellers were unrecruitable. Moreover, their families in the GDR were vulnerable and could be used as insurance.[4]

The Wall expedited communist counter-espionage. Dead drops had to be serviced on East German territory rather than in West Berlin, making them easier to spot and observe. With no personal access to their case officers in the West, agents made greater use of radio transmissions and secret writing. Confounding the 'spy tech' image of the Cold War, secret ink became the prime means of communication, with messages concealed in letters and postcards, or within the pages of magazines. The Stasi's Department M, its postal interception branch, thus grew in size and importance. It has been said that the Stasi now began to reap the full benefits of its 'immense surveillance capability'. In theory, it could scrutinise everyone entering or leaving the GDR, use its growing informer networks to report on attempted recruitments, and employ its growing radio detection facilities to intercept transmissions.[5]

With remarkable stupidity, the BND habitually posted parcels containing communications equipment, money and instructions to its spies in East Germany until at least 1963. The Stasi intercepted many such parcels and made the consequent arrests. By this time, postcodes had been introduced in West Germany, making it easier to monitor postal traffic. Together with Main Department II (counter-espionage), Department M identified places in the Federal Republic where there were concentrations of cover addresses used by intelligence services.[6] Counter-espionage penetrations continued to account for Western spies too. Just one example is provided by the head of the Berlin network of the DST, France's domestic security service, who was somehow pressured into working for the Stasi.[7]

In 1962 the Berlin branch of Main Department IX investigated more than double the number of alleged spies and couriers than it had the previous year. In 1963 the increase was seven-fold compared to 1961; in 1964 it was four-fold. Many of these arrests were enabled by information that had originated from Heinz Felfe and Hans Clemens, KGB moles inside the BND. Clemens, recruited by the Soviets as agent 'Khanni' in 1950 'for material reward', at a time when he was merely an unemployed former SS captain, had in fact recruited Felfe, his biggest success.[8] Felfe, the KGB's agent 'Kurt', was arrested late in 1961 after spending years delivering an average of 'twelve rolls of Minox film per month'.[9] His imprisonment in West Germany freed the Stasi from concerns about exposing him, enabling arrests to be made. Despite the excellence of Felfe's information, however, Paul Maddrell argues that the BND 'lost most of its spies in East Germany owing to the construction of the Berlin Wall'.

Using HA IX summaries, Maddrell gives a breakdown of the 258 'important cases' of spies arrested from August 1961 to December 1965: 156 (sixty percent) were 'agents' of the BND, fifty-four (twenty-one percent) the United States, twenty-seven (ten percent) the BfV, and twenty (eight percent) of France. Just one spy for Britain was arrested, a retired railway worker codenamed 'Paul' who was probably reporting to the army's Berlin Intelligence Staff. This was not because the British were dazzlingly successful at concealing spies, but rather that, by this time, they were simply letting the BND get on with it.[10] Arguably for the first time in its history, the Stasi was now effectively defending the East German state against espionage and subversion. It could rely on much institutional help. By this point, around 2,000 of the GDR's 6,000 police detectives were accredited to work on spy cases.[11]

In its first reports on the effects of the Wall, the Stasi surveyed the landscape of Western espionage. It was noted that France's Sûreté Nationale, still active in Berlin from a headquarters on Müllerstrasse, 'uses violence in interrogations', which was no great surprise.[12] The Americans, it was said, were making increasing use of lie detectors in debriefings, and false flag recruitments in which they would pose as the BfV. Agents of the US in East Germany now had tape recorders which could play their radio messages at ten times the normal speed; miniature cameras 'built into glasses case, wristwatch, cigarette lighter, and fountain pen'; bugging devices, 'attached to tape recorders which run for 24 hours', which were installed at telephone exchanges and 'in chandeliers and pocket torches'; and these same agents were concealing 'technical devices, codes, and instructions' inside 'cans of beef, tins of paint, bars of chocolate, accordions, vacuum cleaners'. The BND's favourite secret containers were said to be 'cars and toy railway sets'. All of these concealments meant that the Stasi's technical branch, named Department K at this point, was to make better use of 'quartz lamp, magnets [and] X-rays' for searching objects. But the BND, it was noted, could still observe Berlin traditions. More focused on the Stasi than were the other Western services, it was 'spying on officers of MfS by means of… bar visits, drinking bouts, and suchlike'. For their part, the British were said to have ruled out clandestine 'meetings in bars'; the newest alternative was to meet agents in lorries 'with perfectly installed meeting rooms' that 'drive around Berlin'.

Yet in a typical Cold War lose-lose, the Wall helped Western counter-espionage too. According to Markus Wolf, for Western spy-catchers:

> the sealed border was an unexpected boon because it filtered out large numbers of ordinary people and allowed allied [sic] counterintelligence to concentrate its resources on the much smaller number of citizens now allowed to cross, usually

on some form of state business, such as trade officials, approved academics, and ordinary citizens occasionally given permission to cross on urgent family business.[13]

HVA agents needed new identity papers to cross the borders, and tricky cover stories had to be invented to satisfy the West German border guards as to why these particular East Germans were allowed to leave the GDR. Like their Western counterparts, Soviet Bloc agencies were now less able to get spies through or maintain safe contact with them. This was despite the maintenance of secluded 'border locks' on the inter-German frontiers, where agents and equipment could be smuggled.

Much of the Soviet Bloc's desired penetration had already been achieved, however. For instance, in July 1961 the KGB was able to report to Nikita Khrushchev on the NATO council meeting held in Oslo, and on side meetings where the foreign ministers of the US, Britain, France and West Germany had discussed the Berlin crisis. In the words of KGB chairman Alexander Shelepin, such information came from an abundance of highly placed sources 'employed in the foreign ministries, general staffs, and other government agencies of the Western powers as well as the NATO structure'.[14]

Just one of the NATO sources enjoyed by the Soviets was Hugh Hambleton, a British-Canadian who had studied at the Sorbonne and begun his NATO career in its economics directorate. In another instance, Jack Dunlap, a staff sergeant at America's SIGINT agency, the NSA, who was recruited in 1960 and run by the GRU, was:

> able to provide instruction books, repair manuals, mathematical models and design plans for the United States' most secret cipher machines. He also had access to CIA estimates on Soviet forces and missiles in Eastern Europe, especially the German Democratic Republic.[15]

Moreover, the KGB's penetrations of North America in the 1960s were often effected by spies who had entered the West as refugees before the Wall went up, having adopted bogus German identities – either from dead people or from 'live doubles' who had been paid or blackmailed into giving their documents and life story to the KGB. This was the case with agents 'Konov' ('Gerhard Max Kohler'), 'Douglas' ('Rudolf Albert Hermann'), 'Bogun' ('Peter Carl Fisher') and 'Rybakov' ('Heinz Feder').[16]

One Stasi department to suffer notably from the closed borders was Main Department III, responsible for securing the economy. In 1960 a state campaign called 'Freeing from Interference' (Störfreimachung) had been devised, which aimed to end the GDR's dependence on buying goods and materials from the Federal Republic. It required an expansion of HA III's agent networks inside West German businesses – a move that had already been called for, without much success, in 1955 and 1957. Hampered by its underqualified staff and problems with recruiting sources in West Germany, the only thing HA III could do was cobble together an unhelpful report on the tremendous difficulties of 'freeing from interference', which it presented to the newly formed Economic Council of the GDR.[17]

The practice of kidnapping declined. Although in the following decades there were some abductions of defectors, 'escape helpers' and errant athletes, the Wall increased the SED regime's sense of security and limited the possible damage caused by Western propaganda, for East Germans could no longer react to it in any meaningful way. Some of the Stasi's arch-kidnappers, like the personnel of Main Department VIII (observations), now concentrated on surveillance of 'hostile-negative persons' inside the GDR, where 'political-ideological diversion' was fast becoming the chief concern. HA VIII also observed the new borders. In December 1961 a communication from Major General Bruno Beater hailed 'changes in the defensive work' of the Stasi, with the setting up of observation posts and mobile surveillance squads along the length of the Berlin Wall. Personnel of HA VIII were deployed together with the Volkspolizei on every access road to West Berlin, and covert watching posts were established at all border crossings. This meant an increase in the number of employees, who arrived at HA VIII in the person of trusted young SED and Free German Youth members recruited from the army, police, and other state agencies.[18]

As kidnapping declined, ransoming increased. One of the most lucrative cases was said to be that of Count Benedikt von Hoensbroech, scion of a Dutch-German aristocratic family who became stranded in East Berlin when the borders were being sealed, and was subsequently arrested. Sniffing money, the Stasi helped to organise a ransom demand of 450,000 deutschmarks for Hoensbroech's return to western Europe. The Federal government paid 40,000 DM of this fee. So began the practice of selling humans, an activity that was to net the GDR billions of deutschmarks over the succeeding years.

70

Conclusions

'I love everyone.'

Erich Mielke to the Volkskammer, 13 November 1989[1]

From the building of the Berlin Wall onwards, the Stasi story is one of steady expansion. Now that a concrete border was taking care of some problems around *Republikflucht* and Western infiltration, the Stasi increasingly involved itself in activities that went far beyond acknowledged intelligence and security tasks. The Stasi wasn't weakened by the presence of the Wall; it was strengthened by it, doubling in size between 1972 and 1989.[2]

In the early 1960s Walter Ulbricht again attempted to lighten the mood in East Germany. His softening gestures were prompted partly by the anti-Stalin tone of the twenty-second congress of the Soviet communist party. The Stasi was fine with this relaxation; it saw the reforms of Ulbricht's New Economic System as 'an opportunity for amplified activities in the national economy'.[3] Sure enough, after a few years of relative liberalisation the policy pendulum swung again, with the SED taking a decidedly authoritarian turn, signalled by the party's so-called 'Demolition Plenum' of 1965. Among other things, the party began to crack down on questioning voices – writers, artists and intellectuals.

Meanwhile some 'enemy' organisations disappeared of their own accord, like the CDU and FDP Ostbüros, which were wound down. In its turn, the Stasi started using subtler means to tackle state enemies. It increased its general surveillance of society and the amount of secret reports it delivered to the top SED executives. By the mid-1960s the Stasi had acquired responsibility for passport control, holidaymakers, Berlin's system of visitor passes, and youth affairs. It oversaw the training, and the doping, of sportspeople, and ran such sporting entities as Mielke's beloved Dynamo football club. It ran the Wandlitz Politbüro settlement, where the SED's high-ups lived. Its martial side found expression in a new guerrilla warfare section, in the growth of its Dzerzhinsky Guards Regiment, and in its ownership of intelligence and reconnaissance for the border troops. Its school at Potsdam was upgraded to award doctorates, generating thousands of earnest theses ground out by Stasi officers.

There was no repeat of June 1953: in the words of Mary Fulbrook, 'the East German police state became peculiarly efficient in diverting, controlling, and suppressing most spontaneous popular unrest.'[4] The Stasi's numbers helped. When the Berlin Wall went up, the Stasi had about 19,000 employees. By 1971 it had more than 45,000. By backing-up the unpopular policies of the SED, in operations that became a substitute for sensible political-economic governance, the Stasi certainly prolonged the existence of the GDR, almost certainly by decades.

The Stasi had to react to a series of international events: Czechoslovakia's Prague Spring, which led to tighter control of youth and political discourse in East Germany; the early 1970s détente between East and West Germany, which saw the GDR gain international recognition and immense funding from the Federal Republic; and the signing of the Helsinki Accords in 1975, which raised the expectation of ordinary East Germans that they would be treated fairly and allowed to travel. They were not. Instead, the Stasi refined its subtler means of oppressing, like its use of Zersetzung (demoralisation) tactics to sow doubt and division in the growing dissident movement.

Much of this work consisted of spreading rumours and opinions that would dissuade people from oppositional activity. Thus the Stasi's moles ideally were persuasive, articulate people who could influence others, for much of their job was to put forward arguments on behalf of the Stasi and SED. Frequently, Stasi orders required employees and collaborators to 'smear' people or organisations. As well as being a formidable information-gatherer, the Stasi became perhaps the world's leading smearer. In time, opposition and reform campaigns in the GDR crystalised around the churches, the peace movement, and youth sub-cultures. The Stasi had its grasses and persuaders in all of them.

Meanwhile, Markus Wolf's HVA got involved in the developing world. This trajectory was first hinted at in the late 1950s, when East German SIGINT experts had been deployed at listening posts in Morocco and Tunisia, in support of the Algerian rebellion against French colonial rule.[5] Subsequently the HVA helped the KGB to foster Soviet communism, and train security services, in such countries as Cuba, Mozambique, Angola and Ethiopia. Guerrilla fighters from Rhodesia, Namibia, South Africa and the Middle East were taught how to shoot rockets by Stasi instructors. The Stasi lent support to terrorists – Carlos the Jackal, Wadie Haddad, West Germany's murderous Red Army Faction – and came to regard the Irish Republican Army as an ideological partner.[6] At the same time, Wolf's spies stole ridiculous amounts of economic, scientific and technological information; not that it helped the East German economy as intended, for the GDR's dilapidated and under-resourced manufacturers were unable to make products to Western specifications. The

HVA attracted unwelcome publicity at the end of 1973 with the exposure of its spy Günter Guillaume, a crisis that forced the resignation of West German chancellor Willy Brandt. But its penetrations of Western agencies provide a masterclass in these activities – such cases as Gabriele Gast at the BND, Klaus Kuron and Hans Tiedke at the BfV, and Rainer Rupp at NATO. The defection of the HVA's Werner Stiller in 1979 provided a rare intelligence windfall for the other side.

Its expanding remit reflected the Stasi's position as 'a central pillar of the power structure of communism'.[7] The Stasi came indelibly to represent the menace and wrongs of a surveillance state. Erich Mielke, Walter Ulbricht and his replacement as national leader, Erich Honecker, kept giving the Stasi more money and duties, more powers and people. The way the Stasi was able to leak into everyday life is perhaps best illustrated by its Officers on Special Assignment (Offiziere im besonderen Einsatz, OibE).

Deployed increasingly from the early 1960s onwards, OibE were undercover Stasi officers who, unknown even to senior Stasi colleagues, worked in managerial positions at government ministries, industrial concerns, and civil, religious and cultural organisations. Some of the OibE were outed after the collapse of East Germany. One of the most well-known was Alexander Schalck-Golodkowski, an undercover Stasi colonel who spent years acquiring embargoed goods and hard currency for the GDR from his official position at the head of an import-export concern.

The OibE ensured the Stasi had a view of everything that was happening across diverse walks of life. They could also influence the decision-making at their place of work, giving the Stasi a say in how organisations conducted their business. This is another difference between the Stasi and other intelligence services. In America, for example, there remains 'no guarantee that policy-makers will take heed of intelligence disseminations or even read the [CIA] estimates'.[8] By contrast, the Stasi's views were always communicated loudly and clearly to all concerned parties, and were heeded. The Stasi was always in the room.

The Stasi's proliferation also shows up in its in-house terminology. Stasi bosses were great coiners of terminology and jargon – a trait that tends to go hand-in-hand with authoritarianism or zealotry, with their need to define and isolate subjects, and to present themselves, falsely, as intellectually robust. As the Stasi's duties diversified, so its language evolved into a baffling array of phrases, acronyms and abbreviations. Stasi collaborators – IM – were subdivided into IMA, IMF, PIM and many more, to denote slightly varying roles. Sources of information – Quellen – became an A-Quelle or an O-Quelle; and so on. These arcane terms, and dozens more, which once were fiercely guarded secrets of the

Cold War, are now discoverable via a brief visit to the MfS Lexikon, a website run by Germany's national archive.

Most of the people written about in this book are dead. But Stasi history still matters, a lot, and especially in Germany, where recriminations, accusations and denials around its work can still play out in the courts, resulting in fines, prison sentences, and ruined careers and reputations. Nevertheless, only a very small percentage 'of those directly involved in Stasi activities [have] paid even the relatively mild penalty' of losing a job in the public sector.[9] In short, most Stasi people got away with it.

When more details of Stasi espionage emerged in the 1990s, great anger was felt towards those West Germans who had agreed to spy for East Germany. Criminal proceedings were initiated against the 1,553 West Germans who were still on the Stasi's books as collaborators when the Berlin Wall fell. Most of these proceedings – 1,134 – were dropped, largely due to lack of evidence. By 1998, sentences had been passed on 181 former West Germans, 118 of whom received a fine or suspended sentence; just 63 went to prison for two years or more.[10]

For most people, the thousands of West and East Germans who spied in the GDR were political resisters engaged in daring but supportable activity against an oppressive state; an unwanted state, imposed by Moscow. Adding to Soviet culpability is the fact that Joseph Stalin started the Cold War. It was his fault, his aggression and expansionism: he was the one who didn't want his armies to come home after the Nazis' defeat. But this book also suggests that, having entered Stalin's Cold War, Western countries adopted policies and behaviours which today can be questioned.

Did the actions of Western intelligence services give the Stasi a reason for doing some of the things it did? Yes. If Western intelligence services had behaved differently, would the terrible experiences of many ordinary Germans at the hands of the Stasi have been avoided? Yes. The gathering of information by the Ostbüros, and the interference organised by the likes of the KgU, were an expression of moral and political opposition to the Soviet and SED authorities. Whatever the terminology used by those authorities, they were far from democratic and, in some cases, were killing people extrajudicially. This, therefore, was resistance activity. Yet it gave the Stasi real enemies to fight, and there were lots of unrepentant Nazis working for the West. There should not have been. And if the US and other Western countries had provided political campaign groups with overt, rather than covert, funding, it might have saved some unnecessary trouble. At least as much would have been achieved, and the communists would have lost some of their justification for acting so harshly.

Although a few Western agents were sent into eastern Germany in summer 1945, the mass infiltration of spies into foreign territory was initiated by the communists. Then, during the 1950s, both sides in the Cold War put similar numbers of spies into the other's territory, the West to meet its defence needs. The number of Western spies in the Soviet Bloc declined after 1961 because of the Berlin Wall. The honourable practices of Western democracy saw a high number of communist spies continuing to operate in the West.

The initiation of covert propaganda is more debatable. It could be argued that East German propaganda belonged to a history of communist interference in foreign countries that fired up after the Russian Revolution. But in terms of covert propaganda concerning Germany, the East Germans were arguably a bit slow off the mark. The SED had its propagandists, but Britain discussed and launched a covert propaganda effort before the East Germans did.

It isn't absolving the Stasi to argue that the picture of it that emerges from this book is somewhat different to the 'all-seeing eye' and 'red terror' Stasi of Western infamy. Often the Stasi acted cautiously, mindful of its public image. It is important to understand that many Stasi operations were unlike the streets-running-with-blood terror of the American Cold War imagination. Their subtlety was their danger. Much of the Stasi's early activity targeted professional people working in responsible positions; it was concerned with removing perceived opponents from the institutions of the young GDR, rather than from the streets. Moreover, the Stasi had to walk lines, treading carefully around certain constraints. Faced with finite resources and genuine security threats, it had to pick its battles. Meanwhile, the Western powers kept seeking the weak points in East Germany's defences, the places where counter-espionage didn't work. A major example is the telecommunications department of the SED Central Committee, in which the CIA had spies long after the Berlin Wall appeared.

The Stasi didn't begin life as a mass surveyor of society. In its earlier years it had a narrower focus, although not for benevolent reasons. From a security perspective it had real enemies. Only after the Berlin Wall did the Stasi become an all-round participant in East German life. Before that it carried out specific intelligence and secret police tasks that moved in phases. Phase one, establish a pro-Moscow territory and ensure the primacy of the SED, usually by 'disappearing' politicians and state servants. Phase two, deal with criminal Nazis. Phases three and four, enforce nationalisation and collectivisation, which are unpopular, and tackle Western spies and other interference. Phase five, put down the rebels of 1953. Phase six, rid the country of enemy spies and increase the collection of secret information from abroad. Phase seven, secure the borders. While there were some horrific occurrences in the Stalinist years, it is difficult to say whose lives were more affected by the Stasi: Germans of the 1950s or those of the 1980s. The 1950s are rightly seen as the time of brutality, but at that point the Stasi was more constrained by circumstances. In the 1980s, some of East Germany's citizens enjoyed living there, but the Stasi was able to interfere in almost every aspect of their lives.

This book raises age-old questions about divided Germany: why did millions of Germans stay in the GDR during the Stalinist years? Why didn't they all leave? Mostly because it was the place they came from. There were local and family ties, and hundreds of thousands of Neubauern had been given land to tend. To a much lesser extent, people remained due to their socialist convictions. They were told that they were building a new kind of German nation where everything would come good. They were told they would be servants of America if they left. There was a fatalistic and shellshocked atmosphere in the postwar years, and tremendous political apathy; some East Germans believed that life wouldn't improve even if they did leave. There was no clarity around what would happen in terms of German reunification; at certain moments it looked imminent. And, in torrents of propaganda, people were urged to stay. Those who left, or tried to, were demonised at best, prosecuted or even killed at worst. To leave was nonconformist, to say the least, and most members of any society tend to conform. To leave was to disobey the government. Ordinarily, most citizens do not do so.

Nevertheless, the Stalinist years saw East Germany afflicted by terrible economic failings and grinding hardship. In this context it is interesting that Markus Wolf, unable to bring himself to criticise Marxist economics, believed that East Germany failed because it didn't respect freedom of expression and thought. Wolf believed the SED was unpopular because it didn't allow more cultural freedom, more varied and abundant entertainment. He had a point. Over time, the absence of cultural freedom, varied entertainment, and the possibility of travel – at least around one's own country – aggravates a population almost as much as a hungry belly does. They are as necessary for a contented population as food.

Wolf also insisted on the moral equivalence of Cold War intelligence services. He didn't think his HVA was worse than any other; in fact he thought it was better, because it enshrined the concept of peace. Spying indeed can prevent war; the East Germans didn't discover anything new there. But for Wolf:

> The intelligence world, East and West, was a realm of moral shadows. Its practices were often unethical, its methods dirty. Given this fact, it seems to me that the

CIA was at a peculiar disadvantage in having to take part in a sort of democratic pantomime to satisfy the requirements of the American Constitution, regardless of whether or not they were relevant to intelligence work. No secret service can ever be democratic nor, however much politicians may wish it, open to constant scrutiny and still perform its tasks properly.

It is true that all governments need the facility to gather secret information secretly. It can even be argued that a certain amount of opacity is part of good, not bad, governance. But there are some bottom lines, which Wolf chose to ignore. Just one fact will suffice to illustrate this point. In East Germany, hundreds of people were executed or sentenced to life in prison for their espionage, or 'agent activity'. In West Germany, over the same period, there were no death sentences for espionage, and just one life sentence was passed; and thanks to a successful appeal, the recipient only spent a couple of years in prison.

Some of the Stasi's abusive practices might occur in any police force. The types of oppression dished out by the Stasi were arguably mirrored in the West by the ways in which law enforcement agencies treated people of colour. For example, in early 1960s France, north Africans, and no other citizens, were subject to curfews, and were routinely the victims of extreme authoritarian violence. The Maigret detective novels of Georges Simenon, which cover the period from the early 1930s to the 1970s, are full of references to French police beating up suspects. In twentieth century Britain, the dishonesty of some police officers led to serious miscarriages of justice. One of the worst examples was the 'fitting up' of black youths by a minority of corrupt detectives. This shocking practice lingered into the 1980s and beyond, and saw completely innocent British citizens go to prison. But these, of course, were aberrations, and are challenged as such. The Stasi behaved this way on the orders of its government; to ensure its government couldn't be deposed.

The Stasi was not the first or the last agency to acquire such power. The display text in a room at the Doge's palace in Venice, referring to the city's Council of Ten, which was established in 1310, reads: 'Its authority covered all sectors of public life – from religious orthodoxy to foreign policy, from espionage to state security – and this range of powers gave rise to the legend of the Council as a ruthless, all-seeing tribunal at the service of the ruling oligarchy, a court whose sentences were handed down rapidly after hearings held in secret.'

Such agencies will always remain a possibility. And it shouldn't be forgotten that some good came from the Cold War. The NATO system saw the countries of Europe united and peaceful in a way that was unimaginable in previous centuries.

A last word

Germany's emergence from its postwar troubles is one of the greatest national success stories. Although the west of the country continues to fare better than the east, contemporary Germany continues to be one of the best representations of Western democracy – at least if looked at through a filter of idealism, and stubborn hope. A buoyant economy that provides affordable basics but still has room for the innovation and competition that spur progress; a sufficient amount of good food; a relatively small (although still too large) gap between the wealthy and the poor; a high degree, usually, of public order and safety; a free and occasionally ethical press; a good standard of affordable education; a good standard of affordable healthcare; freedom of religion; freedom of culture and entertainment; the ambition to protect the interests of social minorities and vulnerable groups; the ambition to protect the environment; a carefully worked out legal system, with many practitioners who care deeply about its efficacy and rectitude; influential civil society organisations, which in theory are able to challenge individuals and entities to ensure that power isn't assumed or abused. Almost miraculously, all of this emerged from the animosities of the Cold War divide. This is Western liberal democracy in action. There is no place in it for the likes of the Stasi.

Appendices

Appendix 1
Structure and tasks of K5

The secret police force known as K5, which existed roughly from 1946 to 1949, was a branch of the Kriminalpolizei (criminal investigation department).* It had a headquarters staff at Berlin and smaller staffs throughout the Länder police forces. K5 was created mostly to fulfil 'Orders from the occupation authorities'. Another definition was provided in April 1947 by its first chief, Fritz Lange, who wrote that K5 was to tackle crimes that 'endanger the construction of our young democracy'.

At that time the German Administration of the Interior (DVdI) planned to divide K5 into eight 'working groups' (Arbeitsgruppen). They would be responsible for preventing and investigating offences, and making arrests, in the following areas:

Group A. Orders of occupying powers:
1. Violations of orders from the occupying powers, [fulfil] requests for investigations and arrests, processing of special cases or checking cases processed in lower-level units.
2. Verbal and written violations of the commands and orders of the occupying powers and newly established authorities.
[Criminal Law] Basis: SMAD orders and directives, Allied Control Council laws and directives.

Group B. Orders of German authorities, central administrations, Länder administrations and authorities:
1. Violations of orders from German authorities, [fulfil] requests for investigations and arrests from central and Länder administrations and authorities. Close cooperation with the Central Administration for Justice.
2. Checking for Parteigenossen [former Nazi party members] in the central administrations and authorities. Preventing their establishment in administrations and authorities.
Basis: SMAD Order 124, ACC Directives 24, 38.

---

* Sources for this appendix: BArch P, DVdI 7/352, Ref. K 5, An Leiter K, 11 April 1947, Entwurf Ref. K 5 – Straftaten anderer Art, 18; BStU ZA AS 229/66, K5 annual report for Saxony 1947, 8 January 1948, 372-3; Tantzscher, 'Die Vorläufer'; Ronald Wiedmann, 'K5', MfS Lexikon.

3. Monitoring all departments and sections of the criminal police to ensure the proper completion of their tasks.
4. Prosecution of offences based on ACC Law No. 10 (Crimes against Humanity).

Group C. Assassinations and explosives violations:
1. Attacks against public figures, institutions, etc.
2. Explosives and weapons offences.

Group D. Sabotage (sabotage of reconstruction, prosecution of sabotage in industry, commerce, transport, etc.)

Group E. Combating illegal fascist organisations:
1. Combating illegal fascist organisations (Werewolf, Edelweiss organisations, etc.)
2. Registration and observation of former Nazi activists, organisations, reactionaries, etc. Creation of a National Socialist index in the Länder.
3. Misinforming by former [Nazi] Parteigenossen.

Group F. Combating other anti-democratic activities:
1. Combating the spread of anti-democratic rumours and 'slogans'.
2. Combating the damage and removal of democratic propaganda.

Group G. Other violations of democratic reconstruction:
1. Executive intervention in special cases concerning DVdI and K5 employees throughout the Soviet zone.

Group H: Registry and archive:
1. Preparation of special statistics for K5.
2. Registry and archive.
3. Special files.
4. Collecting all intelligence material and statistics for crimes falling under A-G, evaluation, comparison of personal descriptions, working methods and means used, in close cooperation with other departments of [the Kriminalpolizei], in particular K7 [wanted persons, searches for persons, identifications].

In practice the structure of K5 departments varied. An organisational chart from October 1947, probably from K5 headquarters at the DVdI, shows the working groups organised as follows:

Groups A1 and A2: Violations of SMAD orders
Group A3: Possession of explosives and weapons

Groups B1 and B2: Order 201 and Allied Control Council Law No. 10

Group B3: Remaining Nazi organisations

Groups C1 and C2: Attacks on officials and sabotage

Group C3: Combating rumours and 'slogans' [and later] 'Schumacherites' and 'Trotskyists'

Group D: 'Other violations'

[and from February 1948:]

Group C4: Monitoring/investigation of radio manufacturers and repairers

Group D2: Not specified

In Saxony, K5 appears to have had a simpler structure. The Land organisational chart at the start of 1948 shows five K5 sections:

1. Political crimes including violations of SMAD orders.
2. Violations of Allied Control Council laws and directives.
3. Sabotage ('of the reconstruction').
4. 'Anti-democratic activity'.
5. Technical support: surveillance, data collection, postal interception.

The same document classifies the crimes to be dealt with by K5:

1. Violations of orders from the occupation authorities.
2. Violations of orders from German authorities.
3. Explosives and weapons offences, unauthorised possession of weapons.
4. Concealment [stashing] of weapons and explosives.
5. Order 201, ACC Directive 38, ACC Directive 24.
6. Cases tried under ACC Law No. 10 [crimes against humanity].
7. Illegal fascist, militarist, reactionary organisations.
8. Fascist leaflets, daubing of slogans and agitation attempts.
9. Anti-Semitism.
10. Assassination attempts against public figures.
11. Dangerous acts of sabotage.
12. Politically motivated arson.
13. Other illegal organisations.
14. Leafletting, daubing of slogans.
15. Resistance against state authority, demonstrations, strikes, sabotage of granted fundamental rights.
16. Illegal border activity, activities among re-settlers, travellers, private detective agency work [banned under] SMAD Order 136.
17. Falsifying identities.
18. Other cases to be prosecuted as needed – conduct of staff in administrations,

escape of prisoners from detention centres, employees going missing from administrations, continuing application of illegal Nazi laws, prohibited research work [ACC Law No. 23], violation of other orders.

Above all, K5 existed to fulfil commands from the Soviet authorities and security forces, and from top-ranking SED members. Its biggest mission was the enforcing of SMAD Order 201. In carrying out such tasks, K5 contributed, in the words of Monika Tantzscher, to 'the systematic development and expansion of a political police' in the Soviet occupation zone.

Appendix 2
Stasi officer ranks

Rank group	Before 1952	After 1952	Abbreviation
Generals		Armeegeneral	
	Generalinspekteur	Generaloberst	GO
	Chefinspekteur	Generalleutnant	GL
		Generalmajor	GM
Officers	Inspekteur	Oberst	
	Kommandeur	Oberstleutnant	OSL
	Oberrat	Major	Maj.
	Rat	Hauptmann	Hptm.
	Oberkommissar	Oberleutnant	Oltn.
	Kommissar	Leutnant	Ltn.
	Unterkommissar	Unterleutnant	Ultn.

Source: Roland Wiedmann, *Die Diensteinheiten des MfS 1950-1989: Eine organisatorische Übersicht* (MfS-Handbuch) (Berlin: BStU, 2012), 523.

Appendix 3
Stasi budgets 1954-1961

In millions of marks (foreign currency budget not included). Italics = planned

Year	Grants from national budget	Income (e.g. through visa sales)	Expenses	Change in expenses vs. previous year (in per cent)
1954	*377.5*	*51.3*	*428.8*	–
1955	*709.4*	*109.4*	*818.8*	*(91.0)*
1956	*780.1*	*102.0*	*882.1*	*7.7*
1957	*247.1*	*40.7*	*287.8*	*(-67.4)*
1958	286.9	41.1	328.0	14.0
1959	321.4	44.0	365.3	11.4
1960	377.5	51.3	428.7	17.4
1961	397.8	53.0	450.8	5.2

Source: Krzysztof Persak and Łukasz Kamiński (eds.), *A Handbook of the Communist Security Apparatus in East Central Europe 1944-1989* (Warsaw: Institute of National Remembrance, 2005), 173, based on Jens Gieseke, *Die DDR-Staatssicherheit: Schild und Schwert der Partei* (2000).

Appendix 4
Organisational charts

Chart 1. Stasi leaders, October 1952

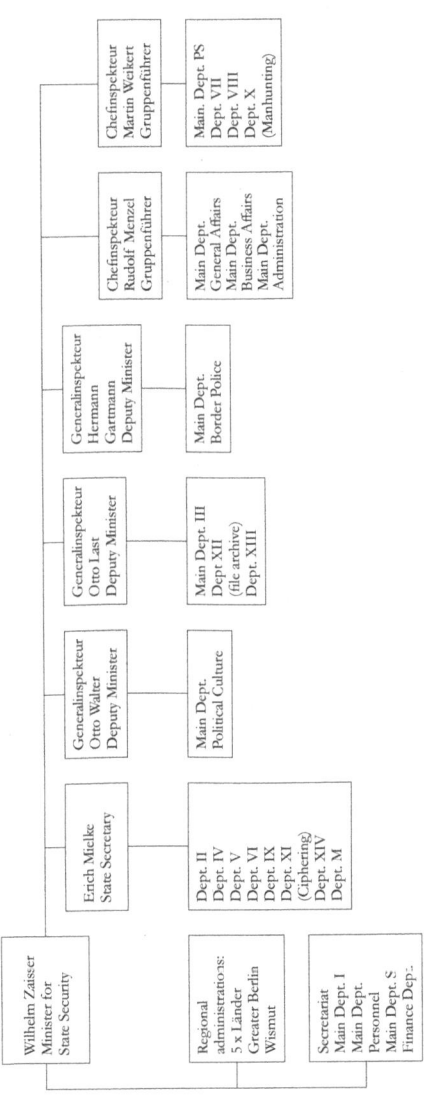

Source: Wiedmann, *Die Diensteinheiten*, 497.

Chart 2. Stasi leaders, May 1956

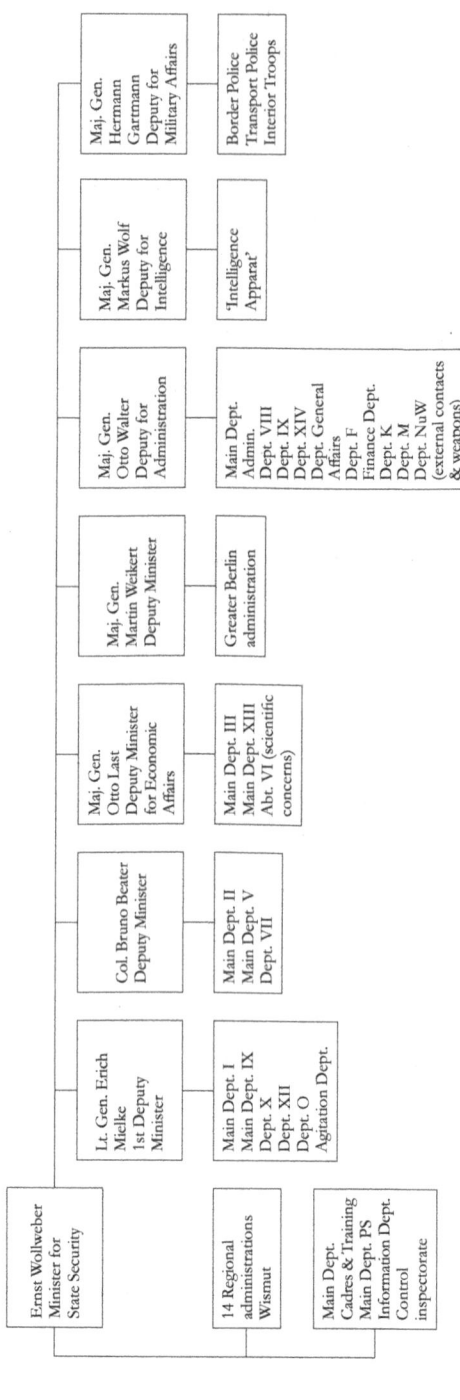

Ernst Wollweber
Minister for
State Security

Lt. Gen. Erich
Mielke
1st Deputy
Minister

Col. Bruno Beater
Deputy Minister

Maj. Gen.
Otto Last
Deputy Minister
for Economic
Affairs

Maj. Gen.
Martin Weikert
Deputy Minister

Maj. Gen.
Otto Walter
Deputy for
Administration

Maj. Gen.
Markus Wolf
Deputy for
Intelligence

Maj. Gen.
Hermann
Gartmann
Deputy for
Military Affairs

14 Regional
administrations
Wismut

Main Dept.
Cadres & Training
Main Dept. PS
Information Dept.
Control
inspectorate

Main Dept. I
Main Dept. IX
Dept. X
Dept. XII
Dept. O
Agitation Dept.

Main Dept. II
Main Dept. V
Dept. VII

Main Dept. III
Main Dept. XIII
Abt. VI (scientific
concerns)

Greater Berlin
administration

Main Dept.
Admin.
Dept. VIII
Dept. IX
Dept. XIV
Dept. General
Affairs
Dept. F
Finance Dept.
Dept. K
Dept. M
Dept. NuW
(external contacts
& weapons)

'Intelligence
Apparat'

Border Police
Transport Police
Interior Troops

Source: Wiedmann, *Die Diensteinheiten*, 501.

Chart 3. HVA leaders, August 1956

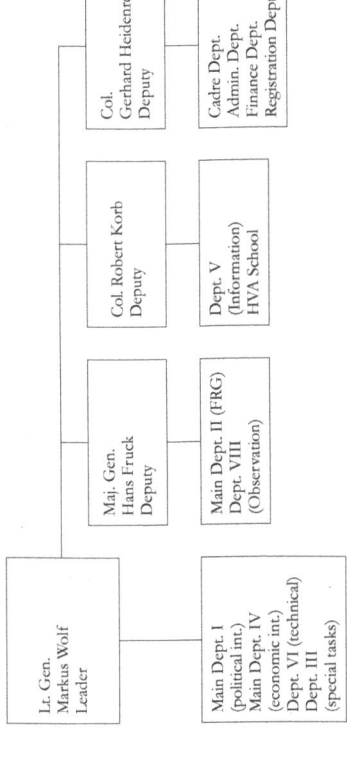

Source: Wiedmann, *Die Diensteinheiten*, 513.

Chart 4. Main Department II (Counter-espionage), 1958

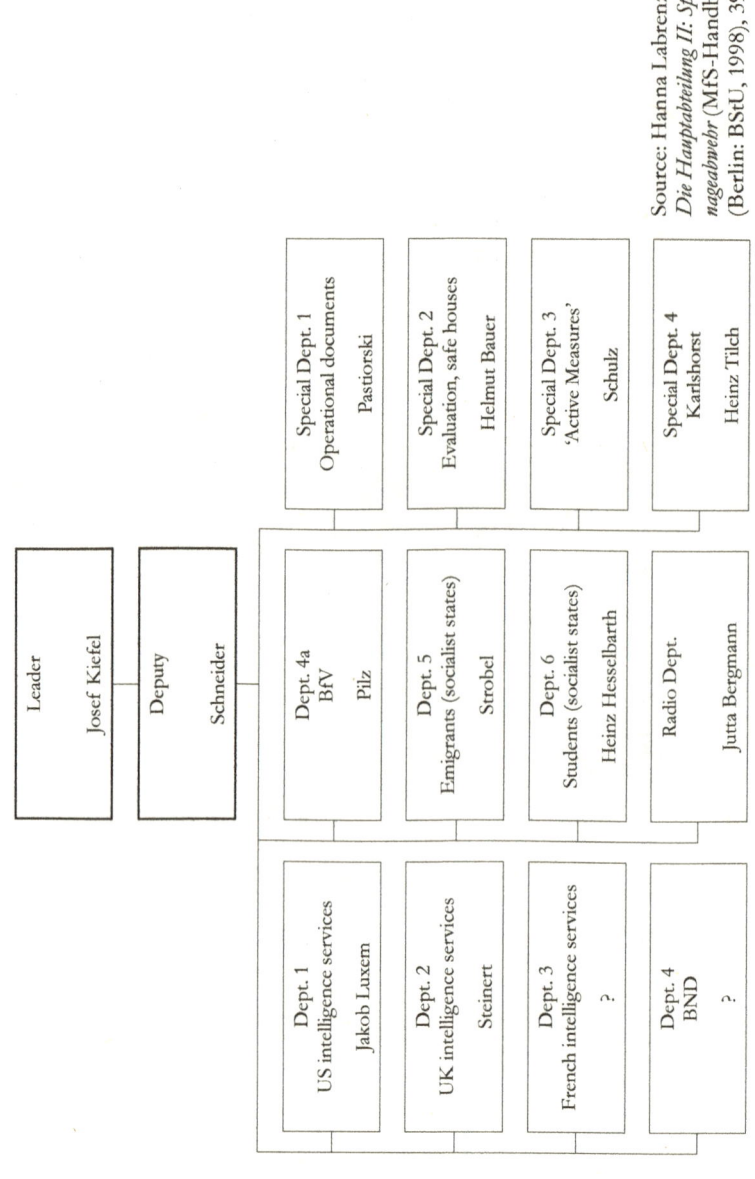

Leader		
Josef Kiefel		

Deputy		
Schneider		

Dept. 1 US intelligence services — Jakob Luxem	Dept. 4a BfV — Pilz	Special Dept. 1 Operational documents — Pastiorski
Dept. 2 UK intelligence services — Steinert	Dept. 5 Emigrants (socialist states) — Strobel	Special Dept. 2 Evaluation, safe houses — Helmut Bauer
Dept. 3 French intelligence services — ?	Dept. 6 Students (socialist states) — Heinz Hesselbarth	Special Dept. 3 'Active Measures' — Schulz
Dept. 4 BND — ?	Radio Dept. — Jutta Bergmann	Special Dept. 4 Karlshorst — Heinz Tilch

Source: Hanna Labrenz-Weiss, *Die Hauptabteilung II: Spionageabwehr* (MfS-Handbuch) (Berlin: BStU, 1998), 39.

Chart 5. Stasi leaders, December 1960

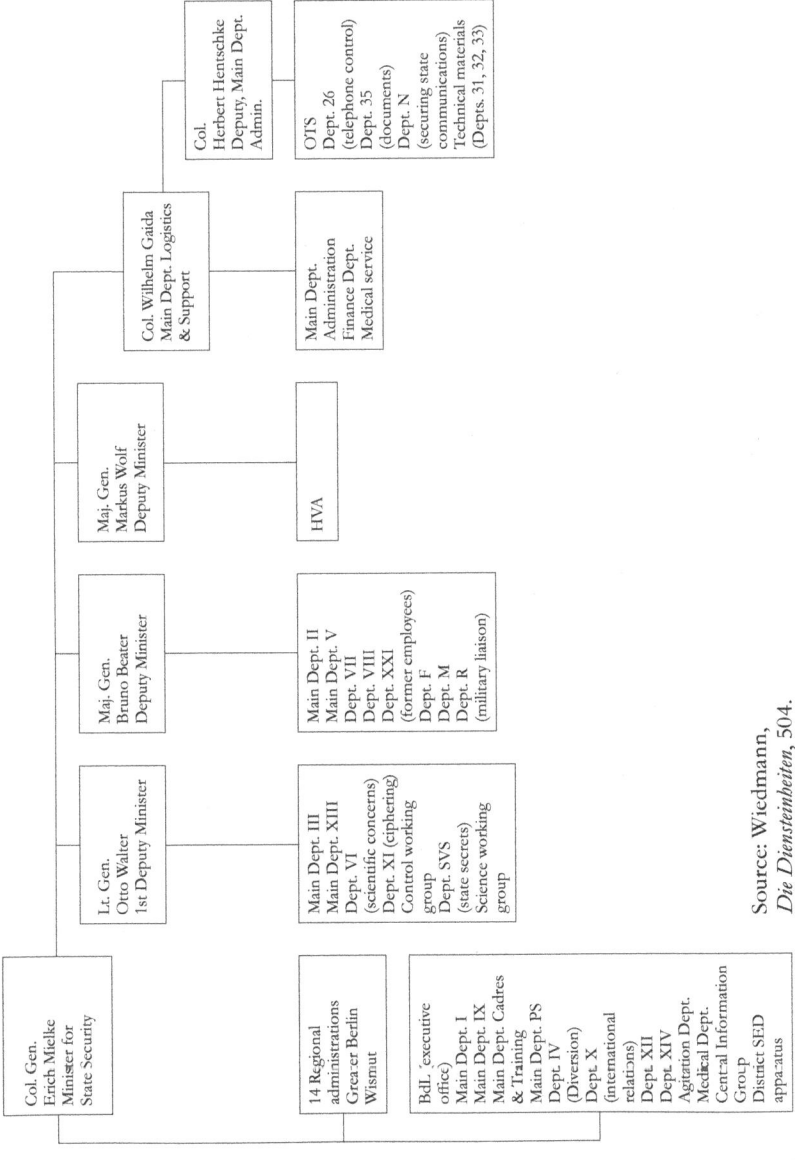

Col. Gen.
Erich Mielke
Minister for
State Security

Lt. Gen.
Otto Walter
1st Deputy Minister

Maj. Gen.
Bruno Beater
Deputy Minister

Maj. Gen.
Markus Wolf
Deputy Minister

Col. Wilhelm Gaida
Main Dept. Logistics
& Support

Col.
Herbert Hentschke
Deputy, Main Dept.
Admin.

14 Regional
administrations
Greater Berlin
Wismut

BdL (executive
office)
Main Dept. I
Main Dept. IX
Main Dept. Cadres
& Training
Main Dept. PS
Dept. IV
(Diversion)
Dept. X
(international
relations)
Dept. XII
Dept. XIV
Agitation Dept.
Medical Dept.
Central Information
Group
District SED
apparatus

Main Dept. III
Main Dept. XIII
Dept. VI
(scientific concerns)
Dept. XI (ciphering)
Control working
group
Dept. SVS
(state secrets)
Science working
group

Main Dept. II
Main Dept. V
Dept. VII
Dept. VIII
Dept. XXI
(former employees)
Dept. F
Dept. M
Dept. R
(military liaison)

HVA

Main Dept.
Administration
Finance Dept.
Medical service

OTS
Dept. 26
(telephone control)
Dept. 35
(documents)
Dept. N
(securing state
communications)
Technical materials
(Depts. 31, 32, 33)

Source: Wiedmann,
Die Diensteinheiten, 504.

Selected bibliography

Articles and papers

Christopher Andrew, 'Intelligence and International Relations in the Early Cold War', *Review of International Studies*, Vol. 24 No. 3 (1998)

Richard Bessel, 'Policing in East Germany in the wake of the Second World War', *Crime, Histoire & Sociétés/Crime, History & Societies*, Vol. 7, No. 2 (2003)

Thomas Boghardt, 'America's Secret Vanguard: US Army Intelligence Operations in Germany, 1944-47', *Studies in Intelligence*, Vol. 57, No. 2 (2013)

Thomas Boghardt, 'Our man in Berlin: The secret life of Willy Brandt', *Army History*, No. 122 (2022)

Gary Bruce, 'The Prelude to Nationwide Surveillance in East Germany: Stasi Operations and Threat Perceptions, 1945-1953', *Journal of Cold War Studies*, Vol. 5, No. 2 (2003)

Gary Bruce, *'Aufklärung und Abwehr*: The lasting legacy of the Stasi under Ernst Wollweber', *Intelligence and National Security*, 21:3 (2006)

Francesco Alexander Cacciatore, 'Re-evaluating the émigrés: intelligence collection and policy-making in the early Cold War', *Journal of Intelligence History*, Vol.20, No.2 (2021)

Kenneth J. Campbell, 'Markus Wolf: One of History's Most Effective Intelligence Chiefs', *American Intelligence Journal*, Vol. 29, Nr. 1 (2011)

Simon Case, 'The Joint Intelligence Committee and the German Question, 1947-61', PhD thesis, Queen Mary, University of London

Luke Daly-Groves, 'Control not morality? Explaining the selective employment of Nazi war criminals by British and American intelligence agencies in occupied Germany', *Intelligence and National Security*, Vol. 35 Issue 3 (2019)

Karsten Dümmel, Melanie Piepenschneider (eds.), *Was war die Stasi? Einblicke in das Ministerium für Staatssicherheit der DDR* (Konrad-Adenauer-Stiftung, 2019)

Michael Fredholm, 'Soviet active measures in west, southeast, and east Asia with regard to Afghanistan, 1980-1982', *Journal for Intelligence, Propaganda and Security Studies*, Vol. 13, No. 1 (2020)

Frank Hagemann, 'Der Untersuchungsausschuss Freiheitlicher Juristen 1949-1969', dissertation, Keil University, 1994

Frank Hagemann, 'Die Drohung des Rechts: Der Kampf des Untersuchungsausschusses Freiheitlicher Juristen' in Gerhard Finn et al., *Unrecht überwinden: SED-Diktatur und Widerstand* (Sankt Augustin: Konrad-Adenauer-Stiftung, 1996)

Hope M. Harrison, 'Ulbricht and the concrete 'Rose': New archival evidence on the dynamics of Soviet-East German relations and the Berlin Crisis, 1958-61', Cold War International History Project Working Paper #5 (Washington: Woodrow Wilson International Center for Scholars, 1993)

Enrico Heitzer, '...die Masse soweit bringen, dass sie nachdenkt...': Ein Widerstandsgruppe in Altenburg in der Zeit der SBZ und frühen DDR', *Deutschland Archiv* 39 (2006)

Enrico Heitzer, 'SMT-Verfahren im Zusammenhang mit der Kampfgruppe gegen Unmenschlichkeit (KgU)' in *Sowjetische Militärjustiz in der SBZ/DDR (1945-1955)* (Halle: Hallische Beträge zur Zeitgeschichte, 2007)

Enrico Heitzer, '"Kalter Krieger": Zur Tätigkeit der Kampfgruppe gegen Unmenschlichkeit in West-Berlin und der Bundesrepublik' in Wolfgang Benz (ed.), *Ein Kampf um Deutungshoheit: Politik, Opferinteressen und historische Forschung* (Berlin: Metropol Verlag, 2013)

Enrico Heitzer, 'Humanitäre Organisation und Nachrichtendienst: Die Kampfgruppe gegen

Unmenschlichkeit (1948-1959) im Bundesnotaufnahmeverfahren', *Zeitschrift für Geschichtswissenschaft* (2016)

Monty Johnstone, 'The CPGB, the Comintern and the War, 1939-1941: Filling in the Blank Spots', *Science & Society*, Vol. 61, No. 1 (1997)

Michael Kuhlmann, '"Wir waren Kalte Krieger! Ich auch!" RIAS Berlin und der Aufstand des 17. Juni 1953 in der DDR', *Journal for Intelligence, Propaganda and Security Studies*, Vol. 17 Nr. 1/2023 (2023)

Detlef Kühn, 'Lothar Weirauch und der Nachrichtendienst der West-KPD', *ZdF* 11 (2002)

Paul Maddrell, 'Britain's exploitation of occupied Germany for scientific and technical intelligence on the Soviet Union', PhD thesis, Corpus Christie College, University of Cambridge, 1998

Paul Maddrell, 'The Western secret services, the East German Ministry of State Security and the building of the Berlin Wall', *Intelligence and National Security*, Vol. 21 No. 5 (2006)

Paul Maddrell, 'Exploiting and Securing the Open Border in Berlin: the Western Secret Services, the Stasi, and the Second Berlin Crisis, 1958-1961', Cold War International History Project Working Paper #58 (Washington: Woodrow Wilson International Center for Scholars, 2009)

Paul Maddrell, 'British Intelligence through the Eyes of the Stasi: What the Stasi's Records Show about the Operations of British Intelligence in Cold War Germany', *Intelligence and National Security*, Vol. 27 No. 1 (2012)

Paul Maddrell, 'Im Fadenkreuz der Stasi: Westliche Spionage in der DDR, Die Akten der Hauptabteilung IX', *VfZ* 2/2013 (2013)

Paul Maddrell, 'The economic dimension of Cold War intelligence-gathering: The West's spies in the GDR's economy', *Journal of Cold War Studies*, Vol. 15 No. 3 (2013)

Eduard Mark, 'Revolution by Degrees: Stalin's National-Front Strategy for Europe, 1941-1947', Working Paper No. 31, Cold War International History Project (Washington: Woodrow Wilson International Center for Scholars, 2001)

McIlroy et al., 'Forging the Faithful: The British at the International Lenin School', *Labour History Review* (2003)

Susanne Muhle, 'Wie das MfS Menschen entführen liess', Bundeszentrale für politische Bildung (2016)

Helmut Müller-Enbergs, 'Die DDR-Nachrichtendienste: Juristische Aufarbeitung, Erinnerungen und Darstellungen', *Jahrbuch für Historische Kommunismusforschung* (1996)

Helmut Müller-Enbergs, 'Spione beim Klassenfeind', Bundeszentrale für politische Bildung (2016)

David E. Murphy, 'Spies in Berlin: A hidden key to the Cold War', *Foreign Affairs* Vol. 77 No. 4 (1998)

Norman Naimark, 'To Know Everything and To Report Everything Worth Knowing: Building the East German Police State, 1945-1949', Cold War International History Project Working Paper No. 10 (Washington: Woodrow Wilson International Center for Scholars, 1994)

Christian Ostermann, 'The United States, the East German Uprising of 1953, and the Limits of Rollback', Cold War International History Project Working Paper No. 11 (Washington: Woodrow Wilson International Center for Scholars, 1994)

Arnold Paucker, *German Jews in the Resistance 1933-1945: The Facts and the Problems* (Berlin: Gedenkstätte Deutscher Widerstand, 2005)

Kevin P. Riehle, 'Early Cold War evolution of British and US defector policy and practice', *Cold War History* (2018)

Kevin Riehle, 'Soviet Intent at the Dawn of the Cold War: Igor Gouzenko's Revelations About GRU Intelligence Taskings' in *Journal of Intelligence History*, Vol. 22 No. 2 (2023)

Uwe Spiekermann (ed.), *The Stasi at Home and Abroad: Domestic Order and Foreign Intelligence*, Bulletin of the German Historical Institute, Supplement 9 (Washington DC: GHI, 2014)

Monika Tantzscher, 'Die Vorläufer des Staatssicherheitsdienstes in der Polizei der Sowjetischen Besatzungszone: Ursprung und Entwicklung der K 5', *JHK* (1998)

Thomas Widera, 'Aktive Selbstorganisation und der Polizeiaufbau in Dresden 1945', *ZdF* 19 (2006)

Hugh Wilford, 'The Information Research Department: Britain's secret Cold War weapon revealed', *Review of International Studies* (1998)

Publications of the Bundesarchiv and Die Bundesbeauftragte für die Unterlagen des Staatssicherheitsdienstes der ehemaligen Deutschen Demokratischen Republik (BStU)

Anon., *Hauptverwaltung A (HV A): Aufgaben-Strukturen-Quellen* (MfS-Handbuch) (Berlin: BStU, 2013)

Anon., *Der Deutsche Bundestag 1949 bis 1989 in den Akten des Ministeriums für Staatssicherheit (MfS) der DDR* (Berlin: BStU, 2013)

Anon., *Das geteilte Berlin und die Stasi: Spionage, Opposition und Alltag* (Berlin: BStU, 2018)

Anon., *Die Stasi im Westen: Spionage in der Bundesrepublik Deutschland und West-Berlin* (Berlin: BStU, 2017)

Christine André and Doris Hubert, *Stasi: The exhibition of the GDR's State Security* (Berlin: BStU, 2011)

Thomas Auerbach, *Vorbereitung auf den Tag X: Die geplanten Isolierungslager des MfS* (Berlin: BStU, 1995)

Thomas Auerbach, Matthias Braun, Bernd Eisenfeld, Gesine von Prittwitz, Clemens Vollnhals, *Hauptabteilung XX: Staatsapparat, Blockparteien, Kirchen, Kultur, 'politischer Untergrund'* (MfS-Handbuch) (Berlin: BStU, 2008)

Klaus Bästlein, Annette Rosskopf, Falco Werkentin, *Beiträge zur juristischen Zeitgeschichte der DDR* (Berlin: BStU, 2009)

Johannes Beleites, *Abteilung XIV: Haftvollzug* (MfS-Handbuch) (Berlin: BStU, 2009)

Peter Boeger, Elise Catrain (eds.), *Stasi in Sachsen: Die DDR-Geheimpolizei in den Bezirken Dresden, Karl-Marx-Stadt und Leipzig* (Berlin: BStU, 2017)

Peter Boeger, Elise Catrain (eds.), *Stasi in Sachsen-Anhalt: Die DDR-Geheimpolizei in den Bezirken Halle und Magdeburg* (Berlin: BStU, 2016)

Peter Boeger, Elise Catrain (eds.), *Stasi in Thüringen: Die DDR-Geheimpolizei in den Bezirken Erfurt, Gera und Suhl* (Berlin: BStU, 2018)

Peter Boeger, Elise Catrain (eds.), *Stasi in Dresden: Die Geheimpolizei im DDR-Bezirk* (Berlin: BStU, undated)

Wolfgang Buschfort, *Die Ostbüros der Parteien in den 50er Jahren* (Berlin: BStU, 2006)

Elise Catrain (ed.), *Stasi in Mecklenburg-Vorpommern: Die DDR-Geheimpolizei in den Bezirken Neubrandenburg, Rostock und Schwerin* (Berlin: BStU, 2019)

Roger Engelmann, Silke Schumann, *Kurs auf die entwickelte Diktatur: Walter Ulbricht, die Entmachtung Ernst Wollwebers und die Neuausrichtung des Staatssicherheitsdienstes 1956/57* (Berlin: BStU, 1995)

Roger Engelmann, Frank Joestel, *Grundsatzdokumente des MfS* (MfS-Handbuch) (Berlin: BStU, 2010)

Roger Engelmann, Frank Joestel, *Die Hauptabteilung IX: Untersuchung* (Berlin: BStU, 2016)

Stephan Fingerle, Jens Gieseke, 'Partisanen des Kalten Krieges: Die Untergrundtruppe der Nationalen Volksarmee 1957-1962 und ihre Übernahme durch die Staatssicherheit' (Berlin: BStU/Abt. Bildung und Forschung, 1996)

Jens Gieseke, *Das Ministerium für Staatssicherheit 1950 bis 1989/90: Ein kurzer historischer Abriss* (Berlin: BStU, 1998)

Maria Haendcke-Hoppe-Arndt, *Die Hauptabteilung XVIII: Volkswirtschaft* (MfS-Handbuch) (Berlin: BStU, 1997)

Karsten Jedlitschka, Jens Niederhut, Philipp Springer, Christian Appl, *Verschluss-Sachen: Dokumente, Fotos und Objekte aus dem Archiv der Staatssicherheit* (Berlin: BStU, 2017)

Hubertus Knabe, *Die Rechtsstelle des MfS* (MfS-Handbuch) (Berlin: BStU, 1999)

Hanna Labrenz-Weiss, *Die Hauptabteilung II: Spionageabwehr* (MfS-Handbuch) (Berlin: BStU, 1998)

Hanna Labrenz-Weiss, *Abteilung M: Postkontrolle* (MfS-Handbuch) (Berlin: BStU, 2005)

Hanna Labrenz-Weiss, *Die KD Nordhausen: Arbeitsstruktur und Wirkung der Kreisdienststelle des Ministeriums für Staatssicherheit im Grenzkreis Nordhausen* (BF informiert 37, 2017)

Siegfried Mampel, *Der Untergrundkampf des Ministeriums für Staatssicherheit Gegen den Untersuchungsausschuss Freiheitlicher Juristen in West-Berlin* (Berlin: BStU, 1999)

Wilhelm Mensing, *SED-Hilfe für West-Genossen: Die Arbeit der Abteilung Verkehr beim Zentralkomitee der SED im Spiegel der Überlieferung des Ministeriums für Staatssicherheit der DDR (1946–1976)* (Berlin: BStU, 2010)

Helmut Müller-Enbergs, *Geschichte der HV A und ihrer Militärspionage: Analysen und Fallstudien* (Berlin: BStU, 2021)

Daniela Münkel (ed.), *Staatssicherheit: Ein Lesebuch zur DDR-Geheimpolizei* (Berlin: BStU, 2015)

Arno Polzin, *Der Wandel Robert Havemanns vom Inoffiziellen Mitarbeiter zum Dissidenten im Spiegel der MfS-Akten* (BF informiert 26, 2005)

Andreas Schmidt, *Hauptabteilung III: Funkaufklärung und Funkabwehr* (MfS-Handbuch) (Berlin: BStU, 2010)

Angela Schmole, *Abteilung 26. Telefonkontrolle, Abhörmassnahmen und Videoüberwachung* (MfS-Handbuch) (Berlin: BStU, 2009)

Angela Schmole, *Hauptabteilung VIII: Beobachtung, Ermittlung, Durchsuchung, Festnahme* (MfS-Handbuch) (Berlin: BStU, 2011)

Silke Schumann, *Die Parteiorganisation der SED im MfS* (MfS-Handbuch) (Berlin: BStU, 2002)

Konstanze Soch (ed.), *Stasi in Brandenburg: Die DDR-Geheimpolizei in den Bezirken Cottbus, Frankfurt (Oder) und Potsdam* (Berlin: BStU, 2020)

Walter Süss, *Das Verhältnis von SED und Staatssicherheit: Eine Skizze seiner Entwicklung* (BF informiert 17, 1997)

Regina Teske, *Staatssicherheit auf dem Dorfe: Zur Überwachung der ländlichen Gesellschaft vor der Vollkollektivierung 1952 bis 1958* (BF informiert 27, 2006)

Gudrun Weber in collaboration with Bernd Florath, *"Nun falten Sie den Zettel...": Wahlen in der DDR in der Überlieferung der Staatssicherheit (1949-1961)* (Berlin: BStU, 2019)

Stephan Wolf, *Hauptabteilung I: NVA und Grenztruppen* (MfS-Handbuch) (Berlin: BStU, 2005)

Tobias Wunschik, *Hauptabteilung VII: Ministerium des Innern, Deutsche Volkspolizei* (MfS-Handbuch) (Berlin: BStU, 2009)

Books

Jefferson Adams, *Historical Dictionary of German Intelligence* (Lanham, Toronto, Plymouth: The Scarecrow Press, Inc., 2009)

Keith R. Allen, *Befragung – Überprüfung – Kontrolle: Die Aufnahme von DDR-Flüchtlingen in West-Berlin bis 1961* (Berlin: Ch. Links, 2013)

Christopher Andrew and Oleg Gordievsky, *KGB: The Inside Story of its Foreign Operations from Lenin to Gorbachev* (London: Sceptre, 1991)

Christopher Andrew, Vasili Mitrokhin, *The Mitrokhin Archive: The KGB in Europe and the West* (London: Allen Lane, 1999)

Henry Ashby Turner, *Germany from Partition to Unification* (New Haven: Yale University Press, 1992)

Bernd-Rainer Barth, Jens Gieseke, *Wer war wer in der DDR?* 5. Ausgabe. Band 1 (Berlin: Links Verlag, 2010)

Helmut Bärwald, *Das Ostbüro der SPD* (Krefeld: SINUS, 1991)

Klaus Behling, *Die Kriminalgeschichte der DDR: Vom Umgang mit Recht und Gesetz im Sozialismus, Politische Prozesse, skurrile Taten, Alltagsdelikte* (Berlin: Edition Berolina, 2017)

K. Behnke and J. Fuchs (eds.), *Zersetzung der Seele: Psychologie und Psychiatrie im Dienst der Stasi* (Hamburg: Rotbuch Verlag, 1995)

Richard Bessel, Ralph Jensen (eds.), *Die Grenzen der Diktatur: Staat und Gesellschaft in der DDR* (Göttingen: Vandenhoeck & Rupprecht, 1996)

Vadim J. Birstein, *SMERSH: Stalin's Secret Weapon* (London: Biteback Publishing, 2011)

Gerhard Block, *Verraten und verkauft: Memoiren eines Unverbesserlichen* (Berlin: NoRa, 2004)

Günter Bohnsack, Herbert Wehner, *Auftrag Irreführung* (Hamburg: Cartsen, 1992)

Douglas Botting, *In The Ruins of the Reich* (London: Methuen, 2005)

Beatrix Bouvier, Horst-Peter Schulz, *'...die SPD aber aufgehört hat zu existieren'* (Bonn: J.H.W. Dietz, 1993)

Gary Bruce, *Resistance with the People: Repression and Resistance in Eastern Germany 1945-1955* (Lanham, Boulder, New York, Oxford: Rowman & Littlefield, 2003)

Gary Bruce, *The Firm: The Inside Story of the Stasi* (Oxford, New York: Oxford University Press, 2010)

Wolfgang Buschfort, *Das Ostbüro der SPD* (Munich: Oldenbourg Wissenschaftsverlag, 1991)

David Childs and Richard Popplewell, *The Stasi: The East German Intelligence and Security Service* (Basingstoke, New York: Palgrave, 1996)

Mike Dennis, *The Rise and Fall of the German Democratic Republic* (London, New York: Routledge, 2000)

Mike Dennis, *The Stasi: Myth and Reality* (London, New York: Routledge, 2003)

Torsten Diedrich, *Der 17. Juni 1953* (Berlin: Dietz Verlag, 1991)

F.S.V. Donnison, *Civil Affairs and Military Government North West Europe 1944-1946* (London: HM Stationery Office, 1961)

R. Engelmann, C. Vollnhals (eds.), Justiz im Dienste der Parteiherrschaft: Rechtspraxis und Staatssicherheit in der DDR (Berlin: Ch. Links, 1999)

Roger Engelmann et al.: *Das MfS-Lexikon* (Berlin: Ch. Links, 2016)

Roger Faligot and Pascal Krop, *La Piscine: The French Secret Service since 1944* (Oxford: Basil Blackwell Ltd, 1989)

Hans Fallada, *Nightmare in Berlin*, translated by Allan Blunden (Melbourne, London: Scribe US, 2017)

Jan von Flocken and Michael F. Scholtz, *Ernst Wollweber: Saboteur, Minister, Unperson* (Berlin: Aufbau, 1994)

Christoph Franceschini, Thomas Wegener Friis, Erich Schmidt-Eenboom, *Spionage Unter Freunde: Partnerdienstbeziehungen und Westaufklärung der Organisation und des BND* (Berlin: Ch. Links, 2017).

Karl Wilhelm Fricke, *Politik und Justiz in der DDR* (Cologne: Verlag Wissenschaft und Politik, 1979)

Karl Wilhelm Fricke, *Die Staatssicherheit der DDR* (Cologne: Verlag Wissenschaft und Politik, 1984)

Karl Wilhelm Fricke, *Opposition und Widerstand in der DDR* (Cologne: Verlag Wissenschaft und Politik, 1989)

Karl Wilhelm Fricke, *MfS Intern: Macht, Strukturen, Auflösung der DDR-Staatssicherheit: Analyse und Dokumentation* (Cologne: Verlag Wissenschaft und Politik, 1991)

Karl-Wilhelm Fricke and Roger Engelmann, *'Konzentrierte Schläge': Staatssicherheitsaktionen und politische Prozesse in der DDR 1953-1956* (Berlin: Ch. Links, 1998)

Mary Fulbrook, *History of Germany, 1918-2000: The Divided Nation* (Oxford: Blackwell, 2002)

Mary Fulbrook, *Anatomy of a Dictatorship: Inside the GDR 1949-1989* (Oxford: Oxford University Press, 2009)

Jens Gieseke, *Mielke-Konzern: Die Geschichte der Stasi 1945-1990* (Stuttgart: Deutsche Verlags Anstalt, 2001)

Jens Gieseke, *The GDR State Security: Shield and Sword of the Party* (Berlin: BStU, 2006), translated by Mary Carlene Forszt

Jens Gieseke, *The History of the Stasi: East Germany's Secret Police, 1945-1990* (New York, Oxford: Berghahn, 2015), translated by David Burnett

Anthony Glees, *The Secrets of the Service: British Intelligence and Communist Subversion 1939-51* (London: Jonathan Cape, 1987)

Anthony Glees, *The Stasi Files: East Germany's Secret Operations Against Britain* (London: Free Press, 2004 ed.)

Werner Grossmann, *Bonn im Blick: die DDR-Aufklärung aus der Sicht ihres letzten Chefs* (Berlin: Das Neue Berlin, 2001)

Manfred Hagen, *DDR – June '53* (Stuttgart: Franz Steiner Verlag, 1992)

Georg Herbstritt, *Bundesbürger im Dienst der DDR-Spionage: Eine analytische Studie* (Göttingen: Vandenhoeck & Ruprecht, 2007)

Roger Hermiston, *The Greatest Traitor: The Secret Lives of Agent George Blake* (London: Aurum, 2013)

Peter Hübner, Böhlau Köln (eds.), *Eliten im Sozialismus: Beiträge zur Sozialgeschichte der DDR* (Potsdam: Zentrum für Zeithistorische Forschung, 1999)

Keith Jeffery, *MI6: The History of the Secret Intelligence Service, 1909-1949* (London: Bloomsbury, 2011)

Tony Judt, *A History of Europe Since 1945* (London: Pimlico, 2007)

Brigitte Kaff (ed.), *'Gefährliche politische Gegner': Widerstand und Verfolgung in der sowjetischen Zone/DDR* (Düsseldorf: Droste, 1995)

Hubertus Knabe, *Die unterwanderte Republik: Stasi im Westen* (Berlin: Propyläen, 1999)

Hubertus Knabe, *Die Täter sind unter uns: Über das Schönreden der SED-Diktatur* (Berlin: Propyläen Verlag, 2007)

John O. Koehler, *Stasi: The Untold Story of the East German Secret Police* (Boulder, Oxford: Westview, 1999)

Ilko-Sascha Kowalczuk et al. (eds.), *Der Tag X: Die 'Innere Staatsgründung' der DDR als Ergebnis der Krise 1952/1954* (Berlin: Ch. Links, 1995)

Walter Krivitsky, *I Was Stalin's Agent* (Cambridge: Ian Faulkner Publishing Ltd, 1992)

Manfred Krug, *Abgehauen* (Düsseldorf: Econ, 1996)

Barbara Kuhle, Wolfgang Titz, *Speziallager Nr. 7 Sachsenhausen 1945-1950* (Berlin: Brandenburgisches Verlagshaus, 1990)

Franziska Kuschel, *Schwarzhörer, Schwarzseher und heimliche Leser: Der DDR und die Westmedien* (Göttingen: Wallstein, 2016)

Raymond W. Leonard, *Secret Soldiers of the Revolution: Soviet Military Intelligence, 1918-1933* (Westport, London: Greenwood Press, 1999)

Keith Lowe, *Savage Continent: Europe in the Aftermath of World War II* (London: Penguin, 2013)

Andrew Lownie, *Stalin's Englishman: The Lives of Guy Burgess* (London: Hodder & Stoughton, 2016)

Kristie Macrakis, *Seduced by Secrets: Inside the Stasi's Spy-Tech World* (Annapolis: Naval Institute Press, 2014)

David C. Martin, *Wilderness of Mirrors: Intrigue, Deception, and the Secrets that Destroyed Two of the Cold War's Most Important Agents* (New York: Skyhorse, 2018)

Klaus Marxen, Gerhard Werle (eds.), *Strafjustiz und DDR-unrecht Dokumentation 4/1: Spionage* (Berlin: De Gruyter Recht, 2004)

I. Merkel (ed.), *'Wir sind doch nicht die Meckerecke der Nation!' Briefe an das Fernsehen der DDR* (Berlin: Schwarzkopf & Schwarzkopf, 1998)

P. Merseburger, *Willy Brandt 1913-1992: Visionär und Realist* (Stuttgart: Deutsche Verlags-Anstalt, 2002)

Allan Merson, *Communist Resistance in Nazi Germany* (London: Lawrence and Wishart Ltd, 1985)

Kai-Uwe Merz, *Kalter Krieg als antikommunistischer Widerstand: Die KgU 1948-1959* (Munich: R. Oldenbourg Verlag, 1987)

Barbara Miller, *Narratives of Guilt and Compliance in Unified Germany: Stasi informers and their impact on society* (London: Routledge, 1999)

Armin Mitter, Stefan Wolle, *Untergang auf Raten* (Munich: Bertelsmann Verlag, 1993)

Jörn Mothes et al. (eds.), *Beschädigte Seelen: DDR-Jugend und Staatssicherheit* (Bremen: Edition Temmen, 1996)

Susanne Muhle, *Auftrag – Menschenraub: Entführungen von Westberlinern und Bundesbürgern durch das Ministerium für Staatssicherheit der DDR* (Göttingen: Vandenhoeck & Ruprecht, 2015)

Klaus D. Müller et al., *Die Vergangenheit lässt uns nicht los: Haftbedingungen politischer Gefangener in der SBZ/DDR und deren gesundheitliche Folgen* (Berlin: Berliner Wissenschafts-Verlag, 1998)

David E. Murphy, Sergei A. Kondrashev, George Bailey, *Battleground Berlin: CIA vs KGB in the Cold War* (New Haven, London: Yale University Press, 1997)

Norman Naimark, *The Russians in Germany: A History of the Soviet Zone of Occupation, 1945-1949* (Cambridge, Mass., London: The Belknap Press of Harvard University Press, 2001 ed.)

Christian Ostermann, *Uprising in East Germany, 1953: The Cold War, the German Question, and the first major upheaval behind the Iron Curtain* (Budapest: Central European Press, 2001)

Bruce Page, David Leitch, Phillip Knightley, *The Philby Conspiracy* (New York: Doubleday & Company, 1968)

Stanley G. Payne, *The Spanish Civil War, the Soviet Union and Communism* (Newhaven, London: Yale University Press, 2004)

Krzysztof Persak and Łukasz Kamiński (eds.), *A Handbook of the Communist Security Apparatus in East Central Europe 1944-1989* (Warsaw: Institute of National Remembrance, 2005)

N. Podewin, *Walter Ulbricht: Eine neue Biographie* (Berlin: Dietz Verlag, 1995)

Douglas Porch, *The French Secret Services: A History of French Intelligence from the Dreyfus Affair to the Gulf War* (New York: Farrar, Straus and Giroux, 1995)

Gordon W. Prange, *Target Tokyo: The Story of the Sorge Spy Ring* (New York: McGraw Hill Book Company, 1984)

Donald Rayfield, *Stalin and His Hangmen: An Authoritative Portrait of a Tyrant and Those Who Served Him* (London: Penguin, 2005)

Michael Richter, *Die Ost-CDU 1948-1952: Zwischen Widerstand und Gleichschaltung* (Düsseldorf: Drost, 1991)

Ariane Riecker, Annett Schwarz, Dirk Schneider, *Stasi intim: Gesprächer mit ehemaligen MfS-Angehörigen* (Leipzig: Forum, 1990)

Hubert Rottleuthner (ed.), *Steuerung der Justiz in der DDR* (Cologne: Bundesanzeiger Verlag, 1994)

Julius Ruiz, *The 'Red Terror' and the Spanish Civil War: Revolutionary Violence in Madrid* (New York: Cambridge University Press, 2014)

John C. Schmeidel, *Stasi: Shield and Sword of the Party* (London, New York: Routledge, 2014)

Erich Schmidt-Eenboom, *Schnüffler ohne Nase: Der BND – die unheimliche Macht im Staate* (Dusseldorf, Vienna, New York: Econ, 1993)

Silke Schumann, *Parteierziehung in der Geheimpolizei: zur Rolle der SED im MfS der fünfziger Jahre* (Berlin: Ch. Links, 1997)

Victor Serge, *Unforgiving Years*, translated by Richard Greeman and The Victor Serge Foundation (New York: New York Review of Books, 2008)

David R. Shearer, *Policing Stalin's Socialism: Repression and social order in the Soviet Union, 1924-1953* (New Haven, London: Yale University Press, 2009)

Bob Steers (ed.), *FSS Field Security Section* (Heathfield: Robin Steers, 1996)

Donald P. Steury (ed.), *On the Front Lines of the Cold War: Documents on the Intelligence War in Berlin, 1946 to 1961* (Washington DC: Center for the Study of Intelligence, 1999)

Pavel Sudoplatov and Anatoli Sudoplatov with Jerrold L. and Leona P. Schecter, *Special Tasks: The Memoirs of an Unwanted Witness – a Soviet spymaster* (London: Warner Books, 1994)

Bruno Thoss (ed.), *Volksarmee schaffen – ohne Geschrei: Studien zu den Anfängen einer 'verdeckten Aufrüstung' in der SBZ/DDR 1947-1952* (Munich: R. Oldenbourg, 1994)

Jan Valtin, *Out of the Night* (New York: Alliance Book Corporation, 1941)

Boris Volodarsky, *Stalin's Agent: The Life and Death of Alexander Orlov* (New York, Cambridge: Cambridge University Press, 2015)

Armin Wagner, *Walter Ulbricht und die geheime Sicherheitspolitik der SED* (Berlin: Ch. Links, 2002)

Franz Walter et al. (eds.), *Die SPD in Sachsen zwischen Hoffburg und Diaspora* (Bonn: Dietz, 1993)

Hermann Weber, *DDR: Grundriss der Geschichte 1945-1990* (Hannover: Fackelträger, 1991)

Hermann Weber, *Zur Situation der Sozialdemokratie in der SBZ/DDR zwischen 1945 und dem Beginn der 50er Jahre* (Schüren: Presseverlag, 1992)

Thomas Wegener Friis et al. (eds.), *East German Foreign Intelligence: Myth, reality and controversy* (London, New York: Routledge, 2012)

Falco Werkentin, *Politische Strafjustiz in der Ära Ulbricht* (Berlin: Ch. Links, 1995)

Nigel West, *Mask: MI5's Penetration of the Communist Party of Great Britain* (Abingdon, New York: Routledge, 2005)

Nigel West, *Historical Dictionary of Sexpionage* (Lanham MD: Scarecrow Press, 2009)

Nigel West, *Historical Dictionary of International Intelligence* (Lanham MD: Rowman & Littlefield, 2015)

Rebecca West, *The Meaning of Treason* (London: Virago Press Limited, 1982)

Manfred Wilke, *Der Weg zur Mauer: Stationen der Teilungsgeschichte* (Berlin: Ch. Links, 2011)

Markus Wolf with Anne McElvoy, *Memoirs of a Spymaster: The Man Who Waged a Secret War Against the West* (London: Pimlico, 1998)

Edgar Wolfrum, *Geschichtspolitik in der Bundesrepublik Deutschland: Der Weg zur bundesrepublikanischen Erinnerung 1948-1990* (Darmstadt: Wissenschaftliche Buchgesellschaft, 1999)

Notes

These notes refer to Stasi documents with the prefix 'BArch', the designation for Germany's Bundesarchiv, and those with the prefix 'BStU', the designation of the state agency formerly responsible for Stasi materials. The prefixes of document collections used by other researchers are as given in those researchers' work.

Introduction

1   Manfred Krug, *Abgehauen* (Düsseldorf: Econ, 1996), 122-125, quoted in Jens Gieseke, *The GDR State Security: Shield and Sword of the Party* (Berlin: BStU, 2006), 47, translated by Mary Carlene Forszt, amended by author.
2   Paul Maddrell, 'The Western secret services, the East German Ministry of State Security and the building of the Berlin Wall', *Intelligence and National Security*, Vol. 21, No. 5 (2006), 830.
3   Jens Gieseke, *The History of the Stasi: East Germany's Secret Police, 1945-1990*, translated by David Burnett (New York, Oxford: Berghahn, 2015), 7.
4   Christopher Andrew, Vasili Mitrokhin, *The Mitrokhin Archive: The KGB in Europe and the West* (London: Allen Lane, 1999), 30.
5   Gieseke, *The History*, 47.
6   Gieseke, *The GDR*, 7-8.
7   Klaus D. Müller et al., *Die Vergangenheit lässt uns nicht los: Haftbedingungen politischer Gefangener in der SBZ/DDR und deren gesundheitliche Folgen* (Berlin: Berliner Wissenschafts-Verlag, 1998), 129-143, cited in Anthony Glees, *The Stasi Files: East Germany's Secret Operations Against Britain* (London: Free Press, 2004 edition), 44-45.
8   John Hooper, 'East Germany jailed 75,000 escapers', *The Guardian*, 7 August 2001.
9   Glees, *The Stasi Files*, 47.
10 Helmut Müller-Enbergs, 'Die DDR-Nachrichtendienste: Juristische Aufarbeitung, Erinnerungen und Darstellungen', *Jahrbuch für Historische Kommunismusforschung*, 1996, 401-412, available at https://www.kommunismusgeschichte.de/jhk/article/detail/die-ddr-nachrichtendienste-juristische-aufarbeitung-erinnerungen-und-darstellungen, accessed 4. 12.2023.
11 Andrew and Mitrokhin, *The Mitrokhin Archive*, 40.
12 J. Boulter, 'The Successful Spy: an interview with Alan Judd', *Crime Time*, 23 November 2020.
13 Paul Maddrell writes that 'numerous case reports show that Line IX [the Stasi's investigation department] was careful and critical in assessing material obtained from an arrestee... The context in which the [Stasi's counter-espionage] reports were written also supports the assumption that they are reliable.' Paul Maddrell, 'Im Fadenkreuz der Stasi: Westliche Spionage in der DDR, Die Akten der Hauptabteilung IX', *VfZ* 2/2013 (Munich, Berlin: Institut für Zeitgeschichte), 147-149.
14 Hooper, 'East Germany jailed'.
15 Glees, *The Stasi Files*, 38.
16 Helmut Müller-Enbergs, 'Spione beim Klassenfeind', Bundeszentrale für politische Bildung, 7 October 2016, available at https://www.bpb.de/themen/deutsche-teilung/stasi/222253/spione-beim-klassenfeind/, accessed 4.12.2023.

17 Blair Worden, *The English Civil Wars 1640-1660* (London: Weidenfeld & Nicolson, 2009), Preface.
18 'Secrets, Lies and British Spies', ITV television, broadcast 29 January 2023.
19 Mary Fulbrook, *Anatomy of a Dictatorship: Inside the GDR 1949-1989* (Oxford: Oxford University Press, 2009 ed.), 45.

Part I. Death to Spies: The Descent of Eastern Germany

1 Quoted by Milovan Djilas in *Conversations with Stalin*, translated by Michael B. Petrovic (London: Rupert Hart-Davis, 1962), 105.
2 Quoted in Tony Judt, *A History of Europe Since 1945* (London: Pimlico, 2007), 131, requoted in Keith Lowe, *Savage Continent: Europe in the Aftermath of World War II* (London: Penguin, 2013), 331.

1. *Stunde Null*

1 Quotations in this section are from the US edition of *Nightmare in Berlin* (*Der Alpdruck*), translated by Allan Blunden (Melbourne, London: Scribe US, 2017), passim.
2 Unless otherwise stated, quotations in this section are from Lowe, *Savage Continent*, passim.
3 In his book *Auschwitz: The Nazis and the Final Solution* (London: BBC, 2005).
4 R.D. Laing, *Wisdom, Madness and Folly: The Making of a Psychiatrist* (Edinburgh: Canongate, 2001), 66.
5 Central Statistical Office, *Statistical Digest of the War* (London: HMSO, 1951), 51, cited in Lowe, *Savage Continent*, 408.
6 Lowe, *Savage Continent*, 335-336.

2. Circles of Hell: Postwar Germany

1 Friends of the author in conversation.
2 F.S.V. Donnison, *Civil Affairs and Military Government North West Europe 1944-1946* (London: HM Stationery Office, 1961), 250.
3 Major A.G. Moon, Imperial War Museum Documents 91/13/1, typescript memoir, cited in Lowe, *Savage Continent*, 109.
4 Guy Liddell diaries, entry for 3 December 1945, KV-4/467, UK National Archives, 19.
5 Richard Bessel, 'Policing in East Germany in the wake of the Second World War', *Crime, Histoire & Sociétés/Crime, History & Societies*, Vol. 7, No. 2, 2003, citing Mecklenburgisches Landeshauptarchiv (MLHA), Kreistag/Rat des Kreises Demmin, Nr. 46, ff. 'Tätigkeitsbericht über die Verwaltung des Kreises Demmin vom Mai bis November 1945', 21 November 1945, 62-64.
6 Ibid.
7 Public Records Office FO 938/310, cited in Lowe, *Savage Continent*, 404.
8 *Newsweek*, 11 June 1945, 56, cited in ibid., 58.
9 Werner Ratza, 'Anzahl und Arbeitsleistungen der deutschen Kriegsgefangenen' in Erich Maschke (ed.), *Zur Geschichte der deutschen Kriegsgefangenen des zweiten Weltkrieges* (Bielefeld: Ernst & Werner Gieseking, 1962-74), 207-226, cited in ibid., 117.
10 Douglas Botting, *In The Ruins of the Reich* (London: Methuen, 2005), 183, cited in ibid., 46.
11 Botting, *Ruins*, 282, cited in ibid., 413.
12 Ann J. Merritt, Richard L. Merritt, *Public Opinion in Occupied Germany: The OMGUS Surveys 1945-1949* (Chicago, London: Urbana, 1970), 32, cited in Gieseke, *The History*, 23.

3. SMERSH

1 Donald Rayfield, *Stalin and His Hangmen: An Authoritative Portrait of a Tyrant and Those Who Served Him* (London: Penguin, 2005), 382-383.

2   Captain Mikhail Koryakov of the 1st Ukrainian Front, quoted in Vadim J. Birstein, *SMERSH: Stalin's Secret Weapon* (London: Biteback Publishing, 2011), 301, citing Koryakov, *I'll Never Go Back*, translated from the Russian by Nicholas Wreden (London: George G. Harrap & Co., 1948), 61.
3   Birstein, *SMERSH*, 289, citing Perry Biddiscombe, *The SS Hunter Battalions: The Hidden History of the Nazi Resistance Movement 1944-45* (Stroud: Tempus, 2006).
4   Ibid., citing V.A. Kozlov, 'Deyatel'nost' upolnomochennykh i operativnykh grupp NKVD SSSR v Germanii v 1945-1946 gg.' in S.V. Mironenko (ed.), *Spetsial'nye lagerya NKVD/MVD SSSR v Germanii 1945-1950 gg. Sbornik dokumentov I stsatei* (Moscow: ROSSPEN, 2001), 315.
5   Ibid., citing Moscow Conference, October 1943: Joint Four-Nation Declaration, http://www.yale.edu/lawweb/avalon/imt/moscow.htm, retrieved 5 January 2011.
6   Ibid., 247-255.
7   Ibid., 369.
8   Ibid., 355.
9   Ibid., 354, citing Zhukov and Telegin's telegram to the GSOVG troops, dated June 30, 1945, quoted in Nikita Petrov, *Pervyi predsedatel' KGB Ivan Serov* (Moscow: Materik, 2005), 49-50.
10   Ibid., citing Zhukov's Order No. 00138/op, dated September 9, 1945, quoted in Petrov, *Pervyi predsedatel' KGB*, 54.
11   Ibid., citing Serov's report to Stalin about Abakumov, dated September 8, 1946, quoted in Document No. 19 in Petrov, *Pervyi predsedatel' KGB*, 245-246.
12   Birstein, *SMERSH*, 355-356.
13   Quoted in A.I. Romanov, *Nights Are Longest There: A Memoir of the Soviet Security Services*, translated by Gerald Brooke (Boston: Little, Brown and Company, 1972), 144, cited in Birstein, *SMERSH*, 349.

4. Anti-fascist Unity: The New Politics

1   This claim is discussed in Anthony Glees, *The Secrets of the Service: British Intelligence and Communist Subversion 1939-51* (London: Jonathan Cape, 1987), 261.
2   Stalin's planning is discussed in ibid., passim. For Stalin's self-protective intentions, see Kevin Riehle, 'Soviet Intent at the Dawn of the Cold War: Igor Gouzenko's Revelations About GRU Intelligence Taskings', *Journal of Intelligence History*, Vol. 22, No. 2, 2023, 216-244.
3   Quoted in Vladimir K. Volkov, 'The German Question as Stalin Saw It (1947-1952)', paper prepared for the Stalin Conference of the Cold War International History Project, Yale University, 23-26 September 1999, 11-14, requoted in Eduard Mark, 'Revolution by Degrees: Stalin's National Front Strategy for Europe, 1941-1947', Working Paper No. 31, Cold War International History Project (Washington: Woodrow Wilson International Center for Scholars, 2001), 17.
4   Norman Naimark, *The Russians in Germany: A History of the Soviet Zone of Occupation, 1945-1949* (Cambridge, Mass, London: The Belknap Press of Harvard University Press, 2001 ed.), 274.
5   Gary Bruce, *Resistance with the People: Repression and Resistance in Eastern Germany 1945-1955* (Lanham, Boulder, New York, Oxford: Rowman & Littlefield, 2003), 23, citing SAPMO-BA, ZPA, RY1/I2/3, 1-2.
6   Monika Tantzscher, 'Die Vorläufer des Staatssicherheitsdienstes in der Polizei der Sowjetischen Besatzungszone: Ursprung und Entwicklung der K-5', *JHK*, 1998, 125-156.
7   'Verlauf der Gründungssitzung am 13. und 14.7.45. Gedächtnisprotokoll von Erich Gniffke' quoted in Siegfried Suckut, 'Zur Krise und Funktionswandel der Blockpolitik in der sowjetisch Besetzten Zone Deutschlands um die Mitte des Jahres 1948', *Vierteljahrshefte für Zeitgeschichte* 31 (1983), 674-718, cited in Bruce, *Resistance*, 76.
8   Beatrix Bouvier and Horst-Peter Schulz, '…die SPD aber aufgehört hat zu existieren' (Bonn: J.H.W. Dietz, 1993), 235; Hermann Weber, *Zur Situation der Sozialdemokratie in der SBZ/DDR zwischen 1945 und dem Beginn der 50er Jahre* (Schüren: Presseverlag, 1992), 129, 186, cited in ibid., 24-26.

9   Naimark, *The Russians*, 259.
10   Recollection of Peter Stafford-Hill in Bob Steers (ed.), *FSS Field Security Section* (Heathfield: Robin Steers, 1996), 163-165.
11   Naimark, *The Russians*, 49, cited in Bruce, *Resistance*, 28.
12   Bruce, *Resistance*, 29, citing SAPMO-BA, ZPA, I 2/12/22, 66, 'minutes of a KPD meeting of 7 January 1946 regarding the economic programme'.
13   Ibid., 30, citing CDU protocol reproduced in Siegfried Suckut, 'Der Konflikt um die Bodenreform-Politik in der Ost-CDU 1945', *Deutschland Archiv* 15 (1982), 1083.
14   Peter Hermes, *Die CDU und die Bodenreform in der SBZ im Jahre 1945* (Saarbrücken: Verlag der Saarbrücker Zeitung, 1963), 68, cited in Bruce, *Resistance*, 30.
15   Bruce, *Resistance*, 31.

5. The Police Reborn

1   Tantzscher, 'Die Vorläufer', 126.
2   Lowe, *Savage Continent*, 69.
3   Tantzscher, 'Die Vorläufer', 129.
4   Bessel, 'Policing', 2.
5   Thomas Widera, 'Aktive Selbstorganisation und der Polizeiaufbau in Dresden 1945', *ZdF* 19, 2006, 78.
6   Tantzscher, 'Die Vorläufer', 128.
7   MI5 file on Hans Kahle, KV-2/1565, UK National Archives, 21.
8   Ibid., KV-2/1566, 12. Kahle died after a stomach operation in 1947.
9   Norman Naimark, 'To Know Everything and To Report Everything Worth Knowing: Building the East German Police State, 1945-1949', Cold War International History Project Working Paper No. 10 (Washington: Woodrow Wilson International Center for Scholars, 1994), 3, citing Order No. 112, 23 May 1946, GARF f.7184, opis (op.) 2, delo (d.) 2, list 1, 249.
10   Bessel, 'Policing', 5.
11   Ibid.
12   Naimark, 'To Know', 5, citing BStU, MfSZ, 400/66, 31.
13   Ibid., citing Order No. 112, 23 May 1946, GARF f.7184, op.2, d. 2, list 1, 250.
14   Lowe, *Savage Continent*, 107.
15   Tantzscher, 'Die Vorläufer', 133.
16   Ibid., 132.
17   Lowe, *Savage Continent*, 334.
18   Widera, 'Aktive Selbstorganisation', 78.
19   Ibid., 83. Information and quotations in the following section come from Widera, passim. Any errors in translation or interpretation are the fault of the author.

6. Ordering the Occupation Zone

1   Kirsten Poutros, 'Von den Massenvergewaltigungen zum Mutterschutzgesetz: Abtreibungspolitik und Abtreibungspraxis in Ostdeutschland, 1945-1950' in Richard Bessel and Ralph Jensen (eds.), *Die Grenzen der Diktatur: Staat und Gesellschaft in der DDR* (Göttingen: Vandenhoeck & Ruprecht, 1996), 174, cited in Bruce, *Resistance*, 46.
2   John O. Koehler, *Stasi: The Untold Story of the East German Secret Police* (Boulder, Oxford: Westview, 1999), 54.
3   David Childs and Richard Popplewell, *The Stasi: The East German Intelligence and Security Service* (Basingstoke, New York: Palgrave, 1996), 34-36.
4   Gieseke, *The GDR*, 9.
5   Pavel Sudoplatov and Anatoli Sudoplatov with Jerrold L. and Leona P. Schecter, *Special Tasks: The Memoirs of an Unwanted Witness – a Soviet Spymaster* (London: Warner Books, 1994), 48.
6   Birstein, *SMERSH*, 404.

7   Ibid., 403.
8   Jens Gieseke, *Das Ministerium für Staatssicherheit 1950 bis 1989/90: Ein kurzer historischer Abriss* (Berlin: BStU, 1998), 6; and Gieseke, *The History*, 24.
9   Koehler, *Stasi*, 126.
10 Lucio Caracciolo, 'Der Untergang der Sozialdemokratie in der SBZ', *VfZ* 36 (1998), 298, cited in Bruce, *Resistance*, 36.
11 Bruce, *Resistance*, 38.
12 Caracciolo, 'Der Untergang', 312, quoted in ibid., 38.
13 Bruce, *Resistance*, 41, citing Franz Neumann Archiv VII/8 and ADsD, SPD-PV-Ostbüro 0394.
14 Quoted in Helmut Bärwald, *Das Ostbüro der SPD* (Krefeld: SINUS, 1991), 32, requoted in Bruce, *Resistance*, 39.
15 Ibid., 29 and 40.
16 Wolfgang Buschfort, *Das Ostbüro der SPD* (Munich: Oldenbourg Wissenschaftsverlag, 1991), 17.
17 Lowe, *Savage Continent*, 337.

7. Denazification

1   Donnison, *Civil Affairs*, 359.
2   Glees, *Secrets*, 421-422.
3   Keith Jeffery, *MI6: The History of the Secret Intelligence Service, 1909-1949* (London: Bloomsbury, 2011), 654.
4   Douglas Porch, *The French Secret Services: A History of French Intelligence from the Dreyfus Affair to the Gulf War* (New York: Farrar, Straus and Giroux, 1995), 277.
5   Jeffery, *MI6*, 664.
6   Luke Daly-Groves, 'Control not morality? Explaining the selective employment of Nazi war criminals by British and American intelligence agencies in occupied Germany', *Intelligence and National Security*, Volume 35 Issue 3 (2019), 333.
7   Unless otherwise stated, this section draws on Donnison, *Civil Affairs*, 360-378.
8   Peter Eden quoted in Helen Fry, *Denazification: Britain's Enemy Aliens, Nazi War Criminals and the Reconstruction of Post-war Europe* (Stroud: The History Press, 2010), 90.
9   Tantzscher, 'Die Vorläufer', 142.
10 Lord Pakenham in Hansard, CLII., H. of L., 5th Series, Col. 625-631, 12 November 1947, quoted in Donnison, *Civil Affairs*, 376.
11 Gieseke, *The History*, 17.
12 Barbara Kuhle and Wolfgang Titz, *Speziallager Nr. 7 Sachsenhausen 1945-1950* (Berlin: Brandenburgisches Verlagshaus, 1990), 13, cited in Bruce, *Resistance*, 48.
13 Gieseke, *The History*, 18.
14 Excerpts reprinted in Karl Wilhelm Fricke, *Politik und Justiz in der DDR* (Cologne: Verlag Wissenschaft und Politik, 1979), 106-109, quoted in Bruce, *Resistance*, 69.
15 Gieseke, *The History*, 19-21.
16 Falco Werkentin, *Politische Strafjustiz in der Ära Ulbricht* (Berlin: Ch. Links, 1995), 23, cited in Bruce, *Resistance*, 69.
17 David E. Murphy, Sergei A. Kondrashev, George Bailey, *Battleground Berlin: CIA vs KGB in the Cold War* (New Haven, London: Yale University Press, 1997), 38.
18 Koehler, *Stasi*, 127.
19 Childs and Popplewell, *The Stasi*, 39.
20 Gieseke, *The History*, 121.

8. The German Administration of the Interior

1   ACC Law 31 in *Official Gazette of the Control Council for Germany*, No. 8, 1 July 1946, cited in Naimark, 'To Know', 25.

2   Naimark, 'To Know', 16, citing BStU, MfSZ, SdM, AS 323, 15.
3   Ibid., 8, citing BStU, MfSZ, SdM, AS 323, 29.
4   Wolfgang Eisert, 'Zu den Anfängen der Sicherheits- und Militärpolitik der SED-Führung 1948 bis 1952' in Bruno Thoss (ed.), *Volksarmee schaffen – ohne Geschrei: Studien zu den Anfängen einer 'verdeckten Aufrüstung' in der SBZ/DDR 1947-1952* (Munich: R. Oldenbourg, 1994), 147, cited in Bruce, *Resistance*, 45.
5   Bruce, *Resistance*, 45, citing BA-P, DO 1 7/253.
6   Naimark, *The Russians*, 368.
7   Naimark, 'To Know', 7, citing BStU MfSZ., 333, b.10; for Kremlevka see Murphy et al., *Battleground*, 40.
8   Gieseke, *The History*, 27.
9   Ingetraut Melzer, *Staats- und Rechtsgeschichte der DDR* (Berlin: Staatsverlag der DDR, 1983), 51, cited in Bruce, *Resistance*, 45.
10 Andrea Feth, 'Die Volksrichter' in Hubert Rottleuthner (ed.), *Steuerung der Justiz in der DDR* (Cologne: Bundesanzeiger Verlag, 1994), 358, cited in ibid., 69.
11 Karl Wilhelm Fricke, *Opposition und Widerstand in der DDR* (Cologne: Verlag Wissenschaft und Politik, 1989), 50-51, cited in ibid., 49-50.
12 Martin Broszat and Hermann Weber, *SBZ-Handbuch* (Munich: R. Oldenbourg Verlag, 1990), 422-423, cited in ibid., 50.

9. New Cloaks and Daggers

1   Koehler, *Stasi*, 57, citing directive 350.09 (CIC/S-3/PG) of the Headquarters, Counter Intelligence Corps, United States Forces, European Theater, Frankfurt-am-Main.
2   Murphy et al., *Battleground*, 456.
3   Ibid., 20.
4   Ibid., 10-11.
5   Targets of German Mission, 10 January 1947, (MORI No. 144270), Document I-4 in Donald P. Steury (ed.), *On the Front Lines of the Cold War: Documents on the Intelligence War in Berlin, 1946 to 1961* (Washington DC: Center for the Study of Intelligence, 1999), 106-107.
6   Murphy et al., *Battleground*, 12.
7   Ibid., 23.
8   Naimark, *The Russians*, 383.
9   Murphy et al., *Battleground*, 24-26.
10 Ibid., 8.
11 Ibid., 19-20, citing Dana Durand, 'Report on Berlin Operations Base', 8 April 1948, CSHP 24, CIA-HRP., X.
12 Ibid., 19-20.
13 Roger Hermiston, *The Greatest Traitor: The Secret Lives of Agent George Blake* (London: Aurum, 2013), 178.
14 SSU, AB46 to AB-51, 'Project Proposal for CIB: GAMBIT,' 13 July 1946, LBX-435, (S).
15 Guy Liddell diaries, entry for 8 December 1945, KV-4/467, UK National Archives, 26.
16 Information on Kemritz from Murphy et al., *Battleground*, 408-409.
17 Ibid., 411-414.
18 Ibid., 457, citing Durand, 'Report'.
19 Durand, 'Report', 11-12, as reproduced in Steury (ed.), *On the Front Lines*.
20 Jeffery, *MI6*, 649.
21 Murphy et al., *Battleground*, 447.
22 Hugh Wilford, 'The Information Research Department: Britain's secret Cold War weapon revealed', *Review of International Studies* (1998, 24), 353.
23 Jeffery, *MI6*, 665.
24 Simon Case, 'The Joint Intelligence Committee and the German Question, 1947-61', PhD thesis, Queen Mary, University of London, 28.
25 Paul Maddrell, 'Britain's exploitation of occupied Germany for scientific and technical

intelligence on the Soviet Union', PhD thesis, Corpus Christi College, University of Cambridge, 1998, 40-44.

26 Ibid., 162.

27 Ibid., 61.

28 Guy Liddell diaries, entry for 13 February 1948, KV-4/470, UK National Archives, 33-34.

29 Guy Liddell diaries, entry for 8 October 1947, KV-4/469, UK National Archives, 78.

30 Maddrell, 'Britain's exploitation', 8.

31 Quoted in Jeffery, MI6, 659.

32 Jeffery, MI6, 666.

33 Thomas Boghardt, 'America's Secret Vanguard: US Army Intelligence Operations in Germany, 1944-47', Studies in Intelligence, Vol. 57, No. 2 (June 2013).

34 Murphy et al., Battleground, 416-417.

35 Boghardt, 'America's Secret Vanguard'.

36 Naimark, The Russians, 383-384.

37 Tantzscher, 'Die Vorläufer', 136.

38 Boghardt, 'America's Secret Vanguard', citing HQ, CIC Region VIII, 970th CIC Detachment, memorandum for officer in charge, subject: Soviet Penetration of the Political Affairs Section, Civil Administration Branch, OMGBS, 16 Oct 1947, folder "Soviet Apprehension of German Nationals in US Zone XE 182 800," IRR, RG 319, NA.

39 Maddrell, 'Britain's exploitation', 62.

40 Roger Faligot and Pascal Krop, La Piscine: The French Secret Service since 1944 (Oxford: Basil Blackwell Ltd, 1989), 31-33.

41 Murphy et al., Battleground, 47-49.

42 Ibid., 14.

43 Ibid, 69.

44 Andrew and Mitrokhin, The Mitrokhin Archive, 200.

45 Bruce Page, David Leitch, Phillip Knightley, The Philby Conspiracy (New York: Doubleday & Company, 1968), 184.

46 Ibid., 187.

47 Andrew Lownie, Stalin's Englishman: The Lives of Guy Burgess (London: Hodder & Stoughton, 2016), 157.

48 Ibid., 157-158.

49 Ibid., 324.

10. Germany's New Political Police: K5

1 Tantzscher, 'Die Vorläufer', 140.

2 Adapted from Gieseke, The GDR, 10-11, translated by Mary Carlene Forszt, amended by author.

3 Naimark, The Russians, 362.

4 Naimark, 'To Know', 8.

5 Naimark, 'To Know', 12.

6 Childs and Popplewell, The Stasi, 55.

7 Ibid., 38.

8 Markus Wolf with Anne McElvoy, Memoirs of a Spymaster: The Man Who Waged a Secret War Against the West (London: Pimlico, 1998), 40.

9 Naimark, 'To Know', 12, citing FES, SPD Ostbüro, 0046 A-G, report, 27 May 1949.

10 Tantzscher, 'Die Vorläufer', 150.

11 Naimark, 'To Know', 9, citing FES, SPD Ostbüro, 0046 A-G, 27 May 1949.

12 Ibid.

13 Naimark, 'To Know', 11, citing BStU, MfSZ, AS 238/66, 'Allgemeines über die Aufgaben und das Arbeitsbereich des Kommissariats 5', 343.

14 Ibid., 41.

15 Frank Thomas Stössel, *Positionen und Strömungen in der KPD/SED 1945-1954* (Cologne: Verlag Wissenschaft und Politik, 1985), 194, cited in Bruce, *Resistance*, 74.

16 Bruce, *Resistance*, 75, citing Stiftung Archiv der Parteien und Massenorganisationen (SAPMO-BA), ZPA, IV 2/4/383, Reports by SED Party Control Commission, 25 August and 10 September 1948, 236, 244.

17 Franz Walter et al. (eds.), *Die SPD in Sachsen zwischen Hoffburg und Diaspora* (Bonn: Dietz, 1993), 149, cited in Bruce, *Resistance*, 71.

18 Naimark, 'To Know', 11, citing FES, SPD Ostbüro, 0046 A-G, 13 July 1949.

19 Buschfort, *Das Ostbüro*, 21, cited in Bruce, *Resistance*, 76.

20 Naimark, 'To Know', 11, citing US Army CIC Report R-579-48, 11 October 1948, box 24, RG 260, NA, 2.

21 Bruce, *Resistance*, 76, citing Mecklenburgisches Landeshauptarchiv (MLHA), IV L 2/12/530, memorandum of 18 March 1949 from Dr Scheffler to the High Division for Criminal Matters of the provincial court in Schwerin, 45.

22 Ibid., 77, citing ACDP (Archiv für Christlich-Demokratische Politik in der Konrad-Adenauer-Stiftung, Sankt Augustin), I-298-oo1/3, NL W. Seibert, letter from Seibert to Dertinger 18 February 1947.

23 Michael Richter, *Die Ost-CDU 1948-1952: Zwischen Widerstand und Gleichschaltung* (Düsseldorf: Drost, 1991), 80, cited in Bruce, *Resistance*, 81.

24 Bruce, *Resistance*, 78, citing AdsD, t/c 16 1947, internal report.

25 Martin McCauley, *The German Democratic Republic since 1945* (London: MacMillan, 1983), 34, cited in Bruce, *Resistance*, 109.

26 Bruce, *Resistance*, 66.

27 Bessel, 'Policing', 66.

28 Ibid., 65, citing Bundesarchiv-Potsdam Abteilungen (BA-P), DO 1 7/205, .34. 10 August 1947, 'Zur Lage in der Polizei' from Otto Hanschke to Pfeiffer, SED Instrukteur for Brandenburg.

29 Frank Thomas Stössel, *Positionen und Strömungen in der KPD/SED 1945-1954* (Cologne: Verlag Wissenschaft und Politik, 1985), 169, cited in Bruce, *Resistance*, 84.

11. Order No. 201

1 Donnison, *Civil Affairs*, chapter XX.

2 Tantzscher, 'Die Vorläufer', 145.

3 Werkentin, *Politische Strafjustiz*, 23, cited in Bruce, *Resistance*, 69.

4 BA-P, DO 1 7/441, Protocol of the meeting of Mecklenburg Volkspolizei, 3 February 1948, 32, quoted in ibid., 69.

5 'Working Group C 3': see Ronald Wiedmann, Stasi-Unterlagen-Archiv, MfS Lexikon, https://www.stasi-unterlagen-archiv.de/mfs-lexikon/detail/k-5/, accessed 8.2.23.

6 Bruce, *Resistance*, 67, citing BStU ZA AS 229/66, K-5 annual report for Saxony 1947, 8 January 1948, 385.

7 Ibid., 101 and 596.

8 Bruce, *Resistance*, 85.

9 200 in Brandenburg, 120 in Mecklenburg, 155 in Saxony-Anhalt, 150 in Thuringia, 250 in Saxony. Tantzscher, 'Die Vorläufer', 144.

10 Naimark, 'To Know', citing BStU, MfSZ, AS 229/66, 'Jahresbericht Dezernat K-5' [same source as note 6].

11 Tantzscher, 'Die Vorläufer', 148.

12 Bruce, *Resistance*, citing BA-P, DO 1 7/270, 21 October 1947, 40.

13 Ibid., 42, citing ADsD, SPD-PV-Ostbüro, 0420 B/I, 15 August 1951, report by Helmut Wenke.

14 Ibid., 75, citing Brandenburgisches Landeshauptarchiv (BLHA), Ld.Br. Rep.332, L IV 2/4/187, SED Landesvorstand Brandenburg, 10 May 1948.

15 Buschfort, *Das Ostbüro*, 21, cited in Bruce, *Resistance*, 85.

16 Bruce, *Resistance*, 41, citing ADsD (Archiv der sozialen Demokratie in der Friedrich-Ebert-Stiftung Bonn Bad Godesberg), SPD-PV-Ostbüro, 0421, 25 July 1956, report on the arrest of the Rieke Group, Gardelegen, 2.

17 Ibid., 42, citing ADsD, SPD-PV-Ostbüro, 0421, 25 July 1956, report on Arthur Liebknecht's arrest by Soviet security organs, 2.

18 Ibid., citing interview with Hermann Kreutzer, 24 April 1995.

19 Thomas Boghardt, 'Our man in Berlin: The secret life of Willy Brandt', *Army History*, Winter 2022, No. 122, 10.

20 Bruce, *Resistance*, 72, citing AdsD, SPD-PV-Ostbüro 0421.

21 Ibid., 74, citing AdsD, SPD-PV-Ostbüro 0368a-c.

22 Ibid., citing Fricke, *Opposition*, 39.

23 Ibid., 43, citing Fricke, *Politik*, 118.

24 Konrad-Adenauer-Stiftung, 1996, cited in Bruce, *Resistance*, 92.

25 Soviet official in Thuringia, quoted in Murphy et al., *Battleground*, 506.

26 Richter, *Die Ost-CDU*, 83-86, cited in Bruce, *Resistance*, 86-87.

27 Ibid., 81 and 87.

28 Ibid., 82 and 86.

29 Murphy et al., *Battleground*, 420.

30 Richter, *Die Ost-CDU*, 81, cited in Bruce, *Resistance*, 87.

31 Michael Richter, 'Vom Widerstand der christlichen Demokraten in der DDR' in Brigitte Kaff (ed.), '*Gefährliche politische Gegner': Widerstand und Verfolgung in der sowjetischen Zone/DDR* (Düsseldorf: Droste, 1995), 50, cited in ibid., 87.

32 Tantzscher, 'Die Vorläufer', 146.

33 Ibid., 148.

34 Ibid., 149.

35 Ibid., 154.

36 Gieseke, *The GDR*, 13.

37 John C. Schmeidel, *Stasi: Shield and Sword of the Party* (London, New York: Routledge, 2014), 56, citing W. Dittmann and W. Zimmermann (eds.), *Otto Dibelius: So habe ich es erlebt – Selbstzeugnisse* (Berlin: Christlicher Zeitschriften Verlag, 1980), 265-70, and 'Abteilung K-5 Landesregierung Sachsen-Anhalt an die Deutsche Verwaltung des Innerns im sowjetischen Besatzungszone, Hirtenbrief des Doktor Dibelius'.

12. Developments in the Zone

1 Naimark, *The Russians*, 382.

2 'Memorandum des Chefs der SMA-Verwaltung des Landes Thüringen I. Kolesnicenko für B. Ponomarev zu Fragen der politischen Praxis in Deutschland (Auszug)' in Bernd Bonwetsch et al. (eds.), *Sowjetische Politik in der SBZ 1945-1949: Dokumente zur Tätigkeit der Propagandaverwaltung (Informationsverwaltung) der SMAD unter Sergei Tjulpanow*, Archiv für Sozialgeschichte, Beiheft 20 (Bonn: 1998), 183-98, cited in Gieseke, *The History*, 22.

3 Ibid., quoted in Gieseke, *The GDR*, 10, translated by Mary Carlene Forszt.

4 Gieseke, *The History*, 22.

5 Ibid., 19, and Naimark, *The Russians*, 395.

6 Bruce, *Resistance*, 84.

7 Henry Ashby Turner, *Germany from Partition to Unification* (New Haven: Yale University Press, 1992), 63, cited in ibid.

8 Suckut, 'Zur Krise', 33-34, cited in ibid., 87.

9 Dietrich Staritz, *Geschichte der DDR 1949-1985* (Frankfurt am Main: Suhrkamp Verlag, 1985), 23, quoted in Bruce, *Resistance*, 95.

10 Bruce, *Resistance*, 96-97.

11 Suckut, 'Zur Krise', 441-445, cited in Bruce, *Resistance*, 100.

12 Bruce, *Resistance*, 100.

13 Naimark, *The Russians*, 374.

14 Wolfgang Eisert, 'Zu den Anfängen der Sicherheits- und Militärpolitik der SED-Fuhrung 1948 bis 1952' in Thoss (ed.), *Volksarmee schaffen*, 173, cited in Bruce, *Resistance*, 83.
15 Rüdiger Wenzke, 'Auf dem Wege zur Kaderarmee: Aspekt der Rekrutierung, Sozialstruktur und personellen Entwicklung des ensteheden Militärs in der SBZ/DDR bis 1952/1953' in Thoss (ed.), *Volksarmee schaffen*, 209, cited in Bruce, *Resistance*, 43.
16 Bessel, 'Policing', 6.
17 BA-P, DO 1 7/38, Secretariat report on CDU meeting at Luchau 3 September 1948, 34, cited in Bruce, *Resistance*, 88.
18 *Die Neue Zeitung*, 31 December 1948.
19 Bruce, *Resistance*, 88, citing POLAD (Office for the Political Advisor) Secret Intelligence Report No. 495, 10 September 1948, NA, RG 59, 740.00119, Control (Germany), 9-1048, 1.
20 Naimark, 'To Know', 16, citing BStU, MfSZ, SdM, AS 331, 1.
21 Ibid., citing BStU, MfSZ, SdM, AS 323, 8.
22 Ibid.
23 Ibid., 17, citing BStU MfSZ, SdM, AS 323, 8.
24 Bessel, 'Policing', citing BAB, DO-1-7, No. 229, 'Eidesstattliche Erklärung der VP-Rekruten', 26.
25 Naimark, 'To Know', 17, citing BStU MfSZ, SdM, AS 323, 1-4.
26 Bruce, *Resistance,* 94, citing AdsD, SPD-PV-Ostbüro 0360/1.
27 See quote of CDU member Peter Bloch in Bruce, *Resistance*, 80.
28 Bruce, *Resistance*, 32-33.

13. The Cold War Hits New Depths

1 Francesco Alexander Cacciatore, 'Re-evaluating the émigrés: intelligence collection and policy-making in the early Cold War', *Journal of Intelligence History*, 2021, Vol. 20, No. 2, 133.
2 Murphy et al., *Battleground*, 66-70.
3 Sudoplatov et al., *Special Tasks*, 232.
4 Ibid., 233.
5 Ashby Turner, *Germany*, 23-24, cited in Bruce, *Resistance*, 82.
6 Naimark, 'To Know', 21, citing RP-321-48, NA, RG 260, box 24, 2.
7 Attributed to Paul Markgraf and Richard Gyptner, quoted in Naimark, 'To Know', 21, citing BStU, MfSZ, SdM 323, 15.
8 Naimark, 'To Know', 22, citing SAPMO-BA, ZPA, EA 0890/2, 260.
9 Ibid., 25, citing SMAD protocol, 9 March 1949, *Rossiiskii Tsentr Khraneniia I Izucheniia Dokumentov Noveishei Istorii* f.17, op.128, d.682, list 1, 123.
10 Ibid., 22, citing 7854th Military Intelligence report R-424-48, October 1948, NA, RG 260, box 24, 1-3.
11 Murphy et al., *Battleground*, 61.
12 Ibid., 74.
13 CIA information report, 30 December 1948, reproduced in Murphy et al., *Battleground*, 60.
14 Murphy et al., *Battleground*, 57-61.

14. Clean and Dirty Spying

1 National Archives and Records Administration (NARA), RG 263, Intelligence Publication Files, 1945-1950, ORE 22-48 (Addendum), 'Possibility of Direct Soviet Military Action during 1948-49', cited in Cacciatore, 'Re-evaluating', 132; CIA ORE 29-48, 'Possible Program of Future Soviet Moves in Germany', 28 April 1948, Document II-6 in Steury (ed.), *On the Front Lines*, 159.
2 David C. Martin, *Wilderness of Mirrors: Intrigue, Deception, and the Secrets that Destroyed Two of the Cold War's Most Important Agents* (New York: Skyhorse, 2018), 89.
3 Cacciatore, 'Re-evaluating', 133.
4 Ibid., 131.

5   Ibid., 126 and 144.
6   Jeffery, *MI6*, 667-668.
7   Wolf and McElvoy, *Memoirs*, 52-54.
8   Detlef Kühn, 'Lothar Weirauch und der Nachrichtendienst der West-KPD', *ZdF* 11 (2002).
9   Jeffery, *MI6*, 665.
10 Case, 'The Joint Intelligence Committee', 64.
11 Murphy et al., *Battleground*, 66-68.
12 Ibid., 72.
13 Faligot and Krop, *La Piscine*, 49.
14 Murphy et al., *Battleground*, 75.
15 Ibid., 415.
16 Ibid., 415-416.
17 Information in this section comes from Wilhelm Mensing, *SED-Hilfe für West-Genossen: Die Arbeit der Abteilung Verkehr beim Zentralkomitee der SED im Spiegel der Überlieferung des Ministeriums für Staatssicherheit der DDR (1946-1976)* (Berlin: BStU, 2010).
18 MI5 file on Richard Stahlmann, KV-2/3698, UK National Archives, 43.
19 Ibid., 42-43.
20 Ibid., 28.
21 Jerome Wilson, 'The Mastermind of Shipping Sabotage', *Reader's Digest*, December 1957.
22 Heinz Kühne, *Kuriere-Spitzel-Spione: Der ehemalige Leiter der Berliner Filiale des Ostbüros berichtet über den Spitzel- und Spionageapparat der SPD* (Berlin: Dietz Verlag, 1949).
23 Unless otherwise stated, quotes and the information discussed in this section come from Wilfred Burchett, *War-mongers Unmasked No. 5: Cold War in Germany* (Melbourne: World Unity Publications, 1950), Ch.1 and 2, and passim.
24 *Neues Deutschland*, 14 April 1949.

15. The Murder That Wasn't

1   Unless otherwise stated, information in this chapter comes from BArch, MfS, AS, 222-66, Bd. 2.
2   *Welt am Sonntag*, 24 July 1949.
3   *Der Tag*, 28 July 1949.
4   *Die Welt*, 27 July 1949.
5   *Sozialdemokrat*, 9 August 1949.
6   *Hamburger Echo*, 23 July 1949.

16. The Final Steps Towards the Stasi

1   'Die Aufgaben der Volkspolizei', 15 October 1948 (BStU MfSZ, Sekretariat des Ministers, AS 323, p.8), quoted in Norman Naimark, *The Russians*, 369.
2   Naimark, 'To Know', 13, citing BStU MfSZ, 400/66, 126.
3   Naimark, *The Russians*, 365.
4   Naimark, 'To Know', citing BStU MfSZ, AS 229/66, 266-267.
5   Naimark, *The Russians*, 365.
6   Naimark, 'To Know', 15.
7   Ibid., 14.
8   Ibid., 15, citing BStU, MfSZ, AS 238/66, 'Polizei und Bevölkerung' manuscript, 204-205.
9   Gieseke, *The GDR*, 12.
10 Gieseke, *The History*, 28.

Part II. United at Birth: The GDR and the Stasi

17. The Firm

1   'Gangster und Mörder im Kampf gegen unsere Republik. Bericht des Generalinspekteurs der Hauptverwaltung zum Schutz der Volkswirtschaft, Erich Mielke' ('Gangsters and murderers fighting our republic: report of the Inspector General of the Main Directorate for the Protection of the National Economy, Erich Mielke'), *Neues Deutschland*, 28 January 1950, quoted in Gieseke, *The History*, 12.
2   Schmeidel, *Stasi*, 8.
3   Mielke, 'Gangster und Mörder'.
4   'Die Hintermänner' ('The Backers'), *Neues Deutschland*, 29 January 1950.
5   Provisorische Volkskammer der Deutschen Demokratischen Republik, Protokoll der 10. Sitzung, 213, cited in Gieseke, *The History*, 11.
6   Ibid., cited in Gieseke, *The GDR*, 15.
7   Gieseke, *The History*, 13.
8   Roger Engelmann, Frank Joestel, *Grundsatzdokumente des MfS* (MfS-Handbuch) (Berlin: BStU, 2010), 5-6.
9   Gieseke, *The History*, 124.
10 The latter figure is given in Childs and Popplewell, *The Stasi*, 76, the former in Jens Gieseke, 'German Democratic Republic' in Krzysztof Persak and Łukasz Kamiński (eds.), *A Handbook of the Communist Security Apparatus in East Central Europe 1944-1989* (Warsaw: Institute of National Remembrance, 2005), 174.
11 Jefferson Adams, *Historical Dictionary of German Intelligence* (Lanham, Toronto, Plymouth: The Scarecrow Press, Inc., 2009), 143.
12 Roland Wiedmann, Hauptabteilung PS on Stasi-Unterlagen-Archiv, MfS Lexikon, available at https://www.stasi-unterlagen-archiv.de/mfs-lexikon/detail/hauptabteilung-ps-personenschutz/, accessed 13.4.2024.
13 Maria Haendcke-Hoppe-Arndt, *Die Hauptabteilung XVIII: Volkswirtschaft* (MfS-Handbuch) (Berlin: BStU, 1997, 13-14).
14 Ibid.
15 Tobias Wunschik, *Hauptabteilung VII: Ministerium des Innern, Deutsche Volkspolizei* (MfS-Handbuch) (Berlin: BStU, 2009), 36.
16 Angela Schmole, *Hauptabteilung VIII: Beobachtung, Ermittlung, Durchsuchung, Festnahme* (MfS-Handbuch) (Berlin: BStU, 2011), 69.
17 Ibid.
18 Roger Engelmann, Frank Joestel, *Die Hauptabteilung IX: Untersuchung* (Berlin: BStU, 2016), 44-45.
19 Childs and Popplewell, *The Stasi*, 81.
20 BStU, MfS, BdL-Dok. 3098, 'Dienstordnung des Staatssekretariats für Staatssicherheit', 17 September 1954.
21 Gieseke, *The History*, 32.
22 Gary Bruce, *The Firm: The Inside Story of the Stasi* (Oxford, New York: Oxford University Press, 2010), 37.
23 Mike Dennis, *The Stasi: Myth and Reality* (London, New York: Routledge, 2003), 80.
24 BStU, MfS, BV Karl-Marx-Stadt, AIM, No. 1573/72, 37.
25 Childs and Popplewell, *The Stasi*, 49.
26 BStU, MfS, OV Wismut, AIM, No. 728/69, 20.
27 Benjamin Schulz, 'Wie die Stasi SS-Leute aus Auschwitz erpresste', *Der Spiegel*, 24 August 2014.
28 Pseudonymous interview in Bruce, *The Firm*, 67.
29 Bruce, *The Firm*, 54.
30 BStU, MfS, BdL 2635, No. 101157, 'Vorläufige Geschäfts- und Büroordnung des Ministeriums fur Staatssicherheit'.

31 Jens Gieseke, "'Genossen erster Kategorie'": Die hauptamtlichen Mitarbeiter des Ministeriums für Staatssicherheit als Elite' in Peter Hübner, Böhlau Köln (eds.), *Eliten im Sozialismus: Beiträge zur Sozialgeschichte der DDR* (Potsdam: Zentrum für Zeithistorische Forschung, 1999), 222-223.

18. Party, Partners, and the Law

1   The above quotes come from Stasi materials cited in Childs and Popplewell, *The Stasi*, 69.
2   Arno Polzin, *Der Wandel Robert Havemanns vom Inoffiziellen Mitarbeiter zum Dissidenten im Spiegel der MfS-Akten* (Berlin: BF informiert 26/2005), 50-51.
3   BStU, ZA, KL-SED 570, 6-26.
4   Silke Schumann, *Parteierziehung in der Geheimpolizei: zur Rolle der SED im MfS der fünfziger Jahre* (Berlin: Ch. Links, 1997), 135.
5   Gieseke, *The GDR*, 15.
6   Dennis, *The Stasi*, 191.
7   Schmeidel, *Stasi*, 119.
8   Ibid., 78.
9   Dennis, *The Stasi*, 63.
10 Klaus Marxen, "Recht' im Verständnis des Ministeriums für Staatssicherheit der DDR' in Roger Engelmann and Clemens Vollnhals (eds.), *Justiz im Dienste der Parteiherrschaft: Rechtspraxis und Staatssicherheit in der DDR* (Berlin: Ch. Links, 1999), 16, quoted in Dennis, *The Stasi*, 61.
11 Cited in Clemens Vollnhals, "'Die Macht ist das Allererste": Staatssicherheit und Justiz' in Engelmann and Vollnhals, *Justiz im Dienste*, 227, re-cited in Dennis, translated by Mike Dennis and Peter Brown.
12 Dennis, *The Stasi*, 62.
13 Schmeidel, *Stasi*, 40.
14 Ibid.
15 Ibid., citing the GDR Criminal Code (*Strafgesetzbuch*), 1988 (StGB).
16 Jens Gieseke, *Mielke-Konzern: Die Geschichte der Stasi 1945-1990* (Stuttgart: Deutsche Verlags Anstalt, 2001), 174-178, cited in Schmeidel, *Stasi*, 41.

19. A New European Country

1   Information in this section comes from Childs and Popplewell, *The Stasi*, 66.
2   Childs and Popplewell, *The Stasi*, 96.
3   Siegfried Suckut, 'Die Entscheidung zur Gründung der DDR', *VfZ* 39 (1991), 134, cited in Bruce, *Resistance*, 128.
4   Bruce, *Resistance*, 139, citing ACDP, III-013-630/3, report 5 March 1952.
5   Ibid., citing AdsD, SPD-PV-Ostbüro 0357 I, report on the conduct of the election in the GDR, 3 November 1950.
6   Ina Merkel (ed.), *'Wir sind doch nicht die Meckerecke der Nation!' Briefe an das Fernsehen der DDR* (Berlin: Schwarzkopf & Schwarzkopf, 1998), 14, 22, 25, cited in Dennis, *The Stasi*, 216.
7   Wolf and McElvoy, *Memoirs*, 42.
8   Murphy et al., *Battleground*, 106.
9   Childs and Popplewell, *The Stasi*, 96.
10 Lowe, *Savage Continent*, 61.
11 BArch, MfS, BdL-Dok Nr. 3356, 'Instruktion für die Beobachtung – Abteilung VIII', 4 December 1954, 4.
12 Schmeidel, *Stasi*, 41.
13 Gieseke, *The History*, 25.
14 Ibid., 126.
15 Football Focus, BBC One television, 16 November 2013.

16 Nancy Thorndike Greenspan, *Atomic Spy: The Dark Lives of Klaus Fuchs* (New York: Viking, 2020), 353-354.
17 Bruce, *Resistance*, 103.
18 Thomas Ammer, *Universität zwischen Demokratie und Diktatur* (Cologne: Verlag Wissenschaft und Politik, 1969), 48-53, cited in Bruce, *Resistance*, 91.

Interlude: The DNA of the Stasi

1 Comintern official, Report on National School, 1932, RGASPI, 495/100/842; Special Bureau, 23 January 1933 and Party Day, 24 January 1933, RGASPI, 531/2/61, quoted in McIlroy et al., 'Forging the Faithful: The British at the International Lenin School', *Labour History Review* (2003), 109.

20. Conspiracy

1 The discussion in this section is based upon, and quotations taken from, Victor Serge, *Unforgiving Years*, translated by Richard Greeman and The Victor Serge Foundation (New York: New York Review of Books, 2008), part I, The Secret Agent.
2 Michael Fredholm, 'Soviet active measures in west, southeast, and east Asia with regard to Afghanistan, 1980-1982', *Journal for Intelligence, Propaganda and Security Studies*, Vol. 13, No. 1 (2020), 69.
3 See for example the MI5 files on the FPA, KV 2/1099-1101, UK National Archives, passim.
4 Christopher Andrew and Oleg Gordievsky, *KGB: The Inside Story of its Foreign Operations from Lenin to Gorbachev* (London: Sceptre, 1991) 99.

21. Chekists: The OGPU and NKVD

1 V.I. Lenin, *The State and Revolution* (London: Allen & Unwin, 1919), ch.5, pts. 2 and 3, quoted in Andrew, *KGB*, 54.
2 Rayfield, *Stalin*, 60.
3 Ibid.
4 Ibid., 275.
5 Ibid., 79.
6 This figure was quoted in the text of an exhibition at the British Library in 2007. See also, for example: www.balticworlds.com/culture-and-displacement-in-the-age-of-war-and-revolution, accessed 14.10.2021.
7 David R. Shearer, *Policing Stalin's Socialism: Repression and social order in the Soviet Union, 1925-1953* (New Haven, London: Yale University Press, 2009), 335.
8 Publicly released NKVD statistics put the number of deaths at 682,000 shot and 116,000 who died in the labour camps. Both figures almost certainly are too low.
9 Three books in particular are recommended for their coverage of the purge and are sources for the information in this section: *Policing Stalin's Socialism* by David R. Shearer, *Terror by Quota* by Paul R. Gregory, and *Stalin's Loyal Executioner* by Marc Jansen and Nikita Petrov.
10 Norbert Podewin, *Walter Ulbricht: Eine neue Biographie* (Berlin: Dietz Verlag, 1995), 133-134, cited in Dennis, *The Stasi*, 19.

22. RU

1 Andrew and Mitrokhin, *The Mitrokhin Archive*, 366-367.
2 See for example Gordon W. Prange, *Target Tokyo: The Story of the Sorge Spy Ring* (New York: McGraw-Hill Book Company, 1984), passim.
3 Raymond W. Leonard, *Secret Soldiers of the Revolution: Soviet Military Intelligence, 1918-1933* (Westport, London: Greenwood Press, 1999), 20.
4 Gieseke, *The History*, 155.

5 Leonard, *Secret Soldiers*, 18.
6 MI5 debriefing of Walter Krivitsky, reproduced partially in Nigel West, *Mask: MI5's Penetration of the Communist Party of Great Britain* (Abingdon, New York: Routledge, 2005), 265.
7 Ibid., 247-300.

23. The Comintern and the OMS

1 West, *Mask*, 243-244.
2 Leonard, *Secret Soldiers*, 17.
3 See for example Walter Krivitsky, *I Was Stalin's Agent* (Cambridge: Ian Faulkner Publishing Ltd, 1992), 39-87.
4 Monty Johnstone, 'The CPGB, the Comintern and the War, 1939-1941: Filling in the Blank Spots', *Science & Society*, Vol. 61, No. 1 (1997), 31.
5 MI5 debriefing, 291.
6 Paul McMahon, *British Spies & Irish Rebels: British Intelligence and Ireland 1916-1945* (Woodbridge: The Boydell Press, 2018), 209.
7 MI5 debriefing, 267.
8 McIlroy et al., 'Forging', 103.
9 Ibid., 101.
10 MI5 debriefing, 290.
11 Julia Köstenberger, 'Die Internationale Lenin-Schule (1926-1938)', in Michael Buckmiller, Klaus Meschkat (eds.), *Biographisches Handbuch zur Geschichte der Kommunistischen Internationale: Ein deutsch-russisches Forschungsprojekt* (Berlin: Akademie Verlag, 2007), 287.

24. Stasi Creation Myths

1 Allan Merson, *Communist Resistance in Nazi Germany* (London: Lawrence and Wishart Ltd, 1985), 34.
2 Rebecca West, *The Meaning of Treason* (London: Virago Press Limited, 1982), 69.
3 See for example the permanent exhibition on the rise of the Nazis at NS-Dokumentationszentrum der Stadt Köln.
4 Merson, 88.
5 Ibid., 51.
6 Childs and Popplewell, *The Stasi*, 20-21.
7 Merson, 112-113.
8 Arnold Paucker, *German Jews in the Resistance 1933-1945: The Facts and the Problems* (Berlin: Gedenkstätte Deutscher Widerstand, 2005), 18-23.
9 Arlene Riecker, Annett Schwarz, Dirk Schneider, *Stasi intim: Gespräcber mit ehemaligen MfS-Angehörigen* (Leipzig: Forum, 1990), 167-168, quoted in Gieseke, *The GDR*, 21, translated by Mary Carlene Forszt.
10 Quoted in Stanley G. Payne, *The Spanish Civil War, the Soviet Union and Communism* (Newhaven, London: Yale University Press, 2004), 165.
11 See Boris Volodarsky, *Stalin's Agent: The Life and Death of Alexander Orlov* (New York, Cambridge: Cambridge University Press, 2015), Part II 'In Spain', 135-353.

25. First Class Comrades: The Stasi's Early Leaders

1 As well as obvious online sources, the main background sources for these biographies are:

Jefferson Adams, *Historical Dictionary of German Intelligence* (Lanham, Toronto, Plymouth: The Scarecrow Press, Inc., 2009).
Heike Amos, *Politik und Organisation der SED-Zentrale 1949-1963: Struktur und Arbeitsweise*

von Politbüro, Sekretariat, Zentralkomitee und ZK-Apparat (Berlin, Hamburg, Munster: LIT Verlag, 2003).

Thomas Auerbach, *Einsatzkommandos an der unsichtbaren Front: Terror- und Sabotagevorbereitung des MfS gegen die Bundesrepublik* (Berlin: Links Verlag, 1999).

Bernd-Rainer Barth, Jens Gieseke, *Wer war wer in der DDR?* 5. Ausgabe. Band 1 (Berlin: Links Verlag, 2010).

Gabriele Baumgartner, Dieter Hebig (eds.), *Biographisches Handbuch der SBZ/DDR 1945-1990* (Munich: Saur, 1996).

David Childs and Richard Popplewell, *The Stasi: The East German Intelligence and Security Service* (Basingstoke, New York: Palgrave, 1996).

Torsten Diedrich et al., *Im Dienste der Partei – Handbuch der bewaffneten Organe der DDR* (Berlin: Links Verlag, 1998).

Roger Engelmann et al.: *Das MfS-Lexikon* (Berlin: Links Verlag, 2016).

Stephan Fingerle, Jens Gieseke, 'Partisanen des Kalten Krieges: Die Untergrundtruppe der Nationalen Volksarmee 1957-1962 und ihre Übernahme durch die Staatssicherheit' (Berlin: BStU/Abt. Bildung und Forschung, 1996).

Jan von Flocken and Michael F. Scholtz, *Ernst Wollweber: Saboteur, Minister, Unperson* (Berlin: Aufbau, 1994).

Karl Wilhelm Fricke, *Der Wahrheit verpflichtet: Texte aus fünf Jahrzehnten zur Geschichte der DDR* (Berlin: Links Verlag, 2000).

Klaus Froh, Rüdiger Wenzke (eds.), *Die Generale und Admirale der NVA: Ein biographisches Handbuch*, 5th edition (Berlin: Links Verlag, 2007).

Gottfried Hamacher et al. (eds.), *Gegen Hitler: Deutsche in der Résistance, in den Streitkräften der Antihitlerkoalition und der Bewegung 'Freies Deutschland'* (Berlin: Dietz, 2005).

Heiko Haumann, 'Hermann Diamanski: Ein deutsches Schicksal zwischen Auschwitz und Staatssicherheitsdienst. Perspektiven der Erinnerung', in Birgit E. Klein, Christiane E. Müller (eds.), *Memoria – Wege jüdischen Erinnerns: Festschrift für Michael Brocke zum 65* (Berlin: Metropol, 2005).

Andreas Herbst, 'Friedrich Dickel – GRU-Agent, NVA-General und Innenminister der DDR', in Hans Ehlert, Armin Wagner (eds.), *Genosse General! Die Militärelite der DDR in biografischen Skizzen* (Berlin: Links Verlag, 2003).

Andreas Herbst et al., *So funktionierte die DDR* (Reinbek: Rowohlt, 1994).

Andreas Herbst et al., *Die SED – Geschichte, Organisation, Politik: Ein Handbuch* (Berlin: Dietz, 1997).

Thomas Horstmann, *Logik der Willkür: Die Zentrale Kommission für Staatliche Kontrolle in der SBZ/DDR von 1948 bis 1958* (Cologne: Böhla, 2002), originally Bamberg University dissertation, 2000.

Bernd Kaufmann et al.: *Der Nachrichtendienst der KPD 1919-1937* (Berlin: Dietz, 1993).

Hubertus Knabe, *West-Arbeit des MfS: Das Zusammenspiel von 'Aufklärung' und 'Abwehr'*, in collaboration with Bernd Eisenfeld (Berlin: Links Verlag, 1999).

Michael Kubina, "Was in dem einen Teil verwirklicht werden kann mit Hilfe der Roten Armee, wird im anderen Teil Kampffrage sein", Zum Aufbau des zentralen Westapparates der KPD/SED 1945–1959', in Manfred Wilke (ed.), *Die Anatomie der Parteizentrale: Die KPD/SED auf dem Weg zur Macht* (Berlin: Akademie Verlag, 1998).

Wilhelm Mensing, 'Zwischen Ost und West – Kuriere und Schleuser im Dienst von KPD und SED', *Zeitschrift des Forschungsverbundes SED-Staat* Ausgabe, 18/2005.

Werner Röder, Herbert A. Strauss (eds.), *Biographisches Handbuch der deutschsprachigen Emigration nach 1933* (Munich: Saur, 1980).

Matthias Uhl, 'Richard Stahlmann (1891–1974): Ein Handlanger der Weltrevolution im Geheimauftrag der SED', in Dieter Krüger, Armin Wagner (eds.), *Konspiration als Beruf: Deutsche Geheimdienstchefs im Kalten Krieg,* (Berlin: Links Verlag, 2003).

Boris Volodarsky, *Stalin's Agent: The Life & Death of Alexander Orlov* (Oxford: Oxford University Press, 2015), 214-218.

Armin Wagner, *Walter Ulbricht und die geheime Sicherheitspolitik der SED: Der Nationale*

Verteidigungsrat der DDR und seine Vorgeschichte (1953 bis 1971) (Berlin: Links Verlag, 2002), originally Potsdam University dissertation, 2001.

Hermann Weber, Andreas Herbst (eds.): *Deutsche Kommunisten: Biographisches Handbuch 1918 bis 1945* 2., Überarbeitete und stark erweiterte Auflage (Berlin: Dietz, 2008).

Erich Wollenberg, 'Der Apparat – Stalins fünfte Kolonne', *Ost-Probleme* Nr. 19 (Bonn: Bundesministerium für gesamtdeutsche Fragen, 1951).

2   Jan von Flocken and Michael F. Scholtz, *Ernst Wollweber*, quoted in Childs and Popplewell, *The Stasi*, 27.

3   See, for example, 'De activiteiten van een communistische sabotagegroep in Antwerpen en Rotterdam: De organisatie Wollweber (1933-1939)' by Hans Dankaart and Rudi van Doorslaer, available at https://www.marxists.org/nederlands/thema/wereldoorlog2/1979sabotage.htm, accessed 12.1.2022.

4   Extract from MI6 letter in MI5 file for Richard Stahlmann, KV-2/3698, UK National Archives, 10.

Part III. Stalinism in Action

1   BStU, ZA, KL-SED 570, fo. 24, quoted in Gieseke, *The GDR*, 20, translated by Mary Carlene Forszt, amended by author.

26. Rostock, 1950

1   Engelmann and Joestel, *Die Hauptabteilung IX*, 50-53.

2   'Stalinism' has been described as a form of 'militarised socialism', its features being 'the high priority traditionally assigned to defense and heavy industry and the policy of relative economic autarky; the pervasive bureaucratization of public life and a political style that favors discipline and obedience over consensus-building and pluralism; a pronounced ideological disdain for markets, material incentives, and the private realm in general, in favor of moral-ideological suasion and self-sacrifice in the name of a greater public good to be attained in the indefinite future; the relatively favorable social status and prestige attached to military careers and the place of officers among social and political elites; the permeation of education and culture with patriotism, national security values, conservative nationalism, and a high premium on conformism; finally a foreign policy predicated on confrontation, a rhetorical and eventually material support for military revolutionary elites and, since the late 1930s, a heavy reliance on Soviet military might for attaining foreign policy objectives'. Mark von Hagen, 'Army, Society and Reformism in Soviet History' in David Holloway, Norman Naimark (eds.), *Reexamining the Soviet Experience: Essays in Honor of Alexander Dallin* (Boulder, London: Westview Press, 1996), 52.

3   Engelmann and Joestel, *Die Hauptabteilung IX*, 40.

4   Gieseke, *The GDR*, 16.

5   Quoted in ibid., 18.

6   Recollections of Richard J. Zatka in *Zeitzeugen: Inhaftiert in Berlin-Hohenschönhausen* (Berlin: Gedenkstätte Berlin-Hohenschönhausen, 1998), 14, extracted in Gieseke, *The GDR*, 16, translated by Mary Carlene Forszt.

7   Bruce, *Resistance*, 258-261.

8   Karsten Jedlitschka, Jens Niederhut, Philipp Springer, Christian Appl, *Verschluss Sachen: Dokumente, Fotos und Objekte aus dem Archiv der Staatssicherheit* (Berlin: BStU, 2017), 14-16.

9   Engelmann and Joestel, *Die Hauptabteilung IX*, 40.

10 Ibid., 12.

11 'Boykotthetze gegen demokratische Einrichtungen und Organisationen, Mordhetze gegen demokratische Politiker, Bekundung vo Glaubens-, Rassen-, Volkerhass, militärische Propaganda sowie Kriegshetzeas', cited in Susanne Muhle, *Auftrag – Menschenraub: Entführungen von Westberlinern und Bundesbürgern durch das Ministerium für Staatssicherheit der DDR* (Göttingen: Vandenhoeck & Ruprecht, 2015), 201.

12 Engelmann and Joestel, *Die Hauptabteilung IX*, 40.
13 Muhle, *Auftrag*, 201.

27. Cleansing the SED

1 Dennis, *The Stasi*, 25.
2 BStU, MfS, AU, Nr. 192/56, Bd. 2, 134.
3 Engelmann and Joestel, *Die Hauptabteilung IX*, 38.
4 Fricke, *Opposition*, 42, cited in Bruce, *Resistance*, 74.
5 Koehler, *Stasi*, 126.
6 Ibid., 125.
7 Margarete Bauer was held in the Brandenburg/Havel detention centre. Engelmann and Joestel, *Die Hauptabteilung IX*, 38.
8 Hubertus Knabe, *Die Täter sind unter uns: Über das Schönreden der SED-Diktatur* (Berlin: Propyläen Verlag, 2007), 294.

28. Neutering the National Front

1 Karl Wilhelm Fricke, *Opposition*, 68, cited in Bruce, *Resistance*, 128.
2 Richter, 'Vom Widerstand', 228, 239, cited in ibid.
3 Wolfgang Buschfort, *Die Ostbüros der Parteien in den 50er Jahren* (Berlin: BStU, 2006), 49.
4 Kaff (ed.), *'Gefährliche politische'*, 226, cited in Bruce, *Resistance*, 128.
5 Bruce, *Resistance*, 138, citing BA-P, DO 1 11/1121, 139.
6 Hermann Weber, *DDR: Grundriss der Geschichte 1945-1990* (Hannover: Fackelträger, 1991), 45, cited in Bruce, *Resistance*, 139.
7 Gudrun Weber in collaboration with Bernd Florath, *"Nun falten Sie den Zettel…": Wahlen in der DDR in der Überlieferung der Staatssicherheit (1949-1961)* (Berlin: BStU, 2019), 24-26.
8 BStU, MfS, AS 221/66, Bd. 1, 18-20.
9 BStU, MfS, AS 11/51, Bd. 2, 113-124.
10 Bruce, *Resistance*, 140, citing BA-P, DO 1 11/752 and 11/1121, 20 September and 18 October 1950.
11 Bruce, *Resistance*, 141-144.
12 Richter, 'Vom Widerstand', 118, cited in ibid., 128.
13 Konrad-Adenauer-Stiftung, cited in ibid., 150-151.
14 BStU, MfS, HA XX 6, 31, MfS Dienststelle Salzwedel, 16 August 1950, quoted in Weber and Florath, *"Nun falten Sie den Zettel…"*, 24.
15 Peter Bloch, *Zwischen Hoffnung und Resignation* (Cologne: Verlag Wissenschaft und Politik, 1986), 165, cited in Bruce, *Resistance*, 131.
16 Bruce, *Resistance*, 132-133.
17 Bruce, *Resistance*, 123, citing BStU, ZA, GVS 27/50, #101092, Directive I/IVa/50, 2 November 1950.
18 Richter, *Die Ost-CDU*, 363, cited in Bruce, *Resistance*, 132.
19 Franz-Josef Kos, 'Der Erfurter Schauprozess und die beiden Nachfolgeprozesse 1952/53' in Kaff (ed.), *'Gefährliche Politische Gegner'*, 126-130, cited in ibid., 163.
20 Richter, 'Vom Widerstand', 48-52, cited in ibid., 163.
21 Willi Brundert, *Es begann im Theater…'Volksjustiz' hinter dem eisernen Vorhang* (Berlin: J.H.W. Dietz, 1958), 49, cited in ibid., 129-130.
22 Bruce, *Resistance*, 138.
23 Bessel, 'Policing', 4.
24 Fricke, *Politik*, 215, cited in Bruce, *Resistance*, 137.
25 Richter, *Die Ost-CDU*, 278-9, cited in Bruce, *Resistance*, 131.
26 BArch, MfS, BdL-Dok, 2365, Richtlinie I/IV/50, 9 October 1950, and 2366, Richtlinie I/IVa/1950, 9 November 1950.
27 Murphy et al., *Battleground*, 112-113.

28 Bruce, *Resistance*, 131, citing ADL, #2929 report by CDU's Werner Westermann regarding resistance group 'Michael' in Halberstadt, Saxony-Anhalt, 30 March 1951.

29 Schmeidel, *Stasi*, 91-92.

30 Schmole, *Hauptabteilung VIII*, 70.

31 Christine André and Doris Hubert, *Stasi: The exhibition of the GDR's State Security* (Berlin: BStU, 2011), 31.

32 Koehler, *Stasi*, 107-109.

29. Enemies

1   BStU, ZA, GVS 8/50 #101091, 'Richtlinien über die Erfassung von Personen, die eine feindliche Tätigkeit durchführen und die von den Organen des Ministeriums für Staatssicherheit festgestellt wurden', 20 September 1950.

2   BStU, MfS, BdL-Dok. 2508. – Abschrift, 4 S. – MfS-DSt-Nr. 101091, 'Richtlinien zur Erfassung der durch die Organe des Ministeriums für Staatssicherheit der DDR verhafteten Personen', 20 September 1950. Gary Bruce notes the importance assigned to 'agents of the USA'.

3   Gieseke, *The History*, 32.

4   Gary Bruce, 'The Prelude to Nationwide Surveillance in East Germany: Stasi Operations and Threat Perceptions, 1945-1953', *Journal of Cold War Studies*, Vol. 5, No. 2 (2003), 15.

5   Schmeidel, *Stasi*, 29, citing Richtlinie 21: Über die Suche, Anwerbung und Arbeit mit Informatoren, geheimen Mitarbeitern und Personen, die konspirativen Wohnungen unterhalten (1953), translated by Schmeidel, amended by author.

6   Engelmann and Joestel, *Hauptabteilung IX*, 42.

7   Konstanze Soch (ed.), *Stasi in Brandenburg: Die DDR-Geheimpolizei in den Bezirken Cottbus, Frankfurt (Oder) und Potsdam* (Berlin: BStU, 2020), 125.

8   Engelmann and Joestel, *Hauptabteilung IX*, 50.

9   Murphy et al., *Battleground*, 470.

10 Ralf Langroth, 'Finstere Pläne für den Tag X', *Der Spiegel*, 16 April 2021.

11 Ibid.

12 Bruce, *Resistance*, 123, citing BStU, ZA, Tgb. Nr. 423/51, Directive 7/51, Mielke to Hermann Gartmann, Chefinspekteur of MfS Brandenburg.

13 BArch, MfS, AS, Nr. 171-56, Bd 2, 27.

14 Ibid., 123.

15 Langroth, 'Finstere Pläne'.

16 'Utilization of the Mass of Soviet Refugees', 19 April 1948 (MORI No. 144243), Document I-6 in Steury (ed.), *On the Front Lines*, 110.

17 Andrew and Mitrokhin, *The Mitrokhin Archive*, 230-231; Murphy et al., *Battleground*, 241-244.

18 Kai-Uwe Merz, *Kalter Krieg als antikommunistischer Widerstand: Die KgU 1948-1959* (Munich: R. Oldenbourg Verlag, 1987), 60, cited in Bruce, *Resistance*, 94.

19 Ibid.

20 Elise Catrain (ed.), *Stasi in Mecklenburg-Vorpommern: Die DDR-Geheimpolizei in den Bezirken Neubrandenburg, Rostock und Schwerin* (Berlin: BStU, 2019), 10-14.

21 Enrico Heitzer, '...die Masse soweit bringen, dass sie nachdenkt...': Ein Widerstandsgruppe in Altenburg in der Zeit der SBZ und frühen DDR', *Deutschland Archiv* 39 (2006), 245-254.

22 BStU, MfS, AS 555/57, Bd. 1, 194-201, Verwaltung Thüringen des MfS: Bericht über westliche Feindorganisationen, 27.3.1952.

23 'CIA finanzierte Sabotage und Anschläge in der DDR', *Der Spiegel*, 20 February 2015.

24 BStU, MfS, ZAIG, No. 18533, Propagandabroschüre zum Volksaufstand des 17. Juni 1953, 22.

25 Merz, *Kalter Krieg*, 159.

26 Murphy et al., *Battleground*, 108.

27 Thomas Boghardt review of the Enrico Heitzer book *Die Kampfgruppe gegen Unmenschlichkeit (KgU): Widerstand und Spionage im Kalten Krieg 1948-1959*, Studies in Intelligence, Vol 59, No. 4, December 2015.

28 Thomas Auerbach, Matthias Braun, Bernd Eisenfeld, Gesine von Prittwitz, Clemens Vollnhals, *Hauptabteilung XX: Staatsapparat, Blockparteien, Kirchen, Kultur, 'politischer Untergrund'* (MfS-Handbuch) (Berlin: BStU, 2008), 105.

29 Enrico Heitzer, "'Kalter Krieger": Zur Tätigkeit der Kampfgruppe gegen Unmenschlichkeit in West-Berlin und der Bundesrepublik' in Wolfgang Benz (ed.), *Ein Kampf um Deutungshoheit: Politik, Opferinteressen und historische Forschung* (Berlin: Metropol Verlag, 2013), 162-169.

30 Ibid., 173-178.

31 Enrico Heitzer, 'Humanitäre Organisation und Nachrichtendienst: Die Kampfgruppe gegen Unmenschlichkeit (1948-1959) im Bundesnotaufnahmeverfahren', *Zeitschrift für Geschichtswissenschaft* (2016), 152.

32 Keith R. Allen, *Befragung – Überprüfung – Kontrolle: Die Aufnahme von DDR-Flüchtlingen in West-Berlin bis 1961* (Berlin: Ch. Links, 2013), 16.

33 Ibid.

34 Fricke, *Politik*, 251, cited in Bruce, *Resistance*, 137; Gieseke, *The History*, 33.

35 'CIA finanzierte'.

36 Enrico Heitzer, 'SMT-Verfahren im Zusammenhang mit der Kampfgruppe gegen Unmenschlichkeit (KgU)' in *Sowjetische Militärjustiz in der SBZ/DDR (1945-1955)* (Halle: Hallische Beträge zur Zeitgeschichte, 2007), 60.

37 BArch, MfS, BdL-Dok, Nr. 62, Befehl Nr. 60/52, 24.4.52.

38 Murphy et al., *Battleground*, 107-108.

39 Heitzer, 'SMT-Verfahren', 52.

40 Koehler, *Stasi*, 288.

41 Ibid., 132-133.

42 Heitzer, "'Kalter Krieger"', 168.

43 'CIA finanzierte'.

44 Heitzer, 'SMT-Verfahren', 52-71.

45 Siegfried Mampel, *Der Untergrundkampf des Ministeriums für Staatssicherheit Gegen den Untersuchungsausschuss Freiheitlicher Juristen in West-Berlin* (Berlin: BStU, 1999), 21.

46 Koehler, *Stasi*, 137.

47 Frank Hagemann, 'Die Drohung des Rechts: Der Kampf des Untersuchungsausschusses Freiheitlicher Juristen' in Gerhard Finn et al., *Unrecht überwinden: SED-Diktatur und Widerstand* (Sankt Augustin: Konrad-Adenauer-Stiftung, 1996), 17.

48 Frank Hagemann, 'Der Untersuchungsausschuss Freiheitlicher Juristen 1949-1969', dissertation, Kiel University, 1994, 59.

49 Mampel, *Der Untergrundkampf*, 31.

50 Hagemann, 'Die Drohung', 18.

51 SVR file 70465, Vol. 1, MGB annual report 1952, 138-139, quoted in Murphy et al., *Battleground*, 118.

52 Koehler, *Stasi*, 137.

53 Engelmann and Joestel, *Hauptabteilung IX*, 50.

54 'Operations against East Germany', https://www.globalsecurity.org/intell/ops/ddr.htm, accessed 12.12.2021.

55 Murphy et al., *Battleground*, 212.

56 BStU, MfS, AS 88/59, 36-37, Westpresse zur 'Grünen Woche', Info Nr. M1/56.

57 Christiane Kohl, 'Donner, Blitz und Teddy', *Der Spiegel*, 3 March 1996.

58 Koehler, *Stasi*, 140

59 Adams, *Historical Dictionary*, 468.

60 Murphy et al., *Battleground*, 117.

61 Ibid.

62 Katja Iken, 'Von West nach Ost verschleppt', *Der Spiegel*, 25 January 2017.

63 Gieseke, *The GDR*, 16.
64 Murphy et al., *Battleground*, 124-125.
65 Ibid., 210.

30. Re-ordering the Stasi

1 Bruce, *Resistance*, 70, citing MLHA, IV L 2/12/525, Landesleitung der SED Mecklenburg, Sicherheit, 16, transcript of Ulbricht's speech August 1950.
2 Unless otherwise stated, information in this section comes from BStU, MfS, BdL-Dok. 1. – Original, 2 S. – MfS-DSt-Nr. 100001, 'Befehl Nr. 1/50 über die Schaffung einer Abteilung Erfassung und Statistik und über das In-Kraft-Treten der Richtlinien'; BStU, MfS, BdL-Dok. 2505.- Abschrift, 5 S. – MfS-DSt-Nr. 101091, 'Richtlinien über die Erfassung von Personen, die eine feindliche Tätigkeit durchfuhren und die von den Organen des Ministeriums für Staatssicherheit der DDR festgestellt wurden'; BStU, MfS, BdL-Dok. 2508. – Abschrift, 4 S. – MfS-DSt-Nr. 101091, 'Richtlinien zur Erfassung der durch die Organe des Ministeriums für Staatssicherheit der DDR verhafteten Personen'.
3 Engelmann and Joestel, *Hauptabteilung IX*, 39-40.
4 Ibid., 41.
5 BStU, MfS, BdL 2032, #100855 'Dienstanweisung: Übergabe von Untersuchungsvorgängen an die Staatsanwaltschaft und die Gerichte', 20.3.1952.
6 BStU, MfS, BdL 74, #100034, 'Befehl Nr. 74/52 zum Beschluss des Ministerrates vom 27. Marz 1952: Strafrechtliche Untersuchungstatlgkelt', 15.5.1952.
7 BStU, MfS, BdL 66, # 100034, 'Strafrechtliche Untersuchungstätigkeit', 15.5.1952.
8 Unless otherwise stated, quotes and information in the following section come from Engelmann and Joestel, *Hauptabteilung IX*, 47.
9 Ibid., 50-53.
10 BStU, MfS, BV Neubrandenburg, AU, Nr. 109/53, Bd. 2, 282-289.
11 Engelmann and Joestel, *Hauptabteilung IX*, 54.
12 Ibid., 56.
13 BStU, ZA, GVS 9/50, #101091, 20.9.1950, 'Richtlinien über die Erfassung der geheimen Mitarbeiter, der Informatoren und der Personen, die konspirative Wohnungen unterhalten'; GVS MfS 18/52, 20.11.1952, 'Richtlinie 21 über die Suche, Anwerbung und Arbeit mit Informatoren, geheimen Mitarbeitern und Personen, die konspirative Wohnungen unterhalten'. Unless otherwise stated, information in this section comes from these two documents.
14 Gieseke, *The History*, 79.
15 Helmut Müller-Enbergs, Stasi-Unterlagen-Archiv, MfS Lexikon, available at https://www.stasi-unterlagen-archiv.de/mfs-lexikon/detail/geheimer-mitarbeiter-gm/, accessed 9.2.2022.
16 Andrew and Mitrokhin, *Mitrokhin Archive*, 216.
17 Richtlinie 21 vom 20.11.1952.
18 Bruce 'The Prelude', 20.
19 Dennis, *The Stasi*, 97.
20 Gieseke, *The History*, 87.
21 Bruce, *The Firm*, 86, citing BStU-Schwerin, AIM 47/55, 22 June 1950, translation by Gary Bruce amended by author.
22 Ibid., citing BStU-Schwerin, AIM 47/55, 20 December 1954, translation by Gary Bruce amended by author.
23 Ibid., citing BStU-Schwerin, AIM 444/56, 3 June 1953.
24 Ibid., citing Richtlinie 21/52, reproduced in Helmut Müller-Enbergs, *Inoffizielle Mitarbeiter*.
25 Ibid., 87.
26 Ibid., 87.
27 Ibid., 124.

28 Information in this section comes from Hanna Labrenz-Weiss, *Abteilung M: Postkontrolle* (MfS-Handbuch), (Berlin: BStU, 2005).
29 Ibid., 13.

31. Ulbricht's Acceleration of Socialism

1   *Gesetz über den Fünfjahrplan zur Entwicklung der Volkswirtschaft der Deutschen Demokratischen Republik 1951-1955* (Berlin: Amt für Information der Regierung der DDR, 1952), translated by Randall Bytwerk at the German Propaganda Archive, available at https://research.calvin.edu/german-propaganda-archive/5yrplan.htm, accessed 29.2.24.
2   Schmeidel, *Stasi*, 19.
3   Childs and Popplewell, *The Stasi*, 50.
4   Jens Gieseke, *Das Ministerium*, 11-12.
5   Vladimir Migev, 'The Bulgarian Peasants' Resistance to Collectivization 1948-1958', *Bulgarian Historical Review* No. 25 (1997), 59-68, cited in Bruce, *Resistance*, 259.
6   Armin Mitter, '"Am 17.6.1953 haben die Arbeiter gestreikt, jetzt aber streiken wir Bauern": Die Bauern und der Sozialisumus' in Ilko-Sascha Kowalczuk et al. (eds.), *Der Tag X: Die 'Innere Staatsgründung' der DDR als Ergebnis der Krise 1952/54* (Berlin: Ch. Links, 1995), 86, cited in Bruce, *Resistance*, 168.
7   Torsten Diedrich, *Der 17. Juni 1953* (Berlin: Dietz Verlag, 1991), 40-41, cited in Bruce, *Resistance*, 166.
8   CIA Intelligence Report, 'East Germany, Supply and Distribution of Foodstuffs', 3 December 1952, Document IV-10 in Steury (ed.), *On the Front Lines*, 285-286.
9   Bruce, *Resistance*, 163, citing Resolution of the Second Party Congress reproduced in *Dokumente der Sozialistischen Einheitspartei Deutschlands* (Vol. IV) (Berlin: Dietz Verlag, 1954), 70.
10 Bruce, *Resistance*, 151.
11 Quoted in Werkentin, *Politische Strafjustiz*, 68, requoted in Bruce, *Resistance*, 162.
12 Bruce, *Resistance*, 227, citing ACDP, VII-013-1743, CDU Potsdam report, 18 July 1953.
13 Manfred Hagen, *DDR – June '53* (Stuttgart: Franz Steiner Verlag, 1992), 26, cited in Bruce, *Resistance*, 160.
14 Diedrich, *Der 17. Juni*, 40-41; Ilko-Sascha Kowalczuk and Armin Mitter, 'Die Arbeiter sind zwar geschlagen worden, aber sie sind nicht besiegt! Die Arbeiterschaft während der Krise 1952/53' in Kowalczuk et al., *Der Tag X*, 44, cited in ibid.
15 Quoted in Armin Mitter and Stefan Wolle, *Untergang auf Raten* (Munich: Bertelsmann Verlag, 1993), 27, requoted in Bruce, *Resistance*, 170.
16 Ibid.
17 Quoted in Murphy et al., *Battleground*, 146.
18 BStU, MfS, BdL/Dok., Nr. 5120, 1-3.
19 Bruce 'The Prelude', 18, citing Fricke, *Politik*, 173.
20 BStU, MfS, AS, Nr. 300/57, Bd. 4, 24-28.
21 David Clay Large, *Berlin* (New York: Basic Books, 2000), 425.
22 CIA Intelligence Report, 'SED Directives on Refugees', 4 March 1953, Document IV-13 in Steury (ed.), *On the Front Lines*, 296.
23 Rüdiger Wenzke, 'Auf dem Wege zur Kaderarmee: Aspekt der Rekrutierung, Sozialstruktur und personellen Entwicklung des enstehenden Militärs in der SBZ/DDR bis 1952/53' in Thoss (ed.), *Volksarmee schaffen*, 243, cited in Bruce, *Resistance*, 125.
24 Bruce, *Resistance*, citing ACDP VII-013-1361.
25 Bruce, *The Firm*, 34.
26 Gieseke, *The History*, 36.
27 Bruce, *The Firm*, 31.
28 Ibid.
29 Gieseke, *The GDR*, 19.
30 Dennis, *The Stasi*, 81.

31 Gieseke, *The History*, 37.
32 Childs and Popplewell, *The Stasi*, 76.
33 Helmut Müller-Enbergs, 'Warum wird einer IM? Zur Motivation bei der inoffiziellen Zusammenarbeit mit dem Staatssicherheitsdienst' in Klaus Behnke and Jürgen Fuchs (eds.), *Zersetzung der Seele: Psychologie und Psychiatrie im Dienst der Stasi* (Hamburg: Rotbuch Verlag, 1995), 102-129, cited in Dennis, *Stasi*, 90.
34 Georg Herbstritt, Stasi-Unterlagen-Archiv, MfS Lexikon, available at https://www.stasi-unterlagen-archiv.de/mfs-lexikon/detail/hauptabteilung-ii-spionageabwehrha-ii/, accessed 19.3.2023.
35 Hanna Labrenz-Weiss, *Die Hauptabteilung II: Spionageabwehr* (Berlin: BStU, 1998), 35.
36 Roland Wiedmann and Arno Polzin, Stasi-Unterlagen-Archiv, MfS Lexikon, available at https://www.stasi-unterlagen-archiv.de/mfs-lexikon/detail/abteilung-v/, accessed 27.2.2022.
37 Auerbach et al., *Hauptabteilung XX*, 81.
38 Haendcke-Hoppe-Arndt, *Die Hauptabteilung XVIII*, 15.
39 Wunschik, *Hauptabteilung VII*, 39.
40 Gieseke, *The History*, 33.
41 MfS ZA, Allgemeine Sachablage, No. 940/67, quoted in Dennis, *The Stasi*, 154, translated by Mike Dennis and Peter Brown.
42 For the Cheka method see Andrew and Mitrokhin, *The Mitrokhin Archive*, 51-52.
43 MfS ZA, HA IX, No. 23540, 1976, quoted in Dennis, *The Stasi*, 154.
44 Childs and Popplewell, *The Stasi*, 109.
45 Schmeidel, *Stasi*, 68.
46 Ibid., 57.
47 Christoph Klessmann, *Die doppelte Staatsgründung* (Göttingen: Vandenhoeck & Rupprecht, 1982), 267, cited in Bruce, *Resistance*, 161.
48 SVRA file 68881, Vol. 1, 214-221, cited in Murphy et al., *Battleground*, 134.
49 Sefton Delmer, 'The courage of Mr Meyer', *Daily Express*, 2 February 1953.
50 Dennis, *The Stasi*, 152.
51 Schmeidel, *Stasi*, 82.
52 Von Flocken and Scholtz, *Ernest Wollweber*, 140, 52, cited in Childs and Popplewell, *The Stasi*, 52.
53 Rudolf Herrnstadt, *Das Herrnstadt-Dokument: Das Politbüro der SED und die Geschichte des 17. Juni 1953*, edited by Nadja Stulz-Herrnstadt (Hamburg: 1990), 58, quoted in ibid., 53.
54 Ibid., 74 & 54.
55 Quoted in Bruce, *Resistance*, 171.
56 *Neues Deutschland*, 11 June 1953.

32. Spy Wars

1 Paul Maddrell, 'British Intelligence through the Eyes of the Stasi: What the Stasi's Records Show about the Operations of British Intelligence in Cold War Germany', *Intelligence and National Security*, Vol. 27, No. 1, February 2012, 51-52.
2 Murphy et al., *Battleground*, 210.
3 Maddrell, 'Im Fadenkreuz', 153.
4 Report by a US committee convened in 1954, quoted in Bernard Porter, *Plots and Paranoia: A History of Political Espionage in Britain 1790-1988* (London: Unwyn Hyman, 1989), 189.
5 Email to author from Thomas Wegener Friis, Director of the Center for Cold War Studies, University of Southern Denmark.
6 Faligot and Krop, *La Piscine*, 34.
7 Ibid., 36.
8 Murphy et al., *Battleground*, 101.
9 Guy Liddell diaries, entry for 7 March 1952, KV-4/474, UK National Archives, 45-49.
10 Boghardt, 'Our man', 9.

11 Recollection of Peter Stafford-Hill in Steers (ed.), *FSS*, 163.

12 Murphy et al., *Battleground*, 100-101.

13 Ibid., 99.

14 This account of Churchill's opinions is given in Guy Liddell diaries, entry for 29 December 1951, KV-4/473, UK National Archives, 207.

15 Guy Liddell diaries, entry for 1 January 1950, KV-4/472, UK National Archives, 4-5.

16 Ibid., entry for 4 January 1952, KV-4/474, UK National Archives, 5.

17 Ibid., entry for 3 May 1950, KV-4/472, UK National Archives, 78.

18 Ibid., entry for 1 January 1949, KV-4/471, UK National Archives, 4.

19 Uncredited author, *Das geteilte Berlin und die Stasi: Spionage, Opposition und Alltag* (Berlin: BStU, 2018), 5-6.

20 Case, 'The Joint Intelligence Committee', citing 80D EFE41/63, RC (Germany) 45th Meeting, 30 June 1947; CAB159/1, JIC(47) 32nd Meeting, 30 May 1947; CAB159/2, JIC(47) 74th Meeting, 31 October 1947; CAB159/2, JIC(47) 82nd Meeting, 26 November 1947.

21 Maddrell, 'Britain's exploitation', 112.

22 Boghardt, 'Our man', 13.

23 Michael Kuhlmann, '"Wir waren Kalte Krieger! Ich auch!" RIAS Berlin und der Aufstand des 17. Juni 1953 in der DDR', *Journal for Intelligence, Propaganda and Security Studies*, Vol. 17, Nr. 1/2023, 99-103.

24 BArch, MfS, AS, Nr. 301-61, correspondence between HA II, Abteilung II at BV Neubrandenburg, and Abteilung II at BV Gross-Berlin.

25 Andrew and Mitrokhin, *The Mitrokhin Archive*, 570.

26 Naimark, *The Russians*, 382.

27 Kühn, 'Lothar Weirauch', 57.

28 Adams, *Historical Dictionary*, 220.

29 Uncredited author, *Hauptverwaltung A (HV A): Aufgaben-Strukturen-Quellen* (MfS-Handbuch) (Berlin: BStU, 2013), 56.

30 Adams, *Historical Dictionary*, 220.

31 Gieseke, *The History*, 164.

32 Wolf and McElvoy, *Memoirs*, 105.

33 Müller-Enbergs, 'Die DDR-Nachrichtendienste', 410.

34 Andrew and Mitrokhin, *The Mitrokhin Archive*, 513.

35 Koehler, *Stasi*, 317.

36 Unless otherwise stated, information in the following section comes from Labrenz-Weiss, *Hauptabteilung II*, 32-35.

37 Engelmann and Joestel, *Hauptabteilung IX*, 42.

38 BStU, ZA, DSt 101164, Rundbrief Mielkes an die Länderverwaltungen des MfS vom 6.6.1952, cited in ibid., 33.

39 Decision of Politburo TsK VKP(b) 23 October 1950, RGASPI f.17 op.162, d.44 l.132; reproduced in David R. Shearer and Vladimir Khaustov, *Stalin and the Lubianka: A Documentary History of the Political Police and Security Organs in the Soviet Union, 1922-1953* (New Haven, London: Yale University Press, 2015), 282.

33. Gehlen

1 Parliamentarisch-Politischer Pressedienst (Bonn), Informationsbrief 90/54, 11 August 1954.

2 Childs and Popplewell, *The Stasi*, 149.

3 Case, 'The Joint Intelligence Committee', 112-114.

4 BArch, MfS, HA II, Nr. 25945, 161, 'Aussagen des Inhaftierten Agenten Haase, Werner'.

5 Parliamentarisch-Politischer Pressedienst 90/54.

6 Hermann Zolling and Heinz Höhne, *The General Was A Spy: The Truth about General Gehlen and his Spy Ring* (New York: 1972), cited in Childs and Popplewell, *The Stasi*, 150.

7 Armin Wagner, 'BND military espionage in East Germany, 1946-1994', in Thomas Wegener

Friis et al. (eds.), *East German Foreign Intelligence: Myth, Reality and Controversy* (London, New York: Routledge, 2012), 221.

8   Erich Schmidt-Eenboom, 'The rise and fall of West German intelligence operations against East Germany' in Wegener Friis et al. (eds.), *East German Foreign Intelligence*, 35.

9   E.H. Cookridge, *Gehlen: Spy of the Century* (London: 1972), cited in Childs and Popplewell, *The Stasi*, 152.

10   Childs and Popplewell, *The Stasi*, 150.

11   Dennis, *The Stasi*, 193.

12   Erich Schmidt-Eenboom, *Schnüffler ohne Nase: Der BND – die unheimliche Macht im Staate* (Dusseldorf, Vienna, New York: Econ, 1993), 59-60, cited in ibid.

13   Unless otherwise stated, information in the following section comes from Schmidt-Eenboom, 'The rise and fall', 35-37, and Wagner, 'BND military espionage', 223.

14   James H. Critchfield, *Partners at the Creation: The Men Behind Post-war Germany's Defense and Intelligence Establishments* (Annapolis: Naval Institute Press, 2003). 42-60, cited in Wagner, 'BND military espionage', 223.

15   Kristie Macrakis, *Seduced by Secrets: Inside the Stasi's Spy-Tech World* (Annapolis: Naval Institute Press, 2014), 260.

16   Andreas Schmidt, *Hauptabteilung III: Funkaufklärung und Funkabwehr* (MfS-Handbuch) (Berlin: BStU, 2010), 171.

17   Unless otherwise stated, information in this section comes from BArch, MfS, HA-II, Nr. 25945, passim.

18   Reproduced in BArch, MfS, HA-II, Nr. 51298, 264.

34. Sabotage and Kidnappings

1   Unless otherwise stated, information in the following section comes from Childs and Popplewell, *The Stasi*, 116-117; John O. Koehler, *Stasi*, 418.

2   See for example its personal file on Ernst Wollweber, KV-2/3054, passim.

3   *Daily Colonist*, Victoria, BC, 15 March 1953.

4   *Sunday Graphic*, 1 March 1953.

5   Gieseke, *The GDR*, 26.

6   Julius Ruiz, *The 'Red Terror' and the Spanish Civil War: Revolutionary Violence in Madrid* (New York: Cambridge University Press, 2014), 136-138.

7   Susanne Muhle, 'Wie das MfS Menschen entführen liess', Bundeszentrale für politische Bildung, 7.10.2016, available at https://www.bpb.de/themen/deutsche-teilung/stasi/223062/wie-das-mfs-menschen-entfuehren-liess/, accessed 23.3.2022.

8   Koehler, *Stasi*, 126.

9   Uncredited author, *Der Deutsche Bundestag 1949 bis 1989 in den Akten des Ministeriums für Staatssicherheit (MfS) der DDR* (Berlin: BStU, 2013), 312-313, citing BStU, MfS, BV Potsdam, AOP 100/52, Vol. 3, 290.

10   Cited in Iken, 'Von West nach Ost'.

11   Childs and Popplewell, *The Stasi*, 81.

12   Muhle, *Auftrag*, 152.

13   Mampel, *Der Untergrundkampf*, 36-41, cited in Bruce, 'The Prelude', 23.

14   Muhle, 'Wie das MfS Menschen entführen liess'.

15   Andrew and Mitrokhin, *The Mitrokhin Archive*, 571 and 871-872.

35. The Institute: The Birth of East German Foreign Intelligence

1   Steury (ed.), *On the Front Lines*, 231.

2   Decision of the KI Collegium, 'O Sozdanii Predstavitelstva Kollegii Pri Vneshne-politichskoi Ravvedke GDR', 19 July 1951, SVRA, quoted in Murphy et al., *Battleground*, 135-136.

3   Murphy et al., *Battleground*, 135.

4 Wolf and McElvoy, *Memoirs*, 44-45.
5 Unless otherwise stated, information in this section comes from Helmut Müller-Enbergs, *Geschichte der HV A und ihrer Militärspionage: Analysen und Fallstudien* (Berlin: BStU, 2021); Uncredited author, *Hauptverwaltung A*; and Barth and Gieseke, *Wer war wer*.
6 Wolf and McElvoy, *Memoirs*, 44-45.
7 Schmeidel, *Stasi*, 9.
8 Macrakis, *Seduced*, 20-21.
9 Adams, *Historical Dictionary*, 486.
10 Macrakis, *Seduced*, 23-24.
11 Werner Grossmann, *Bonn im Blick: die DDR-Aufklärung aus der Sicht ihres letzten Chefs* (Berlin: Das Neue Berlin, 2001), reproduced in 'Solide Arbeit beim Klassenfeind', *Der Spiegel*, 4 February 2001.
12 Childs and Popplewell, *The Stasi*, 118.
13 Ibid., 118.
14 Dennis, *The Stasi*, 198.
15 Wolf and McElvoy, *Memoirs*, 117.
16 Uncredited author, *Der Deutsche Bundestag*, 235-236.
17 BStU, MfS, BV Leipzig, AIM 671/53, 75-77, Bericht, Abteilung II, 14.4.1953.
18 Wolf and McElvoy, *Memoirs*, 59.
19 Memorandum, 10 April 1953, from Richard Helms, acting deputy director, plans, to Allen Dulles, director, Central Intelligence, reproduced in Murphy et al., *Battleground*, 140.
20 Murphy et al., *Battleground*, 141.
21 Reproduced in BArch, MfS, HA II, No. 25945, 182-183.
22 'HVA [sic] Meeting Chaired by Wolf, 2 February 1953', MORI No. 145205, reproduced in Steury (ed.), *On the Front Lines*, 261-268.
23 'HVA [sic] Meeting Chaired by Wolf, 7 March 1953', MORI No. 145348, reproduced in ibid., 269-272.
24 According to Murphy et al., *Battleground*, 141, 'In later years KGB officers who had worked closely with IWF and its successor organization noted that Wolf was conveniently absent when the storm broke.'
25 Adams, *Historical Dictionary*, 479.
26 Wolf and McElvoy, *Memoirs*, 58.

36. 'A Fascist Putsch': The Uprising of 1953

1 Rayfield, *Stalin*, 446.
2 Christian Ostermann, *Uprising in East Germany, 1953: The Cold War, the German Question, and the first major upheaval behind the Iron Curtain* (Budapest: Central European Press, 2001), 3.
3 Herrnstadt, *Das Herrnstadt-Dokument*, 87, quoted in Childs and Popplewell, *The Stasi*, 52.
4 Report No. 708/i, 19 Feb 1953, SVRA file 45513, Vol. 7, 97-99, quoted in Murphy et al., *Battlefield*, 156.
5 Report No. 44/B to the Presidium of the CC CPSU, 6 May 1953, SVRA file 3581, Vol. 7, quoted in ibid., 156-158.
6 Dennis, *The Stasi*, 26.
7 Mitter and Wolle, *Untergang*, 87-89, cited in Bruce, *Resistance*, 177.
8 Bruce, *Resistance*, 179, citing BA-P, DO 1 11/304, report by the political department of the Berlin Volkspolizei Präsidium, 259.
9 Ibid.
10 Bruce, *Resistance*, 199, citing BA-P DO 1 11/45, extracts from Bezirke police situation reports.
11 Bruce, *Resistance*, 221.
12 Armin Mitter, 'Die Ereignisse im Juni und Juli 1953 in der DDR', *Aus Politik und Zeitgeschichte*, B5 (1991), 36, cited in ibid., 221.
13 Bruce, *Resistance*, 180-182, citing SAPMO-BA, ZPA, JIV 2/202/14, report 17 June 1953.

14 Ibid.

15 Murphy et al., *Battleground*, 167.

16 Ibid., 169.

17 François Fejitö, *A History of the People's Democracies* (2nd edition, London: 1974), 36, quoted in Childs and Popplewell, *The Stasi*, 51.

18 Mitter and Wolle, *Untergang*, 104, cited in Bruce, *Resistance*, 182.

19 Unless otherwise stated, information in the following section comes from Bruce, *Resistance*, 182-193, citing SAPMO-BA, ZPA, JIV 2/202/14, report 17 June 1953; BA-P, DO 1/11/305, report by *Bezirk* Halle Volkspolizei; BA-P DO 1 11/45, extracts from *Bezirke* police situation reports; BA-P, DO 1 11/304, report by the political department of the Berlin Volkspolizei Präsidium; BA-P, DO 1/11/305, report by *Bezirk* Cottbus Volkspolizei.

20 BStU, MfS, BV Dresden, 1. Stellvertreter des Leiters, Nr. 4, 17.

21 Fulbrook, *Anatomy*, 185.

22 BStU, MfS, BV Leipzig, AKG, Nr. 133, 1.

23 'Der Tag, an dem Stalin brannte', *Der Spiegel*, 3 July 2013.

24 BStU, MfS, BV Erfurt, AU, Nr. 206/53, Bd. 2, 66-67.

25 Report by Lt-General Fedenko to Lt-General Pavlovsky, Soviet army, 27 June 1953, reproduced as Document #26 in Christian Ostermann, *The Post-Stalin Succession Struggle and the 17 June 1953 Uprising in East Germany* (Washington: National Security Archive, 1996), cited in Bruce, *Resistance*, 220. Fedenko estimated the number of strikers as 132,169 on 17 June and 218,700 on 18 June. These are almost certainly underestimates.

26 BStU, MfS, OV Wismut, AU, Nr. 83/53, 53.

27 Bruce, *Resistance*, 220-222, citing BA-P, DO 1/11/305, reports by *Bezirke* Frankfurt/Oder, Cottbus and Halle Volkspolizei.

28 Peter Boeger and Elise Catrain, *Stasi in Thüringen: Die DDR-Geheimpolizei in den Bezirken Erfurt, Gera und Suhl* (Berlin: BStU, 2018), 14.

29 Gieseke, *The History*, 41; *The GDR*, 23.

30 Roger Engelmann, *DDR im Blick* jahrgang 1953, Das Bundesarchiv, available at https://www.ddr-im-blick.de/jahrgaenge/jahrgang-1953/report/einleitung-1953/, accessed 30.1.2024.

31 Weber and Florath, *"Nun falten Sie den Zettel..."*, 193.

32 Wolf and McElvoy, *Memoirs*, 58.

33 Murphy et al., *Battleground*, 286-288.

34 SVRA file 68881, Vol. 2, 328-329, quoted in Murphy et al., *Battleground*, 171-172.

35 Ibid., 172.

36 Bruce, *Resistance*, 194, citing BA-P, DO, 1 11/758, report by Weidlich, head of investigation department of Volkspolizei, 2 July 1953.

37 Gieseke, *Mielke-Konzern*, 60-61.

38 Gieseke, *The History*, 41.

39 BStU, MfS, BV Gera, AU, Nr. 128/53, Bd. 2, 4; BStU, MfS, BV Erfurt, AU, Nr. 206/53, Bd. 3, 15.

40 BStU, MfS, BV Suhl, AU, Nr. 48/53, 172-178.

41 Bruce, *Resistance*, 194, citing SAPMO-BA, ZPA, DY 30 IV 2/5/560, 1 July 1953.

42 Sven Felix Kellerhof, 'Ermordet, weil die SED "feindliche Provokateure" brauchte', *Welt*, 21.11.2022.

43 Boeger and Catrain, *Stasi in Thüringen*, 14.

44 Karl Wilhelm Fricke, 'Todesstrafe für Magdeburger 'Provokateur", Deutschland Archiv 26 (1993), 527-531, cited in Bruce, *Resistance*, 215.

45 Bruce, *Resistance*, 225, citing BA-P, DO 1 11/24, summary of letter from Karl Maron to Ulbricht, 5 January 1954.

46 BStU, MfS, SdM, Nr. 249, 1.

47 BStU, MfS, BV Karl-Marx-Stadt, Abt. XX, Nr. 309, 446.

48 BStU, MfS, BV Dresden, AU, Nr. 239/53, 27.

49 Soch (ed.), *Stasi in Brandenburg*, 14-17.

50 BStU, MfS, BV Dresden, AU, Nr. 237/54, GA, 1-31.

51 Heizer, '"Kalter Krieger"', 168. For the assessment of West German opinion see Edgar Wolfrum, *Geschichtspolitik in der Bundesrepublik Deutschland: Der Weg zur bundesrepublikanischen Erinnerung 1948-1990* (Darmstadt: Wissenschaftliche Buchgesellschaft, 1999), 78.

52 BStU, MfS, AU, Nr. 487/53, Bd. 16, 12-32.

53 Murphy et al., *Battleground*, 169-170.

54 Case, 'The Joint Intelligence Committee', 149-153, citing Churchill's private opinions as quoted in Ivone Kirkpatrick, *The Inner Circle* (London: Macmillan, 1959), 255.

55 Quoted in Kuhlmann, '"Wir waren Kalte Krieger"', 100.

56 CIA SE-47, Probable Effect on Recent Developments in Eastern Germany on Soviet Policy with Respect to Germany, 24 July 1953, Document III-2 in Steury (ed.), *On the Front Lines*, 223.

57 Wagner, 'BND military espionage', 223.

58 BStU, MfS, AU, Nr. 15/54, Bd. 8, 200-201.

59 BStU, MfS, AU, Nr. 15/54, 202-204.

60 Engelmann, *DDR im Blick*.

61 Gieseke, *The History*, 41.

62 Von Flocken and Scholtz, *Ernst Wollweber*, 146, quoted in Childs and Popplewell, *The Stasi*, 52.

63 Helmut Müller-Enbergs, *Der Fall Rudolf Herrnstadt: Tauwetterpolitik vor dem 17. Juni* (Berlin: 1991), 54-55, quoted in ibid., 52.

64 Colonel I.A. Fadeikin by V Ch to MVD Moscow, 12:25 p.m., 17 June 1953, SVRA, quoted in Murphy et al., *Battleground*, 167.

65 Von Flocken and Scholtz, *Ernst Wollweber*, 144, quoted in Childs and Popplewell, *The Stasi*, 59.

66 Fricke, *Die DDR-Staatssicherheit*, Ch.2, quoted in ibid.

67 Quoted in Bärwald, *Das Ostbüro*, 78, requoted in Bruce, *Resistance*, 185.

68 Bruce, *Resistance*, 226.

69 Ibid., 194, citing BA-P, DO, 1 11/758, report by Weidlich, head of investigation department of Volkspolizei, 2 July 1953.

70 Bruce, *Resistance*, 226.

71 Ibid., 130, citing ACDP, VII-013-1743, report on meetings of CDU Kreis secretaries, 13 July 1953.

72 Kowalczuk and Mitter, 'Die Arbeiter', 44, cited in Bruce, *Resistance*, 224.

73 Bruce, *Resistance*, 232, citing SAPMO-BA, ZPA, IV 2/4/391, Resolution of the Central Committee of the SED, 221.

74 Armin Mitter, "Am 17.6.1953", 117, cited in Bruce, *Resistance*, 225.

75 Bruce, *Resistance*, 228, citing ADL, LDPD #25366, LDPD report for *Kreis* Eisleben, 20 July 1953.

76 Bruce, *Resistance*, 228.

77 Ibid.

78 Engelmann and Joestel, *Die Hauptabteilung IX*, 60.

79 Diedrich, *Der 17. Juni 1953*, 184, cited in Bruce, *Resistance*, 233.

80 Childs and Popplewell, *The Stasi*, 58.

81 Gieseke, *The History*, 24.

82 Koehler, *Stasi*, 60.

83 Mitter and Wolle, *Untergang*, 146, cited in Bruce, *Resistance*, 233.

84 Quoted in Bruce, *Resistance*, 233-234, citing BStU, ZA, A/S 43/58, Vol. 9, 388.

85 Helmut Müller-Enbergs, Stasi-Unterlagen-Archiv, MfS Lexikon, available at https://www.stasi-unterlagen-archiv.de/mfs-lexikon/detail/geheimer-hauptinformator-ghi/, accessed 9.2.2022.

86 BStU, MfS, BdL-Dok. 18, # 100072, Befehl Nr. 279/53 'Bildung von Informationsgruppen und zum Informationsdienst'.

37. Main Department XV: Foreign Intelligence Joins the Stasi

1   Childs and Popplewell, *The Stasi*, 144.
2   Nigel West, 'Counter-intelligence in post-war Europe, 1945-1965' in Wegener Friis et al. (eds.), *East German Foreign Intelligence*, 15.
3   Childs and Popplewell, 173.
4   Wolf and McElvoy, *Memoirs*, 205.
5   Bernd Lippmann, 'Foreign intelligence under the roof of the Ministry for State Security' in Wegener Friis et al. (eds.), *East German Foreign Intelligence*, 142.
6   BStU, MfS, AS, Nr. 173/66, 3-6.
7   BStU, MfS, ZAIG 7373, Bl.2ff., cited in Lippmann, 'Foreign intelligence', 143.
8   Unless otherwise stated, information in this section comes from Müller-Enbergs, *Geschichte*, and BStU, *Hauptverwaltung A*.
9   Wolf and McElvoy, *Memoirs*, 49-50.
10 Grossmann, *Bonn im Blick*, 30-32.
11 'Solide Arbeit beim Klassenfeind', quoting ibid.
12 Macrakis, *Seduced*, 147.
13 Wolf and McElvoy, *Memoirs*, 237-238.
14 Boghardt, 'Our man', 13.
15 Wolf and McElvoy, *Memoirs*, 76-78.
16 Ibid., 78-79.
17 Ibid.
18 Childs and Popplewell, *The Stasi*, 131.
19 Gary Bruce, '*Aufklärung und Abwehr*: The lasting legacy of the Stasi under Ernst Wollweber', *Intelligence and National Security*, 21:3 (2006), 375-376.
20 Ibid., 376.
21 Ibid.
22 Wollweber's words were '50% das Gesicht dem Westen zu'; they are translated and their meaning discussed by Bruce in ibid., 377.
23 Ernst Wollweber, 'Aus Erinnerungen. Ein Porträt Walter Ulbrichts, documented by Wilfriede Otto', *Beiträge zur Geschichte der Arbeiterbewegung* 32 (1990), 350, quoted in ibid., 378.
24 BStU, ZA, SdM 1921, Referat des Staatssekretärs Wollweber auf der Dienstbesprechung am 5.8.1955., translated and quoted in ibid., 379-384.
25 Wolf and McElvoy, *Memoirs*, 61.
26 Indictment of Markus Wolf, Oberlandesgericht Düsseldorf, 6 December 1993, reproduced in Klaus Marxen and Gerhard Werle (eds.), *Strafjustiz und DDR-unrecht Dokumentation 4/1: Spionage* (Berlin: De Gruyter Recht, 2004), 30-31.
27 Ibid, 31.
28 Koehler, *Stasi*, 221-225.
29 Indictment of Markus Wolf, Marxen and Werle (eds.), *Strafjustiz*, 31.

Part IV. *Grossaktionen*: Spy-catching with the Stasi

38. A Crisis of Spies

1   Sudoplatov et al., *Special Tasks*, 25.
2   Childs and Popplewell, *The Stasi*, 30.
3   Jan Valtin, *Out of the Night* (New York: Alliance Book Corporation, 1941), 9.
4   'Augen auf, der Feind greift an!', *Tagliche Rundschau*, 7 November 1953.
5   Bruce, *The Firm*, 88.
6   Bruce, *Resistance*, 225, citing BStU, ZA, SdM 1921, protocol of SfS conference 21 August 1953.
7   Ibid., 235, citing BStU, ZA, SdM 2613, transcript of Wollweber speech at SED activists meeting at SfS, 2 November 1953.

8   Ibid., citing BStU, ZA, SdM 2612 (1953).

9   Such as Service Instruction (Dienstanweisung) No. 38/53 of December 1953.

10 Bruce, *Resistance*, 235, citing BStU, ZA, SdM 1921, note on conference of 13 August 1954, 169.

11 Engelmann and Joestel, *Die Hauptabteilung IX*, 64.

12 Paul Maddrell, 'Western espionage and Stasi counter-espionage in East Germany, 1953-1961' in Wegener Friis et al. (eds.), *East German foreign intelligence*, 25-26.

13 Paul Maddrell, 'The Western secret services', 830.

14 Maddrell, 'Western espionage', 26.

15 Maddrell, 'The Western secret services', 832, citing NSC-158, 'United States Objectives and Actions To Exploit the Unrest in the Satellite States', 29 June 1953, Folder 'President's Papers 1953(5)', White House Office, OSANSA: Records, 1952-61, Special Assistant Series, Presidential Subseries, Box 1, Dwight D. Eisenhower Library (DDEL), Abilene, Kansas, USA.

16 Ibid., citing 'A National Psychological Plan with Respect to Germany', PSB D-21, 9 October 1952, Folder 'Master Book of PSB Documents, Vol. II(1)', White House Office, NSC Staff, 1948-61: NSC Registry Series, 1947-62, Box 14, DDEL.

17 Kevin P. Riehle, 'Early Cold War evolution of British and US defector policy and practice', *Cold War History* (2018), citing 'Propaganda Defection Campaign,' Minutes of the 124th meeting of JIC (Germany), 24 March 1952, DEFE 41/67, UK National Archives.

18 Ibid., citing JIC report, 'Russian and Satellite Defectors and Refugees,' JIC(49)107, 21 February 1952, 2, CAB 301/136, UK National Archives; Joint Secretaries' memo, 'Policy on Defectors,' 26 September 1950, RG 59, Entry A1 1583D, Box 117, National Archives and Records Administration, College Park, Maryland.

19 Karl-Wilhelm Fricke and Roger Engelmann, *'Konzentrierte Schläge': Staatssicherheitsaktionen und politische Prozesse in der DDR 1953-1956* (Berlin: Ch. Links, 1998), 252-254, this item translated by Mary Carlene Forszt.

20 Engelmann and Joestel, *Die Hauptabteilung IX*, 60.

21 BStU, MfS, SdM 1574, Statut des Staatssekretariats für Staatssicherheit, 6 October 1953.

39. 'Concentrated Blows'

1   Von Flocken and Scholtz, *Ernst Wollweber*, 146, quoted in Childs and Popplewell, *The Stasi*, 60.

2   Fricke and Engelmann, *Konzentrierte Schläge*, 42.

3   In CIA analyses of the June events and their aftermath, there are accurate predictions of, for example, concessions being made to the East German public. But there are no apparent warnings that a wave of arrests would take place targeting Western spies and agents. See, for example, the documents in part III of Steury (ed.), *On the Front Lines*.

4   See, for example, Fricke and Engelmann, *Konzentrierte Schläge*, and Gieseke, *The History*.

5   Engelmann and Joestel, *Hauptabteilung IX*, 57, citing BStU, MfS, AS, #102/66, Protokoll der Dienstbesprechung mit den Leitern der Untersuchungsabteilungen der BV/V des SfS am 1.12.1953.

6   Wilson, 'The mastermind'.

7   Fricke and Engelmann, *Konzentrierte Schläge*, 119.

40. The First *Grossaktion:* Feuerwerk, October-December 1953

1   BArch, MfS, HA II, Nr. 25945, 12.

2   Unless otherwise stated, information in this section comes from BArch, MfS, BdL-Dok, Nr. 191, Einsatzbefehl 333753; BArch, MfS, BdL-Dok, Nr. 193, Operativplan Aktion Feuerwerk, 26.10.1953; Fricke and Engelmann, *Konzentrierte Schläge*, 42-47.

3   BArch, MfS, BdL-Dok, Nr. 3356, Instruktion für die Beobachtung – Abteilung VIII,

4.12.1954; BArch, MfS, BdL-Dok, Nr. 3339, Instruktion über Festnahmen, Verhaftung, Durchsuchung und Sicherstellung, 14.4.1956.

4　BArch, MfS, HA-II, Nr. 51298, 10.

5　BArch, MfS, BdL-Dok, Nr. 192, 31.10.1953.

6　*Neues Deutschland*, 10 November 1953.

7　BArch, MfS, HA II, Nr. 51298, 20-43 and 101-141.

8　Ibid., 77.

9　Ibid., 141.

10　Ibid., 144.

11　BArch, MfS, HA II, Nr. 25945, 168.

12　BArch, MfS, HA II, Nr. 51298, 152-155.

13　This and the following quotes taken from the records of the 1st Criminal Division of the GDR Supreme Court, quoted in Fricke and Engelmann, *Konzentrierte Schläge*, 42-47.

14　In Fricke and Engelmann, *Konzentrierte Schläge*.

15　BStU, MfS, BdL-Dok. 2089, MfS-DSt-Nr. 100880, Dienstanweisung Nr. 38/53, Zusammenarbeit der Organe des Staatssekretariats für Staatssicherheit mit den Organen der Staatsanwaltschaft, 1.12.1953.

16　BStU, MfS, BdL-Dok. 3032, MfS-DSt-Nr. 100891, Richtlinie für die operative Erfassung und Statistik in den Organen des Staatssekretariats für Staatssicherheit des MdI der DDR, 12.12.1953.

41. An Outbreak of Kidnapping

1　Labrenz-Weiss, *Hauptabteilung II*, 35.

2　Muhle, *Auftrag*, 93.

3　Ibid., 221.

4　Ibid.

5　Ibid., 220.

6　*Die Welt*, 12 June 1954, quoted in ibid., 225.

7　Muhle, *Auftrag*, 226.

8　Fricke, *Opposition und Widerstand*, 305-310.

9　Carey Goldberg, 'KGB's True Confessions Spark Emigrants' Anger', *Los Angeles Times*, 24 July 1992.

10　Andrew and Mitrokhin, *The Mitrokhin Archive*, 470.

42. The Second *Grossaktion*: Pfeil, August 1954

1　Fricke and Engelmann, *Konzentrierte Schläge*, 47.

2　Schmole, *Hauptabteilung VIII*, 71.

3　BArch, MfS, BdL-Dok, 3085, Dienstanweisung Nr. 44/54, 27.7.1954.

4　Ibid., Hauptabteilung II/4 to Bezirk Karl-Marx-Stadt, 27.7.1954.

5　Fricke and Engelmann, *Konzentrierte Schläge*, 47-48.

6　Unless otherwise stated, information in this section comes from BArch, MfS, HA II, Nr. 46702.

7　As in the case of Heinz Brandt in 1961.

8　BArch, MfS, HA II, Nr. 40653, 19.8.1954.

9　BArch, MfS, AS, Nr. 96-55, Bd.1, 19.10.1954.

10　*Neues Deutschland*, 25 July 1954, reporting on arrests made in Aktion Raket.

11　Information in this section comes from Fricke and Engelmann, *Konzentrierte Schläge*, 130-134.

43. New Friends: The KGB

1　Sudoplatov et al., *Special Tasks*, 110.

2　West, 'Counter-intelligence', 14.

3   Uhl, 'The professionalization', 205.
4   West, 'Counter-intelligence', 16.
5   Ibid., 14-15.
6   Information in this section comes from Sudoplatov et al., *Special Tasks*, 246-248, and Andrew and Gordievsky, *KGB*, 431-432.
7   Bruce, *Resistance*, 238, citing BStU, ZA, GVS 1922/54, #100095, SfS report on preparations for elections, 12 October 1954.
8   BArch, MfS, HA II, Nr. 51298, 261.
9   BStU, MfS, AS 39/55, Bd. 1, 2-21.
10 Weber and Florath, "*Nun falten Sie den Zettel…*", 28.

44. The Third *Grossaktion*: Blitz, December 1954-April 1955

1   BArch, MfS, AS, Nr. 171-56, Bd.1, 7, 'Kurze Einschätzung über den bisherigen Verlauf der Aktion "Blitz"'.
2   Adams, *Historical Dictionary*, 42.
3   BArch, MfS, AS, Nr. 171-56, 119.
4   Maddrell, 'British Intelligence', 67.
5   Murphy et al., *Battleground*, 295.
6   Koehler, *Stasi*, 281.
7   Maddrell, 'Western espionage', 28.
8   BArch, MfS, BdL-Dok, 3093, Dienstanweisung 54/54, 16.11.1954.
9   Ibid.
10 BArch, MfS, AS, Nr. 171-56, 78.
11 BArch, MfS, AS, Nr. 171-56, 72-73, Plan zur Aktion "Blitz".
12 Unless otherwise stated, information in this section comes from BArch, MfS, AS, Nr. 171-56, passim.
13 Buschfort, *Das Ostbüros*, 60-63.
14 Ibid., 58.

45. The Holes and Corners of Blitz

1   BArch, MfS, AS, Nr. 171-56, 99.
2   Ibid., 27.
3   Ibid., 83.
4   Maddrell, 'Western espionage', 28.
5   BArch, MfS, AS, Nr. 171-56, 115-117.
6   Ibid., 19.
7   Ibid., 11.
8   BArch, MfS, HA II, Nr. 51298, 43.
9   BArch, MfS, AS, Nr. 171-56, 59.
10 Ibid., 109.
11 BArch, MfS, BdL-Dok, 3093, Dienstanweisung 54/54, 16.11.1954.
12 BArch, MfS, AS, Nr. 171-56, 3-4.
13 Ibid., 58.

46. Wrath

1   Unless otherwise stated, information in this section comes from the Stasi files reproduced in 'Sekretärin im Vizier der Stasi', Das Bundesarchiv, Stasi Mediathek, available at https://www.stasi-mediathek.de/geschichten/sekretaerin-im-visier-der-stasi/sheet/0-0/type/cover/, accessed 29.12.2021; and Koehler, *Stasi*, 269-273.
2   BStU, MfS, AOP, No. 57/56, Vol. 2, 188-189.
3   BStU, MfS, AOP, No. 57/56, 18-20.

4   Information in this section comes from BArch, MfS, AU, No. 292-51.
5   Carola-Stern-Stiftung, available at https://web.archive.org/web/20160303215028/http://www.carola-stern-stiftung.de/person_03.htm, accessed 30.5.2023.
6   Unless otherwise stated, information on Lisa Stein and Franz S comes from Muhle, *Auftrag*, 318-9; Franziska Kuschel, *Schwarzhörer, Schwarzseher und heimliche Leser: Der DDR und die Westmedien* (Göttingen: Wallstein, 2016), 88; Wilson, 'The Mastermind'; *Berliner Zeitung*, 30 May 1955.
7   BArch, MfS, AS, Nr. 96-55, Bd 2.
8   Fricke and Engelmann, *Konzentrierte Schläge*, 162.
9   Information in this section comes from Iken, 'Von West nach Ost'; Karl Wilhelm Fricke, *Akten-Einsicht: Rekonstruktion einer politischen Verfolgung* (Berlin: 1997), 179, cited in Muhle, *Auftrag*, 194; Engelmann and Joestel, *Hauptabteilung IX*, 69.
10   Muhle, *Auftrag*, 318.

47. Liquidating the Müller Network in Aktion Frühling

1   Information in this chapter comes from BArch, MfS, HA II, Nr. 43063, GV 'Anwerbung', 1953-55.
2   Gary Bruce, 'Participatory repression? Reflections on popular involvement with the Stasi' in Uwe Spiekermann (ed.), *The Stasi at Home and Abroad: Domestic Order and Foreign Intelligence*, Bulletin of the German Historical Institute, Supplement 9 (Washington DC: GHI, 2014), 51.

48. Treacherous Trials

1   Unless otherwise stated, information in this section comes from Fricke and Engelmann, *Konzentrierte Schläge*, 140-148, quotes translated by author.
2   BArch, MfS, HA-II, Nr. 51298, 275-302.
3   BArch, MfS, AS, Nr. 171-56, 17.
4   Ibid., 16.
5   Unless otherwise stated, information in this section comes from Fricke and Engelmann, *Konzentrierte Schläge*, 159-164.
6   BArch, MfS, AS, Nr. 171-56, Bd. 1, 83.

49. 'His Trench Coat Was Splattered With Blood'

1   BArch, MfS, AP, Nr. 21893-80, Bd. 2, 58. Information in this section comes from ibid., passim, and from BArch, MfS, AP, Nr. 21893-80, Bd.1, passim.
2   Information on Hans Wax and the Special Tasks Group from Labrenz-Weiss, *Die Hauptabteilung II*, 37; Kohl, 'Donner, Blitz und Teddy'.
3   As confirmed later by Denmark's deputy intelligence chief, P.A. Mørch. Christoph Franceschini, Thomas Wegener Friis, Erich Schmidt-Eenboom, *Spionage Unter Freunde: Partnerdienstbeziehungen und Westaufklärung der Organisation und des BND* (Berlin: Ch. Links, 2017), 223-224.
4   Jedlitschka et al., *Verschluss-Sachen*, 34-36.

50. The Stasi of the *Grossaktionen* Years

1   Quoted in Bruce, '*Aufklärung und Abwehr*', citing BStU, ZA, SdM 1921, 'Protokoll von der Dienstbesprechung mit den Leitern der Bezirksverwaltungen und den Abteilungsleitern im Staatssekretariat vom 21.8.1953.'
2   Bruce, '*Aufklärung und Abwehr*', 374.
3   Haendcke-Hoppe-Arndt, *Die Hauptabteilung XVIII*, 21.
4   Ibid.

5　Ibid., 20.

6　Fricke, *Die DDR-Staatssicherheit*, Ch. 2; Gieseke, *The History*, 36.

7　Müller-Enbergs, *Inoffizielle Mitarbeiter*, Teil 1, 165f.

8　Gieseke, *The History*, 46.

9　BStU, MfS, BdL/Dok., Nr. 288, Bl. 2., Befehl Nr. 236/55 von Staatssekretär Wollweber, 10.8.1955, quoted in Engelmann and Joestel, *Die Hauptabteilung IX*, 67.

10　Engelmann and Joestel, *Die Hauptabteilung IX*, 67.

11　H. Reinke, 'Staatssicherheir und Justiz' in Bundesministerium der Justiz (ed.), *Im Namen des Volkes? Über die Justiz im Staat der SED: Wissenschlaftlicher Begleitband zur Austellung des Ministeriums der Justiz* (Leipzig: Forum Verlag, 1996), 243, quoted in Dennis, *The Stasi*, 68.

12　Thomas Auerbach, *Vorbereitung auf den Tag X: Die geplanten Isolierungslager des MfS* (Berlin: BStU, 1995), 14.

13　BStU, MfS, SdM 1574, 3-6, Geschäftsordnung fur das Kollegium beim Staatssekretär des Staatssekretariats für Staatssicherheit, 6 July 1954.

14　Bruce, *'Aufklärung und Abwehr'*, citing Armin Wagner, *Walter Ulbricht und die geheime Sicherheitspolitik der SED* (Berlin: Ch. Links, 2002), 63-67.

15　Labrenz-Weiss, *Die Hauptabteilung II*, 38.

16　Wunschik, *Hauptabteilung VII*, 40.

17　BStU, ZA, GVS, 1500/55, #100104, Directive 14/55, 8 June 1955, cited in Bruce, *Resistance*, 240.

18　BStU, ZA, SdM 1924, proposal for the creation of the Agitation Department of the SfS, 10 July 1954, 107, cited in Bruce, *Resistance*, 235.

19　'Wer die Deutsche Demokratische Republik verlässt, stellt sich auf die Seite der Kriegstreiber', *Notizbuch des Agitators*, November 1955, translated by Randall Bytwerk at the German Propaganda Archive, available at https://research.calvin.edu/german-propaganda-archive/notiz3.htm, accessed 31.10.23.

20　BStU, MfS, AS 81/59, 111-112, Ergebnisse der Agitation des MfS, Info Nr. 65/56.

21　Engelmann and Joestel, *Die Hauptabteilung IX*, 61.

22　Schmole, *Hauptabteilung VIII*, 73-74.

23　BStU, ZA, AS 43/58, Vol. 3, SfS Informationsdienst report 31 May 1955, cited in Bruce, *Resistance*, 239.

24　BStU, ZA, SdM 1921, 73, cited in ibid., 242.

25　Maddrell, 'Western espionage', 23.

26　Ibid., 24.

27　Macrakis, *Seduced*, 256, 258.

28　Bruce, *The Firm*, 110.

29　Schmeidel, *Stasi*, 24.

30　Macrakis, *Seduced*, 247.

31　Karl Wilhelm Fricke, *MfS Intern: Macht, Strukturen, Auflösung der DDR-Staatssicherheit: Analyse und Dokumentation* (Cologne: Verlag Wissenschaft und Politik, 1991), 62, cited in Dennis, *Stasi*, 72.

32　J. Beleites, 'Der Untersuchungshaftvollzug des Ministeriums für Staatssicherheit der DDR' in Engelmann and Vollnhals (eds.), *Justiz im Dienst*, 457, cited in ibid., 69.

33　Ibid., 460-461, cited in ibid., 70.

34　Karl Wilhelm Fricke, *Die Staatssicherheit der DDR* (Cologne: Verlag Wissenschaft und Politik, 1984), 37, cited in ibid., 70.

35　Statement of Horst Schumm at a press conference in West Berlin, 1981, quoted in ibid.,130, cited in ibid., 72.

36　B. Eisenfeld, 'Rolle und stellung der Rechtsanwälte in der Ära Honecker im Spiegel kaderpolitischer Entwicklungen und Einflüsse des MfS' in Engelmann and Vollnhals (eds.), *Justiz im Dienst*, 371-372, cited in ibid., 70.

37　Engelmann and Joestel, *Die Hauptabteilung IX*, 83-84.

38　BStU, MfS, HA IX, Nr. 4981, Bl. 44, Richtlinie 4/59 des Ministers für die Arbeit der

Untersuchungsabteilungen des Ministeriums für Staatssicherheit, Anlage 1, Die Arbeit mit Zelleninformatoren, quoted in ibid., 84.

39 Schmeidel, *Stasi*, 39.
40 Ibid.
41 Ibid., 89.
42 Gerhard J quoted in Thomas Wernicke, *Staats-Sicherheit – ein Haus in Potsdam* (Potsdam: Potsdam-Museum, 1992), 39, requoted in Dennis, *Stasi*, 72, translated by Mike Dennis and Peter Brown.
43 Wolf and McElvoy, *Memoirs*, 262-263.
44 Mark Lynton, *Accidental Journey: A Cambridge internee's memoirs of WWII* (Woodstock, New York: The Overlook Press, 1998), 211.
45 Schmeidel, *Stasi*, 21-22.
46 Ibid.
47 Information in this section comes from Labrenz-Weiss, *Abteilung M*, 12-20.
48 Information in this section comes from Angela Schmole, *Abteilung 26. Telefonkontrolle, Abhörmassnahmen und Videoüberwachung* (MfS-Handbuch) (Berlin: BStU, Berlin 2009), 21-22.
49 Murphy et al., *Battleground*, 208.

51. Investigations, Observations, Arrests

1 BArch, MfS, BdL-Dok, Nr. 3337, Instruktion für die Mitarbeiter der Agenturermittlung.
2 Unless otherwise stated, information in this chapter comes from ibid.; BArch, MfS, BdL-Dok, Nr. 3339, Instruktion über Festnahmen, Verhaftung, Durchsuchung und Sicherstellung, 14.4.1956; BArch, MfS, BdL-Dok, Nr. 3356, Instruktion für die Beobachtung – Abteilung VIII, 4.12.1954.
3 Schmole, *Hauptabteilung VIII*, 74.
4 Ibid., 70-71.

52. Reflections on the *Grossaktionen*

1 Andrew and Mitrokhin, *The Mitrokhin Archive*, 600.
2 Murphy et al., *Battleground*, 442 and 500.
3 Adams, *Historical Dictionary*, 383.
4 Quoted in Andrew and Mitrokhin, *The Mitrokhin Archive*, 521.
5 Jeffery, *MI6*, 661.
6 Faligot and Krop, *La Piscine*, 47.
7 Ibid., 76.
8 Engelmann and Joestel, *Die Hauptabteilung IX*, 66.
9 *Fuldaer Zeitung*, 1 December 1953.
10 Childs and Popplewell, *The Stasi*, 61.
11 Guy Liddell diaries, entry for 11 September 1952, KV-4/474, UK National Archives, 136-137.
12 Quoted in Case, 'The Joint Intelligence Committee', 157.
13 BStU, MfS, ACE 81/59, 205-280.
14 Murphy et al., *Battleground*, 296.
15 Franceschini et al., *Spionage Unter Freunden*, 225.
16 Thomas Gaevert, 'Die Supergeheimen: Der Militärische Nachrichtendienst der DDR', promotion for SWR2 feature, 10 January 2018.
17 Murphy et al., *Battleground*, 257-267.
18 Maddrell, 'Im Fadenkreuz', 154.
19 Koehler, *Stasi*, 285-286.
20 BArch, MfS, AS, Nr. 171-56, Bd. 1, 294-299, 'Disposition zum Referat über die Tatsache, dass Westberlin die Ausgangsbasis, der ausländischen imperialistischen und bonner Geheimdienste und Agentenzentralen ist', 23.5.1955.
21 Information in this section comes from BArch, MfS, AS, Nr. 114-57, Bd. 2, passim.

Part V Up to the Wall

1 CIA Current Intelligence Weekly Summary, 5 February 1959, in Steury (ed.), *On the Front Lines*, 415.

53. Spies, Again

1 Maddrell, 'Western espionage', 28.
2 H. Rositzke, *The CIA's Secret Operations: Espionage, Counter-espionage and Covert Action* (Boulder: Westview Press, 1977), 39-43, cited in ibid.
3 CIA Division Project Clearance Sheet, DTLINEN, Fiscal Year 1957, 1 July 1956 through 30 June 1957, 14.
4 Adams, *Historical Dictionary*, 411.
5 Murphy et al., *Battleground*, 331.
6 Ibid., 34.
7 Adams, *Historical Dictionary*, 259.
8 Wolf and McElvoy, *Memoirs*, 48.
9 Murphy et al., *Battleground*, 431-438.
10 Wagner, 'BND military espionage', 224, citing summary of BND 'Garrison Files GDR', BAK B 206/107-116.
11 CIA Current Intelligence Weekly Summary, 7 May 1959, Document IV-1 in Steury, *On the Front Lines*, 233-236.
12 Adams, *Historical Dictionary*, 267.
13 Murphy et al., *Battleground*, 258.
14 Wagner, 'BND military espionage', citing National Security Archive, Washington DC, Memo: Soviet missiles in East Germany, 22 April 1959, in Microfiches – The Berlin Crisis, 1958-1962, Washington DC, 1991, Doc. 01211.
15 Hermann Zolling and Heinz Hölle, *Pullach intern: General Gehlen und die Geschichte des Bundesnachrichtendienst* (Hamburg: Hoffmann und Campe, 1971), 10, quoted in Wagner, 'BND military espionage', 224.
16 BStU, Mfs, ACE 79/59, Vol. 1a, 20-55, Analyse (Nr. 1/56) über Tätigkeit und Einfluss von SPD und SPD-Ostbüro.
17 Footnotes 14-22 to the online reproduction of the above document at Das Bundesarchiv, available at https://www.ddr-im-blick.de/jahrgaenge/jahrgang-1956/report/analyse-nr-156-ueber-taetigkeit-und-einfluss-von-spd-und-spd-ostbuero/#FN56-0788, accessed 31.1.2024.
18 Schmidt-Eenboom, 'The rise and fall', 44.
19 Ibid., 39.
20 Ibid.
21 Paul Maddrell, 'The economic dimension of Cold War intelligence-gathering: The West's spies in the GDR's economy', *Journal of Cold War Studies*, Vol. 15, No. 3, 2013, 77.
22 Wagner, 'BND military espionage', 219.
23 Maddrell, 'Britain's exploitation', 220.
24 Ibid., 192, citing SAPMO, DY 3011V 2/202/56, 'Über die zurückkehrenden SU-Spezial-isten', 31.12.54.
25 CIA Division Project Clearance Sheet, DTLINEN, 4-9.
26 BStU, Mfs, ACE 80/59, Vol. 1a, Info Nr. M111/56, Aktionen westlicher Organisationen und Einrichtungen gegen die DDR, 166-180.
27 Murphy et al., *Battleground*, 220.
28 Ibid., 211.
29 Wolf and McElvoy, *Memoirs*, 89-91.
30 BStU, MfS, ACE 80/59, Vol. 1b, 92, quoting UfJ leaflet, Information No. 30/56, 22 June 1956.
31 BStU, MfS, ACE 81/59, 205-280, quoting FDP leaflet.

54. Special Tasks

1   West, *The Meaning of Treason*, 350.
2   Hansard, Volume 548 c2345, debated on Wednesday 15 February 1956.
3   Sven Felix Kellerhof, 'Stasi-Mord aufgeklärt', *Die Welt*, 8 April 2008.
4   Klaus Taubert, 'Stiller Tod im "Gelben Elend"', *Der Spiegel*, 25 June 2010.
5   BStU, MfS, ACE 79/59, Vol. 1a, 20-55.
6   Unless otherwise stated, information in this section comes from Labrenz-Weiss, *Die Hauptabteilung II*, 37; Kohl, 'Donner, Blitz und Teddy'; Koehler, Stasi, 203-219.
7   Adams, *Historical Dictionary*, 187.
8   Koehler, *Stasi*, 221.
9   Adams, *Historical Dictionary*, 187.
10 Muhle, 'Wie das MfS Menschen entführen liess'.
11 Muhle, *Auftrag*, 200.
12 Koehler, *Stasi*, 238.
13 Quoted in ibid., 239.
14 See Klaus Behling, *Die Kriminalgeschichte der DDR: Vom Umgang mit Recht und Gesetz im Sozialismus, Politische Prozesse, skurrile Taten, Alltagsdelikte* (Berlin: Edition Berolina, 2017).
15 See Muhle, *Auftrag*, 240-245. Note that Muhle uses pseudonyms.
16 Ibid., 228, citing BStU, MfS, AU 312/57, Agitationsplan, Abt. Agitation.
17 Koehler, *Stasi*, 268-269.

55. Changing Times

1   Gieseke, *The History*, 39.
2   Roger Engelmann, Silke Schumann, *Kurs auf die entwickelte Diktatur: Walter Ulbricht, die Entmachtung Ernst Wollwebers und die Neuausrichtung des Staatssicherheitsdienstes 1956/57* (Berlin: BStU, 1995), 37, quoted in Gieseke, *The History*, 115.
3   Werkentin, *Politische Strafjustiz*, 409, cited in Bruce, *Resistance*, 260.
4   Peter Maxwill, 'Erich Mielkes ganz kurze Prozesse', *Der Spiegel*, 17 July 2012.
5   Adams, *Historical Dictionary*, 368.
6   Engelmann and Joestel, *Die Hauptabteilung IX*, 62.
7   Ibid., 73.
8   Ibid., citing BA, IV 2/1/171, Protokoll des 30. Plenums des ZK, 30.1.-1.2.1957.
9   Weber, *DDR*, 80, cited in Bruce, *Resistance*, 260.
10 BArch, MfS, ZAIG 167, 'Bericht über die Festnahme Kapitänleutnants Horst Ludwig 23. Januar 1959', 1-6, reproduced in *DDR im Blick* jahrgang 1959, Das Bundesarchiv, availableathttps://www.ddr-im-blick.de/jahrgaenge/jahrgang-1959/report/bericht-ueber-die-festnahme-kapitaenleutnants-horst-ludwig/, accessed 14.4.2024.
11 Murphy et al., *Battleground*, 295.
12 Uncredited author, *Die Stasi im Westen: Spionage in der Bundesrepublik Deutschland und West-Berlin* (Berlin: BStU, 2017), 7.
13 Stephan Wolf, Hauptabteilung I, Stasi-Unterlagen-Archiv, MfS Lexikon, available at https://www.stasi-unterlagen-archiv.de/mfs-lexikon/detail/hauptabteilung-i-nva-und-grenztruppenha-i/, accessed 15.2.2024.
14 Stephan Wolf, *Hauptabteilung I: NVA und Grenztruppen* (MfS-Handbuch) (Berlin: BStU, 2005), 54.
15 Ibid., 61.
16 Fulbrook, *Anatomy*, 45.
17 BStU, MfS, BV Leipzig, Leiter, Nr. 731, Bd. 4, 2.
18 BStU, MfS, SdM, Nr. 1201, 138-144.
19 Martin, *Wilderness*, 89.
20 BStU, MfS, AU, Nr. 73/57, 94.
21 BStU, MfS, BV Leipzig, Leiter, Nr. 731, Bd. 4, 34-40.

22 Fulbrook, *Anatomy*, 188-190.

23 Gieseke, *The History*, 45, citing 'Brief des 1. Sekretärs des ZK an die Genossen und Mitarbeiter der Staatssicherheit', 5.11.1956', SAPMO-BA, DY 30 IV 2.12/102, 315f. Translation by David Burnett.

24 Walter Janka, *Schwierigkeiten mit der Wahrheit* (Reinbek: Rowohlt, 1990), 90-91, translated by Mary Carlene Forszt.

25 *Neues Deutschland*, 24 July 1957.

26 Karl Wilhelm Fricke, 'Anklage: Staatsverrat', Deutschlandsfunk Archiv, 9 March 2007, available at https://www.deutschlandfunk.de/anklage-staatsverrat-100.html, accessed 10.11.2023.

27 Childs and Popplewell, *The Stasi*, 99.

28 Unless otherwise stated, information in this section comes from Polzin, *Der Wandel*, passim.

29 BStU, MfS, AOP, Nr. 5469/89, 44.

30 Auerbach et al., *Hauptabteilung XX*, 122.

31 Childs and Popplewell, *The Stasi*, 228.

32 Adams, *Historical Dictionary*, 220.

33 BStU, MfS, BdL/Dok. 002379, Richtlinie 1/56 des Stellvertreters des Ministers Beater, 3.11.1956, 1-9.

34 Recollections of Dietrich Garstka in 'Flucht einer Abiturklasse von Storkow/Mark nach Bensheim', available at https://arbeitsplattform.bildung.hessen.de/netzwerk/geschichtswerkstatt/storkow/storkow.pdf, accessed 24.7.2024.

35 BStU, MfS, SdM, Nr. 2613, 78-80.

36 Patrik von zur Mühlen, 'Widerstand in einer thüringischen Kleinstadt 1953 bis 1958: Der "Eisenberger Kreis"' in Ulrike Poppe et al. (eds.), *Zwischen Selbtsbehauptung und Anpassung* (Berlin: Ch. Links, 1995), 164-169, cited in Bruce, *Resistance*, 231.

37 Adams, *Historical Dictionary*, 414.

38 Peter Boeger, Elise Catrain (eds.), *Stasi in Sachsen: Die DDR-Geheimpolizei in den Bezirken Dresden, Karl-Marx-Stadt und Leipzig* (Berlin: BStU, 2017), 113.

39 Schmeidel, *Stasi*, 57, citing Dienstanweisung 9/56 Künftige Arbeit auf der Line V/6.

40 Childs and Popplewell, *The Stasi*, 106.

41 Schmeidel, *Stasi*, 58.

42 Auerbach et al., *Hauptabteilung XX*, 90-94.

56. Mielke Wins

1 Murphy et al., *Battleground*, 308.

2 Hubertus Knabe, *Die unterwanderte Republik: Stasi im Westen* (Berlin: Propyläen, 1999), 77, quoted in Bruce, 'Aufklärung', 386.

3 Bruce, 'Aufklärung', 387.

4 Quoted in Engelmann and Schumann, *Kurs auf die entwickelte Diktatur*, 20.

5 BStU, MfS, BdL-Dok. 212 – MfS-DSt-Nr. 100966, 'Dienstanweisung Nr. 16/57: Massnahmen zur Verbesserung der operative Arbeit in den Betrieben, Ministerien und Hauptverwaltungen, Universitäten, Hochschulen und wissenschaftlichen Instituten sowie in den Objekten der Landwirtschaft', 30 May 1957; and Haendcke-Hoppe-Arndt, *Die Hauptabteilung XVIII*, 23.

6 Murphy et al., *Battleground*, 300.

7 Beatrice de Graaf, 'How the MfS' worldview affected the intelligence cycle: a study based on operations against the Netherlands' in Wegener Friis et al. (eds.), *East German Foreign Intelligence*, 173.

8 In an operational order of 1962 cited in Bruce, *The Firm*, 73.

9 Dennis, *The Stasi*, 30.

10 Murphy et al., *Battleground*, 291.

11 BStU, MfS, SdM, Nr. 423, 17.

12 Childs and Popplewell, *The Stasi*, 178.

13 Hubertus Knabe, *Die Rechtsstelle des MfS* (MfS-Handbuch) (Berlin: BStU, 1999), 7-14.

14 Muhle, *Auftrag*, 191.

15 Engelmann and Joestel, *Die Hauptabteilung IX*, 74-75.

16 Ibid., 78.

17 Ibid., 77-78.

18 Weber and Florath, "Nun falten Sie den Zettel…", 229.

19 Fitzroy Maclean, *Eastern Approaches* (London: Penguin, 1991 reissue), 327.

20 Rayfield, *Stalin*, 252.

21 Childs and Popplewell, *The Stasi*, 67.

22 Siegfried Schwarz, 'Eine DDR-Zeitschrift mit gesamtdeutschem Anspruch', Deutschland Archiv, 5.98, 783-790, quoted in Michael F. Scholz, 'Active measures and disinformation as part of East Germany's propaganda war, 1953-1972' in Wegener Friis et al. (eds.), *East German Foreign Intelligence*, 114.

23 *Zehn Jahre Deutsche Demokratische Republik* (Berlin: Ministerrat der DDR, 1959), translated by Randall Bytwerk at the German Propaganda Archive, available at https://research.calvin. edu/german-propaganda-archive/ddr10.htm, accessed 29.2.24.

24 Scholz, 'Active measures', 120.

25 Murphy et al., *Battleground*, 200.

26 Information in this section comes from Klaus Bästlein, "'Nazi-Blutrichter als Stützen des Adenauer-Regimes": Die DDR-Kampagnen gegen NS-Richter und- Staatsanwälte, die Reaktionen der bundesdeutschen Justiz und ihre gescheiterte "Selbstreinigung" 1957-1968' in Klaus Bästlein, Annette Rosskopf, Falco Werkentin, *Beiträge zur juristischen Zeitgeschichte der DDR* (Berlin: BStU, 2009), 53-92.

27 Bästlein, "'Nazi-Blutrichter"', 64.

28 Buschfort, *Die Ostbüros*, 43-45.

57. More Dirty Operations

1   Information in this section from Kohl, 'Donner, Blitz und Teddy'.

2   Adams, *Historical Dictionary*, 87.

3   *Time*, 2 February 1959, available at https://content.time.com/time/subscriber/article/ 0,33009,894095,00.html, accessed 16.11.2023.

4   Unless otherwise stated, information in this section comes from Adams, *Historical Dictionary*; Muhle, *Auftrag*, 140-148; Koehler, *Stasi*, 141. The interpretation of this information is the author's own.

5   Mampel, *Der Untergrundkampf*, 49.

6   Quoted in Hagemann, 'Die Drohung', 21.

7   Mampel, *Die Untergrundkampf*, 35-36.

8   Ibid., 87-88.

9   Koehler, *Stasi*, 137.

10 Mampel, *Die Untergrundkampf*, 58-59.

11 Muhle, *Auftrag*, 495-496.

12 For example in *Berliner Morgenpost*, 10 March 1992.

13 Mampel, *Die Untergrundkampf*, 63-67.

14 Ibid., 108.

15 West, 'Counter-intelligence', 15.

16 Information in this section comes from Muhle, 'Wie das MfS Menschen entführen liess'.

58. The Informer Age: The 1958 Guideline on Collaborators and Stasi Reporting

1   Quoted in Fricke, *MfS Intern*, 13, requoted in Fulbrook, *Anatomy*, 47.

2   BStU, MfS, BdL-Dok. 3098, 'Dienstordnung des Staatssekretariats für Staatssicherheit', 17.9.1954.

3   Bruce, *The Firm*, 88, citing Richtlinie 1/58, 1 October 1958.
4   Gieseke, *The History*, 90.
5   'Der Geheime Informator "Richard": Ein Spitzel im Dienst der Staatssicherheit', Das Bundesarchiv Stasi Mediathek, available at https://www.stasi-mediathek.de/geschichten/der-geheime-informator-richard/sheet/0-0/type/cover/.
6   Barbara Miller, *Narratives of Guilt and Compliance in Unified Germany: Stasi Informers and their Impact on Society* (London: Routledge, 1999), 40, quoted in Bruce, *The Firm*, 88.
7   Gieseke, *The History*, 100-101.
8   Jörn Mothes et al. (eds.), *Beschädigte Seelen: DDR-Jugend und Staatssicherheit* (Bremen: Edition Temmen, 1996), 174-178, quoted in Gieseke, *The GDR*, translated by Mary Carlene Forszt, amended by author.
9   BArch, MfS, AOP, Nr. 30954, Bd.1, 5-15.
10 Roger Engelmann, ZAIG, Stasi-Unterlagen-Archiv, MfS-Lexikon, available at https://www.stasi-unterlagen-archiv.de/mfs-lexikon/detail/zentrale-auswertungs-und-informationsgruppe-zaig/, accessed 8.4.2024.
11 DDR im Blick Jahrgänge 1956, 1959, Das Bundesarchiv, available at https://www.ddr-im-blick.de/jahrgaenge/, accessed 9.4.2024.
12 BStU, MfS, ACE 81/59, 205-280.
13 BStU, MfS, ACE 85/59, 158-163.
14 BStU, MfS, ZAIG 47, 124-140.
15 BStU, MfS, ZAIG 149, 78-106.
16 BStU, MfS, ZAIG 47, 40-55.
17 BStU, MfS, ZAIG 149, 78-106.

59. Enlightenment: The Growth of East German Foreign Intelligence

1   *The Star*, 10 December 1957.
2   *The Sunday Times*, 11 November 1957.
3   Georg Herbstritt, *Bundesbürger im Dienst der DDR-Spionage: Eine analytische Studie* (Göttingen: Vandenhoeck & Ruprecht, 2007), 70.
4   Benjamin B. Fischer, 'Deaf, dumb and blind: the CIA and East Germany' in Wegener Friis et al. (eds.), *East German Foreign Intelligence*, 50.
5   Andreas Förster, 'Rosenholz: Schatz oder Schätzen', *Berliner Zeitung*, 20 March 2004.
6   Kenneth J. Campbell, 'Markus Wolf: One of History's Most Effective Intelligence Chiefs', *American Intelligence Journal*, Vol. 29, Nr. 1 (2011), 156.
7   Wolf and McElvoy, *Memoirs*, 86.
8   Childs and Popplewell, *The Stasi*, 127.
9   Information in this section comes from BStU, *Hauptverwaltung A*, ch. 3 and 4; Müller-Enbergs, *Geschichte der HVA*, ch. 3.2 and 3.3.
10 Maddrell, 'Britain's exploitation', 70.
11 Maddrell, 'The economic dimension', 85-86.
12 Macrakis, *Seduced*, 42.
13 Ibid., 25-6, citing BStU, Minister's Orders, No. 14/56, 8 June 1956.
14 BArch, MfS, BdL-Dok, Nr. 2225, Dienstanweisung Nr. 18/56, Massnahmen zur Bearbeitung der Bundeswehr, des Bundesverteidigungsministeriums und seiner nachgeordneten Dienststellen, der NATO-Stäbe und der Soldatenverbände in der Bundesrepublik, 17.8.1956.
15 Adams, *Historical Dictionary*, 392.
16 Glees, *The Stasi Files*, passim.
17 Childs and Popplewell, *The Stasi*, 166.
18 Thomas Wegener Friis, 'East German espionage in Denmark' in Wegener Friis et al., *East German Foreign Intelligence*, 149.
19 Stephan Fingerle, Jens Gieseke, 'Partisanen des Kalten Krieges: Die Untergrundtruppe der Nationalen Volksarmee 1957-1962 und ihre Übernahme durch die Staatssicherheit' (Berlin:

BStU/Abt. Bildung und Forschung, 1996), 7.

20 Gieseke, *The History*, 177.

21 From a draft resolution of the SED Security Commission, probably issued 1960-1961, reproduced in Fingerle, Gieseke, 'Partisanen', 39.

22 Quotations in this section from Wolf and McElvoy, *Memoirs*, passim.

23 Adams, *Historical Dictionary*, 361; Koehler, *Stasi*, 193-194.

24 Macrakis, *Seduced*, 187.

25 Childs and Popplewell, *The Stasi*, 92.

26 Klaus Eichner and Gotthold Schramm (eds.), *Kundschafter im Westen* (Berlin: Edition Ost, 2003), preface by Raussendorf.

27 Koehler, *Stasi*, 195.

28 Dennis, *The Stasi*, 197.

29 Koehler, *Stasi*, 198-199.

30 Marxen and Werle (eds.), *Strafjustiz*, 240-241; 'Objektiv begrenzt', *Der Spiegel*, 4 October 1992.

31 Childs and Popplewell, *The Stasi*, 153.

32 Friedrich-Wilhelm Schlomann, *Operationsgebiet Bundesrepublik* (Munich: Universitas, 1984), 235-236, cited in Macrakis, 'The crown jewels', 194.

33 Adams, *Historical Dictionary*, 360.

34 Dennis, *The Stasi*, 198, citing Informations- und Dokumentationszentrum Berlin, 1998.

35 Gieseke, *The History*, 171.

60. Tradecraft and Technologies

1 Wilson, 'The mastermind'.

2 Information in this section comes from Faligot and Krop, *La Piscine*, 223; Schmeidel, *Stasi*, 126-127; Macrakis, *Seduced*, 187.

3 Leopold Trepper, *The Great Game: Memoirs of a Spymaster* (London: Sphere Books edition, 1979), 140-141.

4 Wolf and McElvoy, *Memoirs*, 189.

5 MfS-BdL/Dok. No. 000652, 25 July 1960 and BStU, MfS/JHS, MF 214, Henschke, 'Effective Planning and Meeting Operational Technological Needs at the MfS According to the Demands of Increased Work against the Enemy', thesis, May 1968, cited in Macrakis, *Seduced*, 147-148.

6 Macrakis, *Seduced*, 161.

7 Ibid., 180-190.

8 Ibid., 236, thanking H. Keith Melton for the information.

9 Ibid., 205.

10 'Intelligence Report', *Daily Express*, 27 January 1957.

11 'Intelligence Report', *Daily Express*, 14 January 1957.

12 Guy Liddell diaries, entry for 29 March 1951, KV-4/473, UK National Archives, 53.

13 Macrakis, 'The crown jewels', 200-201.

61. Love Rats

1 Information in this section comes from Wolf and McElvoy, *Memoirs*, 124-125.

2 Nigel West, *Historical Dictionary of International Intelligence* (Lanham MD: Rowman & Littlefield, 2015), 293.

3 Wolf and McElvoy, *Memoirs*, 128.

4 Adams, *Historical Dictionary*, 22.

5 Andrew and Gordievsky, *KGB*, 454.

6 Wolf and McElvoy, *Memoirs*, 136.

7 Ibid., 135.

8 Nigel West, *Historical Dictionary of Sexpionage* (Lanham MD: Scarecrow Press, 2009), 164.

9   Wolf and McElvoy, *Memoirs*, 138; Adams, *Historical Dictionary*, 273.
10   West, *Historical Dictionary of Sexpionage*, 164; Adams, ibid.
11   Macrakis, 'The crown jewels', 194, citing BStU, Rosenholz and SIRA: 'Ilona' Reg. Nr. XV/3980/63.

62. A Torrent of Spies

1   Unless otherwise stated, information in this section comes from Helmut Müller-Enbergs, 'Political intelligence: foci and sources, 1969-1989' in Wegener Friis et al. (eds.), *East German Foreign Intelligence*, 91-112; Wegener Friis, 'East German espionage', 146-161; Macrakis, 'The crown jewels', 185-203; Macrakis, *Seduced*, 79-117; Müller-Enbergs, *Geschichte der HVA*, 48-67.
2   Dennis, *The Stasi*, 124.
3   Gerhard Block, *Verraten und verkauft: Memoiren eines Unverbesserlichen* (Berlin: NoRa, 2004).
4   Uncredited author, *Der Deutsche Bundestag*, 250-265.
5   Wolf and McElvoy, *Memoirs*, 111.
6   Adams, *Historical Dictionary*, 163.
7   Ibid., 154.
8   Murphy et al., *Battleground*, 297.
9   Wolf and McElvoy, *Memoirs*, 75.
10   BStU, MfS, SdM 1909, 219, Informationsdienst zur Beurteilung der Situation in Westdeutschland und Westberlin.
11   BStU, MfS, SdM 1909, 209, Generalmajor Wolf, 25.4.1957: Information für die Mitglieder des Kollegiums; uncredited author, *Der Deutsche Bundestag*, 57-58.
12   Uncredited author, *Der Deutsche Bundestag*, 182-183.
13   Ibid., 201-202.
14   Information in this section comes from Müller-Enbergs, *Geschichte der HVA*, 52-68.
15   BStU, ZA, HA KuSch, Bündel Abt. Planung 10 III, 'Kaderbestandsmeldungen', cited in Gieseke, *The History*, 160; Lippmann, 'Foreign intelligence', 136.
16   Murphy et al., *Battleground*, 331.
17   Matthias Uhl, 'The professionalization of Soviet military intelligence and its influence during the Berlin Crisis under Khrushchev' in Wegener Friis et al. (eds.), *East German Foreign Intelligence*, 271-280.
18   Steury (ed.), *On the Front Lines*, 255-258, cited in Murphy, *Battleground*, 210, also citing USAREUR Intelligence Estimate 1965 (U), 15 February 1965, 354.
19   Janusz Piekalkiewicz, *Weltgeschichte der Spionage* (Munich: Südwest, 1988), cited in ibid., 208.
20   Wolf and McElvoy, *Memoirs*, 161.

63. Exposing Nazis

1   Andrew and Mitrokhin, *The Mitrokhin Archive*, 199.
2   BStU, *Hauptverwaltung A*, 30-31.
3   Wolf and McElvoy, *Memoirs*, 233-236.
4   Protocol of 9th Central Committee plenum, July 1960, SAPMO-BA, DY 30, IV/2/1/123, quoted in Scholz, 'Active Measures', 115.
5   Helmut Müller-Enbergs, Stasi Unterlagen Archiv, MfS Lexikon, available at https://www.stasi-unterlagen-archiv.de/mfs-lexikon/detail/kontaktperson-kp/, accessed 10.2.2022.
6   Murphy et al., *Battleground*, 496.
7   Ibid., 371.
8   Scholz, 'Active Measures', 114.
9   Josef Frolik, *The Frolik Defection: The Memoirs of an Intelligence Agent* (London: Leo Cooper, 1975), 58.
10   Bästlein, '"Nazi-Blutrichter"', 59.

11 Jens Gieseke, 'Antifaschistischer Staat und postfaschistische Gesellschaft: die DDR, das MfS und die NS-Täter' in *Historical Social Research*, 35(3) (2010), 85.

12 Wolf and McElvoy, *Memoirs*, 234.

13 Ibid., 50.

14 Boghardt, 'Our man', 13.

15 Günter Bohnsack and Herbert Wehner, *Auftrag Irreführung* (Hamburg: Cartsen, 1992), 27, cited in Scholz, 'Active measures', 117.

16 Sefton Delmer, *Black Boomerang* (London: Martin Secker & Warburg Limited, 1962), 181.

17 Scholz, 'Active measures', 118.

18 Childs and Popplewell, *The Stasi*, 154.

19 Wolf and McElvoy, *Memoirs*, 236.

20 Boghardt, 'Our man', 14.

21 Scholz, 'Active measures', 117.

22 Information in this section comes from Koehler, *Stasi*; Adams, *Historical Dictionary*.

64. Securing the Border

1 CIA CIWS, The Problem of Western Access to Berlin, 30 April 1959, (MORI No. 45593), Document VI-14 in Steury (ed.), *On the Front Lines*, 451.

2 Hope M. Harrison, 'Ulbricht and the concrete 'Rose': New archival evidence on the dynamics of Soviet-East German relations and the Berlin Crisis, 1958-61', Cold War International History Project Working Paper #5 (Washington: Woodrow Wilson International Center for Scholars, 1993), 6.

3 For example, see ibid., passim.

4 Paul Maddrell, 'The Western secret services', 829.

5 Childs and Popplewell, *The Stasi*, 93.

6 BStU, MfS, AS, Nr. 109/65, Bd. 2, 86.

7 Childs and Popplewell, *The Stasi*, 93.

8 BStU, MfS, AS, Nr. 109/65, 93-94.

9 BStU, MfS, AS, Nr. 109/65, Vol. 10, 151-159.

10 Ibid., 256-267.

11 BStU, MfS, AS, Nr. 109/65, Bd. 2, 98.

12 Ibid., 67-111 and 308-316.

13 BStU, MfS, AS, Nr. 109/65, Vol. 10, 226-231 and 233-239.

14 BStU, MfS, AS, Nr. 204/62, Bd. 9, 238-260.

15 *Der Kurier*, 19 December 1956, cited in BStU, MfS, ZAIG, Nr. 1, 1-14.

16 Mitter and Wolle, *Untergang auf Raten* (Munich: Bertelsmann Verlag, 1993), 343, cited in Bruce, *Resistance*, 261.

17 Bruce, *Resistance*, 261; Koehler, *Stasi*, 67; David Childs, *The GDR: Moscow's German Ally* (London: Unwin Hyman, 1988), 61, cited in Bruce, *Resistance*, 261.

18 Wolf and McElvoy, *Memoirs*, 102-103.

19 Quoted in Manfred Wilke, *Der Weg zur Mauer: Stationen der Teilungsgeschichte* (Berlin: Ch. Links, 2011), 202.

20 BStU, ZA, SdM 1198, 8-20, quoted in Gieseke, *The GDR*, 32, translated by Mary Carlene Forszt.

21 Koehler, *Stasi*, 66.

22 Daniela Münkel, Einleitung, *DDR im Blick* Jahrgang 1961, Das Bundesarchiv, available at https://www.ddr-im-blick.de/jahrgaenge/jahrgang-1961/report/einleitung-1961/, accessed 10.4.2024.

23 Engelmann and Joestel, *Die Hauptabteilung IX*, 89.

24 Haendcke-Hoppe-Arndt, *Die Hauptabteilung XVIII*, 27.

25 BStU, MfS, AS, Nr. 204/62, 61-78.

26 Haendcke-Hoppe-Arndt, *Die Hauptabteilung XVIII*, 26.

65. The Western Powers Prepare

1   CIA CIWS, Internal Situation in East Germany, 11 December 1958 (MORI No. 45626), Document VI-2 in Steury (ed.), *On the Front Lines*, 386.
2   Maddrell, 'Western espionage', 29.
3   Maddrell, 'The Western secret services', 833, citing BStU, ZA, MfS-HA IX, MF-11171, Tätigkeitsbericht für November 1957, 9.12.1957.
4   Maddrell, British Intelligence', 70.
5   Maddrell, 'The Western secret services', 834-838.
6   Maddrell, British Intelligence', 62.
7   Ibid., 59-60.
8   Paul Maddrell, 'Exploiting and Securing the Open Border in Berlin: the Western Secret Services, the Stasi, and the Second Berlin Crisis, 1958-1961', Cold War International History Project Working Paper #58 (Washington: Woodrow Wilson International Center for Scholars, 2009), 5-6.
9   BStU, MfS, AS, Nr. 109/65, Bd. 9, 54.
10 Ibid., 55-73.
11 Maddrell, 'The economic dimension', 97-107.
12 Maddrell, 'Im Fadenkreuz', 164.
13 Adams, *Historical Dictionary*, 133.
14 BStU, ZA, MfS-HA IX, Nr. 4350, 226-235, translated by Paul Maddrell.
15 Maddrell, 'The economic dimension', 102.
16 Wegener Friis, 'East German espionage', 148-149.
17 Case, 'The Joint Intelligence Committee', 257.
18 Murphy et al., *Battleground*, 309.
19 Maddrell, 'British Intelligence', 67.

66. A Decision is Made

1   Engelmann and Joestel, *Die Hauptabteilung IX*, 87.
2   BStU, MfS, SdM, Nr. 1218, 196, Oberstleutnant Heinitz, 28.2.1961: Stellungnahme zum Schreiben des Ministers für Justiz vom 14.2.1961. quoted in ibid., 90.
3   BStU, MfS, AS, Nr. 96/66, 365, HA IX/4, Major Leipold, Bericht über das Ergebnis der vom Leiter der Hauptabteilung IX angewiesenen Überprüfungen in den Abteilungen IX der Bezirksverwaltungen, 12.6.1961, quoted in ibid.
4   Engelmann and Joestel, *Die Hauptabteilung IX*, 91.
5   Matthias Uhl, 'The professionalization', 210-211.
6   Murphy et al., *Battleground*, 330-331.
7   Uhl, 'The professionalization', 211.
8   Ibid., 210-211.
9   CIA SNIE 100-7-59, Soviet Tactics on Berlin, 11 June 1959, Document VI-16 in Steury (ed.), *On the Front Lines*, 479-480.
10 BStU, MfS, AS, Nr. 109/65, Bd. 8, 3-6.
11 BStU, MfS, AS, Nr. 204/62, Bd. 3, 1-23.
12 Harrison, 'Ulbricht and the concrete 'Rose'', 51.
13 BStU, MfS, SdM, Nr. 2861, 231-240.

67. Old Tricks

1   Buschfort, *Die Ostbüros*, 67.
2   Ibid., 63-64.
3   John L. Steele, 'Assassin Disarmed By Love', *Life*, 7.9.1962; Andrew and Gordievsky, *KGB*, 467-468.
4   Porch, *The French Secret Services*, 371.

5   Faligot and Krop, *La Piscine*, 163-166; Porch, *The French Secret Services*, 371-372 and 442.

6   Susanne Muhle, *Auftrag*, 234, citing BStU, MfS, AOP 234/61, Massnahmeplan, HA I/DGP, 30.7.1959.

7   Quoted in R.J. Evans, *Rituals of Retribution: Capital Punishment in Germany, 1600-1987* (London: Penguin, 1997), 852, requoted in Dennis, *The Stasi*, 39-40, translated by Peter Brown, amended by author.

8   https://www.stasi-mediathek.de/geschichten/erziehung-mit-der-guillotine/sheet/0-0/type/cover/, accessed 26.4.2023.

9   Unless otherwise stated, information in this section comes from BStU, MfS, GH, Nr. 9/89, Bd. 4, 118-119,'Beurteilung zu Manfred Smolka'; BStU, MfS, AOP, Nr. 234/61, 12, 'Beschluss über das Anlegen des Operativ-Vorgangs "Verräter"'; BStU, MfS, GH, Nr. 9/89, Bd. 8, 214-218, 'Gutachten über den durch Manfred Smolka verursachten Schaden'; BStU, MfS, AOP, Nr. 234/61, 116-117, 'Abschrift eines Briefes Smolkas an einen Bekannten bei der Grenzpolizei'; BStU, MfS, GH, Nr. 9/89, 26-29, 'Bericht über die Festnahme des ehemaligen Grenzpolizisten Manfred Smolka'; BStU, MfS, GH, Nr. 9/89, 469-471, 'Vorschlag zur Durchführung eines Prozesses gegen den ehemaligen Grenzpolizisten Manfred Smolka'; BStU, MfS, HA IX, Tb, Nr. 111-126, 'Schlusswort Manfred Smolkas beim Strafprozess vor dem Bezirksgericht Erfurt'.

10 Muhle, *Auftrag*, 235-237.

11 BStU, MfS GH 9/89, Festnahmebericht, HA I/DGP/4., cited in Muhle, *Auftrag*, 235.

12 Muhle, *Auftrag*, 237, 238, 501.

13 Manfred Wilke, 'Ein widerständiges Leben: Heinz Brandt', Deutschland Archiv (Bundeszentrale für politische Bildung), 11.1.2019, available at https://www.bpb.de/themen/deutschlandarchiv/299741/ein-widerstaendiges-leben-heinz-brandt/, accessed 27.4.2023.

14 Ibid.

15 Quoted in 'Von der Stasi entführt: Das Beispiel Heinz Brandt', *Der Mitteldeutsche Rundfunk*, 15 September 2015, available at https://www.mdr.de/geschichte/ddr/politik-gesellschaft/stasi/entfuehrung-heinz-brandt-100.html, accessed 27.4.2023.

16 Unless otherwise stated, information in the following section comes from BStU, MfS, ZAIG 900, 11-17, available at https://www.ddr-im-blick.de/jahrgaenge/jahrgang-1964/report/ig-metall-und-heinz-brandt-ueber-seine-ausreise-2/, accessed 30.4.23; and Muhle, *Auftrag*, passim.

17 1964 interview with Brandt quoted in ibid.

18 Quoted in Wilke, 'Ein widerständiges Leben'.

19 Information in this section comes from Muhle, *Auftrag*, 160-165.

20 Muhle, 'Wie das MfS Menschen entführen liess'.

68. 'The Anti-fascist Protective Barrier'

1   Mary Fulbrook, *History of Germany, 1918-2000: The Divided Nation* (Oxford: Blackwell, 2002), 158.

2   Peter Merseburger, *Willy Brandt 1913-1992: Visionär und Realist* (Stuttgart: Deutsche Verlags-Anstalt, 2002), 182-185, cited in Maddrell, 'The Western secret services', 836-837.

3   BStU, MfS, ZAIG, Nr. 31066, 353-362.

4   Koehler, *Stasi*, 69.

5   *Da schlug's 13* (Berlin: Kreisleitung Berlin-Mitte der SED, Abteilung Agitation und Propaganda, 1963), translated by Randall Bytwerk at the German Propaganda Archive, available at https://research.calvin.edu/german-propaganda-archive/schlugs13.htm, accessed 29.2.24.

6   CIA CIWS, Berlin, 17 August 1961, (MORI No. 28205), Document VII-6 in Steury (ed.), *On the Front Lines*, 525; CIA CIWS, Berlin, 24 August 1961, (MORI No. 28206), Document VII-8 in ibid., 535.

7   Fulbrook, *Anatomy*, 191-192.

8   BStU, MfS, AS, Nr. 204/62, Bd. 7, 39.

9   '...das halbe Jahr nach dem Mauerbau eine der repressivsten Phasen in der gesamten
    Geschichte der DDR war'; Engelmann and Joestel, *Die Hauptabteilung IX*, 95.
10 CIA, Dispatch, Berlin Since 13 August, 6 November 1961, (MORI No. 14411), Document
    VII-14 in Steury (ed.), *On the Front Lines*, 570.
11 Gieseke, *Mielke-Konzern*, 75.
12 BStU, MfS, AS, Nr. 204/62, Bd. 10, 173-197.
13 Uhl, 'The professionalization', 209.
14 Engelmann and Joestel, *Die Hauptabteilung IX*, 91.
15 BStU, MfS, HA XX/4 332, 67, Jahresanalyse der Hauptabteilung V/4 für das Jahr 1960 und
    die sich daraus ergebende politisch-operative Aufgabenstellung für 1961.
16 BStU, MfS, ZAIG, Nr. 31066, 344-346.
17 CIA, Dispatch, in Steury (ed.), *On the Front Lines*, 569.
18 Bruce, *The Firm*, 117, citing BStU-Schwerin, AOP 866/62, 15 June 1962, Beschluss über
    Einstellen eines OV.
19 Engelmann and Joestel, *Die Hauptabteilung IX*, 92.
20 BStU, MfS, BdL-Dok. 2633, 1-4.
21 BStU, MfS, BdL-Dok. 3030, 'Veränderungen im System der operativen Erfassung',
    20.5.1960.
22 BStU, MfS, BdL-Dok. 670, 'Befehl Nr. 584160: Verbesserung der Informationsarbeit des
    Ministeriums für Staatssicherheit', 7.12.1960.
23 Adams, *Historical Dictionary*, 264.
24 Uncredited author, 'Aktenvermerk über Unzulänglichkeiten bei der Durchführung der
    Aktion "Licht"', Das Bundesarchiv Stasi Mediathek, available at https://www.stasi-
    mediathek.de/medien/aktenvermerk-ueber-unzulaenglichkeiten-bei-der-durchfuehrung-
    der-aktion-licht/blatt/37/, accessed on 11.2.2024.
25 Information in this section comes from BStU, MfS, HA XX 6521, Teil 2, 41-183; BStU,
    MfS, HA IX/MF/11844, 1-2.
26 Engelmann and Joestel, *Die Hauptabteilung IX*, 94.
27 Information in this section comes from BArch, MfS, HA II-6, Nr. 395, OV 'Blitz', 1960-62;
    and Peter Erler, 'Tod im Gewahrsam der Staatssicherheit: Suizide und andere Sterbefälle
    am Haftort Berlin-Hohenschönhausen, 1951 bis 1989. Eine vorläufige Übersicht', *ZdF*,
    38/2015, 65-87.
28 Mike Dennis, *The Rise and Fall of the German Democratic Republic* (London, New York:
    Routledge, 2000), 100.
29 Uncredited author, *Das geteilte Berlin*, 6; Daniela Münkel, Einleitung, *DDR im Blick* jahrgang
    1961.
30 BStU, MfS, ZAIG, Nr. 31066, 122-129.
31 Wolf and McElvoy, *Memoirs*, 105.
32 Bruce, *The Firm*, 153.
33 Childs and Popplewell, *The Stasi*, 89.
34 Daniela Münkel, Einleitung, *DDR im Blick* Jahrgang 1961.
35 Fulbrook, *Anatomy*, 192-193.
36 Bruce, *The Firm*, 153.
37 'Arbeitsgemeinschaft 13. August', December 2004, cited 'with caution' in Gieseke, *The
    History*, 146.

69. Spies, Still

1   CIA, Dispatch, in Steury (ed.), *On the Front Lines*, 571-572.
2   Murphy et al., *Battleground*, 386. For the figure of 100 agents see CIA, Memorandum for
    Washington on Berlin, 14 September 1961, (MORI No. 14414), Document VII-10 in Steury
    (ed.), *On the Front Lines*, 549.
3   Indicated by the chief of Danish intelligence, H.M. Lunding. Franceschini et al., *Spionage
    Unter Freunde*, 226.

4   E. Schmidt-Eenboom, *Schnüffler*, 108-110, cited in Maddrell, 'The Western secret services',
    842.
5   Maddrell, 'Western espionage', 30.
6   Labrenz-Weiss, *Abteilung M*, 17.
7   Faligot and Krop, *La Piscine*, 225.
8   Andrew and Mitrokhin, *The Mitrokhin Archive*, 571-572.
9   Aleksandr Korotkov quoted in Murphy et al., *Battleground*, 508.
10 Maddrell, 'Western espionage', 30; Maddrell, 'British Intelligence', 70.
11 Wunschik, *Hauptabteilung VII*, 46.
12 Information in this section comes from Paul Maddrell's translations of BStU, ZA, MfS-HA
    IX Nr. 4350, 226-235 and 341-360.
13 Wolf and McElvoy, *Memoirs*, 104.
14 Quoted in Murphy et al., *Battleground*, 368-369.
15 Andrew and Gordievsky, *KGB*, 462-463.
16 Andrew and Mitrokhin, *The Mitrokhin Archive*, 248-253.
17 Haendcke-Hoppe-Arndt, *Die Hauptabteilung XVIII*, 27.
18 Schmole, *Hauptabteilung VIII*, 75.

70. Conclusions

1   Quoted in Gieseke, *The GDR*, 96.
2   Glees, *The Stasi Files*, 3.
3   Gieseke, *The GDR*, 35.
4   Fulbrook, *Anatomy*, 31.
5   Porch, *The French Secret Services*, 387.
6   Glees, *The Stasi Files*, 126.
7   Gieseke, *The History*, 7.
8   Cacciatore, 'Re-evaluating', 145, citing Anne Karalekas, *History of the Central Intelligence
    Agency* (Laguna Hills: Aegean Park Press, 1997), 56-57.
9   Glees, *The Stasi Files*, 20.
10 Müller-Enbergs, 'Die DDR-Nachrichtendienste'.

Index

OLDCASTLE BOOKS

POSSIBLY THE UK'S SMALLEST INDEPENDENT PUBLISHING GROUP

Oldcastle Books is an independent publishing company formed in 1985 dedicated to providing an eclectic range of titles with a nod to the popular culture of the day.

Imprints include our lists about the film industry, KAMERA BOOKS & CREATIVE ESSENTIALS. We have dabbled in the classics, with PULP! THE CLASSICS, taken a punt on gambling books with HIGH STAKES, provided in-depth overviews with POCKET ESSENTIALS and covered a wide range in the eponymous OLDCASTLE BOOKS list. Most recently we have welcomed two new sister imprints with THE CRIME & MYSTERY CLUB and VERVE, home to great, original, page-turning fiction.

oldcastlebooks.com

  kamera BOOKS creative ESSENTIALS

| OLDCASTLE BOOKS | CREATIVE ESSENTIALS | THE CRIME & MYSTERY CLUB
| POCKET ESSENTIALS | PULP! THE CLASSICS | VERVE BOOKS
| KAMERA BOOKS | HIGHSTAKES PUBLISHING |